macromedia®

FLASH™ MX
professional
2004
application development

training from the source

jeanette stallons

macromedia®
PRESS

Macromedia® Flash™ MX professional 2004: application development Training from the Source

Jeanette Stallons

 Published by Macromedia Press, in association with Peachpit Press, a division of Pearson Education.

Macromedia Press

1249 Eighth Street
Berkeley, CA 94710
510/524-2178
800/283-9444
510/524-2221 (fax)
Find us on the World Wide Web at:
http://www.peachpit.com
http://www.macromedia.com

To report errors, please send a note to errata@peachpit.com

Printed and bound in the United States of America

ISBN 0-321-23834-6

9 8 7 6 5 4 3 2 1

Credits

Author

Jeanette Stallons

Macromedia Press Editor

Wendy Sharp

Developmental Editor

Carol Person

Copy Editor

Peggy Gannon

Production Coordinator

Becky Winter

Compositors

Rick Gordon, Emerald Valley Graphics

Myrna Vladic, Bad Dog Graphics

Indexer

Joy Dean Lee

Cover

George Mattingly, GMD

Technical Review

Robert Crooks, Macromedia, Inc.

Dedication

This book is dedicated to Russ, Bumpy, and Muffin.

Table of Contents

Introduction

Macromedia Flash MX Professional 2004 lets you design and deliver rich, cross-platform, low-bandwidth user interfaces and applications. You can create and import graphics and text; add animation and interactivity; retrieve dynamic data from text files, XML files, web services, and ColdFusion, Java, or .NET services; and persist data on both the client and the server. To view Flash applications, users need the Macromedia Flash Player. Almost all online users already have the Flash Player in their browsers. (See http://www.macromedia.com/software/player_census/flashplayer for statistics.)

This *Training from the Source* book focuses exclusively on teaching you, a programmer, what you need to know about the Macromedia Flash interface and the ActionScript language. After you finish this book, you will be able to build a real-world rich Internet application that interacts dynamically with the user and exchanges data with XML files, web services, and application server classes. It takes you step-by-step through the development of a Flash application, grounding you in the basics of the Flash interface and the ActionScript 2.0 language (based on the ECMAScript-262 Edition 4 proposal), and then moves on to explain the Flash object model and how to architect your applications using ActionScript's new class-based programming model. After learning the fundamentals, you build an application using the new Flash application framework that consists of screens, user interface components, data access components, and data binding.

To complete the lessons in this book, you must have the Professional version of Flash MX 2004. To complete Lessons 13 through 16 (which connect to remote server functionality), you will also need a web server, an application server, and either Microsoft Access or MySQL. Three versions of the lesson files are provided (ColdFusion, C#, and Java) so you can use either a ColdFusion, J2EE, or .NET application server.

Any known errata are posted on the web site: http://www.trainingfromthesource.com. Please send any additional errata you find to jeanette@stallons.com and/or errata@peachpit.com.

Prerequisites

The lessons in this book assume you have no prior Flash experience, but that you do have programming experience in some language (for example Java, JavaScript, ColdFusion, C#, ActionScript, or another language) and are familiar with programming constructs like loops, conditional logic, and functions. A background in object-oriented programming is not required or assumed, but it is definitely beneficial because ActionScript is an object-oriented language.

In Lessons 13 and 14, you learn to access remote application functionality that resides on a ColdFusion, J2EE, or .NET platform from Flash. In this course, you do not write the server-side functionality; it is provided. You only need to place the files in the correct locations on the server. Although a background in building web applications with ColdFusion, Java, or C# is not required to complete these lessons, it is helpful. Brief instructions for installing and setting up an application server are located in the appendix.

If you have prior Flash experience, you might want to skip Lesson 1 or just take a quick look at the sections on version detection and Flash projects, both of which are new to Flash MX 2004. If you have prior experience with ActionScript, you might also want to skip Lessons 2 through 4, but be sure to read about exception handling, which is new to ActionScript, in Lesson 2.

Outline

This Macromedia training course steps you through the exercises in each lesson, presents the major features and tools in Flash MX Professional 2004, and guides you toward developing the skills you need to create Flash applications. This curriculum should take approximately 24 hours to complete and includes the following 16 lessons:

Lesson 1: Learning the Flash Interface

Lesson 2: Learning ActionScript Fundamentals

Lesson 3: Learning the Flash Player Object Model

Lesson 4: Creating Button and MovieClip Objects

Lesson 5: Creating Classes

Lesson 6: Creating Components

Lesson 7: Building Applications with Screens

Lesson 8: Using the Flash Application Framework

Lesson 9: Learning the UI Component Framework

Lesson 10: Using UI Component APIs

Lesson 11: Creating Visual Objects Dynamically

Lesson 12: Retrieving Data from XML Files

The Project

In this book you build two separate projects. In the first six lessons, you create a Flash application containing a mortgage calculator that calculates a mortgage payment, given a house price, down payment amount, interest rate, and loan length. In Lesson 6, you convert the application elements into a Flash component that can be easily distributed and reused by other developers.

In Lessons 7 through 16, you build a multipage Flash application for Macromediestate, a fictional real estate company. The application includes login/logout functionality that checks user input against a database on the server using a web service; a dynamic home page that displays text from an XML file and an image from an external JPG; a search interface that enables users to retrieve houses from a database using a web service or Flash Remoting; and the mortgage calculator you built in the first six lessons.

Standard Elements

Each lesson in this book begins by outlining the major focus of the lesson and introducing new features or concepts. Learning objectives and the approximate time needed to complete all the exercises are also listed at the beginning of each lesson. The lessons are divided into short exercises that explain the importance of each skill you learn. Every lesson builds on the concepts and techniques used in the previous ones.

Some features you will see in each lesson:

Tips. Alternative ways to perform tasks and suggestions to consider when applying the skills you are learning.

Notes. Additional background information to expand your knowledge, as well as advanced techniques you can explore to further develop your skills.

Boldface terms. New vocabulary that is introduced and emphasized in each lesson.

Italic text. Text you need to type in is printed in italics.

Code text: All text in code font is ActionScript code including the names of variables, properties, and methods.

Menu commands and keyboard shortcuts. There are often multiple ways to perform the same task in Flash. The different options will be pointed out in each lesson. Menu commands are shown with angle brackets between the menu names and commands: Menu > Command >

Subcommand. Keyboard shortcuts are shown with a plus sign between the names of keys to indicate that you should press the keys simultaneously; for example, Shift+Tab means that you should press the Shift and Tab keys at the same time.

DVD-ROM. The files you need to complete the exercises for each lesson are located in the fpad2004 folder on the enclosed DVD, which can be found at the back of the book.

Appendix. This contains setup instructions for installing and configuring the software needed to complete all lessons in this book.

File Structure

You can save the fpad2004 folder located on the DVD-ROM to any location on your computer (even your Desktop). All lessons in this book refer to opening files from and saving files to this folder, wherever you might have saved it. Some of the files contained in the fpad2004 folder, though, need to be placed in specific folders for the application server you are using. Instructions for placing these files in the correct locations are included in the appendix and in the relevant lessons.

Within the fpad2004 folder, you will find individual lesson folders (for example; lesson01, lesson 02, and so on) as well as mmestate, data, and services folders.

lessons. The lesson folders contain the files necessary to perform the exercises. Each lesson folder has a start, intermediate, and complete subfolder. The start folder contains all the files you need to complete the lesson. The intermediate folder contains copies of what each file should look like at the end of each exercise. The files in the complete folder show what your files should look like at the end of the lesson. There are multiple versions of the folders for Lesson 13 through Lesson 16, which contain files for different application server setups. For example, lesson13 (ColdFusion port 80), lesson13 (ColdFusion port 8500), and lesson13 (Java port 80). All files in the lesson folders are reference files. You save all the files you create throughout the book in the /fpad2004/mmestate/ folder so you can continue to work on the same files across all the lessons.

mmestate. This folder is your working directory where you save all the files you create. It contains three subfolders: assets, includes, and classes. The assets folder contains all the assets you need for the entire application. (Copies of assets needed for individual lessons are also included in the individual lesson folders.) In Lessons 2 through 4, you create external script files that you place in the includes folder. You place all class files you create in Lessons 5 through 16 in the classes folder.

services. The services folder contains all the application server files that need to be copied to other locations on your computer. It contains subfolders specifying files to place on ColdFusion, J2EE, or .NET servers. Instructions for placing these files in the correct locations are included in the appendix and in the relevant lessons.

data. The data folder contains two versions of the database referenced by the application server code: a Microsoft Access database and an equivalent MySQL database. Instructions for setting up each database are included in the appendix.

Macromedia Training from the Source

The Macromedia Training from the Source and Advanced Training from the Source series are developed in association with Macromedia, and reviewed by the product support teams. Ideal for active learners, the books in the Training from the Source series offer hands-on instruction designed to provide you with a solid grounding in the program's fundamentals. If you learn best by doing, this is the series for you. Each Training from the Source title contains hours of instruction on Macromedia software products. They are designed to teach the techniques that you need to create sophisticated professional-level projects. Each book includes a DVD-ROM that contains all the files used in the lessons, completed projects for comparison and more.

Macromedia Authorized Training and Certification

This book is geared to enable you to study at your own pace with content from the source. Other training options exist through the Macromedia Authorized Training Partner program. Get up to speed in a matter of days with task-oriented courses taught by Macromedia Certified Instructors. Or learn on your own with interactive, online training from Macromedia University. All of these sources of training will prepare you to become a Macromedia Certified Developer.

For more information on authorized training and certification, check out www.macromedia.com/go/training1.

What You Will Learn

As you work through these lessons, you will develop the skills needed to create your own rich Internet applications with Flash MX Professional 2004.

By the end of the course, you will be able to:

- Comfortably navigate the Flash MX 2004 interface
- Build a Flash application interface containing text, images, and user interface controls
- Create familiar programming constructs with ActionScript 2.0
- Use the built-in nonvisual classes including Math, Date, String, Array, and Object
- Create instances of the built-in visual objects to interact with the user
- Write event handling code to respond to user events
- Turn visual elements into MovieClips so they can be manipulated with ActionScript
- Place your code in external files separate from the Flash document
- Create your own class files and build a class-based application
- Turn your MovieClips into components that can be distributed and reused by others
- Build applications using the new screen-based programming metaphor
- Use the built-in code-generating behaviors and create your own

- Create visual objects with code by dynamically loading MovieClips, UI components, images, or other Flash applications
- Manipulate the UI components using their custom APIs and the shared underlying component framework
- Change the appearance of the UI components
- Use visual data binding to bind properties from one component to another
- Retrieve data from XML files using the visual XMLConnector component and the built-in XML class
- Call a web service using the visual WebServiceConnector component and the WebService class
- Use Flash Remoting to access your remote ColdFusion, C#, or Java classes
- Use components to manipulate sets of data
- Persist data on the client using SharedObjects

Minimum System Requirements

Windows

- 600MHz Intel Pentium III processor or equivalent
- Windows 98 SE (4.10.2222 A), Windows 2000, or Windows XP

Macintosh

- 500MHz PowerPC G3 processor
- Mac OS X 10.2.6 and later, 10.3

Cross-Platform

- 256 MB RAM (512 MB recommended)
- 600 MB available disk space
- DVD-ROM drive
- Macromedia Flash MX Professional 2004
- Macromedia Dreamweaver MX 2004 (recommended)
- A web server
- An application server (ColdFusion, J2EE, or .NET)
- Macromedia Flash Remoting MX (this is built into ColdFusion MX and JRun4)
- Microsoft Access or MySQL
- A web browser with Flash Player 7
- A text editor
- An extraction program (like WinZip or StuffIt)

1 Learning the Flash Interface

In this lesson, you become familiar with the Macromedia Flash MX 2004 authoring environment and use it to create the interface for a mortgage calculator. You will create a Flash document, add text, add an image and text fields to it, organize the content into layers, and finally publish it as a Flash application that is embedded in an HTML page. In later lessons, you add the code to calculate the payments.

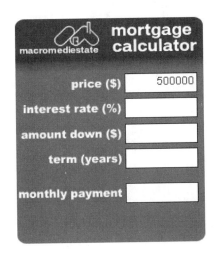

In this lesson, you create the Flash interface for a mortgage calculator.

What You Will Learn

In this lesson, you will:

- Create a Flash document
- Manipulate Flash interface panels
- Use tools in the Tools panel
- Add text to a Flash document
- Publish a Flash document as a SWF and an HTML page
- Embed a Flash application in an existing web page
- Organize content into layers
- Add images to a Flash document
- Create a Flash project

Approximate Time

This lesson takes approximately 90 minutes to complete.

Lesson Files

Asset Files:

/fpad2004/lesson01/start/assets/calculator.png

Starting Files:

/fpad2004/lesson01/start/aboutus.html

Completed Files:

/fpad2004/lesson01/complete/calculator.fla
/fpad2004/lesson01/complete/aboutus.html

Creating a Flash Document

The first step in developing a Flash application—whether for an animation, a presentation, or a full-blown web application—is creating a document. A Flash document contains the visual assets for your application: images, text, and user interface elements. You can also place your code in the document—or you can place your code in external files.

From within Flash, you can create seven types of files. A **Flash document** is the basic Flash file (with the extension FLA that rhymes with *draw*) to which you add content, media assets, and (optionally) code. In Flash MX Professional 2004, you can also create FLAs using an authoring environment architecture different than that for the traditional FLA: A **Flash slide presentation** uses slide screens to create slide-based content and a **Flash form application** uses form screens to create a form-based application. You can also create files that contain only code; **ActionScript files** (AS), **ActionScript Communication files** (ASC), and you can create external **ActionScript JavaScript** files (JSFL) in Flash or in any other text editor. Finally, a **Flash project file** (FLP) is an index for grouping related files (FLA, AS, JSFL, media files, and so on) and implementing version control options.

1. Copy the fpad2004 folder from the DVD-ROM included with this book to your computer.

You can place this folder anywhere on your computer—even on your desktop. If you plan to complete Lessons 13, "Consuming Web Services," and 14, "Accessing Remote Services Using Flash Remoting," which retrieve data from an application server, you should, however, place the fpad2004 folder in your web root. For example, if you are using the stand-alone ColdFusion server, place the folder in C:\CFusionMX\wwwroot\. All instructions in this book refer to opening and saving files to this folder. Starting and completed files for each lesson are located in a corresponding lesson folder. All files in the lesson folders are reference files. You should save all the files you create in the /fpad2004/mmestate/ folder so that you can easily work on the same files across all the lessons.

2. Launch Macromedia Flash MX Professional 2004.

The Flash Start page contains quick links to open recent files, create new Flash files, create files from templates, view tutorials, and update your help files.

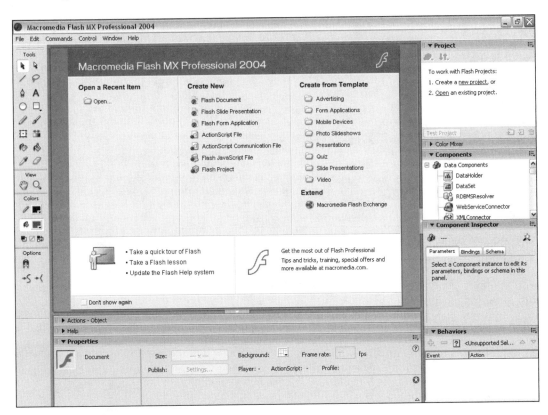

By default, the Start page displays when you open Flash and when you close all open documents. You can close the Start page and not have it display again by clicking the "Don't show again" check box in the lower left corner of the Start page.

Note *You can re-enable the Start page by selecting Edit > Preferences and selecting the Show Start Page radio button on the General tab.*

3. On the Start page, click Flash Document under Create New.

A new Flash document is created. The authoring environment should appear as shown in the following screenshot.

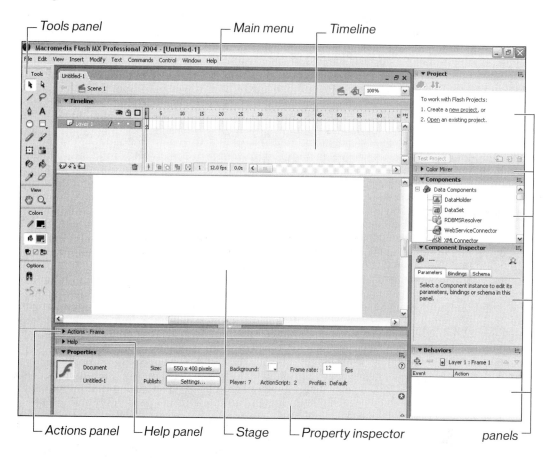

Main menu. The main menu bar allows you to control and edit the Flash authoring environment, including options for manipulating your files and customizing the authoring environment.

Stage. The Stage contains the visible elements of the document such as text, images, and user interface elements.

Timeline. The Timeline represents different phases, or frames, of an animation. In this book, you create application interfaces that are contained in a single frame; you do not create multiframe Flash animations.

Panels. Panels provide access to authoring tools and can be open, closed, minimized, and rearranged.

Tools panel. The Tools panel, also referred to as the **toolbar**, contains tools for creating text and vector graphics. Whenever you select a tool, the Property inspector automatically displays the properties associated with that tool.

Actions panel. The Actions panel, or **ActionScript editor**, is where you add ActionScript code to a document.

Help panel. The Help panel integrates all help information within the Flash authoring environment. New Help content can be downloaded from Macromedia.

Property inspector. The Properties panel, usually referred to as the Property inspector, provides an interface to modify commonly used attributes of documents and objects. It is context-sensitive, and the properties in the panel vary, depending on the type of object selected.

> **Tip** *You can also create a new document by selecting File › New from the main menu. If you prefer to use a more traditional document toolbar, you can make it visible by selecting Window › Toolbars › Main. You create a new document by clicking the New Document icon on the document toolbar.*

4. In the Property inspector, click the Size button.

The Document Properties dialog box opens. You can also access this dialog box by selecting Modify > Document.

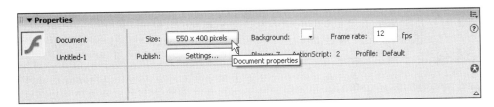

5. In the Document Properties dialog box, set the Dimensions width to *240 px* (pixels) and the height to *280 px* (pixel). Click OK.

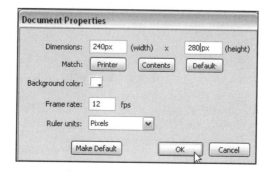

You are setting the height and width of the document to match the size of a calculator image you will import later in this lesson.

Look at the name of the file on the document tab near the top of the window. The asterisk next to the filename indicates that you have made changes to the file and the changes have not yet been saved. When you save the file, the asterisk disappears.

6. Select File › Save and save the document as *calculator.fla* in /fpad2004/mmestate/.

You can also save the file by pressing Ctrl+S (Windows) or Command+S (Macintosh). The new document name appears on the tab. You will use this document as the starting file for the next exercise. It should resemble the finished file: /fpad2004/lesson01/intermediate/calculator_doc.fla.

Manipulating Panels

The Flash authoring environment is comprised mostly of panels, which provide access to specific authoring tools. Each panel focuses on a particular functionality: aligning objects, selecting components, adding code, registering web services, and so on. You can find a list of the main panels in the Window menu. The remaining panels are divided into three categories: Design panels, Development panels, and Other panels.

Each panel can have three states:

- **Open.** The panel is visible in the interface with its content window displayed.
- **Collapsed.** The panel is visible as only a title bar with its content window hidden.
- **Closed.** The panel is not visible in the interface.

The position of the panels can be changed and each panel can be docked or undocked. In the following figure, the Align panel is undocked; all other panels are docked.

Closed panel ⌐   Open panel ⌐   Collapsed panel ⌐

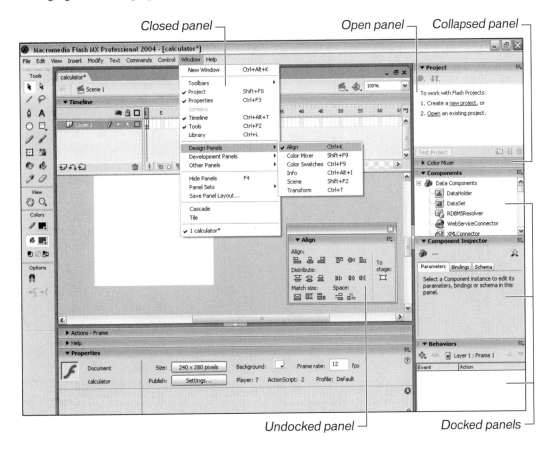

Undocked panel ⌐   Docked panels ⌐

You can customize panel layouts, specifying what panels are shown, where they are located, and their size. After you get a layout you like, you can also save the layout.

In this exercise, you manipulate panels and create a custom panel layout.

1. In Flash, return to calculator.fla in /fpad2004/mmestate/.

This is the document you created in the last exercise. If you did not do that exercise, open /fpad2004/lesson01/intermediate/calculator_doc.fla and save it as */fpad2004/mmestate/calculator.fla*.

2. Open the Color Mixer panel by clicking its name in the title bar.

The Color Mixer panel opens.

3. Undock the Color Mixer panel by placing the cursor over its panel gripper. Click and drag the panel to another location on the screen, and drop the panel in its new location.

The panel gripper is the group of dots to the left of the panel name in the panel title bar.

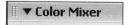

When you pass the cursor over the gripper, it changes to a four-sided pointer. To move the panel, click the gripper; while holding down the mouse button, drag the panel to a new location. Use this method to dock and undock panels, or change the order of the docked panels.

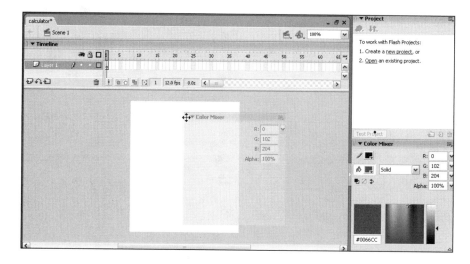

4. Close the Color Mixer panel by clicking the options menu icon in the upper right corner of the panel and selecting Close Panel.

Every panel has a context-sensitive options menu.

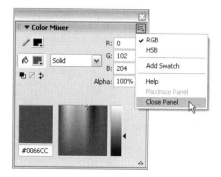

You can also right-click (Windows) or Control-click (Macintosh) the panel's title bar and select Close Panel from the drop-down list to close a panel or if the panel is undocked, you can click the X in the panel's upper right corner.

5. Open the Align panel by selecting Window > Design Panels > Align.

The Align panel appears, undocked, in your authoring environment. Use the Align panel to align multiple items on the Stage.

Note *If you select a panel from the Windows menu that is already open and docked, it is toggled between the open and collapsed states. Selecting an open, undocked panel toggles between open and closed states.*

6. Dock the Align panel on the right side of the screen by placing the cursor over its panel gripper, and click and drag the Align panel over the panels on the right side of the screen. Drop the panel when a black line appears between the docked panels.

When you move a panel over the docked panels, a thick black line appears, indicating where the panel would dock if you let go of the gripper.

If you move a panel over any other dockable region, a black box outline appears, showing you where the panel would dock if you let go of the gripper.

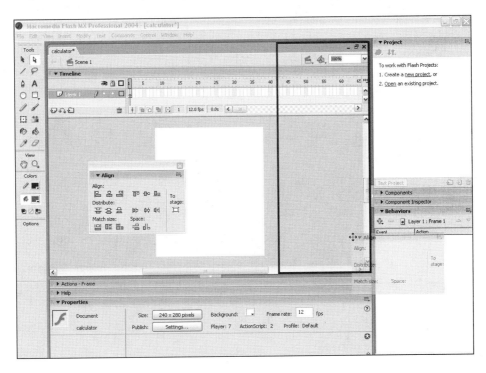

LEARNING THE FLASH INTERFACE

You can also move an undocked panel by clicking and dragging anywhere other than the gripper on its title bar; you can move but not dock a panel using this method.

7. **Rearrange the order of the docked panels on the right by clicking the gripper for one of the panels and dragging the panel up or down in the stack.**

Notice the black line move as you move the panel up and down the stack of docked panels.

8. **Decrease the size of the Project panel by dragging the bottom border of the panel upward.**

When you place the cursor over the border, it should change to a two-sided arrow.

9. **Hide all the docked panels on the right by clicking the arrow button on the left side of the panel grouping.**

This is a quick way to hide all the panels on the right, giving you a larger Stage to work on.

> **Tip** *You can hide all the panels, not just the panels on the right, by selecting Window > Hide Panels or pressing F4. Select Window > Hide Panels or press F4 again to restore the panels.*

10. **Restore the panels by clicking the arrow button and dragging it to the left.**

Release the arrow button when the panels are at the desired width. If you release the arrow button before the panels' minimum required width, the panels default to the minimum width.

> **Tip** *You can restore the panels to their previous width by clicking and releasing the arrow button.*

11. Save the panel set by selecting Window > Save Panel Layout. Give the panel layout the name *fpad2004* and click **OK**.

Make sure to always give panel layouts meaningful names. When you create a custom panel layout, a file with the name of the panel layout is created in the user-specific Flash configuration folder.

For Windows, this folder is <boot drive>:\Documents and Settings\<user>\Local Settings\ Application Data\Macromedia\Flash MX 2004\<language>\Configuration\Panel Sets\.

For Macs, it is <Macintosh HD>/Users <username>/Library/Application Support/Macromedia/ Flash MX 2004/<language>/Configuration/Panel Sets/.

To delete a custom panel set, you must manually delete the file from the configuration folder.

12. Return to the default panel layout by selecting Window > Panel Sets > Default Layout.

The default panel layout contains the Color Mixer panel instead of the Align panel.

13. Switch back to your custom panel layout by selecting Window > Panel Sets > fpad2004.

Your custom panel layout displays the Align panel.

Using the Tools Panel

The Tools panel contains tools for creating text and vector graphics. When you select a tool, the Property inspector automatically displays the properties associated with that tool. In this book, you will use the Text, Selection, and Free Transform tools to build application interfaces.

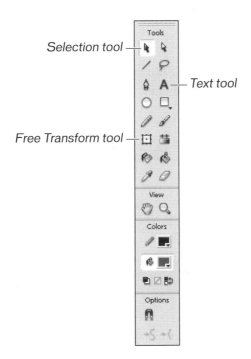

Text tool. Use the Text tool to add text. You can use the Property inspector to adjust the size, typeface, style, spacing, color, direction, and alignment of your text. You can also turn text into a hyperlink by specifying a URL.

Selection tool. Use the Selection tool to move or modify objects on the Stage. To move a single object, click and drag the object using the Selection tool. To select multiple objects, click and drag to select all objects within a rectangular area on the Stage.

Free Transform tool. Use the Free Transform tool to change the size of objects. Depending on the object selected, you can transform, rotate, skew, scale, or distort the object.

> **Tip** *You can change which tools are displayed in the Tools panel by selecting Edit › Customize Tools panel.*

In this exercise, you add text fields to your calculator interface—manipulating their size, content, and location.

1. In Flash, return to calculator.fla in /fpad2004/mmestate/.

This is the document you created in the first exercise of this lesson. If you did not do that exercise, open /fpad2004/lesson01/intermediate/calculator_doc.fla and save it as */fpad2004/mmestate/ calculator.fla.*

2. Click the Text tool in the Tools panel.

The cursor changes to a cross hair (+) with an A next to it.

3. Click anywhere on the Stage to create a text field.

In the Property inspector, make sure the Static Text option is selected in the pop-up menu in the left corner. These text options will be explored in the next exercise.

4. Type the text *price ($)* in the text field.

The text field expands as you type, changing size as you add text.

5. Click anywhere on the Stage to remove focus from the text field.

Do not click the text field itself. Notice that after you draw a text field, the Text tool remains active, as indicated by the cross-hair cursor.

6. Click and drag to create a second text field below the text field on the Stage. Enter the text *interest rate*.

When you click and drag to create a text field, you give the text field a specific width. If you enter less text than needed to fill the text field, the field will have white space. If you enter a lot of text, it wraps to a new line.

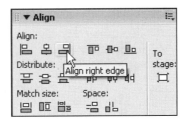

7. Click the Selection tool in the Tools panel. Click and drag a rectangle around both text fields.

When you release the mouse button, a bounding box surrounds both text fields.

Tip *You can also select multiple objects by holding down the Shift key as you click them.*

8. In the Align panel, click the Align right-edge button.

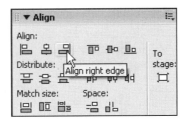

When you click the Align right-edge button, the text fields align to the rightmost edge of the selected items. In general, when you use the Align panel, items align to the edge of the item closest to the alignment you selected. For example, if you select Align top edge, the items will align to the top edge of the item nearest the top of the Stage. To align items relative to the Stage instead of to each other, click the To Stage button on the right side of the Align panel before clicking a specific align button.

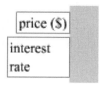

Tip *If you place the cursor over a button in a panel, a tooltip is displayed.*

9. Click anywhere on the Stage to deselect the text fields.

Do not click on the text fields. The document is now selected, as reflected in the Property inspector.

10. Click the Text tool and then click the interest rate text field. Change its value to *interest rate (%)*.

You can also edit a text field by double-clicking the text field using the Selection tool.

11. Resize the interest rate text field by dragging the text field handle.

The text field handle is the box that appears in the upper right corner when the text field is selected.

Drag the handle to the left or the right. Notice the size of the text field changes but the size of the text inside the text field does not change.

12. Double-click the interest rate text field handle in the upper right corner.

interest|rate (%)

When you double-click the text field handle, the size of the text field changes to fit the text.

Note *When the size of the text field is manually set, the text field handle is a square. When the size is automatically set, the text field handle is a circle.*

If you have a line break after the first word, remove it so all the text is on one line.

13. With the interest rate text field still selected, change the X and Y coordinates to *0* and *100* in the Property inspector.

In order for any value set in the Property inspector to be applied to the selected object, you must remove focus from that value in the Property inspector. You can press Enter or Tab, select another value field in the Property inspector, or select an object on the Stage.

14. With the interest rate text field still selected, change the width (the W: field) to *300* in the Property inspector.

This step changes the size of the text field and proportionately changes the size of the text inside the text field, which is usually not what you want. To change the size of the text field without changing the size of the text, use the text handle as in Step 11 or 12.

interest rate (%)

15. With the interest rate text field still selected, click the Free Transform tool in the Tools panel. Drag one of the handles to change the text field's size.

interest rate (%)

Like changing the width in the Property inspector, this method also changes the size of the text field and the text.

16. Press Ctrl+Z until your text field is back to its original size and position.

price ($)
interest rate (%)

You can also undo your previous steps by selecting Edit > Undo last step, where *last step* is whatever operation you last performed. Make sure that the text fields are set to size automatically and are aligned to their right edges.

17. Save the document as *calculator.fla* in /fpad2004/mmestate/.

You will use this as the starting file for the next exercise. It should resemble the finished file: /fpad2004/lesson01/intermediate/calculator_tools.fla.

Adding Text

In the last exercise, you used the Text tool to create static text—text visually placed on the Stage that does not and cannot change during application runtime. You can also use the Text tool to create input and dynamic text. The three different types of text are as follows:

- **Static.** A text field placed on the Stage that cannot change during application runtime. Static text is often used for labels, titles, or descriptive blocks of text.

- **Input.** A text field in which users can input text in the application. You can create and modify input text fields using ActionScript as well as capture and programmatically use any text entered by the user. Input text fields are much like HTML text input controls.

- **Dynamic.** A text field whose content and properties can be modified programmatically during the application runtime with ActionScript. Dynamic text fields can also be created with ActionScript.

You can change the type of text field in the Property inspector using the drop-down list near the upper left corner.

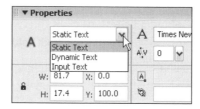

When you add text to a document, you must decide whether you want the text displayed in the application using embedded fonts or device fonts:

Embedded fonts. The specified font is downloaded with the application. Using embedded fonts ensures that the exact font is available and used in the application. Embedding fonts adds to the file size.

Device fonts. Fonts on the client computer are used to display the text in the application. Using device fonts decreases the file size of the download, because the Flash Player communicates with the client's operating system to display the Flash text with a font installed on their computer. If the font you specified is not available on the client's computer, a font with the closest match is used.

> **Note** *You can use device fonts only with horizontal text; you cannot use them with vertical text.*

You set the font behavior settings in the Property inspector. The default font behavior depends on the type of text:

Static text. By default, static text uses embedded fonts because only a subset of characters needs to be included in the file.

Input and dynamic text. By default, input and dynamic text fields use device fonts because you do not know ahead of time what characters will be displayed in the text field, so you would have to download all the font characters.

In this exercise, you create input and dynamic text fields for your calculator. Input text fields are used to get the house price, the down payment, the loan interest rate, and the length of the loan in years from the user. A dynamic text field is used to display the calculated monthly payment.

1. **In Flash, return to calculator.fla in /fpad2004/mmestate/.**

This is the document you created in the last exercise. If you did not do that exercise, open /fpad2004/lesson01/intermediate/calculator_tools.fla and save it as */fpad2004/mmestate/ calculator.fla.*

2. **Create three additional static text fields:** *amount down ($)*, *term (years)*, **and** *monthly payment*.

Place these fields under the two existing text fields.

3. **Using the Selection tool, select all five text fields and modify their properties in the Property inspector. Change the font to Arial Black and the size to 14.**

You should see a "Use device fonts" check box in the Property inspector. By default, this check box is not selected because static fields use embedded fonts. To use device fonts instead, select this check box.

4. **With all the text fields still selected, use the Align panel to align their right edges and distribute them from their vertical centers.**

The Distribute Vertical Center button is the second button in the second row in the Align panel.

5. With all the text fields still selected, use the arrow keys on your keyboard to move the text fields to the left edge of the document.

The arrow keys provide a way to fine-tune object placement, which is not easy using the mouse.

6. Click anywhere on the Stage to deselect the text fields, click the Text tool, and create a new text field to the right of the price ($) field.

You will change this text field into an input text field and format it in the next steps.

7. In the Property inspector, set the Text type to Input Text and check the "Show border around text" button.

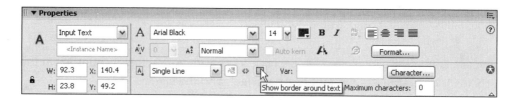

The user will enter the house price in this text field.

> **Tip** *Always use a visual cue for an input text field so a user can see the text field and know that he or she needs to input data.*

8. Still in the Property inspector, click the Character button and confirm that No Characters is selected in the Character Options dialog box. Click OK to close the dialog box.

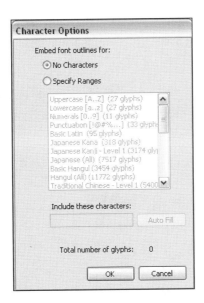

When you see a Character button in the Property inspector, device fonts will be used to display the text entered by the user in the text field.

Note *To use embedded fonts, click the Character button, select the Specify Ranges radio button in the Character Options dialog box, and either select one or more character ranges or specify individual characters to include.*

9. With the Selection tool, make a copy of the input text field (Ctrl+S (Windows) or Command+S (Macintosh)) and drag the copy to a new location.

This is a quick way to create copies of objects. Notice that when you drag the copy, guidelines appear to aid you in aligning the object with existing objects. You can turn off the guidelines by selecting View > Snapping > Snap Align.

Tip *You can also make a copy of objects by using the File > Edit menu or the keyboard shortcuts Ctrl+C and Ctrl+V (Windows) or Command+C and Command+V (Macintosh) to copy and paste.*

10. Make three more copies of the input text field and align all the fields using the Align panel so they appear as shown in the following screenshot.

price ($)

interest rate (%)

amount down ($)

term (years)

monthly payment

Leave a little extra space above the monthly payment text field to set it off from the input text fields.

11. Select the input text field next to monthly payment and change it to dynamic text in the Property inspector.

You do not want the monthly payment text field to be an input field because the monthly payment will be calculated from the input fields.

12. Double-click the price ($) text field and enter *5000000*.

The text appears aligned to the left edge of the text field.

13. Select the five input and dynamic text fields. In the Property inspector, select Arial font and click the Align Right button.

The text in the price text field is now aligned to the right inside the text field. Text added to the other text fields by the user will also appear aligned to the right.

14. Save the document as *calculator.fla* in /fpad2004/mmestate/.

You will use this as the starting file for the next exercise. It should resemble the finished file: /fpad2004/lesson01/intermediate/calculator_text.fla.

Publishing a Flash Document

Documents created in the Flash environment are FLA files, which is short for FLAsh files. FLA files are your authoring files where you add application elements and write code for the user to interact with the elements.

For users to view your files with their Flash Player, the FLA files need to be compiled into SWF files (pronounced as "swif" files). SWF stands for Small Web Format. These SWF files are referred to as Flash applications. They are also commonly referred to as movies because Flash was originally an animation tool and is still used to create animations or movies.

You can test your Flash applications by publishing the FLA file—which creates the corresponding SWF file. The Flash application can be viewed by doing any of the following:

- Browsing a web page (HTML, CFM, JSP, and so on) that contains the embedded SWF file. The browser must have the Flash Player plug-in.

- Browsing the SWF file in a web browser. The browser must have the Flash Player plug-in. This method is not advised, however, because you cannot view a SWF in some browsers on some platforms—even with the Flash plug-in installed.

- Opening the SWF as a stand-alone application using the Flash Player. To view the SWF outside a browser, users must have a stand-alone version of the Flash Player installed.

- Publishing the SWF as a projector file (EXE or HQX) and running the executable. A copy of the Flash Player is included in the projector file so the user does not need the Flash Player installed.

Note *The latest version of the Flash Player can be downloaded from http://www.macromedia.com/downloads/.*

The following screenshot shows the workflow to publish and view a Flash application on the Internet.

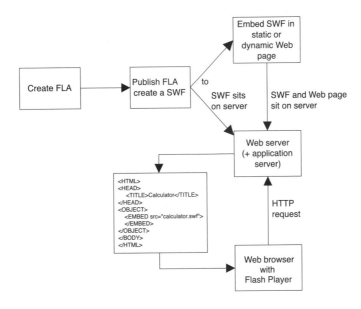

Creating SWFs and HTML Pages Containing SWFs

There are two ways to publish a FLA document to create a SWF:

- **Directly.** Select File > Publish. By default, this procedure creates a SWF and an HTML file in the same folder as the FLA. The HTML file contains `<object>` and `<embed>` tags to include the SWF. The types of files created when you publish a FLA and the properties of those files can be modified in a Publish Settings dialog box.

- **Indirectly.** Select Control > Test Movie or press Ctrl+Enter (Windows) or Command+Return (Macintosh). A SWF is created and saved in the same folder as the FLA document; a window opens to display the SWF, the Flash application.

Both methods create a SWF corresponding to the *current* state of the open FLA document—not the last saved state.

> **Note** *The FLA document is not automatically saved when you publish using either method.*

In this exercise, you publish your calculator application as a SWF and as a SWF embedded in a new HTML page.

1. In Flash, return to calculator.fla in /fpad2004/mmestate/.

Return to the document you created in the last exercise or open /fpad2004/lesson01/intermediate/ calculator_text.fla and save it as *calculator.fla* in /fpad2004/mmestate/.

2. Publish the document by selecting Control › Test Movie or pressing Ctrl+Enter (Windows) or Command+Return (Macintosh).

Publishing the FLA creates a SWF corresponding to the current state of the FLA but does not save the current FLA file if you have made changes to it.

3. Enter text in the input text fields and then close the SWF window.

You can close the SWF window by clicking the x in the upper right corner of the window or by pressing Ctrl+W (Windows) or Command+W (Macintosh). You can also leave the SWF open and return to the FLA by clicking the appropriate tab at the top of the window.

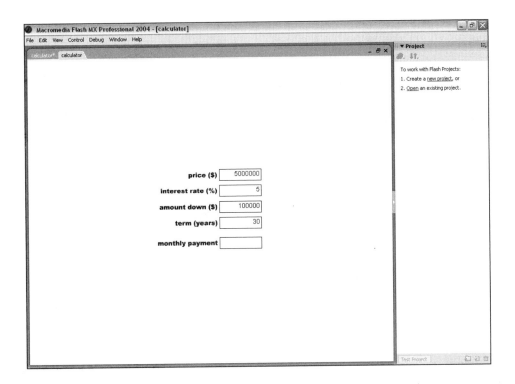

4. Select File > Publish Settings.

The Publish Settings dialog box opens.

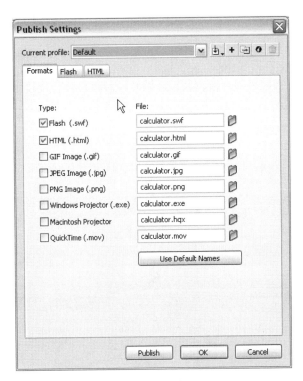

The Flash and HTML check boxes are checked by default on the Formats tab. When you publish the document, SWF and HTML files with the same name as the FLA but with different file extensions are created in the same folder as the FLA. You can publish the files with different names or in different locations by changing the filename and path in the File field next to each file in the Type field.

> **Tip** *Each FLA has a default publish settings profile. If you change the publish settings, the profile is updated and the new settings are retained for the FLA; you do not need to change the settings every time you publish the document. You can also create multiple publish settings profiles for a FLA, which is handy when you publish files to multiple locations. To create a new profile, click the Create New Profile button at the top of the Publish Settings dialog box and give the new profile a name. The new profile appears in the Current Profile pop-up menu. You can then change the settings for that profile and switch back and forth between the profiles.*

> **Tip** *You can also reuse profiles across multiple FLAs. To make a profile available to other FLAs, you must export the FLA by clicking the Import/Export Profile button and name the profile. This export process creates an XML file in the configuration Publish Profiles directory. For Windows, this folder is ‹boot drive›:\Documents and Settings\‹user›\Local Settings\Application Data\Macromedia\Flash MX 2004\‹language›\Configuration\Publish Profiles\. For Macs, it is ‹Macintosh HD›/Users‹username›/Library/ Application Support/ Macromedia/Flash MX 2004/‹language›/Configuration/Publish Profiles/. After exporting the profile, you can then use it for other FLAs by opening the Publish Settings dialog box for a new FLA and importing the profile by clicking the Import/Export Profile button and selecting the profile you saved.*

5. Click Publish and then OK to close the dialog box.

The SWF and HTML files that you specified in the Publish Settings dialog box (calculator.swf and calculator.html) are created.

6. Select File > Publish Preview and then select Default (HTML).

When you select File > Publish Preview > {file type}, the files specified in the Publish Settings dialog box are created and the file type you select from the pop-up menu is opened in the appropriate program: A SWF is displayed within the Flash authoring environment; all other types of files are displayed in a browser. In this case, SWF and HTML files are created, and calculator.html is displayed in a browser window. (The system default browser is used.)

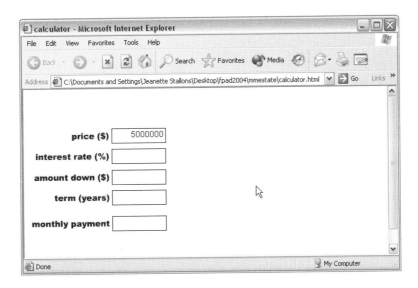

This method browses to the file using the local file system. If you saved the fpad2004 folder in your web root, you could also browse to it directly on your web server.

7. Select View > Source. Briefly examine the code and then close the window.

The code contains the `<object>` and `<embed>` tags needed to display the Flash application in a browser window using the Flash Player plug-in.

```
<object classid="clsid:d27cdb6e-ae6d-11cf-96b8-444553540000"¬
codebase="http://download.macromedia.com/pub/shockwave/cabs/flash/¬
swflash.cab#version=7,0,0,0" width="240" height="280" id="calculator"¬
align="middle">
<param name="allowScriptAccess" value="sameDomain" />
<param name="movie" value="calculator.swf" />
<param name="quality" value="high" />
<param name="bgcolor" value="#ffffff" />
<embed src="calculator.swf" quality="high" bgcolor="#ffffff" width="240"¬
height="280" name="calculator" align="middle" allowScriptAccess="sameDomain"¬
type="application/x-shockwave-flash" pluginspage="http://www.macromedia.com/¬
go/getflashplayer" />
```

Adding Flash Player Version Detection

What happens if a user tries to view your Flash application but doesn't have the Flash Player plug-in installed? Or what if a user doesn't have the correct plug-in version? The results vary depending on their browser. If the user does not have *any* version of the Flash Player installed, most browsers either open a Security Warning dialog box with instructions to install the latest version from Macromedia or display a link so the user can download the plug-in. The information needed by the browser for the download is included in the `<object>` and `<embed>` tags created for the Flash application in the HTML page.

If a user has the wrong version of the Flash Player, your application will usually display, but will not function correctly. To make sure the user has the right version, you can have Flash add code that checks for a specific version of the Flash Player in the HTML page that is created when you publish the FLA. Then, if users try to view a Flash application and they do not have the correct version, they are prompted to update.

In this exercise, you publish your Flash application in an HTML page that has Flash Player version detection implemented.

1. In Flash, return to calculator.fla in /fpad2004/mmestate/.

Return to the document you created in the last exercise or open /fpad2004/lesson01/intermediate/ calculator_text.fla and save it as calculator.fla in /fpad2004/mmestate/.

2. Select File > Publish Settings. Click the HTML tab, select the Detect Flash Version check box, and click the Settings button.

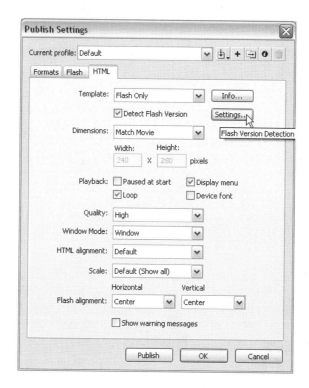

A Version Detection Settings dialog box opens.

3. Look at the settings in the Version Detection Settings dialog box and then click **OK.**

When you publish the FLA with these default settings selected, a group of files is created that together check and make sure the user has Flash Player 7.0.0 or later. You can change these Version Detection Settings to check for other major and/or minor revision numbers of the Flash Player.

The following files will be created when you publish the FLA:

calculator.swf. This is the same swf Flash application file created without version detection selected.

calculator.html. This is a new version of the HTML file and contains an embedded Flash application, flash_detection.swf, which checks to see whether the user has a specific version or later of the Flash Player. If an appropriate Flash Player version is detected, calculator_content.html is displayed. If an appropriate Flash Player version is not detected, calculator_alternate.html is displayed.

calculator_content.html. This is the same as the HTML file created when you published your FLA without version detection: calculator.html.

calculator_alternate.html. This is an HTML file containing a message that a later version of the Flash Player is required to view the content and includes a download link.

flash_detection.swf. This is a Flash application file that checks to see whether the user has a specific version or later of the Flash Player installed.

alternate.gif. This is a Get Macromedia Flash Player image that is used in calculator_alternate.html.

4. Click **OK** to close the **Publish Settings** dialog box.

Because you did not click Publish, the six files specified in Step 3 are not yet created.

5. Select File > Publish Preview > Default (HTML).

The six files listed in Step 3 are created, and calculator.html is displayed in a browser window. If you have the correct version of the Flash Player installed, you are redirected to calculator_content.html where you see the calculator application. If you do not have the correct version of the Flash Player installed, you are redirected to calculator_alternate.html. The calculator_alternate.html page is shown here.

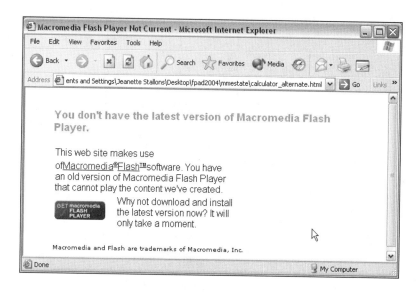

Embedding SWFs in Existing Web Pages

In the previous exercises, you published your SWF application in *new* HTML pages. You can also embed your Flash applications in existing HTML or application server pages (such as ColdFusion, JSP, or ASP).

One way to embed the SWF is to simply publish your Flash document as HTML (as you did previously), view the source code for the generated HTML file, and copy and paste the generated code into your existing web page. A second, more direct way is to use the tools in Dreamweaver MX or later to add the necessary code. Dreamweaver also provides tools for playing the Flash application from within the authoring environment without going to a browser, modifying parameters of the embedded Flash application with the Property inspector, and editing the FLA source file.

In this exercise, you embed the Flash calculator application in an existing HTML page for the Macromediestate website.

1. Open Dreamweaver MX 2004.

You will use Dreamweaver to embed your Flash calculator application into an existing HTML web page for the Macromediestate website.

2. In Dreamweaver, open aboutus.html in /fpad2004/lesson01/start/.

Make sure that you are in Dreamweaver's Design mode by clicking the Design button in the upper left corner.

3. Save the file as *aboutus.html* in /fpad2004/mmestate/. In the Update Links dialog box, click Yes. Browse the HTML page by pressing F12.

This is an HTML page for the Macromediestate website.

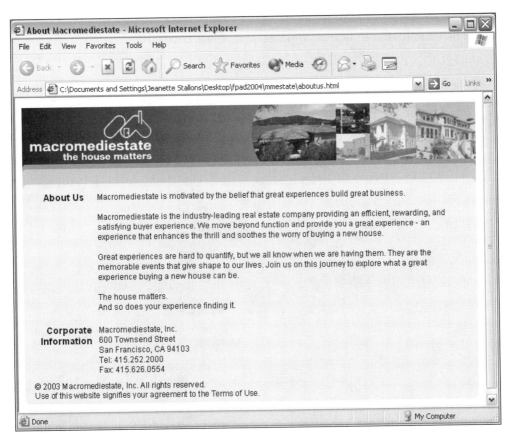

4. Close the browser window and return to Dreamweaver. Place your cursor in the largest empty table cell in the lower right corner of the page.

You will insert the Flash calculator application you are building into this area of the page.

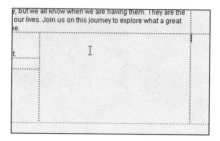

5. Select Insert > Media > Flash. In the Select File dialog box, browse to and select calculator.swf, located in /fpad2004/mmestate/. Click OK.

This process embeds the Flash application in the existing HTML page. In Dreamweaver's Design mode, a gray box with a Flash logo represents the SWF; the gray box is the same size as the embedded Flash application.

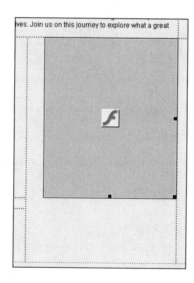

6. Click the embedded Flash application to select it and click the Play button in the Dreamweaver Property inspector.

You see a live version of the embedded Flash application in the Dreamweaver authoring environment. Enter some text in the input fields.

If you do not see the Play button, make sure the inserted SWF file is selected and then click the expander arrow in the bottom right corner of the Property inspector.

Tip *You can also click the Edit button in the Dreamweaver Property inspector to open the SWF source FLA for editing in the Flash authoring environment.*

7. Click the Stop button in the Property inspector.

The live preview of the Flash calculator embedded in the HTML page ends.

8. Save the document and browse the application by pressing F12.

You should see your Flash calculator embedded in the HTML page in a browser window.

9. Return to Dreamweaver and select the Flash application. Change the application's width to *180,* the height to *210,* and the background color to *#EFEFEF* in the Property inspector.

This step changes the size of the embedded Flash application and makes its background color the same color as the background of the table.

10. Save the document and then press F12 to browse the document.

Your Flash calculator is now smaller and has a gray background.

Organizing Content into Layers

As your Flash documents become more complex, it is useful to organize the content in separate layers to make it easier to find and select a particular item. Layers are different tiers of content that sit on top of each other.

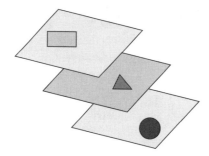

The order of the layers reflects the stacking order of objects in those layers. Stacking order only matters if you have visible objects that overlap on the Stage. Moving a layer up in the stack places the contents of that layer higher in the stacking order, above the objects in the layers beneath it. Layers in Flash are a design-time feature; they do not exist and cannot be manipulated programmatically at runtime. When the FLA document is compiled into a SWF, the layers are "flattened" and objects are simply located at different depths relative to one another.

Document layers are shown in the Layers pane on the left side of the Timeline panel. Within the Layers pane, you can create, name, arrange, and delete layers. You can also lock and hide layers and organize the layers into folders. The following screenshot shows the content layers organized together in the Layers pane.

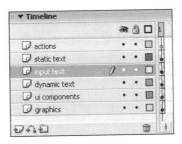

To place content into a particular layer, you must select the appropriate layer *before* adding an item to your document. If you place an item in the wrong layer, simply cut the misplaced item, select the correct layer, and paste the item.

Creating and Arranging Layers

In this exercise, you create a new layer, add content to it, and then change its location in the layer stacking order.

1. In Flash, return to calculator.fla in /fpad2004/mmestate/.

Return to the document you created in the adding text exercise or open /fpad2004/lesson01/ intermediate/calculator_text.fla and save it as *calculator.fla* in /fpad2004/mmestate/.

2. In the Timeline panel, click Layer 1 to select it.

When you select a layer, all the content located in that layer is surrounded by a highlight bounding box. Right now all your content is located in Layer 1.

3. Create a new layer by clicking the Insert Layer button in the lower left corner of the Layer pane in the Timeline panel.

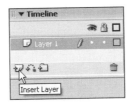

Layer 2 is created. The new layer is added above whatever layer was selected. You can also add a new layer when you right-click (Windows) or Control-click (Macintosh) an existing layer and select Insert Layer from the pop-up list. This process also adds the new layer above the selected layer.

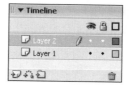

Look at the circles in the first frame of the Timeline; the filled circle means all your elements are in Layer 1. Layer 2, which has an empty circle, has no content.

4. With Layer 2 selected in the Layer pane, use the Text tool to create a static text field at the bottom of the Stage.

This procedure creates a new text field in Layer 2.

5. Type *TEST* in the new text field. Use the Property inspector to change the font to bold, with a size of **30** and a color of light gray.

You need a light color for the text so that you when you drag the text on top of the existing text fields in the next step, you can see which text field is on top.

6. Select the new text field and drag it on top of one of the existing static text fields.

The new text in Layer 2 appears above the text in Layer 1 because Layer 2 is located above Layer 1 in the Layer pane of the Timeline panel.

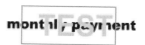

7. In the Timeline panel, click Layer 1 to select it. Drag and drop Layer 1 above Layer 2 so that Layer 1 is the first layer in the stack.

Your new text should now appear below all the other text.

monthly payment

8. Save the document as *calculator.fla* in /fpad2004/mmestate/.

It should resemble the finished file: /fpad2004/lesson01/intermediate/calculator_layersA.fla.

Placing Content in Layers

In this exercise, you create new layers for the calculator application and place the appropriate content in each layer.

1. In Flash, return to calculator.fla in /fpad2004/mmestate/.

Return to the document you created in the last exercise or open /fpad2004/lesson01/intermediate/ calculator_layersA.fla and save it as *calculator.fla* in */fpad2004/mmestate/*.

2. Double-click Layer 1 and rename it *static text*.

Make sure you always give your layers descriptive names.

3. Click Layer 2 and drag and drop it in the trash can in the lower right corner of the Layer pane.

You can also delete a layer by right-clicking (Windows) or Control-clicking (Macintosh) the layer and selecting Delete Layer from the pop-up menu.

4. Create four new layers called *input text*, *dynamic text*, *background*, and *actions*.

It does not matter what order the layers are in right now; you will change their order later.

5. Increase the height of the Layer pane by placing the cursor on the border between the Layer pane and the Stage and dragging the border downward until you can see all the layers in the list.

Your cursor turns into a set of parallel lines with arrows when it is in the right position to drag the border.

6. Increase the width of the Layer pane by placing the cursor on the border between the Layer pane and the Timeline and dragging the border to the right.

7. Click the Insert Layer Folder button in the lower left corner of the Layer pane.

This step adds a layer folder above the layer you had highlighted.

8. Rename the layer folder text and drag and drop the three text layers into the text layer folder.

By placing layers in a folder, you can manipulate them as a group, hiding or locking all the layers at once. You can also collapse the folder so that only the folder and not the individual layers are visible in the Layer pane. This process helps you organize and navigate the Layer pane when you have lots of layers.

9. Click the actions layer to select it and drag and drop it above all the other layers so it is the first layer in the stack. Next, if necessary, move the background layer so that it is the bottom layer.

In the next exercise, you import an image into the Flash document and place it in this background layer. In Lesson 2, "Learning ActionScript Fundamentals," you start writing code for your calculator. You will place the code in the actions layer.

> **Note** For documents that contain code, it is a best practice to place all the code in a layer called actions, which is the first layer in the Layer pane.

10. Select the four input text fields on the Stage and select Edit > Cut.

You need to remove these fields from the static text layer and place them in the input text layer.

11. Click the input text layer in the Timeline panel and select Edit > Paste in Place.

This procedure pastes the fields exactly where they were on the Stage but in a new layer.

12. Move the one dynamic text field to the dynamic text layer.

Use the procedure given in Steps 10 and 11. You now have all the content in an appropriate layer.

13. Hide the static text layer by clicking the bullet in the Eye column. Click it again to make the layer visible.

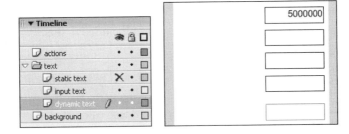

It is often useful to hide layers to make it easier to work on individual graphics when there are many graphics in the work area on the Stage.

14. Lock the text folder by clicking the bullet in the Lock column. Try to edit or move any of the text.

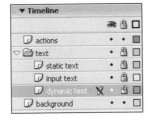

You lock layers to prevent their content from being inadvertently edited. When you lock a folder, all the layers inside the folder are locked. You can toggle back and forth between locked and unlocked states by clicking the bullet in the Lock column.

15. Save the document as *calculator.fla* in /fpad2004/mmestate/.

It should resemble the finished file: /fpad2004/lesson01/intermediate/calculator_layersB.fla.

Adding Images

Flash provides a wide range of tools to create, import, edit, and manipulate different graphics. When you import an image into a Flash document, the image is placed on the Stage and added to the document's Library panel as a bitmap symbol. (You can also import images directly to the library without placing a copy on the Stage.) Each document has its own library that contains the assets used in that document (such as bitmaps, graphics, sounds, and buttons). The library is simply another Flash panel that provides an interface to the Flash document's associated assets.

When you import a graphic from a program that supports layers such as Fireworks, you have the option to flatten or retain the layers when you import it into Flash.

You can use multiple copies of an asset in a document by clicking the asset in the library and dragging an instance of the asset onto the Stage. Because all copies refer to the same asset, using multiple copies of the asset in your document does not increase the file size. In fact, an asset that exists in the library but is not used in the document is not included in the SWF when the FLA is published and hence, does not contribute to the file size of the application.

If you edit an asset in the library, all instances of the asset used in the document are modified.

In this exercise, you import a background image for your Flash calculator.

1. In Flash, return to calculator.fla in /fpad2004/mmestate/.

Return to the document you created in the last exercise or open /fpad2004/lesson01/intermediate/ calculator_layersB.fla and save it as *calculator.fla* in /fpad2004/mmestate/.

2. Test the application by pressing Ctrl+Enter (Windows) or Command+Return (Macintosh). In the SWF window, select View › Bandwidth Profiler or Ctrl+B (Windows) or Command+B (Macintosh).

The Bandwidth Profiler shows you the size of your application, and gives you a sense of the time it will take to download. Your application should be roughly 2KB in size.

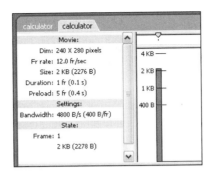

You can change the bandwidth setting used for the download time calculations by selecting View > Download Settings and selecting a new bandwidth. You can simulate the download for the specified download setting by selecting View > Simulate Download.

3. Close the SWF and select the background layer in the Layer pane.

You will place the image you import for the calculator in the next step in this background layer.

Note *It is a good practice to create layers for like elements on the Stage.*

4. Select File > Import > Import to Library. In the File Open dialog box, select calculator.png from /fpad2004/mmestate/assets/ and click Open.

A Fireworks PNG Import Settings dialog box appears. Because you are importing a graphic file that contains layers, you have the option to retain the layers when you import the graphic. If you are not going to edit the layers in Flash, you should flatten all the layers into one when you import the graphic.

Tip *You can also add images from other applications to the Stage and library by copying and pasting them into Flash.*

5. In the Fireworks PNG Import Settings dialog box, select the "Import as a single flattened bitmap" check box and click OK.

Your bitmap, calculator.png, is added to the library, but is not yet placed on the Stage.

6. Select Window > Library to open the Library panel. Click calculator in the Library panel to get a preview of the bitmap symbol.

When you import an image, it becomes a **bitmap** symbol in the library. You can also create **graphic** symbols. Create a graphic symbol when you want to combine multiple items including graphics created by the drawing tools, static text, bitmap symbols, and so on that you want to manipulate and reuse as a single entity. To create a graphic symbol, select the item(s), and either right-click (Windows) or Control-click (Macintosh) and select Convert to Symbol; you can also select Modify > Convert to Symbol. In the Convert to Symbol dialog box, select Graphic Behavior and give the symbol a name. The new graphic symbol appears in the library. You will learn about the other two behaviors listed in the dialog box, button and movie clip, in Lesson 4, "Creating Buttons and MovieClip Objects."

7. Test the application.

Your application should still only be about 2KB, even though the bitmap has been added to the library. Because you did not add the bitmap symbol to the document, it is not compiled in the SWF even though it is in the library for the FLA.

8. Close the SWF. Make sure the background layer is selected, and click calculator.png in the library and drag it to the Stage.

A copy of the bitmap symbol is now visible on the Stage.

9. In the Property inspector, set the X and Y coordinates of the bitmap to *0* and then test the application.

Your application should now be about 6KB.

10. Close the SWF and unlock the text folder in the Timeline panel.

You need to rearrange the text fields in relation to the new bitmap image.

11. Move the text fields as necessary to make them visible under the logo and change the font color for the static text fields to white.

12. Drag another instance of the calculator.png bitmap from the library to the Stage and then retest the application.

Your application should still be only 6KB. Adding additional instances of the bitmap symbol to the Stage does not increase the file size.

13. Select View > Bandwidth Profiler to turn off the profiler. Close the SWF file.

When you turn on the Bandwidth Profiler, it displays each time you test an application until you deselect the option.

14. Delete the second copy of the calculator bitmap from the Stage.

Deleting all instances of an asset from the Stage does not remove the asset from the library. Anything added to the library remains in the library until you delete it from the library.

15. Lock the background layer and the text layer folder.

Locking these layers prevents you from accidentally moving the background image or the text fields when you are trying to select other elements on the Stage.

16. Save the document as *calculator.fla* in /fpad2004/mmestate/.

It should resemble the finished file: /fpad2004/lesson01/intermediate/calculator_image.fla.

17. From Dreamweaver or in a browser window, browse to /fpad2004/mmestate/ aboutus.html.

You should see your new and improved calculator interface in the Macromediestate web page.

Creating a Flash Project

A Flash Project helps you manage and organize files located in various directories in one place within the Flash authoring environment. A Project panel provides a quick visual way to view and open files without navigating directories in the File Open dialog box.

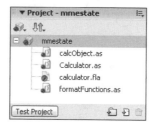

When you create a Flash project, an FLP file is created, which is an XML file that contains the names and locations of files you want to include in your project. The Project panel is populated using this XML file.

After you create the project file, you can add files from any location on your computer. The files do not have to be located in the same directory, which allows you to group files together in the project that are located in different directories on your computer. The Flash project does not have to reflect a particular directory structure. You also have the ability to manually create folders for the project in the Project panel, so you can make your project files match your physical directory structure if you want.

If you are working with a team of developers on the same files, you can share a single Flash project file and use version control for the files in the Flash project.

Version Control

Flash's version control capabilities are similar to those available in Dreamweaver MX and later. Local/Network and FTP access protocols are provided along with a plug-in interface to allow integration with SourceSafe (Windows only).

> **Tip** *Although there are no plug-ins provided for WebDAV, RDS, SVN, CVS, or other version control systems, Macromedia provides information on the plug-in interface if you want to write your plug-in. For more information, go to http://www.macromedia.com/ support/dreamweaver/downloads/scheaderfile.html.*

To use version control, you must create a site or point to an existing site. A **site** is a collection of files and folders on a server that corresponds to your web site. Site definitions are shared between Dreamweaver MX 2004 and Flash MX Professional 2004. You can create a new site or edit an existing site for the project from within Flash by selecting File > Edit Sites or by clicking the Version Control button in the Project panel.

After you define a site for a Flash project, you can check in and check out files using version control from the Project panel. Status icons appear next to the filenames in the Project panel:

Green check mark. You have the file checked out. You can make changes on your local file copy.

Red check mark. Someone else has the file checked out. You cannot make changes to the file until the file is checked back in and you check it out. Just as with Dreamweaver, two people cannot have the same file checked out at the same time. If you attempt to check out a file that is already checked out by someone else, you will be asked if you want to override the other person's checkout.

Lock. The file is checked into the version control system, and no one has it checked out. Your local version of the copy is locked and you cannot make changes to it.

No icon. You have added the file to the project, but the file has not yet been uploaded to the server. In order to check in a file to the server if you are using a shared project file, you must first check out the project file and then add the file to the project. Finally, you need to check in both the project file and the new file.

You can refresh the Project panel, which checks the status of the files on the server and updates their icons in your Project panel. The refresh mechanism does not, however, add new files to the Project panel, even if someone has added a new file to a shared project file. The Project panel does not have automatic updating or syncing functionality. So if you want to see whether new files have been added to the Flash project by other team members, you need to check out the project FLP file from the server. Any new files in the project will appear in your Project panel, but will have a missing file icon. To add a missing file, select the missing file, right-click (Windows) or Control-click (Macintosh), and select "Get file from Version Control."

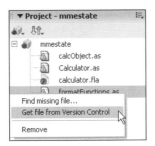

In this exercise, you create and add files to a Flash project, create a site that points to a folder in your web root, and set up source control for the project.

1. In Flash, return to calculator.fla in /mmcourses/fpad2004/.

Return to the document you created in the last exercise or open /fpad2004/lesson01/intermediate/ calculator_image.fla and save it as calculator.fla in /fpad2004/mmestate/.

2. In the Project panel, click the new project link.

The Project panel is docked on the right side of the screen.

A New Project dialog box opens. You can also create a new project by selecting File > New in the main menu and select Flash Project.

3. In the New Project dialog box, name the project *fpad2004*, browse to your /fpad2004/ folder, and click Save.

Your new project is displayed in the Project panel. Right now, it is empty; you need to add files to it.

> **Tip** *You should not use spaces in your project filename because most FTP servers do not accept filenames with spaces.*

4. Right-click (Windows) or Control-click (Macintosh) anywhere on the Stage of calculator.fla. In the pop-up menu select Add To Project: fpad2004.

Your file is added to the project and displayed in the Project panel.

You can also add files to a project by clicking the Add File(s) to Project icon at the bottom of the Project panel. You can only add individual files; you cannot add directories of files.

5. Click the Version Control button in the Project Panel and select Edit Sites.

You cannot implement version control without defining a site for the project.

Tip *If you already have a Dreamweaver MX 2004 site created, you do not have to create a new site for the Flash project. You can right-click (Windows) or Control-click (Macintosh) the name of a file you want to check in and select Check In. You are prompted to select an existing site to assign to the project.*

6. In the Edit Sites dialog box, click New. In the Site Definition dialog box, enter the following information:

- Site Name: *fpad2004*.

- Local Root: Browse to the location of your /fpad2004/ folder.

- Email: Enter your e-mail address.

- Check Out Name: Enter your name.

- Connection: Select Local/Network.

- Remote Directory: Enter *<location of your webroot>/mmcourses/fpad2004/*. Create the mmcourses and fpad2004 folders if necessary. An example location for the remote directory is C:\Inetpub\wwwroot\fpad2004\.

7. Click OK in the Site Definition dialog box. Click Done in the Edit Sites dialog box.

You can now check files in and out of your remote location, which in this case, is just another directory on your computer under your web root.

8. In the Project panel, click the Project button and select Settings. In the Project Settings dialog box, select fpad2004 from the Site drop-down list and then click OK.

This assigns a site to the project: the remote location for the source files.

9. In the Project panel, select both the project file and calculator.fla. Right-click (Windows) or Control-click (Macintosh) and select Check In from the pop-up menu.

Both files are checked in, and lock icons appear next to their names in the Project panel. This procedure creates copies of the files to the remote folder you specified for the site.

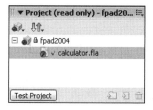

10. Close calculator.fla.

You must close your local version of the file before you can check it out from the remote server.

11. In the Project panel, right-click (Windows) or Control-click (Macintosh) calculator.fla and select Check Out.

A green check mark appears next to the filename in the Project panel. The file is now checked out to you. Only you can edit the file.

12. Double-click calculator.fla in the Project panel to open it.

This step opens your local version of the file, which you can now edit. When you are done making changes to the file, check it back in to the remote site.

What You Have Learned

In this lesson, you have:

- Created a new Flash document (pages 2–6)
- Created a custom panel layout (pages 6–11)
- Used the Selection, Text, and Free Transform tools (pages 11–16)
- Added static, input, and dynamic text to a Flash document (pages 16–20)
- Published a Flash document as a SWF and a new HTML page (pages 21–25)
- Added Flash Player version detection to an HTML page (pages 25–28)
- Embedded a Flash application in an existing web page (pages 28–32)
- Organized Flash content into layers (pages 32–38)
- Added an image to a Flash document (pages 38–41)
- Created a Flash project with version control (pages 42–47)

2 Learning ActionScript Fundamentals

Using ActionScript, Macromedia Flash's scripting language, you can write code to perform calculations, manipulate the visual interface and respond to user actions, retrieve and manipulate data from outside data sources, persist data on the client's computer, and much more. ActionScript is an ECMAScript-based language; it belongs to the same family of scripting languages as JavaScript and CFScript. All ECMAScript languages are similar in syntax, so if you know either of these languages, the basic ActionScript code should be familiar to you. ActionScript 2.0, introduced with Macromedia Flash MX 2004, is based on the ECMA-262 Edition 4 proposal (see www.ecma-international.org) and adds case-sensitivity, strict variable typing, and keywords to create a class-based architecture to the language. Previous versions of ECMAScript and ActionScript were prototype-based languages, based on objects and prototypes instead of classes and instances.

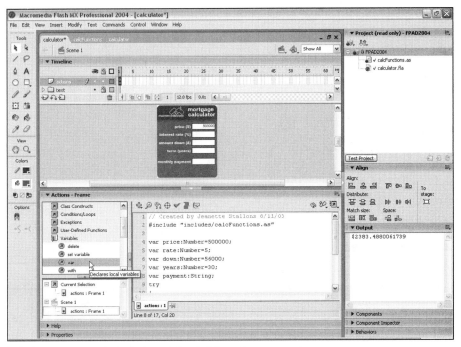

In this lesson, you write ActionScript code to calculate mortgage payments.

When you create a Flash application, you can put code in three places: in the FLA document, in an external file included in the FLA, or in a class file that is imported into your application. In this lesson, you use the Actions panel to place code inside a Flash document and to include code from an external file. In Lesson 5, "Creating Classes," you create separate class files and import the classes into your application.

In this lesson, you create code to calculate monthly mortgage payments by creating typed variables and using loops, conditional logic, functions, and exception handlers. In the next lesson, you hook up the code to the Flash interface, getting values for the price, rate, down payment, and loan years from user input.

What You Will Learn

In this lesson, you will:

- Use the Actions panel
- Create variables and assign them values
- Display data in the Output panel
- Loop over data
- Use conditional logic
- Create a function
- Place code in an external ActionScript file and include it in your FLA
- Handle exceptions using try and catch

Approximate Time

This lesson takes approximately 90 minutes to complete.

Lesson Files

Asset Files:
none

Starting Files:
/fpad2004/lesson02/start/calculator.fla

Completed Files:
/fpad2004/lesson02/complete/calculator.fla
/fpad2004/lesson02/complete/includes/calcFunctions.as

Exploring the Actions Panel

You add code inside the Flash authoring environment using the Actions panel.

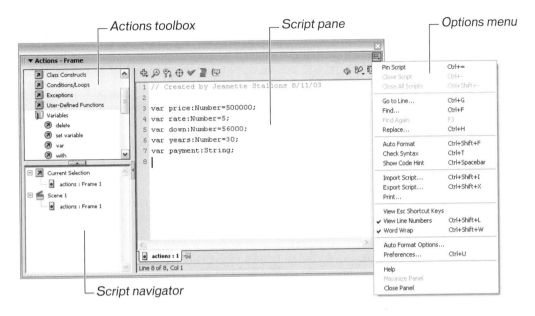

Actions toolbox   *Script pane*   *Options menu*

Script navigator

The Actions panel has three parts. The left side contains two panes: the Actions toolbox and a Script navigator. The large pane on the right is the Script pane in which you enter your code.

Actions toolbox. Lists all constructs of the ActionScript language, including keywords, statements, operators, and built-in classes and components plus their properties, methods, and events. (Objects and classes are covered in Lesson 3, "Learning the Flash Player Object Model.") You can double-click or drag and drop items from the Actions toolbox to the Script pane to insert them into your code. You can also right-click (Windows) or Control-click (Macintosh) any item in the toolbox to view a help reference for that entry.

Script navigator. Visual representation of the structure of your FLA file, showing where you can place code and where you already have code. You can place code in the main Timeline for the document (including different frames or layers) or on an object. It is a best practice to keep all your code in external files or as much of your code together in one place as possible. There are many ways and places to enter code in a document but in this lesson, you place all the code in the main Timeline for the document.

Script pane. The pane where you enter code. The toolbar at the top of the Script pane has buttons to check code syntax, format the code, and find and replace items in the code. You can customize how code appears using the Script pane options menu.

Options menu. Contains options to customize the ActionScript editor, import code, check syntax, search and replace, and more. You can change the size and color of fonts for specific constructs, turn on word wrap, show line numbers, and so on.

51

In this exercise, you explore the Actions panel.

1. In Flash, return to calculator.fla in /fpad2004/mmestate/.

This is the document you created in the last exercise of Lesson 1, "Learning the Flash Interface." If you did not do that exercise, open /fpad2004/lesson02/start/calculator.fla and save it as *calculator.fla* in /fpad2004/mmestate/.

2. Collapse the Property inspector, select the actions layer in the Timeline and open the Actions panel.

The Actions panel is initially docked near the bottom of your window. If you do not see it, select Windows > Development Panels > Actions from the main menu.

In the Actions panel's Script navigator, you should see the current selection for code placement is actions: Frame 1. When you enter code in the Script pane, you are placing the code in Frame 1 of the actions layer.

3. Increase the size of the Actions panel by clicking and dragging the border between the Actions panel and the Stage.

This is the same technique you used to change the size of docked panel sets in Lesson 1.

> **Tip** To maximize the size of the ActionScript editor, you can undock the Actions panel and make it almost full screen. You can then toggle it open and closed by pressing F9 or selecting Window > Development Panels > Actions.

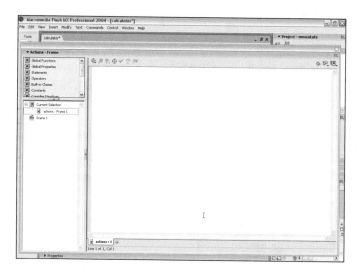

4. Click the options menu icon in the upper-right corner of the Actions panel and select View Line Numbers. Repeat to turn on Word Wrap.

The options menu icon is in the panel's title bar. You can also select View Line Numbers from the View Options menu icon located beneath the options menu icon.

5. Increase the size of the Actions toolbox by clicking and dragging the border between the Actions toolbox and the Script navigator.

You can hide the Actions toolbox by clicking the arrow button on the border between it and the Script navigator.

Learning Basic ActionScript Syntax

Now that you know where to put code, you are ready to learn the ActionScript language. The most basic rules of the ActionScript syntax are outlined here.

Case-sensitivity. ActionScript 2.0 is a case-sensitive language, although previous versions of ActionScript were not. All keywords, variable names, function and method names, and so on are case-sensitive. Case-sensitivity is implemented at both compile time and, if you publish for Flash Player 7, at runtime. If you use ActionScript 2.0 and publish for Flash Player 6, case-sensitivity is only implemented at compile time. If you use ActionScript 1 and publish for Flash Player 6 or earlier, case-sensitivity is not implemented.

White space and line breaks. ActionScript ignores white spaces, tabs, and newlines that appear outside of string values.

Optional semicolons. All ActionScript statements (except compiler directives and class and function definitions) should be terminated with a semicolon (;). The semicolon is used to separate statements from each other. Although it is not a best practice, you can omit the semicolons if you place statements on separate lines; Flash will add the semi-colons automatically.

Comments. Use comments liberally to explain the logic and variables so anyone can easily understand your code. Comments are not compiled and do not affect the size of your SWF. Code inside a comment is not executed. You can create two types of comments: single line and multiline. Use // to create a single-line comment. Any characters after the // to the end of the line are part of the comment.

```
// Created by JMS 8/11/03
```

Surround multiline comments with /* and */. All code across multiple lines between these two sets of characters is part of the comment.

```
/*
Flash calculator application to calculate mortgage payments
Created by JMS 8/11/03
*/
```

Reserved words. ActionScript has many reserved words including break, case, class, continue, and so on, that should not be used as identifiers for variables, functions, methods, or anything else. By default, reserved words appear blue in the ActionScript editor. If you name variables or functions with many of the reserved words, you sometimes get a compile time error. Even if you do not get an error, you might get unexpected runtime behavior or compile time errors with future versions of Flash. You can see a list of all ActionScript reserved words (along with all the ActionScript operators) by expanding the index entry in the Actions toolbox.

In this exercise, you explore the Actions panel, add code from the Actions toolbox, check syntax, add comments, and pin scripts.

1. In Flash, return to calculator.fla in /fpad2004/mmestate/.

Return to the file you used in the last exercise or open /fpad2004/lesson02/start/calculator.fla and save it as *calculator.fla* in /fpad2004/mmestate/.

2. In the Actions toolbox in the Actions panel, click Statements and then Variables to expand that branch of the toolbox.

You are not creating variables quite yet. Right now, just explore the Actions toolbox. You learn to create variables in the next exercise.

3. Double-click the `var` entry to add it to your code.

You use the `var` keyword to declare variables.

You can also add items from the Actions toolbox to the Script pane by clicking an entry and dragging and dropping it onto the Script pane.

4. Right click/Control-click `var` in the Script pane. Select View Help from the context menu.

This procedure opens the Help panel with the entry in the ActionScript dictionary displayed for the selected item—the keyword `var` in this case.

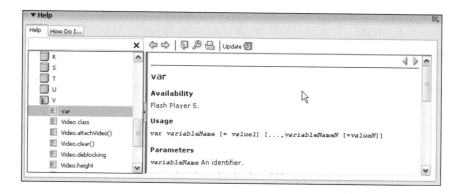

Tip *You can print the contents of the Help panel by selecting Print from the Help panel's options menu.*

The Help panel contents are HTML files displayed using an embedded browser. On Windows, the Help files are located at <boot drive>\Documents and Settings\<username>\Local Settings\ Application Data\Macromedia\Flash MX 2004\<language>\Configuration\HelpPanel\Help\ and Internet Explorer is used to display them within Flash. On Macintosh, the Help files are located at <Macintosh HD>/Users <username>/Library/Application Support/Macromedia/Flash MX 2004/ <language>/Configuration/ HelpPanel/Help/ and an embedded browser in Flash displays the files. You can change the size of the text in the Help panel by changing the font-size in the style sheet. On Windows, the style sheet is /HelpPanel/_sharedassets/help_pc.css. On Macintosh, it is /HelpPanel/ _sharedassets/help_mac.css. On Windows, you can also change the font size by placing the cursor within the Help panel, pressing Ctrl, and then scrolling the mouse wheel.

5. Collapse the Help panel and click the Check Syntax button at the top of the Script pane.

This procedure runs the syntax checker on your script and reports any syntax errors. The syntax checker also runs automatically when you test or publish the document. Because you did not finish your variable declaration, you get an error. An alert window appears if there are syntax errors in the code and the errors are displayed in the Output panel.

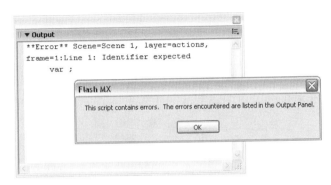

The Output panel appears when you check your code syntax or if you have errors when you test the application. It also appears if you use the `trace()` function. The `trace()` function is used to output variables in the next exercise.

6. Click OK to close the alert window. Dock the Output panel anywhere on the right side of your screen.

After you dock the Output panel in the authoring environment, it appears docked next to the SWF every time you test an application—even if nothing is displayed in it. This is handy because you don't have to keep closing the Output panel after every application test.

7. In the Script pane, delete the **var** statement and add a single-line comment.

```
// Created by Jeanette Stallons 8/11/03
```

Use your name and the current date in the comment. Notice that the code in the comment is gray by default.

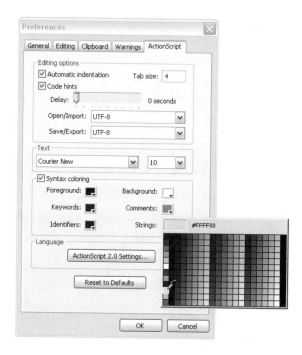

8. In the Timeline, click the input text layer.

You should no longer see code in the Script pane, and the current selection in the Script navigator should now be input text: Frame 1. Any code in the input text layer is displayed. In the bottom portion of the Script navigator, you should see actions: Frame 1 under Scene 1. Under Scene 1, all locations or objects that have any associated code are listed, which enables you to see where there is code and to quickly switch back and forth between any of the code.

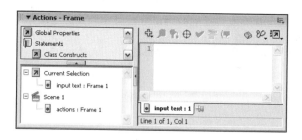

9. In the Script navigator, click actions: Frame 1 and then click the "Pin active script" button at the bottom of the Script pane.

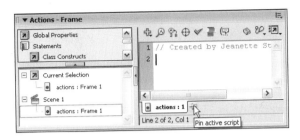

When you click actions: Frame 1 in the Script navigator, your code is displayed. When you click the Pin active script button, the code in Frame 1 of the actions layer is *pinned* to the editor and is displayed as a tab at the bottom of the Script pane. This code is now displayed when you open the Actions panel—regardless of which object, layer, or frame is selected. If you navigate to any other code from the Script navigator, you can return to the pinned script by clicking its tab on the bottom of the Script pane.

> **Tip** *You can also pin multiple scripts and switch back and forth between them using the tabs at the bottom of the Script pane.*

10. Save the document as *calculator.fla* in /fpad2004/mmestate/.

It should resemble the finished file: /fpad2004/lesson02/intermediate/calculator_comment.fla.

Creating Variables

Flash and ActionScript have grown in their functionality and their sophistication. To maintain backward compatibility for the Flash Player, you can often do things the "old way" as well as the "new way". This flexibility makes learning and reading code more difficult especially for creating variables. There are now several ways to declare and use variables. This book uses the latest and greatest way to declare variables, introduced with ActionScript 2.0, in which variables are strictly typed when you create them.

To create a new variable in Flash, use the `var` keyword and then specify a variable name and variable type as shown in the following code:

```
var username:String;
var age:Number;
```

You can also combine variable declarations on one line:

```
var username:String, age:Number;
```

After you create a variable, you can assign it a value using the assignment operator (=):

```
username="Alex";
age=9;
```

You can also combine the declaration and assignment statements, providing initial values for the variables:

```
var username:String="Alex";
var age:Number=9;
```

Note the use of quotation marks to denote a literal string value and no quotation marks to specify a number.

Naming Variables

Use the following rules when naming variables:

- Variable names are case-sensitive. Case-sensitivity is new to Flash Player 7, so old code might not use variable names and other identifiers consistently.
- Variable names can contain only letters, numbers, underscores (_), and dollar signs ($).
- The first letter of the variable name can be a letter, _ , or $ but cannot be a number.

> **Tip** It is common practice to use lower-case when naming variables. Use capital letters only for the first letters in multiple words, for example, `firstname` or `firstName`.

Using the `var` Keyword

When you use the `var` keyword, you are declaring a new variable instead of just assigning it a new value. You don't *need* the `var` keyword when defining a variable, however, you always should! Unlike many programming languages, you do not get an error if you assign a value to a variable without first declaring it. Flash creates the variable for you:

```
username="Alex"; //Does not generate an error even if you do not
        //first define the variable
```

You should always use the `var` keyword to define your variables. Why?

- For code readiblity. Using the `var` keyword differentiates when a variable is defined versus when it is assigned a new value later in the code.
- It is common practice to define all your variables at the top of code, giving you one place to locate all that code's variables.
- If you declare a variable with the `var` keyword, you can now also specify the variable type with ActionScript 2.0.

- It is a good habit to get into because when you create a function later in this lesson, you must use the `var` keyword to make your variables local to the function.

Strictly Typing Variables

You do not *have* to specify a variable type when you declare a variable. If you don't, the values you assign to a variable are not constrained to one data type. For example, you can set the variable `username` equal to the string `"Alex"` and then later set it equal to the number 9:

```
var username="Alex";
username=9;     //Changing data type does not generate an error
```

Strict data typing, the capability to define variable types and have data typing enforced at compile time, is new to Flash MX 2004 and ActionScript 2.0. You can now specify the data type for a variable when you declare it:

```
var username:String;
username=9;     //Generates an error at compile time
```

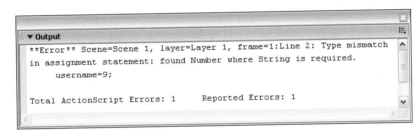

Note *Unlike many programming languages, data typing in Flash is enforced only at compile time, not at runtime.*

There are five main primitive data types in Flash: String, Number, Boolean, undefined, and null. Everything else in Flash is a type of object; you can assign a variable type of any of the built-in object types or any custom class you create. Objects and the Flash object model are covered in the next lesson. Creating your own classes is covered in Lesson 5.

Tip *In ActionScript, the Number type encompasses all types of numbers including integers and floating point numbers. If a number has a decimal point, it is maintained to double precision (15 significant figures). There is also a special number value, NaN (stands for not-a-number), which represents a noncalculable number but is still of type Number. There are also Infinity and –Infinity values.*

Because ActionScript 2.0 is case-sensitive, make sure you use the proper case when specifying your variable type. When you type the `var` keyword followed by a variable name and a colon, a pop-up menu appears, displaying a list of data types (including primitives, built-in classes, and framework classes) to choose from.

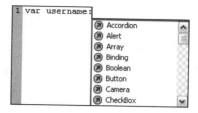

The built-in data types are also listed in the Actions toolbox under Types.

Variable typing is not required, so why use it? There are two main benefits: 1) It provides a more robust programming framework for developing applications. When you attempt to assign a variable an incorrect value or pass a function the wrong argument type, you get an error message, which makes debugging much easier; 2) You get code-hinting in the ActionScript editor. If you type a variable, when you enter the variable name followed by a period, you see a pop-up menu of all the properties and methods for that object. (Objects and the Flash object model are covered in the next lesson.)

In this exercise, you create variables for your calculator application. You create variables to hold the values for the house price, the interest rate of the loan, the down payment, the number of years for the loan, and a string to display the monthly payment. You strictly type all these values and assign some of them initial values.

1. In Flash, return to calculator.fla in /fpad2004/mmestate/.

Return to the file you created in the last exercise or open /fpad2004/lesson02/intermediate/ calculator_comment.fla and save it as *calculator.fla* in /fpad2004/mmestate/.

2. In the Actions panel, create a variable called `price` of type *Number* and is equal to 500000.

```
var price:Number=500000;
```

After you type the colon, select Number from the data type pop-up menu.

3. Create three more variables called `rate, down,` and `years` of type *Number* with initial values of *5, 56000,* and *30,* respectively.

```
var rate:Number=5;
var down:Number=56000;
var years:Number=30;
```

4. Create a variable called `payment` of type *String* that has no initial value.

```
var payment:String;
```

You do not have to assign an initial value to a variable when you declare it.

> **Tip** | It is a best practice to define all variables at the top of your code.

5. Save the document as *calculator.fla* in /fpad2004/mmestate/.

It should resemble the finished file: /fpad2004/lesson02/intermediate/calculator_varsA.fla.

Assigning Values to Variables

In the previous exercise, you used the assignment operator (=) to assign values to variables:

```
username="Alex";
age=9;
var loggedin:Boolean=false;
```

You can also assign a value to multiple variables in one statement:

```
username=login="Alex";
```

When you assign a value to a variable, you can assign a literal value or an expression. A **literal value** is a value that does not need to be evaluated. Literal string values are denoted with quotation marks; for example, "Alex". No quotation marks are used around numbers or Boolean values (true or false). When a variable is set equal to an **expression**, the expression on the right side is first evaluated and then the result is assigned to the variable.

```
var username:String="Alex";
var login=username;
```

You can also use more complicated expressions:

```
var fullName:String="Alex"+"Stallons";
var age:Number=(20%9+10)/3+5;
```

The following table shows the arithmetic operators in ActionScript. In general, the operators are listed starting with those having the highest order of precedence when evaluating expressions. Some of the operators have the same order of precedence in which case precedence is left-to-right in the expression. As in all programming languages, use parentheses to group sections of code to override normal operator precedence and to make your code more readable.

Operator	Name	Details
x++	postfix increment	x++ is equivalent to x=x+1. Same as ++x when used alone. In an expression, returns x+1.
x--	postfix decrement	x-- is equivalent to x=x-1. Same as --x when used alone. In an expression, returns x-1.
++x	prefix increment	++x is equivalent to x=x+1. Same as x++ when used alone. In an expression, returns x.
--x	prefix decrement	--x is equivalent to x=x-1. Same as x-- when used alone. In an expression, returns x.
-	negation	Switches the operand's sign. For example: -5.
*	multiply	Yields a number or NaN.
/	divide	Yields a number, NaN, Infinity, or -Infinity.
%	modulo division	Returns the remainder or NaN. 10%4 is equal to 2.
+	addition	If one or more operands is a string, the values are concatenated.
-	subtraction	Yields a number or NaN.
=	assignment	Assigns a value to a variable.
+=	add and assignment	x+=2 is equivalent to x=x+2.
-=	subtract and assignment	x-=2 is equivalent to x=x-2.
*=	multiply and assignment	x*=2 is equivalent to x=x*2.
/=	divide and assignment	x/=2 is equivalent to x=x/2.
%=	modulo division and assignment	x%=2 is equivalent to x=x%2.

Displaying Variables

When you test an application from the Flash authoring environment, you can use a `trace()` function to display the value of any variable or expression in an Output panel. Simply add a `trace()` function in your code where you want the value of a variable traced:

```
var username:String="Alex";
trace(username);
```

The code above displays the string "Alex" in the Output panel.

You can display more than one value by concatenating literal strings, variables, and/or expressions:

```
var username:String="Alex";
var age:Number=9;
trace(username+" is"+age);
```

Tip *Flash's built-in Debugger can also be used to display and modify variable values, watch variables, set and remove breakpoints, and step though lines of code. For more information, see Debugging in the ActionScript Reference Guide in the Help panel.*

Manipulating Data Types

You can use the `typeof` operator to get the type of a variable:

```
var username:String;
trace (typeof username); //Outputs "string"
```

The `typeof` operator returns a string of the name of the data type; possible return values include string, number, boolean, function, movieclip, or object.

Tip *The data types returned by the `typeof` operator are all lowercase strings, unlike the data types you use to type variables which all have the first letter as uppercase.*

You can explicitly change the type of a literal, variable, or expression before assigning it to a typed variable by using built-in `String()`, `Number()`, and `Boolean()` functions.

```
var age:Number=Number("9");
```

You can find the casting functions in the Actions toolbox under Global Functions > Conversion Functions.

> **Tip**   *User input into TextFields is always of type `String`. You always need to convert the input data to the type `Number` before using it in any calculations. You learn how to address and manipulate values input from the screen in Lesson 3, "Learning the Flash Player Object Model."*

You can also cast data using the `parseInt()` and `parseFloat()` functions (located in the Actions toolbox under Global Functions > Mathematical Functions), which convert a string containing numbers, letters, and characters into an integer or decimal number, respectively:

```
var age:Number=Number("9a");          //Assigns NaN (Not a number)
var age:Number=parseInt("9.5a");      //Assigns the integer 9
var age:Number=parseFloat("9.5a");    //Assigns the number 9.5
```

In this exercise, you create additional variables for your calculator application: a monthly interest rate and the calculated mortgage amount. You strictly type these values and assign them values from complex expressions. You output values of the variables using the `trace()` function.

1. In Flash, return to calculator.fla in /fpad2004/mmestate/.

Return to the file you created in the last exercise or open /fpad2004/lesson02/intermediate/ calculator_varsA.fla and save it as *calculator.fla* in /fpad2004/mmestate/.

2. Create a variable called `monthlyrate` of type *Number* and equal to the variable `rate` divided by 100 divided by 12.

```
var monthlyrate:Number=rate/100/12;
```

This expression calculates a monthly interest rate as a decimal value. The `rate` variable is an annual percentage rate (for example, 5%). You divide the rate by 100 to get an annual rate in decimal form (0.05). You divide by 12 to get a monthly interest rate (0.00417).

3. Create a variable called `mortgage` of type *Number* and equal to the house price (`price`) minus the down payment (`down`) and multiply by the monthly interest rate (`monthlyrate`).

```
var mortgage:Number=(price-down)*monthlyrate;
```

Make sure you use parentheses so the subtraction operation precedes the multiplication operation.

This calculation provides a *rough* estimate of the mortgage payment, estimating it as the monthly interest on the original loan amount. It neglects the fact that the loan amount will decrease with time and does not account for payment on the principal value itself. An actual mortgage that accounts for both of these factors is calculated in the next exercise using a loop and in Lesson 3 using an exponential expression.

4. Set the variable `payment` equal to the string "$" plus the variable `mortgage`.

```
payment="$"+mortgage;
```

You do not need a `var` keyword because the `payment` variable has already been defined. You are only assigning the `payment` variable a value.

5. Trace the value of the variable `payment` and test the application.

```
trace(payment);
```

You should see $1850 in the Output panel.

6. Save the document as *calculator.fla* in /fpad2004/mmestate/.

It should resemble the finished file: /fpad2004/lesson02/intermediate/calculator_varsB.fla.

Creating Loops

When creating an application, you often need to create a block of code that is executed multiple times. For example, you might need to perform a calculation a set number of times or loop though all the elements in an array and perform an operation with each element.

There are four types of loops in ActionScript: `for`, `while`, `do-while`, and `for-in`. The first three will be covered in this exercise. The `for-in` loop, is used only with objects and will be covered in Lesson 3.

for loop

Use a `for` loop to execute a block of code a set number of times. You create a `for` loop using the `for` keyword, specifying three loop conditions (initial, test, and update), separated by semicolons in parentheses, and including the block of code to be repeated in curly braces.

```
for (initial condition; test condition; update condition)
{
        [code]
}
```

The **initial condition** declares the variable to be used as the loop index and gives it an initial value (for example, `var i=0`). The **test condition** is an expression which uses the loop index to be evaluated to see whether the loop should continue (for example, `i<3`). The **update condition** is an expression which specifies how the loop index should be updated each time through the loop (for example, `i=i+1` or `i++`).

An example of a `for` loop that traces the values 0, 1, and 2 on separate lines in the Output panel is shown here.

```
for (var i=0;i<3;i++)
{
        trace(i);
}
```

Note In this example, the variable `i` is declared but not typed with a data type. It is a best practice to use only the variables `i`, `j`, and `k` as loop indices in which case the `Number` type is usually left off the definition of the loop index because the variables are never used anywhere else in the code.

You can also nest loops.

```
for (var i=0;i<2;i++)
{
        for (var j=0;j<2;j++)
        {
                trace(i+" "+j);
        }
}
```

This code results in the following output in the Output panel.

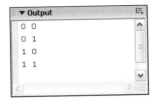

You can also use multiple iterators in a loop as shown in the following code. This code yields a slightly different output because i and j are increased each time through the loop. They are not incremented independently.

```
for (var i=0,j=0;i<2,j<2;i++,j++)
{
      trace(i+" "+j);
}
```

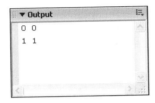

while loop

The logic in a for loop can also be written as a while loop. The for loop has a more concise structure and is generally preferred but when the loop index variable is updated in a complicated or non-predictable fashion, a while loop must be used.

> **Note** When you compile a FLA file, the ActionScript is compiled into bytecode. Equivalent for and while loops produce the same bytecode. The Flash Player is a virtual machine (software that allows the same application program to be run on multiple platforms without any changes) that interprets this bytecode.

You create a while loop using the while statement, as shown here.

```
var i:Number=0;
while (i<3)
{
      trace(i);
       i++;
}
```

The output for this code is 0,1,2 in the Output panel. The variable i has the value of 3 after the loop.

do-while loop

A do-while loop is a variant of the while loop. Use a do-while loop if you want the body of the loop to execute *at least* once. You create a do-while loop by moving the loop condition to the end of the loop body so the interpreter does not get to the test condition until after the code has been executed the first time. In the following example, the value 4 is traced to the Output panel, even though 4 is not less than 3. The variable i has the value of 5 after the loop.

```
var i:Number=4;
do
{
        trace(i);
        i++;
}
while (i<3);
```

Note *If any loop runs for more than 15 seconds, an alert window appears with the message: "A script in this movie is causing the Flash Player to run slowly. If it continues to run, your computer may become unresponsive. Do you want to abort the script?"*

In this exercise, you use a for loop to correctly calculate the mortgage payment. The actual equation for the mortgage calculation is shown here.

$$\text{mortgage} = \frac{(\text{price - down payment}) * \text{monthly interest rate}}{1-(1+\text{monthly interest rate})^{-\text{number of loan months}}}$$

You don't need to worry about the math, but in case you must know, you can calculate the second value in the denominator using a for loop, multiplying (1+monthly interest rate) by 12 times the number of loan years and then taking the inverse of this value. You take the inverse at the end because $x^{-N} = (1/x)^N$. (After you learn about the Flash object model and built-in classes in the next lesson, you can also calculate this value directly using a method of a Math class that calculates exponentials.)

1. In Flash, return to calculator.fla in /fpad2004/mmestate/.

Return to the file you created in the last exercise or open /fpad2004/lesson02/intermediate/ calculator_varsB.fla and save it as *calculator.fla* in /fpad2004/mmestate/.

2. After the monthlyrate variable declaration, create a variable called x that is of type *Number* and set it equal to 1.

```
1  // Created by Jeanette Stallons 8/11/03
2  var price:Number=500000;
3  var rate:Number=5;
4  var down:Number=56000;
5  var years:Number=30;
6  var payment:String;
7  var monthlyrate:Number=rate/100/12;
8  var x:Number=1;
9  var mortgage:Number=(price-down)*monthlyrate;
10 payment="$"+mortgage;
11 trace(payment);
```

3. After the line where the variable **x** is defined, create a `for` loop that loops from 1 to 12 times the *number* of years for the loan (`years`). Increment the loop by one each time.

```
8  var x:Number=1;
9  for (var i=1;i<=years*12;i++)
10 {
11 }
12 var mortgage:Number=(price-down)*monthlyrate;
13 payment="$"+mortgage;
14 trace(payment);
```

The variable i has not been strictly typed as a Number in this case (though it certainly could) because the variable i is never and should never be used anywhere in code except as a counter in loops.

4. Inside the loop, set the variable **x** equal to itself times (**1+monthlyrate**).

```
for (var i=1;i<=years*12;i++)
{
        x=x*(1+monthlyrate);
}
```

This code calculates $x = (1 + \text{monthly interest rate})^{\text{number of loan months}}$.

5. Change the line of code calculating the **mortgage** so that the variable **monthlyrate** is divided by (**1-1/x**).

```
var mortgage:Number=(price-down)*monthlyrate/(1-1/x);
```

This code calculates the actual mortgage using the equation given before Step 1.

6. Test the application.

You should get $2383.4880061739 in the Output panel, which is the actual mortgage amount. The amount calculated in the last exercise was, unfortunately, an overly optimistic estimate.

7. Save the document as *calculator.fla* in */fpad2004/mmestate/*.

It should resemble the finished file: /fpad2004/lesson02/intermediate/calculator_loop.fla.

Using Conditional Logic

When creating an application, you often need to create blocks of code that execute only if certain conditions are met. For example, in the calculator application, make sure that valid numbers are entered for the house price, interest rate, down payment, and years for the loan. If invalid fields are entered, your application does not work and a mortgage cannot be calculated. You should always validate the values entered and respond accordingly, by either calculating the mortgage or displaying a message for the user to enter new values.

Conditional Structures

You create conditional structures in ActionScript using if, else if, and else statements.

```
if (condition)
{
      [code]
}
else if (condition)
{
      [code]
}
else
{
      [code]
}
```

The inclusion of else and else if blocks is optional. You can have any number of else if blocks, but can only have one else block.

The conditions used in the if and else if statements must be Boolean expressions that evaluate to true or false. You can use a simple Boolean variable as the condition, as shown here.

```
var test:Boolean=true;
if (test)
{
      trace("true");
}
```

You can also use a string or a number instead of a Boolean. In this case, the Flash Player casts the data to a Boolean for evaluation. All nonempty strings and nonzero numbers convert to true. The following code displays a value of true in the Output panel.

```
if ("Alex")
{
      trace("true");
}
```

You can also create more complicated expressions to be evaluated using comparison and logical operators.

Comparison Operators

The following table contains the ActionScript comparison operators. The variables a and b in the usage column are simple variables.

Operator	Name	Usage	Description	Example
==	equality	a==b	True if a is equal to b	5=="5" evaluates to true
!=	inequality	a!=b	True if a is not equal to b	5!="5" evaluates to false
===	strict equality	a===b	True if a is the same data type and is equal to b	5==="5" evaluates to false
!==	strict inequality	a!==b	True if a is not the same data type as b and/or equal to b	5!=="5" evaluates to true
<	less than	a<b	True if a is less than b	5<"5" evaluates to false
>	greater than	a>b	True if a is greater than b	5>"5" evaluates to false
<=	less than or equal	a<=b	True if a is less than or equal to b	5<="5" evaluates to true
>=	greater than or equal	a>=b	True if a is greater than or equal to b	5>="5" evaluates to true

All string comparisons are case-sensitive. All characters have a numeric Unicode code point which is used for comparisons. For letters, this means that uppercase letters come before lowercase letters and A comes before Z.

If the two operands for any comparison operator (except the strict equality and strict inequality operators) are not the same data type, the Flash Player casts them to similar types. Numbers are always favored. If you have one operand that is a number and one that is a string, the string is cast to a number for the comparison. Likewise, if one operand is a Boolean and the other is not, the Boolean is cast to a number. This automatic casting occurs even if your variables are strictly typed.

> **Tip** Make sure that you use the equality operator and not the assignment operator in a conditional expression. For example, use if (myname=="Alex") and not if (myname="Alex"). If you use the assignment operator, the variable myname is assigned the new value, Alex, and the expression always evaluates to true. The expression will only evaluate to false if you assign the variable a value of zero or an empty string ("").

In this exercise, you add conditional logic to the mortgage calculation code to display error messages if the value of the down payment is greater than the house price or if the interest rate is less than 0.

1. In Flash, return to calculator.fla in /fpad2004/mmestate/.

Return to the file you created in the last exercise or open /fpad2004/lesson02/intermediate/ calculator_loop.fla and save it as *calculator.fla* in /fpad2004/mmestate/.

2. Right before the line in which the `monthlyrate` variable is defined, create an `if` statement that checks to see whether the down payment is greater than the house price. If it is, set the variable `payment` equal to the string `"Invalid price or down payment"`.

```
4  var  down:Number=56000;
5  var  years:Number=30;
6  var  payment:String;
7  if  (down>price)
8  {
9      payment="Invalid price or down payment";
10 }
11 var  monthlyrate:Number=rate/100/12;
12 var  x:Number=1;
```

3. Surround the rest of the code, except the `trace()` statement, with an `else` block.

```
7  if  (down>price)
8  {
9      payment="Invalid price or down payment";
10 }
11 else
12 {
13     var  monthlyrate:Number=rate/100/12;
14     var  x:Number=1;
15     for  (var  i=1;i<=years*12;i++)
16     {
17         x=x*(1+monthlyrate);
18     }
19     var  mortgage:Number=(price-down)*monthlyrate/(1-1/x);
20     payment="$"+mortgage;
21 }
22 trace(payment);
```

4. Test the application.

Because you have not changed the values of the price or down payment, you should still see $2383.4880061739 in the Output panel.

5. Return to the FLA and change the `price` to *50000*. Test the application.

You should get the string "Invalid price or down payment" in the Output panel.

6. Between the `if` and `else` blocks, add an `else if` block that sets the variable `payment` equal to `"Invalid rate"` if `rate` is less that zero.

```
else if (rate<0)
{
        payment="Invalid rate";
}
```

7. Change the `price` back to *500000*, set the `rate` to *-5*, and test the application.

You should get the string "Invalid rate" in the Output panel.

8. Return to the FLA, change the `rate` back to *5*, and save the document as *calculator.fla* in /fpad2004/mmestate/.

You will use this file as the starting file for the next exercise. It should resemble the finished file: /fpad2004/lesson02/intermediate/calculator_logicA.fla.

Logical Operators

You can also combine Boolean expressions with logical operators to create complex expressions to be evaluated. The following table contains logical operators in ActionScript.

Operator	Name	Usage	Description
!	not	!a	True if a is not true
!		(a<b)	True if a is not less than b
&&	and	a&&b	True if a and b are both true
||	or	a||b	True if a or b is true

Flash does short-circuit Boolean algebra; if the first condition in a complex expression fails, there is no further evaluation. For example, in the expression `if(a&&b)`, if a is false, b is never evaluated.

Conditional Operator

If you have a simple `if/else` statement, you can use the conditional operator (`?:`) to shorten your code to one line. The conditional operator uses the following syntax to write conditional logic.

```
condition ? expression1 : expression2
```

If the condition evaluates to true, expression1 is evaluated. If the condition evaluates to false, expression2 is evaluated. Here is a simple `if/else` statement.

```
if (name=="Alex")
{
        trace("valid user");
}
else
{
        trace("invalid user");
}
```

This statement can be rewritten using the conditional operator, as shown here.

```
name=="Alex" ? trace("valid user") : trace("invalid user");
```

When the conditional operator is evaluated, the value of expression1 or expression2 is also returned. In the previous case, this value was not needed or used anywhere. In the following example, the return value is assigned to a variable `message`, which is then displayed.

```
var message:String;
message=(name=="Alex") ? "valid user" : "invalid user";
trace(message);
```

Switch Statement

In ActionScript, as in most programming languages, you can use a `switch/case` statement to create concise conditional logic when you have a single expression to evaluate and have different code blocks to execute for different expression values.

Here is the syntax for a `switch` statement that checks for the value of a simple expression, the value of the variable `myname`.

```
1  var myname:String="Alex";
2  switch (myname)
3  {
4      case "Alex":
5          trace("I am 9");
6          break;
7      case "Brett":
8          trace("I am 1");
9      case "Gabrielle":
10         trace("I am 2");
11     default:
12         trace("I am old");
13 }
```

In this case, where `myname` is equal to "Alex", only the string "I am 9" is displayed in the Output panel. Because the keyword `break` is used inside the case, none of the subsequent cases are executed. If you do not use a `break` statement and a case executes to true, all the code in all the following cases are executed until a break is encountered. If none of the cases execute to true before a default case is encountered, the default case is executed. The use of a default case is optional.

Outcomes for different values of myname are displayed in the following table.

Value of myname	Output
Jeanette	I am old
Alex	I am 9
Brett	I am 1
	I am 2
	I am old
Gabrielle	I am 2
	I am old

Note *The switch statement uses strict equality (===) when comparing the value of the expression to case values. This distinction is pertinent only if you are not using a strictly typed variable. In this example, the variable myname was typed as a String. It you try to assign it a value of 1, you get a type mismatch error at compile time.*

In this exercise, you create complex conditional logic, adding logic to verify the down payment assigned is a number and the interest rate is not greater than 100.

1. In Flash, return to calculator.fla in /fpad2004/mmestate/.

Return to the file you created in the last exercise or open /fpad2004/lesson02/intermediate/ calculator_logicA.fla and save it as *calculator.fla* in /fpad2004/mmestate/.

2. Add another condition to the if statement to check and make sure the price variable is of type number. Use the typeof operator.

```
if (down>price || (typeof price!="number"))
{
      payment="Invalid price or down payment";
}
```

Remember, string comparisons are case-sensitive so make sure the word "number" is lowercase.

3. Change the `price` to the text ab, without quotes. Test the application.

You should get the string "Invalid price or down payment" in the Output panel because the price is not of type `number`. If you put the text ab in quotes, "*ab*", you get a compiler time error: "Type mismatch in assignment statement: found String where Number is required." The type mismatch is not caught at compile time if you leave the quotes off, because ab could be the name of a variable to be evaluated.

4. Add another condition to the `else if` statement to check and make sure the `rate` is not greater than *100*.

```
else if (rate<0 || rate>100)
{
        payment="Invalid rate";
}
```

5. Change the `price` back to *500000*, set the `rate` to *110*, and then test the application.

You should get the string "Invalid rate" in the Output panel.

6. Return to the FLA, change the `rate` back to *5*, and save the document as *calculator.fla* in /fpad2004/mmestate/.

It should resemble the finished file: /fpad2004/lesson02/intermediate/calculator_logicB.fla.

Creating Functions

Reusable sets of statements should be organized into functions. For the calculator application, the mortgage calculation is a good candidate for a function because it needs to recalculate every time the user changes a value in one of the input text fields.

Defining Functions

To create a function, use the `function` keyword followed by the name of the function, a comma-separated list of the function parameters in parentheses, and then the group of statements to be executed surrounded by curly braces.

```
function printName(firstname:String,lastname:String):Void
{
        trace(firstname+" "+lastname);
}
```

As shown here, you can type each of the individual function parameters and the return type of the function. To assign a function's return type, use a colon followed by the return variable type after the argument parentheses and before the curly braces. If the function does not return a value, assign it a return type of Void.

Note *Typing the argument parameters and return type of the function is a best practice, but is not required.*

You can call the function from anywhere in your code by invoking the function name, passing to it any required arguments.

```
printName("Alex","Stallons");
```

Tip *It is a general practice to name your functions in lowercase, using capital letters only for the first letters of multiple words.*

You can create the skeleton code for a function by selecting Statements > User-Defined Functions > function from the Actions toolbox.

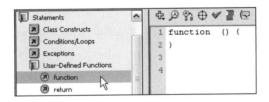

Tip *You can change the way auto-generated code is formatted by selecting Auto Format Options from the options menu in the Actions panel.*

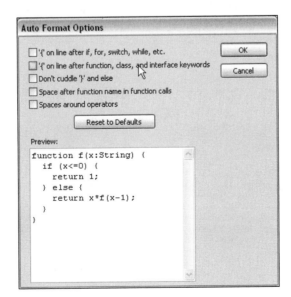

Returning Values from Functions

If the function returns a value to the caller, you need to do two things: indicate the appropriate return type in the function signature and use a `return` statement inside the function body.

```
function getRectArea(sideA:Number,sideB:Number):Number
{
        return sideA*sideB;
}
```

To call a function that returns a value, set a variable equal to the function invocation to capture the results.

```
var side1:Number=5;
var side2:Number=7;
var area:Number=getRectArea(side1,side2);
```

Although not required, it is a best practice to define the functions at the top of the code or include them in an external file. Placing code in an external file is covered in the next exercise.

In this exercise, you encapsulate the logic for the mortgage calculation inside a function: `calcMortgage()`. You call the function from your script, passing to it the necessary arguments corresponding to the house price, interest rate, down payment, and loan years; and then print the returned mortgage calculation.

1. In Flash, return to calculator.fla in /fpad2004/mmestate/.

Return to the file you created in the last exercise or /fpad2004/lesson02/intermediate/ calculator_logicB.fla and save it as *calculator.fla in* /fpad2004/mmestate/.

2. Define a function at the top of your code called `calcMortgage` that returns a value of type **Number**.

```
function calcMortgage():Number
{
}
```

> Tip   *You can create the function skeleton by selecting Statements > User-Defined Functions > function from the Actions toolbox.*

3. Cut all the code from inside the `else` block—except the last line assigning the variable `payment`—and paste it inside the function declaration.

```
1   // Created by Jeanette Stallons 8/11/03
2   function calcMortgage():Number
3   {
4       var monthlyrate:Number=rate/100/12;
5       var x:Number=1;
6       for (var i=1;i<=years*12;i++)
7       {
8           x=x*(1+monthlyrate);
9       }
10      var mortgage:Number=(price-down)*monthlyrate/(1-1/x);
11  }
12
13  var price:Number=500000;
14  var rate:Number=5;
```

4. Define four function parameters–`price`, `rate`, `down`, and `years`–that are all of type *Number*.

```
function calcMortgage(price:Number,rate:Number,down:Number,
years:Number):Number
```

5. Add a `return` statement as the last line in the function to return the variable `mortgage`.

```
return mortgage;
```

This finishes the creation of the function to calculate a mortgage.

6. Inside the `else` block, replace the variable `mortgage` in the statement assigning a value to `payment` with a call to the `calcMortgage()` function. Pass to it the four arguments: `price`, `rate`, `down`, and `years`.

```
23  else if (rate<0 || rate>100)
24  {
25      payment="Invalid rate";
26  }
27  else
28  {
29      payment="$"+calcMortgage(price,rate,down,years);
30  }
31  trace(payment);
```

7. Test the application.

Even though you have restructured your code, you have not changed the values of the variables, so you should still get $2383.4880061739 in the Output panel.

8. Save the document as *calculator.fla* in /fpad**2004**/mmestate/.

It should resemble the finished file: /fpad2004/lesson02/intermediate/calculator_functionA.fla.

Creating Variables Local to Functions

To define variables in ActionScript, you use the var keyword followed by the name of the variable and the variable type. You use the same method to define variables inside functions. When you use the var keyword to declare a variable inside a function definition, the variable's scope is limited to the function. If you do not use the var keyword, the scope of the variable is the main document or Timeline.

If the variable is created in the main document, regardless of whether you use var or not, the variable is available to functions. Inside a function, however, the var keyword makes the variable available only inside the function.

Note *You can use the var keyword anywhere inside a function definition. var declarations do not have to be the first lines of code inside the function definition as they do in some languages.*

Always use the var keyword to limit the scope of function variables and avoid unintentionally overwriting variables in the main document. If a function requires access to the main document variables, pass the variables to the function as arguments. If the code that calls a function needs access to data created inside the function, pass the data back using the return statement.

Here is an example of a well-constructed function in which the variable area is local to the function.

```
function getRectArea(sideA:Number,sideB:Number):Number
{
      var area:Number=sideA*sideB;
      return area;
}
var area:Number=10000;
getRectArea(2,3);
trace(area);                          //Outputs 10000
```

Here is an example of a poorly written function in which the variable area is *not* local to the function and overwrites the value of a variable with the same name in the main document.

```
function getRectArea(sideA:Number,sideB:Number):Number
{
      area=sideA*sideB;
      return area;
}
var area:Number=10000;
getRectArea(2,3);
trace(area);                          //Outputs 6
```

Creating Function Literals

In addition to creating a stand-alone function with a unique name, you can also create a variable and set it equal to a function. The function in this case is referred to as a **function literal** because you never give it an explicit name.

```
var area:Function=function(sideA:Number,sideB:Number):Number
{
     return sideA*sideB;
};
trace(area(2,3));                    //Outputs 6
```

Note the data type `Function` is used for strict typing. This statement is equivalent to first defining the function and then setting the variable equal to the function.

```
function getRectArea(sideA:Number,sideB:Number):Number
{
     return sideA*sideB;
}
var area:Function=getRectArea;
trace(area(2,3));                    //Outputs 6
```

The difference between the two functions is that in the first case, you never assign the function a name. If you do not need to reference or call the function from anywhere in your code, you don't need to define it as a stand-alone function with a unique name. Using function literals is common when defining methods and event handlers for objects—a topic introduced in the next lesson.

Beware, however, that unlike functions, you have to define variables before you can use them in your code, so you must define function literals *before* you can use them.

Creating Optional Parameters

There are two ways to handle optional parameters. 1) You can explicitly define them as function parameters and then check to see whether they have a value of `undefined` or not. 2) You can choose not to define them as function parameters, and refer to them as elements in an arguments array inside the function body. (You learn about ActionScript arrays in the next lesson.)

When parameters are explicitly defined in the function definition, and a call to the function does not pass in the specified number of arguments, each unspecified argument is assigned a value of `undefined`.

```
function test(a:String,b:String,c:String):Void
{
     trace(a+","+b+","+c);
}
test("Alex");    //Outputs Alex,undefined,undefined
```

In this case, you can use conditional logic to test for the existence of arguments and respond accordingly if they do not exist.

```
1  function test(a:String,b:String,c:String):Void
2  {
3      trace(a+","+b+","+c);
4      if (a)
5      {
6          trace(a);
7      }
8      if (b)
9      {
10         trace(b);
11     }
12     if (c)
13     {
14         trace(c);
15     }
16 }
```

You can pass only the first or only the first and second arguments simply by leaving off the rest of the arguments.

```
test("Alex");
test("Alex","R");
```

You can pass only the first and third arguments by specifing the middle argument as undefined, null, or as an empty string.

```
test("Alex",undefined,"Stallons");
test("Alex","","Stallons");
```

You cannot use commas to leave out the value of the second argument.

Another way to deal with optional arguments is to use an arguments array that is automatically created each time a function is called. (Arrays are covered in the next lesson.) The arguments array contains all the arguments passed to the function. The benefit of accessing arguments as elements in the arguments array is that the function signature (the name and number of parameters specified in the definition) does not show optional arguments. It is a general practice to include only required arguments as function parameters.

In this exercise, you test the scoping of variables within a function. Then, you create a displayMortgage() function, which encapsulates the logic for displaying the mortgage calculation inside a function.

1. In Flash, return to calculator.fla in /fpad2004/mmestate/.

Return to the file you created in the last exercise or open /fpad2004/lesson02/intermediate/ calculator_functionA.fla and save it as *calculator.fla in* /fpad2004/mmestate/.

2. To test the scoping of variables within the function, first remove the `var` keyword from in front of the variable `i` inside the `calcMortgage()` function.

```
for (i=1;i<=years*12;i++)
```

3. Outside the function and before the `if` block, define a variable called `i` of type *Number*, set it equal to *100*, and then trace its value.

```
17 var years:Number=30;
18 var payment:String;
19 var i:Number=100;
20 trace(i);
21 if  (down>price || (typeof price!="number"))
22 {
```

4. After the `else` block, trace `i` again.

```
29 else
30 {
31     payment="$"+calcMortgage(price,rate,down,years);
32 }
33 trace(i);
34 trace(payment);
```

5. Test the application.

You should get the following values displayed in the Output panel: 100, 361, $2383.4880061739.

Because you did not use the `var` keyword to define the variable `i` inside the function, it is in the scope of the main document and overwrites the value of the existing main document variable `i`.

6. Fix your code by returning a `var` keyword in front of the variable `i` inside the function. Delete the variable declaration for `i` and the two traces you added in the main document.

This returns the variable `i` to the scope of the function.

7. After your `calcMortgage()` function, create a second function called `displayMortgage` that returns a value of type *Void* and has four parameters—`price`, `rate`, `down`, and `years`—that are all of type *Number*.

```
function displayMortgage(price:Number,rate:Number,down:Number,
years:Number):Void
{
}
```

In the next steps, you will place all the code that checks for valid data, calls the `calcMortgage()` function, and displays the mortgage payment inside this new function.

8. Cut all the code declaring the **payment** variable, the **if/else if/else** block, and the **trace** statement. Paste it inside the **displayMortgage()** function declaration.

```
function displayMortgage(price:Number,rate:Number,down:Number,
years:Number):Void {
      var payment:String;
      if (down>price || (typeof price!="number"))
      {
            payment="Invalid price or down payment";
      }
      else if (rate<0 || rate>100)
      {
            payment="Invalid rate";
      }
      else
      {
            payment="$"+calcMortgage(price,rate,down,years);
      }
      trace(payment);
}
```

You should indent the code as shown here so it easier to see where the various code blocks start and end.

9. At the end of the main code, call the **displayMortgage()** function.

```
displayMortgage(price,rate,down,years);
```

10. Test the application.

Even though you have restructured your code, you have not changed the values of any of the variables, so you should still get $2383.4880061739 in the Output panel.

11. Save the document as *calculator.fla* in /fpad2004/mmestate/.

It should resemble the finished file: /fpad2004/lesson02/intermediate/calculator_functionB.fla.

Including External ActionScript Files

Up to now, you have placed all your code in the FLA file. You can also place code in an external file and then include that file in the FLA when it gets published.

Placing your code in external files has three main benefits.

- Lets you reuse your code in multiple Flash files or applications.
- Separates the visual elements of the Flash application from the code so multiple people can work on the application at the same time.
- Allows your code to be versioned and differenced in a source control system.

You can create and edit external ActionScript files in Flash or any other text editor. Flash has an integrated Script window that is separate from the Actions panel and the normal authoring environment, and is used exclusively to create and edit external code files. The Script window has the Actions toolbox and the Script pane, just like the Actions panel, but lacks the Script navigator, which is not applicable for a code file.

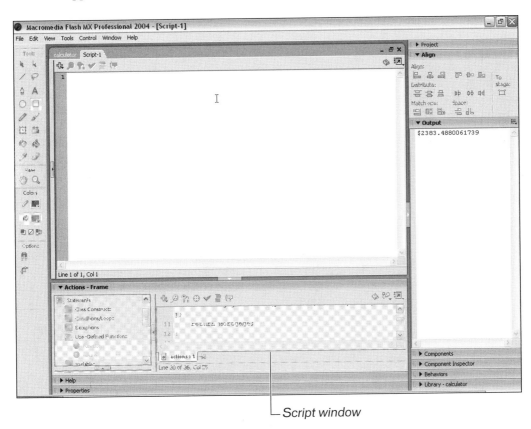

Script window

Note *When you edit a script in the Script window, the Flash authoring environment is inaccessible and is grayed-out.*

It is best practice to use the file extension AS for your external code files to indicate that the file contains ActionScript code.

To include an AS file in a FLA document, use the `#include` compiler directive:

```
#include "{path}filename.as"
```

The path is relative to the location of the FLA file:

```
#include "includes/filename.as"
```

Note *You must use quotation marks around the path/filename and you cannot place a semicolon at the end of the statement.*

The external code is included when the FLA is compiled into a SWF. If you change the code in an external file, you must republish any SWFs that include that code.

In this exercise, you remove your `calcMortgage()` and `displayMortgage()` functions from the FLA file and place them in an external AS file. You then include the AS file in the calculator.fla document.

1. In Flash, return to calculator.fla in /fpad2004/mmestate/.

Return to the file you created in the last exercise or open /fpad2004/lesson02/intermediate/ calculator_functionB.fla and save it as *calculator.fla* in /fpad2004/mmestate/.

2. Select all the code for the `calcMortgage()` and `displayMortgage()` functions and cut it to the Clipboard.

You will place the functions in an external AS file.

3. Select File > New and then select ActionScript File. Click OK.

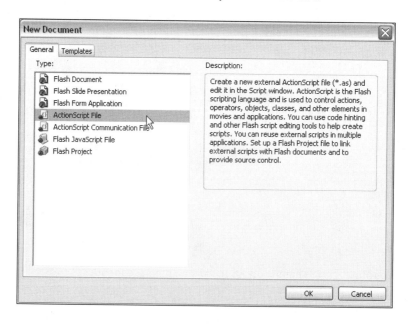

A Script window appears. The Flash authoring environment is grayed-out and is not active.

4. Paste your code in the Script window and save the document as *calcFunctions.as* in /fpad2004/mmestate/includes/.

You are placing the AS file in a subdirectory called includes, so that it is in a different directory than the FLA, giving you practice using a more complicated relative path when including a file in the FLA.

The finished file should resemble: /fpad2004/lesson02/intermediate/includes/calcFunctions_include.as.

5. Click the calculator.fla tab at the top of the screen to return to the FLA file.

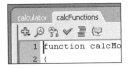

The Macintosh version of Flash does not have document tabs. If you do not have document tabs, select Window > calculator.fla to return to that file.

6. After the comment, include the calcFunctions.as file using the correct relative path.

```
#include "includes/calcFunctions.as"
```

Do not put a semicolon at the end of the statement.

7. Test the application.

Even though your functions are now contained in an external file, you have not changed the values of the variables, so you should still get $2383.4880061739 in the Output panel.

8. Save the document as *calculator.fla* in /fpad2004/mmestate/.

It should resemble the finished file: /fpad2004/lesson02/intermediate/calculator_include.fla.

Handling Exceptions

Earlier, you used conditional logic to make sure your calculator rate, price, and down payment fields would result in the calculation of a valid mortgage payment. If you had an invalid value or values, you returned a string error message that was traced to the Output panel. This simple exception handling worked fine in this case. In real life, though, you want to handle error situations more gracefully. Instead of assigning the error to the mortgage payment field, you should stop program execution, display the message in an appropriate place, highlight for the user what needs to be fixed, and so on. Using conditional logic and different return values can get messy when working with complicated program flow so you should use a standard `try/catch` exception handling framework to handle exceptions gracefully.

In general, an error is considered a fatal condition—something that stops the program from running entirely. An exception is a nonfatal condition—something you can check for and handle appropriately. In ActionScript, all exceptions must be generated and thrown explicitly by the developer. No exceptions are thrown automatically by the Flash Player. This exception throwing differs from other languages, in which some exceptions are thrown by the runtime environment.

ActionScript's exception handling framework, new in ActionScript 2.0, has four keywords: `try`, `catch`, `finally`, and `throw`, which are similar to those used by other languages. You enclose the code that might have exceptions inside a `try` block. If an exception occurs in this code, it is caught by a `catch` block. Any code inside a `finally` block is executed, regardless of whether exceptions are thrown or not. The inclusion of `catch` and `finally` blocks are optional, but you must have at least one `catch` or `finally` block.

The general syntax for a handling exceptions is shown here.

```
try
{
      [code to attempt that has at least one throw statement in it]
}
catch(variable)
{
      [code to be executed if an exception is caught]
}
finally
{
      [code to be executed in all situations]
}
```

First the code inside the `try` block is executed. If no exception is thrown from any of the code, all the code inside the `try` block is executed. If an exception is thrown from any of the code inside the `try` block, execution of the `try` block code stops and control is passed to the `catch` block (if one exists). When you create the `catch` block, you specify a name for the variable thrown to it; the generic name `variable` is used in the preceding code. If there is no `catch` block to handle the exception, the variable thrown is displayed in the Output panel. After the code in the `catch` block is executed (if there is one), the code in the `finally` block is executed (if a `finally` block exists). Code in a `finally` block is *always* executed, regardless of whether an exception is thrown or not and whether there is a `catch` block or not.

So how do you throw something to be caught by a `catch` block? You use the `throw` keyword followed by the variable you want to throw. Here is a very simple example that requires an order total to be less than $1000.

```
var total:Number=1500;//You learn to get this data from user next lesson
var e:String;
try
{
        if (total>1000) {
            throw "Error. Your order must be less than $1000.";
        }
        submitOrder();
        displayReceipt();

}
catch(e)
{
        trace(e);
}
```

In this case, the order is never submitted, and a receipt is not displayed. Instead, an error message is displayed. Note that when the exception is thrown to the catch block, it is assigned to the variable e defined after the catch keyword. This is much like the definition of a function parameter.

Another advantage of using exception handling is that you do not have to handle errors where they are thrown. You can throw an error in a function call, but handle it in the calling page. If a function does not handle an exception, it "bubbles up" until an exception handler is found. If no catch handler is found, all code execution stops.

```
function calcPrice(){
        var total:Number=1500;
        if (total>1000) {
                throw "Error. Your order must be less than $1000.";
        }
        trace("total");
}
var e:String;
try
{
        calcPrice();
        submitOrder();
        displayReceipt();
}
catch(e)
{
        trace(e);
}
```

Execution of the function stops as soon as the exception is encountered and thrown. The total is not traced to the Output panel, and the order is not submitted. Only the error message is displayed from the `catch` handler.

You can also throw and catch different types of exceptions that can be handled by different `catch` blocks. You don't have to have just one `catch` block, as shown here. To do this, you need to create and throw different types of objects. In Lesson 5, you throw instances of a built-in Error class and your own custom classes.

In this exercise, you use exception handling to throw exceptions from your `displayMortgage()` function and catch them in the calling page.

1. In Flash, return to calculator.fla in /fpad2004/mmestate/.

Return to the file you created in the last exercise or open /fpad2004/lesson02/intermediate/ calculator_include.fla and save it as *calculator.fla* in /fpad2004/mmestate/.

2. Before the call to the `displayMortgage()` function, declare a variable e of type *String*.

```
var e:String;
displayMortgage(price,rate,down,years);
```

3. Place the line of code calling the `displayMortgage()` function inside a `try` block.

```
7  var years:Number=30;
8  var e:String;
9  try
10 {
11     displayMortgage(price,rate,down,years);
12 }
```

4. After the `try` block, add a `catch` block. Pass a variable called e to the `catch` block and trace the value of e inside the `catch` block.

This variable e will hold whatever variable is thrown to the `catch` block. You should declare and type this variable so that compile time checking can occur on the variable passed to the `catch` block.

```
catch(e)
{
    trace("Error: "+e);
}
```

5. Return to calcFunctions.as in /fpad2004/mmestate/.

Return to the file you created in the last exercise or open /fpad2004/lesson02/intermediate/includes/ calcFunctions_include.as and save it as *calcFunctions.as* in /fpad2004/mmestate/includes/.

6. Inside the `displayMortgage()` function, change the two lines of code returning invalid strings to instead throw the strings back to the calling page.

In this example, you are throwing simple strings out of the function back to the calling page.

```
15      if   (down>price || (typeof price!="number"))
16      {
17              throw "Invalid price or down payment";
18      }
19              else if (rate<0 || rate>100)
20      {
21              throw "Invalid rate";
22      }
23      else
```

7. Move the `trace` statement inside the `else` block.

```
else
{
        payment="$"+calcMortgage(price,rate,down,years);
        trace(payment);
}
```

8. Save the document as *calcFunctions.as* in /fpad2004/mmestate/includes/.

It should resemble the finished file: /fpad2004/lesson02/intermediate/includes/calcFunctions _trycatch.as.

9. Return to calculator.fla and change your rate to *120*.

```
var rate:Number=120;
```

The `displayMortgage()` function checks to make sure that the rate is between 0 and 100 and throws an error if it is not in this range.

10. Test the application.

You should get the string "Error: Invalid rate" in the Output panel. The string "Invalid rate" was thrown from inside the function; and because the function call was inside a `try` block, it was caught and handled by the associated `catch` block.

11. Return to calculator.fla and move the `displayMortgage()` function call below the `try/catch` block. Cut the `try/catch` block and the declaration for the variable e to the clipboard.

```
 7  var years:Number=30;
 8  var e:String;
 9  try
10  {
11
12  }
13  catch(e)
14  {
15      trace("Error: "+e);
16  }
17  displayMortgage(price,rate,down,years);
```

12. Return to calcFunctions.as and paste the code inside the `displayMortgage()` function before the `if` statement.

You are going to place the `if` statement inside the `try` block. Originally, the `try/catch` block was outside the function so that you could see an error thrown from a function back to the calling page. In this specific case, though, it is better to encapsulate the `try/catch` logic inside the `displayMortgage()` function; you want the error handling to occur every time a new mortgage is calculated and displayed.

13. Move the `if/else if/else` block inside the `try` block. Save the file.

```
12  function displayMortgage(price:Number,rate:Number,down:Number,years:Number):Void
13  {
14      var payment:String;
15      var e:String;
16      try
17      {
18          if (down>price || (typeof price!="number"))
19          {
20              throw "Invalid price or down payment";
21          }
22          else if (rate<0 || rate>100)
23          {
24              throw "Invalid rate";
25          }
26          else
27          {
28              payment="$"+calcMortgage(price,rate,down,years);
29              trace(payment);
30          }
31      }
32      catch(e)
33      {
34          trace("Error: "+e);
35      }
36  }
```

14. Return to calculator.fla and test the application.

You should still get the string "Error: Invalid rate" in the Output panel.

15. Return your `rate` to 5 and test the application.

You should get the previous value of $2383.4880061739 in the Output panel.

16. Save the document as *calculator.fla* in /fpad2004/mmestate/.

It should resemble the finished file: /fpad2004/lesson02/intermediate/calculator_trycatch.fla.

What You Have Learned

In this lesson, you have:

- Learned to add code to your FLA using the Actions panel (pages 51–59)
- Created strictly typed variables (pages 59–63)
- Displayed data in the Output panel when testing an application (pages 63–67)
- Executed blocks of code multiple times using loop structures (pages 67–71)
- Created conditional logic structures to control program flow (pages 72–78)
- Created functions to reuse code (pages 78–86)
- Placed code in an external ActionScript file to enable reuse in multiple FLA files and editing independent of the FLA (pages 86–89)
- Handled exceptions using try, catch, and throw (pages 89–95)

3 Learning the Flash Player Object Model

In the last lesson, you learned the general syntax and constructs of the ActionScript language, which gave you the tools to create variables and control program flow with loops, logic, and exception handling. To manipulate more complex data and interact with the user and visual elements on the Stage, however, you need to become familiar with the Flash Player object model. Besides the primitive data types you learned in Lesson 2, "Learning ActionScript Fundamentals," everything in Macromedia Flash is an object. For example, you can have array objects, date objects, button objects, and so on that you manipulate using their properties and methods. The objects that are native to Flash and recognized by the Flash Player at application runtime make up the Flash Player object model.

This lesson introduces (or reviews, for some) the concepts and building blocks of object-oriented programming (OOP). After you understand the concept of classes, objects, properties, methods, and events, you move on to get a high-level view of the Flash Player object model and then look at specific built-in objects and what they are used for.

In this lesson, you make your calculator functional, calculating payments for values that the user input in the calculator interface.

In the first part of this lesson, you work with several nonvisual classes. You rewrite some of the calculator code in a more concise manner using the `Math` class, you use the Date class to display the current date, and then you create a function to strip out all non-numeric characters using the `String` class. Next, you create an array and a custom object using the `Array` and `Object` classes to hold all the values needed to calculate the mortgage. Finally, you reference and manipulate instances of the built-in `TextField` class, and capture and use the values entered into the calculator by the user to calculate the mortgage payment.

What You Will Learn

In this lesson, you will:

- Learn or review the concepts of object-oriented programming
- Get familiar with the Flash built-in classes
- Use static methods of the Math class
- Create and use instances of the Date class
- Manipulate strings using the String wrapper class
- Create and manipulate Array objects
- Create custom objects with custom properties and methods
- Manipulate visual TextField objects
- Respond to user events for the TextField class
- Add event listeners for TextField objects

Approximate Time

This lesson takes approximately 2 hours to complete.

Lesson Files

Asset Files:
none

Starting Files:
/fpad2004/lesson03/start/calculator.fla
/fpad2004/lesson03/start/includes/calcFunctions.as

Completed Files:
/fpad2004/lesson03/complete/calculator.fla
/fpad2004/lesson03/complete/includes/calcObject.as
/fpad2004/lesson03/complete/includes/formatFunctions.as

Introducing Object-Oriented Programming

The general constructs of object-oriented programming (OOP) are introduced in this first section. If you are familiar with OOP skip to "Getting Familiar with Built-in ActionScript Classes."

Note *In this lesson, you use the built-in classes. You learn to create your own classes and extend the built-in classes in Lesson 5, "Creating Classes."*

In traditional procedural languages, an application is made up of data (stored in databases or persisted in memory), and you write functions or procedures to manipulate this data. The data and the procedures, are entirely separate, and a procedure might manipulate different pieces of data. In object-oriented languages, however, an application is a collection of interacting objects. Each object contains its own data and its own behaviors—the procedures to manipulate the data. All the program code and logic is contained inside individual objects. In a procedural system, any change to the logic can result in code having to be changed in many places. In a well-architected, object-oriented system, any change to the logic results in code having to be changed in only one object, and this change does not affect the rest of the system. Architecting an application in an object-oriented manner is more maintainable, flexible, and extendable than traditional structured architectures.

The following sections provide definitions of the main concepts in OOP using a bicycle, as an example.

Classes

A **class** is a blueprint from which you make instances. The class defines all the characteristics (properties) and behaviors (methods) that are common to all instances of the class.

You have a set of specifications or a blueprint (the class) that you use to build all bicycles (the objects). The blueprint ensures that all bicycles have two wheels, a seat, handle bars, and so on. The blueprint does not specify the frame brand, its color, or its size. A bicycle must have all these properties but the properties don't have to be the same for every bicycle.

Objects

An **object** is an instance of a class. An object doesn't exist until you create it from a class definition. When you create an instance of a class, it is called **instantiating** an object. An object has its own values for the variables (properties) specified in the class definition. The word object is used interchangeably with the word instance.

The most common way to create a new object from a class is to use the `new` keyword followed by the name of the class.

```
var instancename:Classtype=new Classtype();
```

This code creates a new instance called `instancename` of a class called Classtype and invokes the class's **constructor** function, a special function of the class that is called when the object is created. The constructor function might set initial values for properties, run other initialization code, or do nothing at all. This is one way to create object instances. You can also create objects visually in Flash or using special object methods.

Creating a Bicycle object could be translated to the following code:

```
var myBike:Bicycle=new Bicycle();
```

This code creates a new bicycle, but no initial values are specified for its color, size, and so on. There must have been some default values specified in the blueprint, however, so the bicycle could still be built. If you want to specify the properties (color, size, and so on) for your bicycle before it is built, you can pass them to the constructor function as arguments. The constructor function definition specifies what arguments you can pass to the constructor and in what order. The following code creates a new blue bicycle with a 17-inch frame:

```
var myBike:Bicycle=new Bicycle("blue","17");
```

Properties

A **property** is a variable attached to an object. All objects in a class have the same set of properties, but they might have different values. Properties are the characteristics of an object instance.

Properties of a Bicycle object might include `frameType`, `yearMade`, `frameColor`, and `frameSize`. Different Bicycle objects can have different values of these properties. For example, one `Bicycle` object can have a `frameColor` of blue and a `frameSize` of 17 inches, whereas another Bicycle instance has a `frameColor` of silver and a `frameSize` of 19 inches.

Tip *Most property names are adjectives or nouns.*

You access properties using dot notation. The following code sets and displays the `frameColor` of a Bicycle object.

```
myBike.frameColor="blue";
trace(myBike.frameColor);
```

Methods

A **method** is a function attached to an object. It is an action or procedure that can be performed on a particular object. A method is aware of the object and all the properties that the object contains and can access them internally. The properties and methods are called the **members** of a class.

Methods of the Bicycle class might include `setColor(color)`, `getColor()`, `goSlower(speed)`, `goFaster(speed)`, and `changeGear(gear)`. Each of these methods knows the existing color for a particular object, the gear the bicycle is in, the pedal cadence, and so on, and can change these properties if necessary.

Tip *Most method names are verb-adjective or verb-noun constructs.*

You access methods using dot notation. Use the following code to set and display the `frameColor` of the Bicycle object using the `setColor()` and `getColor()` methods.

```
myBike.setColor("blue");
trace(myBike.getColor());
```

When you call a method of an object, it is referred to as **invoking** a method. Methods that get and set a particular property value are often called **getters** and **setters**. The set method accomplishes the same thing as setting the `frameColor` property. In many cases, however, you do not want developers to access properties of an object. For maintainability and security, you want to make the properties available only through methods, protecting them from being changed from outside the class. Creating methods is covered in Lesson 5.

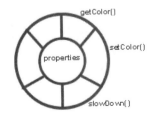

Static Members

In addition to properties and methods, which act upon an object, a class can also have **static** properties or methods. A static member has the same value for every instance of the class. Static methods are referred to as **class methods**, and static properties as **class properties** or **constants**. Properties and methods that are unique for each instance are sometimes called **instance properties** and **instance methods**.

You invoke static properties and methods directly on the class, not on an object (an instance of the class).

A static property of the Bicycle class might be NUMWHEELS, which is a property that has the same value for *all* Bicycle objects (for example, 2). Each Bicycle instance does not need its own copy of the NUMWHEELS property because each bicycle has the same value. You can access a class property using dot notation with the name of the class.

```
Bicycle.NUMWHEELS=2;
trace(Bicycle.NUMWHEELS);          //Outputs 2
```

NUMWHEELS=2
frameSize=17
frameColor=Black

NUMWHEELS=2
frameSize=15
frameColor=Blue

NUMWHEELS=2
frameSize=19
frameColor=Silver

Tip *Names of static properties are usually in all capital letters.*

Events

An event is something that can happen to the object and that the object can react to. There are two types of events: user events and system events.

A **user event** is carried out by the user while interacting with the Flash application. A user might click a button, change the size of the window, or select an option from a drop-down list.

A **system event** is fired automatically when a system process occurs; for example, after data loads from a text or XML file.

User events for the Bicycle class might include brake, pedal, and turn. These events are all things the rider can do to the Bicycle object. When the event occurs, a particular method of the object can be called to respond to the event. For example, when the user brakes, the goSlower() method of the Bicycle object should be invoked

Getting Familiar with Built-In ActionScript Classes

Now that you are familiar with OOP terminology, let's look at Flash's built-in classes. ActionScript has about 40 built-in classes that all descend from the general Object class. Classes can be broken into two main categories: core classes which are the same or similar to those specified in the ECMAScript specification and classes that are unique to Flash. In the Actions toolbox the built-in classes are organized into the core classes and four categories of classes unique to Flash.

Movie. Classes for visual objects and for nonvisual objects that provide control over or information for the visual objects. There are three classes of visual objects: TextField, Button, and MovieClip.

Media. Classes that provide control of sound and video.

Client-server. Classes that let you communicate with external files.

Authoring. Classes used in Flash JavaScript files, which you use to customize the Flash authoring environment.

In this book, you are going to use most of the core classes and some of the movie and client-server classes. Keep in mind that these categories only provide a way of organizing the classes in the Actions toolbox. They have nothing to do with the actual object model hierarchy, which is shown in the following chart.

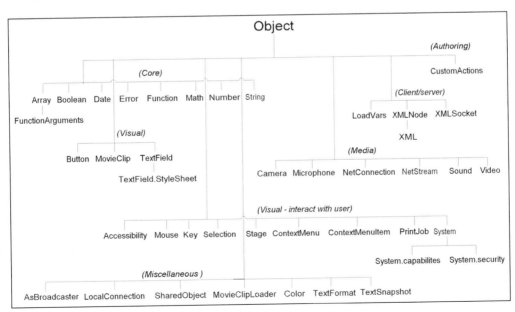

The way you instantiate an object and use its members varies from class to class. The various techniques are outlined in the following table. Although some classes fall in more than one category, they are listed in only one category for clarity (the one most of their members fall under). You will get experience using classes from each of these categories throughout the book.

Class Description	Members Invoked On	Classes
Use static members without having to create object instances	Class	Accessibility, AsBroadcaster, CustomActions, Key, Math, Mouse, Selection, Stage, System, System.capabilities, System.security
Use instance members on objects instantiated in ActionScript using the new keyword	Object	Array, Color, ContextMenu, ContextMenuItem, Date, Error, LoadVars, LocalConnection, NetConnection, NetStream, Object, PrintJob, MovieClipLoader, Sound, TextField.StyleSheet, TextFormat, XML, XMLNode, XMLSocket
Use instance members on objects instantiated in ActionScript using a class method	Object	Camera, Microphone, SharedObject, TextSnapshot, Video
Use instance members without having to explicitly instantiate an object	Object	Boolean, String, Number, Function, FunctionArguments
Use instance members on objects instantiated visually on the Stage or with ActionScript	Object	TextField, MovieClip
Use instance members on objects that can only be instantiated visually	Object	Button

In this exercise, you locate and explore the built-in classes listed in the Actions toolbox.

1. In Flash, open the Actions panel and make sure the Actions toolbox is visible.

It does not matter what file you have open; you are just exploring the Actions toolbox.

2. Click Built-in Classes to expand that branch of the tree.

Explore the various branches under Built-in Classes. You will use properties and methods of some of these built-in classes in the various exercises in this lesson.

Using Static Methods of the Math Class

The first class you will use is the Math class, which has properties that correspond to common mathematical constants such as Pi and e. The Math class has methods for common mathematical operations such as taking the square root, taking the absolute value, rounding to the nearest integer, and so on.

The Math class is one of the simplest built-in classes to use because you do not have to create an instance of it to use its properties or methods. All the Math class members are static. You can find the Math class in the Actions toolbox under Built-in Classes > Core; static properties are listed under Constants and static methods are listed under Methods.

A static property of the Math class is used here to calculate the area of a circle.

```
var radius:Number=4;
var circleArea:Number=Math.PI*radius*radius;
```

You can rewrite the same expression using the static method pow( ) of the Math class.

```
var circleArea:Number=Math.PI*Math.pow(radius,2);
```

In this exercise, you use static methods of the Math class. First, you use the round( ) method to round the calculated mortgage to two decimal places. Next, you use the pow( ) method to calculate the following term raised to a power in the mortgage calculation, $(1+\text{monthly interest rate})^{-\text{number of loan months}}$, instead of using a loop as you did in the last lesson.

1. In Flash, return to calcFunctions.as in /fpad2004/mmestate/includes/.

This is a file you created in the last exercise of Lesson 2. If you did not do that exercise, open /fpad2004/lesson03/start/includes/calcFunctions.as and save it as *calcFunctions.as* in /fpad2004/mmestate/includes/.

2. In the `calcMortgage()` function before the `return` statement, use the `round()` method of the Math class to round the `mortgage` to two decimal places. To do this, multiply the `mortgage` by 100, round it, and then divide it by 100.

The `round()` method has only one argument: the number to be rounded. Because the Math class methods are all static methods, you do not have to create an instance of the Math class. You simply use the class name followed by the method.

```
mortgage=Math.round(mortgage*100)/100;
```

After you enter the period (.), a code-hinting pop-up menu of all the properties and methods of the Math class appears. Press *r* on the keyboard to go directly to the class members starting with r and then use the keyboard's down arrow key to move to the `round()` method.

Tip *If code-hinting does not appear, make sure you used the correct case when you typed Math. All of ActionScript is case-sensitive.*

3. Save the document as *calcFunctions.as* in /fpad2004/mmestate/includes/.

You need to save the file so that the latest version will be included when you publish the application.

4. Return to calculator.fla in /fpad2004/mmestate/ and test the application.

This is the document you created in the last exercise of Lesson 2. If you did not do that exercise, open /fpad2004/lesson03/start/calculator.fla and save it as *calculator.fla* in /fpad2004/mmestate/.

You should get the mortgage rounded to two decimal places: $2383.49, in the Output panel.

5. Return to the `calcMortgage()` function in calcFunctions.as and delete or comment out the code defining the variable x and the `for` loop.

You are deleting this code, so you can use the `pow()` method of the Math class to calculate the term $(1+\text{monthly interest rate})^{-\text{number of loan months}}$ instead of using with the `for` loop, as you did previously.

Your function should appear as shown in the screenshot.

```
1  function calcMortgage(price:Number,rate:Number,down:Number,years:Number):
   Number
2  {
3      var monthlyrate:Number=rate/100/12;
4      var mortgage:Number=(price-down)*monthlyrate/(1-1/x);
5      mortgage=Math.round(mortgage*100)/100;
6      return mortgage;
7  }
```

6. Replace (1-1/x) in the line of code calculating the `mortgage` with
*(1-Math.pow(1+monthlyrate,-years*12)).*

```
var mortgage:Number=
(price-down)*monthlyrate/(1-Math.pow(1+monthlyrate,-years*12));
```

The `pow()` method computes and returns x to the power of y: x^y. The first argument is the number to be raised to a power. The second argument is the number specifying a power the first parameter is raised to.

In case you are interested in the math, here is the equation you are using to calculate the mortgage.

$$\text{mortgage} = \frac{(\text{price - down payment}) * \text{monthly interest rate}}{1-(1+\text{monthly interest rate})^{-\text{number of loan months}}}$$

7. Save the document as *calcFunctions.as* in */fpad2004/mmestate/*.

You will use this file as the starting file for the next exercise. It should resemble the finished file: /fpad2004/lesson03/intermediate/includes/calcFunctions_math.as.

8. Return to calculator.fla and test the application.

You should get exactly the same mortgage calculation as before, $2383.49, in the Output panel.

Creating and Using Instances of the Date Class

Next you will use the Date class. The Date class has no accessible properties, but has many methods enabling you to get and set parts of a date including the day, month, year, hours, minutes, seconds, and so on. You can access the user's system clock to get current date and time values or you can create a Date object with specific values.

To use any of the methods of the Date class, you must first create a Date object, an instance of the Date class. To do this, you call the class constructor function using the new keyword.

```
var today:Date=new Date();
```

Use strict data typing to type your variable when you declare it, exactly as you did for your primitive variables in the last lesson. This code creates a Date object that will refer to the user's system clock to retrieve any values. You can retrieve or set any of these values using methods of the Date class for that instance. Date class methods are listed in the Actions toolbox under Built-in Classes > Core > Date > Methods.

All the getter methods return values as numbers. If you want to display the month or day of the week as a string, you must write code. A method of the Date class is used here to display the current day of the week as a number: 0 for Sunday, 1 for Monday, and so on.

```
trace(today.getDay());
```

The methods including UTC in the name (for Universal Time Clock) get or set values according to universal time, which is set relative to the user's local time.

As well as creating an instance of the Date class that gets its values dynamically from the user's system clock, you can also create a Date object with specific values. You can do this by passing specific values to the constructor function. If you pass any arguments to the constructor, you must pass a year and month. The other arguments are optional.

```
new Date(year:Number,month:Number,date:Number,hour:Number,min:Number,
sec:Number,ms:Number);
```

Use the following rules when specifying your values:

Year. Use all four digits (A value of 0 to 99 indicates 1900 though 1999)

Month. Specify an integer from 0 (January) to 11 (December)

Date. Specify an integer from 1 to 31

Hour. Specify an integer from 0 (midnight) to 23 (11 pm)

In the following code, a new Date object is created with values for the year and month.

```
var startDate:Date=new Date(2003,10);
```

You can trace the date and see that if no value for the date parameter is passed to the constructor as a third argument, the day of the month is set equal to 1. If no hours, minutes, or milliseconds are specified, they are set equal to 0.

```
trace(startDate);
```

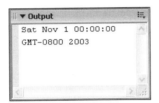

In this exercise, you create an instance of the Date class and then print out the current date in a custom format.

1. In Flash, return to calculator.fla in /fpad2004/mmestate/.

Return to the file you used in the last exercise or open /fpad2004/lesson03/start/calculator.fla and save it as *calculator.fla* in /fpad2004/mmestate/.

2. At the end of the code, declare a new variable called today that is of type *Date*.

```
var today:Date;
```

You are placing this at the end of the code to keep it separate from all the calculator variables and functions, which you are going to manipulate later.

3. Set the variable today equal to a new instance of the Date class. Use the new keyword followed by the class name and parentheses to call the constructor with no arguments.

```
var today:Date=new Date();
```

This code creates a Date object corresponding to the user's system clock. It does not hard-code the date value. Whenever you use a method of the object, the current values from the user's system clock are used.

4. Trace the variable **today** and test the application.

```
trace(today);
```

You should see today's date in the Output panel formatted, as shown here.

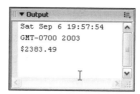

Even though the date is a complex object and not a string, you get a string value displayed in the Output panel because the date (and many of the other built-in classes) has a **toString()** method that is automatically invoked when using the **trace()** function to display data in the Output panel.

5. Change the **trace()** function to trace only the current month. Use the **getMonth()** method.

```
trace(today.getMonth());
```

You should get the number of the current month displayed in the Output panel. It might seem like this is off by one, but remember that January is month 0 and December is month 11. This is not as odd as it seems because arrays in Flash are zero-based. You will work with arrays later in this lesson.

6. Add one to the value returned from the **getMonth()** method. Test the application.

```
trace(today.getMonth()+1);
```

You should now get the "correct" month number displayed in the Output panel.

7. Add the string **"/"** inside the **trace()** function and then the current day of the month. Use the **getDate()** method. Test the application.

```
trace((today.getMonth()+1)+"/"+today.getDate());
```

You should now get the month and day in the format 9/6 displayed in the Output panel.

8. Add another string **"/"** to the **trace** and then the current year. Use the **getFullYear()** method. Test the application.

```
trace((today.getMonth()+1)+"/"+today.getDate()+"/"+ today.getFullYear());
```

You should now get the month, day, and year in the format, 9/6/2003, displayed in the Output panel.

9. Delete the two lines of code creating and displaying the date and save the document as *calculator.fla* in /fpad2004/mmestate/.

The finished file should resemble: /fpad2004/lesson03/intermediate/calculator_date.fla.

Manipulating Strings Using the String Wrapper Class

Next you will use the String class, which is a **wrapper** class for the primitive string data type and provides methods to manipulate it. Similarly, there are Number and Boolean classes, which are wrappers for the number and Boolean primitive data types.

Although you can explicitly create instances of the String, Number, and Boolean classes using a constructor with the new keyword, you don't have to. You can directly invoke a method on the variable holding the primitive data type. The Flash interpreter automatically creates an instance of the class, invokes the method, and then deletes the instance after method invocation is complete. When a String object is created, the actual value of the primitive string data type is held in an internal, unnamed property.

As an example, the String class has a method called toUpperCase() that returns an uppercase version of the string.

```
var frameType:String="Kona";
trace(frameType.toUpperCase());        //Outputs KONA
```

All the properties and methods of the String class are listed in the Actions toolbox.

The String class has only one property, length, which returns the length of the string.

```
trace(frameType.length());             //Outputs 4
```

All the String class methods are instance methods, except the fromCharCode() method, which is a static method that generates a string by concatenating the characters represented by specific Unicode character code points.

In this exercise, you create a function formatNumber() that uses properties and methods of the String class to remove any non-numeric characters from string values for the house price and down payment. Although hard-coded in this exercise, the house price and down payment values will be input by the user from the Flash interface in a later exercise, and any dollar signs or commas they might enter need to be stripped out.

1. In Flash, create a new ActionScript file.

Select File > New. In the New Document dialog box, select ActionScript file and click OK.

2. Create a new function called `formatNumber` that returns a *Number* and has one parameter called `start` of type *String*.

```
function formatNumber(start:String):Number
{
}
```

This function will take a string with any characters in it (such as "$500,000") and return the equivalent number (500000). You cannot use the `Number()` function or the `parseInt()` functions to do this. If you pass a string equal to "$500,000" to either of these functions, you get NaN.

3. Inside the function, create a variable called `end` that is of type *String* and is equal to an empty string, `""`.

```
var end:String="";
```

You will loop over the starting string value and place all the numeric characters into this variable called end. In this way, you are building a new string comprised of only the numeric characters.

4. Inside the function, create a `for` loop that loops over the length of the `start` string. Use the `length` property of the String class.

```
for (var i=0;i<start.length;i++)
{
}
```

Remember, you do not have to create an instance of the String class before using any of its properties or methods. You can invoke the properties and methods directly on a variable holding a primitive String data type.

5. Inside the `for` loop, create an `if` statement to check and see whether the character at the ith position in the `start` string is a number. Use the String class `charAt()` method and the `Number()` and `isNaN()` functions.

```
if(!isNaN(Number(start.charAt(i))))
{
}
```

Let's walk through what each of these methods and functions do.

The String class `charAt()` method returns the character at a specific position in a string. The code `start.charAt(i)` returns the character in the ith position; you are looping through and examining each letter in the `start` string. For the `start` string "$500,000", `start.charAt(0)` returns "$", and `start.charAt(1)` returns "5".

The Number() function converts the character (a primitive string) to a primitive number. For the start string "$500,000", Number(start.charAt(0)) returns NaN, and Number(start.charAt(1)) returns 5.

The isNaN() function checks to see if the value is equal to NaN. For the start string "$500,000", isNaN(Number(start.charAt(0))) returns true, and isNaN(Number(start.charAt(1))) returns false.

Finally, the ! checks to see if the opposite is true. For the start string "$500,000", !isNaN(Number (start.charAt(0))) returns false, and !isNaN(Number(start.charAt(1))) returns true. Any characters for which this complete expression is true are characters that you want to keep.

6. Inside the **if** statement, add the character in the ith position to the end variable.

```
end+=start.charAt(i);
```

You are building a new string called end that contains only numeric characters.

7. After the **for** loop, return the number equivalent of the end string. Use the **Number()** function.

```
return Number(end);
```

Your final function should appear as shown in the screenshot.

```
1  function formatNumber(start:String):Number
2  {
3      var end:String="";
4      for (var i=0;i<start.length;i++)
5      {
6          if(!isNaN(Number(start.charAt(i))))
7          {
8              end+=start.charAt(i);
9          }
10     }
11     return Number(end);
12 }
```

8. Save the document as *formatFunctions.as* in /fpad2004/mmestate/includes/.

It should resemble the finished file: /fpad2004/lesson03/intermediate/includes/formatFunctions.as.

9. Return to calculator.fla in /fpad2004/mmestate/.

Return to the file you used in the last exercise or open /fpad2004/lesson03/intermediate/ calculator_date.fla and save it as *calculator.fla* in /fpad2004/mmestate/.

10. Before the existing `include`, include your new file, formatFunctions.as.

```
#include "includes/formatFunctions.as"
```

Remember, don't put a semicolon at the end of the `include` statement.

You did not place the `formatNumber()` function in the calcFunctions.as file because it is a general function, which can be reused in many different applications.

11. After the two `include` statements, declare a variable called `price_txt` of type *String* and set it equal to "$500,000."

```
var price_txt:String="$500,000";
```

12. Change the declaration of the existing `price` variable, so instead of setting it equal to the number 500000, you set it equal to the value returned from the `formatNumber()` function when you pass `price_txt` to it as an argument.

```
var price:Number=formatNumber(price_txt);
```

The `price` variable is still equal to the number 500000, but it is now set from the initial string, "*$500,000.*"

13. Test the application.

You should get exactly the same mortgage calculation as before, $2383.49, in the Output panel.

14. Save the document as *calculator.fla* in /fpad2004/mmestate/.

It should resemble the finished file: /fpad2004/lesson03/intermediate/calculator_string.fla.

Creating and Manipulating Arrays

In the previous exercises, you learned three different ways to use methods of classes, using static methods, instance methods, and instance methods of wrapper classes. Now that you have mastered using methods, you move on to work with some of the built-in classes for manipulating more complex data types. In this exercise, you create and manipulate arrays.

In ActionScript, an array is an object. It is an instance of the Array class that has properties and methods to manipulate individual array instances. As in most programming languages, the first element of an ActionScript array has the index [0].

Creating Array Objects

You create a new Array object using the new keyword to call the constructor function, exactly as you did to create an instance of the Date class.

```
var bikes:Array=new Array();
```

If no elements are specified, an empty array is created. You can populate specific elements of the array by assigning values to particular indices.

```
bikes[0]="Kona";
bikes[1]="Rocky Mountain";
```

Note *You can type an Array object only as an Array data type. You cannot type the items contained in the array as you can in some programming languages.*

If you assign values of noncontiguous indices, the elements in-between are assigned a value of undefined and are counted in the length of the array.

```
bikes[0]="Kona";
bikes[1]="Rocky Mountain";
bikes[3]="VooDoo";
```

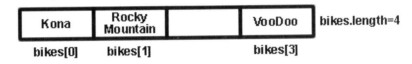

You can also pass individual values to the array constructor function to be used to populate the array.

```
var bikes:Array=new Array("Kona","Rocky Mountain","VooDoo");
```

If you pass only one integer value to the constructor function, though, it is used to set the length of the array—not the value of the first element. All the elements are assigned the value undefined.

```
var bikes:Array=new Array(3);
trace(bikes[0])                        //Outputs undefined
```

Tip *ActionScript does not directly support multidimensional arrays; for example,* my2Darray=new Array(2) *creates a single dimension array of length 2. To create a multidimensional array, you must add an array as an element of an existing array:* my2Darray=new Array(); my2Darray[0]=new Array(2);my2Darray[1]=new Array(2);.

You can also assign an element dynamically.

```
var elementPosition:Number=1;
bikes[elementPosition]="Rocky Mountain";
trace(bikes[1]);                    //Outputs Rocky Mountain
```

Finally, you can use a shortcut notation to create instances of the Array class. Two examples are shown here.

```
var bikes:Array=[];
var bikes:Array=["Kona","Rocky Mountain","VooDoo"];
```

Using Array Class Properties

The Array class has one instance property, length, which contains the length of the array—including any undefined elements.

```
var bikes:Array=new Array("Kona","Rocky Mountain");
bikes[3]="VooDoo";
trace(bikes.length); //Outputs 4
```

The Array class also has five static properties that are used in conjunction with the sort() and sortOn() methods, which are discussed in the next section.

Using Array Class Methods

The methods for the Array class are listed in the Actions toolbox under Built-in Classes > Core > Array > Methods.

For developers new to ActionScript, the array methods can be confusing because some array methods operate on and return the existing array instance whereas others return a new array instance or another value. In the following table, details for each method are displayed, indicating what is returned from each method and whether the method affects the original array.

Method	Return Value	Affects Original?	Description
concat()	new array	no	Appends all the method arguments to the existing array.
join()	new string	no	Converts an array to a string separated by commas (unless another delimiter is specified).
pop()	new string, number, or Boolean	yes	Removes the last element of the array and returns its value. Array is compacted.
push()	new array length	yes	Appends all method arguments to the existing array.
reverse()	reversed array	yes	Reverses the order of the indices.
shift()	new string, number, or Boolean	yes	Removes the first element of the array and returns its value. Array is compacted.
slice()	new array	no	Returns the elements from index start to index end as a new array.
sort()	sorted array	yes	Sorts the array alphabetically. See the Sorting an Array section.
sortOn()	sorted array	yes	Sorts an array of objects by the specified property. Objects are introduced in a later exercise in this lesson.
splice()	new array	yes	Deletes elements from an array and creates a new array containing the deleted elements. Array is compacted.
toString()	new string	no	Returns a comma-delimited list of the array elements converted to strings.
unShift()	new array length	yes	Adds one or more elements to the beginning of an array.

In this exercise, you create an array to hold all the initial values for the calculator. You create and populate the array using several different techniques.

1. In Flash, return to calculator.fla in /fpad2004/mmestate/.

Return to the file you created in the last exercise or open /fpad2004/lesson03/intermediate/ calculator_string.fla and save it as *calculator.fla* in /fpad2004/mmestate/.

2. After the `price_txt` variable declaration, create a new variable called `calculator` that is of type *Array* and make it a new instance of the Array class.

```
var calculator:Array=new Array();
```

Use strict data typing to get code-hinting and compile-time data typing.

3. Populate the array with the values *500000* and *200000* by passing values to the constructor. Trace the `calculator` array and test the application.

```
var calculator:Array=new Array(500000,200000);
trace(calculator);
```

You should get "500000,200000" in the Output panel. Even though the array is a complex object and not a string, you get a string value displayed in the Output panel, similar to how you saw a string value when tracing the complex Date object earlier. If it exists, a `toString()` method of an object is automatically invoked when you attempt to trace a complex object using the `trace()` function.

4. Before the `trace()` function, populate the first and second array indices with the values 5 and 56000.

```
calculator[1]=5;
calculator[2]=56000;
```

You should see "500000,5,56000" in the Output panel. ActionScript arrays are zero-based, so the first index is the second element in the array, and the previous value in the first index is overwritten.

5. After the `trace(calculator)`, add another line of code to trace the `length` of the array and then test the application.

```
trace(calculator.length);
```

Notice that because you typed the calculator variable as an array, you get code-hinting. When you test the application, you should get a length of 3 displayed in the Output panel.

6. Change the line populating the second index to populate the third index. Test the application.

```
calculator[3]=56000;
```

You should get "500000,5,undefined, 56000" in the Output panel and an array length of 4.

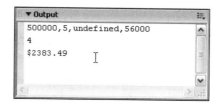

When you populate discontiguous array indices, all elements between are given values of undefined and are counted in the length of the array.

7. Before the `trace` statements, add a new element with the value *30* to the end of the array. Use the `push()` method. Test the application.

```
calculator.push(30);
```

You should see "500000,5,undefined,56000,30" in the Output panel and an array length of 5.

8. Before the `trace` statements, add a new element with the value *0* to the beginning of the array. Use the `unshift()` method. Test the application.

```
calculator.unshift(0);
```

You should see "0,500000,5,undefined,56000,30" in the Output panel and an array length of 6.

9. Save the document as *calculator.fla* in */fpad2004/mmestate/*.

It should resemble the finished file: /fpad2004/lesson03/intermediate/calculator_array.fla.

Sorting an Array

You use the `sort()` method of the Array class to sort a simple array. By default, the sort is alphabetical and case-sensitive: numbers are first, followed by uppercase letters, and then lowercase letters. (The numeric Unicode code points for the characters are used for sorting.)

```
var test:Array=new Array("Gabrielle","alex",2,15);
trace(test.sort());
//Outputs 15,2,Gabrielle,alex
```

You can change how the array is sorted by passing an argument to the `sort()` method, specifying how you want it sorted. There are five static properties (called constants in the Actions toolbox) of the Array class you can use as arguments.

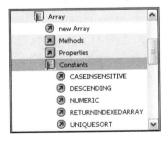

Use one of these static properties as an argument to the `sort()` method.

```
var test:Array=new Array("Gabrielle","alex",2,15);
trace(test.sort(Array.CASEINSENSITIVE));
//Outputs 15,2,alex,Gabrielle
```

You can specify multiple sort conditions by separating multiple sort properties with the | character.

```
var test:Array=new Array("Gabrielle","alex",2,15);
trace(test.sort(Array.CASEINSENSITIVE|Array.NUMERIC));
//Outputs 2,15,alex,Gabrielle
```

Looping Over an Array

You can use the `for` loop to loop over the elements of an array. Just use the array's `length` property in the loop's test condition.

```
for (var i=0;i<test.length;i++)
{
  trace("["+i+"] "+test[i]);
}
```

You can also loop over an array using a `for-in` loop. A `for-in` loop is a special type of loop used to loop over the members of an object. The loop body is executed once for each member of the object. Each loop iteration, the iterator variable (called `item` in the following code) is assigned the name of the property or method in the object. For an Array object, the loop is executed once for each element in the array, and the `item` variable is assigned the number of the array element.

```
for (var item in test)
{
  trace(item+" "+ test[item]);
}
```

Notice that the properties of the built-in array class are not enumerated; you do not see the `length` property or the `unshift()` method listed in the output because most of the properties and methods of the built-in classes have been hidden so they do not appear in a `for-in` loop. All user-defined properties are displayed, but only some or none of the built-in members are.

Tip *To hide user-defined properties or to display specific built-in properties or methods in a* for-in *loop, you can use the undocumented* ASSetPropFlags() *function. You can find information on this function in the Macromedia Press book,* Object Oriented Programming with ActionScript 2.0.

When using a `for-in` loop, the properties of an object are not looped over in any predictable order. For large arrays, a `for` loop is also faster than an equivalent `for-in` loop. Thus, it is usually more desirable to use a `for` loop when looping through an array.

In this exercise, you sort and loop over your `calculator` array.

1. In Flash, return to calculator.fla in /fpad2004/mmestate/.

Return to the file you created in the last exercise or open /fpad2004/lesson03/intermediate/calculator_array.fla and save it as *calculator.fla* in /fpad2004/mmestate/.

2. Before the `trace` statements for the array, sort the array. Use the `sort()` method.

```
calculator.sort();
```

```
 5  var calculator:Array=new Array(500000,200000).
 6  calculator[1]=5;
 7  calculator[3]=56000;
 8  calculator.push(30);
 9  calculator.unshift(0);
10  calculator.sort();
11  trace(calculator);
12  trace(calculator.length);
```

3. Test the application.

You should see "0,30,5,500000,56000,undefined" in the Output panel. By default, the elements are sorted alphabetically, not numerically.

4. Add the argument `Array.NUMERIC` to the `sort()` method. Test the application.

```
calculator.sort(Array.NUMERIC);
```

`Array.NUMERIC` is a static property of the Array class and can be found under Built-in Classes > Core > Array > Constants in the Actions toolbox. You should also see a pop-up display of all the static properties after you type `Array.` in the Actions panel.

You should see "0,5,30,56000,500000,undefined" in the Output panel. The array is correctly sorted numerically.

5. Add a second sort type, `Array.DESCENDING`, to the `sort()` method. Use the | symbol to separate the sort types. Test the application.

```
prices.sort(Array.NUMERIC | Array.DESCENDING);
```

You should get "undefined,500000,56000,30,5,0" in the Output panel. The array is now sorted numerically in a descending order.

6. After the `trace` statements, loop over the `calculator` array using a `for` loop. Loop from 0 to the `length` of the array.

```
for (var i=0;i<calculator.length;i++)
{
}
```

Why is your test condition i less than the calculator length, and not less than or equal to the length? Because arrays are zero-based which means that if the array has three elements, it has indices 0 to 2; one fewer than the length of the array.

7. Inside the loop, trace the number of each array element and its value.

```
trace(i+" "+calculator[i]);
```

Here you are assigning the array element position dynamically. The variable i is set equal to a new value with each loop iteration.

You should see the following in the Output panel.

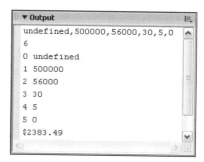

8. Comment out or delete all the code you added in this lesson for manipulating an array, except the variable declaration for `calculator`.

The one line of code you keep is highlighted in the code below.

```
1  // Created by Jeanette Stallons 8/11/03
2  #include "includes/formatFunctions.as"
3  #include "includes/calcFunctions.as"
4  var price_txt:String="$500,000";
5  var calculator:Array=new Array(500000,200000);
6  var price:Number=formatNumber(price_txt);
7  var rate:Number=5;
```

9. Save the document as *calculator.fla* in /fpad2004/mmestate/.

It should resemble the finished file: /fpad2004/lesson03/intermediate/calculator_arraysortloop.fla.

Creating Associative Arrays

In addition to creating arrays with numeric indices, you can create **named** or **associative** arrays, whose elements are identified by a string instead of a number. Using an associative array is useful when you want to store separate but related data in an array, not just variants of the same data. For example, in the last section, we created an array holding the types of bikes. All the elements in the array were the same thing: a name of a bike. What if you wanted to have the array hold all the data for one particular bike instead: type, size, color, and so on? In this case, it does not make sense to have numeric indices because you would have to remember, for example, which piece of data you stored in element 2. Instead, you can use named array indices.

Using named array indices has two main benefits.

- You can assign a meaningful named index to represent what is in an element.
- You can access an element without knowing its position in the array.

> **Tip** *Instead of creating an associative array to hold name/value pairs, you can create a custom object, which is a more common practice.*

To create a named array, you first create an instance of the Array class exactly as you did for a numerically indexed array.

```
var bike:Array=new Array();
```

You can then create a named element by specifying a name instead of a number for the array index.

```
bike["frameType"]="Kona";
```

The named array element is another property of the Array object. You surround the name of the element with quotation marks because it is a literal string.

You can also assign an element name dynamically.

```
var elementName:String="frameSize";
bike[elementName]=17;
trace(bike["frameSize"]);          //Outputs 17
```

You can use dot notation to assign and access a named element, just as you did to access properties of built-in class instances.

```
bike.frameSize=17;
```

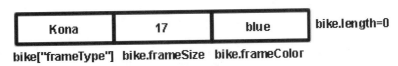

What effect does naming an array element instead of using a number have on the Array object?

- Named elements are not considered in the length of the array. Although not recommended, you can create a mixed array containing both numeric and named elements. In this case, the array length is the number of numerically indexed elements only.

- You cannot access a named element by a number, only by its name.

- You cannot use Array class methods to manipulate named array elements. To delete a named element, you use the keyword: `delete bike.frameSize;`.

- You must use a `for-in` loop to loop through and access all elements of a named or mixed array.

In this exercise, you change your `calculator` array into an associative array.

1. In Flash, return to calculator.fla in /fpad2004/mmestate/.

Return to the file you created in the last exercise or open /fpad2004/lesson03/intermediate/ calculator_arraysortloop.fla and save it as *calculator.fla* in /fpad2004/mmestate/.

2. Remove the two initial array values from the statement declaring the `calculator` array.

Your assignment should appear as shown.

```
var calculator:Array=new Array();
```

You will populate the array elements after the array is created.

3. Change the `price` and the `rate` variable declarations so they are named elements in the `calculator` array. Use array notation to define the elements.

Here is one of the starting lines of code.

```
var price:Number=formatNumber(price_txt);
```

First, delete the `var` keywords and then delete the data typing for the `price` and `rate` variables. Prefix the variables with `calculator`, the name of the array, and then place the element name in quotation marks inside square brackets.

```
calculator["price"]=formatNumber(price_txt);
calculator["rate"]=5;
```

You are getting experience using square bracket notation to assign properties of an associative array.

4. Change the `down` and `years` variable declarations so they are named elements in the `calculator` array. Use dot syntax to define the elements.

```
calculator.down=56000;
calculator.years=30;
```

You are using dot notation to assign properties of an associative array.

5. After the `calculator.years` property assignment, trace the `price` element of the array. Test the application.

```
trace(calculator.price);
```

You can use array or dot notation.

Note *If you* `trace(calculator)`, *you get no output. The* `toString()` *method does not work with an associative array.*

In the Output panel, you see the price 500000 and the error message: "Error: Invalid price or down payment." Why do you get this error? Look at the call to the `displayMortgage()` function. It is trying to pass variables `price`, `rate`, `down`, and `years` that no longer exist.

6. Change the variables passed to the `displayMortgage()` function so they are elements of the `calculator` array. Use dot notation. Test the application.

```
displayMortgage(calculator.price,calculator.rate,calculator.down,
calculator.years);
```

The correct mortgage payment, $2383.49, should be calculated and displayed.

7. Change the `trace()` function to trace the `length` of the array instead of the `price`. Test the application.

```
trace(calculator.length);
```

You get a length of zero. Because the array does not have any numeric indices, it has a length of zero.

8. After the `trace()`, loop over the `calculator` array. Use a `for-in` loop.

```
for (var i in calculator)
{
}
```

You cannot use a regular `for` loop because this is an associative array that no longer has a meaningful `length` property.

9. Inside the loop, trace the name of each array element and its value. Use square bracket notation to dynamically evaluate the named property of the array.

```
trace(i+" "+calculator[i]);
```

You should get the following in the Output panel:

10. Delete the **trace** of `calculator.length` and save the document as *calculator.fla* in **/fpad2004/mmestate/.**

It should resemble the finished file: /fpad2004/lesson03/intermediate/calculator_namedarray.fla.

Creating Custom Objects

In the last exercise, you created an associative array—an Array object with custom properties. After you added named properties to the Array object, however, you could no longer use the properties and methods of the Array class, removing any benefit the object had for being an instance of the Array class.

When you want a collection of name/value pairs associated with one variable and don't need to (or can't) use any of the properties or methods of a built-in class, you can instead create an instance of the general Object class, which allows you to create a complex data type with its own properties and/or methods that you define.

> **Tip** *Remember, all of the built-in classes in Flash are children of the Object class.*

Creating Objects

You create a new Object instance using the new keyword to invoke the Object class constructor.

```
var rectangle:Object=new Object();
```

For arrays, there was also the [] short-cut syntax you could use to access the Array class constructor. Similarly, you can shortcut the call to the Object class constructor using {} notation.

```
var rectangle:Object={};
```

Defining Properties

You usually add properties to an object after you create it. Assign properties using dot or square bracket notation.

```
rectangle["sideA"]=4;
rectangle.sideB=5;
```

You can also assign a property name dynamically.

```
var propertyName:String="sideA";
rectangle[propertyName]=4;
trace(rectangle.sideA);                    //Outputs 4
```

If you use the {} notation, you can also assign properties to an object when you create it (instead of after). Inside the curly braces, you specify property name/value pairs separated by commas.

```
var rectangle:Object={sideA:4,sideB:5};
```

> **Note** *You cannot type the properties of an object as you can in some programming languages.*

In this exercise, you change the `calculator` associative array you created in the last exercise into a general Object class instance. The object properties are the house price, loan rate, down payment, and loan years.

1. In Flash, return to calculator.fla in /fpad2004/mmestate/.

Return to the file you created in the last exercise or open /fpad2004/lesson03/intermediate/ calculator_namedarray.fla and save it as *calculator.fla* in /fpad2004/mmestate/.

2. Change the `calculator` variable declaration so instead of creating a new array, you create a new instance of the Object class. Test the application.

```
var calculator:Object=new Object();
```

You should now see the object properties appear as output from the `for` loop, exactly as they did when they were properties of the associative array. The correct mortgage payment, $2383.49, should be calculated and displayed because you refer to properties of objects exactly as you do named elements of arrays.

3. Change the `include` statement to include *calcObject.as* instead of calcFunctions.as.

```
#include "includes/calcObject.as"
```

You are going to create this file in the next several steps.

4. Cut the code declaring the `calculator` object and its properties and paste the code at the top of the calcFunctions.as file.

Return to the file you used in the last exercise or open /fpad2004/lesson03/intermediate/includes/calcFunctions_math.fla.

5. Change the `calculator` objects' `price` property back to the value of *500000* (instead of `formatNumber(price_txt)`).

```
calculator["price"]=500000;
```

You will use this value as an initial value for the input text field in a later exercise.

6. Save the file as *calcObject.as* in **/fpad2004/mmestate/includes/**.

You are changing the name of the file because calcFunctions.as is no longer an appropriate name. The file will contain all the code for defining the `calculator` object, its properties, and its methods.

The finished file should resemble: /fpad2004/lesson03/intermediate/includes/calcObject_object.as.

7. Return to calculator.fla and save it in **/fpad2004/mmestate/**. Test the application.

The correct mortgage payment, $2383.49, should be calculated and displayed along with values for each of the properties of the `calculator` object.

The finished file should resemble: /fpad2004/lesson03/intermediate/calculator_object.fla.

Defining Methods

In addition to creating properties for a custom object, you can create custom methods. A **method** is just a function that belongs to an object. To create a method, set the name of the method equal to the name of a function or a function literal (which were introduced in Lesson 2). In most cases, function literals are used because the code is not reused anywhere in your code.

Here we add a method called getRectArea() to the rectangle object that calculates the rectangle's area.

```
var rectangle:Object=new Object();
rectangle.sideA=4;
rectangle.sideB=5;
rectangle.getRectArea=function(sideA:Number,sideB:Number):Number
{
      var area:Number=sideA*sideB;
      return area;
};
```

Tip *As a best practice, the names of your object methods should be verbAdjective or verbNoun constructs.*

You do not need to explicitly pass parameters sideA and sideB in the method call, however, because these are properties of the rectangle. You can remove them as parameters to the method and instead refer to them directly inside the method definition.

```
rectangle.getRectArea=function():Number
{
      var area:Number=rectangle.sideA*rectangle.sideB;
      return area;
};
```

You can also take this one step further. You do not have to explicitly refer to the sideA and sideB properties of the rectangle object because this method getRectArea() also belongs to the rectangle object. You can instead refer to the properties as this.sideA and this.sideB. Inside a method definition, this refers to the object the method belongs to.

```
rectangle.getRectArea()=function:Number
{
      var area:Number=this.sideA*this.sideB;
      return area;
};
```

Instead of returning the area as an independent variable, you can make it a property of the rectangle object.

```
rectangle.area;
rectangle.getRectArea()=function:Void
{
      this.area=this.sideA*this.sideB;
};
rectangle.getRectArea();
trace(rectangle.area);                     //Outputs 20
```

Looping Over Objects

You loop over your custom objects using a `for-in` loop. For an Object object, the loop is executed once for each property or method of the Object instance. In the following code, the iterator `item` is assigned the name of the object property or method. The members of an object are not looped through in any predictable order.

```
for (var item in rectangle)
{
        trace(item+" "+rectangle[item]);
}
```

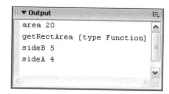

Retrieving an Object's Type

When you need to determine programmatically what type of object you have, you can use the `instanceof` operator.

```
x instanceof class
```

For example, the following code checks to see whether a variable `test` is an instance of the Array class.

```
var test:Array=new Array();
if (test instanceof Array)
{
        trace(test.length);              //Outputs 0
}
```

The variable `test` is an `Array` object, so the expression returns true and the code inside the `if` block is executed. Because all built-in classes are children of the Object class, an array is also an instance of the Object class. The code inside the `if` block is also executed in the following code.

```
var test:Array=new Array();
if (test instanceof Object)
{
        trace(test.length);
}
```

Tip *The class name is case-sensitive.*

In this exercise, you change the `displayMortgage()` and `calcMortgage()` methods from stand-alone functions to methods of the `calculator` object.

1. In Flash, return to calcObject.as in /fpad2004/mmestate/includes/.

Return to the file you used in the last exercise or open /fpad2004/lesson03/intermediate/includes/ calcObject_object.as and save it as *calcObject.as* in /fpad2004/mmestate/includes/.

2. Change the `calcMortgage()` and `displayMortgage()` function definitions so instead of being stand-alone functions, they are methods of the `calculator` object. Save the file.

```
calculator.calcMortgage=function(price:Number,rate:Number,down:Number,
years:Number):Number
calculator.displayMortgage=function(price:Number,rate:Number,
down:Number,years:Number):Void
```

3. Return to calculator.fla and test the application.

Return to the file you created in the last exercise or open /fpad2004/lesson03/intermediate/ calculator_object.fla and save it as *calculator.fla* in /fpad2004/mmestate/.

You should now see the methods appear as output from the `for` loop.

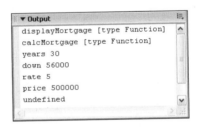

```
▼ Output
displayMortgage [type Function]
calcMortgage [type Function]
years 30
down 56000
rate 5
price 500000
undefined
```

The mortgage payment, however, is no longer calculated and displayed. Why not? Look at the call to `displayMortgage()` in calculator.fla. You are still calling the stand-alone function, not the method of the `calculator` object.

4. In calculator.fla, delete or comment out the `for-in` loop. Next, change the call to `displayMortgage()`, so you are calling the method of the `calculator` object.

```
calculator.displayMortgage(calculator.price,calculator.rate,
calculator.down,calculator.years);
```

5. Return to calcObject.as. Inside the `displayMortgage()` method, change the call to the `calcMortage()` function to call the method. Save the file.

```
payment="$"+this.calcMortgage(price,rate,down,years);
```

You could also use `calculator.calcMortgage(price,rate,down,years)` but `this.calcMortgage(price,rate,down,years)` is more general.

6. Return to calculator.fla and test the application.

You should again get the correct mortgage payment, $2383.49, calculated and displayed.

7. In calcObject.as, delete all parameters from the `calcMortgage()` method definition.

```
calculator.calcMortgage=function():Number
```

Instead of passing arguments to the method, you are going to access properties of the object directly from within the method.

8. Inside `calcMortgage()`, change all occurrences of the `price`, `rate`, `down` and `years` variables to `this.price`, `this.rate`, `this.down`, and `this.years`.

There is one reference to each variable.

```
 7  calculator.calcMortgage=function():Number
 8  {
 9      var monthlyrate:Number=this.rate/100/12;
10      var mortgage:Number=(this.price-this.down)*monthlyrate/(1-Math.pow(1+
        monthlyrate,-this.years*12));
11      mortgage=Math.round(mortgage*100)/100;
12      return mortgage;
13  }
```

9. In the definition for the `displayMortgage()` method, delete all arguments from the call to `calcMortgage()`.

```
payment="$"+this.calcMortgage();
```

10. Delete all parameters from the `displayMortgage()` method definition.

```
calculator.displayMortgage=function():String
```

11. Inside `displayMortgage()`, change all occurrence of the `price`, `rate`, `down` and `years` variables to `this.price`, `this.rate`, `this.down`, and `this.years`. Save the file.

There are a total of five occurrences.

```
18      try
19      {
20          if (this.down>this.price || (typeof this.price!="number"))
21          {
22              throw "Invalid price or down payment";
23          }
24          else if (this.rate<0 || this.rate>100)
25          {
26              throw "Invalid rate";
27          }
28          else
```

12. In calculator.fla, delete all arguments from the call to the `displayMortgage()` method. Test the application.

```
calculator.displayMortgage();
```

You should again get the correct mortgage payment, $2383.49, calculated and displayed.

13. In calcObject.as, create another property of the `calculator` object, call it **mortgage**, and set it equal to *0*.

```
1  var calculator:Object=new Object()
2  calculator["price"]=500000;
3  calculator["rate"]=5;
4  calculator.down=56000;
5  calculator.years=30;
6  calculator.mortgage=0;
7
```

14. Change the return type of the `calcMortgage()` method from **Number** to **Void**.

```
calculator.calcMortgage=function():Void
```

You will rewrite the method, so instead of returning a value, it sets a property of the `calculator` object.

15. Inside the method, delete the `return` statement, remove the `var` keyword from in front of the **mortgage** variable and remove its data type of Number.

```
mortgage=(this.price-this.down)*monthlyrate/(1-Math.pow(1+monthlyrate,
-this.years*12));
```

16. Replace the three instances of the `mortgage` variable in the `calcMortgage()` method definition with `this.mortgage`.

```
this.mortgage=(price-down)*monthlyrate/(1-Math.pow(1+monthlyrate,
-years*12));
this.mortgage=Math.round(this.mortgage*100)/100;
```

17. In the `displayMortgage()` method, call the `calcMortgage()` method right above the line of code currently calling it.

```
19        if (this.down>this.price || (typeof this.price!="number")
20        {
21            throw "Invalid price or down payment";
22        }
23        else if (this.rate<0 || this.rate>100)
24        {
25            throw "Invalid rate";
26        }
27        else
28        {
29            this.calcMortgage();
30            payment="$"+this.calcMortgage();
31            trace(payment);
32        }
```

18. Change the statement assigning a value to `payment`, so instead of calling the `calcMortgage()` function, it uses the `mortgage` property of the `calculator` object.

```
payment="$"+this.mortgage;
```

19. Save the file as *calcObject.as* in /fpad2004/mmestate/

It should resemble the finished file: /fpad2004/lesson03/intermediate/includes/calcObject_methods.as.

20. Return to calculator.fla and save it in /fpad2004/mmestate/. Test the application.

You should again get the mortgage payment, $2383.49, calculated and displayed.

The finished file should resemble: /fpad2004/lesson03/intermediate/calculator_methods.fla.

Manipulating Visual TextField Objects

So far in this lesson, you have learned how to create and manipulate nonvisual objects with ActionScript. You can also use ActionScript to manipulate visual objects on the Stage. In code, you work with visual objects the same way you work with nonvisual objects: by setting properties and invoking methods.

To manipulate visual objects with code, you need to learn two things:

- How to reference the visual objects from your code.

- The types of visual built-in classes that are available and what their properties and methods are so you can manipulate them.

There are three types of built-in visual classes in Flash: the TextField, Button, and MovieClip classes. First, you get familiar with the TextField class. You created instances of the TextField class when you created input and dynamic text fields on the Stage. In this exercise, you will learn how to change these text fields' values and appearances and how to use the values input into them by the user. In the next lesson, you learn about the Button and MovieClip classes, which are more complex visual objects with their own Timelines.

Instance Names

To make TextField objects accessible from ActionScript, you must give them instance names so that you can reference them in your code. You assign instance names for visual objects in the Property inspector.

You can only manipulate dynamic and input TextField objects with ActionScript, not static text fields. You cannot assign instance names to static text fields in the Property inspector.

Tip *You should get in the habit of immediately adding an instance name whenever you add a visual object to the Stage.*

From the Actions panel, you can use the Target tool to view the names of all the visual objects on the Stage and insert them into your code. You click the Insert a target path icon on the Actions panel's toolbar, which opens a dialog box where you can choose from a list of all available object instances.

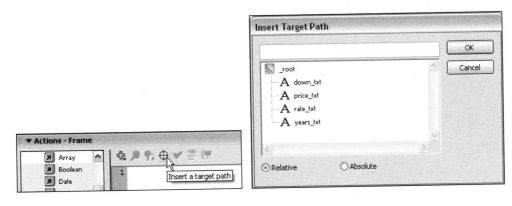

The `_root` reference refers to the main document; it is explained in detail in the next lesson. It indicates that all the TextField objects (denoted by the A symbol) reside in the main document (the main Timeline).

Code-Hinting

You can get code-hinting for a TextField object in two ways. You can assign a data type to the TextField objects in code in exactly the same way you have been typing your nonvisual objects. Here, a TextField object with the instance name price is typed as a TextField.

```
var price:TextField;
```

This variable declaration is allowed, even though you have already instantiated the object visually and assigned an instance name. The declaration simply assigns a data type to be used for compile-time data type checking of the ActionScript code. The data typing also enables code-hinting. Now, if you type the name of the variable followed by a period in your code, you get a pop-up of all the properties and methods for the TextField class.

You can also get code-hinting if you use a _txt suffix to name your TextField. Any time you type _txt. in your code, you get the pop-up containing all the properties and methods for the TextField class.

Tip *On Windows, the code hints for suffixes are defined in <boot drive>\Documents and Settings\<username>\Local Settings\Application Data\ Macromedia\Flash MX 2004\<language>\ Configuration\ActionsPanel\AsCodeHints.xml. On Macintosh, the code hints are defined in <Macintosh HD>/Users <username>/Library/Application Support/Macromedia/Flash MX 2004/<language>/Configuration/ActionsPanel/ AsCodeHints.xml. This file contains code-hinting suffixes that can be used for all of the built-in objects: _array, _date, _string, and so on. You can change the suffixes for the code hints that appear by editing this file.*

Properties

Properties of visual objects can be modified using the Property inspector or with ActionScript. The most commonly modified properties are available to set in the authoring environment using the Property inspector. There are additional properties accessible only with ActionScript. Besides accessing additional properties, you also need to access TextField properties in code to set or modify properties at runtime and capture and respond to user input. If you assign values in both the Property inspector and with ActionScript, the ActionScript values are used because they are set at runtime instead of at compile time.

You can view a complete list of properties for the TextField class in the Actions toolbox. The TextField class can be found under Built-in Classes > Movie.

Some of the TextField properties are described here.

Property	Value	Description
text	a string	Sets the text to display onscreen in the text field.
autoSize	true/false	Makes the TextField object resize automatically to fit the text.
tabIndex	integer	Sets the tab index for input fields to allow the user to tab through them.
maxChars	integer	Limits the number of characters the user can enter in an input field.
password	true/false	Sets the display of input text to a string of asterisks.
textColor	hex color	Indicates the hexadecimal color of the text. In ActionScript, you use 0x instead of # for a hexadecimal color. For example, use 0xFF3300.

Here is a code sample setting TextField properties:

```
message_txt.autoSize=true;
orderID_txt.tabIndex=2;
orderID_txt.maxChars=6;
```

In this exercise, you give instance names to your calculator TextField objects, change their appearance with code, and then use their `text` properties to hook up your calculator interface to the code calculating the mortgage payment.

1. In Flash, return to calculator.fla in /fpad2004/mmestate/.

Return to the file you created in the last exercise or open /fpad2004/lesson03/intermediate/ calculator_methods.fla and save it as *calculator.fla* in /fpad2004/mmestate/.

2. Unlock the text folder in the Layer pane of the Timeline panel.

This step unlocks all the layers in the folder. If a layer is locked, you cannot manipulate the items located in it; you cannot even give them names in the Property inspector.

3. On the Stage, select the text field next to the text price and give it the instance name `price_txt` in the Property inspector. Give the other four text fields the instance names `rate_txt`, `down_txt`, `years_txt`, and `payment_txt`. Relock the text folder and save the file.

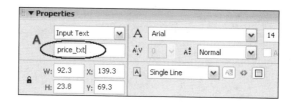

4. Return to calcObject.as.

Return to the file you created in the last exercise or open /fpad2004/lesson03/intermediate/includes/ calcObject_methods.as and save it as *calcObject.as* in /fpad2004/mmestate/includes/.

5. Delete the `trace(payment)` statement from the `else` block.

Instead of displaying the mortgage in the Output panel, you are finally going to display it in the calculator interface.

6. Change the code that assigns a value to the `payment` variable to instead set the `text` property of the `payment_txt` TextField. Save the file.

```
payment_txt.text="$"+this.mortgage;
```

The finished file should resemble: /fpad2004/lesson03/intermediate/includes/calcObject_textfield.as.

7. Return to calculator.fla and test the application.

You should see the mortgage payment, $2383.49, displayed in the monthly payment text field on the calculator. Finally!

8. In calculator.fla, change the `price_txt` variable declaration so its type is `TextField` (from `String`) and it has no initial value.

```
var price_txt:TextField;
```

Instead of assigning a value, you are going to get a value from the user.

9. Define the other four TextField objects, typing them each as a `TextField`.

```
var rate_txt:TextField;
var down_txt:TextField;
var years_txt:TextField;
var payment_txt:TextField;
```

Your code will still execute correctly if you do not explicitly type these objects. By typing them, however, you get code-hinting and also compile-time data type checking for the properties.

10. After these variable declarations, set the `text` properties of the input TextField objects equal to the corresponding `calculator` object property values. Test the application.

```
price_txt.text=calculator.price;
rate_txt.text=calculator.rate;
down_txt.text=calculator.down;
years_txt.text=calculator.years;
```

You are assigning initial values to these input text fields using ActionScript. The user can change these values.

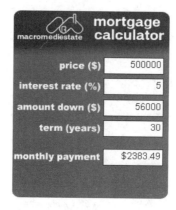

Try changing the value of one of the input fields. Nothing happens. You want the mortgage calculation to be recalculated. You will learn to do this in the next exercise.

11. After the code where you set the `text` properties of the TextField objects, set the `maxChars` property of the `rate_txt` and `years_txt` TextFields to *2*. Test the application.

```
rate_txt.maxChars=2;
years_txt.maxChars=2;
```

Try and change the values in the rate and years fields in the calculator interface. You can no longer enter more than two characters. For simplicity, you are allowing only integer rates.

12. After the code where you set the `maxChars` properties of the TextField objects, set the `backgroundColor` and `borderColor` properties of `price_txt` to *0xFFF1C3* and *0xFFC200*, respectively. Test the application.

These are both light orange colors. The border is a darker orange.

```
price_txt.backgroundColor=0xFFF1C3;
price_txt.borderColor=0xFFC200;
```

You cannot set the `backgroundColor` or the `borderColor` in the Property inspector. You can set these properties only with ActionScript. The default colors are white and black, respectively.

13. Save the document in /fpad2004/mmestate/.

It should resemble the finished file: /fpad2004/lesson03/intermediate/calculator_textfield.fla.

Responding to User Events for TextField Objects

In addition to setting properties for a TextField object, you can respond to user events. Whether or not a particular object can handle an event depends on whether its class has a built-in listener for that event. The events for the TextField class are listed in the Actions toolbox under built-in Classes > Movie > TextField > Events.

There are four user events that can be captured for TextField objects: when the user changes the value in an input text field (onChanged); gives focus to an input text field (onSetFocus); removes focus from an input text field (onKillFocus); and scrolls a dynamic or input text field (onScroller).

To write code to respond to one of these events, you set the name of the event equal to the name of a function or a function literal (which were introduced in Lesson 2), exactly as you did when creating custom methods.

The names of the built-in events are properties of the object. These are often referred to as **event handler properties**. The function that is executed when the event fires is called the **callback function** or the **event handler**.

Here is the general syntax for creating an event handler using a named callback function:

```
function callBackFunction():Void
{
    [Code]
}
instanceName.eventName=callbackFunction;
```

If you won't call the callback function from anywhere else in your code, you do not need to give it an explicit name. Instead, you can set the event handler property equal to the function itself, a function literal. Function literals are often used as event handlers.

```
instanceName.eventName=function():Void
{
    [Code]
};
```

In the following example, an event handler for an input TextField is defined. When the text field loses focus (which occurs when the user moves to another field or object), the following code is executed. The code checks to make sure that the user entered some text in the text field (`length` is a property of the TextField class) and displays a message if text is not entered.

```
name_txt.onKillFocus=function():Void
{
        if (name_txt.length==0)
{
                name_txt.text="A name is required!";
                }
};
```

In this exercise, first you use the `onSetFocus` event of the `TextField` class to change the background color and border color to orange of whatever input text field has focus. Next, you use the `onKillFocus` event to return the colors back to the default values when the user clicks or tabs out of the field. Finally, you use the `onChanged` event to recalculate the mortgage whenever the user changes the value of the input text fields. You finally make your calculator fully functional!

1. In Flash, return to calculator.fla in /fpad2004/mmestate/.

Return to the file you created in the last exercise or open /fpad2004/lesson03/intermediate/ calculator_textfield.fla and save it as *calculator.fla* in /fpad2004/mmestate/.

2. Place the code setting the price_txt backgroundColor and borderColor properties inside an onSetFocus event handler for price_txt. Test the application.

The `onSetFocus` event handler is fired whenever the user clicks in (or gives focus to) the specified text field.

```
price_txt.onSetFocus=function():Void
{
        price_txt.backgroundColor=0xFFF1C3;
        price_txt.borderColor=0xFFC200;
};
```

> **Tip** *You do not have to set the return type of the function literal to Void, but it is a best practice.*

When you test the application, the `price_txt` text field is no longer initially orange. Click the price_txt text field; it turns orange again.

3. Create an onKillFocus event handler for price_txt. Inside the event handler, return the backgroundColor and borderColor properties to their default values of white and black, respectively. Test the application.

The onKillFocus event handler is fired whenever the user clicks out of (or removes focus from) the specified text field. In Flash hexadecimal colors, white is 0xFFFFFF and black is 0x000000.

```
price_txt.onKillFocus=function():Void
{
        price_txt.backgroundColor=0xFFFFFF;
        price_txt.borderColor=0x000000;
};
```

When you test the application, click the price_txt text field; it turns orange again. Click any other text field; the price_txt text field returns to its default colors. Next, you are going to add this behavior to all the other input text fields.

4. Set the **price_txt.onSetFocus** event handler to also be the **onSetFocus** event handler for the other three input text fields. Test the application.

Remember that you can daisy-chain assignment statements.

```
15 price_txt.onSetFocus=rate_txt.onSetFocus=down_txt.onSetFocus=years_txt.onSetFocus=
   function():Void
16 {
17      price_txt.backgroundColor=0xFFF1C3;
18      price_txt.borderColor=0xFFC200;
19 };
```

When you test the application, click the rate_txt text field. The price_txt text field is highlighted. Inside the event handler, you are currently highlighting the price_txt text field, regardless of what field is given focus.

5. Inside the **onSetFocus** event handler, change **price_txt** to **this**. Test the application.

Inside the event handler, this refers to whatever object the handler was called for. When the price_txt text field is clicked, this is the price_txt TextField object. When the rate_txt text field is clicked, this is the rate_txt TextField object.

```
this.backgroundColor=0xFFF1C3;
this.borderColor=0xFFC200;
```

When you test the application, click the rate_txt text field. The rate_txt text field is highlighted. Click the down_txt text field. The down_txt text field is highlighted. None of the fields besides that for the price, however, change back from orange to their original color when they lose focus.

6. Set the `price_txt.onKillFocus` event handler to also be the `onKillFocus` event handler for the other three input text fields. Inside the `onKillFocus` event handler, change `price_txt` to `this`. Test the application.

```
20  price_txt.onKillFocus=rate_txt.onKillFocus=down_txt.onKillFocus=years_txt.onKillFocus=
    function():Void{
21      this.backgroundColor=0xFFFFFF;
22      this.borderColor=0x000000;
23  };
```

When you test the application, click the `rate_txt` text field. The `rate_txt` text field is highlighted. Click the `down_txt` text field. The `down_txt` text field is highlighted, and the `rate_txt` text field returns to its default colors.

7. After the `onKillFocus` event handler, create an `onChanged` event handler for the `price_txt` TextField object.

The `onChanged` event handler is fired whenever the user changes the value in an input text field.

```
price_txt.onChanged=function():Void
{
};
```

8. Inside the `onChanged` event handler, set the `calculator` object's `price` property equal to the value entered in the `price_txt` text field.

```
calculator.price=price_txt.text;
```

The `mortgage` is calculated using the `calculator` object's properties. When the `price_txt` text field is changed onscreen, you need to update the `calculator` object's `price` property because it is used in the mortgage calculation.

9. Inside the `onChanged` event handler, call the `calculator.displayMortgage()` method. Test the application.

```
29  price_txt.onChanged=function():Void
30  {
31      calculator.price=price_txt.text;
32      calculator.displayMortgage();
33  }
```

Change the house price in the calculator interface. You get an invalid price or down payment message because the `price_txt.text` is not of type number, and you are checking to make sure that it is a number in the `displayMortagage()` method. All values input into an input TextField object are of type String.

10. Inside the `onChanged` event handler, change the code setting the `calculator` object's `price` property so it is instead equal to the value returned from your `formatNumber()` function when you pass `price_txt.text` as the argument.

```
calculator.price=formatNumber(price_txt.text);
```

Here is where your `formatNumber()` function really becomes useful. Not only does it convert your `text` property to a number, it also strips out any non-numeric characters the user might enter.

11. Test the application. Change the house price in the calculator interface.

The mortgage should be recalculated and displayed in the monthly payment field. Success! Add a $ or commas to your price. The mortgage is still calculated correctly.

12. Set the `price_txt.onChanged` event handler to also be the `onChanged` event handler for the other three input text fields. Test the application.

```
price_txt.onChanged=rate_txt.onChanged=down_txt.onChanged=
years_txt.onChanged=function():Void
```

Although this event handler is called when any of the fields are changed, the mortgage is recalculated correctly only when a new price is entered. You need to reset the other `calculator` object properties inside the handler for the `rate_txt`, `down_txt`, or `years_txt` text fields as well.

13. Inside the `onChanged` event handler, set the `calculator` object's `rate`, `down`, and `price` properties to the corresponding values in the input text fields. Test the application.

```
24  price_txt.onChanged=rate_txt.onChanged=down_txt.onChanged=years_txt.onChanged=function
    ():Void
25  {
26      calculator.price=formatNumber(price_txt.text);
27      calculator.rate=formatNumber(rate_txt.text);
28      calculator.down=formatNumber(down_txt.text);
29      calculator.years=formatNumber(years_txt.text);
30      try
31      {
32          payment_txt.text=calculator.displayMortgage();
33      }
34      catch(e)
35      {
36          trace("Error: "+e);
37      }
38  };
```

Change the rate in the calculator interface. The mortgage is now recalculated correctly when any of the input text fields are changed.

14. Save the document in /fpad2004/mmestate/.

It should resemble the finished file: /fpad2004/lesson03/intermediate/calculator_events.fla.

Adding Event Listeners for TextField Objects

Besides having an object respond to its own events, you can register other objects to listen for that object's events and execute their own event handlers. You cannot register listeners for all of an object's events, only for the events that have this capability. The events you can register or subscribe listeners for are listed in the Actions toolbox under Built-in Classes > *classname* > Listeners. The TextField class has four events, but you can register listeners for only the `onChanged` and `onScroller` events.

You register an object to listen for a TextField event using the TextField object's `addListener()` method. The listener object can be any type of object: an Object, an Array, another TextField, and so on.

```
var myObject:Object=new Object();
my_txt.addListener(myObject);
```

The `myObject` object will now receive notice any time the `onChanged` or `onScroller` events occur for the `my_txt` TextField. If the `myObject` object has a property defined (set equal to an event handler function) with the same name as any of these TextField events, the event handler is executed when the corresponding event fires for the `my_txt` TextField.

```
myObject.onChanged=function():Void
{
    [code]
};
```

Tip *You cannot specify which TextField event the listener object receives notice for; it automatically receives event notices for all of the TextField events.*

Registering and using listeners is useful when you want an object to respond to other object's events and when you want more than one object to respond to an event.

In this exercise, you register the `calculator` object to be a listener for all the input TextField objects. You then define an `onChanged` event handler for the calculator object. When any of the input text fields are changed, the `calculator` object's `onChanged` event handler is invoked.

1. In Flash, return to calculator.fla in /fpad2004/mmestate/.

Return to the file you created in the last exercise or open /fpad2004/lesson03/intermediate/calculator_events.fla and save it as *calculator.fla* in /fpad2004/mmestate/.

2. Before the `onSetFocus` event handler, register the `calculator` object to listen for `price_txt` events. Use the TextField object's `addListener()` method.

```
12  years_txt.text=calculator.years;
13  rate_txt.maxChars=2;
14  years_txt.maxChars=2;
15  price_txt.addListener(calculator);
16
17  price_txt.onSetFocus=rate_txt.onSetFocus=down_txt.onSetFocus=years_txt.onSetFocus=
    function():Void
18  {
19      this.backgroundColor=0xFFF1C3;
```

3. Register the `calculator` object to also listen for `rate_txt`, `down_txt`, and `years_txt` events.

```
rate_txt.addListener(calculator);
down_txt.addListener(calculator);
years_txt.addListener(calculator);
```

You want the `calculator` object to respond to changes in any of the text fields.

4. Change the existing `onChanged` event handler so that it is the event handler for only the `calculator` object (and not for `price_txt`, `rate_txt`, `down_txt`, or `years_txt` objects).

```
30  calculator.onChanged=function():Void
31  {
32      calculator.price=formatNumber(price_txt.text);
33      calculator.rate=formatNumber(rate_txt.text);
34      calculator.down=formatNumber(down_txt.text);
35      calculator.years=formatNumber(years_txt.text);
36      try
37      {
38          payment_txt.text=calculator.displayMortgage()
39      }
40      catch(e)
41      {
42          trace("Error: "+e);
43      }
44  };
```

5. Change the references to `calculator` inside the function literal to `this`. There should be five instances.

6. Cut the code for the `calculator.onChanged` event handler. Save the file.

Because the `onChanged` event is now defined for the `calculator` object, you are moving it to the file that contains all the code for the `calculator` object.

7. Return to calcObject.as in /fpad2004/mmestate/includes/.

Return to the file you used in the last exercise or open /fpad2004/lesson03/intermediate/includes/ calcObject_textfield.as and save it as *calcObject.as* in /fpad2004/mmestate/includes/.

8. Paste the code you copied at the bottom of the calcObject.as file. Save the file.

It should resemble the finished file: /fpad2004/lesson03/intermediate/includes/calcObject_listener.as.

9. Return to calculator.fla and test the application.

Change the values for each of the text fields. The mortgage is still recalculated successfully. When an event occurs for any of the text fields, the corresponding event handler for the registered `calculator` listener is fired.

10. Save the document as *calculator.fla* in /fpad2004/mmestate/.

It should resemble the finished file: /fpad2004/lesson03/intermediate/calculator_listener.fla.

What You Have Learned

In this lesson, you have:

- Learned or reviewed the concepts of object-oriented programming (pages 99–102)
- Became familiar with the Flash built-in classes (pages 103–104)
- Used static methods of the Math class (pages 105–107)
- Created and used instances of the Date class (pages 107–110)
- Manipulated strings using the String wrapper class (pages 111–114)
- Created and manipulated Array objects (pages 114–126)
- Created objects with custom properties and methods (pages 126–134)
- Manipulated visual TextField objects (pages 134–140)
- Responded to events for the TextField class (pages 141–146)
- Added event listeners for TextField objects (pages 146–148)

4 Creating Button and MovieClip Objects

In Lesson 3, "Learning the Flash Player Object Model," you worked with a handful of the built-in classes. The TextField class had a visual representation and provided a way for a user to interact with it on the screen. Two other built-in classes, the Button and the MovieClip classes, also have a visual component and can be used to interact with the user.

The Button and MovieClip classes are more complex than the TextField class. Instances of both these classes have their own Stage and Timeline that can be manipulated independently of the main document, enabling you to group graphics and text into an object that can be manipulated with code. A Button object's Timeline has four states (or frames), in which you can place content: the Up, Over, Down, and Hit states. The main purpose of a Button object is to provide something for the user to click, roll over, or drag over to make something happen. You cannot place code in a Button object's Timeline.

The MovieClip class is more flexible and powerful than the Button class. It is the building block of all Flash applications. It has a complete Timeline with many frames and its own layers, just like the main document. You can place code in a MovieClip's Timeline, giving you the ability to encapsulate visual elements and the code that controls and manipulates them into an independent MovieClip object that can be reused and distributed among applications and developers.

In the first part of this lesson, you add a Button object to your calculator. You learn to create a Button object, edit its Timeline, and add event handlers to respond to user events. In the second

In this lesson, you convert the calculator into a MovieClip object that users can drag and drop around the screen.

part of this lesson, you convert the entire calculator into a MovieClip object, which gives you the ability to manipulate it as a single entity and also to encapsulate the calculator visual components and code, separating it from the main document.

What You Will Learn

In this lesson, you will:

- Create a Button object
- Edit a Button symbol's Timeline
- Respond to Button object events
- Create a MovieClip object visually
- Set MovieClip properties
- Respond to MovieClip events
- Reference objects in different Timelines
- Create global variables
- Use MovieClip methods to drag and drop objects

Approximate Time

This lesson takes approximately 75 minutes to complete.

Lesson Files

Asset Files:

/fpad2004/lesson04/start/assets/calcButton.png
/fpad2004/lesson04/start/assets/calcButtonOver.png
/fpad2004/lesson04/start/assets/calcButtonDown.png
/fpad2004/lesson04/start/assets/moveme.png

Starting Files:

/fpad2004/lesson04/start/calculator.fla
/fpad2004/lesson04/start/includes/calcObject.as
/fpad2004/lesson04/start/includes/formatFunctions.as

Completed Files:

/fpad2004/lesson04/complete/calculator_button.fla
/fpad2004/lesson04/complete/includes/calcObject_button.as
/fpad2004/lesson04/complete/calculator.fla
/fpad2004/lesson04/complete/includes/calcObject.as
/fpad2004/lesson04/complete/includes/formatFunctions.as

Creating a Button Object

You use the Button class to create Button objects that the user can click, roll over, or drag over to make something happen in the application. The Button class has built-in events (`onPress`, `onRelease`, `onRollover`, and more) that enable these interactions.

You create instances of the built-in Button class visually in the Flash authoring environment. (You cannot create Button objects with ActionScript.) You can either select a graphic and convert it to a Button object or create an empty Button object and add content to it. By creating a Button object from scratch, you have total control over what your button looks like and how it behaves.

Macromedia Flash MX 2004 also has a Button component you can use in your applications. This is a prebuilt button with a specific look and behavior that you can use without building a button yourself.

This Button component is not a native class for the Flash Player. It was built using ActionScript and the native classes and is compiled when you publish the application. You use the prebuilt Button component in later lessons. You should create buttons from scratch using the built-in Button class instead of the Button component when:

- You want a button with a different look and feel than the built-in component. You can easily add an icon or change the size, color, and text font of the prebuilt component, but that is about it.

- You are not using prebuilt components in your application. The built-in components have about ~26 K size overhead for their internal framework. If you use many components, you pay this size price once, and the code is used by all the components. If you only use one button, however, such as in your calculator application, there is no need to incur this size cost.

- You want to create "invisible buttons" that you can place over any text or element on the Stage to give them button functionality.

Using the built-in Button class, you can also easily create rollover or disjointed rollover effects at design time without using code.

Creating a Button Symbol

To create a button from elements on the Stage, you select the element(s) you want to group into a Button object and select Insert > Convert to Symbol. To create a button from scratch, select Insert > New Symbol. Both open the Convert to Symbol dialog box.

You set the name, behavior, and registration point (the 0,0 point for the new button's local coordinate system) of a Button symbol in the Convert to Symbol dialog box. When you click OK, a Button symbol is created and placed in the document library. You can think of this **Button symbol** as a subclass of the general Button class; it is based on the Button class, but has specific contents determining how it looks (images and text). You can reuse this Button symbol throughout your application without increasing the size of the application, exactly as you reused multiple bitmap symbols. You simply drag out multiple copies from the library, give them unique instance names in the Property inspector, and write different event handlers for each of them in your code.

Names and Code-Hinting

You assign Button names in two places: You name the Button symbol in the library and you name instances of the Button symbol in the Property inspector. You can give a Button symbol in the library any name you want; this name is displayed only in the Library panel and is not used for anything else. It is common practice to use the prefix btn when naming Button symbols to indicate the symbol type.

When you create instances of the Button symbol, you must give the instances unique names in the Property inspector. The instance name of a Button object is what you use to manipulate it with ActionScript code.

Like the TextField object, you can get code-hinting for a Button object in two ways: by assigning a data type to the Button object or by using a _btn suffix to name the instance. In the following code, a Button object with the instance name next is strictly typed, providing compile time type checking of its properties, methods, and events; and providing code-hinting.

```
var next:Button;
```

You can also get code hinting if you use a _btn suffix to name your Button object.

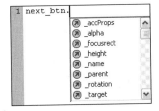

Properties

You can set properties of your Button objects in the Property inspector or with ActionScript. All the properties can be found in the Actions toolbox under Built-in Classes > Movie > Button > Properties.

The following code sets various Button object properties:

```
next_btn._x=200;              //Sets the x position of the button
next_btn._visible=false;      //Makes the button invisible
next_btn._rotation=90;        //Rotates the button by 90 degrees
next_btn._alpha=20;           //Makes the button alpha transparency 20%
```

In this exercise, you create a button for the calculator that the user can click to calculate their mortgage payment. You create the Button object and set properties of the button. In the following exercises, you edit the button's appearance and add event handlers for the button.

1. In Flash, return to calculator.fla in /fpad2004/mmestate/ and save it as *calculator_button.fla.*

This is a file you created in the last exercise of Lesson 3. If you did not do that exercise, open /fpad2004/lesson04/start/calculator.fla and save it as *calculator_button.fla* in /fpad2004/mmestate/.

2. In the Timeline, make a new layer called *button* **above the background layer.**

Remember, it is a good idea to place like objects in their own layer so you can easily find and manipulate them.

3. Select File › Import › Import to Stage. Browse to calcButton.png in /fpad2004/mmestate/ assets/ and click Open. In the Fireworks PNG Import Settings dialog box, select "Import as a single flattened bitmap" and click OK.

You are importing a prebuilt graphic to use for the button instead of creating it yourself.

4. Move the button so it is between the `years_txt` and `payment_txt` text fields on the calculator.

Move the monthly payment text label and dynamic text field down to make room for the new button. Your interface should appear as shown in the screenshot.

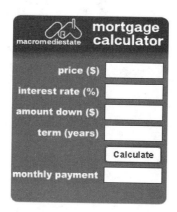

5. Right-click/Control-click the button graphic and select Convert to Symbol.

The Convert to Symbol dialog box appears. You can also get this dialog box by selecting the graphic and selecting Modify > Convert to Symbol from the main menu.

6. In the Convert to Symbol dialog box, give the Button symbol the name *btnCalc*, select Button as the Behavior, and leave the Registration point in the upper left corner. Click OK.

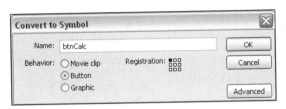

Tip *For Button symbols, prefix the name with _btn to indicate the symbol type.*

The registration point is the 0,0 point for the new Button symbol's local coordinate system. You can move the registration point by clicking one of the small rectangles. The upper left corner is usually recommended for consistency with the main document's registration point, which is also in the upper left corner.

7. Open the Library panel by selecting Window > Library or pressing Ctrl+L (Windows) or Command+L (Macintosh).

You should see your new symbol btnCalc in the library with a button icon next to it. If you click btnCalc in the Library panel, a preview of the button is displayed in the top portion of the panel.

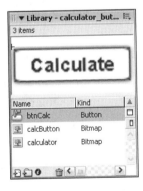

8. In the Property inspector, give the button the instance name *calc_btn*.

You do not have to use the suffix _btn when naming your Button instance because you will strictly type the Button object in the next step to enable code-hinting. The _btn suffix does, however, make it very clear in your code that this variable is a visual Button object.

9. Open the Actions panel and if you don't see your code, select actions: Frame 1 under Scene 1 in the Script navigator. After your existing variable declarations, declare the *calc_btn* variable as a *Button*.

```
var calc_btn:Button;
```

This declaration is not required to reference the button in your code. It just provides compile time checking and code-hinting.

10. Set the _alpha property of the button to *50*. Test the application.

```
calc_btn._alpha=50;
```

When you test the application, your button should be partially transparent.

Explore the Actions panel and see the other properties you can set for a button.

11. Delete or comment out the code setting the _alpha property of `calc_btn`.

You want the button to be fully visible in the calculator.

12. Save the document as *calculator_button.fla* in */fpad2004/mmestate/*.

You will use this file as the starting file for the next exercise. It should resemble the finished file: /fpad2004/lesson04/intermediate/calculator_btnsymbol.fla.

Editing a Button Symbol's Timeline

After you create a Button symbol, you usually want to change how it looks when a user places the pointer over the button or clicks it. By changing the color, the border, the size, the text, or any other property, you provide a visual cue to the user that this button is something they can interact with. You set the **states** for the button by editing its Timeline.

You enter a Button symbol's Timeline by double-clicking the button on the Stage or right-clicking/ Control-clicking the button and selecting Edit in Place. When you enter the button's Timeline this way, the appearance of the authoring environment changes. The rest of the items on the Stage become partially transparent, and you can no longer edit them. You also see a cross hair indicating the registration point (the 0,0 point) of the Button symbol.

You can also enter a button's Timeline by double-clicking the button in the library or right-clicking/Control-clicking the button on the Stage or in the library and selecting Edit. When you enter the button's Timeline this way, you do not see the button in the context of the application; no other items on the Stage are visible.

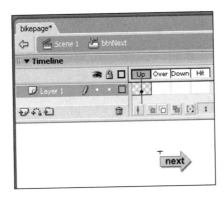

When you enter a buttons' Timeline, the Timeline also changes. You see only four frames, each representing a state of the Button object. You edit the content in these four frames to change what the button looks like when the user interacts with it.

The four button states are as follows:

Up. The button when the user does not have the pointer over it.

Over. The button when the user places the pointer over it.

Down. The button when the user clicks it.

Hit. The button area the user has to click, mouse over, or drag over for the button to respond. There is no visual representation of the Hit state in the application.

After you have finished editing your button, you need to return to the main document. When you are in symbol-editing mode, the name of the Button symbol appears on the Edit bar.

To return to the main document, click Scene 1 in the Edit bar. The label Scene 1 is a holdover from the beginning days of Flash when it was only an animation tool. You could then (and still can) divide your movie into different scenes that are played in sequence. The first scene, by default, is called Scene 1, which is where you have been adding content and code for your application.

If you need buttons that do not change appearance when the user's pointer rolls over them, you can create a single invisible button and then reuse it many times. You create a button with nothing in the Up, Over, and Down states, and a rectangle in the Hit state.

You then place an instance of the button over any item on the Stage that you want the user to interact with, resize the Button instance, and then give it a unique instance name. Buttons with nothing in the Up state appear as blue rectangles in the authoring environment.

In this exercise, you edit the Down, Over, and Hit states of the calculator button's Timeline.

1. In Flash, return to calculator_button.fla in /fpad2004/mmestate/.

Return to the file you created in the last exercise or open /fpad2004/lesson04/intermediate/ calculator_btnsymbol.fla and save it as *calculator_button.fla* in /fpad2004/mmestate/.

2. Double-click the button to enter its Timeline.

You can also enter the button's Timeline by double-clicking the Button symbol in the library or by right-clicking/Control-clicking the Button instance in the library or on the Stage and selecting Edit or Edit in Place. Symbol-editing mode can look different depending on how you access it. In edit-in-place mode, the main document's Stage is partially transparent in the background, so you see your button in the context of the application. In regular edit mode, the background isn't visible.

You should see three visual cues indicating that you are now inside the button's Timeline: The main document is partially transparent and you can't edit it; the name of the Button symbol appears on the Edit bar; and you see a new Timeline with only four frames.

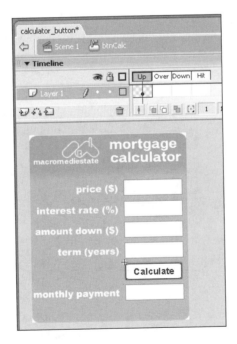

A filled circle in the Up frame indicates that the frame has content. In this exercise, the frame contains the button graphic you converted to a Button symbol in the last exercise.

3. In the Timeline, right-click/Control-click the Over frame and select Insert Blank Keyframe.

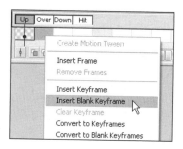

A **keyframe** is a frame that has content that differs from the content in the frame before it. Keyframes have a circle in them in the Timeline. A filled circle means that the keyframe has content. An empty circle means that the keyframe has no content. No circle means that the frame is not a keyframe and will display whatever content was in the keyframe before it in the Timeline.

Look at the Stage. The button graphic is no longer visible on the calculator because the Over frame is selected and displayed and the Over frame currently has no content.

4. Select File > Import > Import to Stage. Browse to calcButtonOver.png in /fpad2004/ mmestate/assets/ and click Open. Select "Import as a single flattened bitmap" and click OK.

You are importing a prebuilt graphic to use for the button's Over state instead of creating it yourself. Move the graphic to the same position on the calculator as the graphic in the Up frame.

5. In the Timeline, right-click/Control-click the Down frame and select Insert Blank Keyframe.

An empty circle appears in the Down frame of the Timeline.

6. Select File > Import > Import to Stage. Browse to calcButtonDown.png in /fpad2004/ mmestate/assets/ and click Open. Select "Import as a single flattened bitmap" and click OK.

Move the graphic to the same position as the graphic in the other two frames.

7. In the Timeline, right-click/Control-click the Hit frame and select Insert Keyframe.

Do not select Insert Blank Keyframe as you did for the other two frames. When you select Insert Keyframe, the frame is populated with the contents of the previous frame, which in this case, is the contents of the Down frame—the calcButtonDown bitmap. The area covered by this bitmap will be the "hotspot" for the user. You can use a plain rectangle to represent the Hit area in this frame; you do not have to use an image of the button. The content you have in the Hit frame never appears on the screen; it only defines the Hit area.

8. Click Scene 1 in the Edit bar to return to the main document Timeline.

You can tell you are back in the main document because the calculator is no longer partially transparent or invisible.

9. From the main menu, select Control > Enable Simple Buttons. Roll over and click the button to see it in action.

When you select Enable Simple Buttons, you get a live preview in the authoring environment of how the buttons will look in your application. You should not leave this functionality enabled because it makes it more difficult to select buttons on the Stage and uses memory to display the live preview.

If your button graphics in the three frames are not in exactly the same place, the button moves as you roll over and/or click it. If your button is moving, go back to the button's Timeline and reposition the graphics as necessary.

10. Select Control > Enable Simple Buttons again to disable it. Test the application.

Roll over and click the button. You should see its appearance change with each action—when you roll over, click, and then move the mouse pointer off the button. Right now, nothing happens when you click the button. In the next exercise, you will calculate a new mortgage when the user clicks the button.

11. Save the document as *calculator_button.fla* in /fpad2004/mmestate/.

You will use this file as the starting file for the next exercise. It should resemble the finished file: /fpad2004/lesson04/intermediate/calculator_btnstates.fla.

Responding to Button Object Events

Now you need to make your button functional. You need to add event handlers for the button so that something happens when the user interacts with it. The events for the Button class are listed in the Actions toolbox under Built-in Classes > Movie > Button > Events.

There are eleven user events for Button objects. The events most commonly used are `onPress` and `onRelease`, which capture when a user clicks and releases the button; and `onRollover` and `onRollout`, when a user's mouse rolls over and off the button. If a user clicks a button, moves the pointer off the button, and then releases the mouse button, the `onRelease` event does not fire; the `onReleaseOutside` event fires instead.

There are three places you can add event handlers for a Button object. You can add code to the main document Timeline as you did for the TextField objects in the last lesson, to the Button object itself, or in a class file. When adding code to a FLA, it is a best practice to add your event handlers to the main document Timeline so that all your code is in one place. You do need to know, however, that you can add code directly to objects because some developers find this method easier conceptually and syntactically. In addition, there are some new built-in code-generating capabilities in Flash (called behaviors) that add the code directly to an object so that the object does not have to be given an instance name, and the instance name does not have to be referenced in the generated code. You learn to place code in class files in Lesson 5, "Creating Classes."

Handling Events in the Document Timeline

You handle a Button object's events on the main document Timeline by defining event handlers exactly as you did for TextField objects in Lesson 3. First you name the Button instance and then you set the event handler property of the Button instance equal to a callback function or event handler, which is often a function literal.

In the following example, when the user moves their mouse over the button, the code inside the onRollOver event handler is executed and a dynamic text field is populated with a message. When the user moves their mouse off the button, the code inside the onRollOut event handler is executed, clearing the message from the dynamic text field.

```
next_btn.onRollOver=function():Void
{
     message_txt.text="Click here to see the next bike";
};
next_btn.onRollOut=function():Void
{
     message_txt.text="";
};
```

In this exercise, you make your calculator button functional. You add an onPress event handler for the button so that the mortgage is recalculated and displayed when the user clicks the button. The event handler for the button is added to the main document Timeline.

1. In Flash, return to calculator.fla in /fpad2004/mmestate/.

Return to the file you created in the last exercise or open /fpad2004/lesson04/intermediate/ calculator_btnstates.fla and save it as *calculator_button.fla* in /fpad2004/mmestate/.

2. Open the Actions panel and select actions: Frame 1 in the Script navigator.

You will replace the calculator object's onChanged event handler with an onPress handler for the button.

3. Delete the four lines of code registering the calculator object as a listener for the TextField objects.

```
14  years_txt.text=calculator.years;
15  rate_txt.maxChars=2;
16  years_txt.maxChars=2;
17  price_txt.addListener(calculator);
18  rate_txt.addListener(calculator);
19  down_txt.addListener(calculator);
20  years_txt.addListener(calculator);
21
22  price_txt.onSetFocus=rate_txt.onSetFocus=down_txt.onSetFocus=years_txt.onSetFocus=
    function():Void
```

4. Return to calcObject.as in /fpad2004/mmestate/includes/.

Return to the file you created in the last exercise of the last lesson or open /fpad2004/lesson04/start/includes/calcObject.as and save it as *calcObject_button.as* in /fpad2004/mmestate/includes/.

5. Change the `onChanged` event handler to an `onPress` event handler for `calc_btn`.

```
calc_btn.onPress=function():Void
{
      this.price=formatNumber(price_txt.text);
      this.rate=formatNumber(rate_txt.text);
      this.down=formatNumber(down_txt.text);
      this.years=formatNumber(years_txt.text);
      this.displayMortgage();
};
```

6. Inside the `onPress` handler, change all references of `this` to `calculator`.

There are five instances. Inside the `onPress` handler, `this` now refers to the `calc_btn` Button instead of calculator.

7. Cut all the code for the `onPress` event handler and save the file as *calcObject_button.as* in /fpad2004/mmestate/includes/.

The finished file should resemble: /fpad2004/lesson04/intermediate/includes/calcObject_button.as.

8. Return to calculator_button.fla and paste the `onPress` event handler at the end of the code.

You are removing this code from the calcObject.as file because the event is no longer a property of the `calculator` object.

9. Change the `include` statement to *include calcObject_button.as* instead of calcObject.as.

```
#include "includes/calcObject_button.as"
```

10. Test the application.

Change one of the input text fields. The mortgage payment is no longer instantly recalculated as it was in the last lesson. Change several input field values and then click the button. A new mortgage is calculated and displayed.

11. Save the document as *calculator_button.fla* in /fpad2004/mmestate/.

The finished file should resemble: /fpad2004/lesson04/intermediate/calculator_btnevents.fla.

Handling Events on a Button Object

In the last exercise, you added Button object event handlers to the main document Timeline. In this exercise, you add event handlers directly *on* the Button object. You can only place code directly *on* Button and MovieClip objects.

To add event handlers on a Button object, click the object on the Stage and open the Actions panel (or have the Actions panel open and click the object on the Stage). Two things change in the Actions panel: The name in the title bar switches from Actions – Frame to Actions – Button, and the name of the selected Button object appears in the Script navigator.

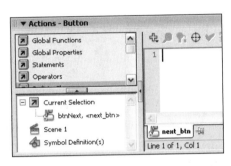

The button's instance name appears under Current Selection. Code (if any) for the object or frame displayed under Current Selection is displayed in the Script pane. Only one object or frame can ever be displayed under Current Selection. In contrast, all objects and frames in the application that have code attached to them appear under Scene 1. Your button will appear under Scene 1 as soon as you add code to it. This list of code locations in the Script navigator is extremely useful, because it shows where all the code in your application is located. You can also switch back and forth between any code by selecting an object or frame from this list.

Once you are in the Actions panel for the object, you can add code. *The only code that you can place on an object is an event handler.* Although you can define multiple event handlers, you cannot have any code outside the event handlers, not even a semicolon to separate them. You can, however, have comments. When you place code directly on an object, you must use a new syntax. You use on, the name of the event in parentheses, and then the code to execute in curly braces.

```
on(event)
{
        [code]
}
```

The name of the event you use for code on an object is not the same name as the event property you use on the main document. In the main document, you use onPress; in the code on the object, you simply use press in parentheses after the on keyword.

The same code that was used in the last section to create event handlers on the main Timeline is rewritten here, placing the event handlers directly on the object.

```
on(rollOver)
{
        message_txt.text="Click here to see the next bike";
}
on(rollOut)
{
        message_txt.text="";
}
```

Note *A Button object does not need an instance name for you to define event handlers on the object itself.*

If you have multiple buttons, you can place the event handlers for each button on the respective button. In this case, you would see all the buttons that have code in the Script navigator.

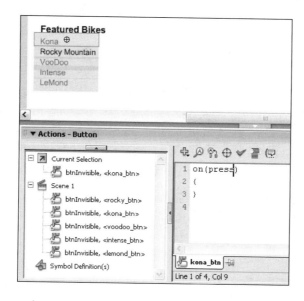

Alternatively, you could name your buttons and then place all the event handler code in the main document Timeline.

Tip *It is considered a best practice to add event handlers to the main document Timeline instead of on individual objects, so that all your code is in one place. Be aware, though, that the new built-in code-generating tools in Flash (called behaviors) add code directly to an object so that the object does not need an instance name and the instance name does not have to be referenced in the code.*

In this exercise, you move your `onPress` event handler from your main document Timeline to the calculator button. This procedure is for illustrative purposes only.

1. In Flash, return to calculator.fla in /fpad2004/mmestate/.

Return to the file you created in the last exercise or open /fpad2004/lesson04/intermediate/ calculator_btnevents.fla and save it as *calculator_button.fla* in /fpad2004/mmestate/.

2. Return to the Stage and click the Calculate button to select it.

The title bar of the Actions panel changes. It now says Actions – Button, indicating that any code displayed in the Actions panel is on this button and not in a Timeline frame.

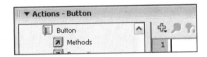

Tip *If your title bar says Actions - Frame, you probably have your code pinned. You need to open the panel and unpin the code. After you unpin the code, the view in the Actions panel will switch to the code for the button because you selected the button on the Stage.*

3. Open the Actions panel and look at the Script navigator.

You should see your `calc_btn` instance of the btnCalc symbol as the Current Selection. Now when you add code to the Script pane, you are adding code to this selection.

4. In the Script pane, type `on(` and then select `press` from the pop-up menu.

```
on(press
```

You get a pop-up menu of all possible event handlers for the button.

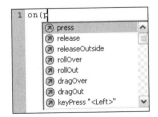

Look at the Script navigator. The button should now be listed under Scene 1. As soon as you type code in the Script pane, the button appears under Scene 1, indicating that this location has code attached to it.

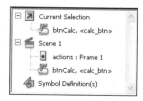

5. Close the parentheses and make open and close curly braces ({ }).

```
on(press)
{
}
```

6. Click actions: Frame 1 under Scene 1 in the Script navigator. Cut all the code from inside the **onPress** event handler and then delete the empty event handler.

You will move the code to the Button object from the Timeline of the main document. Again, this is not necessary for this application, but it will give you experience and an understanding of where and how code can be placed on an object.

7. Click btnCalc, <calc_btn> in the Script navigator. Inside the event handler, paste the code you cut in Step 6. Test the application.

```
1 on(press)
2 {
3       calculator.price=formatNumber(price_txt.text);
4       calculator.rate=formatNumber(rate_txt.text);
5       calculator.down=formatNumber(down_txt.text);
6       calculator.years=formatNumber(years_txt.text);
7       calculator.displayMortgage();
8 }
```

Change calculator input values and click the Calculate button. The mortgage should be successfully recalculated.

8. Save the document as *calculator_button.fla* in /fpad2004/mmestate/.

You will *not* use this file as the starting file for the next exercise. The finished file should resemble: /fpad2004/lesson04/intermediate/calculator_btnobjectcode.fla.

Creating a MovieClip Object Visually

The MovieClip class is the last built-in class that also has a visual component. You can do many things with MovieClip objects that you cannot do with either the TextField or Button objects, including the following:

- Make an object the user can drag and drop.
- Load visual content dynamically into an object using ActionScript.
- Create visual elements at runtime using the MovieClip class drawing methods.
- Create an object that has its own associated code (independent of the document it is embedded in) so you can create reusable application elements that contain both code and visual content and can be reused across multiple documents and applications.
- Create an object that has its own Timeline that you can use to make animations using multiple frames independent of the main document's Timeline

You also create MovieClip objects to make *any* visual element able to be manipulated with ActionScript. For example, if you want to change the size of an image at runtime you need to place the image inside a MovieClip object. The MovieClip can then be manipulated with ActionScript.

There are two ways to create MovieClips: visually in the authoring environment or with ActionScript. In this exercise, you create a MovieClip from objects on the Stage, just as you did for a Button object. You create MovieClips dynamically using ActionScript in Lesson 11, "Creating Visual Objects Dynamically."

To create a MovieClip from elements on the Stage, you use exactly the same process you did to create a Button. Select the element(s) you want to group into a MovieClip and then select Insert > Convert to Symbol. To create an empty MovieClip to which you later add content, select Insert > New Symbol. Both processes open the same dialog box you used when creating a Button.

A **MovieClip symbol** is created in the library. Think of the symbol as a subclass of the general MovieClip class. You can reuse the MovieClip symbol throughout your application or in other applications. Like the Button symbol, the name of the MovieClip symbol is not used anywhere but in the library. It is a common practice to prefix the names of MovieClip symbols with _mc to indicate the symbol type.

You create instances of the MovieClip symbol by dragging them from the Library panel to the Stage. You then give them instance names in the Property inspector and manipulate them with ActionScript code.

Like the TextField and Button objects, you can get code-hinting for a MovieClip object in two ways: by assigning a data type to the MovieClip object or by using a _mc suffix to name the instance. In the following code, a MovieClip object with the instance name `bike` is strictly typed, providing compiler-time type checking of its properties, methods, and events and providing code-hinting.

```
var bike:MovieClip;
```

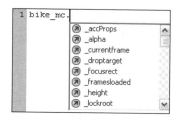

In this exercise, you convert the entire calculator into a MovieClip, which gives you the ability to manipulate the calculator as a single entity: changing its size, repositioning it, dragging and dropping it, and so on.

1. In Flash, open calculator.fla in /fpad2004/mmestate/.

You are *not* using the file you created in the last exercise. Instead, you are using the file you created in the last exercise of Lesson 3 (the last file that did not have a button). If you did not do that exercise, open /fpad2004/lesson04/start/calculator.fla and save it as *calculator.fla* in /fpad2004/mmestate/.

2. In the Timeline panel, unlock the background layer and the text folder. Select the background image on the Stage. Look at the Property inspector.

You cannot give a bitmap (or graphic) symbol an instance name so you cannot manipulate it with ActionScript. In order to manipulate a bitmap (or graphic) symbol with ActionScript, you need to place it inside a MovieClip or a Button.

> **Tip** *In general, if you want to create an object that behaves as a button with Up, Down, and Over states that you set visually at design time, use the Button class. For all other cases when you want to manipulate a visual object with ActionScript, use the MovieClip class.*

3. Select Edit › Select All from the main menu.

This procedure selects all the visual elements on the Stage in all the layers. You will place all these elements inside a MovieClip.

4. Right-click/Control-click on the calculator and select Convert to Symbol. In the Convert to Symbol dialog box, give the symbol the name *mcCalculator*, assign a **MovieClip** behavior, and leave the registration point in the upper left corner. **Click OK.**

> **Tip** *For MovieClip symbols, prefix the name with mc to indicate the symbol type.*

Look at your Timeline: There is no longer any content except in the static text layer (or whatever layer you had first in the text layer folder). By default, all the content gets placed into the uppermost layer; in this case, the static text layer. This layer now contains a single MovieClip object.

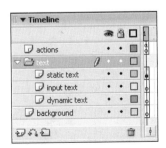

5. Open the library by selecting Window › Library or pressing Ctrl+L (Windows) or Command+L (Macintosh).

You should see your new symbol `mcCalculator` in the library. It has a MovieClip icon next to it.

6. In the Property inspector, give the MovieClip the instance name *calculator_mc*.

You do not have to use the suffix _mc when naming your MovieClip instance. You will strictly type your MovieClip object in the next step (which also enables code-hinting). The _mc suffix make it clear in your code that this variable is a visual MovieClip object.

7. Rename the background layer to *calculator*. Select the MovieClip on the Stage, cut it, select the calculator layer, and then select Edit › Paste in Place.

The single MovieClip object is now in the calculator layer instead of a text layer.

8. Delete the text layer folder by dragging it to the trash can in the Layers pane. Click Yes in the dialog box asking you to confirm the deletion.

There is no longer any content in the text folder, so you can delete it. You can tell that there is no content because all the circles in the first frames of the layers in the Timeline are empty. You can also delete the layer folder by right-clicking/Control-clicking the layer and selecting Delete folder from the pop-up menu.

9. Test the application.

The calculator no longer works. Why not? Because the code still refers to TextField objects in the main document Timeline. The TextFields are now located inside the MovieClip object. You will place the code inside the MovieClip object in the next exercise.

10. Save the document as *calculator.fla* in /fpad2004/mmestate/.

The finished file should resemble: /fpad2004/lesson04/intermediate/calculator_mcsymbol.fla.

Editing a MovieClip Symbol

After you create a MovieClip object, you can edit both its Stage and Timeline. You can change its visual contents, add code that is associated with the MovieClip symbol and not the instance, or add content to its frames that are independent of the main document Timeline.

To edit the MovieClip, you enter symbol-editing mode, just as you did for a Button symbol by double-clicking the MovieClip instance on the Stage or the MovieClip symbol in the library. (You can also right-click/Control-click the MovieClip on the Stage or in the library and select Edit or Edit in Place.) When you enter symbol-editing mode for the MovieClip, the appearance of the authoring environment changes just as it did when editing Button symbols. In edit-in-place mode, all the objects on the main Stage become partially transparent and you can no longer edit them; you can edit only the selected MovieClip symbol. In edit mode, only the MovieClip symbol is visible. The Timeline panel also changes, though not as drastically as it did for a Button symbol.

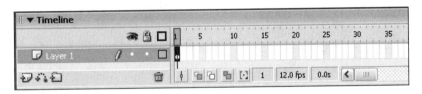

You still see layers and a large number of frames, but these are the MovieClip's frames and layers—not the main document's frames and layers. You can place code in the MovieClip's Timeline, similar to how you added code for your main document; this code is associated with the MovieClip symbol, not a particular instance of the MovieClip.

To leave symbol-editing mode and return to the main document, you click Scene 1 in the Edit bar, just as you did to leave symbol-editing mode for a Button symbol.

In this exercise, you move all the code for the calculator from the main document Timeline to the `mcCalculator` MovieClip symbol Timeline.

1. In Flash, return to calculator.fla in /fpad2004/mmestate/.

Return to the file you created in the last exercise or open /fpad2004/lesson03/intermediate/ calculator_mcsymbol.fla and save it as *calculator.fla* in /fpad2004/mmestate/.

2. Double-click the MovieClip on the Stage to enter its Timeline.

You can click anywhere on the Stage because the background image inside the MovieClip takes up the entire Stage. You can also right-click/Control-click the MovieClip and select Edit in Place.

Look at the Timeline of the MovieClip. When you converted the content contained in the different layers of the main document to a MovieClip symbol, all the layers were flattened into one layer inside the MovieClip. It is better to start with an empty MovieClip and then add content to it so you can organize the content into appropriate layers, which makes it easier to find and manipulate items.

3. Change the name of Layer 1 to *calculator*.

In the interest of time, there are no explicit steps to separate the content inside the MovieClip back into layers, but feel free to do so.

4. Create a new layer inside the MovieClip called *actions*.

Make sure the actions layer is the first layer.

5. Open the Actions panel and select actions: Frame 1 under Scene 1 in the Script navigator. Select all the code and cut it to the Clipboard. Make sure your code is not pinned.

You will move all the code from the main document Timeline to the MovieClip Timeline making the code part of the MovieClip so that if you reuse the MovieClip in another application, you do not need to cut and paste the associated code into the new document. This process separates the code from the main document's code, a necessity when building distributable application components. You want to make the distributable MovieClip a black box, something other developers can use without having to look at, manipulate, or understand the code.

6. In the Timeline panel, click Frame 1 of the actions layer. In the Actions panel, paste the code you cut in Step 5.

All the calculator code is now on the Timeline of the MovieClip. Look at the Timeline panel. You should see an α in the first frame of the actions layer, indicating there is code in that frame.

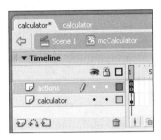

Note the different workflow for adding or editing MovieClip code as opposed to editing a visual part of a MovieClip. If you want to edit a visual part of the MovieClip, you must enter symbol-editing mode, make your changes, and then return to the main document. If you want to make changes to code, though, you do not have to enter symbol-editing mode. The Script navigator in the Actions panel lets you navigate between all the code in the document, regardless of where it is located.

7. In the Script navigator, click the + sign next to mcCalculator to expand it.

You should see an entry for actions: Frame 1 under mcCalculator, indicating there is code inside the mcCalculator MovieClip symbol.

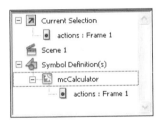

8. Test the application.

The calculator works again. You have now made a reusable entity that has all its visual elements and code encapsulated. It can be reused in this or other documents and distributed to other developers.

9. Save the document in /fpad2004/mmestate/.

The finished file should resemble: /fpad2004/lesson04/intermediate/calculator_mccode.fla.

Setting MovieClip Properties

The MovieClip class has almost thirty properties you can use to manipulate MovieClip objects with ActionScript. These properties can be found under Built-in Classes > Movie > MovieClip > Properties in the Actions toolbox. Many of these properties are similar to the properties of the TextField and Button classes.

Tip Names of many of the MovieClip properties begin with an underscore character to avoid namespace conflicts with custom properties that you might add to MovieClip instances.

You can assign values to MovieClip properties in four places: from inside the MovieClip in its own Timeline; from outside the MovieClip in the Timeline of the document it is embedded in; from outside the MovieClip but *on* the MovieClip instance inside an on() event handler; or from a class file. The first two methods are examined here. You implement the third, which is generally not a best practice, using the same method outlined for the Button object earlier in his lesson. The last method is covered in Lesson 5.

From the main document, you simply use the instance name of the MovieClip followed by a period and the name of the property, exactly as you have done for other objects (nothing new here). You use this method to customize a specific instance of a MovieClip in a particular application.

```
bike_mc._x=100;          //Sets the MovieClip's x position from the
                         //upper left corner of the main document
bike_mc._height=50;      //Sets the MovieClip's height to 50 pixels
bike_mc._yscale=50;      //Scales the MovieClip's height by 50%
                         //from the MovieClip's registration point
bike_mc._alpha=20;       //Makes the MovieClip alpha transparency 20%
```

You can also set a property value from inside the MovieClip, but there you cannot use the instance name followed by the property inside the MovieClip. Code in the Timeline of a MovieClip is part of the MovieClip symbol and is not unique to a specific instance. You must instead use the prefix this. to refer to the MovieClip itself. The prefix this means make *my* height 50 pixels, not set the height of that particular MovieClip instance, bike_mc, to 50 pixels. Place code that you want to apply to all instances of that MovieClip symbol in the MovieClip Timeline.

```
this._height=50;         /Sets the MovieClip's height to 50 pixels
this._width=30;          //Sets the MovieClip's width to 50 pixels
trace(this._xmouse);     //Returns the x coordinate of the mouse position
```

In this exercise, you set properties of the calculator MovieClip both from the main document Timeline (which sets instance properties) and from inside the MovieClip (which sets symbol properties). You change the calculator's size and location.

1. In Flash, return to calculator.fla in /fpad2004/mmestate/.

Return to the file you created in the last exercise or open /fpad2004/lesson04/intermediate/ calculator_mccode.fla and save it as *calculator.fla* in /fpad2004/mmestate/.

2. Return to the main document by clicking Scene 1 on the Edit bar. Select the actions layer of the main Timeline and open the Actions panel.

Make sure your code is not pinned. You should now be editing code for the actions layer of the main document.

3. Declare the `calculator_mc` variable as a MovieClip.

```
var calculator_mc:MovieClip;
```

This declaration is not required to use the instance name in your code. It provides compiler time checking and code-hinting.

4. Set the _x property of the MovieClip to *200* and the `_height` and `_width` to *210* and *180*, respectively. Test the application.

```
calculator_mc._x=200;
calculator_mc._height=210;
calculator_mc._width=180;
```

When you test the application, your calculator should appear smaller and further to the right than it was before. This x position of the MovieClip is set relative to the registration point of the main document, which is in the upper left corner.

> **Tip** *On Windows, when you test an application from the Flash authoring environment, the application is centered on the Stage with lots of white space around it. To see the actual size of the application without this extra space, click the Restore Down button in the upper right corner of the SWF window. All the files in the authoring environment become independent windows that can be manipulated instead of tabs on a Tab bar. On the Macintosh, there is no Tab bar and the files are always displayed in independent windows. Click the Maximize button in the upper right corner of any of the files to return the files to a Tab bar*

5. In the Script navigator of the Actions panel, click actions: Frame 1 under mcCalculator.

You are now editing the code in the actions layer of the MovieClip.

6. After the variable declarations near the top of the code, set the _x property of the MovieClip symbol to *-200*. Test the application.

```
this._x=-200;
```

When you test the application, your calculator should appear far to the left of where it was. (If your document windows are not docked in the authoring environment, it will appear off the screen.) The _x value set inside the MovieClip overrides the value set outside the MovieClip, which means that the code in the main document is evaluated before the code inside any MovieClips in that Timeline.

7. Delete or comment out all the code you added setting MovieClip properties in this exercise.

You are deleting code in the main Timeline and in the actions layer of the MovieClip.

8. Save the document in /fpad2004/mmestate/.

The finished file should resemble: /fpad2004/lesson04/intermediate/calculator_mcproperties.fla.

Responding to MovieClip Events

The MovieClip class has almost twenty events you can use to respond to user and system events with ActionScript, including all the events of the Button classes and more. The events can be found under Built-in Classes > Movie > MovieClip > Events in the Actions toolbox.

You can write event handlers for MovieClips in the same four places you could set MovieClip properties: from inside the MovieClip in its Timeline, from outside the MovieClip in the Timeline of the document, from outside the MovieClip but *on* the MovieClip instance using on() event handlers, or in a class file. The first two methods are examined here. You implement the third, which is generally not a best practice, using the same method outlined for the Button object earlier in this lesson. The last method is covered in Lesson 5.

To define event handlers from the main document, you simply use the instance name of the MovieClip followed by a period and the name of the event property, exactly as you have done for other objects. The following code sets the _alpha property of a MovieClip to 30 when the user's mouse rolls over it.

```
bike_mc.onRollOver=function():Void
{
      this._alpha=30;
};
```

You can also define event handlers inside the MovieClip symbol that you want to apply to all instances of the MovieClip. For example, when you want all instances of the MovieClip to be draggable when a user clicks them. Inside a MovieClip, you refer to the MovieClip with the `this` identifier, just as you did when defining properties.

```
this.onRollOver=function():Void
{
        this._alpha=30;
};
```

The events most commonly used are `onPress` and `onRelease`, which capture when a user clicks and release the MovieClip; and `onRollover` and `onRollout`, which capture when a user rolls over and then off the MovieClip. If a user clicks a MovieClip, moves the pointer off the MovieClip, and then releases their mouse button, the `onReleaseOutside` event fires.

These methods should not be confused with the `onMouseDown`, `onMouseMove`, and `onMouseUp` events, which fire when the user presses the mouse button, moves the mouse, or releases the mouse button *anywhere* on the application (*not* just when the pointer is located over the MovieClip).

In this exercise, you add an event handler for the MovieClip symbol that changes its `_alpha` property when it is pressed. You place the code inside the MovieClip symbol, making it applicable to all the MovieClip instances.

1. In Flash, return to calculator.fla in /fpad2004/mmestate/.

Return to the file you created in the last exercise or open /fpad2004/lesson04/intermediate/ calculator_mcproperties.fla and save it as *calculator.fla* in /fpad2004/mmestate/.

2. In the Script navigator of the Actions panel, click mcCalculator to expand it and then click actions: Frame 1 under mcCalculator

You are now editing the code for the actions layer of the MovieClip symbol.

3. At the end of the code, create an `onPress` event handler for the MovieClip. Inside, the event handler, set the `_alpha` property of the MovieClip to *20*.

```
this.onPress=function():Void
{
        this._alpha=20;
};
```

4. Test the application.

When you place the pointer anywhere over the calculator, it turns to a hand pointer, indicating that there is an event associated with that object onscreen. If you click the calculator, it becomes partially transparent. You can also no longer change the input text fields because any time you place the mouse over the calculator, it is checking for MovieClips events to fire; you can't get to the text fields any more. You will fix this problem in the next exercise by making only a part of the MovieClip clickable by nesting another MovieClip inside the calculator MovieClip and adding an event handler to the nested MovieClip.

5. After the `onPress` handler, create an `onRelease` event handler for the MovieClip. Inside the event handler, set the `_alpha` property of the MovieClip to *100*.

```
58  this.onPress=function()
59  {
60      this._alpha=20;
61  };
62  this.onRelease=function()
63  {
64      this._alpha=100;
65  };
66
```

6. Test the application.

Click the calculator. It becomes partially transparent. Release the mouse button; the calculator returns to full visibility.

7. Save the document in **/fpad2004/mmestate/**.

The finished file should resemble: /fpad2004/lesson04/intermediate/calculator_mcevents.fla.

Referencing MovieClips in Different Timelines

So far in this lesson, you created one MovieClip in the main document. You can also create **nested** MovieClips, creating or placing a MovieClip inside another MovieClip, another MovieClip inside that MovieClip, and so on as deep as you want to go. A MovieClip nested inside another MovieClip is often referred to as a **child** MovieClip, and the container MovieClip is referred to as the **parent**.

After you start nesting MovieClips, though, how do you reference variables in the other MovieClips? Can you? Yes, using either relative or absolute paths to the variables. Although you can reference other MovieClip's variables from different Timelines, you should avoid it as much as possible because it makes the MovieClips dependant upon one another and less reusable. Referencing variables in other MovieClips is most acceptable when the nested MovieClips are never to be used separately from the parent MovieClip.

Main Document MovieClip

Although you did not know it, you have actually been creating nested MovieClips throughout this lesson. The main document is a MovieClip and is the parent MovieClip for your `calculator_mc` child MovieClip. You can use most of the MovieClip class's properties, methods, and events on the main document—though not all.

Just as you reference the code inside a MovieClip's Timeline with `this`, you can use `this` on the main Timeline to refer to the main document. The following statements are equivalent.

```
this._alpha=20;        //Sets _alpha of everything in main document
                       //(except text using device fonts)
_alpha=20;             //Sets _alpha of everything in main document
                       //(except text using device fonts)
```

Using Relative Path References

You can reference variables in MovieClips by using relative or absolute paths. When possible, it is best to use relative paths because they are not as dependent on the document's MovieClip structure. They depend on the relative location of MovieClips to each other, not the absolute positioning of the nested MovieClips within the entire document—which can change when you load SWFs or MovieClips into other MovieClips dynamically (which you will learn how to do in Lesson 11).

The following examples (which illustrate the various relative and absolute identifiers that can be used) are based on the following nested MovieClip architecture.

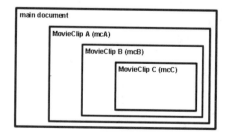

this. Use to reference the current MovieClip. You used this notation when specifying properties and event handlers inside a MovieClip's Timeline.

```
this._alpha=20;                //Assigns _alpha of mcA from mcA
                               //or assigns _alpha of mcB from mcB
                               //or assigns _alpha of mcC from mcC
                               //or assigns _alpha of main document
                               //from main document
```

dot syntax. Use to reference a nested MovieClip from the parent MovieClip.

```
mcA._alpha=20;                 //Assigns _alpha of mcA from main document
this.mcA._alpha=20;            //Assigns _alpha of mcA from main document
mcA.mcB._alpha=20;             //Assigns _alpha of mcB from main document
mcA.mcB.mcC._alpha=20;         //Assigns _alpha of mcC from main document
mcB._alpha=20;                 //Assigns _alpha of mcB from mcA
```

_parent. Use to reference a parent MovieClip from inside a child MovieClip. Using _parent is similar to using "../" when specifying relative file locations.

```
_parent._alpha=20;             //Assigns _alpha of mcB from mcC
                               //or assigns _alpha of mcA from mcB
                               //or assigns _alpha of main document from mcA
```

You can chain multiple _parent identifiers together to move up any number of MovieClip levels.

```
_parent._parent._alpha=20;     //Assigns a property of mcA from mcC
                               //or assigns _alpha of main doc from mcB
```

Using Absolute Path References

You can also reference variables using absolute paths. When you know the document MovieClip structure will not change, you can use absolute paths to avoid chaining together relative path identifiers.

_root. Use to reference the main document Timeline from any nested MovieClip.

```
_root._alpha=20;               //Assigns a property of main document from
                               //mcA, mcB, mcC, or the main document
_root.mcA._alpha=20;           //Assigns a property of mcA from mcA, mcB,
                               //mcC, or the main document
```

The MovieClip class has a property called _lockroot that allows you to set what _root refers to when traversing nested MovieClips. If you set _lockroot=true in a MovieClip, any references to _root from that MovieClip or any embedded MovieClips do not traverse the MovieClip tree up to the main document, but stop at the MovieClip, which sets _lockroot to true.

```
_lockroot=true;                //Place in mcA
_root._alpha=20;               //This code used in mcB or mcC assigns
                               //_alpha of mcA, NOT the main document
```

_level0. Use to reference the main document Timeline from any nested MovieClip. In your application, _root and _level0 are synonymous. You can, however, load SWFs dynamically into different levels of the Flash Player. The first SWF loaded into the Flash Player is automatically loaded into _level0. From this base application, you can dynamically load SWFs into different levels: _level1, _level2, and so on. SWFs in higher levels appear in front of SWFs in lower levels. You can then use a _levelX identifier to absolutely reference variables in other levels.

```
_level0._alpha=20;          //Assigns a property of main document from mcA,
                            //mcB, mcC, or the main document
```

In this exercise, you nest a MovieClip inside the calculator MovieClip. You add an event handler to this child MovieClip to drag and drop its parent MovieClip when the user presses and releases it. By adding the event handler to a nested MovieClip instead of the mcCalculator symbol, you can change the calculator text fields again.

1. In Flash, return to calculator.fla in /fpad2004/mmestate/.

Return to the file you created in the last exercise or open /fpad2004/lesson04/intermediate/ calculator_mcevents.fla and save it as *calculator.fla* in /fpad2004/mmestate/.

2. In the main document, create a new layer called *text* below the actions layer. On the Stage, create the static text *TEST*.

Make the text large enough to be very visible (for example, black, font size 40, bold). You need to add temporary content to the main document so that there is something in addition to the calculator_mc MovieClip. Make sure you use static text, which uses embedded fonts and can be made transparent; input or dynamic text fields use device fonts by default and cannot be made transparent unless you embed fonts.

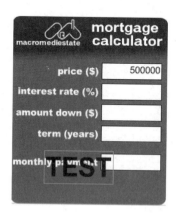

3. Return to symbol-editing mode for the `mcCalculator` MovieClip by double-clicking the calculator. Inside the MovieClip, create a new layer called *move me mc*.

Make sure the new layer is below the actions layer. You will place a new graphic in this layer that you will convert into a MovieClip and write event handlers for, enabling drag and drop of the calculator.

4. Select File › Import › Import to Stage. Browse to moveme.png in /fpad2004/mmestate/ assets/ and click Open. Select "Import as a single flattened bitmap" and click OK.

You are importing a prebuilt graphic to place inside the MovieClip instead of creating the contents with the text and drawing tools in Flash (or any other graphics program).

5. Move the bitmap symbol to the lower right corner of the calculator.

It should appear as shown in the screenshot.

6. Right-click/Control-click the bitmap and select Convert to Symbol. In the Convert to Symbol dialog box, give it the name *mcMoveme*, assign a MovieClip behavior, and leave the registration point in the upper left corner. Click OK.

This step creates a new MovieClip symbol in the library and an instance of the symbol nested in the `mcCalculator` MovieClip symbol.

> **Note** *You could make this bitmap a button because the Button class also has* `onPress` *and* `onRelease` *events. In general, though, you use the Button class only when you want to create an object with Up, Down, and Over states that you set visually at design time. If, for example, you wanted to change what a graphic looks like when the user rolls over or clicks it, you would use an instance of the Button class.*

7. In the Property inspector, give the new MovieClip the name *moveme_mc*.

You must give the instance a name so you can reference it with ActionScript.

8. Open the Actions panel and navigate to actions: Frame 1 for `mcCalculator`. Change the existing `onPress` and `onRelease` handlers from `this` to `moveme_mc`.

```
58  moveme_mc.onPress=function()
59  {
60        this._alpha=20;
61  };
62  moveme_mc.onRelease=function(
63  {
64        this._alpha=100;
65  };
```

To make the input text fields functional again, you need to remove the event handlers from the `mcCalculator` MovieClip.

9. Test the application.

Place your mouse over the `moveme_mc` MovieClip. Your pointer changes to a hand, indicating there is an event handler for that corner of the calculator. Click the MovieClip. Only the `moveme_mc` MovieClip and not the entire `calculator_mc` MovieClip becomes partially transparent.

10. Change the code inside the `onPress` handler so that the `_alpha` property of the main document is changed. Use `_root` to reference it.

```
_root._alpha=20;
```

`_root` refers to the main document Timeline. This code causes everything in the main document to become transparent including the `calculator_mc` MovieClip and the static text you added when the MovieClip is clicked.

11. Change the code inside the `onRelease` handler so that the `_alpha` property of the Timeline in `_level0` is changed.

```
_level0._alpha=100;
```

`_level0` also refers to the main document Timeline because there is only one SWF loaded into the Flash Player. This code causes everything in the main document to return to full visibility when the mouse is released over the MovieClip.

12. Test the application.

Click the `moveme_mc` MovieClip. The entire document, including the `calculator_mc` MovieClip and the static text, becomes partially transparent.

13. Change the code inside the `onPress` and `onRelease` handlers so that the `_alpha` property of only the `calculator_mc` MovieClip is changed. Use absolute paths.

```
_root.calculator_mc._alpha=20;        //Code in onPress
_level0.calculator_mc._alpha=100;     //Code in onRelease
```

Both of these lines of code set the `_alpha` of the `calculator_mc` MovieClip, not the main document that includes the static text.

14. Test the application.

Click the `moveme_mc` MovieClip. Only the `calculator_mc` MovieClip becomes partially transparent, the static text does not.

15. Change the code inside the `onPress` and `onRelease` handlers so that the `_alpha` property of the main document is changed. Use relative paths.

```
_parent._alpha=20;        //Code in onPress
_parent._alpha=100;       //Code in onRelease
```

Both of these lines of code set the `_alpha` of the main document, not just the `calculator_mc` MovieClip. Even though this code is inside an event handler for `moveme_mc`, `_parent` refers to the Timeline of the MovieClip that is the parent (the main document) to the MovieClip the code is on (`mcCalculator`)—regardless that the code is inside an event handler for a different MovieClip. There is no relative way to reference `mcCalculator` from inside the `moveme_mc` event handlers defined on `mcCalculator` symbol's Timeline. If you want to reference `mcCalculator` (not `calculator_mc`), you have to move the event handlers to inside the `moveme_mc` MovieClip or place them directly on the nested MovieClip in `calculator_mc`. The scope of the code on objects is different from the scope for code in a Timeline. You can explore these scopes by tracing `this` and `_parent` inside code blocks in each location.

16. Test the application.

Click the `moveme_mc` MovieClip. The main document becomes partially transparent again, including the static text.

17. Save the document as *calculator.fla* in /fpad2004/mmestate/.

The finished file should resemble: /fpad2004/lesson04/intermediate/calculator_mctargets.fla.

_global Object

In the last section, you learned how to reference variables (relative and absolute) in different Timelines of the application. You can also create **global** variables that you can access from any MovieClip without using a fully qualified reference. To create global variables, you create properties of a built-in _global object. In the following code a global property, global object, and global function are created.

```
_global.appURL="http://localhost/mmestate/";
_global.company={cname:"Macromediestate",city:"San Francisco"};
_global.dateFormatter=function(inDate:Date):String
{
     [code to format date]
};
```

You can create these properties of the _global object anywhere in the application and they can be directly accessed from any MovieClip without any further reference to where the _global property was defined. For example, the following code can be used to display the global company name from any Timeline in the application.

```
trace(_global.appURL);       //Displays global application URL from main
                             //document, mcA, mcB, or mcC
```

You can also leave off the _global identifier when accessing global properties from any Timeline.

```
trace(appURL);               //Displays global application URL from main
                             //document, mcA, mcB, or mcC AS LONG AS they
                             //do not also have a variable called appURL
```

If a variable in a Timeline has the same name as a global variable and no identifier is used when accessing the variable, the variable in the local Timeline is used. Local variables and functions override the global ones if no access qualifier is used to reference the variable.

```
_global.appURL="http://localhost/mmestate/";
tvar String: appURL ="none";
trace(appURL);               //Outputs none
trace(_global.appURL);       //Outputs http://localhost/mmestate/
```

> **Tip** It is a best practice to always use the _global qualifier when referencing global variables. Even though you do not have to use _global, it makes it obvious what variable you are referring to, and avoids any possible naming conflicts with variables of the same name in a MovieClip or function.

Although you can define properties of the `_global` object in any MovieClip, it is difficult to keep track and use the global properties if their definitions are scattered all over the place. It is a best practice to define all global properties in an external file and include that file in the main document or reusable MovieClip that accesses them.

```
#include "myGlobalFunctions.as"
```

In this exercise, you place your `formatNumber()` function into the global scope by making it a property of the `_global` object.

1. In Flash, return to calculator.fla in /fpad2004/mmestate/.

Return to the file you created in the last exercise or open /fpad2004/lesson04/intermediate/calculator_mctargets.fla and save it as *calculator.fla* in /fpad2004/mmestate/.

2. In the Script navigator in the Actions panel, navigate to the code in mcCalculator actions: Frame 1. Cut the line of code including formatFunctions.as.

```
#include "includes/formatFunctions.as"
```

You will move the `include` statement to the main document so it can be used by all code (if there was any more) in the main document.

3. Navigate to the Script pane for the main document Timeline. Paste the `include` statement.

If you did not leave comments in the code in the main Timeline, the actions frame will not appear in the Script navigator under Scene 1. To navigate to the Script pane for the main document Timeline, you must select the actions layer in the Timeline of the main document. If you are still inside the MovieClip, first click Scene 1 on the Edit bar, then click the actions layer.

4. Save the file and test the application.

Change one of the input text fields. You get an error message displayed in the Output panel. Why? The `formatNumber()` function, which is included in the formatFunctions.as file can no longer be found and so the input fields are not correctly formatted in the code.

The finished file should resemble: /fpad2004/lesson04/intermediate/calculator_global.fla.

5. Return to calcObject.as in /fpad2004/mmestate/includes/.

Return to the file you created in the last exercise or open /fpad2004/lesson04/start/includes/ calcObject.as and save it as *calcObject.as* in /fpad2004/mmestate/includes/.

6. In the `onChanged` event handler, prefix the four calls to `formatNumber()` with `_parent`. Save the file.

```
41  calculator.onChanged=function():Void
42  {
43      this.price=_parent.formatNumber(price_txt.text);
44      this.rate=_parent.formatNumber(rate_txt.text);
45      this.down=_parent.formatNumber(down_txt.text);
46      this.years=_parent.formatNumber(years_txt.text);
47      this.displayMortgage();
48  }
```

Because you have included the function definition in the main document, it can now be referenced from within the MovieClip using `_parent`.

7. Return to calculator.fla and test the application.

Change one of the input text fields. The mortgage should be correctly calculated again.

8. Open formatFunctions.as in /fpad2004/mmestate/includes/.

Return to the file you created in the last lesson or open /fpad2004/lesson04/start/includes/ formatFunctions.as and save it as *formatFunctions.as* in /fpad2004/mmestate/includes/.

9. Change the function definition so it is a property of the `_global` object.

```
_global.formatNumber=function(start:String):Number
{
    [code]
};
```

You must change the function from a stand-alone function to a function literal.

10. Save the document as *formatFunctions.as* in /fpad2004/mmestate/includes/.

The finished file should resemble: /fpad2004/lesson04/intermediate/includes/ formatFunctions_global.as.

11. Return to calculator.fla and test the application.

Change one of the input text fields. You get an error message and the mortgage is not recalculated. There is no longer a function in the parent's Timeline called `formatNumber()`. The function is now a property of the _global object.

12. Return to calcObject.as and remove **_parent** from the four calls to `formatNumber()` in the **onChanged** event handler. Save the file.

The compiler will first look for the function in the Timeline of the code in which it is referenced. If it does not find a function with that name, it will look to see if there is a method of the _global object with that name.

13. Return to calculator.fla and test the application.

Change one of the input text fields. The mortgage is recalculated correctly. Because there is no `formatNumber()` in the scope of the Timeline, the one in the global scope is used. You cannot tell by looking at the code, though, where the function is defined. Although optional, it is better to use the _global identifier when referencing variables in the global scope.

14. In calcObject.as, add **_global** in front of the four calls to `formatNumber()` in the **onChanged** event handler. Save the file.

```
41  calculator.onChanged=function():Void
42  {
43      this.price=_global.formatNumber(price_txt.text);
44      this.rate=_global.formatNumber(rate_txt.text);
45      this.down=_global.formatNumber(down_txt.text);
46      this.years=_global.formatNumber(years_txt.text);
47      this.displayMortgage();
48  }
```

The finished file should resemble: /fpad2004/lesson04/intermediate/includes/calcObject_global.as.

15. Return to calculator.fla and test the application.

Change one of the input text fields. The mortgage is calculated correctly.

Using MovieClip Drag-and-Drop Methods

The MovieClip object has almost forty methods, most located in the Actions panel under Built-in Classes > Movie > MovieClip > Methods.

Many of these methods are used to create MovieClips dynamically and are covered in Lesson 11. Other methods (used primarily in animation and not covered in this book) are used to move through different frames in a MovieClip's Timeline giving you the ability to change what is displayed onscreen by changing the frame that is displayed. Although you can also use different frames of the Timeline to display various application states, you will instead use better methods, which use multiple SWFs and screens to represent the states in later lessons. Finally, there are additional methods used to create graphics at runtime located in the Actions panel under Built-in Classes > Movie > MovieClip > Drawing Methods.

You can use the following methods in conjunction with the MovieClip event handlers to create more advanced user interactivity with your application elements.

startDrag(). Initiates dragging on the specified MovieClip so that it begins to follow the motion of the mouse pointer. The MovieClip remains draggable until explicitly stopped by calling the `stopDrag()` method or until another MovieClip is made draggable—only one MovieClip is draggable at a time. You typically start a drag in response to an `onPress` event.

```
bike_mc.onPress=function():Void
{
      this.startDrag();
};
```

stopDrag(). Ends a `startDrag()` method. You typically stop a drag in response to an onRelease event.

```
bike_mc.onRelease=function():Void
{
      this.stopDrag();
};
```

hitTest(). Checks to see whether the MovieClip being dragged overlaps or intersects with specific x and y coordinate parameters or another object. In some cases, it might be fine for the user to drop a MovieClip object anywhere. In other cases, you might want the drag to stop when something happens—like when the object is in a certain location or when it runs into another object. In this case, you use the `hitTest()` to check a condition inside the event handler.

To check and see whether a MovieClip overlaps or intersects with another object, you specify the instance name of the target as a single argument to the method.

```
bike_mc.hitTest(target_mc);
```

To check and see whether a MovieClip overlaps given x and y coordinates, you specify the x and y coordinates as arguments followed by a third argument of true.

```
bike_mc.hitTest(x,y,true);
```

As soon as the edge of the MovieClip hits the specified x and y coordinates, the method returns a value of true. You get the same behavior if you set the third argument to false, which checks to see whether the edge *or* the MovieClip's interior points overlap the x, y coordinates. Setting the third parameter to false is useful when a MovieClip is loaded dynamically into a location, but is not necessary when the user is dragging an existing MovieClip.

The following code checks to see whether the draggable MovieClip `bike_mc` is overlapping with the `target_mc` object when it is dropped. If it is overlapping, the MovieClip it hits is made invisible.

```
bike_mc.onRelease=function():Void
{
      if (this.hitTest(target_mc))
      {
            target_mc._visible=false;
      }
      this.stopDrag();
};
```

In this exercise, you make the calculator MovieClip draggable so the user can place it anywhere on their screen.

1. In Flash, return to calculator.fla in /fpad2004/mmestate/.

Return to the file you created in the last exercise or open /fpad2004/lesson04/intermediate/ calculator_global.fla and save it as *calculator.fla* in /fpad2004/mmestate/

2. Return to the code for actions: Frame 1 of `mcCalculator`. Change the `moveme_mc` `onPress` event handler so instead of setting the `_alpha` of the parent MovieClip, it starts dragging it. Use the `startDrag()` method. Test the application.

```
moveme_mc.onPress=function():Void
{
        _parent.startDrag();
}
```

As you saw in an earlier exercise, `_parent` refers to the main document. This means that the entire document will be dragged including the static text that is not part of the MovieClip.

3. Test the application.

Click the `moveme_mc` MovieClip in the lower right corner of the calculator and move your mouse. The calculator follows your mouse pointer and is dragged around the screen. You cannot drop it. Close the SWF window by clicking the X in its upper right corner.

4. Return to the code for actions: Frame 1 of `mcCalculator`. Change the `moveme_mc` `onRelease` event handler so that instead of setting the `_alpha` of the parent MovieClip, it stops dragging it. Use the `stopDrag()` method. Test the application.

```
moveme_mc.onRelease=function():Void
{
        _parent.stopDrag();
}
```

The main document will stop dragging when the user releases their mouse button.

5. Test the application.

Click the `moveme_mc` MovieClip in the lower right corner of the calculator and then move your mouse. The calculator follows your mouse pointer and is dragged around the screen. Release the mouse button to drop the calculator. Change values in the input text fields. The mortgage is still calculated correctly.

6. Return to main document Stage and delete the text layer containing the static text field.

You no longer need this text field for testing.

7. Save the document as *calculator.fla* in /fpad2004/mmestate/.

The finished file should resemble: /fpad2004/lesson04/intermediate/calculator_mcdrag.fla.

What You Have Learned

What You Have Learned

In this lesson, you have:

- Created a Button object (pages 153–158)
- Created different states of a Button symbol (pages 158–164)
- Responded to Button object events (pages 164–170)
- Created a MovieClip object visually from elements on the Stage (pages 171–174)
- Placed code inside a MovieClip to create a distributable software element (pages 175–177)
- Set MovieClip properties from outside and inside the MovieClip (pages 178–180)
- Responded to MovieClip events (pages 181–183)
- Referenced objects in different Timelines using relative and absolute paths (pages 183–189)
- Created global variables accessible from any Timeline (pages 190–193)
- Created MovieClips that you can drag and drop (pages 194–197)

5 Creating Classes

In Lesson 4, "Creating Button and MovieClip Objects," you created a MovieClip symbol and attached code to that symbol by placing the code in the MovieClip's Timeline. By separating the MovieClip's code from the main document's code, you made a reusable application element. Although functional, there are two main problems with this technique. First, there is no easy way to share and distribute the MovieClip and its attached code; the FLA containing the MovieClip and the associated ActionScript files must be distributed, the MovieClip must be copied to your document's library, and the ActionScript files saved in the appropriate directories so the relative paths specified in the original MovieClip still work.

Second, and more important, with the code embedded inside the MovieClip, it is difficult to change the MovieClip's behavior or appearance. For example, if a developer reused your mortgage calculator and wanted to change the initial values, he would have to edit the code inside the MovieClip's Timeline. The application element is not a black box that can be easily reused by others. What the element needs is an application programming interface (API) consisting of properties and methods that other developers can use without changing the code for the element itself. Defining your program functionality in classes results in a more maintainable and scalable application with elements that can be easily reused.

```
CalcError
1  class errors.CalcError extends Error
2  {
3      private var _selectField:String;
4      function CalcError(message:String, selectField:String)
5      {
6          super(message);
7          this._selectField = selectField;
8      }
9      public function set selectField(field:String):Void
10     {
11         this._selectField = field;
12     }
13     public function get selectField():String
14     {
15         return this._selectField;
16     }
17 }
```

Line 18 of 18, Col 1

In this lesson, you create a CalcError class file; instances of the class are created and used when invalid rates or down payments are entered in the calculator.

In this lesson, you will learn how to create your own classes with their own properties and methods. New to ActionScript 2.0, you can now create classes, create packages of classes, and define classpaths (which tell the compiler where exactly to search for your classes). In addition, you can use all the traditional object-oriented constructs, including the ability to create instance or static properties and methods; define class members as public or private; extend other classes; and create interfaces, implicit getters and setters, and dynamic classes.

You will also learn to create a custom error class and implement each of the standard class constructs for it. When specific calculator errors occur, such as when an improper down payment is entered, an instance of an error class is created. The error is caught and handled using properties and methods you define. In Lesson 6, "Creating Components," you associate class files with visual MovieClip objects, allowing you to rearchitect your calculator so that it has a visual symbol and an associated class file.

What You Will Learn

In this lesson, you will:

- Create a class
- Set classpaths
- Create and reference packages
- Define class properties
- Create a class constructor
- Define class methods
- Control access to class members
- Inherit from other classes
- Create an interface
- Create implicit getter and setter methods
- Create dynamic classes

Approximate Time

This lesson takes approximately 2 hours to complete.

Lesson Files

Asset Files:

none

Starting Files:

/fpad2004/lesson05/start/calculator.fla
/fpad2004/lesson05/start/includes/calcObject.as
/fpad2004/lesson05/start/includes/formatFunctions.as

Completed Files:

/fpad2004/lesson05/complete/calculator.fla
/fpad2004/lesson05/complete/includes/calcObject.as
/fpad2004/lesson05/complete/classes/Formatters.as
/fpad2004/lesson05/complete/classes/errors/CalcError.as

Creating a Class

You define a class in an external ActionScript file using the `class` keyword.

```
class classname
{
}
```

A class can be defined *only* in an external AS file; it cannot be defined in a FLA. There can be no other code other than the class definition in the external file—no straggling variable or function definitions are allowed. You can define one class per file, and the class must have the same name as the file.

You can find the `class` keyword in the Actions panel under Statements > Class Constructs.

The following screenshot shows the class definition for the most basic Bicycle class—one with no properties or methods. You learn to add properties and methods to a class in the following exercises.

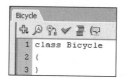

You create new instances of your class using the new keyword, just as you did for many of the built-in classes in Lesson 3, "Learning the Flash Player Object Model." Use strict data typing when you create instances of your custom classes to enable compile time type checking for the properties and methods.

The following code creates a new Bicycle object—a simple object with no properties or methods.

```
var mybike:Bicycle=new Bicycle();
```

In this exercise, you create two new classes, DownPaymentError and RateError. You change your displayMortgage() method to throw instances of these classes instead of throwing strings. By throwing different types of exceptions, you can catch the exceptions in different catch blocks and handle them differently. In Lesson 2, "Learning ActionScript Fundamentals," you used only one catch block that caught any exception thrown.

1. In Flash, return to calculator.fla in /fpad2004/mmestate/.

This is the file you used in the last lesson. If you did not do that exercise, open /fpad2004/lesson05/start/calculator.fla and save it as *calculator.fla* in /fpad2004/mmestate/.

2. Test the application. Type *a* in the down payment text field.

You get $NaN displayed in the monthly payment text field because all input text is passed to the formatNumber() function, which strips out all numeric characters. If you pass *a* to the formatNumber() function, it returns the value of Number(""), the numeric equivalent of an empty string, which is equal to NaN.

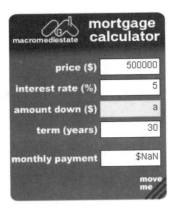

3. Return to calcObject.as in /fpad2004/mmestate/includes/.

This is a file you used in the last lesson. If you did not do that exercise, open /fpad2004/lesson05/ start/includes/calcObject.as and save it as *calcObject.as* in /fpad2004/mmestate/includes/.

4. Inside the `displayMortgage()` method, change the second condition in the `if` statement so that instead of checking the `typeof` the `price`, it checks to see if `this.down` is not a number. Use the `isNaN()` function. Save the file.

```
18      try
19      {
20          if (this.down>this.price || (isNaN(this.down))
21          {
22              throw "Invalid price or down payment";
23          }
```

Make sure you save the file so your changes will be incorporated when you publish the FLA that includes this file.

5. Return to calculator.fla and test the application. Type *a* in the down payment text field.

Now you get the error "Error: Invalid price or down payment" displayed in the Output panel.

6. In a new ActionScript file, define a class called *DownPaymentError*.

```
class DownPaymentError
{
}
```

Make sure you capitalize DownPaymentError with a capital D. It is a best practice to capitalize the first letter of a class name to differentiate it from an instance or instances of a class, which should begin with lowercase letters.

7. Save the file as *DownPaymentError.as* in /fpad2004/mmestate/.

Make sure you use the correct capitalization (the filename must match the class name exactly) and save the file in the same folder as calculator.fla file (not in the includes folder).

You will use this file as the starting file in the next exercise. It should resemble the finished file: /fpad2004/lesson05/intermediate/DownPaymentError_class.as.

8. Return to calcObject.as. Inside the `displayMortgage()` method, change the `throw` statement for an invalid down payment so that it throws a new instance of the DownPaymentError class. Save the file.

Instead of throwing a simple string, you are now throwing an object of a custom class type. Exceptions of different types can be caught by different `catch` blocks.

Use the new keyword to create a new instance of your class.

```
18    try
19    {
20        if (this.down>this.price || (isNaN(this.down))
21        {
22            throw new DownPaymentError();
23        }
24        else if (this.rate<0 || this.rate>100)
```

In this step, you are creating an unnamed instance of the DownPaymentError class. You can define a variable inline if you never need to refer to the variable by name. The line of code in the screenshot is equivalent to the following code, except that you do not have the overhead of creating a variable that you never use again.

```
var downError:DownPaymentError=new DownPaymentError();
throw downError;
```

9. Return to calculator.fla and test the application. Type *a* in the down payment text field.

You should get the error "Error: [object Object]" in the Output panel. If you do not, make sure that you saved calcObject.as before recompiling calculator.fla.

The `catch` block is now receiving a DownPaymentError object instead of a string. Your custom DownPaymentError class does not have a `toString()` method, so it cannot be displayed as a string in the Output panel.

10. Return to calcObject.as. Inside the `displayMortgage()` method, add a new `catch` block before the existing `catch` block that accepts a variable e2 of type *DownPaymentError*.

You can create multiple `catch` blocks by specifying the type of exception each `catch` block should catch. You do this by typing the variable specified in parentheses after the `catch` statement. Use the same notation you use to type variables: name, colon, data type (name:datatype). Place any typed catch blocks before a general catch handler that has no type specified. The general catch block will catch any exceptions that are not caught by any catch blocks defined before it.

```
35    catch(e2:DownPaymentError)
36    {
37    }
38    catch(e)
39    {
40        trace("Error: "+e);
41    }
```

11. At the top of the code inside the `displayMortgage()` method, declare a new variable **e2** as type *DownPaymentError*.

```
var e2:DownPaymentError;
```

12. Inside the `catch` block, set the `text` property of `payment_txt` to *"Fix Amt Down"*, and set focus in the `down_txt` TextField using the `setFocus()` method of the Selection class.

The Selection class, which you have not used yet, has static methods for setting focus in a TextField object. The Selection class can be found in the Actions toolbox under Built-in Classes > Movie > Selection.

You specify one argument to the `setFocus()` method: The instance name of the object you want to give focus to.

```
catch(e2:DownPaymentError)
{
    payment_txt.text="Fix Amt Down";
    Selection.setFocus("down_txt");
}
```

13. Save calcObject.as and return to calculator.fla and test the application. Type *a* in the down payment text field.

You should see the message "Fix Amt Down" in the monthly payment text field. The text in the down payment text field should also be highlighted, indicating to the user that this field needs to be changed.

Note *If the string message does not fit in the text field, you can change the size of the text field in the FLA.*

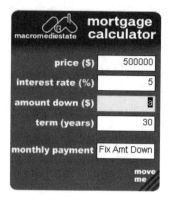

14. Create another new ActionScript file and define a class called *RateError*.

```
class RateError
{
}
```

You will throw an object of this class type when an invalid rate is entered.

15. Save the file as *RateError.as* in /fpad2004/mmestate/classes/.

Make sure you use the correct capitalization (the filename must match the class name exactly) and that you save the file in the *classes* folder, not in the mmestate folder. After your project gets larger, you will not want all your files in one directory.

The finished file should resemble: /fpad2004/lesson05/intermediate/classes/RateError_class.as.

16. Return to calcObject.as. Inside the **displayMortgage()** method, change the **else if** statement so that it checks to see if **this.rate** is not a number. Use the **isNaN()** function.

```
20        if (this.down>this.price || (isNaN(this.down))
21        {
22            throw new DownPaymentError();
23        }
24        else if (isNaN(this.rate))
25        {
26            throw "Invalid rate";
27        }
```

The rate is now always between 0 and 100 because all negative signs are stripped out by the `formatNumber()` function. You also set the `maxChars` property to 2, so that no value greater than 99 can be entered. The only exception that can still occur is the `formatNumber()` can return NaN for any invalid nonnumeric entries in the rate field.

17. Inside the `displayMortgage()` method, change the `throw` statement for an invalid rate to throw a new instance of the RateError class.

```
else if (isNaN(this.rate))
{
      throw new RateError();
}
```

18. Inside the `displayMortgage()` method, add a new `catch` block before the final `catch` block that accepts a variable `e3` of type *RateError*. Inside the `catch` block, set the **text** property of `payment_txt` to *"Fix Rate"* and set the focus in the `rate_txt` TextField using the `setFocus()` method of the Selection class.

```
catch(e3:RateError)
{
      payment_txt.text="Fix Rate";
      Selection.setFocus("rate_txt");
}
```

When a RateError object is thrown, the message "Fix Rate" will be displayed in the monthly payment text field and the rate payment text field will be highlighted.

19. At the top of the code inside the `displayMortgage()` method, declare a new variable `e3` as type *RateError*.

```
var e3:RateError;
```

20. Save calcObject.as. Return to calculator.fla and test the application.

It should resemble the finished file: /fpad2004/lesson05/intermediate/includes/calcObject_class.as.

When you test the application, you should get several error messages in the Output panel. One of the errors should be: The class 'RateError' could not be loaded. The class file is not in the same directory of the FLA and cannot be found. In the next exercise, you set locations where the compiler looks for classes when a FLA is compiled.

Setting Classpaths

In the last exercise, you first saved a class file in the same directory as the FLA and the compiler located it and loaded it correctly. When you saved the class file in a different directory than the FLA, the compiler could not find it. So where can you save your class files? By default, the compiler looks in two places: in the current directory and in a user-specific classes directory. The directories in which the compiler looks for your class files are called the **classpaths**. You can also specify additional directories for the compiler to look in: **per-FLA classpaths** that apply only to a particular FLA or **global classpaths** that apply to all FLAs. If both per-FLA and global classpaths are specified, the per-FLA classpaths are searched first, and then the global classpaths for a class file with the correct filename.

Setting per-FLA Classpaths

You define per-FLA classpaths in the Publish Settings dialog box for the FLA. Select File > Publish Settings, click the Flash tab, and then click the ActionScript 2.0 Settings button.

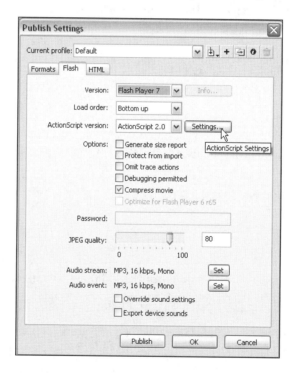

In the ActionScript Settings dialog box, click the Add New Path button to add classpaths. You can specify the classpaths as either absolute or relative to the location of the FLA. When specifying relative paths, use a period (.) to represent the directory of the FLA and then specify locations relative to that directory using forward slashes (/). You can also use the Browse to Path button to locate a specific folder. By default, there are no per-FLA classpaths set. The classpaths in the following screenshot have been added as examples.

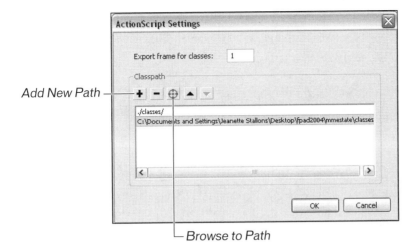

Add New Path ────────

── Browse to Path

Setting Global Classpaths

You define global classpaths by setting preferences for the Flash authoring environment. Select Edit > Preferences, click the ActionScript tab, and then click the ActionScript 2.0 Settings button.

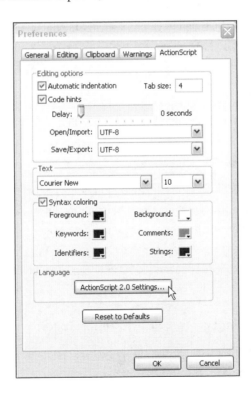

Global classpaths can also be either absolute or relative to the location of the FLA file. If you specify a relative classpath, the actual directory searched will vary depending on the location of the FLA. By default, there are two global classpaths defined.

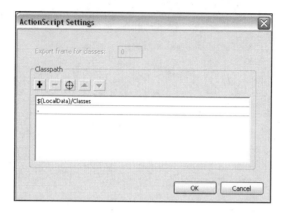

A per-user configuration classes directory. Specified as $(LocalData)/Classes in the classpath settings. For Windows, this points to <boot drive>\Documents and Settings\<username>\Local Settings\Application Data\Macromedia\Flash MX 2004\<language>\Configuration\Classes\. For Macs, this points to <Macintosh HD>/Users <username>/Library/Application Support/Macromedia/Flash MX 2004/<language>/Configuration/Classes/.

Note *Class definitions for the built-in classes are located in the classes folder in the Configuration folder. For more information on these class files, see the exercise in Lesson 6, "Creating Components," on intrinsic classes.*

The current working directory. Specified in relative path notation as ".".

You can also specify $(AppConfig) as a platform-independent, per-application configuration directory. On Windows, this points to <boot drive>\Program Files\Macromedia\Flash MX 2004\<language>\Configuration\. On a Mac, this points to <Macintosh HD>/Applications/ Macromedia Flash MX 2004/ <language>/Configuration/.

In this exercise, you set the /fpad2004/mmestate/classes/ directory as a global classpath.

1. In Flash, return to calculator.fla in /fpad2004/mmestate/.

Return to the file you used in the last exercise or open /fpad2004/lesson05/start/calculator.fla and save it as *calculator.fla* in /fpad2004/mmestate/.

2. Select Edit > Preferences, click the ActionScript tab, and then click the ActionScript 2.0 Settings button.

The ActionScript Settings dialog box appears.

3. Click the Add New Path button.

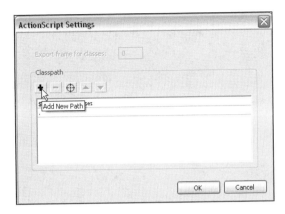

After you click the Add New Path button, the cursor is placed in a new line at the end of the classpath list.

4. Type *./classes* in the text field.

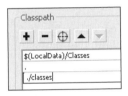

You are using relative notation to specify the classpath. Any time you publish a FLA, the compiler looks for class files in a folder called classes located in the same directory as the FLA.

> **Note** *You cannot specify this relative classpath by simply entering classes. You must specify the relative location starting with the FLA directory, designated by a period (.).*

5. Click the Move Path Up button two times.

The order in which the classpaths are listed will be the order they are searched. You can change the order by selecting a classpath and then clicking the Move Path Up or Move Path Down buttons.

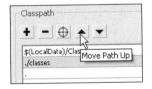

6. Click **OK** in the ActionScript Settings dialog box and then **OK** in the Preferences dialog box. Test the application. Type *a* in the rate text field.

You should see the message "Fix Rate" in the monthly payment text field, and the text in the rate text field should also be highlighted. The compiler successfully found the RateError class file, loaded it, and compiled it.

7. Use Windows Explorer or Macintosh Finder to move DownPaymentError.as to the /mmestate/classes/ folder.

You are moving the file, not simply saving the file to the new location, so that there is no longer a copy in the mmestate folder.

8. Return to calculator.fla and test the application. Type *a* in the down payment text field.

The DownPaymentError class should still be loaded, you should get the message "Fix Amt Down" in the monthly payment text field, and the down payment text field should be highlighted.

The compiler still successfully found and compiled the DownPaymentError class file because it was moved to another global classpath directory.

9. Use Windows Explorer or Macintosh Finder to move RateError.as and DownPaymentError.as to a folder called *errors* in the /fpad2004/mmestate/ classes/ folder.

If you have many classes, you should organize them in subdirectories in the classes folder (or wherever you are storing them).

You will use these files as the starting files in the next exercise. They are equivalent to the files /fpad2004/lesson05/intermediate/classes/errors/RateError_classpath.as and /fpad2004/lesson05/intermediate/classes/errors/DownPaymentError_classpath.as.

10. Return to calculator.fla and test the application.

You should get the following errors in the Output panel "The class 'DownPaymentError' could not be loaded" and "The class 'RateError' could not be loaded." As a result of these errors, you also get an error: This exception clause is placed improperly. In the next exercise, you learn to load classes that are located in subdirectories of classpaths, which will fix these errors.

11. Add the RateError.as and DownPaymentError.as files to your fpad2004 project.

The files are now in their final directory location and can be added to the project file.

Creating and Referencing Packages

As your application grows and/or you make classes you want to share between many applications, you need to organize your classes into directories. You can specify one or several directories as classpaths and organize your class files within subdirectories of these classpath directories; you don't have to specify every folder that contains a class used in your FLA as a classpath. When you organize your classes within subdirectories, you are creating packages of classes. A **package** is a group of related classes. A **package name** is the directory structure from the classpath to the class file, with each directory separated by a period (for example, vehicles.cycles). A **fully qualified class name** is the full name of the class from the classpath including the package name (for example, vehicles.cycles.Bicycle).

If you specify /fpad2004/examples/classes/ as your classpath and then create a subdirectory called *cycles*, you cannot refer to the class Bicycle in a FLA located in /fpad2004/examples/. Instead, you must use its fully qualified class name: cycles.Bicycle.

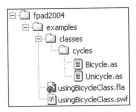

The classes you place in a particular package should be related. For example, all the classes in a package should be for a particular application, organized by types of exceptions, mathematical utilities, and so on.

When you place a class in a package instead of directly in a classpath folder, you must change the class definition. The name of the class defined in the file must be the fully qualified class name, which includes its package name.

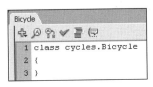

You could have another class Unicycle in the same cycles package.

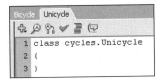

After you place a class file into a package—into a subdirectory of a classpath—you must tell the compiler where the class file is located. The compiler does not automatically search all classpath subdirectories for matching class files. Instead, you must either use the full package name every time you reference the class (called an **implicit import**); or you must first import the class using its fully qualified class name, after which you can refer to it by its simple class name (called an **explicit import**).

Importing Classes Implicitly

You can always import and reference a class by using its fully qualified name anywhere an identifier is expected. For example, when you create a new instance, specify a variable type, or use a static property or method.

```
//Use full class name to specify variable type and instantiate an object
var mybike:cycles.Bicycle=new cycles.Bicycle();
//Reference class using full class name
trace(mybike instanceof cycles.Bicycle);
```

Importing Classes Explicitly

If you use the class name in several places in a file or want to clearly define at the top of the file which classes are imported and used, you can explicitly import the class.

You explicitly import a class using the `import` keyword followed by the fully qualified class name. Any time you reference the class in the code following the `import` statement, you can refer to it by its simple class name—you don't have to use its fully qualified class name. The compiler keeps track of all classes that have been explicitly imported and substitutes the full class names for any abbreviated references found.

```
import cycles.Bicycle;
var mybike:Bicycle=new Bicycle();
trace(mybike instanceof Bicycle);
```

If an imported class is not used in the code that follows it, the class will not be compiled into the resulting bytecode for the SWF.

Tip *The `import` statement applies only to the current frame or object in which it is used. For example, if you import all the classes in the cycles package on Frame 1 of a Flash document, you can reference classes in that package by their simple name only on that frame. If you have code on a different frame or object, you must use another `import` statement or reference the class using its full class name.*

Using Wildcards to Import All Classes in a Directory

If you need to import multiple class files from a single directory, you can use a wildcard in the `import` statement instead of individually importing every class file. All you have to do is substitute an asterisk for the filename, which will import all classes in that directory or package.

```
//The cycles package contains classes Bicycle and Unicycle import cycles.*;
var mybike:Bicycle=new Bicycle();
var hisbike:Unicycle=new Unicycle();
```

Tip *Both the directory and filenames are case-sensitive. If you have a file called /cycles/Bicycle.as, but you import Cycles.Bicycle, the compiler will not find the class you are trying to import.*

You can use the asterisk only as a wildcard for filenames, not for a directory folder. The wildcard imports only classes found in the immediate package directory, and does not traverse subdirectories.

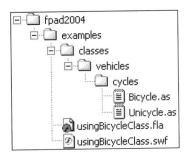

```
//This code does not import class files in the vehicles.cycles package
import vehicles.*;
```

Tip *A package is also a group of classes in a different namespace. At compile time, a package is the hierarchy of folders that contain the class definitions. At runtime, each subdirectory in the package becomes an instance of the Object class, and the class definitions are scoped or belong to that object. For the class cycles.Bicycle, Bicycle belongs to the cycles package inside the /cycles/ subfolder of the classpath, and cycles exists as an instance of the Object class at runtime.*

In this exercise, you import and reference your error classes from a package under the classpath instead of as class files in the classpath. First, you use implicit importing; second, you use explicit importing; finally, you use a wildcard to explicitly import all the classes in the errors package.

1. Return to calcObject.as in /fpad2004/mmestate/includes/.

Return to the file you used in the last exercise or open /fpad2004/lesson05/intermediate/includes/ calcObject_class.as and save it as *calcObject.as* in /fpad2004/mmestate/includes/.

2. Inside the `displayMortgage()` method, change the two `throw` statements to use the fully qualified class names of the two error classes.

In this step, you are implicitly importing the classes using their fully qualified class names whenever they are referenced.

```
20          if (this.down>this.price || (isNaN(this.down))
21          {
22              throw new errors.DownPaymentError();
23          }
24          else if (isNaN(this.rate))
25          {
26              throw new errors.RateError();
27          }
```

3. Change the two `catch` blocks so they also use the fully qualified class names of the two error classes.

```
catch(e2:errors.DownPaymentError)
catch(e3:errors.RateError)
```

4. Change the two variable declarations so they also use the fully qualified class names of the two error classes. Save the file.

```
var e2:errors.DownPaymentError;
var e3:errors.RateError;
```

5. Return to calculator.fla in /fpad2004/mmestate/ and test the application.

Return to the file you used in the last exercise or open /fpad2004/lesson05/start/calculator.fla and save it as *calculator.fla* in /fpad2004/mmestate/.

You should get the following error messages in the Output panel: "The class being compiled, 'DownPaymentError', does not match the class that was imported, 'errors. DownPaymentError'" and "The class being compiled, 'RateError', does not match the class that was imported, 'errors.RateError'". As a result of these errors, you still get the error: This exception clause is placed improperly.

Although you have correctly specified the classes fully qualified class names, you have not changed the class definitions to specify that the classes are part of a package.

6. Return to DownPaymentError.as in /fpad2004/mmestate/classes/errors/. Inside the file, change the class name from DownPaymentError to *errors.DownPaymentError*. Save the file.

Return to the file you used in the last exercise or open /fpad2004/lesson05/intermediate/classes/errors/ DownPaymentError_classpath.as and save it as *DownPaymentError.as* in /fpad2004/mmestate/ classes/errors/.

```
class errors.DownPaymentError
{
}
```

You will use this file as the starting file in the next exercise. It should resemble the finished file: /fpad2004/lesson05/intermediate/classes/errors/DownPaymentError_package.as.

7. Open RateError.as in /fpad2004/mmestate/classes/errors/. Change the class name from RateError to *errors.RateError*. Save the file.

This is the file you used in the last exercise. If you did not do that exercise, open /fpad2004/lesson05/ intermediate/classes/errors/RateError_classpath.as and save it as */fpad2004/mmestate/classes/errors/ RateError.as*.

```
class errors.RateError
{
}
```

You will use this file as the starting file in the next exercise. It should resemble the finished file: /fpad2004/lesson05/intermediate/classes/errors/RateError_package.as.

8. Return to calculator.fla and test the application. Type *a* in the down payment text field.

The classes should be successfully loaded. You should get the message "Fix Amt Down" in the monthly payment text field and the down payment text field should be highlighted.

9. At the top of the code in calcObject.as, explicitly import the *errors.RateError* and *errors.DownPaymentError* classes.

After you explicitly import a class, you can refer to it in the rest of the file using its simple class name.

```
import errors.RateError;
import errors.DownPaymentError;
```

10. Inside the `displayMortgage()` method, change the two `throw` statements so they use the simple class names of the two error classes.

You no longer need to use the fully qualified class names because the classes have been explicitly imported; the compiler will substitute the fully qualified class names for any simple references found.

```
20      if (this.down>this.price || (isNaN(this.down)))
21      {
22          throw new DownPaymentError();
23      }
24      else if (isNaN(this.rate))
25      {
26          throw new RateError();
27      }
28      else
```

11. Change the two `catch` blocks so they also use the simple class names of the two error classes.

```
catch(e:DownPaymentError)
catch(e:RateError)
```

12. Change the two variable declarations so they also use the simple class names of the two error classes. Save the file.

```
var e2:DownPaymentError;
var e3:RateError;
```

13. Return to calculator.fla and test the application. Type *a* in the down payment text field.

The classes should still be successfully loaded. You should get the message "Fix Amt Down" in the monthly payment text field and the down payment text field should be highlighted.

14. Return to calcObject.as and change the first `import` statement so that it uses the asterisk wildcard to import all the classes in the errors subdirectory of a classpath. Delete the second import statement. Save the file.

```
import errors.*;
```

This should be the only `import` statement you have. All classes in the errors subdirectory of a classpath will be imported.

The finished file should resemble: /fpad2004/lesson05/intermediate/includes/calcObject_package.as.

15. Return to calculator.fla and test the application. Type *a* in the down payment text field.

The classes should still be successfully loaded, you should get the message "Fix Amt Down" in the monthly payment text field, and the down payment text field should be highlighted.

Defining Class Properties

In Lesson 3, you defined custom properties for instances of the Object class. These properties were applicable to only that particular Object instance. For example, you could create `mybike` as an instance of the Object class and assign it a property of `defaultColor` with a value of blue.

```
var mybike:Object=new Object();
mybike.defaultColor="blue";
```

If you create another bike object from the Object class, it will not have a property of `defaultColor`. You have to explicitly create and define a `defaultColor` property for that instance. This is not ideal; every time you create a bike object, you want it to have certain properties (such as `defaultColor`) and maybe even default values for some of these properties. In order to achieve this, you must create your own Bicycle class and create properties for it in the class definition; then, every time an instance of the Bicycle class is created, it will have specific properties.

You define properties inside a class definition exactly as you have been defining them in normal scripts; you use the `var` keyword followed by a colon and the variable type.

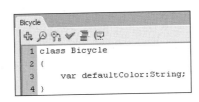

> **Tip** It is a best practice to use lowercase to name all class properties, using mixed case for multiple words.

You can also set the property equal to an initial or default value if desired.

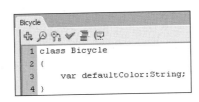

After you create instances of the Bicycle class, you can assign a value to the `defaultColor` property.

```
var mybike:Bicycle=new Bicycle();
trace(mybike.defaultColor);        //Outputs silver
mybike.defaultColor="blue";
trace(mybike.defaultColor);        //Outputs blue
```

> **Note** There is no automatic code hinting generated to show custom properties and methods of custom classes.

Defining Public and Private Properties

You can create two types of properties: public and private.

Public. Properties that can be accessed and referenced from *outside* the class definition (as you did in the last section). The default access behavior for class properties that are not defined with a `public` or `private` attribute is public.

Private. Properties that can be accessed and used only from *within* the class definition.

You specify whether a property is public or private by using a `public` or `private` attribute in front of the variable declaration.

```
Bicycle
1  class Bicycle
2  {
3      public var defaultColor:String="silver";
4      //This is the same as var defaultColor:String="silver";
5  }
```

> **Tip** *Although not required, it is a best practice to always use the `public` attribute to specify your public properties.*

For public properties, you can access the property as an instance property outside the class definition.

```
var mybike:Bicycle=new Bicycle();
trace(mybike.defaultColor);              //Outputs silver
```

You don't always want your properties to be public. For example, if a property is used only inside the class definition, there is no need to make it public. If a property needs to be used by other classes, it must be public.

> **Note** *In ActionScript, there are no equivalents for the Java and C# protected or package/internal access levels.*

If you want developers to be able to access and assign values for a property, but not directly; you can require them to access the property through a method. This process is necessary if the property needs to be manipulated before it is accessed and used by other methods. (You learn to create methods for your classes in a following exercise.) In addition, many strict object-oriented developers prefer this "data hiding" because it provides a layer of abstraction, an interface to the object that does not rely on the internal structure (the properties) of the object itself. If you use methods to access the properties, you can change the names and structure of the object data without breaking the outside code used to access this data. If you set a property directly, a future version of the class might have a property of that name that serves an entirely different purpose internally.

You make a property private by adding the `private` attribute in front of the variable declaration.

You can no longer access the `defaultColor` property from code outside the class definition. If you try, you get the error: The member is private and cannot be accessed.

```
var mybike:Bicycle=new Bicycle();
trace(mybike.frameColor);        //Outputs silver
trace(mybike.defaultColor);      //Gives an error
```

In this exercise, you create an instance property called `message` for the DownPaymentError and RateError classes. You assign a value to the property for the DownPaymentError class after creating an instance of the class. You assign a default value for the `message` property for the RateError class in the class definition. You output the value of the `message` property in the monthly payment text field when an error is thrown instead of assigning a value in the `catch` block.

1. Return to DownPaymentError.as in /fpad2004/mmestate/classes/errors/. Inside the class definition, create a *public* property called *message* that is of type *String*. Save the file.

Return to the file you used in the last exercise or open /fpad2004/lesson05/intermediate/classes/errors/DownPaymentError_package.as and save it as *DownPaymentError.as* in /fpad2004/mmestate/classes/errors/.

```
class errors.DownPaymentError
{
     public var message:String;
}
```

By creating a `message` property for the class, you can use the DownPaymentError class in different situations and assign an appropriate `message` value in each case.

You will use this file as the starting file in the next exercise. It should resemble the finished file: /fpad2004/lesson05/intermediate/classes/errors/DownPaymentError_instanceproperties.as.

2. Return to calcObject.as in /fpad2004/mmestate/includes/.

Return to the file you used in the last exercise or open /fpad2004/lesson05/intermediate/includes/calcObject_package.as and save it as *calcObject.as* in /fpad2004/mmestate/includes/.

3. Inside the `displayMortgage()` method, create a new variable called `downError` before the first **throw** statement. Set it equal to a new instance of the DownPaymentError class.

You are creating a named instance of the class so that you can assign a value to its `message` property before you throw it.

```
18    try
19    {
20        if (this.down>this.price || (isNaN(this.down)))
21        {
22            var downError:DownPaymentError=new DownPaymentError();
23            throw new DownPaymentError();
24        }
```

4. Below this line of code, set the `message` property of the instance equal to the string *"Fix Amt Down"*.

```
downError.message="Fix Amt Down";
```

5. Change the **throw** statement on the next line to throw the `downError` instance of the DownPaymentError class instead of a new instance of the class.

```
20        if (this.down>this.price || (isNaN(this.down)))
21        {
22            var downError:DownPaymentError=new DownPaymentError();
23            downError.message="Fix Amt Down";
24            throw downError;
25        }
```

6. Change the code inside the DownPaymentError `catch` block to set the `text` property of the `payment_txt` TextField equal to the `message` property of the DownPaymentError instance, `e2`. Save the file.

This changes your code so that the message displayed is a property of the error class thrown instead of being hard-coded in the script. It removes the dependency of the script on the particular object thrown, making your code more maintainable and reusable.

```
39        catch(e2:DownPaymentError)
40        {
41            payment_txt.text=e2.message;
42            Selection.setFocus("down_txt");
43        }
```

7. Return to calculator.fla in /fpad2004/mmestate/ and test the application. Type *a* in the down payment text field.

Return to the file you used in the last exercise or open /fpad2004/lesson05/start/calculator.fla and save it as *calculator.fla* in /fpad2004/mmestate/.

You should still get the message "Fix Amt Down" in the monthly payment text field. This message, though, is no longer hard-coded in the script, but it is a property of the error class thrown.

8. Return to RateError.as in /fpad2004/mmestate/classes/errors/. Inside the class definition, create a public property called `message` equal to *"Fix Rate"*. Save the file.

Return to the file you used in the last exercise or open /fpad2004/lesson05/intermediate/classes/errors/RateError_package.as and save it as *RateError.as* in /fpad2004/mmestate/classes/errors/.

In this case, you are creating the `message` property and then assigning a default value in the class definition. All instances of the class that are created will have this value for the property unless a new value is assigned.

```
class errors.RateError
{
        public var message:String="Fix Rate";
}
```

The finished file should resemble: /fpad2004/lesson05/intermediate/classes/errors/RateError_instanceproperties.as.

9. Return to calcObject.as. Change the code inside the RateError `catch` block to set the `text` property of the `payment_txt` TextField equal to the `message` property of the RateError instance, e3. Save the file.

```
44        catch(e3:RateError)
45        {
46                payment_txt.text=e3.message;
47                Selection.setFocus("rate_txt")
48        }
```

The finished file should resemble: /fpad2004/lesson05/intermediate/includes/calcObject_instanceproperties.as.

10. Return to calculator.fla and test the application. Type *a* in the rate text field.

You should still get the message "Fix Rate" in the monthly payment text field, although now this message is not hard-coded in the script, but it is a property of the error class thrown.

Defining Static Properties

All the properties created in the last section were instance properties. An **instance property** is a property associated with a particular instance of a class; each class instance has its own copy of the property and the property can have a value independent of all the other instances. You can also define **static properties**, which are properties associated with the class and have the same value for all instances. These are also referred to as **class properties**. You used both instance and static properties of the built-in classes in Lesson 3.

You create a static property by using the keyword `static` in front of the property declaration inside the class definition. Static properties can be public or private, just like instance properties. If you have both `static` and `private`/`public` attributes for a variable, you can specify the attributes in either order.

```
Bicycle
1  class Bicycle
2  {
3      static public var NUMWHEELS:Number=2;
4      // OR public static var NUMWHEELS:Number=2;
5  }
```

> **Tip** *It is a best practice to name static properties with all uppercase.*

From outside the class definition, you access static properties of the instance exactly as you accessed static properties of built-in classes: by using the name of the class, period, name of the static property (class.staticpropertyname). If you try to access a static property as a property of an instance, you get the error message: Static members can only be accessed directly through classes.

```
var mybike:Bicycle=new Bicycle();
trace(Bicycle.NUMWHEELS);          //Outputs 2
trace(mybike.NUMWHEELS);           //Gives an error
```

In this exercise, you create a static property called `SELECTFIELD` for the DownPaymentError and RateError classes. You assign a default value for the property in the class definitions and then use the value of the static property in the `catch` blocks to select a particular field when an error is thrown.

1. Return to DownPaymentError.as in /fpad2004/mmestate/classes/errors/. Inside the class definition, create a *public static* property called `SELECTFIELD` equal to *"down_txt"* of type *String*. Save the file.

Return to the file you used in the last exercise or open /fpad2004/lesson05/intermediate/classes/errors/ DownPaymentError_instanceproperties.as and save it as *DownPaymentError.as* in /fpad2004/ mmestate/classes/errors/.

```
class errors.DownPaymentError
{
     public var message:String;
     public static var SELECTFIELD:String="down_txt";
}
```

By creating a SELECTFIELD property for the class, you de-couple the dependence of the catch block on the particular error object thrown.

The finished file should resemble: /fpad2004/lesson05/intermediate/classes/errors/ DownPaymentError_staticproperties.as.

2. Return to RateError.as in /fpad2004/mmestate/classes/errors/. Inside the class definition, create a *public static* property called *SELECTFIELD* equal to "*rate_txt*" of type *String*. Save the file.

Return to the file you used in the last exercise or open /fpad2004/lesson05/intermediate/classes/ errors/RateError_instanceproperties.as and save it as *RateError.as* in /fpad2004/mmestate/ classes/errors/.

```
class errors.RateError
{
      public var message:String="Fix Rate";
      public static var SELECTFIELD:String="rate_txt";
}
```

In this step, you are declaring a static property called SELECTFIELD to hold the name of the text field you want highlighted when a rate error occurs. In this calculator application, the value of this property never changes, which is why you can make it a static property. To make this class more reusable, though, this should be an instance property. You are making it a static property in this exercise so that you can get experience creating and referencing static properties. You make it an instance property of a more general error class in a later exercise.

The finished file should resemble: /fpad2004/lesson05/intermediate/classes/errors/ RateError_staticproperties.as.

3. Return to calcObject.as in /fpad2004/mmestate/includes/.

Return to the file you used in the last exercise or open /fpad2004/lesson05/intermediate/includes/ calcObject_instanceproperties.as and save it as *calcObject.as* in /fpad2004/mmestate/includes/.

4. Inside the displayMortgage() method, change the line of code in the DownPaymentError catch block that sets focus to the down_txt field to instead set focus to the TextField specified in the static SELECTFIELD property of the class of the instance caught.

Remember that static properties are properties of the class, not an instance of the class.

```
39    catch(e2:DownPaymentError)
40    {
41        payment_txt.text=e2.message;
42        Selection.setFocus(DownPaymentError.SELECTFIELD);
43    }
```

5. Change the line of code in the RateError `catch` block that sets focus to the `rate_txt` field to instead set focus to the TextField specified in the **SELECTFIELD** property of the class of the instance caught. Save the file.

```
44    catch(e3:RateError)
45    {
46        payment_txt.text=e3.message;
47        Selection.setFocus(RateError.SELECTFIELD);
48    }
```

The finished file should resemble: /fpad2004/lesson05/intermediate/includes/ calcObject_staticproperties.as.

6. Return to calculator.fla in **/fpad2004/mmestate/** and test the application. Type a in the down payment text field.

Return to the file you used in the last exercise or open /fpad2004/lesson05/start/calculator.fla and save it as *calculator.fla* in /fpad2004/mmestate/.

You should get the message "Fix Amt Down" in the monthly payment text field and the down payment text field should still be highlighted, even though the field to select is now being set from a static property of the class of the error instance caught.

Creating a Class Constructor

In the last section, you assigned unique values to instance properties by assigning values in code *after* the instance was created. You can also pass values of properties to the class itself, so that the properties can be set *when* the instance is created. To do this, you need to define a class constructor.

A **class constructor** is a special function that is automatically invoked when an instance of the class is created. You create a constructor by creating a function with the same name as the class inside the class definition. In ActionScript 2.0, you are not required to define a constructor. (You saw this already; you have not created constructors for any of the classes you created so far.) If you do not define a constructor, the compiler automatically creates an empty one for you when the class is compiled.

Defining a Constructor

Use the following rules when creating a constructor:

- A constructor cannot specify a return type.
- A constructor must be public. Although you can explicitly specify the constructor as public using the `public` attribute, this attribute is usually left off.
- If the class is part of a package, the name of the constructor must be the simple name of the class, not the fully qualified class name including the package name.

In the following code, a constructor for the Bicycle class is defined. It assigns the property `frameColor` an initial value.

```
Bicycle
1  class Bicycle
2  {
3      private var defaultColor:String="silver";
4      public var frameColor:String;
5      function Bicycle
6      {
7          frameColor=defaultColor;
8      }
9  }
```

When you create an instance of the Bicycle class, the `frameColor` property is assigned the value of the private `defaultColor` property.

```
var mybike:Bicycle=new Bicycle();
trace(mybike.frameColor);              //Outputs silver
```

Defining Constructor Parameters

You can also specify parameters for your constructor function that the developer must pass to it when they create an instance of the class. You create parameters for the constructor function exactly as you created them for normal functions in Lesson 2. Be sure to type your parameters.

```
Bicycle
1  class Bicycle
2  {
3      public var frameColor:String;
4      function Bicycle(color:String)
5      {
6          frameColor=color;
7      }
8  }
```

When you create an instance of the class, you pass arguments to the constructor function in the parentheses after the name of the class.

```
var mybike:Bicycle=new Bicycle("blue");
trace(mybike.frameColor);        //Outputs blue
```

> **Note**   *Overloaded constructors (multiple constructors with different parameter signatures) are not allowed. You must handle varying numbers of arguments as optional function parameters with conditional logic.*

Using the this Identifier

Inside constructors, you can reference class properties using the `this` keyword (similar to the way you referenced Object instance properties inside a method of that object in Lesson 3).

The use of the `this` keyword is usually optional. If you leave it off, the compiler determines whether a property belongs to the current class scope and adds the `this` keyword to the beginning of the expression for you. Although optional, the explicit use of the `this` keyword provides a visual indicator that you are referencing an instance property rather than a function variable.

You must use the `this` keyword to reference a property inside the constructor if a function parameter has the same name as a property. If you don't use `this` to specify the property, the compiler assigns all references to that named variable inside the constructor to the function parameter variable and your property value will not be assigned.

Tip *You cannot use the `this` keyword outside the constructor or any method definitions (which you'll learn about in the next exercise) in a class definition.*

In this exercise, you create a constructor for the DownPaymentError class to which you pass values for `message` and `selectField` instance properties when instances are created. You also turn this class into a class called CalcError, which is used to create instances when both down payment and rate exceptions occur.

1. Return to DownPaymentError.as in /fpad2004/mmestate/classes/errors/. Change the name of the class to *CalcError*.

Return to the file you used in the last exercise or open /fpad2004/lesson05/intermediate/classes/errors/DownPaymentError_staticproperties.as and save it as *DownPaymentError.as* in /fpad2004/mmestate/classes/errors/.

```
class errors.CalcError
{
      public var message:String;
      public static var SELECTFIELD:String ="down_txt";
}
```

2. Inside the class definition, change the `SELECTFIELD` property so it is a *public* instance property with no default value.

Make sure you change the case of the property so that it is no longer uppercase.

```
class errors.CalcError
{
      public var message:String;
      public var selectField:String;
}
```

3. After the code defining the properties, create a constructor for the class with two parameters called *message* and *selectField* that are both of type *String*.

Remember that to create a constructor, you simply create a function with the same name as the class with no return value specified.

```
1 class errors.CalcError
2 {
3      public var message:String;
4      public var selectField:String;
5      function CalcError(message:String,selectField:String)
6      {
7      }
8 }
```

4. Inside the constructor, set the `message` property equal to the value of the `message` argument passed to the constructor and the `selectField` property equal to the value of the `selectField` argument passed to the constructor.

Use the `this` scope to differentiate the property of the class from the function parameter.

```
function CalcError(message:String,selectField:String)
{
        this.message=message;
        this.selectField=selectField;
}
```

5. Save the file as *CalcError.as* in */fpad2004/mmestate/classes/errors/*.

Make sure that you use correct capitalization.

The finished file should resemble: /fpad2004/lesson05/intermediate/classes/errors/ CalcError_constructor.as.

6. Return to calcObject.as in */fpad2004/mmestate/includes/*.

Return to the file you used in the last exercise or open /fpad2004/lesson05/intermediate/includes/ calcObject_staticproperties.as and save it as *calcObject.as* in /fpad2004/mmestate/includes/.

7. Inside the `displayMortgage()` method, delete the three lines of code creating and throwing the variable `downError` and instead throw an instance of the CalcError class, passing to it the arguments *"Fix Amt Down"* and *"down_txt"*.

The first argument will be assigned to the `message` property of the CalcError instance and its value will be displayed in the mortgage payment text field when an exception occurs; the second argument sets which field should receive focus after an exception occurs and is caught.

```
18    try
19    {
20        if (this.down>this.price || (isNaN(this.down)))
21        {
22            throw new CalcError("Fix Amt Down","down_txt");
23        }
24        else if (isNaN(this.rate))
```

8. Still inside the `displayMortgage()` method, change the line of code throwing an instance of the RateError class to instead throw an instance of the CalcError class, passing to it the arguments *"Fix Rate"* and *"rate_txt"*.

```
24        else if (isNaN(this.rate))
25        {
26            throw new CalcError("Fix rate","rate_txt");
27        }
28        else
```

9. Change the `catch` block that catches instances of the DownPaymentError class to instead catch instances of the *CalcError* class.

```
39    catch(e2:CalcError)
40    {
41        payment_txt.text=e2.message;
42        Selection.setFocus(DownPaymentError.SELECTFIELD);
43    }
```

10. Change the line of code setting focus in this `catch` block to instead set focus to the TextField specified in the `selectField` property of the CalcError instance caught, **e2**.

```
Selection.setFocus(e2.selectField);
```

11. Change the variable declaration for **e2** so it is type *CalcError*. Delete the variable declarations for **e3** and `payment`.

```
var e2:CalcError;
```

12. Delete the `catch` block that catches instances of the RateError class. Save the file.

Here is the code that you should delete.

```
39    catch(e2:CalcError)
40    {
41        payment_txt.text=e2.message;
42        Selection.setFocus(e2.selectField);
43    }
44    catch(e3:RateError)
45    {
46        payment_txt.text=e3.message;
47        Selection.setFocus(RateError.SELECTFIELD);
48    }
49    catch(e)
50    {
```

You will use this file in the following exercises. It should resemble the finished file: /fpad2004/lesson05/intermediate/includes/calcObject_constructor.as.

13. Return to calculator.fla in /fpad2004/mmestate/ and test the application. Type *a* in the down payment text field.

Return to the file you used in the last exercise or open /fpad2004/lesson05/start/calculator.fla and save it as *calculator.fla* in /fpad2004/mmestate/.

You should still get the message "Fix Amt Down" in the monthly payment text field, and the down payment text field should still be highlighted.

Defining Class Methods

In Lesson 3, you defined custom methods of instances of the Object class in addition to defining custom properties. Like the properties, the methods you defined applied only to that single Object instance. For example, you could create `mybike` as an instance of the Object class and assign it a method of `setSpeed()`.

```
var mybike:Object=new Object();
mybike.speed=0;
mybike.setSpeed=function(mph:Number):Void
{
     this.speed=mph;
}
```

If you create another bike object from the Object class, it will not have a method `setSpeed()`. You have to explicitly create and define that method again for the new instance. (You could also define it as a stand-alone function and then assign the function name as the body for each method.) Again, this is not ideal because you want to define the methods for bike objects once and have them automatically available to all instances.

You define methods inside a class definition exactly as you define functions in normal scripts. You use the `function` keyword followed by the name of the method, the names and types of arguments in parentheses, and the data type of the return variable.

```
Bicycle

1 class Bicycle
2 {
3      public var speed:Number=0;
4      function setSpeed(mph:Number):Void
5      {
6           this.speed=mph;
7      }
8 }
```

> **Tip** *It is a best practice to name methods using all lowercase; use mixed case for multiple words.*

After you create an instance of the Bicycle class, you can call the setSpeed() method to change the speed of the Bicycle object.

```
var mybike:Bicycle=new Bicycle();
trace(mybike.speed);              //Outputs 0
mybike.setSpeed(10);
trace(mybike.speed);              //Outputs 10
```

Methods can also return values. In the following code, a getter method is created, which simply returns the value of the Bicycle object's speed property that has been made private.

```
 1  class Bicycle
 2  {
 3      private var speed:Number=0;
 4      function setSpeed(mph:Number):Void
 5      {
 6          this.speed=mph;
 7      }
 8      function getSpeed():Number
 9      {
10          return this.speed;
11      }
12  }
```

Note *It is a best practice to prefix object properties inside the method with the prefix* this.

After you create an instance of the Bicycle class, you can call the method getSpeed() to get the speed of the Bicycle object.

```
var mybike:Bicycle=new Bicycle();
trace(mybike.getSpeed());         //Outputs 0
mybike.setSpeed(10);
trace(mybike.getSpeed());         //Outputs 10
trace(mybike.speed);              //Gives an error
```

Note *Overloaded methods (multiple methods with the same name but different parameter signatures) are not allowed. You must handle varying numbers of arguments as optional method parameters with conditional logic.*

Defining Public and Private Methods

You can specify class methods as private or public, exactly as you could for properties. Use the public or private attribute in front of the method definition. If no access modifier is specified, the method is public by default. Use private methods for methods that are used only inside the class definition and never directly called outside the class definition.

In the following code, instead of setting the speed directly, you can change only the Bicycle object's gear or cadence (how fast the pedals are rotating). Whenever one of the two properties changes, the speed is recalculated using a private method.

```
1  class Bicycle
2  {
3      static private var SOMEFACTOR:Number=0.016;
4      private var speed:Number, gear:Number, cadence:Number;
5      function Bicycle(gear:Number,cadence:Number)
6      {
7          this.gear=gear;
8          this.cadence=cadence;
9          this.setSpeed();
10     }
11     private function setSpeed():Void
12     {
13         this.speed=this.cadence*this.gear*SOMEFACTOR;
14     }
15     public function getSpeed():Number
16     {
17         return this.speed;
18     }
19     public function setGear(gear:Number):Void
20     {
21         this.gear=gear;
22         this.setSpeed();
23     }
24     public function setCadence(rotationsPerMinute:Number):Void
25     {
26         this.cadence=rotationsPerMinute;
27         this.setSpeed();
28     }
29 }
```

Like properties, methods referenced from inside other methods do not need to be prefaced with the this keyword, although they can be.

Tip Although not required, it is a best practice to always use the *public* attribute to specify your public methods.

You can access the public methods to change gear and cadence, but you cannot access the speed directly.

```
var mybike:Bicycle=new Bicycle(2,60);
trace(mybike.getSpeed());              //Outputs 1.92
mybike.setGear(9);
trace(mybike.getSpeed());              //Outputs 8.64
mybike.setSpeed(10);                   //Gives an error
```

In this exercise, you create a `toString()` method for the CalcError class that is automatically called whenever you trace an instance of the CalcError class.

1. Return to calcObject.as in /fpad2004/mmestate/includes/.

Return to the file you used in the last exercise or open /fpad2004/lesson05/ intermediate/includes/ calcObject_constructor.as and save it as *calcObject.as* in /fpad2004/mmestate/includes/.

2. Inside the `displayMortgage()` method, add a `trace` statement inside the CalcError `catch` block that traces the CalcError instance caught, `e2`.

```
39    catch(e2:CalcError)
40    {
41        payment_txt.text=e2.message;
42        Selection.setFocus(e2.selectField);
43        trace(e2);
44    }
```

You will use this file in the next exercise. It should resemble the finished file: /fpad2004/lesson05/ intermediate/includes/calcObject_instancemethods.as.

3. Return to calculator.fla in /fpad2004/mmestate/ and test the application. Type *a* in the down payment text field.

Return to the file you used in the last exercise or open /fpad2004/lesson05/start/calculator.fla and save it as *calculator.fla* in /fpad2004/mmestate/.

You should see "[object Object]" displayed in the Output panel. The variable e that you trace is a complex variable and cannot automatically be represented as a simple string.

4. Return to CalcError.as in /fpad2004/mmestate/classes/errors/.

Return to the file you used in the last exercise or open /fpad2004/lesson05/intermediate/classes/ errors/CalcError_constructor.as and save it as *CalcError.as* in /fpad2004/mmestate/classes/errors/.

5. After the constructor, create a `public` method called `toString` that has no parameters and returns a `String`.

```
public function toString():String
{
}
```

6. Inside the method definition, return the `message` property. Save the file.

```
public function toString():String
{
    return this.message;
}
```

You will use this file in the following exercises. It should resemble the finished file: /fpad2004/lesson05/intermediate/classes/errors/CalcError_instancemethods.as.

7. Return to calculator.fla in /fpad2004/mmestate/ and test the application. Type *a* in the down payment text field.

You should now get the message "Fix Amt Down" in the Output panel and in the monthly payment text field. Whenever you attempt to trace a complex object, the compiler looks to see whether the object has a `toString()` method. If it does, it calls that method to output a string representation of the object.

Defining Static Methods

You specify static methods exactly the same way you specified static properties. Use the `static` attribute in front of the method definition. Use static for methods that do not reference instance properties or set/get only static properties. Static methods cannot access or manipulate instance properties because they are called as methods of the class itself, not from an instance of the class.

You create a static method by using the keyword `static` in front of the method declaration inside the class definition. If you have both `static` and `private/public` attributes, you can specify the attributes in either order.

```
1 class Bicycle
2 {
3     static private var NUMWHEELS:Number=2;
4     static public function getNumWheels():Number
5     {
6         return NUMWHEELS;
7     }
8 }
```

From outside the class definition, you access static methods of the instance exactly as you accessed static methods of built-in classes—by using the name of the class, period, name of the static method (class.staticMethodName).

```
var mybike:Bicycle=new Bicycle();
trace(Bicycle.getNumWheels());        //Outputs 2
trace(mybike.getNumWheels());         //Gives an error
```

In this exercise, you change the global `formatNumber()` function you created in Lesson 2 into a static method of a Formatters class.

1. Return to formatFunctions.as in /fpad2004/mmestate/includes/.

This is the file you created in Lesson 2 but have been referencing in your code in the exercises in all the lessons. If you did not do the last exercise, open /fpad2004/lesson05/start/includes/ formatFunctions.as.

2. Save the file as *Formatters.as* in /fpad2004/mmestate/classes/.

Right now, this file contains a declaration for a global function. To use the global function, you must include this file in your FLA or AS file. You are going to change this global function to be a method of a class instead. To use the method, you must first import the class into your FLA or AS file.

3. Surround the existing function with a definition for a class called *Formatters*.

```
class Formatters
{
        [existing function definition]
}
```

4. Change the function definition to a `public static` method. Save the file.

```
1 class Formatters
2 {
3       public static function formatNumber(start:String):Number
4       {
5             var end:String="";
6             for (var i=0;i<start.length;i++)
7             {
```

You will use this file in the next exercise. It should resemble the finished file: /fpad2004/lesson05/ intermediate/classes/Formatters_staticmethods.as.

5. Return to calculator.fla in /fpad2004/mmestate/.

Return to the file you used in the last exercise or open /fpad2004/lesson05/start/calculator.fla and save it as *calculator.fla* in /fpad2004/mmestate/.

6. In the Actions panel, navigate to the code in actions: Frame 1. Delete the `include` statement. Save the file.

There should be no code in the main Timeline of the application.

The finished file should resemble: /fpad2004/lesson05/intermediate/calculator_staticmethods.fla.

7. Return to calcObject.as in /fpad2004/mmestate/includes/.

Return to the file you used in the last exercise or open /fpad2004/lesson05/intermediate/includes/ calcObject_instancemethods.as and save it as *calcObject.as* in /fpad2004/mmestate/includes/.

8. Below the existing `import` statement, create a second `import` statement that imports the Formatters class.

```
import Formatters;
```

This `import` statement is not required because the Formatters class is located directly in the classpath. However, it is a best practice to import all classes you use at the top of the file so that it is obvious which classes are referenced in the file.

9. Inside the `calculator.onChanged` event handler, change the four `_global` references to `Formatters`. Save the file.

Make sure you use a capital F in Formatters. Because you are calling a static method of the Formatters class, you do not have to create an instance of the class.

```
34  calculator.onChanged=function():Void
35  {
36      this.price=Formatters.formatNumber(price_txt.text);
37      this.rate=Formatters.formatNumber(rate_txt.text);
38      this.down=Formatters.formatNumber(down_txt.text);
39      this.years=Formatters.formatNumber(years_txt.text);
```

The finished file should resemble: /fpad2004/lesson05/intermediate/includes/ calcObject_staticmethods.as.

10. Return to calculator.fla and test the application. Type a in the down payment text field.

Your application should work exactly as before.

Inheriting from Other Classes

Previously, you looked at a Bicycle class and a separate Unicycle class. These classes are not identical, but they definitely have some properties and methods in common. Instead of copying and pasting properties and methods between the class files and maintaining separate versions, you can define a single Cycle class that the Unicycle and Bicycle classes can both **extend**. You assign all the properties and methods common to both classes in the Cycle class and then create individual Unicycle and Bicycle classes that extend the Cycle class. The Unicycle and Bicycle classes **inherit** all the properties and methods of the Cycle class. The Unicycle and Bicycle classes are **subclasses**, or **children**, of the Cycle class. The Cycle class is referred to as the **superclass**, **base** class, or **parent** class.

You create a subclass by using the `extends` keyword in the class definition. You define the parent class in one ActionScript file. Here, the base class Cycle is defined.

```
Cycle
1  class Cycle
2  {
3      static private var NUMWHEELS:Number, SOMEFACTOR:Number;
4      private var speed:Number, gear:Number, cadence:Number;
5      function Cycle()
6      {
7      }
8      static public function getNumWheels():Number
9      {
10         return NUMWHEELS;
11     }
12     public function getSpeed():Number
13     {
14         return this.speed;
15     }
16     private function setSpeed():Void
17     {
18         this.speed=this.cadence*this.gear*SOMEFACTOR;
19     }
20     public function setCadence(rotationsPerMinute:Number):Void
21     {
22         this.cadence=rotationsPerMinute;
23         this.setSpeed();
24     }
25 }
```

In a separate ActionScript file, you define the Bicycle class that extends the Cycle class.

```
Bicycle
1  class Bicycle extends Cycle
2  {
3      function Bicycle(gear:Number,cadence:Number)
4      {
5          this.gear=gear;
6          this.cadence=cadence;
7          SOMEFACTOR=0.016;
8          this.setSpeed();
9          NUMWHEELS=2;
10     }
11     public function setGear(gear:Number):Void
12     {
13         this.gear=gear;
14         this.setSpeed();
15     }
16 }
```

In a separate ActionScript file, you define the Unicycle class that also extends the Cycle class.

```
Unicycle
1  class Unicycle extends Cycle
2  {
3      function Unicycle(cadence:Number)
4      {
5          this.gear=1;
6          this.cadence=cadence;
7          SOMEFACTOR=0.004;
8          this.setSpeed();
9          NUMWHEELS=1;
10     }
11 }
```

The Bicycle and Unicycle classes inherit all the Cycle class's properties and methods, including private and static members.

You can access public properties and methods of a Bicycle instance that were defined for the Bicycle class or the Cycle class from outside the class definition.

```
var mybike:Bicycle=new Bicycle(2,60);
trace(mybike.getSpeed());            //Outputs 1.92. Defined in Cycle class
mybike.setGear(8);                   //Defined in Bicycle class
trace(mybike.getSpeed());            //Outputs 7.68. Defined in Cycle class
```

Other details about class inheritance with ActionScript 2.0 include the following:

- You can extend the built-in classes and your custom classes.
- You cannot inherit from multiple classes.
- You can have multiple layers of inheritance: the Cycle class can inherit from the Vehicle class, and the Bicycle class can inherit from the Cycle class.
- You cannot specify a class as final (unable to be extended) as you can in some languages.

Calling a Parent Class's Constructor Using super()

You can also call a parent class's constructor from within a child class's constructor. Use the notation super() from within the child class constructor, passing any required or optional arguments in the parentheses. An explicit call to the parent class's constructor using super() must be the first line of code in the child class's constructor. If there is no call to a super constructor in a child class's constructor function, a call to its immediate superclass's constructor is inserted by the compiler as the first statement of the construct with *no arguments* passed.

In the following example, the Cycle class is defined with a constructor that takes four arguments: the gear, the cadence, a multiplicative factor to estimate the speed, and the number of wheels.

```
Cycle
 1  class Cycle
 2  {
 3      static private var NUMWHEELS:Number, SOMEFACTOR:Number;
 4      private var speed:Number, gear:Number, cadence:Number;
 5      function Cycle(gear:Number,cadence:Number,someFactor:Number,numwheels:Number)
 6      {
 7          this.gear=gear;
 8          this.cadence=cadence;
 9          SOMEFACTOR=someFactor;
10          this.setSpeed();
11          NUMWHEELS=numwheels;
12      }
13      static public function getNumWheels():Number
14      {
15          return NUMWHEELS;
16      }
17      public function getSpeed():Number
18      {
19          return this.speed;
20      }
21      private function setSpeed():Void
22      {
23          this.speed=this.cadence*this.gear*SOMEFACTOR;
24      }
25      public function setCadence(rotationsPerMinute:Number):Void
26      {
27          this.cadence=rotationsPerMinute;
28          this.setSpeed();
29      }
30  }
```

Only the gear and the cadence need to be specified when creating an instance of the Bicycle class; the other two properties are constants for the Bicycle. The child class constructor (for the Bicycle class) can call the superclass constructor (for the Cycle class) using super(), passing to it any required arguments.

```
Bicycle
 1  class Bicycle extends Cycle
 2  {
 3      function Bicycle(gear:Number,cadence:Number)
 4      {
 5          super(gear,cadence,0.016,2);
 6      }
 7      public function setGear(gear:Number):Void
 8      {
 9          this.gear=gear;
10          this.setSpeed();
11      }
12  }
```

From outside the class definition, you create an instance of the Bicycle class and pass to its constructor two arguments: the bicycle's gear and the cadence. The instance properties are set using these arguments in the constructor of the superclass.

```
var mybike:Bicycle=new Bicycle(2,60);
trace(mybike.getSpeed());          //Outputs 1.92. Defined in Cycle class
mybike.setGear(8);                 //Defined in Bicycle class
trace(mybike.getSpeed());          //Outputs 7.68. Defined in Cycle class
```

In this exercise, you make the CalcError class inherit from the built-in Error class, which has two properties: `name` and `message`, and one method: `toString()`.

1. In Flash, return to CalcError.as in /fpad2004/mmestate/classes/.

Return to the file you used in the last exercise or open /fpad2004/lesson05/ intermediate/ classes/errors/CalcError_instancemethods.as and save it as *CalcError.as* in /fpad2004/ mmestate/classes/errors/.

2. Open the Actions panel and browse the properties and methods for the Error class in the Actions toolbox.

The Error class can be found under Built-in Classes > Core > Error.

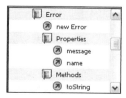

You will use the `message` property and the `toString()` method.

3. In CalcError.as, delete the `toString()` method and the `message` property declaration. Save the file.

Your code should appear as shown in the screenshot.

```
1  class errors.CalcError
2  {
3      public var selectField:String;
4      function CalcError (message:String,selectField:String
5      {
6          this.message=message;
7          this.selectField=selectField;
8      }
9  }
```

In the following steps, you will make this class inherit from the Error class, which already has a `message` property and a `toString()` method.

4. Return to calculator.fla in /fpad2004/mmestate/ and test the application.

Return to the file you created in the last exercise or open /fpad2004/lesson05/intermediate/ calculator_staticmethods.fla and save it as *calculator.fla* in /fpad2004/mmestate/.

You should get the following error in the Output panel: There is no property with the name 'message'. This error is expected because you removed the property declaration for the `message` property. In the next step, you will inherit this property from the built-in Error class.

5. In CalcError.as, change the first line of code defining the CalcError class so that it extends the Error class. Save the file.

Use the extends keyword in the class definition to specify inheritance from another class.

```
class errors.CalcError extends Error
```

Now the code in the constructor assigning a value to the message property will work; the message property is defined for the parent Error class and is inherited by the child CalcError class.

6. Return to calculator.fla and test the application. Type *a* in the rate text field.

You should see the error message "Fix Rate" in the Output panel. The toString() method of the parent Error class is used to display the value of the message property.

7. In CalcError.as, delete the line of code in the constructor assigning a value to the message property. Save the file.

This is the line of code you should delete.

```
this.message=message;
```

You will assign this property by calling the parent Error class's constructor.

8. Return to calculator.fla and test the application. Type *a* in the rate text field.

You should get the error message "Error" in the Output panel. You are no longer assigning a value to the message property, so the default value (equal to the string "Error") defined for the Error class is displayed.

9. In the Actions toolbox, browse to the new Error entry under the Error class. Right-click/Control-click "new Error" and select View Help.

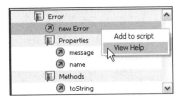

Browse the Help file that opens to find information about what arguments you pass to the Error class's constructor.

10. In CalcError.as, as the first line in the constructor add a call to the parent's constructor passing the `message` variable to it as an argument. Save the file.

Use `super()` to call the parent class's constructor.

```
1  class errors.CalcError extends Error
2  {
3      public var selectField:String;
4      function CalcError(message:String,selectField:String)
5      {
6          super(message);
7          this.selectField=selectField;
8      }
9  }
```

You will use this file in the following exercises. It should resemble the finished file: /fpad2004/lesson05/intermediate/classes/errors/CalcError_inheritance.as.

11. Return to calculator.fla and test the application. Type *a* in the rate text field.

You should get the custom error message "Fix Rate" in the Output panel. The value passed to the CalcError class's constructor is passed to the Error class's constructor using `super()`.

12. Return to calcObject.as in /fpad2004/mmestate/includes/ and delete the `trace` statement in the CalcError `catch` block. Save the file.

Return to the file you used in the last exercise or open /fpad2004/lesson05/intermediate/includes/calcObject_staticmethods.as and save it as *calcObject.as* in /fpad2004/mmestate/includes/.

The finished file should resemble: /fpad2004/lesson05/intermediate/includes/calcObject_inheritance.as.

Creating an Interface

When your applications become large and complex, you might want to create class interfaces. An **interface** is a contract for a class, guaranteeing that the class will have certain methods. The interface says nothing about what the methods do, but simply specifies that if a class implements this interface, it will have certain methods, with certain parameters of certain types, which return a certain type of data. Interfaces can make an application more elegant, scalable, and maintainable. Interfaces are especially useful when designing a large system with many different classes that are to be created by a team of developers; interfaces impose discipline on the team by forcing them to maintain a consistent interface across one or more classes, increasing consistency of code and ensuring that developers won't casually change a class interface in a future version.

The first illustration shows three classes that do similar things but all have display methods with different names, making it difficult to remember which method name to use for each class.

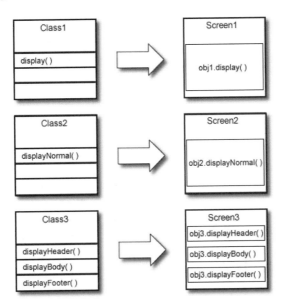

The second illustration shows all three classes implementing an interface that specifies the names to use for each of the methods, making the methods easier and more consistent to use.

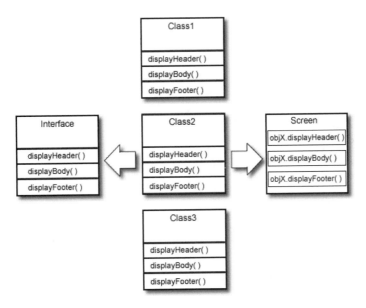

Like class definitions, you can define an interface only in an external ActionScript file located in the classpath. You create an interface by using the `interface` keyword; followed by the name of the interface; and then the names, arguments, and return types of the methods that classes implementing this interface must have. You cannot define function bodies, properties, private methods, or static methods inside an interface; you specify only the names, arguments, and return types of the methods. When a class implements an interface, the compiler checks to make sure that the class has all the public methods specified in the interface, and that each method has the right number and type of parameters and the correct return type. If the class is missing any of the specified methods, or if any of the parameters or method return types does not match exactly, an error is displayed in the Output panel at compile time.

Note *Only public methods can be defined in an interface.*

Here is an example of a Vehicle interface that all types of vehicle classes should implement, including the Cycle class.

```
Vehicle
1  interface Vehicle
2  {
3      function getSpeed():Number;
4  }
```

Note *The function statement does not include curly braces to enclose a function body.*

You specify that a class implements a particular interface using the `implements` keyword. In the following code, the Cycle class implements the Vehicle interface. The Cycle class is guaranteed to have a public method called `getSpeed()` that has no arguments and returns a Number, making the class easier and more predictable to work with on a large complex project.

```
Cycle
1  class Cycle implements Vehicle
2  {
3      static private var NUMWHEELS:Number, SOMEFACTOR:Number;
4      private var speed:Number, gear:Number, cadence:Number;
5      function Cycle(gear:Number,cadence:Number,someFactor:Number,numwheels:Number)
6      {
7          this.gear=gear;
8          this.cadence=cadence;
9          SOMEFACTOR=someFactor;
10         this.setSpeed();
11         NUMWHEELS=numwheels;
12     }
13     public function getSpeed():Number
14     {
15         return this.speed;
16     }
17     static public function getNumWheels():Number
18     {
```

If the Cycle class does not have a method called getSpeed(), or if the method is not public with no parameters and a return type of Number, an error is displayed at compile time. In addition, note that if you define the setSpeed() or getNumWheels() methods in the Vehicle interface, you will get an error unless you change these methods to public nonstatic methods in the Cycle class.

A class that implements an interface is an instance of that interface, as seen by using the instanceof operator in the following code:

```
var mybike:Bicycle=new Bicycle(2,60);
trace (mybike instanceof Cycle);        //Outputs true
trace (mybike instanceof Bicycle);      //Outputs true
trace (mybike instanceof Vehicle);      //Outputs true
trace (mybike instanceof Unicycle);     //Outputs false
```

If you both extend a class and implement an interface, you must extend the class before implementing the interface.

```
class Bicycle extends Cycle implements Vehicle
{
}
You can also implement multiple interfaces. After the implements keyword,
you specify all the interfaces the class implements separated by commas.
class Cycle implements Vehicle,Vehicle2
{
}
```

In this exercise, you create an interface called ErrorInterface that your custom CalcError class must implement. This interface guarantees that all error classes have toString(), getSelectField(), and setSelectField() methods.

1. In Flash, return to CalcError.as in /fpad2004/mmestate/classes/errors/. Change the selectField property so that it is *private* instead of public. Save the file.

Return to the file you created in the last exercise or open /fpad2004/lesson05/intermediate/classes/errors/CalcError_inheritance.as and save it as *CalcError.as* in /fpad2004/mmestate/classes/errors/.

```
private var selectField:String;
```

You are changing the property to private so that you cannot access it directly from outside the class, but instead must use a method.

2. Return to calculator.fla in /fpad2004/mmestate/ and test the application.

Return to the file you created in the exercise on static methods or open /fpad2004/lesson05/intermediate/calculator_staticmethods.fla and save it as *calculator.fla* in /fpad2004/mmestate/.

You should get an error in the Output panel: The member is private and cannot be accessed.

3. Return to CalcError.as. After the constructor, create a new `public` method called *setSelectField* that has one parameter called *field* of type *String*, has no return value, and sets the `selectField` property equal to the `field` argument.

```
public function setSelectField(field:String):Void
{
        this.selectField=field;
}
```

4. Create a second new `public` method called *getSelectField* that has no parameters and returns the *String* value of the `selectField` property. Save the file.

```
public function getSelectField():String
{
        return this.selectField;
}
```

5. Return to calcObject.as in /fpad2004/mmestate/includes/. In the calcError `catch` block of the `displayMortgage()` method, change the reference to the `selectField` property to instead use the `getSelectField()` method. Save the file.

Return to the file you used in the last exercise or open /fpad2004/lesson05/intermediate/includes/ calcObject_inheritance.as and save it as *calcObject.as* in /fpad2004/mmestate/includes/.

The `selectField` property is now private and cannot be accessed directly from outside the class definition. Instead, you need to access it using the `getSelectField()` method.

```
37      catch(e2:CalcError)
38      {
39          payment_txt.text=e2.message;
40          Selection.setFocus(e2.getSelectField());
41      }
```

The finished file should resemble: /fpad2004/lesson05/intermediate/includes/calcObject_interface.as.

6. Return to calculator.fla and test the application. Type *a* in the rate text field.

You should see the error message "Fix Rate" in the monthly payment text field and, most important, the rate text field should be highlighted. The field to select when the error is thrown is now accessed by a method instead of from the property.

7. Create a new ActionScript file and save it as *ErrorInterface.as* in /fpad2004/mmestate/ classes/errors/.

In this file, you will define an interface that all the error classes must implement.

8. Define an interface called *ErrorInterface*.

Because you saved the interface in the /fpad2004/mmestate/classes/errors/ folder and not directly in the classpath, you need to use a fully qualified name for the interface, including the package name, exactly as you did for class definitions.

```
interface errors.ErrorInterface
{
}
```

9. Inside the interface definition, declare a method called **toString()** with no parameters that returns a **String**.

Remember that in an interface, you don't define function bodies inside curly braces.

```
public function toString():String;
```

> **Note**   Using the `public` attribute is optional. All methods defined in an interface must be public.

10. Similarly, declare **setSelectField()** and **getSelectField()** methods with the correct arguments and return types. Save the file.

Look at your CalcError class if you need help remembering which arguments and return types to declare for each method.

```
ErrorInterface   calcObject   calculator   CalcError   calculator

1  interface errors.ErrorInterface
2  {
3      public function toString():String;
4      public function setSelectField(field:String):Void;
5      public function getSelectField():String;
6  }
```

The finished file should resemble: /fpad2004/lesson05/intermediate/classes/errors/ErrorInterface_ interface.as.

11. In CalcError.as, implement the *ErrorInterface* interface. Save the file.

When you have a class that both extends a class and implements an interface, you must define the inheritance first. Remember to also use the fully qualified name for the interface here.

```
class errors.CalcError extends Error implements errors.ErrorInterface
```

12. Return to calculator.fla and test the application. Type *a* in the rate text field.

Everything should still work correctly. You should get your custom error message "Fix Rate" in the monthly payment text field and the rate field should be highlighted.

13. Return to CalcError.as and misspell the name of the `getSelectField()` method. Save the file.

You are introducing an error so that the class no longer correctly implements the methods specified in the interface and you can see what happens.

14. Return to calculator.fla and test the application. Type *a* in the rate text field.

You should get the following error in the Output panel: The class must implement method 'getSelectField' from interface 'errors.ErrorInterface'.

15. Return to CalcError.as and correct the name of the `getSelectField()` method so it is spelled correctly. Save the file.

The finished file should resemble: /fpad2004/lesson05/intermediate/classes/errors/calcError_interface.as.

Creating Implicit Getters and Setters

In an earlier exercise, `getGear()` and `setGear()` methods were defined for the Bicycle class, which get and set the private `gear` property of the Bicycle class. You can use an alternate syntax to create getter and setter methods for properties, which allows developers to reference these methods using dot syntax instead of method notation, even though the property is still being accessed through a method. This method is transparent to the developers; to them it seems as if they are directly accessing the property.

> **Note** *Some developers love implicit getters and setters; others hate them. It is your choice to use them or not.*

Create an implicit setter method by placing the `set` keyword after the `function` keyword in a method definition. An implicit setter method must have one and only one function argument. The name of the method cannot be the same as any property.

The following is a simplified version of the Bicycle class used earlier with an implicit setter used to set the _gear property.

```
1  class Bicycle
2  {
3      private var _gear:Number;
4      function Bicycle(gear:Number)
5      {
6          this._gear=gear;
7      }
8      public function set gear(gear:Number):Void
9      {
10         this._gear=gear;
11     }
12 }
```

Note *Often, the private property name begins with an underscore; then the implicit getter and setter methods use the same name without the underscore.*

Create an implicit getter method by placing the `get` keyword after the `function` keyword in a method definition. An implicit getter method cannot have any function arguments; and the name of the method cannot be the same as any property, though it can have the same name as its partner implicit setter method.

The implicit getter for the _gear property of the Bicycle class is shown here.

```
public function get gear():Number
{
    return this._gear;
}
```

Note *Implicit getter and setter functions must be public.*

From outside the class definition, you can now get and set the `gear` property through the `gear()` getter and setter methods using dot notation.

```
var mybike:Bicycle=new Bicycle(1);
trace(mybike.gear);          //Outputs 1
mybike.gear=8;
trace(mybike.gear);          //Outputs 8
trace(mybike._gear);         //Gives an error
```

In this exercise, you rewrite the `setSelectField()` and `getSelectField()` methods of the CalcError class so they are implicit getters and setters.

1. In Flash, return to CalcError.as in /fpad2004/mmestate/classes/errors/. Change the `selectField` property to `_selectField`.

Return to the file you created in the last exercise or open /fpad2004/lesson05/intermediate/classes/errors/CalcError_interface.as and save it as *CalcError.as* in /fpad2004/mmestate/classes/errors/.

```
private var _selectField:String;
```

You are renaming the property with an underscore so that you can use the name selectField for the getter and setter methods.

2. Change the constructor so that the `_selectField` property is set instead of the `selectField` property, which no longer exists.

```
1  class errors.CalcError extends Error implements errors.ErrorInterface
2  {
3      private var _selectField:String;
4      function CalcError(message:String,selectField:String)
5      {
6          super(message);
7          this._selectField=selectField;
8      }
```

3. Change the `setSelectField()` method so that it is an implicit setter method called *selectField*.

Remember to use the keyword `set` before the method name to declare it as an implicit setter.

```
public function set selectField(field:String):Void
```

4. Inside the implicit setter, set the `_selectField` property instead of the `selectField` property.

```
public function set selectField(field:String):Void
{
    this._selectField=field;
}
```

5. Change the `getSelectField()` method so that it is an implicit getter method called *selectField*.

Remember to use the keyword `get` before the method name to declare it as an implicit setter.

```
public function get selectField():String
```

6. Inside the implicit getter, return the `_selectField` property instead of the `selectField` property.

```
public function get selectField():String
{
        return this._selectField;
}
```

7. Remove the `implements` statement from the class declaration. Save the file.

The CalcError class no longer has `setSelectField()` and `getSelectField()` methods, so will not successfully implement the ErrorInterface interface. You cannot change the interface to include the implicit getters and setters because getter/setter declarations are not permitted in interfaces.

Delete the highlighted code in the screenshot.

```
1  class errors.CalcError extends Error implements errors.ErrorInterface
2  {
3        private var _selectField:String;
4        function CalcError(message:String,selectField:String)
5        {
```

The finished file should resemble: /fpad2004/lesson05/intermediate/classes/errors/CalcError_implicitgetters.as.

8. Return to calculator.fla in /fpad2004/mmestate/ and test the application. Type *a* in the rate text field.

Return to the file you created in the exercise on static methods or open /fpad2004/lesson05/intermediate/calculator_staticmethods.fla and save it as *calculator.fla* in /fpad2004/mmestate/.

The rate text field should no longer be successfully highlighted after the error.

9. Return to calcObject.as in /fpad2004/mmestate/includes/. In the CalcError `catch` block, change the code setting focus to use the implicit getter method. Save the file.

Return to the file you used in the last exercise or open /fpad2004/lesson05/intermediate/includes/calcObject_interface.as and save it as *calcObject.as* in /fpad2004/mmestate/includes/.

Remember to use an implicit getter method, you simply use dot notation with the name of the method. Do not use parentheses after the method name.

```
37        catch(e2:CalcError)
38        {
39             payment_txt.text=e2.message;
40             Selection.setFocus(e2.selectField)
41        }
```

The finished file should resemble: /fpad2004/lesson05/intermediate/includes/ calcObject_implicitgetters.as.

10. Return to calculator.fla and test the application. Type *a* in the rate text field.

The rate text field should now be successfully highlighted after the error.

Creating Dynamic Classes

By default, you cannot define new properties and methods for a specific instance of your custom classes; the class members are defined by the class and are fixed. If you try and add a new property or method to the instance after it is created, you get a compile time error, stating that there is no class member defined with that name. In some cases, though, you might want to add properties and methods to a particular object instance. A **dynamic class** is a class to which you can add properties or methods to its instances.

An example of a dynamic class is the Object class. You can add your own custom properties to an instance of the Object class after it is created. The MovieClip class is also dynamic, enabling you to add objects as properties dynamically at runtime. For example, you might want to create a new TextField or nested MovieClip object inside a MovieClip for each field retrieved from a database. (You will learn to dynamically create and populate MovieClips in Lesson 11, "Creating Visual Objects Dynamically.")

The dynamic built-in classes include the following: Array, ContextMenu, ContextMenuItem, Function, LoadVars, MovieClip, Object, and TextField.

You create a dynamic class by placing the `dynamic` keyword before the `class` keyword in a class definition.

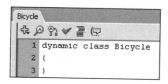

From outside the class definition, you can now define members for a specific instance that are not defined for the class.

```
var mybike:Bicycle=new Bicycle();
mybike.nickname="Pinball wizard";
trace(mybike.nickname);
```

If you had not defined the class as dynamic, you would receive a compile time error: There is no property with the name *nickname*. Because the class is defined as dynamic, members with any name can exist and there is no longer compile time type checking on the property and method names for a class. Class methods, however, are still checked for return type and parameter types.

Note *Subclasses of dynamic classes are automatically dynamic except for subclasses of the Object and MovieClip classes. To make subclasses of the Object and MovieClip classes dynamic, you must explicitly define them as dynamic in their class definitions.*

In this exercise, you make the CalcError class dynamic and add a property to a specific instance of the class. This exercise is not necessary for the application and is purely instructional.

1. In Flash, return to calcObject.as in /fpad2004/mmestate/includes/. Inside the CalcError `catch` block of the `displayMortgage()` method, add a property called `test` to the instance `e2` and set it equal to the string "test".

Return to the file you used in the last exercise or open /fpad2004/lesson05/intermediate/includes/calcObject_implicitgetters.as and save it as *calcObject.as* in /fpad2004/mmestate/includes/.

In this step, you are adding a property to a specific instance of a class after it is created, not to the class itself.

```
37    catch(e2:CalcError)
38    {
39        payment_txt.text=e2.message;
40        Selection.setFocus(e2.selectField);
41        e2.test="test";
42    }
```

2. After defining the `test` property, trace its value. Save the file.

```
trace(e2.test);
```

3. Return to calculator.fla in /fpad2004/mmestate/ and test the application.

Return to the file you created in the exercise on static methods or open /fpad2004/lesson05/intermediate/calculator_staticmethods.fla and save it as *calculator.fla* in /fpad2004/mmestate/.

You should get the following error in the Output panel: There is no property with the name *test*. The class is not dynamic, so you cannot add properties or methods to specific instances.

4. Return to CalcError.as in /fpad2004/mmestate/classes/errors/. Change the class definition to *dynamic*. Save the file.

Return to the file you used in the last exercise or open /fpad2004/lesson05/intermediate/classes/errors/CalcError_implicitgetters.as and save it as *CalcError.as* in /fpad2004/mmestate/classes/errors/.

The `dynamic` keyword must precede the `class` keyword.

```
dynamic class errors.CalcError extends Error
```

5. Return to calculator.fla and test the application. Type *a* in the rate text field.

You should get the string value of the `test` property "test" displayed in the Output panel. The `test` property is specific to that instance of the CalcError class and is not defined for all instances of the class.

6. In CalcError.as, delete the `dynamic` keyword. Save the file.

You are deleting the changes you made in this exercise, which were for instructional purposes only.

The finished file should resemble: /fpad2004/lesson05/intermediate/classes/errors/ CalcError_dynamic.as.

7. In calcObject.as, delete the assignment and `trace` statements for the `test` property. Save the file.

You are deleting the changes you made in this exercise, which were for instructional purposes only.

The finished file should resemble: /fpad2004/lesson05/intermediate/includes/calcObject_dynamic.as.

What You Have Learned

In this lesson, you have:

- Created your own classes (pages 201–207)
- Defined custom classpaths in which to save your classes (pages 208–212)
- Created and referenced packages for your classes (pages 213–218)
- Defined instance and static class properties (pages 219–226)
- Controlled access to class members by defining them as public or private (pages 220–226)
- Created a class constructor that is called when class instances are created (pages 226–232)
- Defined class methods (pages 232–238)
- Created classes that inherit properties and methods from other classes (pages 238–244)
- Defined an interface for other classes to implement (pages 244–250)
- Wrote implicit getter and setter methods to access methods like properties (pages 250–254)
- Created a dynamic class allowing you to add members to a specific instance (pages 254–256)

6 Creating Components

In the last lesson, you created your own classes, enabling you to separate your code from the FLA and to create application functionality that can be reused and distributed to developers as "black boxes" that could be used without having to understand or change the code. The classes you created, though, had no visual elements. In this lesson, you learn to associate a class with a MovieClip symbol so you can control visual elements such as TextFields and MovieClips from a class file.

To distribute this application functionality, you have to share both the FLA containing the MovieClip symbol and the separate class files and install them in the correct locations. Thankfully, there are easier and better ways. After you learn to link the MovieClip symbol and the class file together, you turn the application element into a component. A component is a MovieClip symbol with parameters that can be assigned values from within the Flash authoring environment. Although a component is easier to use, it does not make it easier to distribute. To make it easier to distribute, you compile the MovieClip and its associated class code so that it can be distributed as a single entity without having to distribute the source code. This compiled component can be installed into the Components panel and used by other developers by dragging and dropping instances of the compiled component to the Stage.

In this lesson, you take all your existing calculator code and convert it into a separate class file. To get the code working again, you link the class file to the MovieClip symbol. Next, you turn the MovieClip into a component so initial values for the calculator can be set in the authoring environment. Finally, you create a compiled version of the component that can be installed into the Components panel manually or with an automated installer.

In this lesson, you turn your calculator into a component that can be easily reused and distributed.

What You Will Learn

In this lesson, you will:

- Convert code attached to a MovieClip into a separate class file
- Link a class to a MovieClip symbol
- Create a public API for a class
- Turn a MovieClip symbol into a component
- Define parameters for a component that can be modified in the authoring environment
- Create a compiled version of a component
- Learn about intrinsic class definitions
- Add a component to the Components panel
- Create a custom icon for a component
- Create an automatic installer for a component

Approximate Time

This lesson takes approximately 90 minutes to complete.

Lesson Files

Asset Files:

/fpad2004/lesson06/start/assets/MortgageCalculator.png

Starting Files:

/fpad2004/lesson06/start/calculator.fla
/fpad2004/lesson06/start/includes/calcObject.as
/fpad2004/lesson06/start/MortgageCalculator.mxi

Completed Files:

/fpad2004/lesson06/complete/calculator.fla
/fpad2004/lesson06/complete/classes/MortgageCalculator.as
/fpad2004/lesson06/complete/MortgageCalculator.swc
/fpad2004/lesson06/complete/MortgageCalculator.asi
/fpad2004/lesson06/complete/MortgageCalculator.mxp

Converting Code Inside a MovieClip to a Class File

To make your application elements reusable, you do not want your code embedded inside a layer inside a MovieClip inside a FLA file, as it is now. Instead, you want to create a separate class file that controls all interaction with the MovieClip. While doing this conversion, you implement many of the concepts you learned in the last lesson, including creating a constructor, properties, and methods.

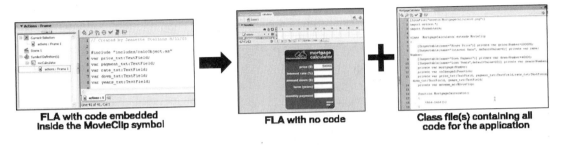

FLA with code embedded Inside the MovieClip symbol   **FLA with no code**   **Class file(s) containing all code for the application**

Before you convert existing scripts into a class definition, here are some things to consider:

Which variables should you define as properties? The variables you declared in your scripts are the obvious choices. For the calculator code, this includes the `price`, `rate`, `down`, `years`, and `mortgage` variables. You also need to declare visual elements as properties, including TextFields and MovieClips whose properties or methods you reference using code. For the calculator code, this includes the `price_txt` and other TextFields as well as the `moveme_mc` MovieClip.

What code should go in the constructor? You should place any "set-up" code inside the constructor—code that sets initial values, call initialization methods, and so on. For the calculator, this includes setting initial values for the `price`, `rate`, `down` and `years` properties and calling the `displayMortgage()` method to calculate the initial mortgage.

Does the class need to extend the MovieClip class? The class you create needs to extend the MovieClip class if it uses any properties or methods of the MovieClip class. Your calculator class needs to extend the MovieClip class because it uses the MovieClip's `startDrag()` and `stopDrag()` methods to make the calculator draggable.

Should members be public or private? You should only make properties and methods public that you want developers to be able to access. For the calculator class, all existing members will be private. All the existing code functionality assumes that any interaction with the calculator comes from the user entering new values in the TextFields.

Do you need additional public methods for manipulating the element? After you encapsulate your code in a class file, take a good look at what functionality you want available to developers. Because you (and everyone else) should not alter the source code, the API for the object needs to be flexible and robust, providing all desirable functionality through public methods. For your calculator, this includes creating a new public method that enables calculator values to be updated from code. You will add this method in a later exercise.

In this exercise, you create a MortgageCalculator class file that contains all the code for the mortgage calculator. When you are done, there should be no remaining code inside the MovieClip symbol.

1. Return to calcObject.as in /fpad2004/mmestate/includes/. Save the file as *MortgageCalculator.as* **in /fpad2004/mmestate/classes/.**

This is the file you used in the last exercise. If you did not do that exercise, open /fpad2004/lesson06/start/includes/calcObject.as.

Make sure you save the file in the classes directory so that it is in a classpath and that you use the correct capitalization when naming the file.

2. Place all the existing code (except the `import` statements) inside a class definition for a class called *MortgageCalculator*.

You cannot import classes inside a class definition, but you can import them at the top of the class file, right before the class definition.

```
import errors.*;
import Formatters;
class MortgageCalculator
{
        [all your existing code]
}
```

You should also indent the code inside the class definition. You can indent the code by selecting it and pressing the Tab key.

3. Delete the line of code defining the `calculator` object.

Your calculator will no longer be an instance of the Object class. Instead, you are creating a MortgageCalculator class file and will instantiate an instance of this class. You should delete the code highlighted in the screenshot.

```
1  import errors.*;
2  import Formatters;
3
4  class  MortgageCalculator
5  {
6        var calculator:Object=new Object();
7        calculator["price"]=500000;
8        calculator["rate"]=5;
```

In the next exercise, you link the class file to the MovieClip symbol so that an instance of the MortgageCalculator class is automatically created when a MovieClip symbol is loaded in the application.

4. At the top of the class definition, create declarations for the `price`, `rate`, `down`, `years`, and `mortgage` variables as *private* properties of type *Number*.

Make sure you define each of the properties on a separate line. You can combine the declarations on one line, but you need this code on separate lines in a later exercise when you define component properties.

```
4  class  MortgageCalculator
5  {
6       private var price:Number;
7       private var rate:Number;
8       private var down:Number;
9       private var years:Number;
10      private var mortgage:Number;
11      calculator["price"]=500000;
12      calculator["rate"]=5;
```

You are making these private properties so they cannot be accessed directly from outside the class. In a later exercise, you will create a public method to change their values so that you or other developers can change the values using code, instead of relying on input from the user.

5. After the property definitions, create a class constructor.

Remember that the constructor must have the same name as the class and must have no return value declared.

```
4  class  MortgageCalculator
5  {
6       private var price:Number;
7       private var rate:Number;
8       private var down:Number;
9       private var years:Number;
10      private var mortgage:Number;
11
12      function MortgageCalculator()
13      {
14      }
15
16      calculator["price"]=500000;
```

6. Inside the constructor, call a method called *init*.

You are going to create the `init()` method in the next steps.

```
function MortgageCalculator()
{
     this.init();
}
```

7. Place the existing code assigning values to the `calculator` object inside a *private* method called *init* with no parameters and no return value.

This `init()` method will contain all the code to be processed when an instance of the class is created. You could place this code inside the constructor function, but most developers prefer to keep the code inside their constructors short and simple, calling other methods when necessary.

```
12      function MortgageCalculator()
13      {
14          this.init();
15      }
16      private function init():Void
17      {
18          calculator["price"]=500000;
19          calculator["rate"]=5;
20          calculator.down=56000;
21          calculator.years=30;
22          calculator.mortgage=0;
23      }
```

8. Inside the `init()` method, change all the references to `calculator` to `this`.

```
private function init():Void
{
        this["price"]=500000;
        this["rate"]=5;
        this.down=56000;
        this.years=30;
        this.mortgage=0;
}
```

9. Locate the definition for the `calcMortgage()` method and make it a *private* method of the class.

You need to change only the line of code defining the method, not the method internals. The following line of code:

```
calculator.calcMortgage=function():Void
```

needs to be changed to:

```
private function calcMortgage():Void
```

```
20          this.down=56000;
21          this.years=30;
22          this.mortgage=0;
23      }
24
25      private function calcMortgage():Void
26      {
27          var monthlyrate:Number=this.rate/100/12;
28          this.mortgage=(this.price-this.down)*month
```

10. Locate the definition for the `displayMortgage()` method and make it a *private* method of the class.

The following line of code:

```
calculator.displayMortgage=function():Void
```

needs to be changed to:

```
private function displayMortgage():Void
```

11. Inside the CalcError `catch` block in `displayMortgage()`, change the line of code selecting the error field so that the argument refers to the class property returned by `e2.selectField`.

To specify the dynamic evaluation of this expression as a property, preface it with `this`. The line of code should appear as shown here:

```
Selection.setFocus(this[e2.selectField]);
```

If you do not make this change, the field is not highlighted when an error is thrown.

12. Locate the `onChanged` event handler definition and move it to the end of the `init()` method declaration.

```
20    private function init():Void
21    {
22        this["price"]=500000;
23        this["rate"]=5;
24        this.down=56000;
25        this.years=30;
26        this.mortgage=0;
27        calculator.onChanged=function():Void
28        {
29            this.price=Formatters.formatNumber(price_txt.text);
30            this.rate=Formatters.formatNumber(rate_txt.text);
31            this.down=Formatters.formatNumber(down_txt.text);
32            this.years=Formatters.formatNumber(years_txt.text);
33            this.displayMortgage();
34        };
```

This code must be placed inside the constructor because it is initialization code; it is assigning an initial value to the onChanged property. The value assigned to it is a function literal.

13. Change the declaration, so that `onChanged` is a property of `this` (the class instance) instead of `calculator`.

```
this.onChanged=function():Void
```

14. At the top of the class definition with the other property declarations, declare onChanged as a *private* property of type *Function*. Save the file.

```
private var onChanged:Function;
```

You must declare onChanged as a property because you assigned it a value in the previous steps. or you will get a compile time error: There is no property with the name 'onChanged'. Its data type is a Function because you set it equal to a function literal.

15. Return to calculator.fla in /fpad2004/mmestate/.

This is the file you used in the last exercise of Lesson 5. If you did not do that exercise, open /fpad2004/lesson06/start/calculator.fla and save it as */fpad2004/mmestate/calculator.fla*.

16. In the Actions panel, navigate to the code in actions: Frame 1 for the mcCalculator MovieClip.

All the code for the MovieClip symbol is located here. You will remove this code from the MovieClip symbol and integrate it into the class file.

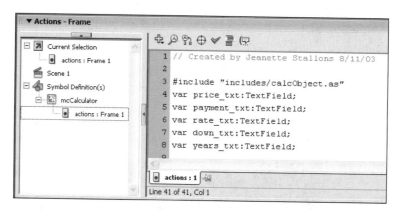

17. Cut the five variable declarations from the MovieClip code and paste them after the existing property declarations in the MortgageCalculator class definition. Make them all *private* properties.

You can also combine these variable declarations so that they are on one line.

```
4  class   MortgageCalculator
5  {
6      private var price:Number;
7      private var rate:Number;
8      private var down:Number;
9      private var years:Number;
10     private var mortgage:Number;
11     private var onChanged:Function;
12     private var price_txt:TextField, payment_txt:TextField,rate_txt:TextField,
   down_txt:TextField, years_txt:TextField;
13
```

18. Return to calculator.fla. Select and cut all the code after the `include` statement and paste it after the existing code inside the `init()` method of the MortgageCalculator class.

You can indent your code by highlighting the code and pressing the Tab key.

19. In the code you just pasted, change all instances of `calculator` to `this`.

There should be nine instances, which are shown here:

```
price_txt.text=this.price;
rate_txt.text=this.rate;
down_txt.text=this.down;
years_txt.text=this.years;
price_txt.addListener(this);
rate_txt.addListener(this);
down_txt.addListener(this);
years_txt.addListener(this);
this.displayMortgage();
```

> **Tip** *You can also use the ActionScript Editor's Find and/or Replace tools to make these replacements. Buttons for each of these tools are located on the toolbar at the top of the Script pane.*

If you want, you can preface all references to the TextField objects with `this` because they are also properties of the MortgageCalculator class.

20. In the lines of code assigning values to the TextField objects, make the right side of each equation an argument to the `String()` function.

The `String()` function casts the numeric value held in the function argument to the corresponding string so that you can assign it to the text property of a TextField, which is inherently typed as a String. If you do not do this casting, you get a type mismatch error when you compile your finished code.

```
25      this.onChanged=function():Void
26      {
27          this.price=Formatters.formatNumber(price_txt.text);
28          this.rate=Formatters.formatNumber(rate_txt.text);
29          this.down=Formatters.formatNumber(down_txt.text);
30          this.years=Formatters.formatNumber(years_txt.text);
31          this.displayMortgage();
32      };
33      price_txt.text=String(this.price);
34      rate_txt.text=String(this.rate);
35      down_txt.text=String(this.down);
36      years_txt.text=String(this.years);
37      rate_txt.maxChars=2;
38      years_txt.maxChars=2;
```

21. At the top of the class definition with the other property declarations, declare *moveme_mc* as a *private* property of type *MovieClip*.

```
private var moveme_mc:MovieClip;
```

You need to define the MovieClip as a property of the class because you define event handlers for it inside the `init()` method. If you do not define the MovieClip as a property and try to assign values to event handler properties, you get a "property does not exist" error when you compile your finished code.

22. Change the line of code defining the MortgageCalculator class so that it extends the MovieClip class. Save the file.

```
class MortgageCalculator extends MovieClip
```

The MortgageCalculator class needs to extend the MovieClip class because you drag and drop it using `startDrag()` and `stopDrag()` methods inside the `moveme_mc` event handler definitions in the `init()` method. If you do not extend the class, the finished code will compile, but the calculator will not be draggable.

You will use this file as the starting file for the next exercise. It should resemble the finished file: /fpad2004/lesson06/intermediate/classes/MortgageCalculator_createclass.as.

23. Return to calculator.fla. Delete all the remaining lines of code in actions: Frame 1 for `mcCalculator`.

Delete the comment, the `include` statement, and any blank lines of code. The `mcCalculator` symbol will not appear in the Actions panel as an item with attached code, and an α will not be displayed in the Timeline. You have now successfully extracted all code from the MovieClip symbol and placed it in a class file.

You will use this file as the starting file for the next exercise. It should resemble the finished file: /fpad2004/lesson06/intermediate/calculator_createclass.fla.

> **Note** *If you try and test the application now, the calculator's text fields will have no initial values. You have not yet connected the class file to the visual object in the FLA file. You do this in the next exercise.*

Linking a Class to a MovieClip Symbol

The last thing you need to do to get your mortgage calculator working again is to link the class file to the MovieClip symbol. Right now, you have not created an instance of the MortgageCalculator class or created a connection between the TextField objects on the Stage and the properties of the class.

Up to now, you instantiated all your custom classes in code using the new keyword. In the case of the MortgageCalculator class, you don't want to instantiate an instance in code; you want the object to be instantiated when the visual MovieClip object appears in the application. You need to somehow link the class you created with a visual object—the mcCalculator MovieClip. Otherwise, the code in the class file that populates the TextFields in the MovieClip and drags and drops the MovieClip will not work.

You make this association by setting the linkage properties for the MovieClip in the library, setting the linkage name equal to the name of the associated class.

You can set the linkage properties for a MovieClip in two ways: either when you create the library symbol (in the Advanced section of the Create Symbol dialog box) or anytime afterward by right-clicking/Control-clicking the symbol in the library and selecting Linkage.

After you set this linkage, any time an instance of the MovieClip is created, the constructor code is automatically run, and an instance of the class is created. If you drag a MovieClip instance from the library to the Stage, the class will be loaded and an instance created when you test the application.

Tip *The class is loaded before the first frame of the symbol's Timeline, ensuring that the class will be loaded before it is referenced.*

In this exercise, you link the MortgageCalculator class file to the mcCalculator MovieClip so that an instance of the MortgageCalculator class is instantiated when an instance of the mcCalculator symbol is created.

1. In Flash, return to calculator.fla in /fpad2004/mmestate/.

Return to the file you created in the last exercise or open /fpad2004/lesson06/intermediate/ calculator_createclass.fla and save it as *calculator.fla* in /fpad2004/mmestate/.

2. Open the document's library.

To open the Library panel for the FLA, press Ctrl+L (Windows) or Command+L (Macintosh) or select Window > Library.

3. In the library, right-click/Control-click mcCalculator and select Rename. Change the name of the symbol to *MortgageCalculator*.

This is a more descriptive name and matches the name of the class file. This name change is not necessary, but reduces the number of distinct names being used, making things less confusing.

4. Right-click/Control-click the MortgageCalculator symbol in the library and select Linkage.

The linkage Properties dialog box appears.

5. Select the Export for ActionScript check box.

When you select this check box, the Identifier and AS 2.0 Class text fields in the dialog box become editable. By default, the Identifier field is populated with the name of the symbol. Leave it as MortgageCalculator. (The name of the Identifier will be the name displayed for the component in the Components panel in a later exercise. The Identifier is also used when creating instances of the symbol dynamically with code, which is covered in a later lesson.)

Note *If you do not enter a class file, selecting the Export for ActionScript check box enables the library item to be included in the compiled SWF, even if an instance of the symbol is not placed on the Stage. You can create instances of symbols at runtime (which is covered in Lesson 11, "Creating Visual Objects Dynamically") without having to have an instance on the Stage.*

6. **In the AS 2.0 Class text field, enter *MortgageCalculator*.**

In this field, you enter the fully qualified name of the class you want to associate with the symbol. When an instance of the symbol is created, an instance of this class is also created.

Remember, a fully qualified class name does not include the filename's extension. It is the class name including the package—basically the class location relative to a classpath. In this case, the file MortgageCalculator.as is located directly in a classpath folder, so the entry in this text field is simply MortgageCalculator.

MortgageCalculator.as is the class file you used in the last exercise. If you did not do that exercise, open /fpad2004/lesson06/intermediate/classes/MortgageCalculator_createclass.as and save it as *MortgageCalculator.as* in /fpad2004/mmestate/classes/.

7. **Click OK. Save the file.**

It should resemble the finished file: /fpad2004/lesson06/intermediate/calculator_linkage.fla.

8. **Test the application. Type *a* in the rate text field.**

Depending upon your version of Flash MX 2004, you probably get an error in the Output panel: Error: Fix Rate. If you get this error, it means that the error thrown is no longer recognized as a member of the CalcError class. This is a bug. To get the application working again, you need to specify the full class name instead of the simple class name in the `catch` block. If you did not get this error, you can skip the rest of the steps.

9. **Return to MortgageCalculator.as in /fpad2004/mmestate/classes/. Inside the CalcError `catch` block, change the type of the variable *e2* from CalcError to *errors.CalcError*. Save the file.**

```
catch(e2:errors.CalcError)
```

You will use this file as the starting file for the next exercise. It should resemble the finished file: /fpad2004/lesson06/intermediate/classes/MortgageCalculator_linkage.as.

10. **Return to calculator.fla and test the application.**

Your calculator should work again! You should see the mortgage payment, $2383.49 displayed in the monthly payment text field on the calculator.

Creating a Public API

After you encapsulate all your code in a class file, you need to look at what functionality you want to make available to developers. Because the public application programming interface is the only way to access and manipulate the objects, the class API needs to be flexible and robust, providing all desirable functionality through its public methods.

For example, right now there is no way for developers to set values for the calculator programmatically (unless they change the calculator code). The values used to calculate the mortgage can be set only at runtime by the user changing the values in the text fields. What if you want to change the values based on some other application event? For example, the user selects a particular house, and you want that house's price to automatically populate the house price text field in the mortgage calculator. To manipulate the calculator at runtime via code, you need to create a public method to access and manipulate private members.

In this exercise, you create a new public method for the MortgageCalculator class that enables you to change the values displayed in the calculator text fields, and recalculate and display the new mortgage.

1. In Flash, return to MortgageCalculator.as in /fpad2004/mmestate/classes/.

Return to the file you used in the last exercise or open /fpad2004/lesson06/ intermediate/classes/ MortgageCalculator_linkage.as and save it as *MortgageCalculator.as* in /fpad2004/mmestate/classes/.

2. Create a new *public* method called *update* with four arguments called *price*, *rate*, *down*, and *years* that are all of type *Number* and that has no return value.

This method will enable developers to change the calculator's corresponding properties, calculate a new mortgage, and display the new input text field's values and the mortgage in the calculator interface.

```
public function update(price:Number,rate:Number,down:Number,
years:Number):Void
{
}
```

> **Note** *You can create this method anywhere inside the class definition after the constructor function. As a best practice, the constructor function should be defined as the first method.*

3. Inside the `update()` method, set the `price` property equal to the `price` parameter.

```
this.price=price;
```

4. Do the same for the `rate`, `down`, and `years` parameters.

```
104    public function update(price:Number,rate:Number,down:Number,years:Number):Void
105    {
106        this.price=price;
107        this.rate=rate;
108        this.down=down;
109        this.years=years;
110    }
```

After setting the properties for the MortgageCalculator instance, you need to display these new values in the calculator interface. You do this by setting the `text` properties of the TextField objects. You already wrote the code to do this; it is currently inside the `init()` method. Instead of duplicating this code, you should pull it out and encapsulate it in a method that can then be called multiple times as necessary.

5. Create a new *private* method called *displayFields* with no arguments and that has no return value.

```
private function displayFields():Void
{
}
```

This method will contain the code to display the current `price`, `rate`, `down`, and `years` properties in the calculator interface.

6. Locate the four lines of code setting the `text` properties of the TextField objects in the `init()` method. Cut and paste them inside the `displayFields()` method.

Cut the lines of code shown in the screenshot.

```
26        this.onChanged=function():Void
27        {
28            this.price=Formatters.formatNumber(price_txt.text);
29            this.rate=Formatters.formatNumber(rate_txt.text);
30            this.down=Formatters.formatNumber(down_txt.text);
31            this.years=Formatters.formatNumber(years_txt.text);
32            this.displayMortgage();
33        };
34        price_txt.text=String(this.price);
35        rate_txt.text=String(this.rate);
36        down_txt.text=String(this.down);
37        years_txt.text=String(this.years);
38        rate_txt.maxChars=2;
39        years_txt.maxChars=2;
```

Your remaining code should look like the following;

```
private function displayFields():Void
{
    price_txt.text=String(this.price);
    rate_txt.text=String(this.rate);
    down_txt.text=String(this.down);
    years_txt.text=String(this.years);
}
```

7. Inside the `init()` method, call the `displayFields()` method right after assigning values to the `price`, `rate`, `down`, `years`, and `mortgage` properties.

This is the replacement method call for the lines of code you deleted in the previous step. This code displays the initial values of the `price`, `rate`, `down`, and `years` properties in the calculator interface.

```
20        private function init():Void
21        {
22            this["price"]=500000;
23            this["rate"]=5;
24            this.down=56000;
25            this.years=30;
26            this.mortgage=0;
27            this.displayFields();
28            this.onChanged=function():Void
29            {
```

8. As the last line inside the `update()` method, call the `displayFields()` method.

After assigning new calculator properties via code, you need to display the new values in the calculator interface.

```
110        public function update(price:Number,rate:Number,down:Number,years:Number):Void
111        {
112            this.price=price;
113            this.rate=rate;
114            this.down=down;
115            this.years=years;
116            this.displayFields();
117        }
```

9. After you call the `displayFields()` method, call the `displayMortgage()` method. Save the file.

This method recalculates the new mortgage and displays the new value.

```
110        public function update(price:Number,rate:Number,down:Number,years:Number):Void
111        {
112            this.price=price;
113            this.rate=rate;
114            this.down=down;
115            this.years=years;
116            this.displayFields();
117            this.displayMortgage();
118        }
```

You will use this file as the starting file for the next exercise. It should resemble the finished file: /fpad2004/lesson06/intermediate/classes/MortgageCalculator_api.as.

10. Return to calculator.fla in /fpad2004/mmestate/ and test the application.

Return to the file you created in the last exercise or open /fpad2004/lesson06/intermediate/ calculator_linkage.fla and save it as *calculator.fla* in /fpad2004/mmestate/.

Your calculator should work exactly as before; you have not added or subtracted any of the basic functionality, just rearranged it. In the next step, you will change the values displayed and calculated from code outside the class definition. This is a powerful addition, giving you and others the ability to interact with the calculator from outside without knowing or having to touch the inside. Your calculator is now a black box of code that can be easily reused; instances are manipulated using the API.

11. In calculator.fla, locate the name of the calculator instance on the Stage.

Click the instance on the Stage and look at the Property inspector; the instance is called `calculator_mc`.

12. Click the Actions layer in the Timeline panel and open the Actions panel. Add code to call the `update()` method of `calculator_mc`. Pass any values you want for the `price`, `rate`, `down`, and `years` arguments.

Although you can pass any values, they must be in the order defined in the class definition: `price`, `rate`, `down`, and `years`. Do not put quotes around any of the arguments because they are all defined as numbers.

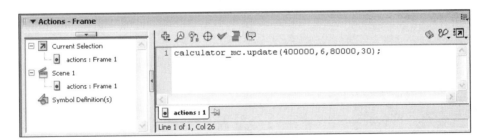

13. Save the file and test the application.

You should see the values you passed to the method displayed in the calculator and the correct mortgage for these values calculated.

You will use this file as the starting file for the next exercise. It should resemble the finished file: /fpad2004/lesson06/intermediate/calculator_api.fla.

Creating a Component

For developers to reuse your MovieClip, they still need to import the MortgageCalculator MovieClip symbol into their library and place the class file(s) in an appropriate location(s) in a classpath. To customize the element, though, they no longer need to change the code for the calculator; they can use the public API. Any customization, however, must be done with code. For your calculator, the developer must call the `update()` method to change the initial values displayed. (They could also change the class file, which is strongly NOT encouraged!)

To make the MovieClip symbol more reusable, you can turn it into a component—another type of library item. What makes a component different from a MovieClip symbol is that you can specify parameters that can be set by the developer in a panel in the authoring environment, alleviating the need to do all initial customization of the symbol with code.

Turning a MovieClip Symbol into a Component

You turn a MovieClip symbol into a Component symbol by right-clicking/Control-clicking the MovieClip symbol in the library and selecting Component Definition. In the Component Definition dialog box, you need to specify the name of the associated class file.

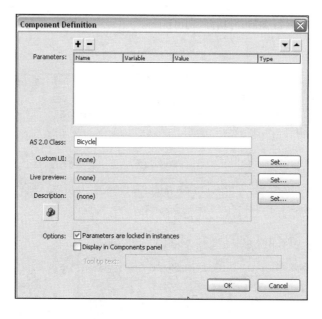

If you want to display parameters and make them editable from within the authoring environment, you need to edit your class file, adding metadata for the specific properties you want to appear in the Property inspector and Component inspector. You add parameters to your component in the following exercise.

In this exercise, you turn your MortgageCalculator MovieClip symbol into a component.

1. In Flash, return to calculator.fla in /fpad2004/mmestate/.

Return to the file you created in the last exercise or open /fpad2004/lesson06/intermediate/ calculator_api.fla and save it as *calculator.fla* in /fpad2004/mmestate/.

2. Right-click/Control-click the MortgageCalculator symbol in the library and select Component Definition.

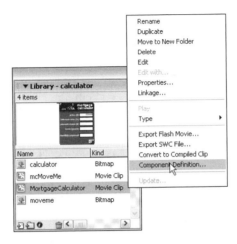

The Component Definition dialog box appears.

3. In the AS 2.0 Class text field, enter *MortgageCalculator*.

In this field, you enter the fully qualified name of the class that contains the parameters to be used for the component.

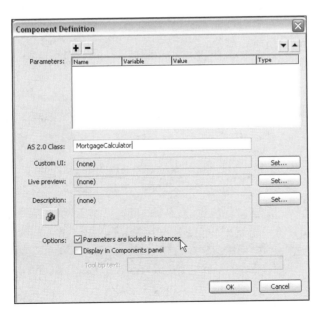

Note *To create a component or a compiled component (which you will do in a later exercise), you must enter the class file in the Component Definition dialog box in addition to entering it in the Linkage dialog box (which you did earlier in this lesson).*

None of the other options in this dialog box are relevant when your component code is contained in a class file; the options are here to preserve backward compatibility with Flash MX components. When you create a class and link it to your MovieClip symbol, you must specify parameters for the component in the class file. You cannot add them manually using this dialog box because they will not stick—they will not be there the next time you open the dialog box. After you specify parameters in your class file, though, they will appear in the Component Definition dialog box. You add component parameters this way in the next exercise.

4. Click OK. Look at the library.

The MortgageCalculator symbol is now listed as a Component symbol and has a new icon.

5. Save the file and test the application.

Your calculator should work exactly as before. So far you have gained nothing by turning it into a component. In the next exercise, you will specify parameters for the component that developers can use to set values for the calculator instead of having to call the update() method in code.

The finished file should resemble: /fpad2004/lesson06/intermediate/calculator_component.fla.

Defining Component Parameters

Component parameters are class properties that can be edited from the Property inspector and Component Inspector panel in the authoring environment. You create component parameters by adding metadata to your class file. **Metadata** is data you add to a class file that is not part of the code, but provides additional information about the code. In this case, the metadata will specify which properties you want to be editable from the authoring environment.

Before each property that you want to appear in the authoring environment inspectors, add the metadata tag [Inspectable] immediately before the property. You can place the metadata tag on the same line as the property declaration or on the line above it.

In the following example, only the gear and cadence properties are defined as parameters.

```
class Bicycle
{
     static private var NUMWHEELS:Number, SOMEFACTOR:Number;
     private var speed:Number;
     [Inspectable]
     private var gear:Number=0;
     [Inspectable] private var cadence:Number;
}
```

Note *Both public and private properties can be defined as inspectable.*

The inspectable parameters will appear in the Component Definition dialog box after the class is registered here.

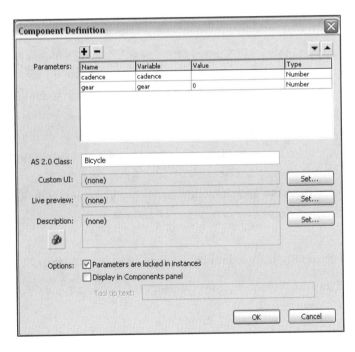

The parameters now appear in the Parameters tab of the Property inspector, where the developer can set their values at design time.

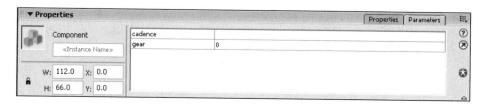

The parameters also appear in the Component Inspector panel. The parameters can be set on the Parameters tab of the panel.

Why the same thing in two places? The Component Inspector panel, which is new in Macromedia Flash MX 2004, is the central place for manipulating components. Not only does the Component Inspector panel have a tab to view and set parameters, but it also has tabs for setting bindings between components and schema for component data. These features are introduced in Lesson 8, "Using the Flash Application Framework," when you use some of the built-in components. (You can also set up and use these capabilities for your components, but that is beyond the scope of this book.) In addition, you can specify certain properties to appear in the Component Inspector panel and not in the Property inspector. This capability allows you to have an abbreviated list of the most commonly used parameters in the Property inspector and a larger complete list of parameters in the Component Inspector panel.

You can also add attributes to the [Inspectable] metadata tag, including the following:

name. A string specifying the display name for the property in the Inspector panels. If not specified, the property's name is used.

defaultValue. A default value for the component parameter. If this attribute is not specified and there is a default value assigned for the property in the class definition when the property is declared (as for the gear property shown previously), this default value is used. If the attribute is not specified and no initial value is defined in the class file, no initial value is specified in the Inspector panels.

```
class Bicycle
{
      static private var NUMWHEELS:Number, SOMEFACTOR:Number;
      private var speed:Number;
      [Inspectable] private var gear:Number=1;
      [Inspectable(defaultValue=60,name="Pedal rotation/minute")]
      private var cadence:Number;
}
```

Note *There are additional properties for the* `[Inspectable]` *metadata tag that you can find in the Help files.*

In this exercise, you define your calculator `price`, `rate`, `down`, and `years` properties as component parameters whose values can be set in the Flash authoring environment.

1. In Flash, return to MortgageCalculator.as in /fpad2004/mmestate/classes/.

Return to the file you used in the last exercise or open /fpad2004/lesson06/intermediate/classes/ MortgageCalculator_api.as and save it as *MortgageCalculator.as* in /fpad2004/mmestate/classes/.

2. Before the `price` property declaration, include an `[Inspectable]` metadata tag to make the property a parameter. Save the file.

```
[Inspectable] private var price:Number;
```

You can place the metadata tag on the same line or the line above the property declaration. It will apply to whatever property immediately follows it in the code.

3. In Flash, return to calculator.fla in /fpad2004/mmestate/.

Return to the file you created in the last exercise or open /fpad2004/lesson06/intermediate/ calculator_component.fla and save it as *calculator.fla* in /fpad2004/mmestate/.

4. Right-click/Control-click the MortgageCalculator symbol in the library and select Component Definition.

You should not see any parameters in the dialog box. When you open the Component Definition dialog box, the specified class file is parsed for any `[Inspectable]` tags. The next time you open this dialog box, these properties will appear as parameters.

5. Click **OK** to close the dialog box. Right-click/Control-click the MortgageCalculator symbol in the library again and select Component Definition.

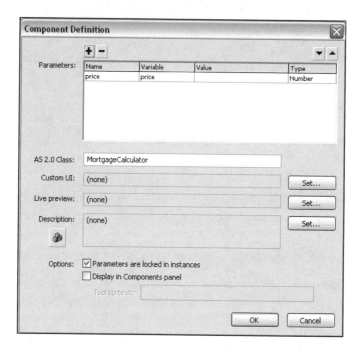

You should now see the `price` property displayed as a component parameter. Note that by default, the parameter is given the same name as the property and has no default value.

6. Click **OK** to close the dialog box and then click the `calculator_mc` MovieClip on the Stage. Open the Property inspector and click the Parameters tab.

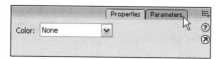

You should see the `price` parameter you defined.

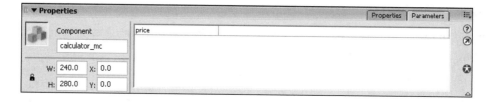

7. Expand the Component Inspector panel.

The Parameters tab should be selected. You should see the same parameters defined in the Component Inspector panel that you saw in the Property inspector.

8. Enter a value of *150000* for the `price` parameter. Test the application.

Your value of 150000 is not displayed in the calculator. Why not? Because you still have a line of code in the calculator.fla file that calls the `update()` method with different values. Anything set with ActionScript always takes precedence over anything set in the authoring environment.

9. Return to calculator.fla and remove the line of code calling the `update()` method. Test the application.

You still don't see the 150000 displayed in the calculator, but you see the default values defined in the class constructor. These values also take precedence over the default values defined in the authoring environment. To successfully apply your author time assigned parameters, you need to assign default values either when you declare the properties or in the [`Inspectable`] metadata tags—but not in the constructor.

10. Return to MortgageCalculator.as. Delete the five lines of code assigning initial property values in the `init()` method called by the constructor.

Delete the code shown in the screenshot.

```
20      private function init():Void
21      {
22          this["price"]=500000;
23          this["rate"]=5;
24          this.down=56000;
25          this.years=30;
26          this.mortgage=0;
27          this.displayFields();
28          this.onChanged=function():Void
```

11. In the `price` property declaration statement, assign the property a default value of *200000*.

```
[Inspectable] private var price:Number=200000;
```

12. Add a `name` attribute to the `[Inspectable]` metadata tag and give it a value of *"House Price."*

```
[Inspectable(name=House Price)] private var price:Number=200000;
```

Now, the parameter name will be displayed in the Inspector panels using the more descriptive string, House Price, instead of the property name, price.

13. Before each of the `rate`, `down`, and `years` property declarations, add an `[Inspectable]` metadata tag with `name` attributes equal to *"Interest Rate,"* *"Down Payment,"* and *"Loan Years,"* respectively.

```
[Inspectable(name="Interest Rate")] private var rate:Number;
[Inspectable(name="Down Payment")] private var down:Number;
[Inspectable(name="Loan Years")] private var years:Number;
```

14. Add a `defaultValue` attribute to the `[Inspectable]` metadata tag for the `rate` property and give it a value of *6*.

```
[Inspectable(name="Interest Rate",defaultValue=6)]
private var rate:Number;
```

Make sure that you use a capital V in defaultValue.

15. Assign default values of *40000* and *20* years to the `down` and `years` properties. Save the file.

You can assign the default value using the `defaultValue` attribute of the `[Inspectable]` tag or by setting the property equal to an initial value when you declare it. You get the same result either way. If you define the initial value when declaring the property, this value is automatically assigned to the `defaultValue` attribute of the `[Inspectable]` tag.

> **Note** You can also define a *type* attribute for the `[Inspectable]` tag, but it isn't necessary because the types you assigned when declaring the properties are automatically used.

```
[Inspectable(name="Down Payment")] private var down:Number=40000;
[Inspectable(name="Loan Years",defaultValue=20)]
private var years:Number;
```

The finished file should resemble: /fpad2004/lesson06/intermediate/classes/ MortgageCalculator_parameters.as.

16. Return to calculator.fla. Right-click/Control-click the MortgageCalculator symbol in the library and select Component Definition. Click OK to close the dialog box. Right-click/Control-click the MortgageCalculator symbol in the library again and select Component Definition.

You should now see the `price`, `down`, `rate`, and `years` properties displayed as component parameters with descriptive labels and default values.

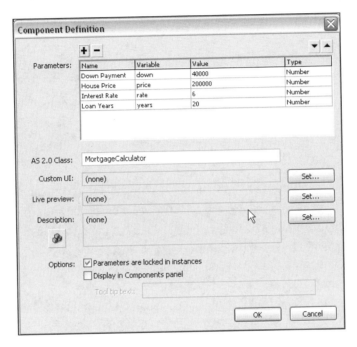

Note *The parameters are listed alphabetically; there is no way to rearrange them.*

17. Click OK to close the dialog box. Open the Component Inspector panel and change the default parameter values. Save the file and test the application.

The parameter values you set in the authoring environment should now be used in the calculator!

You will use this file as the starting file for the next exercise. It should resemble the finished file: /fpad2004/lesson06/intermediate/calculator_parameters.fla.

Creating a Compiled Component

You have turned a MovieClip symbol into a component with parameters that can be set visually in the authoring environment, but the component still cannot be easily distributed for reuse in other applications and by other developers. In this exercise, you learn how to create a compiled version of the component—a single entity that has all the visual elements and code wrapped into one element and that can be installed within the Components panel for easy drag-and-drop use in the Flash authoring environment.

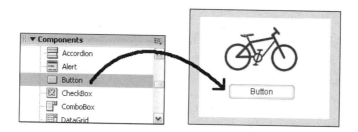

You create a compiled component by right-clicking/Control-clicking the component symbol in the library and selecting Export SWC File. You specify the name of the file and where to save it. A SWC file (pronounced swick) is created, which can be installed into the Components panel in the Flash authoring environment. Instances of the component can then be used in applications by simply dragging them to the Stage. No more worrying about importing an item into a FLA's library and placing class files in the correct locations. The MovieClip and class files are precompiled and ready for use!

What's in a SWC?

The SWC file is a zipped archive file containing an XML manifest file, a SWF of the compiled component, an image to associate with the component, and a list of all the classes used and their members so the compiler can use these for type checking. You can unzip the SWC and look at the files using WinZip or any other compression utility that supports PKZip format. You will find the following files in a SWC:

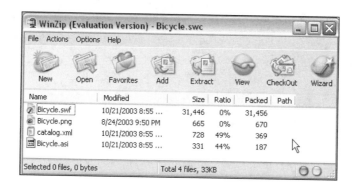

- **catalog.xml.** An XML file listing the contents of the component package and its individual components. It serves as a directory to the other files in the SWC.

- **A SWF file.** The compiled version of the component.

- **Intrinsic class definition files.** ActionScript files containing intrinsic class definitions for all the classes used in the component. These intrinsic class files are used only for type-checking and are not compiled by the authoring tool. You learn more about intrinsic class files in the next exercise.

- **A PNG file.** This file contains an icon to represent the component in the Components panel. The image must measure 18 pixels square and be saved in PNG format. If no icon is supplied, a default component icon is included and displayed in the SWC.

> **Tip** *You can include a Live Preview SWF to change the way the component appears on the Stage in the authoring environment, a SWF to use as a custom Property inspector for the components in the authoring environment, a debugging file (SWD) to integrate with the built-in Debugger, and other files such as a ReadMe file containing the component API. For more information, see the "Creating Components" chapter of the* Using Components *book in the Help panel.*

Obtaining Other SWCs

Flash MX Professional 2004 ships with 30 prebuilt compiled components, including various user interface, data, and media components. (You use many of these components in the rest of the book.) Additional components are available from the following sources:

- The Macromedia exchange at www.macromedia.com/exchange/flash/

- DevNet Resource Kits as part of DevNet subscriptions or individual purchase. More info is available at www.macromedia.com/devnet/subscriptions/

- Third-party companies

> **Note** *Most of these SWCs are distributed as MXP files that can automatically be installed in the Flash authoring environment. You learn to create MXP files in the last exercise of this lesson.*

In this exercise, you create a compiled version of your calculator component, a SWC that can be easily distributed to others. In the next exercise, you will install the component into the Components panel.

1. Return to calculator.fla in /fpad2004/mmestate/.

Return to the file you created in the "Defining Component Parameters" exercise or open /fpad2004/lesson06/intermediate/calculator_parameters.fla and save it as *calculator.fla* in /fpad2004/mmestate/.

2. Right-click/Control-click the MortgageCalculator component in the library and select Export SWC File.

The Export File dialog box appears.

3. Save the SWC as *MortgageCalculator.swc* in /fpad2004/mmestate/.

You are saving the SWC in your application folder. In the next exercise, you will copy it to another location to make it appear in the Components panel in the authoring environment.

You will use this file as the starting file for the next exercise. It should resemble the finished file: /fpad2004/lesson06/intermediate/MortgageCalculator_compile.swc.

4. Using your Windows Explorer or Macintosh Finder, navigate to the MortgageCalculator.swc file you just created and unzip it using a compression utility program such as WinZip or StuffIt.

If you are using Windows and have WinZip installed, you can right-click the file, select Open With, and then choose WinZip executable. Click the Extract button to extract the files. You should get the six files described as follows.

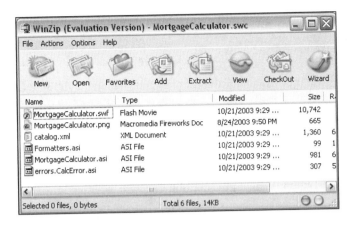

- **Catalog.xml.** An XML file listing the contents of the component.

- **MortgageCalculator.swf.** The compiled version of the component. When you add an instance of the component to an application and then test the application, the component does not need to be recompiled—it is already compiled and is just referenced. This SWF is also used in the authoring environment to preview on the Stage what the component will look like in the application.

- **MortgageCalculator.png.** An icon that appears next to the name of the component in the Components and Library panels.

- **errors.CalcError.asi.** An intrinsic class definition for the Errors.CalcError class.

- **Formatters.asi.** An intrinsic class definition for the Formatters class.

- **MortgageCalculator.asi.** An intrinsic class definition for the MortgageCalculator class.

Note that there is one intrinsic class file (an ASI file) created for each class used in the component. These files do not contain the full source code for the classes, but are only intrinsic class definitions specifying the class members. You will learn about intrinsic class definitions in the next exercise.

You will use the MortgageCalculator.asi file in the next exercise. It should resemble the finished file: /fpad2004/lesson06/intermediate/MortgageCalculator_compile.asi.

Understanding Intrinsic Class Definitions

An **intrinsic class** definition, which enumerates the members in a class, is used by the compiler for type-checking. For properties, the name and access modifiers (public or private) are specified. For methods, the name, access modifiers (public, private, static), return type, and number and type of each argument are specified. An intrinsic class definition resembles an interface (which you created in Lesson 5) in that the method declarations do not include any function bodies. They are unlike interfaces in that you declare all members in them: properties as well as all private and static members.

As you saw in the last exercise, intrinsic class definitions are automatically created for classes when you create a compiled version of component. You will look at what's in these files in this exercise.

Intrinsic class definitions are also available for all the built-in classes (such as Date, Array, and MovieClip). For both your compiled components and the built-in classes, full source code is not needed; the code is already compiled into a SWF for compiled components and is built into the Flash Player for the built-in classes. Intrinsic class definitions are needed for both, though, to implement compile time checking of the names, data types, and access types for properties, methods, and method arguments.

Intrinsic class files also serve as documentation of the API for the compiled component or built-in class. For compiled components, the developer using the SWC does not have access to the source code and hence does not know what properties and methods are available. By looking at the intrinsic class definitions, they can see what public properties and methods are available. Likewise, the intrinsic class definitions for the built-in classes are a great reference and provide a comprehensive listing of the class properties and methods.

Creating an Intrinsic Class

You create an intrinsic class by placing the `intrinsic` keyword before the `class` keyword in a class definition.

```
intrinsic class Bicycle
{
    private var speed:Number;
    public function getSpeed():Number;
    public function setSpeed(speed:Number):Void;
}
```

The `intrinsic` attribute indicates to the compiler that no function bodies are required in the class definition and that no bytecode should be generated for the class. The intrinsic attribute is unique to ActionScript 2.0 and is not found in other object-oriented languages. With this definition, the compiler now has the information it needs to do type-checking for the custom class compiled in the component.

Viewing Intrinsic Class Definitions for Built-in Classes

Intrinsic class definitions for all the Flash MX 2004 built-in classes can be found in the following directories: On Windows, <boot drive>\Program Files\Macromedia\Flash MX 2004\<language>\ First Run\Classes\; on Macintosh, <Macintosh HD>/Applications/Macromedia Flash MX 2004/ <language>/ First Run/Classes/.

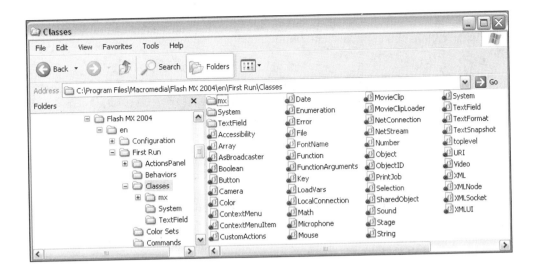

Flash MX 2004 also comes with a large number of prebuilt components that you will use in the following lessons. Full class definitions for each of these components can also be found in these folders.

Here is the intrinsic class definition for the String class.

```
// **********************************************************************
// ActionScript Standard Library
// String object
// **********************************************************************

intrinsic class String
{
        function String(string:String);
        function valueOf():String;
        function toString():String;
        function toUpperCase():String;
        function toLowerCase():String;
        function charAt(index:Number):String;
        function charCodeAt(index:Number):Number;
        function concat():String;
        function indexOf(value:String, startIndex:Number):Number;
        function lastIndexOf(value:String, startIndex:Number):Number;
        function slice(index1:Number,index2:Number):String;
        function substring(index1:Number,index2:Number):String;
        function split(delimiter:String):Array;
        function substr(index1:Number,index2:Number):String;
        static function fromCharCode():String;
        var length:Number;
}
```

In this exercise, you examine the intrinsic class definition for the MortgageCalculator class that was created when you compiled the component into a SWC.

1. Using your Windows Explorer or Macintosh Finder, navigate to the files you unpacked from the SWC in the last exercise.

There were three files intrinsic class files created—one for each class used in the component.

> **Note** It is not necessary to use an ASI file extension when naming intrinsic class files.

2. Open MortgageCalculator.asi using Notepad or any other Text Editor.

Open the file created in the last exercise or open /fpad2004/lesson06/intermediate/MortgageCalculator_compile.asi and save it as *MortgageCalculator.asi* in /fpad2004/mmestate/.

```
import errors.CalcError;
import Formatters;

intrinsic class MortgageCalculator extends MovieClip
{
    public function MortgageCalculator();
    private function calcMortgage():Void;
    private function displayFields():Void;
    private function displayMortgage():Void;
    [Inspectable(name="Down Payment")] private var down:Number;
    private var down_txt:TextField;
    private function init():Void;
    private var mortgage:Number;
    private var moveme_mc:MovieClip;
    private var onChanged:Function;
    private var payment_txt:TextField;
    [Inspectable(name="House Price")] private var price:Number;
    private var price_txt:TextField;
    [Inspectable(name="Interest Rate", defaultValue=6)] private var rate:Number;
    private var rate_txt:TextField;
    public function update(price:Number, rate:Number, down:Number, years:Number):Void;
    [Inspectable(name="Loan Years",defaultValue=20)] private var years:Number;
    private var years_txt:TextField;
};
```

Notice that the intrinsic class definition does not include any method bodies, but does contain information about each property and method. In addition, you can also see what classes are imported or extended, what properties are defined as parameters, whether or not the class is dynamic, whether the class implements an interface, and so on.

Adding Components to the Components Panel

So far in this lesson, you have made your reusable application element into a component that is easier to use—both by creating an API and specifying parameters that can be set at author time. You still, however, have not made it easier to distribute and reuse across files. In this exercise, you learn how to install a SWC into the Components panel so that it can be dragged and dropped into any Flash document.

To make a component appear in the Components panel, you must place the SWC in a specific directory. On Windows, it is <boot drive>\Program Files\Macromedia\Flash MX 2004\<language>\First Run\Components\; on a Macintosh, it is <Macintosh HD>/Applications/Macromedia Flash MX 2004/<language>/First Run/Components/.

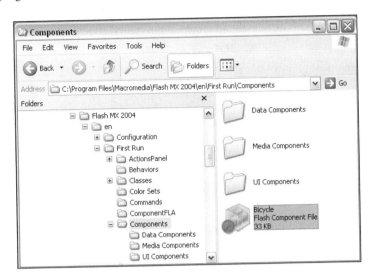

After you place your compiled component in the correct folder and restart Flash, your component will appear in the Components panel and you can drag and drop it to the Stage.

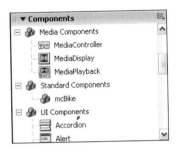

Note *The name of the component that appears in the Components panel will be whatever name you specified as the Identifier in the linkage dialog box before compiling the component.*

When you launch Flash, the components in the First Run folder are copied to a user-specific folder. On Windows, it is <boot drive>:\Documents and Settings\<user>\Local Settings\Application Data\Macromedia\Flash MX 2004\<language>\Configuration\Components\; on a Macintosh, it is <Macintosh HD>/Users <username>/Library/Application Support/Macromedia/Flash MX 2004/<language>/Configuration/ Components/.

If you don't want to restart Flash after adding a new component, you can place a copy of the SWC in the Configuration folder as well as the First Run folder, and then reload the Components panel by clicking the Components panel options menu and selecting Reload.

In this exercise, you add your MortgageCalculator component to the Components panel.

1. Return to Flash and expand the Components panel. Look at its contents.

These are all the prebuilt components that come with Flash MX Professional 2004. You will learn about these components and use many of them in the following lessons.

2. Using your Windows Explorer or Macintosh Finder, copy MortgageCalculator.swc from /fpad2004/mmestate/.

You will paste a copy of the SWC into the appropriate Components directories so it appears in the Components panel.

3. Navigate to the /First Run/Components/ folder.

On Windows, it is <boot drive>\Program Files\Macromedia\Flash MX 2004\<language>\First Run\ Components\; on a Macintosh, it is <Macintosh HD>/Applications/Macromedia Flash MX 2004/ <language>/First Run/Components/.

4. In the Components folder, create a new folder called *fpad2004 Components*.

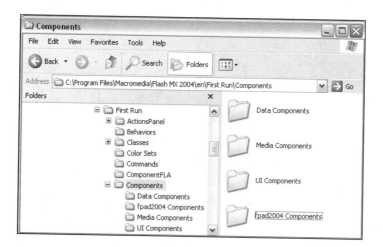

The folders listed in this directory are reflected in the structure of the Components panel.

5. **Paste the SWC into the fpad2004 Components folder.**

The MortgageCalculator will appear in the Components panel under the heading fpad2004 Components.

6. **Copy the fpad2004 Components folder.**

You are copying the entire folder, so you can paste it in the /Configuration/Components/ folder, alleviating the need to restart Flash to have the component appear in the Components panel.

7. **Using your Windows Explorer or Macintosh Finder, navigate to the /Configuration/ Components/ folder.**

On Windows, it is <boot drive>:\Documents and Settings\<user>\Local Settings\Application Data\ Macromedia\Flash MX 2004\<language>\Configuration\Components\; on a Macintosh, it is <Macintosh HD>/Users <username>/Library/Application Support/Macromedia/Flash MX 2004/ <language>/Configuration/Components/.

8. **Paste the fpad2004 Components folder.**

Placing the folder containing the component in the /Configuration/Components/ folder alleviates the need for you to quit and restart Flash to have the component appear in the Components panel.

9. **Return to Flash. Click the Components panel options menu and select Reload.**

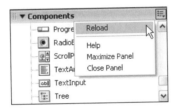

The components for the Components panel are reloaded, and you should now see your component, MortgageCalculator, under fpad2004 Components.

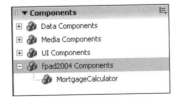

Note *If you do not create a custom directory in the Components panel, but add the SWC directly to the Components folder, the component will appear in the Components panel under a heading of Standard Components.*

10. Create a new Flash document. Drag an instance of the MortgageCalculator component from the Components panel to the Stage. Test the application.

The calculator should work exactly as it did in the calculator.fla file. Close the new untitled document without saving after you finish.

Creating a Custom Icon for the Components Panel

When you create a compiled component and install it in the Components panel, the default component icon is placed next to the component's name. You can also specify a custom icon to be displayed for your component by adding an `[IconFile]` metadata tag to your class file before compiling the SWC.

You add the metadata tag `[IconFile("`*`filename`*`.png")]` at the top of your class file—before the class definition, replacing filename.png with the name of your image file.

```
[IconFile("Bicycle.png")]
class Bicycle{
      [class code]
}
```

In the preceding example, the image file must be in the same directory as the FLA file containing the visual part of the component. You can also specify a relative path to the image file from the FLA directory.

> **Note** *You can name your image file using any name you want, but it is common practice to use the same name as the class file, the Identifier, and the compiled component.*

In this exercise, you specify a custom icon to be used for the MortgageCalculator component in the Components panel.

1. In Flash, return to MortgageCalculator.as in /fpad2004/mmestate/classes/.

Return to the file you used in the previous exercises or open /fpad2004/lesson06/intermediate/ classes/MortgageCalculator_parameters.as and save it as *MortgageCalculator.as* in /fpad2004/ mmestate/classes/.

2. Before the `import` statements, include an `[IconFile]` metadata tag. Save the file.

Refer to the image file MortgageCalculator.png located in /fpad2004/mmestate/assets/ using a relative path.

```
[IconFile("assets/MortgageCalculator.png")]
```

This is the final version of the MortgageCalculator.as file. It should resemble the finished file: /fpad2004/lesson06/intermediate/classes/MortgageCalculator_icon.as.

3. Return to calculator.fla. Right-click/Control-click the MortgageCalculator component in the library and select Export SWC File.

Return to the file you used in the previous exercises or open /fpad2004/lesson06/intermediate/calculator_parameters.fla and save it as *calculator.fla* in /fpad2004/mmestate/.

You need to recompile the component because you changed the class file source code.

4. Save the SWC as *MortgageCalculator.swc* in /fpad2004/mmestate/.

Overwrite the existing SWC version you created previously.

This is the final version of the compiled component. It should resemble the finished file: /fpad2004/lesson06/intermediate/MortgageCalculator_icon.swc.

5. Look at the MortgageCalculator component in the Library panel.

The custom calculator icon now appears next to the component.

The custom icon does not yet appear next to the component in the Components panel, however. You need to copy the new SWC to the appropriate folders and reload the panel.

6. Using your Windows Explorer or Macintosh Finder, copy the SWC and paste it over the existing SWC in the /First Run/Components/ and /Configuration/Components/ folders.

Remember, on Windows, they are <boot drive>\Program Files\Macromedia\Flash MX 2004\ <language>\First Run\Components\ and <boot drive>:\Documents and Settings\<user>\Local Settings\Application Data\Macromedia\Flash MX 2004\<language>\Configuration\Components\.

On a Macintosh, they are <Macintosh HD>/Applications/Macromedia Flash MX 2004/<language>/ First Run/Components/ and <Macintosh HD>/Users <username>/Library/Application Support/ Macromedia/Flash MX 2004/<language>/Configuration/Components/.

> **Note** *If you do not need to make the compiled component available to multiple users, you can just copy it to the Configuration folder.*

7. **Return to Flash. Click the Components panel options menu and select Reload.**

The components for the Components panel are reloaded, and you should now see your custom calculator image next to your MortgageCalculator component.

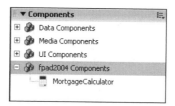

Creating Automatic Installers for Components

You have now created a reusable application element—a compiled component that can be easily distributed and reused by developers and in other documents. No more importing from another FLA's library! This mode of distribution requires that the other developers know where and how to install the SWC or that you send instructions to walk them through the process. You can make the distribution even easier by packaging the SWC as an extension that can automatically be installed into Flash.

An **extension** is a piece of software that can be added to a Macromedia application to enhance the application's capabilities. In Flash, it can be a compiled component (SWC), templates, reusable ActionScript code snippets, additional symbol libraries, and more. You package and install extensions using the Macromedia Extension Manager.

To package a component as an extension, you need to create an MXI file. An MXI file is an XML file containing information for installing the SWC; it includes a name and description for the extension, which files need to be included in the extension, where the files need to be installed on the end user's computer, and so on. You can find example MXI files in the /Program Files/Macromedia/ Extension Manager/Samples/ folder. A description of the MXI file format can be found at the Macromedia site: http://download.macromedia.com/pub/exchange/mxi_file_format.pdf.

After you create an MXI file for your SWC, you use the Extension Manager to package your component as a self-installing extension. The extension filename ends with the MXP file extension and contains all the files needed for the end user to install and use the extension.

You can obtain additional extensions for Flash from the Macromedia Exchange: http://www.macromedia.com/exchange/.

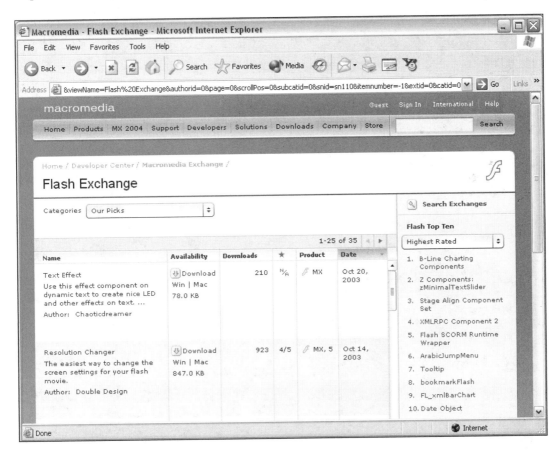

The Macromedia Exchange is a repository of extensions for all Macromedia's products created by Macromedia and third-party developers. Some extensions are free, some are for sale, and all have been through an approval process by Macromedia before posting.

In this exercise, you first look at an MXI file that has been precreated for your MortgageCalculator component. Next, you package the component as an MXP extension using the Extension Manager. Finally, you uninstall your existing MortgageCalculator component and then reinstall it using the MXP file you created.

1. Using your Windows Explorer or Macintosh Finder, navigate to MortgageCalculator.mxi in /fpad2004/lesson06/start/.

This is the XML file needed to package the component. It contains information about what to name the extension, a description for the extension, which files need to be included in the extension, where the files need to be installed on the end user's computer, and so on.

2. Copy the file to /fpad2004/mmestate/.

The MXI file needs to be in the same directory as the SWC.

3. Using Notepad or another text editor, open MortgageCalculator.mxi and examine the code.

```
MortgageCalculator - Notepad
File  Edit  Format  View  Help
<macromedia-extension
        name="Mortgage Calculator"
        version="1.0"
        type="flashcomponent"
        requires-restart="true">

        <!-- Describe the author -->

        <author name="Jeanette Stallons" />

        <!-- List the required/compatible products -->

        <products>
                <product name="Flash" version="7" primary="true" />
        </products>

        <!-- Describe the extension -->

        <description>
        <![CDATA[
        This is a mortgage calculator component that calculates and displays the mortgage for given values of
house price, interest rate, down payment, and number of load years. These properties can be input into the
calculator at run time by the end user, set at author time using the Component or Property inspector, or set
using a public method in code.<br>
        ]]>
        </description>

        <!-- Describe where the extension shows in the UI of the product -->

        <ui-access>
        <![CDATA[
        This item is accessed from the Components panel.
        ]]>
        </ui-access>

        <!-- Describe the files that comprise the extension -->

        <files>
                <file source="MortgageCalculator.swc" destination="$Flash/Components/fpad2004 Components" />
        </files>

</macromedia-extension>
```

Note that the `requires-restart` attribute is set to true; the installer installs the component into the Configuration folder, which requires only that you reload the Components panel—but many users will not know they need to do that. Hence, it is better to force a restart of Flash, thus ensuring that the extension appears in the authoring environment.

You can use this file as a template to package other components. All you need to change is the extension name, author, description, and source filename.

4. Using your Windows Explorer or Macintosh Finder, delete the fpad2004 Components directory in the First Run and Configuration folders.

You are deleting the SWC so that you can install it automatically using the Extension Manager.

Remember, on Windows, these folders are <boot drive>\Program Files\Macromedia\Flash MX 2004\<language>\First Run\Components\ and <boot drive>:\Documents and Settings\<user>\ Local Settings\Application Data\Macromedia\Flash MX 2004\<language>\Configuration\ Components\.

On a Macintosh, these folders are <Macintosh HD>/Applications/Macromedia Flash MX 2004/ <language>/First Run/Components/ and <Macintosh HD>/Users <username>/Library/ Application Support/Macromedia/Flash MX 2004/<language>/Configuration/Components/.

5. Return to Flash. Click the Components panel options menu and select Reload.

You should no longer see MortgageCalculator component in the Components panel.

6. From the main menu, select Help › Manage Extensions.

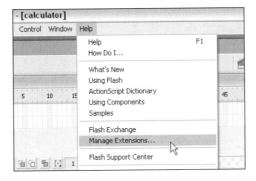

The Macromedia Extension Manager opens.

If this extension is grayed-out and not accessible, you need to install the Macromedia Extension Manager version 1.6 or later; the Extension Manager is not a part of Flash MX 2004. You can download the Extension Manager from http://www.macromedia.com/exchange/em_download/.

7. In the Extension Manager, select Flash **MX** Professional **2004** from the pop-up menu.

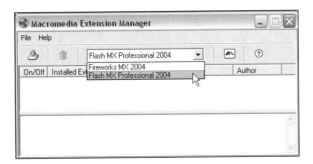

8. Select File > Package Extension.

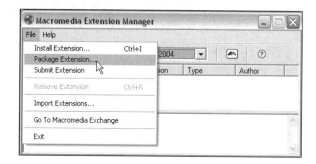

The Select Extension to Package dialog box appears.

9. Browse to MortgageCalculator.mxi in /fpad2004/mmestate/. Click OK.

The Save Extension Package As dialog box appears.

10. Save the extension as *MortgageCalculator.mxp* in /fpad2004/mmestate/. Click Save.

You should see a dialog box that tells you the extension was successfully installed.

This is the final version of the extension. It should resemble the finished file: /fpad2004/lesson06/intermediate/MortgageCalculator.mxp.

11. Select File > Install Extension.

The Select Extension to Install dialog box appears.

Note *You can also install an extension by double-clicking the MXP file from your computer's file system.*

12. Select the MortgageCalculator.mxp extension in /fpad2004/mmestate/ and click Install.

You should see a disclaimer dialog box.

13. Click Accept.

A dialog box appears, informing you that the extension has been successfully installed and that you need to close and restart Flash.

14. Click OK.

You should see your MortgageCalculator extension in the Extension Manager.

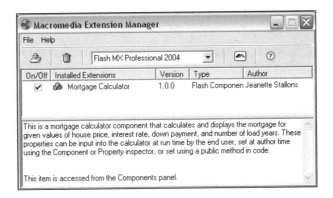

15. Return to Flash. Click the Components panel options menu and select Reload.

You should now see your MortgageCalculator component in the Components panel again.

Creating Components Using the Macromedia Architecture

In this lesson, you learned what components are and the fundamentals for creating them. As mentioned, there are many prebuilt components that come with Flash MX Professional 2004, ranging from simple push buttons and radio buttons to more complex combo boxes, data grids, calendars, and connectors to get data from XML files or web services. All these components are built using version 2 of the Macromedia Component Architecture, which consists of a set of base classes that provide a broadcast/listener event model, depth and focus management, accessibility implementation, skinning mechanisms, and more. The low-level classes for this architecture are the UIObject and UIComponent classes. You can base your components off these classes, providing similar types of functionality and appearances to your components without writing it yourself.

For more information on building components using the Macromedia Component Architecture (V2), see the following sources:

- The Using Components book in the Flash Help files.
- Macromedia Developer Center article: "Exploring Version 2 of the Macromedia Flash MX 2004 Component Architecture" available at http://www.macromedia.com/devnet/mx/flash/articles/ component_architecture.html.
- Macromedia Developer Center article: "Building and Testing Components in Macromedia Flash MX 2004" available at http://www.macromedia.com/devnet/mx/flash/articles/ buildtest_comp.html.

What You Have Learned

In this lesson, you have:

- Converted code attached to a MovieClip into a class file (pages 259–266)
- Linked a class to a MovieClip symbol (pages 266–269)
- Created a public API for a class (pages 270–273)
- Turned a MovieClip symbol into a component (pages 274–276)
- Defined parameters for a component that can be modified in the authoring environment (pages 276–283)
- Created a compiled version of a component (pages 284–287)
- Learned about intrinsic class definitions (pages 287–290)
- Added a component to the Components panel (pages 290–294)
- Created a custom icon for a component (pages 294–296)
- Created an automatic installer for a component (pages 296–301)

7 Building Applications with Screens

You have created a one-page application and turned it into a component. But, what do you do if you want to build a multipage application, one in which you can move between displays in a nonlinear fashion? One option is to build your application using screens, a programming metaphor new to Macromedia Flash MX 2004 and unique to the Professional version. Screens give you the ability to visually organize your application pages in the authoring environment. A second option is to create each unique application page or functionality as its own MovieClip or SWF that can be loaded into a main application SWF. This method will be covered in Lesson 11, "Creating Visual Objects Dynamically." Finally, an old technique, not used in this book, is to use separate frames of the Timeline to represent different application states. You then use Timeline functions to move between different frames in the Timeline.

Screens are part of the new application-building framework introduced in Flash MX Professional 2004 to aid in rapid application development. This framework consists of various classes, components, and development tools to provide additional functionality over that native to the Flash Player. The main features of the application framework include screens, user interface components, data connector components, behaviors, and built-in data binding. In this lesson, you learn to create applications with screens. In Lesson 8, "Using the Flash Application Framework," you are introduced to the other pieces of the application framework.

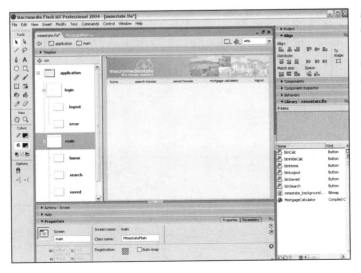

In this lesson, you lay out the structure of the Macromediestate application using screens and create the navigation to enable movement between the application pages.

Up to now, you worked on the MortgageCalculator component. Now that you have finished that project, you need a new one. From here on out, you will build a web site for Macromediestate, the fictitious real estate company that was introduced in Lesson 1, "Learning the Flash Interface." The finished Macromediestate application will include login/logout functionality, a home page displaying dynamic data, an interface to search and display homes for sale, the ability for the user to save his or her favorite homes, and the integration of the mortgage calculator you built in the first part of the book.

What You Will Learn

In this lesson, you will:

- Create a Form-based application using screens
- Set the visibility of a screen in the authoring environment
- Set the initial runtime visibility of a screen
- Architect an application with screens
- Look at the Form screen API
- Place code in the Timeline of a screen
- Place code on a screen object
- Place code in a class associated with a screen

Approximate Time

This lesson takes approximately 70 minutes to complete.

Lesson Files

Asset Files:

/fpad2004/lesson07/start/assets/mmestate_background.png
/fpad2004/lesson07/start/assets/navbuttons.fla

Starting Files:

None

Completed Files:

/fpad2004/lesson07/complete/mmestate.fla
/fpad2004/lesson07/complete/classes/MmestateMain.as

Creating a Form-Based Application

In the last lesson, you learned how to link a MovieClip (which contains the visual elements) to a class file (which contains the code to manipulate the visual elements). This is exactly what a screen is, a MovieClip with a linked class file, with the additional functionality of a thumbnail version of the screen displayed in a Screen Outline pane in the authoring environment. This special pane appears only for screens when you create a new screens-based application. This Screen Outline pane allows you to visually architect and manipulate the structure of a multipage application.

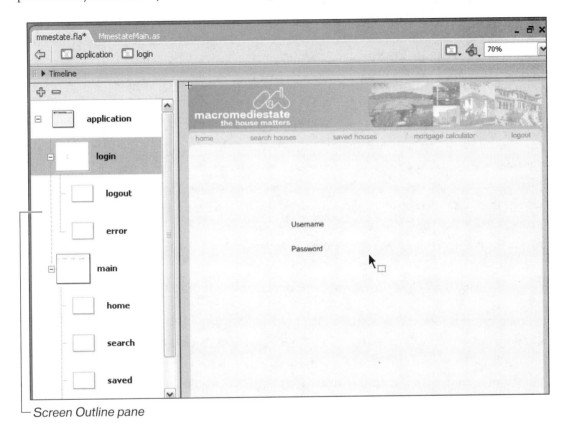

— Screen Outline pane

There are two types of screens-based applications: form screens and slide screens.

A **Flash Form Application** lets you create structured screens-based applications but does not provide any framework for navigating between the screens. A Flash Form Application is ideal for creating typical, rich Internet applications that have nonlinear navigation. You lay out and organize the content in different screens (which can be overlaid or nested) and then you link the screens together, rolling your own navigation using ActionScript. Form-based applications use the form screen as the default screen type.

A **Flash Slide Presentation** has built-in functionality for linear navigation between the screens. It is ideal for creating Flash documents containing sequential content, such as a slide show or a multimedia presentation. By default, you navigate between slide screens using the keyboard's arrow keys. You can design the screen navigation so that screens replace or overlay one another when the next slide is viewed. Slide-based applications use the slide screen as the default screen type.

> **Note** *You can also mix slide screens and form screens within one screens-based application, allowing you to create even more complex structures in a presentation or application.*

Both types of screens descend from the built-in MovieClip class, but have additional functionality with many more properties and methods defined in their associated classes (mx.screens.Form or mx.screens.Slide) and the classes they inherit from. Screens are actually based on the same architecture as the prebuilt components mentioned briefly in the last lesson, inheriting from the UIObject and UIComponent classes. You learn more about the architecture and functionality defined for the prebuilt components in Lesson 9, "Learning the UI Component Framework."

To create a screens-based application, you select Flash Form Application or Flash Slide Presentation when you create a new document. You must create a screens-based application from scratch; you cannot convert an existing application. After you create a screens-based application, you manipulate the screens using the Screen Outline pane where you can add, delete, and rename screens—as well as change their position relative to other screens or nest them within other screens. Each screen is a unique instance that cannot be reused by any other application. You can set parameters for a screen in the Property inspector. You can also use ActionScript to manipulate and control screens.

> **Note** *Screen instances do not appear in the Library panel and cannot be reused.*

In this exercise, you create a new Form-based application and begin creating the Macromediestate application. You import a background image that is used for the entire application and also begin creating a `login` screen, which will be the first screen a user sees. You create nested `logout` and `error` screens, which overlay messages on the `login` screen when the user has logged out or entered incorrect information. In this exercise, you add text and image content to the screens.

1. Select File > New. In the New Document dialog box, select Flash Form Application and click OK.

The new Form application document opens in an authoring environment that looks different from the normal Flash documents that you saw in the previous six lessons. The Timeline panel is collapsed and there is a new Screen Outline pane on the left side of the Stage.

Collapsed Timeline panel

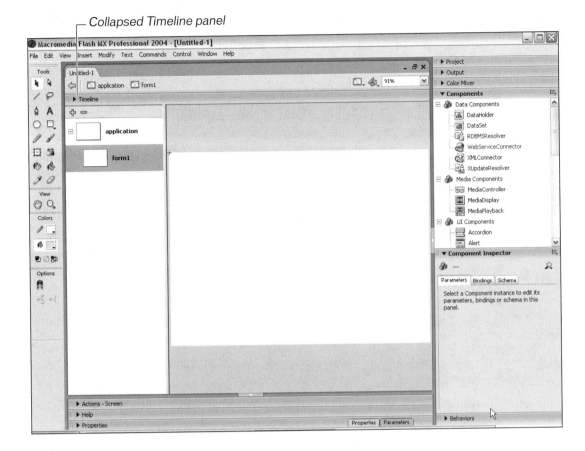

2. Click the `application` screen in the Screen Outline pane.

The `application` screen is the root screen or container for the application. You can change its name, but you cannot delete it. The `application` screen is the parent screen; all other screens must be children screens. You place content you want to appear on every screen on the `application` screen.

3. Select Modify > Document. In the Document Properties dialog box, make the document *700* px (pixels) wide and *600* px (pixels) tall. Click OK.

You are matching the document size to the size of the background image you will import for the `application` screen in the next step. By default, all child Form screens have the same size and same registration point (in the upper left corner) as the `application` screen. You can change the size and location of an individual Form screen with code.

4. Select File > Import > Import to Stage. In the Import dialog box, navigate to mmestate_background.png in /fpad2004/mmestate/assets/. Click Open (Windows) or Import (Macintosh). Select "Import as single flattened bitmap" and then click OK.

Whatever you place in the `application` screen will be visible on all children screens.

5. Click the `form1` screen in the Screen Outline pane.

The background image you imported should become grayed-out, indicating that it is on a screen that no longer has focus and cannot be edited.

6. Double-click `form1` in the Screen Outline pane and rename it *login*.

The name you specify in the Screen Outline pane is also used as the instance name and linkage name for the screen object. For this reason, it is a best practice to name your screen instance using all lowercase or camelcase, exactly as you have been doing for other class instances.

7. On the Stage for the `login` screen, create a static text field with the text *Username* using Arial font, black, size 14.

In this exercise, you add only the text that will appear on the `login` screen. You add the input fields and a button in the next lesson.

8. Beneath that text field, create a second static text field with the text *Password* using Arial font, black, size 14.

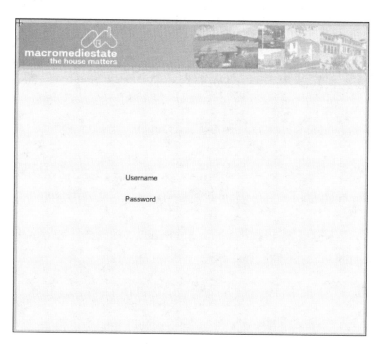

Use the Align panel to align the fields appropriately.

9. Right-click/Control-click the `login` screen in the Screen Outline pane and select Insert Nested Screen.

You will create two nested screens for the `login` screen: a `logout` screen and an `error` screen. Because they are nested screens, the content of both screens will always be displayed in addition to the content in the parent `login` screen and never be displayed independently. The `logout` screen will be displayed over the top of the `login` screen when the user has logged out of the application so the user can log back in if they want. The `error` screen also appears over the top of the `login` screen and will display whenever the user enters an invalid username or password; this functionality will be added in a later lesson.

10. Double-click `form2` in the Screen Outline pane and rename it *logout*. On the Stage for the screen, create a static text field above the existing text fields in the `login` screen with the text *You are now logged out*. Use Arial font, blue (#007ED6), size **14**.

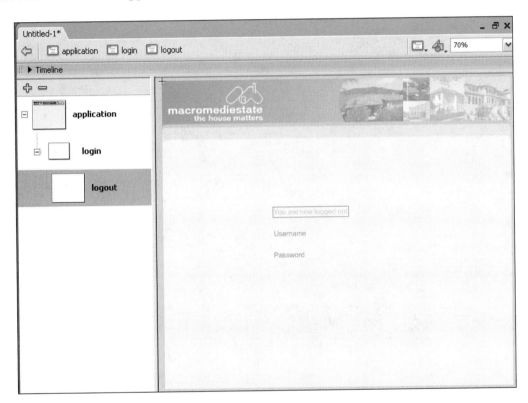

Because these fields are located in different screens, you cannot use the Align panel to align them. Instead, you can align them by eye or you can cut and paste the logout text from the `logout` screen into the `login` screen, align the fields, and then cut the logout text from the `login` screen and use Paste in Place to put it back in the `logout` screen.

11. Right-click/Control-click the `login` screen in the Screen Outline pane and select **Insert Nested Screen**.

You will now create the nested `error` screen.

12. Double-click `form3` in the Screen Outline pane and rename it *error*. On the Stage, create a static text field directly on top of the `logout` screen text field with the text *You have entered an invalid username or password. Please try again*. Use Arial font, red (#FF0000), size 14.

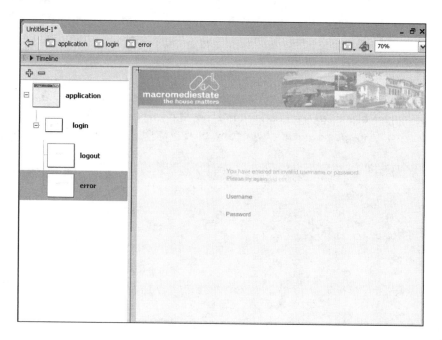

Use the Align panel to align the fields appropriately.

13. Test the application.

You should see all the content in all the screens displayed.

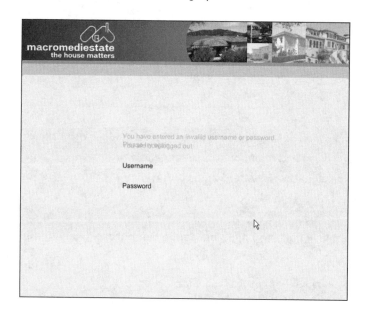

14. Select the `application` screen in the Screen Outline pane and click the Insert Screen button.

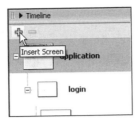

You can also right-click/Control-click a screen and select Insert Screen. When you insert a new screen, the new screen is placed directly below the selected screen and at the same level (it is not nested). The exception is that if you have the root `application` screen selected, a new child screen is created because there can be only one root `application` screen.

15. In the new `form4` screen, use the Text tool to add the text *TEST* with a font size of **42**. Place it on top of the username text field.

Leave the font color red.

16. Test the application.

You should see this new content displayed *over* the content in the other layers. This is because the stacking order of the screen content is determined by the screen positions in the Screen Outline pane. The content in screens located at the top of the Screen Outline pane is displayed at the bottom; the content in screens located at the bottom of the Screen Outline pane is displayed at the top.

17. Click the `form4` screen in the Screen Outline pane and drag and drop it above the `login` screen.

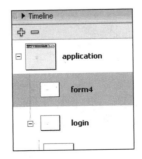

18. Test the application.

The TEST content should now be displayed *beneath* the content in the other layers.

19. Select the `form4` screen in the Screen Outline pane and click the Delete Screen button.

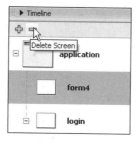

The `form4` screen is deleted. You can also right-click/Control-click the screen and select Delete Screen.

20. Save the file as *mmestate.fla* in /fpad2004/mmestate/.

You will use this file as the starting file for the next exercise. It should resemble the finished file: /fpad2004/lesson07/intermediate/mmestate_screens.fla.

Setting Screen Visibility in the Authoring Environment

There are two different places that you can and will need to set visibility for a particular screen: in the authoring environment and at runtime. Right now in the authoring environment, all content in every screen is displayed on the Stage at the same time. This is a convenient way to place content that will be displayed at the same time—such as the `login` and the nested `logout` screen—but it is difficult to work with content that will *never* be displayed at the same time—such as the `logout` and `error` screens. You can *hide* screens in the authoring environment, so that their content is not visible unless that screen is selected in the Screen Outline pane.

You hide a screen by right-clicking/Control-clicking the screen in the Screen Outline panel and selecting Hide Screen.

In this exercise, you hide the `login`, `logout`, and `error` screens in the authoring environment so that the contents of each screen are displayed only when that particular screen is selected in the Screen Outline pane.

1. Return to mmestate.fla in /fpad2004/mmestate/.

Return to the file you created in the last exercise or open /fpad2004/lesson07/intermediate/ mmestate_screens.fla and save it as *mmestate.fla* in /fpad2004/mmestate/.

Right now, *all* content in *all* screens is displayed on the Stage. This is not desirable because all this content will never be displayed at the same time and it is difficult to design the application visuals.

2. Select the `logout` screen in the Screen Outline pane. Right-click/Control-click it and select Hide Screen.

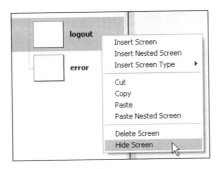

The contents of the `logout` screen are no longer visible unless the `logout` screen is selected.

3. Select the `error` screen in the Screen Outline pane.

The logged-out text should no longer be visible on the Stage.

4. Right-click/Control-click the `error` screen and select Hide Screen.

Similarly, you need to hide the `error` screen so that its contents are not displayed when you select the `logout` screen. The content in these two screens is never displayed simultaneously.

5. Select the `application` screen in the Screen Outline pane.

The error text should no longer be visual on the Stage.

6. Right-click/Control-click the `login` screen and select Hide Screen.

Right now, the `login` screen is the only main page in the application so hiding this screen is not necessary. In a later exercise, though, you will add more screens. Because the `login` screen will not be displayed on every screen in the application, its contents will most likely overlap with other content; thus, you also want to hide it in the authoring environment so its contents are displayed only when it is selected.

7. Select the `application` screen in the Screen Outline pane.

The login page text should no longer be visible on the Stage.

8. Select the `logout` screen in the Screen Outline pane.

The username and password text fields are still visible. Why? Because the content of a parent screen is always displayed when a child screen is selected.

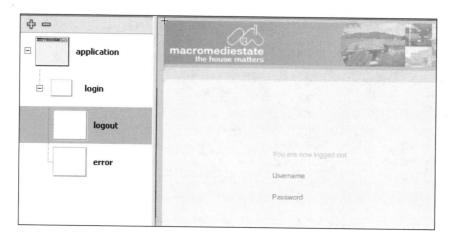

9. Save the file.

It should resemble the finished file: /fpad2004/lesson07/intermediate/mmestate_hide.fla.

10. Test the application.

Even though you have hidden screen content in the authoring environment, the content on every screen is still displayed at runtime. You learn to set the initial runtime visibility of screens in the next exercise.

Setting Initial Runtime Visibility of a Screen

In the last exercise you learned to control the display of the screens in the authoring environment so that the content for all the screens was not displayed at one time. In this exercise, you learn to set the visibility of the screens *at runtime* so that the content for all the screens is not shown at one time in the application. You can set the *initial* visibility of a screen in two ways: in the authoring environment at design time or in code to be executed at runtime.

At design time, you can set the initial visibility of a screen by setting the `visible` parameter to true or false in the Parameters tab of the Property inspector. The visibility of a screen can also be set in code; any value set in code that is executed immediately will override any value set in the authoring environment. In later exercises in this lesson, you will learn about the Form screen application programming interface and how to manipulate a screen visibility and much more by using code.

In this exercise, you make the `login` and `application` screens the only screens initially visible; the `logout` and `error` screens will not be initially visible.

1. Return to mmestate.fla in /fpad2004/mmestate/.

Return to the file you created in the last exercise or open /fpad2004/lesson07/intermediate/ mmestate_hide.fla and save it as *mmestate.fla* in /fpad2004/mmestate/.

2. Select the `logout` screen in the Screen Outline pane. Click the Parameters tab in the Property inspector and set the screen's `visible` parameter to *false*.

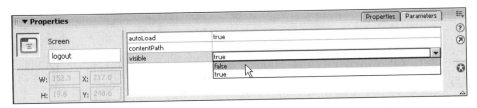

The logout message will no longer be initially visible in the application when you test it. You make the `logout` screen visible again in a later exercise when you add navigation buttons to the application.

3. Select the `error` screen in the Screen Outline pane. In the Parameters tab of the Property inspector, set its `visible` parameter to *false*.

The error message will no longer be initially visible in the application. You make the `error` screen visible again in Lesson 13, "Consuming Web Services," when you add application logic to check login values against a database.

4. Save the file.

It should resemble the finished file: /fpad2004/lesson07/intermediate/mmestate_visible.fla.

5. Test the application.

Now only the content in the `application` and `login` screens is initially displayed.

Architecting an Application with Screens

Now that you have a little practice creating and manipulating screens, you are ready to lay out the structure for the rest of the application. Right now, the Macromediestate application consists only of the `login` screen; you need to build the rest.

Here are some considerations to keep in mind when you are architecting an application with screens:

Content to display on every screen. Place the content you want displayed on every page in the application in the `application` screen. This content usually includes any header text, logos, and possibly a footer. It might also contain navigation if your application does not require a login. If your application requires a login, you will not want the navigation on the `application` screen because you do not want it visible and functional until after the user has successfully logged in.

Content to be displayed on multiple screens, but not all screens. If you have content to be displayed on more than one screen, place this content on a screen and then make all screens that should display this content (along with their own content) nested screens.

In this exercise, you look at the finished Macromediestate Flash application (the SWF not the FLA!) and then finish creating and laying out the necessary screens in your application to achieve comparable functionality. You will add navigation to traverse these pages in a later exercise in this lesson; you add additional content to these screens throughout the rest of the book.

1. Open mmestate.swf in /fpad2004/lesson16/complete/.

Open the SWF. You are opening the finished Macromediestate application that you will build throughout the rest of this book. Examine the finished application to figure out how you should originally architect it using screens. Think about what content should be placed on different screens, what screens should be sibling screens, and what ones should be nested screens.

Try logging into the application using a random username and password and see what happens. Log in successfully to the application using *fpad* for both the username and password. Be sure to navigate to all the different parts of the application.

> **Note** *If you did not install the application server files and the database, some parts of the application will not be functional.*

2. Return to mmestate.fla in /fpad2004/mmestate/.

Return to the file you created in the last exercise or open /fpad2004/lesson07/intermediate/ mmestate_visible.fla and save it as *mmestate.fla* in /fpad2004/mmestate/.

3. Select the `application` (or `login`) screen in the Screen Outline pane and click the Insert Screen button.

A new screen is created at the same level as the `login` screen.

4. Double-click the new form in the Screen Outline pane and rename it *main*.

This screen will contain the content to be displayed on all the pages in the application after a user successfully logs in. In this application, this content includes all the navigation buttons.

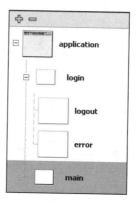

5. Select File > Import > Open External Library.

You will import prebuilt navigation buttons from the library of another FLA document.

6. In the Open as Library dialog box, browse to navbuttons.fla in /fpad2004/mmestate/ assets/ and click Open.

You should now see the Library panel for navbuttons.fla. The document itself has not been opened, just its library, so that you can drag out items from its library to use in other documents. Notice that the background color of the Library panel is gray, which is a visual cue that indicates that it is not the library of the currently selected document.

7. Drag out an instance of the `btnHome` button and place it in the gray bar under the Macromediestate logo. Name the instance *home_btn* in the Property inspector.

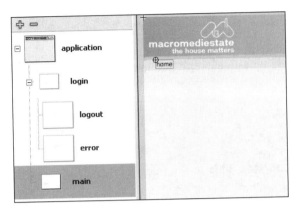

8. Similarly, drag out instances of the `btnSearch`, `btnSaved`, `btnCalc`, and `btnLogout` buttons and place them in the gray bar under the logo. Give them the instance names *search_btn*, *saved_btn*, *calc_btn*, and *logout_btn* in the Property inspector.

Use the Align panel to align the fields appropriately.

9. In the Property inspector, set the `visible` parameter of the `main` screen to *false*.

You do not want the `main` screen to be initially visible. You do not want it to be visible until after the user has successfully logged in to the application.

10. Right-click/Control-click the `main` screen in the Screen Outline pane and select Insert Nested Screen.

A new nested screen is created under the `main` screen. You will create a nested screen for each of the screens in the application that are displayed after a user successfully logs in.

11. Double-click the new form in the Screen Outline pane and rename it *home*. Right-click/Control-click the screen and select Hide Screen.

You do not want this content to always be displayed in the authoring environment.

12. On the Stage for the home screen, create a static text field in the upper left corner with the text *We provide*. Use Arial font, black, size 12.

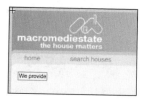

In Lesson 8, you will load the content that will go next to this field dynamically from an XML file.

13. Create a second static text field in the middle left part of the Stage and type in the text *Our mission*. Use Arial font, black, size 12.

You will also load the content to go next to this field dynamically from an XML file.

14. Create a third static text field in the lower left corner with the text *Our info*. Use Arial font, black, size 12.

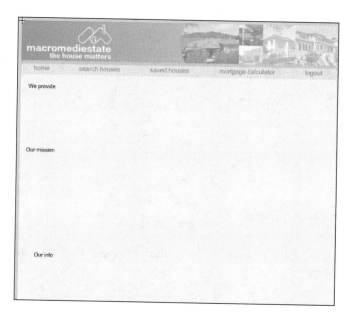

This field is for contact information. You could now add all the contact information (which does not change) right next to this text field. Instead of typing it all in, though, you will load it from the XML file as well. Use the Align panel to right-align the three fields.

15. Select the `main` screen in the Screen Outline pane. Right-click/Control-click and select Insert Nested Screen.

Next you will create a nested screen for the search page.

16. Double-click the new form in the Screen Outline pane and rename it *search*. Right-click/Control-click the screen and select Hide Screen. In the Property inspector, set the `visible` parameter to *false*.

This step sets up the screen for the search page. You will add content to this screen in a later lesson.

17. Right-click/Control-click the `search` screen in the Screen Outline pane and select Insert Screen.

Next you will create a nested screen for the saved page.

18. Double-click the new form in the Screen Outline pane and rename it *saved*. Right-click/Control-click the new screen and select Hide Screen. In the Property inspector, set the `visible` parameter to *false*.

This step sets up the screen for the saved search page. You will add content to this screen in later lessons.

19. Right-click/Control-click the `saved` screen in the Screen Outline pane and select Insert Screen.

Next you will create a nested screen for the mortgage calculator screen.

20. Double-click the new form in the Screen Outline pane and rename it *calculator*. Right-click/Control-click the new screen and select Hide Screen. In the Property inspector, set the `visible` parameter to *false*.

This step sets up the screen to display the mortgage calculator.

21. From the Components panel, drag out an instance of the MortgageCalculator component and place it on the Stage.

It does not matter exactly where you place the calculator; it is draggable and the user can drag it where they like. This screen will not close automatically when the user navigates to another page. It will stay visible until the user closes it.

> **Note** The MortgageCalculator component will exist in the Components panel only if you did the last exercise of Lesson 6, "Creating Components." To install the component, follow the installation steps in the last exercise of Lesson 6.

22. Save the file and test the application.

It should resemble the finished file: /fpad2004/lesson07/intermediate/mmestate_layout.fla.

Make sure you only see the login screen. None of the new content including the navigation buttons should be visible. You hook up the buttons and make them functional in a later exercise.

Using the Form Screen API

To manipulate a screen object using code, you need to become familiar with the application programming interface for the Form screen class (mx.screens.Form), consisting of all the properties and methods you can use to manipulate a Form screen. The inheritance for this class is as follows:

MovieClip > UIObject > UIComponent > View > Loader > Screens > Form

You can find the source code for all these classes in the Classes folder in the First Run and Local Settings folders. For Windows, these two directories are <boot drive>:\Program Files\Macromedia\ Flash MX 2004\<language>\First Run\Classes\ and <boot drive>:\Documents and Settings\<user>\ Local Settings\Application Data\Macromedia\Flash MX 2004\<language>\Configuration\Classes\. For Macintosh, these directories are <Macintosh HD>/Applications/Macromedia Flash MX 2004/ <language>/First Run/Classes/ and <Macintosh HD>/Users <username>/Library/Application Support/Macromedia/Flash MX 2004/<language>/Configuration/Classes/.

Here is a general sketch of the functionality provided by each of these classes.

UIObject. Full class name is mx.core.UIObject, and it inherits from the MovieClip class. It is the base class for all the prebuilt components and has no visual component. It provides additional functionality over the MovieClip class for implementing styles, broadcasting events, and resizing by scaling.

UIComponent. Full class name is mx.core.UIComponent, and it inherits from the UIObject class. It is also a base class for all the prebuilt components and has no visual component. It provides additional functionality for receiving focus and keyboard input, enabling and disabling components, and resizing by layout.

View. Full class name is mx.core.View, and it inherits from the UIComponent class. It is the base class for all view and container components and provides the functionality for managing loaded content.

Loader. Full class name is mx.controls.Loader, and it inherits from the View class. It is a container component into which you can dynamically load content (JPGs or SWFs), monitor the loading progress, and rescale the content.

Screens. Full class name is mx.screens.Screen, and it inherits from the Loader class. It has a user-friendly API for keeping track of and managing its children screens.

Form. Full class name is mx.screens.Form, and it inherits from the Screens class. It has properties and methods with the word *form* in them for keeping track of and managing its children screens.

The properties, methods, and events for the Form class are listed in the Actions toolbox under Screens > Form. The members listed in the toolbox are those specifically for the Form class as well as many for its parent classes.

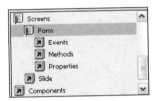

Descriptions for a few common properties, methods, and events are included here:

Visible. A property (from the UIObject class) that sets whether a Form screen is visible at runtime when its parent screen is visible. This is the parameter you previously set in the Property inspector.

contentPath. A property (from the Loader class) that contains a string path to a JPG or SWF to be loaded into the screen.

numChildForms. A property (from the Form class) that returns the number of child forms that the Form screen contains.

Load(). A method (from the Loader class) that loads the content specified in the contentPath property into the screen.

addEventListener(). A method (from the UIEventDispatcher class) that registers a listener object for a particular screen event.

getChildForm(index). A method (from the Form class) that returns a child Form screen at the given index.

Reveal. An event (from the UIObject class) broadcast when a screen is made visible.

Load. An event (from the UIObject class) broadcast when a screen is finished loading into the Flash Player.

To become familiar with the Forms API, open the /fpad2004/lesson07/intermediate/mmestate_layout.fla and browse the form screens branch of the actions toolbox in the Actions panel.

Placing Code in the Timeline of a Screen

Just as with a normal MovieClip, there are three places to add code associated with a screen: in the Timeline of a screen, in event handlers on a screen object, or in a separate class file associated with a screen. You will add your code in each of these locations in the next three exercises.

By default, the Timeline panel is not open when creating Form-based applications. The Timeline is initially hidden to simplify the interface and not confuse more traditional, non-Flash programmers.

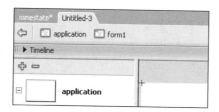

When you open the Actions panel for a particular screen, you are placed *on* the object—that place you learned about in Lesson 4, "Creating Button and MovieClip Objects," for MovieClips in which you have to place all your code inside an event handler for that class instance. You can tell because the title of the Actions panel is Actions – Screen instead of Actions – Frame.

In Lesson 4, you learned that when you open the actions panel for a particular screen, you are placed *on* the object. You have to add all your code for MovieClips inside an event handler for that class instance.

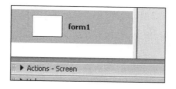

To add code to the Timeline instead of on the object, you need to select a layer or the first frame in a layer (which is usually called actions) and then add code to the Actions panel. Any code added to the Timeline of a screen is executed when that screen is loaded, which is when the application is loaded into the Flash Player.

In this exercise, you create a script to make the navigation buttons functional, enabling navigation between the different screens in the applications. You place your script in the Timeline. You will move the code to the screen object and then to an external class file in the next two exercises.

1. Return to mmestate.fla in /fpad2004/mmestate/.

Return to the file you used in the last exercise or open /fpad2004/lesson07/intermediate/ mmestate_layout.fla and save it as *mmestate.fla* in /fpad2004/mmestate/.

2. Select the `main` screen in the Screen Outline pane.

You will add the navigation code to the Timeline of the `main` screen. The advantage of putting code in the Timeline of the `main` screen is that all the code and the visual elements for one part of the application are all contained and associated with that screen. This structure works well if your code does not interact with any of the other screens in the application. Unfortunately, the Actions panel for a Form-based application does not show all the places in the application that have code attached to them as it did in a normal Flash document so you have to open the Actions panel and then click each screen in the Screen Outline pane to see if it has any associated code.

You can also add this code to the Timeline of the `application` screen. The advantage of placing the code in the Timeline of the `application` screen is that if you have code for multiple screens, all the code is in one place.

3. Click the title bar of the Timeline panel to open it. Rename Layer 1 as *actions*.

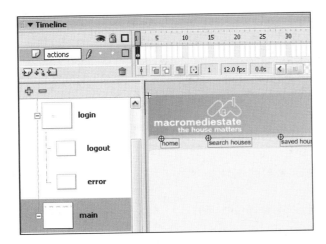

Note that you can still organize content within a screen in different layers, just as you did in a normal document.

4. Open the Actions panel. Look at its title bar.

Because you have a layer in the Timeline selected, the focus of the Actions panel has shifted to the first frame in the Timeline; the title of the Actions panel should be Actions – Frame.

5. Create an `onPress` event handler for `logout_btn`.

```
logout_btn.onPress=function():Void{};
```

6. Inside the event handler definition, set the **visible** property of the **logout** screen to *true*. Use an absolute path to the **logout** screen.

```
_root.application.login.logout.visible=true;
```

7. Still inside the event handler definition, set the **visible** property of the **login** screen to *true* and the **visible** property of the **main** screen to *false*. Use absolute paths.

```
logout_btn.onPress=function():Void
{
        root.application.login.logout.visible=true;
        root.application.login.visible=true;
        _root.application.main.visible=false;
};
```

To test this code you need to temporarily change the initial visibilities of the login and main screens to false and true, respectively, because right now you have no way to get past the login screen in the application. You change these values in the next step.

8. Use the Property inspector to change the **visible** parameter of the **login** screen to *false* and the **visible** parameter of the **main** screen to *true*. Test the application.

You should see the main screen instead of the login screen.

9. Click the logout button.

The navigation buttons should disappear, and you should see the login and logout screens.

10. Return to the code in the Timeline of the **main** screen and create an **onPress** event handler for **home_btn**.

```
home_btn.onPress=function():Void {};
```

11. Inside the event handler definition, set the **visible** property of the **search** and **saved** screens to *false* and the **home** screen to *true*. Use relative paths.

Keep in mind that inside the event handler, the scope is still the main screen.

```
home_btn.onPress=function():Void
{
        search.visible=false;
        saved.visible=false;
        home.visible=true;
};
```

12. After this event handler, create an **onPress** event handler for **search_btn**.

```
search_btn.onPress=function():Void {};
```

13. Inside the event handler definition, set the **visible** properties of the home and **saved** screens to *false* and the **search** screen to *true*. Use relative paths.

```
search_btn.onPress=function():Void
{
        search.visible=true;
        saved.visible=false;
        home.visible=false;
};
```

14. After this event handler, create an **onPress** event handler for **saved_btn**.

```
saved_btn.onPress=function():Void {};
```

15. Inside the event handler definition, set the **visible** properties of the home and **search** screens to *false* and the **saved** screen to *true*. Use relative paths.

```
saved_btn.onPress=function():Void
{
        search.visible=false;
        saved.visible=true;
        home.visible=false;
};
```

16. After this event handler, create an **onPress** event handler for **calc_btn**.

```
calc_btn.onPress=function():Void {};
```

17. Inside the event handler definition, set the **visible** property of the **calculator** screen to *true*. Use a relative path.

```
calc_btn.onPress=function():Void
{
        calculator.visible=true;
};
```

18. Test the application. Try out all the buttons, except the logout button, and make sure they work.

Don't click the logout button or you will not be able to get back to the main screen. Notice that when you click the calculator button and then click another navigation button, the calculator does not disappear. You want the user to be able to use the calculator when they look at other application pages that include house prices. You do need some way, though, to close the calculator, which is a functionality that is not built into the component. You need to add a button with this functionality to the `calculator` screen.

19. Select the `calculator` screen in the Screen Outline pane. From the navbuttons Library panel, drag out an instance of the `btnHideCalc` button and drop it below the mortgage calculator button in the navigation bar. Give it an instance name of `hide_btn`.

You should have the navbuttons library open from a previous exercise. If you closed it, you can reopen it by selecting File > Import > Open External Library and opening navbuttons.fla located in /fpad2004/mmestate/assets/.

20. Return to the code in the Timeline of the `main` screen and add an `onPress` event handler for `hide_btn`.

Be sure to scope `hide_btn` appropriately. It is located in the `calculator` screen, not in the `main` screen, where the code is located.

```
calculator.hide_btn.onPress=function():Void {};
```

21. Inside the event handler definition, set the `visible` property of the `calculator` screen to *false*. Use a relative path.

```
calculator.hide_btn.onPress=function():Void
{
        calculator.visible=false;
};
```

22. Save the file and test the application. Try out your new hide calculator button and make sure it works.

Click the mortgage calculator button; the calculator should appear. Click the home button; the calculator should still be visible. Click the hide calculator button; the calculator should disappear.

The finished file should resemble: /fpad2004/lesson07/intermediate/mmestate_timelinecode.fla.

Placing Code on a Screen Object

In the last exercise, you added code to the Timeline of a screen. The whole Forms-based application development environment, though, tries to steer you away from this workflow. When you select a screen and then open the Actions panel, any code you enter is added to the screen object and must reside inside an event handler for that screen. This is analogous to how you added code *on* instances of MovieClips in Lesson 4.

To add code to a screen instead of the Timeline, you simply select the screen in the Screen Outline pane and then open the Actions panel. Remember, though, that any code placed here must be inside a screen event handler. The code inside an event handler will be executed whenever the event fires; this can be when the screen loads, is made visible, is clicked, and so on.

In this exercise, you move the script controlling the navigation buttons you created in the Timeline to an event handler *on* the `main` screen instance. In the next exercise, you will move the code to an external class file.

1. Return to mmestate.fla in /fpad2004/mmestate/.

Return to the file you created in the last exercise or open /fpad2004/lesson07/intermediate/ mmestate_timelinecode.fla and save it as *mmestate.fla* in /fpad2004/mmestate/.

2. Return to the code in the Actions panel for the first frame of the `main` screen. Select all the code and cut it.

You will move this code to the inside of an event handler *on* the `main` screen instance.

3. Collapse the Timeline panel.

You will no longer use the Timeline to add code to the application.

4. Select the `main` screen in the Screen Outline pane.

The title bar of the Actions panel should change from Actions – Frame to Actions – Screen.

5. Open the Actions panel (if it is collapsed) and create a `reveal` event handler.

```
on(reveal)
{
}
```

6. Paste the code you copied inside the **reveal** event handler.

```
on(reveal)
{
        [all existing code]
}
```

Remember that when placing code directly on an object and not in the Timeline, all code must be inside an event handler, and you must use the `on(event){}` syntax.

7. Save the file and test the application.

Your navigation buttons should work as they did before.

Right now, the code defining the event handlers is executed when the screen is made visible for the first time (which in this case happens to be when the screen is loaded into the Flash Player). The code can also be executed multiple times if the screen's `visible` property is changed with code; the code will be executed anytime the screen's `visible` property is changed from false to true.

8. Return to the code on the **main** screen object and change the **reveal** event to a **load** event.

```
1  on (load)
2  {
3         logout_btn.onPress=function():Void
4         {
```

The code defining the event handlers does not need to be executed every time the screen is made visible; it only needs to be executed once.

9. Save the file and test the application.

Your navigation buttons should work the same as before.

The finished file should resemble: /fpad2004/lesson07/intermediate/mmestate_objectcode.fla.

Placing Code in a Form Screen Subclass

In the last two exercises you added code directly to the FLA. You might want to separate your code from the FLA, enabling multiple developers to work on the application and also allowing your source code to be placed in a source control system. You can separate the code from the FLA in two ways, both of which you have already learned about. One method is to place the script in an external file and then include that file in the appropriate place in the FLA using `#include`. This method enforces the separation, but it does not improve the architecture, readability, and maintainability of the application. These factors can all be improved by implementing a more object-oriented technique of separating the code from the FLA by placing it in a class file.

In Lesson 6 you leaned how to associate a class file with a MovieClip symbol in the library. The linked class file is automatically associated with the symbol and instantiated whenever an instance of the MovieClip symbol is loaded into the Flash Player. You can make the same type of association between a screen object and a class file. Instead of specifying a linkage to the class file in the library, though (because screens do not appear in the library), you assign the class name in the Property inspector.

By default, a screen is linked to the mx.screens.Form class, which gives it its base functionality as a Form screen. If you specify a new class to associate with a screen, you need to make sure that the class extends the mx.screens.Form class to maintain the functionality of the screen as a Form screen object. In addition to creating a constructor for your class, you can also create an init() method, which is automatically invoked by the parent UIObject constructor when the class is instantiated; you do not have to explicitly call the init() method. UIObject's constructor calls the init() method defined at the lowest subclass (in this case your mx.screens.Form subclass). If you create an init() method, you should call the parent class's init() method using super.init() from the form screen subclass's init() method to ensure that all the form screen's base classes finish initializing (and are in usable states).

In this exercise, you move the navigation code to an external class file that subclasses the mx.screens.Form class and then associate that class with the main screen.

1. Create a new ActionScript file and save it as *MmestateMain.as* in /fpad2004/ mmestate/classes/.

Make sure you use the appropriate capitalization.

2. Inside the file, define a class called *MmestateMain*.

```
class MmestateMain
{
}
```

You saved the class in the classes folder, which is a classpath so you do not need to specify a package for the class.

3. Make the class extend the mx.screens.Form class.

```
class MmestateMain extends mx.screens.Form
```

The class must extend the mx.screens.Form class to maintain the functionality of the screen as a Form screen object.

4. Inside the class definition, create the skeleton code for a class constructor with no parameters. Save the file.

```
function MmestateMain()
{
}
```

5. After the constructor, define a *public* method called `init` with no parameters and no return value. Save the file.

If an `init()` method exists for a screen subclass, the method is automatically invoked; you do not have to explicitly call it. You will place all the code that should initially be executed inside the `init()` method instead of directly inside the constructor. It is a best practice to keep the amount of code inside the constructor to a minimum.

```
public function init():Void
{
}
```

6. Inside the `init()` method, call the parent class's `init()` method.

```
super.init();
```

7. Click the Check Syntax button. Save the file.

You should not get any errors.

It is a good idea to always check a class file for errors before you try and link it to a screen. If you attempt to link a class that has errors, the linkage to the screen will fail with a message stating that no such class exists.

8. Return to mmestate.fla in /fpad2004/mmestate/.

Return to the file you created in the last exercise or open /fpad2004/lesson07/intermediate/ mmestate_objectcode.fla and save it as *mmestate.fla* in /fpad2004/mmestate/.

9. Select the `main` screen and then open the Property inspector. Click the Properties tab and look at the name of the class associated with the screen.

You should see mx.screens.Form.

10. Change the name of the class linked to the `main` screen to *MmestateMain* and press enter.

Note *If you did not add the ./classes classpath in Lesson 5, "Creating Classes," this step will fail and you will see a message stating that this class does not exist. Instructions for setting the classpath can be found in the "Setting Classpaths" exercise in Lesson 5.*

11. Click the Parameters tab of the Property inspector.

Unfortunately, when you assign a new class to a screen, the screen parameters no longer appear in the Property inspector. If you want to assign values, you now must do it via code.

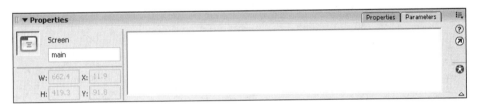

12. Open the Actions panel for the `main` screen and select all the code inside the `load` event handler; cut the code to the Clipboard.

You will place this code in the external class file.

13. Delete the remaining lines of code and save the file.

Delete the lines of code defining the load event handler.

14. Return to the MmestateMain class definition and paste the code inside the `init()` method.

```
 9      public function init():Void
10      {
11          super.init();
12          logout_btn.onPress=function():Void
13          {
14              _root.application.login.logout.visible=true
15              _root.application.login.visible=true;
```

You can highlight the code and press the Tab key to indent it appropriately.

15. Above the constructor, define each of the `main` screen Button instances as *private* properties of type *Button* for the class.

```
private var logout_btn:Button, home_btn:Button, search_btn:Button,
saved_btn:Button, calc_btn:Button;
```

You can make these separate variable declarations or combine them into one, as shown here. You are not defining the `hide_btn` Button because it is not a property of the main screen; it is a property of the calculator screen.

> **Note** To manipulate these Buttons in other class files, you would make them public.

16. Define the `calculator` screen as a *private* property of type *mx.screens.Form*.

```
private var calculator:mx.screens.Form;
```

17. Inside each of the event handlers in the `init()` method (except for `calculator.hide_btn`), prefix each of the relative screen references with `_parent`.

There should be ten references.

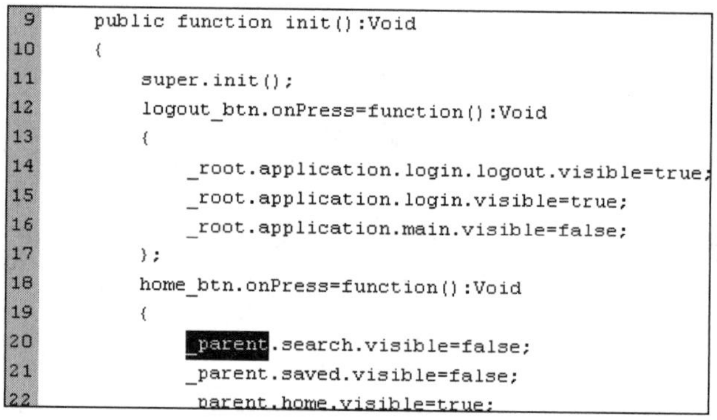

```
9    public function init():Void
10   {
11       super.init();
12       logout_btn.onPress=function():Void
13       {
14           _root.application.login.logout.visible=true;
15           _root.application.login.visible=true;
16           _root.application.main.visible=false;
17       };
18       home_btn.onPress=function():Void
19       {
20           _parent.search.visible=false;
21           _parent.saved.visible=false;
22           _parent.home.visible=true;
```

Inside the constructor you are assigning a function literal to be the value of a class property. The code inside the function literal (inside the event handler definition) is scoped to the property itself (for example, `logout_btn`), not to the class instance (the `main` screen in this case). You can change the references to absolute references, or you can give them the proper scope by prefixing each of them with `_parent`, which refers to the class instance they reside in—in this case, the `main` screen.

18. Inside the `calculator.hide_btn` event handler, change `calculator` to `_parent`. Save the file.

```
calculator.hide_btn.onPress=function():Void
{
    _parent.visible=false;
};
```

19. Click the Check Syntax button.

You should get only one error: There is no property with the name 'hide_btn'. This is because you defined calculator as type mx.screens.Form, and this class definition does not have a property called hide_btn. The rigorous way to fix this error is to create a new class file, MmestateCalc, which defines a public property called hide_btn, to link this class to the `calculator` screen, and then define calculator as type MmestateCalc instead of mx.screens.Form. A quicker, less rigorous solution is to change the type of the `calculator` screen from mx.screens.Form to a general Object. Because the latter solution is faster and because you do not need to place any other code in a class for the `calculator` screen, you will use this solution in the next step. Feel free, though, to define and link a class instead.

20. Change the type of the `calculator` property from mx.screens.Form to *Object*. Click the Check Syntax button. Save the file.

```
private var calculator:Object;
```

You should no longer get any errors.

21. Return to mmestate.fla and test the application. Click the various buttons in the navigation bar.

Your navigation should work exactly as it did before. The only difference in your application is that now your code is contained in an external class file associated with a particular screen.

22. Return to mmestate.fla. In the Property inspector, change the `visible` parameter for the `login` screen to *true*. Save the file.

You need to change back the initial screen visibilities so that the `login` screen is initially visible and the `main` screen is not. You build the button functionality to advance from the `login` screen to the `main` screen in the next lesson.

The finished file should resemble: /fpad2004/lesson07/intermediate/mmestate_classcode.fla.

23. Return to MmestateMain.as. Inside the `init()` method, set the `visible` property of the screen instance to *true*. Save the file.

```
this.visible=false;
```

Because you have linked the `main` screen to a class, you must set its visibility with code. If you test the application now, you should only see the login screen.

The finished file should resemble: /fpad2004/lesson07/intermediate/classes/ MmestateMain_classcode.as.

What You Have Learned

In this lesson, you have:

- Created a Form-based application using screens (pages 305–312)
- Set the visibility of a screen in the authoring environment (pages 312–314)
- Set the initial runtime visibility of a screen (pages 315–316)
- Architected an application with screens (pages 316–322)
- Became familiar with the Form screen API (pages 322–323)
- Added code in the Timeline of a screen (pages 324–328)
- Added code on a screen object (pages 329–330)
- Added code in a class associated with a screen (pages 330–335)

8 Using the Flash Application Framework

Macromedia Flash MX Professional 2004 comes with a powerful new application framework that helps you rapidly build Flash applications. This framework consists of various class files, prebuilt components, and development tools to provide additional functionality to the Flash Player. The main features of the application framework include screens, user interface (UI) components, data connector components, behaviors, and built-in data binding. In the last lesson, you learned how to create applications with screens. In this lesson, you are introduced to each of the other pieces of the application framework.

Flash MX Professional 2004 ships with twenty-one prebuilt UI components that range from simple push buttons and check boxes to more complex list boxes, tree controls, and calendars. In addition to UI components, Flash MX Professional 2004 also has prebuilt data connector components that you can use to retrieve and manipulate data from remote XML files and web services without writing any code. Once you have added UI and data components to your application, there are three ways that you can interact with them; you can write code, you can use prebuilt behaviors, or you can add data bindings. A behavior is a prewritten bit of code that can be customized and applied to an object on the Stage using the Behaviors panel in the authoring environment. Data bindings enable you to populate and update a component's display—also without writing any code.

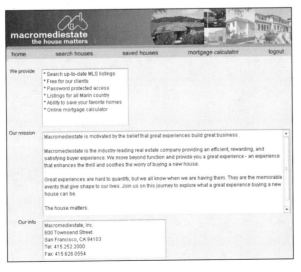

In this lesson, you create the home page of the Macromediestate application using UI components, a data connector component, a prebuilt behavior, and data bindings.

In this lesson, you continue to work with the Macromediestate web site. To the login page, you add TextInput and Button components and a behavior to advance the user to the home page. You don't make the login form fully functional until a later lesson. To the home page, you add TextArea and XMLConnector components, a behavior to trigger data retrieval from the XML file, and data bindings between the TextArea and XMLConnector components to display the data from the XML file in the various text fields. You also create a custom behavior to log all data binding operations to the Output panel when they occur.

What You Will Learn

In this lesson, you will:

- Use prebuilt user interface components to build an application interface
- Retrieve external data using data connector components
- Add application functionality using prebuilt behaviors
- Create a custom behavior
- Bind together the data in components using data binding

Approximate Time

This lesson takes approximately 60 minutes to complete.

Lesson Files

Asset Files:
/fpad2004/lesson08/start/assets/homepagetext.xml

Starting Files:
/fpad2004/lesson08/start/mmestate.fla
/fpad2004/lesson08/start/classes/MmestateMain.as

Completed Files:
/fpad2004/lesson08/complete/mmestate.fla
/fpad2004/lesson08/complete/DataLogger.xml

Using UI Components to Build an Application Interface

In Lesson 6, "Creating Components," you were introduced to the concept of components: MovieClips with parameters that can be set in the authoring environment. These components can also be compiled into SWCs and then easily used by dragging them from the Components panel. Flash MX Professional 2004 ships with thirty prebuilt compiled components that include various user interface, data, and media components; twenty-one of these components are user interface components that range from simple push buttons and radio buttons to more complex combo boxes, data grids, and calendars.

In this exercise you add prebuilt UI controls to your application. You add TextInput components and a Button component to the `login` screen and TextArea components to the `home` screen. This exercise is meant to be an introduction to adding user interface components to your application. Lesson 9, "Learning the UI Component Framework," and Lesson 10, "Using UI Component APIs," are all about the details of using and manipulating these components.

1. Return to mmestate.fla in /fpad2004/mmestate/.

This is the file you created in the last exercise of Lesson 7. If you did not do that exercise, open /fpad2004/lesson08/start/mmestate.fla and save it as *mmestate.fla* in /fpad2004/mmestate/.

2. Select the `login` screen in the Screen Outline pane.

You will add two TextInput components (where the user can enter a username and password) and a Button component (where the user can submit the form).

3. From the Components panel, drag out a TextInput component and drop it next to the Username text on the Stage.

4. In the Property inspector, name the instance `username_ti`.

The use of _ti in the instance name is optional. The _ti is simply a visual reminder to the developer that this variable is a TextInput component; it does not provide any code-hinting.

5. Drag another TextInput component from the Components panel and drop it next to the Password text on the Stage. In the Property inspector, name the instance `password_ti` and change the `password` parameter to *true*.

By setting the password parameter to true, the characters typed in the component's text field will appear as asterisks.

6. Drag a Button component from the Components panel and place it under the two TextInput components.

You can use the Align panel to line up the text and components.

7. In the Property inspector, name the Button instance `login_pb` and set the `label` parameter to *Login*.

The label parameter sets the text displayed on the button. The default label text is Button. You will learn more about the Button API in Lesson 10.

8. Select the home screen in the Screen Outline pane.

You will now add TextArea components to the home screen to hold multiline text strings whose values will be retrieved from an XML file in the next several exercises.

9. From the Components panel, drag a TextArea component and drop it next to the "We provide" text on the Stage. In the Property inspector, name the instance `provide_ta`.

You will learn more about the TextArea API in the Lesson 10.

10. Resize the TextArea component by selecting the Free Transform tool in the Tools panel and dragging one of the handles on the component to make it wider and longer.

Make the TextArea component wider and longer.

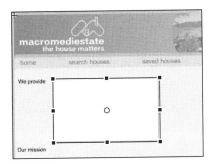

11. Drag out another TextArea component and drop it next to the "Our mission" text on the Stage. In the Property inspector, name the instance `mission_ta`. Resize it appropriately using the Free Transform tool.

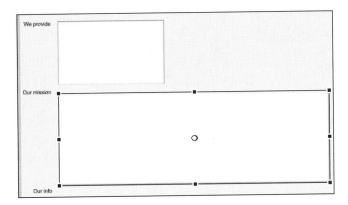

12. Drag out another TextArea component and drop it next to the "Our info" text on the Stage. In the Property inspector, name the instance `info_ta`. Resize it appropriately using the Free Transform tool.

You can use the Align panel to line up the text and components.

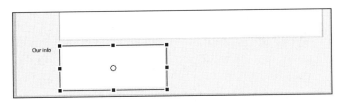

13. Save the file.

You will use this file as the starting file for the next exercise. It should resemble the finished file: /fpad2004/lesson08/intermediate/mmestate_uicomponents.fla.

Retrieving External Data Using Data Connector Components

There are many ways to retrieve external data in Flash. You can use a variety of remote data sources; you can read data from text files or XML files, or access data returned from remote web services or application server classes.

From Flash, you can access remote data using all code; or for XML files and web services, you can also use prebuilt data connector components. These data connector components let you retrieve and manipulate data without writing any code. You can drag and drop the data components from the Components panel as you did for the UI components.

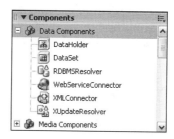

The data connector components differ from the prebuilt UI components in that they have no visual runtime appearance. Their visual representation on the Stage is purely for design time use, allowing you to select the component and set parameters in the Property inspector or Component Inspector panel.

The data source you use for your remote data depends upon the skill sets, technologies, and resources that you, your fellow developers, and your company have access to. Listed below is a brief overview of the possible external data sources you can connect to from Flash. Lessons 12, 13, and 14 cover retrieving data using XML, web services, and Flash Remoting in greater detail. Be aware that for security reasons, the data source of these methods must reside on the exact domain as the Flash application accessing it (unless you create a security policy file on another domain that specifies that your domain can request data from it).

Text files. To retrieve data from a text file, use the built-in LoadVars class. The text file must contain variable name/value pairs separated by ampersands. After the text file is loaded and read, the variables become new properties of the LoadVars instance. An advantage of this method is that text file data sources are simple to create and require no additional software. A disadvantage is that you cannot represent complex data in a text file in a way that can be translated into a complex

Flash object without additional parsing and translation. A second disadvantage is that there is no prebuilt component to use in the authoring environment to retrieve and bind the return data to other components.

```
&provide=* Search up-to-date MLS listings&

&mission=Macromediestate is motivated by the belief that
great experiences build great business.&

&info=600 Townsend Street<br>San Francisco, CA
94103<br>Tel: 415.252.2000<br>Fax: 415.626.0554&
```

XML files. There are two ways you can retrieve data from an XML file: using code or using the prebuilt data connector component, XMLConnector. If you want to separate all your code from your FLA, you can access and manipulate data from XML files using the built-in XML class. Data from the remote XML file is loaded into a local XML object whose nodes and attributes can be accessed programmatically. An advantage of this method is that XML files are easy to create and do not require additional software. In addition, the XML language provides a natural way to represent complex data structures that are directly translated into a complex Flash object. Yet another advantage is that you have the option to use the built-in XMLConnector component to retrieve and manipulate XML data from the authoring environment without writing any code. Retrieving data from XML files is covered in Lesson 12, "Retrieving Data from XML Files."

```
<?xml version="1.0" encoding="UTF-8"?>
<text>

  <provide>* Search up-to-date MLS listings</provide>

  <mission>Macromediestate is motivated by the belief
that great experiences build great business.</mission>

  <info><![CDATA[Macromediestate, Inc.<br>600
Townsend Street<br>San Francisco, CA 94103<br>Tel:
415.252.2000<br>Fax: 415.626.0554]]></info>

</text>
```

Web services. You can retrieve data from web services with code using the mx.services.WebService class (whose source code is contained in the compiled WebServicesClasses component), or you can use the prebuilt data connector component, WebServiceConnector. You usually use web services to access dynamic data that changes often and that you do not want cached in an XML file for any length of time. An advantage of this method is that you might already have web services written to access application functionality on your server (or other third-party web services), so you can directly consume the same web service on your server with Flash and you don't have to create special text or XML files. A potential disadvantage is that in order to access data from any web services, you must have an application server installed on your web server; due to security restrictions you cannot directly access third-party web services (unless the host server has a Flash security policy file in place granting you access), but must access a web service on your server that acts as a proxy to the remote web service. Another advantage is that web services have defined, standard protocols for describing complex data, and the data returned is directly translated into the corresponding Flash objects. And finally, another advantage is that you can use the built-in WebServiceConnector component to retrieve and manipulate data from web services in the authoring environment without writing any code. Retrieving data from Web services is covered in Lesson 13, "Consuming Web Services."

```
<cfcomponent>
  <cffunction name="getHomepagetext" access="remote"
returntype="array">
    <cfset text=ArrayNew(1)>
    <cfset text[1]="' Search up-to-date MLS listings">
    <cfset text[2]="Macromediestate is motivated by the
belief that great experiences build great business.">
    <cfset text[3]="600 Townsend Street<br>San
Francisco, CA 94103<br>Tel: 415.252.2000<br>Fax
415.626.0554">
    <cfreturn text>
  </cffunction>
</cfcomponent>
```

Remote ColdFusion, Java, or .NET classes. If you have existing server-side functionality, you don't have to convert all these classes into web services to access them from Flash. You can access the classes directly using Flash Remoting, which is a programming tool and runtime environment for connecting Flash to remote application server services. Flash Remoting is a separate product and is not built into Flash MX 2004. It has two pieces: a client-side piece that includes the necessary classes (and debugging tools) for the Flash authoring environment and a server piece that is the remoting gateway. The remoting gateway handles all the Flash remoting requests and translates all the data between Flash and the application server. Currently, you must connect to your remote services using code. A visual connector component similar to those for connecting to web services and XML files, however, will be available soon. Flash Remoting is usually used to access dynamic data in similar situations as those used to access web services. Flash Remoting, however, does not require that you convert your server classes to web services; this is advantageous if your system is tightly coupled and doesn't need to be converted to more loosely coupled web services. Flash Remoting calls also require less bandwidth than web service calls do; Flash Remoting transmits data over HTTP using AMF (Action Message Format), a binary protocol, instead of the more verbose SOAP used by web services. Flash Remoting is built into Macromedia's ColdFusion and JRun application servers; for .NET or non-JRun Java servers, Flash Remoting is available as a separate product and can be installed on top of these application servers. Retrieving data from remote application server classes using Flash Remoting is covered in Lesson 14, "Accessing Remote Services Using Flash Remoting."

In this exercise, you add an XMLConnector component to the home screen and set it up to retrieve data from an XML file that contains data to populate the TextArea components on the home page. You are only setting up the component; in the following exercises, you actually retrieve the data and display it in the UI components. This exercise is meant only as an introduction to the data connector components, which are part of the application-building framework.

1. Return to mmestate.fla in /fpad2004/mmestate/.

Return to the file you created in the last exercise or open /fpad2004/lesson08/intermediate/ mmestate_uicomponents.fla and save it as *mmestate.fla* in /fpad2004/mmestate/.

2. Select the home screen.

It makes sense to add the XMLConnector to the home screen because this screen will use the data returned from the XML file. You could also add the component to any of the other screens. If the returned data is to be accessed by more than one screen in the application, it would be preferable to add it to the `application` screen.

3. From the Components panel, drag out an instance of the XMLConnector component and drop it anywhere on the Stage.

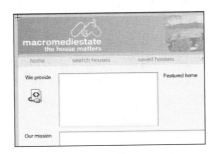

Some developers prefer to place instances of the data connector components off the Stage, usually immediately above the Stage or to its left. Depending on how your Stage is displayed (Fit in Window, Show All, 25%, and so on), items off the Stage might not be visible.

4. In the Property inspector, name the XMLConnector instance home_xc, set the URL parameter to *assets/homepagetext.xml*, and the `direction` parameter to *receive*.

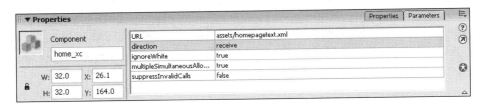

You are using a relative reference to the XML file. You can also use an absolute reference to the file.

Note *Make sure you set the `direction` parameter to receive. If you leave the `direction` parameter equal to the default value of send/receive, your call to the XML file will not work!*

5. Save the file.

You will retrieve the data using this component and display the return data in the UI components in the following exercises.

Your finished file should resemble: /fpad2004/lesson08/intermediate/mmestate_datacomponents.fla.

Using Behaviors

A **behavior** is a prewritten bit of code that can be customized and applied to an object on the Stage using the Behaviors panel in the authoring environment—without you ever going to the Actions panel. Behaviors allow noncoders to add interactivity to a Flash application without writing a single line of code. For programmers, behaviors serve as a tool for rapid prototyping of applications and as a learning tool (you can apply a behavior and then look at the code to see what it does and how it works). You can also make the Behaviors panel work as a partially functional snippets panel, which you will see in the following exercise where you create your own behavior.

Flash MX 2004 ships with almost forty prebuilt behaviors ranging from behaviors to provide functionality to make links to other web sites, load sounds and graphics, control playback of embedded videos, manipulate MovieClips, control screen navigation, and to trigger data access for the data connector components. All these behaviors are found in the Behaviors panel. The behaviors displayed in the panel depend on the object you have selected on the Stage.

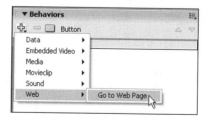

To apply a behavior, you first select the object on the Stage. You can select a button, a MovieClip, a screen, a frame in the Timeline, or any other object. You then open the Behaviors panel and select the behavior you want to apply.

Next, you might need to select targets or provide other parameter values in a dialog box. When the behavior is applied, code is written for that object in the Actions panel, and the specific behavior applied appears in the Behaviors panel list. For many of the behaviors, a default event is used when creating the code. You can change the event that triggers the behavior by selecting a new event for the applied behavior in the Behaviors panel list.

After you apply a behavior, you can open the Actions panel and look at the code that was created. Many of the behaviors are event handlers that generate code, saying do x when x event occurs for this object. In most cases, the code is placed on the object itself, not in the document or object Timeline. Although this causes code to be scattered in multiple places in the document, the instance names of the objects do not have to be referenced in the generated code. Therefore, the code does not have to be updated if the name of the instance the behavior is applied to ever changes. In the few cases that the code is added to the Timeline instead of in an event handler, you must manually change the code if you change the instance names of any objects referenced by that code. (You could also delete the existing behavior and then create a new one.)

Note *The Behaviors panel is not a code-snippet panel; you cannot drag a behavior from the Behaviors panel to the Script Editor pane. As a result, you cannot use behaviors to add code to an ActionScript file.*

In this exercise you use behaviors to accomplish two tasks: navigate to the `main` screen when the login button is clicked and generate the code to trigger the XMLConnector component to retrieve data from the remote XML file.

1. Return to mmestate.fla in /fpad2004/mmestate/.

Return to the file you created in the last exercise or open /fpad2004/lesson08/intermediate/ mmestate_datacomponents.fla and save it as *mmestate.fla* in /fpad2004/mmestate/.

2. Select the Login button on the Stage of the `login` screen.

You want to apply screen behaviors to this button that set the visibility of particular screens; the code should only be executed when the button is clicked. You can, of course, also write this functionality with code, but you don't know the API for the Button component yet; you will learn about the APIs for many of the components in Lesson 10.

3. Open the Behaviors panel. Click the Add Behavior button and select Screen > Hide Screen.

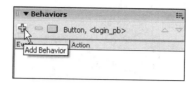

When you click the Login button, you want the `login` screen to disappear. For now, you will go straight to the `home` screen. You add functionality for verifying usernames and passwords against a remote data source in Lesson 13.

Note *The only behaviors in the Screen category that apply to Form screens are Show Screen and Hide Screen, which set the visibility of a particular screen. The remaining Screen behaviors apply only to slide screens.*

4. In the Select Screen dialog box, select the `login` screen and leave the Relative radio button selected.

You can have the generated code use absolute or relative references. The relative reference to the selected target is displayed at the top of the dialog box.

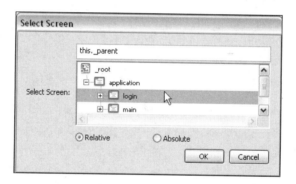

Note *If you change the structure of your application's screens, the generated code will NOT be automatically updated.*

5. Click OK.

The behavior appears in the Behaviors panel. By default, the behavior is assigned to the `click` event for the Button component, which is exactly what you want.

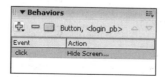

6. Place your mouse over the Hide Screen field in the Action column of the Behaviors panel.

You will see the screen to hide shown in a pop-up text field.

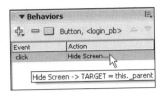

7. Click the Add Behavior button again and select Screen › Show Screen.

When you click the Login button, you want the home screen visible. If you select to show the home screen using the Show Screen behavior, the home screen does not display because a parent screen (the main screen in this case) has to also be visible for a child screen (the home screen in this case) to be visible. Because the visibility of the home screen is set to true in the Property inspector already, it automatically displays when the main screen is made visible. Thus, you only need to add a behavior to show the main screen.

8. In the Select Screen dialog box, select the main screen and leave the Relative radio button selected. Click OK.

The behavior appears in the Behaviors panel.

9. Open the Actions panel for the Login button on the login screen and look at generated code.

The code is added on the login_pb instance. It has a bit of conditional logic added to make it robust enough to handle many different situations. It also uses a setVisible() method instead of the visible property to set a screen's visibility.

10. Save the file and test the application. Click the Login button.

The login screen should disappear, and now you should see the home screen. In the next steps you will add a behavior to trigger the call to the remote XML file.

11. Select the home screen in the Screen Outline pane.

This step ensures that you have the screen selected, not an object on the screen selected. You want to apply the trigger behavior to the screen, so that the XML data is retrieved when the screen is loaded.

12. Open the Behaviors panel. Click the Add Behavior button and select Data › Trigger Data Source.

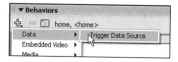

13. In the Trigger Data Source dialog box, browse to home_xc on the **home** screen and leave the Relative radio button selected.

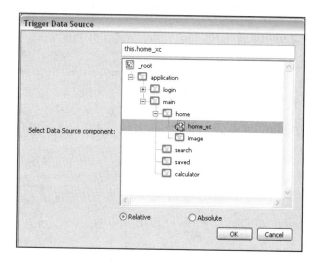

14. Click OK.

The Trigger Data Source behavior appears in the Behaviors panel.

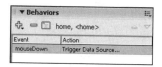

By default, the behavior was assigned to the mousedown event for the screen. You want the behavior to use the load event, so that the code is executed when the screen loads and the data is immediately available on the home page after the user logs in.

15. Double-click mousedown in the Event field. Select load from the pop-up menu.

16. Save the file and test the application. Click the Login button.

You should not see any text in the TextArea components. You have retrieved the data from the XML file, but you have not yet populated the components with the results.

The finished file should resemble: /fpad2004/lesson08/intermediate/mmestate_usingbehaviors.fla.

17. When viewing the SWF, select Debug › List Variables.

If you select this option all the variables used in the application are displayed in the Output panel. Looking at the application variable values here is the simplest method you can use to verify that your call to the XML file has been successful and that the data has been returned to the Flash application. You will display the data in components in the last exercise in this lesson.

18. From the Output panel's options menu, select Find.

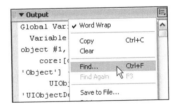

19. Enter *Macromediestate* in the Find dialog box. Click Find Next and close the Find dialog box.

You should see the data retrieved from the XML file.

```
#283] {
    <?xml version="1.0" encoding="UTF-8"?>

    <text>
        <provide>
            * Search up-to-date MLS listings&lt;br&gt; * Free for
our clients&lt;br&gt; * Password protected access&lt;br&gt; *
Listings for all Marin country&lt;br&gt; * Ability to save your
favorite homes&lt;br&gt; * Online mortgage calculator&lt;br&gt;
        </provide>
        <mission>
            Macromediestate is motivated by the belief that great
experiences build great business.&lt;br&gt; &lt;br&gt;
Macromediestate is the industry-leading real estate company
```

Creating a Custom Behavior

In addition to using the prebuilt behaviors, you can create your own behaviors. Every behavior is defined by an XML file located in the Flash MX 2004 Behaviors folder.

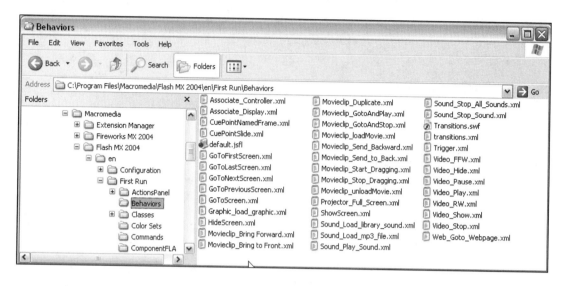

The easiest way to create a custom behavior is to copy an existing XML file in the Behaviors folder and then customize it. If you are not familiar with XML and XML files, don't worry—you can still create a custom behavior; all you need to know is what to substitute where in the file.

XML documents provide an easy-to-use, user-friendly method to format information within a basic text file and contain information in a well-structured, hierarchical manner. XML files are not scripts to be executed by a compiler; they simply provide information that can be easily parsed. An XML document consists of elements (or nodes) and attributes just like in HTML, which is no surprise because HTML is a dialect of the more general XML language. Elements are tag containers that can hold textual information, attribute name/value pairs, and other elements.

The skeleton code for an XML document defining the most basic behavior is shown here.

```
<?xml version="1.0"?>
<flash_behavior version="versionnumber">
 <behavior_definition category="category_name" name="behavior_name">
   <actionscript>
     <![CDATA[
 //The code to insert including any comments
     ]]>
   </actionscript>
 </behavior_definition>
</flash_behavior>
```

Here are descriptions for each of the basic elements:

flash_behavior. This is the root element for the XML file. Every XML document must have one and only one root element and the root element must be the first element in the document. All other elements must be contained inside this element.

behavior_definition. You specify as attributes to this element the behavior name (what you want the name of the behavior to be in the Behaviors panel) and the category (the category under which you want the behavior to be listed in the Behaviors panel). If you specify a category that does not yet exist, the category is automatically created.

actionscript. You place all the code you want inserted for the selected object inside this node. You should enclose the code inside `<![CDATA[` and `]]>` tags, which keeps you from having to escape the characters inside the tags. These tags basically say, don't parse the code inside me.

You can also add `property` nodes to the XML file to specify properties for the behavior whose values are to be selected by the user and which you can refer to in the `actionscript` node. To create the dialog boxes required to gather these properties from the user, you add a `dialog` node. Check out the XML files for other prebuilt behaviors for examples on how to specify values and attributes for these nodes.

After you create a behavior XML document, you need to save it in the Flash MX 2004 Behaviors folder. Just like the Components folder in Lesson 6, the Behaviors folder resides in two places: in the Flash application's First Run directory and in a user-specific Flash directory. Any behavior you place in the First Run Components directory is automatically copied to the user-specific directory when Flash is started. If you place a behavior directly in the user-specific folder, the Behaviors panel can be reloaded without restarting Flash. For Windows, these two directories are <boot drive>:\ Program Files\Macromedia\Flash MX 2004\<language>\First Run\Behaviors\ and <boot drive>:\ Documents and Settings\<user>\Local Settings\Application Data\Macromedia\Flash MX 2004\ <language>\Configuration\Behaviors\. For Macintosh, these directories are <Macintosh HD>/ Applications/Macromedia Flash MX 2004/<language>/First Run/Behaviors/ and <Macintosh HD>/ Users <username>/Library/Application Support/Macromedia/Flash MX 2004/<language>/ Configuration/Behaviors/.

In this exercise, you create a simple custom behavior that adds a line of ActionScript code that enables the tracing of all data connector component operations to the Output panel.

1. In Flash, select File › New. Browse to Trigger.xml in the Flash MX 2004 user-specific Behaviors folder and click Open.

For Windows, this folder is <boot drive>:\Documents and Settings\<user>\Local Settings\ Application Data\Macromedia\Flash MX 2004\<language>\Configuration\Behaviors\. For Macintosh, this is <Macintosh HD>/Users <username>/Library/Application Support/ Macromedia/Flash MX 2004/<language>/Configuration/Behaviors/.

USING THE FLASH APPLICATION FRAMEWORK

In order to see XML files in the Open dialog box, you might need to change the type of file displayed by selecting the All option in the Files of type drop-down (Windows).

The XML file opens in the Flash.

2. Save the file as *DataLogger.xml* in the same directory.

You will now change the code from the Trigger behavior to generate a new behavior for logging data procedures.

3. Examine the code.

The first line of code is the XML declaration and should always be included. It defines the XML version of the document. In this case, the document conforms to the 1.0 specification of XML.

```
<?xml version="1.0"?>
```

4. Delete the six lines of comments after the XML declaration.

You can add your own comments if you want.

5. In the `behavior_definition` element, delete the `dialogID` attribute name/value pair, change the `category` to *"Snippets"* and the `name` to *"Data Logger"*.

Note   *Attribute values must always be surrounded with quotation marks in XML documents.*

6. Delete the `properties` and `dialog` elements, including their nested elements.

You will not gather any parameters from the user. Delete the code shown in the following screenshot.

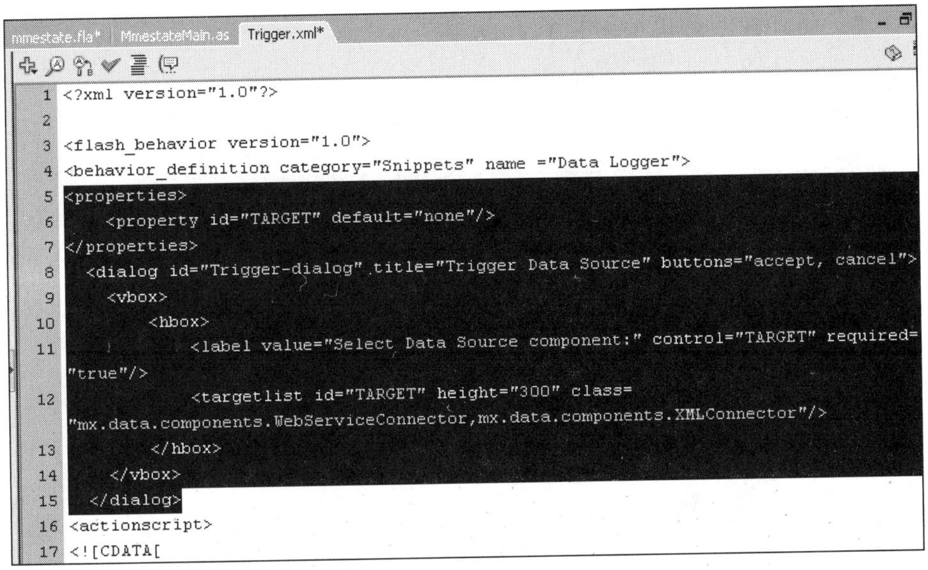

```
1  <?xml version="1.0"?>
2
3  <flash_behavior version="1.0">
4  <behavior_definition category="Snippets" name ="Data Logger">
5  <properties>
6      <property id="TARGET" default="none"/>
7  </properties>
8   <dialog id="Trigger-dialog" title="Trigger Data Source" buttons="accept, cancel">
9     <vbox>
10        <hbox>
11            <label value="Select Data Source component:" control="TARGET" required=
   "true"/>
12            <targetlist id="TARGET" height="300" class=
   "mx.data.components.WebServiceConnector,mx.data.components.XMLConnector"/>
13        </hbox>
14     </vbox>
15    </dialog>
16  <actionscript>
17  <![CDATA[
```

7. In the `actionscript` element, change the comment to the following: //Traces all
operations for data connector components and data bindings.

When the behavior is applied, this comment will appear in the code describing the purpose
of the inserted code.

8. In the `actionscript` element, delete the code `$TARGET$.trigger();` and replace
it with: `_global.__dataLogger=new mx.data.binding.Log();`.

Your `actionscript` element should appear as shown here.

```
<actionscript>
<![CDATA[
    //Traces all operations from data connector components and data ¬
    bindings
    // Macromedia 2003
    _global.__dataLogger=new mx.data.binding.Log();
]]>
</actionscript>
```

When the behavior is applied, this code is inserted. It defines a new global variable called
__dataLogger, which is an instance of the mx.data.binding.Log class. When you create an
instance of this class, all operations for the data connector component operations are traced to
the Output panel. This log information is extremely helpful when debugging applications using
data connector components. This code also traces all data-binding operations. Data binding
between components is covered in the next exercise.

9. Save the file as DataLogger.xml.

It should resemble the finished file: /fpad2004/lesson08/intermediate/DataLogger.xml, whose contents are shown in the following screenshot.

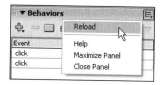

```
1  <?xml version="1.0"?>
2  <flash_behavior version="1.0">
3  <behavior_definition category="Snippets" name ="Data Logger" >
4  <actionscript>
5  <![CDATA[
6      // Traces all operations for data connector components and data bindings
7      // Macromedia 2003
8      _global.__dataLogger=new mx.data.binding.Log();
9  ]]>
10 </actionscript>
11 </behavior_definition>
12 </flash_behavior>
```

10. Return to mmestate.fla in /fpad2004/mmestate/.

Return to the file you created in the last exercise or open /fpad2004/lesson08/intermediate/ mmestate_usingbehaviors.fla and save it as *mmestate.fla* in /fpad2004/mmestate/.

11. Open the Behaviors panel. From the options menu, select Reload.

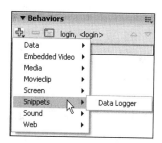

12. Click the Add Behavior button.

You should see your new Snippets category.

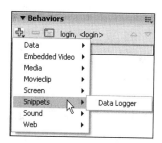

13. Select the `application` screen in the Screen Outline pane and then open the Actions panel.

You will watch the code get created when you apply the behavior.

14. In the Behaviors panel, click the Add Behavior button and select Snippets › Data Logger.

You should see the new code applied to the selected screen in the Actions panel. Note that by default, the `mousedown` event is selected for the screen.

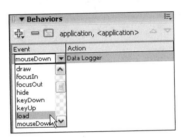

```
1
2   on (mouseDown) {
3
4       // Traces all operations for data connector components and data bindings
5       // Macromedia 2003
6       _global.__dataLogger=new mx.data.binding.Log();
7
8   }
```

15. In the Behaviors panel, click the `mousedown` event and select `load`.

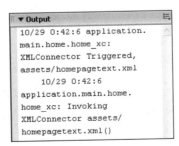

The code in the Actions panel is updated and now uses the `load` event; this code will now be executed when the application screen loads.

16. Save the file and test the application.

You should see statements about your XML connection in the Output panel.

```
▼ Output
10/29 0:42:6 application.
main.home.home_xc:
XMLConnector Triggered,
assets/homepagetext.xml
    10/29 0:42:6
application.main.home.
home_xc: Invoking
XMLConnector assets/
homepagetext.xml()
```

The finished file should resemble: /fpad2004/lesson08/intermediate/mmestate_createbehavior.fla.

Using Data Binding

Now you know how to add UI components to an application and how to add, set up, and trigger the data retrieval for a data connector component. The last step is to hook up the data retrieved from the data connector component so it is displayed in the UI components. You do this using data binding, which enables you to bind one property of a component to another (in either or both directions) so that when the value of the watched property changes, the property bound to it is automatically updated (and its display refreshed, if necessary). Data binding is the infrastructure that makes this happen automatically without you writing any code. You can specify bindings between components rapidly and without code in the FLA using the Bindings tab in the Component Inspector panel. You use the Bindings tab to add, view, and remove bindings.

To create a binding, you select a component and then click the Add Binding button.

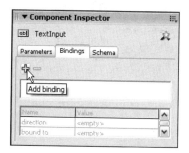

Bindable properties are the component properties that can be bound to other component properties. All bindable properties for a component appear in the Add Binding dialog box.

The properties in this dialog box are also specified as bindable in the component's code. In Lesson 5, "Creating Classes," you learned how to specify inspectable properties for a component (properties that appear as parameters in the Property inspector and Component Inspector panels) by using the [Inspectable] metadata tag in the class file. Similarly, you define bindable properties for a component using a [Bindable] metadata tag in the class file. The component properties that commonly contain dynamic data (like the text property of the TextInput component that contains the string displayed in the text field) were made bindable for the prebuilt components. All bindable properties are also listed in the Schema tab of the Component Inspector panel.

The Schema Tree pane, the top part of the Schema pane, contains a list of all the bindable properties. The Schema Attributes pane, the bottom part of the Schema pane, contains detailed information about a selected schema item. A component's schema describes the structure and type of bindable properties, but is independent of the actual data. You can edit the schema as necessary. For example, to bind results from an XMLConnector component, you need to specify a structure for the results parameter, which is an XML object. You can specify the schema by hand or you can import a sample schema (for XML files, you can import a copy of the remote XML file); a schema of the XML document's structure will be generated for you. You will create a schema using this method in this exercise.

After you specify a property for the binding in the Add Binding dialog box, the binding appears in the Binding List pane, the top part of the Bindings tab. Next, you need to specify the second property for the binding (what the property should be bound to) by clicking in the "bound to" field in the Binding Attributes pane, the lower part of the Bindings pane.

If you change the location of a component after a binding has been defined (such as by placing one or more of the components on another screen or placing a component inside a MovieClip), the bindings are dynamically updated. Remember, though, any behaviors referencing the components need to be updated; while data bindings are dynamically updated, behaviors are not.

In addition to providing the capability to copy property values from one component property to another, data binding provides an architecture for performing transformations on the data being copied. In the Binding Attributes pane, you can specify how the source property should be formatted or validated before being copied to the destination property.

Data bindings are similar to behaviors in that they provide a way to rapidly build application logic without writing any code. They differ from behaviors in that no actual code is created in the Actions panel. The binding information can be found only in the Bindings tab of the Component Inspector panel, which means that you now have application functionality contained in the FLA. To follow the application logic, you have to click each object and see what bindings exist in the Bindings tab of the Component Inspector panel for that object. Although visual data binding is great for building small applications or rapidly prototyping applications, if you are building large applications, you might want to set up bindings entirely in code.

To create data bindings via code, you use the mx.data.binding package of classes whose source code is contained in the compiled DataBindingClasses component. This process enables you to still use data binding without building the event handling to watch and update properties yourself, but also separates all your application logic from the FLA file. To use the data binding classes, you must put a copy of the DataBindingClasses component into your document's library. To do this, you open the library for classes.fla by selecting Window > Other Panels > Common Libraries > Classes and drag a copy of the DataBindingClasses component to the Stage. You can then delete the DataBindingClasses component from the Stage; the component has no runtime visual appearance. You can find more information about creating bindings with code in the Component Dictionary in the Help panel.

In this exercise you use the Bindings tab in the Component Inspector panel to bind the data from the XMLConnector component to the TextArea components on the home screen.

1. Return to mmestate.fla in /fpad2004/mmestate/.

Return to the file you created in the last exercise or open /fpad2004/lesson08/intermediate/ mmestate_createbehavior.fla and save it as *mmestate.fla* in /fpad2004/mmestate/.

2. Select the XMLConnector component on the home screen.

You will bind the results from the call to the XML file using the XMLConnector component to the relevant TextArea components.

3. Click the Schema tab in the Component Inspector panel.

You should see `params` and `results` properties. The `params` property specifies data to send to the server when retrieving the XML document; none in this example. The `results` property is the object that holds the XML data returned from the server.

Currently, these are the only two properties of the component that you can bind to any other components. Because the XML object returned is complex, you need to specify a schema for the return results so that specific node or attribute values can be bound to other components.

4. Select the `results` property and click the "Import a Schema from a sample XML file" button.

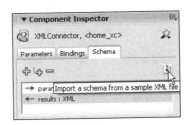

This dialog box allows you to automatically construct the schema, or structure, of the returned XML document. You could also create the schema manually using the "Add a field under the selected field" button and specifying attribute values for the field in the lower part of the Schema pane of the Component Inspector panel.

5. In the Open dialog box, browse to homepagetext.xml in /fpad2004/mmestate/assets/ and click Open.

You should now see a detailed schema for the `results` property of the XMLConnector component in the Schema pane.

Any of these specific values from the XML object can now be bound to other components.

6. Click the Bindings tab and then click the Add Binding button.

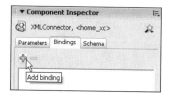

7. In the Add Binding dialog box, select provide : String and click OK.

You will bind the value in the `provide` node of the XML object (which is a String) to a TextArea component.

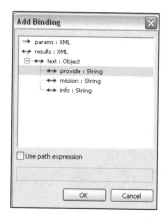

8. In the Binding Attribute pane of the Component Inspector panel, change the `direction` parameter for this binding to *out*.

The binding only needs to be one way, from the XMLConnector component to the TextInput component.

9. Double-click the text field next to the **bound to** parameter.

Now you need to specify what you want to bind to the `provide` node.

10. In the Bound To dialog box, select the **provide_ta** TextArea component on the **home** screen and click **OK**.

Note that by default, the `text` property of the TextArea component is selected. The TextArea component has only one bindable property. You will learn more about the structure of the TextArea component in Lesson 10.

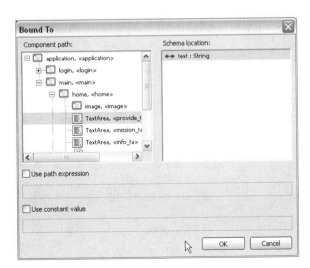

You have now created a binding between the `provide` node of the XML file to the `text` property of the `provide_ta` TextArea component. Any time the data in the `provide` node in the `results` property of the XMLConnector object changes, the value in the `text` property of the TextArea component is automatically updated.

11. Follow the same steps (Steps 6 through 10) to add a second binding which binds the `mission` node of the `results` XML object to the `mission_ta` TextArea component.

12. Follow the same steps (Steps 6 through 10) to add a third binding which binds the `info` node of the `results` XML object to the `info_ta` TextArea component.

13. Test the application. Click the Login button.

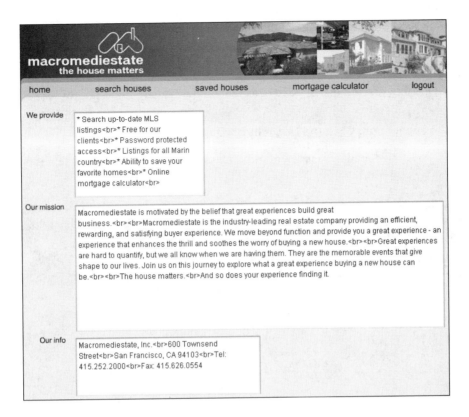

Your TextArea components should now be populated with the data from the external XML file—and you have accomplished this without adding any code. Whether you consider this a good thing or bad thing, it does have a time and place for use, so you should know how to use it. The data display at this point, however, is not the most attractive. In the next step, you change the component so it can render HTML text. You learn to further change the appearance of the components in Lessons 9 and 10.

Look at the Output panel. You should now see information about the bindings. The data binding events are traced because you created an instance of mx.data.binding.Log in your code in the last exercise, which also outputs all data binding operations.

```
▼ Output
10/29 1:11:19 application.main.home.home_xc:
XMLConnector Triggered, assets/homepagetext.xml
    10/29 1:11:19 application.main.home.home_xc:
Invoking XMLConnector assets/homepagetext.xml()
10/29 1:11:20 application.main.home.home_xc: Data of
property 'results' has changed
10/29 1:11:20 application.main.home.home_xc: Data of
property 'results' has changed
10/29 1:11:20 application.main.home.home_xc: Data of
property 'results' has changed
10/29 1:11:20 Executing binding from application.main.
home.home_xc:results:text.info to application.main.
home.info_ta:text:-
    10/29 1:11:20 Assigning new value
```

14. Return to the home screen. For each of the three TextArea components, use the Property inspector to change the `editable` parameter to *false* and the `html` parameter to *true*. Save the file.

The finished file should resemble: /fpad2004/lesson08/intermediate/mmestate_bindings.fla.

15. Test the application. Click the Login button.

Your HTML text is now rendered correctly in the TextArea components and the text is no longer editable.

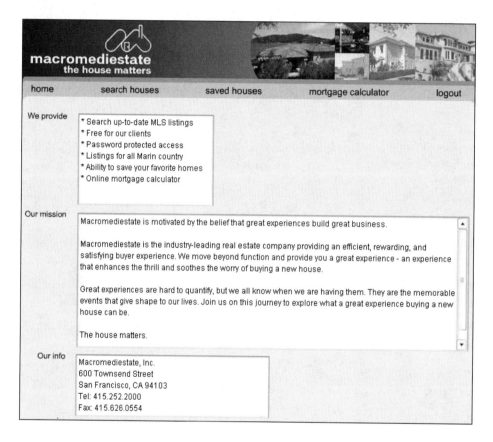

What You Have Learned

In this lesson, you have:

- Used prebuilt user interface components to build an application interface (pages 339–341)
- Retrieved external data using data connector components (pages 342–346)
- Added application functionality using prebuilt behaviors (pages 346–351)
- Created a custom behavior (pages 352–357)
- Bound together the data in components using data binding (pages 358–366)

9 Learning the UI Component Framework

In Macromedia Flash MX Professional 2004, there are twenty-one prebuilt user interface (UI) components that can be used as building blocks for application interfaces, greatly speeding the development of rich Internet applications. The UI components provide common user interface elements such as radio buttons, check boxes, drop-down boxes and so on, so that you do not have to build components with these functionalities.

In Lesson 8, "Using the Flash Application Framework," you were introduced to the UI components. You dragged them to the screen, used the Property inspector or Component Inspector panel to manipulate them, and used data binding in the authoring environment to bind them together. In this lesson, you learn the general methods for manipulating all UI components including how to respond to component events, how to set focus and tab order between the components, and how to customize the component's appearances. In Lesson 10, "Using UI Component APIs," you learn how to manipulate specific UI components using their individual APIs.

In this lesson, you work on the login and home pages of the Macromediestate application. For the login page, you disable and re-enable the Login button, write event handling code for logging

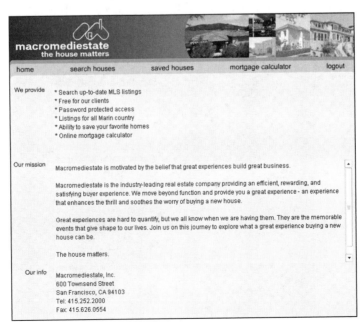

In this lesson, you customize the TextArea components on the home page.

into the application, set initial focus in the username text field, change the text properties of the button label, and change the color of the text entered in the TextInput components. For the home page, you customize the TextArea components to display without a border and with a background color that matches the application.

What You Will Learn

In this lesson, you will:

- Learn about the V2 component architecture
- Handle component events
- Manage focus and tab order for components
- Change the look of components with code
- Edit component graphics

Approximate Time

This lesson takes approximately 90 minutes to complete.

Lesson Files

Asset Files:

/fpad2004/lesson09/start/assets/homepagetext.xml

Starting Files:

/fpad2004/lesson09/start/mmestate.fla
/fpad2004/lesson09/start/classes/MmestateMain.as

Completed Files:

/fpad2004/lesson09/complete/mmestate.fla
/fpad2004/lesson09/complete/classes/MmestateLogin.as
/fpad2004/lesson09/complete/classes/MmestateApp.as

Introducing UI Component Basics

Components were first introduced in Flash MX; in Flash MX 2004, components have been re-architected and now have a more robust and extensible architecture for working with prebuilt components and for building your own. All the components (including the screen objects you used in the last lesson) extend the UIObject and UIComponent classes: MovieClip > UIObject > UIComponent. The following screenshot shows the overall component architecture.

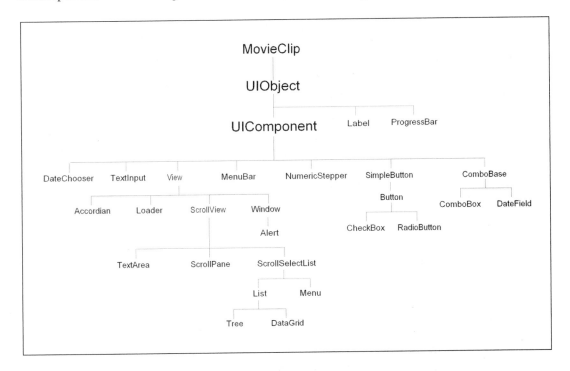

Because all the components are based on the same base classes, the first component adds about 25K to your application size that is not added again as you add additional components. Hence, if you are using only one component in your application, it might not make sense to use a prebuilt V2 architecture component, but it does as soon as you use several components. In addition to providing prebuilt functionality, the prebuilt components also provide a consistent user experience. The UI controls all work similarly and have the same styles (which you learn to customize later in this lesson).

From the authoring environment you add precompiled versions of the UI components to your applications. To aid in building your own components and applications, the class files for the components are included with Flash and are located in the Classes folder in the First Run and the user-specific Configuration folders. The source FLAs that contain the graphics for each of the components are located in the ComponentFLA folder.

Note *Most of the V2 components require Flash Player version 6.0.79 or higher. The media, DataSet, XUpdateResolver, and RDBMSResolver components require Flash Player 7 or higher.*

UIObject

The UIObject class (mx.core.UIObject) directly extends the MovieClip class and is the base class for all components. It provides additional functionality over the MovieClip class for implementing styles, broadcasting events, and scaling. It also hides the MovieClip class API defining an API that is not tied to the Timeline, which many application developers do not need to use or even be familiar with. As a result, there are often two properties or methods (one from the MovieClip class and one from the UIObject class) that can be used to accomplish the same task. Although you can use either class member, it is considered a best practice to use the UIObject member instead of the analogous MovieClip member when working with component instances. The following properties, methods, and events of the UIObject class are available to and commonly used by all components.

Properties. Common read-only properties include those for retrieving the component's size and position: x, y, `height`, `width`, `left`, `right`, `top`, and `bottom`. In order to set any of these values, you need to use the appropriate method (see the following methods section); you should not use the analogous MovieClip properties. You can also get or set the scale of the component using `scaleX` and `scaleY` and set the visibility (which you set for individual screens last lesson) using the `visible` property.

Methods. Common methods include those for moving the component: `move()`, setting its size: `setSize()`, and setting or getting a style property for it: `setStyle()` and `getStyle()`. You set component styles using these methods later in this lesson. There are also methods for dynamically creating and destroying components that will be covered in Lesson 11, "Creating Visual Objects Dynamically." Another method commonly used for all components is `addEventListener()`, which is actually a method of the UIEventDispatcher class, which works with the UIObject class; it registers an object to listen for events broadcast by a component instance. You learn more about event handling in the following exercises.

Events. Common events include: hide, load, move, resize, reveal, and unload. You used several of these in the last lesson. The load and unload events refer to when the object is actually loaded into the Player whereas the reveal and hide events refer to when the visibility of the component is changed.

UIComponent

The UIComponent class (mx.core.UIComponent) extends the UIObject class and is a base class for all components that have any interaction with the user. It provides additional functionality for receiving focus and keyboard input, enabling and disabling user-interaction with components, and resizing components by sizing and positioning internal components.

Properties. The UIComponent class has two properties available to all UI components: `enabled` for setting whether an instance can receive focus and user input and `tabIndex` for setting the tab order used when a user tabs through the application.

Methods. The UIComponent class has two methods available to all UI components: `setFocus()` for setting the instance that has focus and `getFocus()` for getting the instance that has focus.

Events. The UIComponent class has four additional events that can be broadcast to listeners: `focusIn`, `focusOut`, `keyDown`, and `keyUp`.

All the members of the UIObject and UIComponent classes can be found in the Using Components book in the Help panel. The classes are not listed in the Actions toolbox, though many of their members are listed under each of the individual component entries.

In this exercise, you use several of the properties and methods of the base component classes for a component instance. First, you use several positioning properties and methods. Second, you add functionality to disable the Login button until text has been entered in both input text fields.

1. Return to mmestate.fla in /fpad2004/mmestate/.

This is the file you created in the last lesson. If you did not do that exercise, open /fpad2004/lesson09/ start/mmestate.fla and save it as */fpad2004/mmestate/mmestate.fla*.

2. Select the `login` screen and open the Actions panel.

In this exercise, you are going to add your code to the FLA. In the next exercise, you learn more about the component event handling model and then move the code for the `login` screen to an external class file.

In the Actions panel's Script Navigator, expand the selection for the `login` screen. You should see code on the `login_pb` button.

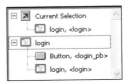

3. Create a `load` event handler on the `login` screen.

```
on(load){}
```

4. Inside the event handler, set the x property of the `login` screen to *300*. Trace the x value before and after you set it. Test the application.

```
trace(this.x);
this.x=300;
trace(this.x);
```

The `login` screen's position should not have moved and you should get a value of 0 for both traces; you cannot set this read-only property.

One way to change the position of the `login` screen is to change your code to set the **_x** property instead of the **x** property. This code would use the MovieClip API to set the _x property directly, which also sets the UIObjects' x property. It is not a good practice, however, to bypass the UIComponent API; instead, you should use the UIObject method, `move()`.

5. Change your code to use the `move()` method to set the x property. Test the application.

```
this.move(300,0);
```

The `login` screen's position should be moved and you should get a value of 300 for the second trace of x.

6. Delete the existing code inside the event handler. Replace it with a function called *setLoginState* that has no parameters and no return value.

```
function setLoginState():Void{}
```

You will use this function to enable and disable the Login button.

7. Inside the function, set the **enabled** property of `login_pb` to *false*.

This is a property of the UIComponent class.

```
login_pb.enabled=false;
```

8. Surround this statement inside the function with conditional logic so that the button is disabled if the **text** property of either TextInput component is blank.

```
1  on(load)
2  {
3      function setLoginState():Void
4      {
5          if(username_ti.text=="" || password_ti.text=="")
6          {
7              login_pb.enabled=false;
8          }
9      }
10 }
```

9. Add an `else` block to re-enable the button.

```
else
{
        login_pb.enabled=true;
}
```

10. After the function definition, call the function to initially disable the Login button.

```
setLoginState();
```

11. Save the file and test the application.

The Login button is disabled and you cannot click it.

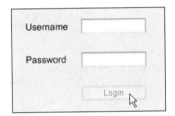

Enter text in both text fields. Right now, the button never becomes re-enabled. In the next exercise, you learn how to programmatically call your `setLoginState()` function when text has been entered in the text fields.

You will use this file as the starting file for the next exercise. It should resemble the finished file: /fpad2004/lesson09/intermediate/mmestate_baseclasses.fla.

Handling UI Component Events

Some events common to all components were introduced in the last exercise. These included `hide`, `load`, `move`, `resize`, `reveal`, `unload`, `focusIn`, `focusOut`, `keyDown`, and `keyUp`. In addition, many components have additional component-specific events. For example, the Button comment has a `click` event. Component specific events are introduced with each component's API in Lesson 11.

There are several ways you can handle component events: You can place code directly on a component in the FLA, or you can register a function or an object as listeners for the component events.

Using Events on Component Instances

You can place code inside the FLA directly on an object using the `on(eventname)` syntax introduced for MovieClips in Lesson 4, "Creating Buttons and MovieClip Objects," and used for screens in Lesson 7, "Building Applications with Screens."

```
on(load)
{
    [code to execute]
}
```

An event object parameter called `eventObj` is always passed to the event handler. It has two properties you can reference inside the event handler, `type` and `target`, which refer to the name of the event fired and the name of the component broadcasting the event, respectively.

Registering a Function as an Event Listener

You need a different way of handling events once you place your code in the Timeline or in an external class file. In these places, you specify listener objects for specific events. Each component **broadcasts** events when they occur to any object **registered** as a **listener**. A listener can be a function or a method of an object that is called when an event is broadcast.

To register the listener object to listen for events broadcast by a specific component, you use the `addEventListener()` method, a method of the mx.events.UIEventDispatcher class that works with the UIObject class. The `addEventListener()` method take two arguments, the first is the name of the event that you want the listener object to listen for and the second is the listener object. You must define the listener object and its event handler before you register it as a listener for the component.

In the following code, a function is specified as a listener for `my_component` using `addEventListener()`.

```
function myHandler():Void
{
    [code to execute]
}
my_component.addEventListener("load", myHandler);
```

Using this method, you can assign the same function to handle multiple events from the same component or events from multiple components. In a class file, the function you specify as the second argument can also be a method of the class.

To prevent your callback functions from being confused with or conflicting with any of Flash built-in events and event callbacks (many of which start with "on"), use the following best practices:

1. Don't start your function name with the word "on."

2. Don't name your function the same name as the event.

Additionally, some developers recommend using a name that is a combination of the component name and the event name.

In this exercise, you return to the code in the `login` screen and add event handlers so that when the user enters text in the text fields, the `setLoginState()` function is called to check and see if the Login button should be re-enabled. To do this, you register the `setLoginState()` function as a listener for the `keyUp` event of the TextInput components. After you have this code working, you move it to an external class file.

1. Return to mmestate.fla in /fpad2004/mmestate/.

Return to the file you created in the last exercise or open /fpad2004/lesson09/intermediate/ mmestate_baseclasses.fla and save it as *mmestate.fla* in /fpad2004/mmestate/.

2. Return to the code for the **login** screen. At the end of the code inside the event handler, assign the function **setLoginState()** to be a listener for the **keyUp** event for the **username_ti** component.

```
1  on(load)
2  {
3      function setLoginState():Void
4      {
5          if(username_ti.text=="" || password_ti.text=="")
6          {
7              login_pb.enabled=false;
8          }
9          else
10         {
11             login_pb.enabled=true;
12         }
13     }
14     setLoginState();
15     username_ti.addEventListener("keyUp",setLoginState);
16 }
```

The `keyUp` event is an event for the UIComponent class available to all UI components. It is fired whenever the user releases a key inside the text field.

3. Assign the function **setLoginState()** to also be a listener for the **keyUp** event for the **password_ti** component.

```
password_ti.addEventListener("keyUp",setLoginState);
```

4. Save the file and test the application. Enter text in both fields.

As soon as you enter text in both fields, the Login button should become re-enabled.

Your working file should resemble the file: /fpad2004/lesson09/intermediate/ mmestate_functionlistener_intermediate.fla.

5. Create a new ActionScript file and save it as *MmestateLogin.as* in /fpad2004/ mmestate/classes/.

You are going to place all the code associated with the login screen in an associated class file. In the next exercise, you also move the code associated with the Login button to this class file so that it contains all the logic for the login interface.

6. Define a class called MmestateLogin that extends mx.screens.Form and has an empty constructor.

```
class MmestateLogin extends mx.screens.Form
{
        function MmestateLogin(){}
}
```

7. Return to the code on the `login` screen in mmestate.fla and cut the `setLoginState()` function to the Clipboard. Return to MmestateLogin.as and paste the function inside the class definition after the constructor.

Make sure you do not place it inside the constructor. This function is now a method of the class.

```
 1 class MmestateLogin extends mx.screens.Form
 2 {
 3       function MmestateLogin()
 4       {
 5       }
 6       function setLoginState():Void
 7       {
 8           if(username_ti.text=="" || password_ti.text=="")
 9           {
10               login_pb.enabled=false;
11           }
12           else
13           {
14               login_pb.enabled=true;
15           }
16       }
17 }
```

8. Make the function a *private* method of the class.

```
private function setLoginState():Void{}
```

9. Return to the code on the `login` screen in mmestate.fla and cut the remaining code inside the `load` event handler to the Clipboard. Delete the load handler.

There should not be any code attached to the `login` screen.

10. Return to MmestateLogin.as and paste the code inside the constructor.

You can also prefix the call to the `setLoginState()` method with `this`.

11. Above the constructor, define the following private properties: `login_pb` of type *mx.controls.Button* and `username_ti` and `password_ti` of type *mx.controls.TextInput*.

```
private var login_pb:mx.controls.Button;
private var username_ti:mx.controls.TextInput;
private var password_ti:mx.controls.TextInput;
```

This code defines the visual elements as properties so that you do not get errors when the class file is compiled. It also enables code-hinting for the Button and TextInput components in the class file.

Note *In order for code-hinting to work, you must define your properties on separate lines. You will not get code hints if you combine the property declarations in one statement separated by commas.*

To avoid having to include the full package names of the Button and TextInput classes, you can also explicitly import the mx.controls package before the class definition, which allows you to reference all the UI components in the class file by their simple class names.

```
import mx.controls.*;
private var login_pb:Button, username_ti:TextInput, password_ti: TextInput;
```

12. Click the Check Syntax button to make sure you have no errors in the file and then save the file.

It will save you a lot of time if you always make sure your class compiles before trying to link it to a screen.

13. Return to mmestate.fla. Select the `login` screen in the Screen Outline pane. Click the Properties tab in the Property inspector and set the screen's class name to *MmestateLogin*. Press the Enter/Return key.

You have moved all the code associated with the `login` screen to an associated class file. You will move the code associated with the Login *button* to this class file as well in the next exercise so that the class file contains all the logic for the login interface.

14. Save the file and test the application.

The finished file should resemble: /fpad2004/lesson09/intermediate/mmestate_functionlistener.fla.

Your application no longer works correctly; the Login button is no longer initially disabled. Why not? There are actually two problems. The first is quite subtle: The components nested inside the login screen have not loaded yet when the code inside the constructor for the login screen is executed. To fix this, you need to change it so that the code is not executed until all the contents of the screen have been loaded. You do this by placing the code inside a callback function for the load event of the screen. The second problem is one of scope; you examine this later in this exercise.

15. Return to MmestateLogin.as. Create a new private method called *loginLoad*. Cut all the code from inside the constructor and paste it inside `loginLoad()`.

```
11    private function loginLoad():Void
12    {
13        setLoginState();
14        username_ti.addEventListener("keyUp",setLoginState)
15        password_ti.addEventListener("keyUp",setLoginState)
16    }
```

In this case, you definitely don't want to name your method load because the Loader class from which the Screen class inherits has a `load()` method that is automatically invoked during the instantiation process. If you create a `load()` method and register it a listener for the screen's load event, the `load()` method will run twice when the screen is loaded.

Note *You could also place the code inside a method called onLoad, which would be called automatically without using addEventListener() because it is a built-in event for the MovieClip class. This, however, is not a best practice because the time that the onLoad callback is invoked varies. (Using the onLoad directly also bypasses the screen class interface).*

16. Inside the constructor, assign the `loginLoad()` method to be the listener for the screen's `load` event.

```
this.addEventListener("load",loginLoad);
```

17. Inside the `setLoginState()` method, trace `this`.

```
19    private function setLoginState():Void
20    {
21        trace(this);
22        if(username_ti.text=="" || password_ti.text==""
23        {
```

Make sure you do not place the `trace()` statement inside the `if` statement. You are using this `trace()` statement to test the scope inside the method when it is called.

18. Click the Check Syntax button to make sure you have no errors in the file and then save the file.

The finished file should resemble: /fpad2004/lesson09/intermediate/classes/ MmestateLogin_functionlistener.as.

19. Return to mmestate.fla and test the application.

Enter text in both of the fields. Your button does not become enabled as it should. Look at the name of the TextInput component traced to the Output panel. The scope inside the `setLoginState()` method is now that of the calling component, not the screen itself.

You might think a solution to the problem is to preface all of the components inside the `setLoginState()` method with `_parent`. This will work when text is entered in the text fields. It will not work, however, for the first call to the `setLoginState()` method from within the constructor because the scope in that case is the screen itself, not one of the components so the `_parent` references would be incorrect. One solution is to rewrite your code so you don't initially call the `setLoginState()` method. A second solution is to reference the method differently as the event callback so that the scope of the method is the screen instead of an individual component. You do this in the next exercise.

Using an Object as an Event Listener

Instead of specifying a function as the listener for the `addEventListener()` method, you can also specify an object. This is a more flexible technique because you can create multiple methods of the same object to handle different events.

You can use an existing object (such as a component or screen instance) as the listener object or you can create a new object. There are two ways the object can respond to events: The object must either have a property with the same name as the component's event you want it to listen for, or the object must have a property called `handleEvent`. Code for the first method in which the listener object has a property with the same name as the event is shown here:

```
var listener:Object=new Object();
listener.load=function():Void
{
        [code to execute]
};
```

You then use the `addEventListener()` method to register the listener object to listen for events broadcast by a specific component, just as you did when registering a function. Instead of specifying the function name as the second argument, though, you specify the name of the listener object.

```
my_component.addEventListener("load",listener);
```

You can also specify a single argument for the callback function to hold an event object, which automatically gets passed to the event handler. Just as you saw when placing events directly on a component, the event object has two properties, type and target, which refer to the name of the event fired and the name of the component broadcasting the event, respectively.

```
listener.load=function(evtObj):Void
{
        trace(evtObj.type+" "+ evtObj.target);
};
```

You need to be careful using this method, however, if you use a component as the listener object. The component might already have a method with the same name as the event (which is the case for the load event for the Loader class). A better solution is to define a handleEvent property for the listener object.

If a listener object has a handleEvent property, the callback function for that property is invoked whenever *any* event fires that the listener object is registered for. You handle multiple events with one callback function. Inside the callback, you use conditional logic to respond based on which event was fired. Instead of having all the handler code in-line in the handleEvent callback, you can call other functions for each event; the handleEvent callback acts as a dispatcher for other functions or methods.

Note *Macromedia's recommendation for event handling is to use a listener object with a* handleEvent *property that acts as an event dispatcher to other functions.*

In the following code, the handleEvent callback function is invoked whenever the reveal or the load event for the component my_component fires.

```
listener:Object=new Object();
listener.handleEvent=function(evtObj:Object):Void
{
        switch (evtObj.type)
        {
                case "load":
                        [code to execute or function to call]
                        break;
                case "reveal":
                        [code to execute or function to call]
                        break;
        }
}
my_component.addListener("reveal",listener);
my_component.addListener("load",listener);
```

> **Note** *There is one additional way to handle events. You can specify a property of the component with the same name as the event plus the string "Handler." The callback function is automatically invoked and you do not have to use addEventListener() to explicitly specify a listener. For example, to create an event handler to be executed when a component loads, create a property for the component called loadHandler.*

In this exercise, you work with the class file associated with the login screen. First, you get your code from the last exercise working so that the keyUp event handling works again. Next, you replace the behaviors on the Login button in the FLA that set screen visibilities with your own event handling code in the login screen class file. Finally, you add a reveal event handler to clear the password text field every time the user logs out.

1. Return to MmestateLogin.as in /fpad2004/mmestate/classes/.

Return to the file you created in the last exercise or open /fpad2004/lesson09/intermediate/classes/ MmestateLogin_functionlistener.as and save it as *MmestateLogin.as* in /fpad2004/mmestate/classes/.

2. After the constructor, create a new private method called handleEvent with one parameter called evtObj of type *Object* and no return value.

```
private function handleEvent(evtObj:Object):Void
{
}
```

3. Inside the handleEvent() method, create an if statement that checks if the type property of evtObj is equal to the string *load*. If it is, call the loginLoad() method.

```
if(evtObj.type=="load")
{
        loginLoad();
}
```

4. In the constructor, change the listener for the load event from the loginLoad() method to the screen object (this).

this.addEventListener("load",this);

5. Inside the `handleEvent()` method, create a second `if` statement that checks if the `type` property of `evtObj` is equal to the string *keyUp*. If it is, call the `setLoginState()` method.

```
12        private function handleEvent(evtObj:Object)
13        {
14            if (evtObj.type=="load")
15            {
16                loginLoad();
17            }
18            if (evtObj.type=="keyUp")
19            {
20                setLoginState();
21            }
22        }
```

6. In the `loginLoad()` method, change the code assigning listeners to the TextInput controls so that the listener is `this`, the `login` screen, instead of the `setLoginState()` function.

```
username_ti.addEventListener("keyUp",this);
password_ti.addEventListener("keyUp",this);
```

When the `keyUp` event fires, the `handleEvent()` method is invoked.

7. Return to mmestate.fla in /fpad2004/mmestate/and test the application.

Return to the file you created in the last exercise or open /fpad2004/lesson09/intermediate/ mmestate_functionlistener.fla and save it as *mmestate.fla* in /fpad2004/mmestate/.

The Login button should now be initially disabled again. The code inside the `loginLoad()` method is called when the `load` event for the `login` screen fires. Enter code in both of the text fields. The Login button is re-enabled; when the `keyUp` event is fired, the `login` screen instance that is listening for the event responds.

Look at the Output panel; you should now see the name of the screen and not one of the TextInput components displayed. The scope inside the event callback function differs depending on how you specify it as a listener: either directly as a function or as a property of an listener object.

8. Return to mmestate.fla. Select the `login_pb` button on the `login` screen and then open the Actions panel.

You should see all the code that was added to the button when you added behaviors to it last lesson. These behaviors hid the `login` screen and showed the `main` screen when the button was clicked.

9. Open the Behaviors panel. Select the first behavior attached to the button and click the Delete Behavior button.

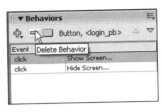

Most of the code should disappear from the Actions panel.

10. Delete the remaining button behavior. Save the file.

There should be no code left in the Actions panel.

The finished file should resemble: /fpad2004/lesson09/intermediate/mmestate_objectlistener.fla.

11. Return to MmestateLogin.as. Inside the `loginLoad()` method, assign the class instance associated with the `login` screen (which is `this`) to be a listener for the `click` event for the `login_pb` Button component.

```
24    private function loginLoad():Void
25    {
26        setLoginState();
27        username_ti.addEventListener("keyUp",this);
28        password_ti.addEventListener("keyUp",this);
29        login_pb.addEventListener("click",this);
30    }
```

This code *must* be inside the `load` event handler for the screen. Otherwise, the Button subcomponent will not yet exist.

12. Create a *private* method called `login_pbClick` with no parameters or return value.

```
private function login_pbClick():Void{}
```

13. Inside the `login_pbClick()` method, set the `visible` property of the `login` screen to *false* and the `main` screen to *true*. Use appropriate relative references. Save the file.

```
this.visible=false;
_parent.main.visible=true;
```

Because the method is called as a property of the listener object and not directly as the method, the scope inside the callback will be the screen and not the component.

14. Inside the `handleEvent()` method, create a third `if` statement that checks if the `type` property of `evtObj` is equal to the string *click*. If it is, call the `loginClick()` method.

```
if(evtObj.type=="click")
{
        login_pbClick();
}
```

If you want, you can replace your multiple `if` statements with a `switch`/`case` construct.

15. Return to mmestate.fla and test the application. Enter text in both text fields and click the Login button.

The `login` screen should disappear and you should see the `main` screen (and the home screen because its initial visibility is set to true). The navigation code is no longer embedded as a behavior in the FLA but is now contained in the class file.

16. Click the Logout button.

You are returned to the `login` screen, but the text fields are still populated with the values you entered previously. This is not good; you need to clear the password field.

17. Return to MmestateLogin.as. Inside the constructor, register the screen instance to be a listener for its `reveal` event.

```
7     function MmestateLogin()
8     {
9         this.addEventListener("load",this);
10        this.addEventListener("reveal",this);
11    }
```

Note the two different ways used to register callbacks for the reveal and load events.

18. Create a private method called `loginReveal` with no parameters or return value.

```
private function loginReveal ():Void{}
```

19. Inside the `loginReveal()` method, set the password text field equal to an empty string.

```
password_ti.text="";
```

The code to clear the password text field needs to be in a `reveal` handler and not a `load` handler, because it needs to execute every time the screen becomes visible—not just once when the screen initially loads.

20. Move the line of code calling the `setLoginState()` method from inside the `loginLoad()` method to inside the `loginReveal()` method after you clear the password.

```
37    private function loginReveal():Void
38    {
39        password_ti.text="";
40        setLoginState();
41    }
```

You want the Login button to be disabled every time the `login` screen is made visible, *not* just the first time it is loaded.

21. Inside the `handleEvent()` method, create a fourth `if` statement that checks if the `type` property of `evtObj` is equal to the string *reveal*. If it is, call the `loginReveal()` method.

```
if(evtObj.type=="reveal")
{
    loginReveal();
}
```

22. Remove the `trace()` from inside the `setLoginState()` method. Save the file.

You are done testing scopes.

The finished file should resemble: /fpad2004/lesson09/intermediate/classes/ MmestateLogin_objectlistener.as.

23. Return to mmestate.fla and test the application. Enter text in both fields and click the Login button and then click the logout button.

The password text field should now be cleared of the value you entered and the Login button should be disabled again.

Managing Focus between Components

What if you want to set which component initially has focus and/or change the order in which the user can tab between the components? Flash's new component architecture implements a FocusManager class (mx.managers.FocusManager), which takes care of focus automatically. It keeps track of the currently focused item and how the focus changes based on user events including various keystrokes and mouse-clicks. It uses the Selection class built in to the Flash Player (which you used in Lesson 5, "Creating Classes," to give focus to fields in the mortgage calculator). By default, no form field has initial focus and the tab order is set by the stacking order of the components on the Stage. You can use the FocusManager class API to customize this default behavior.

An instance of the FocusManager class called `focusManager` is automatically created when you add a component to the application. It is created at the document root. If you are referencing the `focusManager` with code not located on the main document Timeline (such as from inside a MovieClip, a screen, or code attached to one of these objects), you can use an absolute reference to the `_root` or `_level0` scope or you can use the `getFocusManager()` method to retrieve the instance. Both of the following lines of code will retrieve the active FocusManager class instance.

```
trace(_root.focusManger);
trace(getFocusManager());
```

Note   *You can have multiple instances of the FocusManager class if you create multiple windows using the mx.managers.PopUpManager class, which gives you the ability to create modal or non-modal overlapping windows. (If a window is modal, you cannot interact with any of the other windows while it has focus.) You can find more information on the PopUpManager class in the Using Components book in the Help panel.*

Assigning Focus

To assign focus to a particular component, you use the FocusManager class `setFocus()` method with one argument—the name of the component you want to set focus to.

```
focusManager.setFocus(my_component);
```

There is also a partner `getFocus()` method that you can use to retrieve the object that currently has focus.

Note   *When testing a SWF in the authoring environment, you will not see the I-beam cursor in a text field component even if you have given it focus. The field does, though, have focus and you can type text in it without first having to click in the field.*

Setting the Tab Order

In a Flash application, when a user presses the Tab key to navigate, the FocusManager class determines which component receives focus. By default, the FocusManager class assigns the tab order based on the order that the components were placed on the Stage. The assigned order is based on the depth or stacking order of the objects; items placed on the Stage first have a lower depth (unless you change their stacking order using the options under Modify > Arrange, such as the option Send to Back). If you are using a form-based application and have components in multiple screens displayed, tabbing will start on the lowest depth screen (the one highest up in the Screen Outline pane) and then sequentially move through components on the other screens.

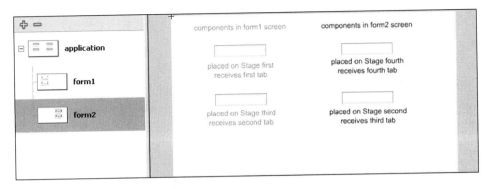

You can change the order in which focus moves between components several ways. You can change the order with code at runtime by setting the `tabIndex` property for all components that should receive focus. When a user presses the Tab key, the `focusManager` instance looks for an enabled object with a `tabIndex` property that is higher than the current value of `tabIndex`. Once the `focusManager` reaches the highest `tabIndex` property, it returns to zero (or the lowest tab index number assigned).

```
my_textInput1.tabIndex=0;
my_textInput2.tabIndex=1;
my_button.tabIndex=2;
```

You can also set the tab order at author time using the Accessibility panel—Select Window > Other Panels > Accessibility. You then have to select each component on the Stage and assign it a tab index value between 1 and 66535 in the Accessibility panel.

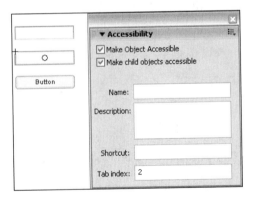

When you tab to a component giving it focus, a ring is shown around the component. This "halo" effect is discussed in greater detail later in this lesson.

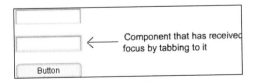

Enabling Automatic Form Submittal

You can also use the FocusManager class to enable a form to be submitted when the user presses Enter (Windows) or Return (Macintosh) instead of explicitly having to click the Button component. To do this, you set the `defaultPushButton` property equal to the instance name of the desired Button component. A `click` event for the default component is broadcast whenever the Return or Enter key is pressed.

```
focusManager.defaultPushButton=submitButton;
```

When you test your FLA in the authoring environment, you must select Control > Disable Keyboard Shortcuts for the default button to work. It will always work fine if you publish the application and view it in a browser window.

> **Note** *When you assign a Button component to be the default button, the button border is highlighted, indicating it is the default button. This highlighting is part of the Halo design (which is discussed later in this lesson) and is not the focus glow you see when you tab to a component. You have to modify the button skin or subclass the button to turn off this highlighting. Modifying graphics skins is covered in a later exercise. If you subclass the button, you need to disable the emphasized state of the button so that it is never true.*

In this exercise, you set the initial focus on the `login` screen to the username TextInput component. You investigate and change the tabbing order between the components.

1. Return to mmestate.fla and test the application.

Return to the file you used in the last exercise or open /fpad2004/lesson09/intermediate/ mmestate_objectlistener.fla and save it as *mmestate.fla* in /fpad2004/mmestate/.

You do not see the I-beam cursor in any of the text fields. Type some letters. The letters do not appear in any of the text fields. Right now, you have to manually click in one of the text fields before you can add text to it.

2. Return to MmestateLogin.as in /fpad2004/mmestate/classes/.

Return to the file you created in the last exercise or open /fpad2004/lesson09/intermediate/classes/ MmestateLogin_objectlistener.as and save it as *MmestateLogin.as* in /fpad2004/mmestate/classes/.

3. Inside the `loginReveal()` method, use the `setFocus()` method of the `focusManager` object to set focus in the `username_ti` component. Save the file.

```
37    private function loginReveal():Void
38    {
39        getFocusManager().setFocus(username_ti);
40        password_ti.text="";
41        setLoginState();
42    }
```

You need to use the getFocusManager() method to reference the focusManager instance because this code is not in the _root or main document Timeline where the focusManager instance is created.

4. Return to mmestate.fla and test the application.

Even though you have set focus to the username text field, you do not see the I-beam cursor in the field. Go ahead and type anyway without clicking in the field. Your text should appear. The text field has focus, the I-beam cursor is just not displayed when you test your application from within the authoring environment.

5. Press the Tab key.

If nothing happens, you need to disable keyboard shortcuts in the testing environment.

6. If tabbing did not work, select Control › Disable Keyboard Shortcuts.

This menu item is only visible when viewing SWFs in the authoring environment and should always be turned off when testing applications; otherwise all kinds of keyboard functionality will not work.

7. Tab between the two components. Enter text into both text fields and then tab between the three components.

The FocusManager class automatically enables tabbing between the components with the tab order set by the components' depth on the Stage; in this case, their depths were set by the order you dragged them to the screen. Also notice that a green "halo" appears around a component when you tab to it. This is part of the Halo theme that has been applied to the components; you learn more about themes and the Halo theme later in this lesson.

8. Return to MmestateLogin.as. Inside the loginLoad() method, set the tabIndex property for the username_ti component to 1.

```
username_ti.tabIndex=1;
```

9. Set the tabIndex property of password_ti to 0 and that for login_pb to 2. Save the file.

The tabbing order is currently correct because you placed the components on the Stage in the correct order. You are temporarily changing the tab order so that you get experience setting tab order with the focusManager.

10. Return to mmestate.fla and test the application.

Enter text in both text fields and then tab between the three components. The tabbing order is now reversed.

11. Return to MmestateLogin.as and delete the `tabIndex` properties you assigned in Steps 8 and 9. Save the file.

The file should resemble: /fpad2004/lesson09/intermediate/classes/MmestateLogin_focus.as.

Changing the Look of Components with Code

You can change the appearance of components in your user interface by using code or by editing the underlying graphics. Using ActionScript, you can change the color and formatting of the components. For example, you can change the background color of a TextInput component, the size of the font on a Button component, and so on. If you want to make more drastic changes to the components, you can also skin them, changing the actual graphic symbols (or in some cases the class file code which creates the graphic symbols), which make up the components.

Using ActionScript, you can set styles for individual components, a group of component instances, all instances of one type of component, or all components in a document. If you set styles for a component in more than one place, the order of the style precedence is shown here.

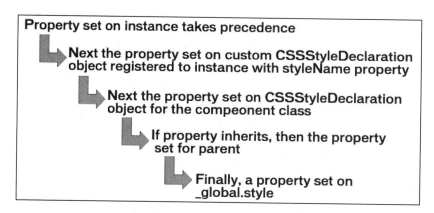

Property set on instance takes precedence

    Next the property set on custom CSSStyleDeclaration object registered to instance with styleName property

        Next the property set on CSSStyleDeclaration object for the compeonent class

            If property inherits, then the property set for parent

                Finally, a property set on _global.style

Setting Style Properties for Component Instance

You customize the appearance of a particular component instance using the UIObject `setStyle()` method, which is available for all the UI components. You specify the property and the desired value of the property as arguments to the method:

```
my_component.setStyle("property", value);
```

The style properties supported by the components are based on a subset of the Cascading Style Sheets specification of the W3C, and include font styles, border colors, and many more. The StyleManager class (mx.styles.StyleManager) keeps track of the styles and colors you can apply to a given component as properties of that component. You can find many of these styles listed in the /First Run/Classes/mx/styles/StyleManager.as class file. Others are defined in the individual component class files.

The available properties for customizing component text with their default values in parentheses are: color (black), fontFamily (_sans), fontSize (10), fontStyle (normal; other option is italic), fontWeight (normal; other option is bold), marginLeft (0), marginRight (0), textAlign (left), textDecoration (none; other option is underlined), and textIndent (0).

There are additional properties that set the appearance (colors, borders, and so on) of the UI components. Some properties are general and apply to most of the UI components. Others are specific to individual UI components. See the Using Components book in the Help panel for complete lists of properties for individual components. Here are some examples of additional style properties: borderColor (black), the color of a section of the border around components; shadowColor (dark gray), the color of the border shadow around components; borderStyle (solid; other options are none, inset, or outset), the kind of component border to use for the component; scrollTrackColor (light gray), the color of the scroll track for a scroll bar.

Note *Remember that colors are specified as hexadecimal numbers in the format: 0xFFCC00. The six characters following the "0x" are the hex codes for color in HTML.*

In this exercise, you change the appearance of the Login button, making the label text larger and bold.

1. Create a new ActionScript file and save it as *MmestateApp.as* in /fpad2004/mmestate/ classes/.

You are going to place all the code that sets styles for any object in the application in a class file associated with the application screen. This is a good practice, so that you can see all the styles you set for all objects in one place. It also makes your code much easier to debug.

2. Define a class called *MmestateApp* that extends *mx.screens.Form* with an empty constructor. Save the file.

```
class MmestateApp extends mx.screens.Form
{
        function MmestateApp(){}
}
```

3. Return to mmestate.fla in /fpad2004/mmestate/.

Return to the file you used in the last exercise or open /fpad2004/lesson09/intermediate/ mmestate_objectlistener.fla and save it as *mmestate.fla* in /fpad2004/mmestate/.

4. Select the `application` screen and open the Actions panel. Cut the line of code enabling data binding debugging and delete the rest.

```
2  on (load) {
3
4      // Traces all operations for data connector components
    and data bindings
5      // Macromedia 2003
6      _global.__dataLogger=new mx.data.binding.Log();
7
8  }
```

There should be no code left inside the FLA associated with the `application` screen. You will move this code to the class file.

5. Select the `application` screen in the Screen Outline pane. Click the Properties tab in the Property inspector and set the screen's class name to *MmestateApp*. Press Enter/Return. Save the file.

It should resemble the finished file: /fpad2004/lesson09/intermediate/mmestate_instancestyle.fla.

6. Return to MmestateApp.as and paste the code you cut in Step 4 inside the constructor.

There should be the one line of code.

7. Inside the constructor, define the class instance to listen for its own `load` events.

```
this.addEventListener("load",this);
```

8. After the constructor, create a new method called `handleEvent` with one parameter called `evtObj` of type *Object* and no return value.

```
private function handleEvent(evtObj:Object):Void
{
}
```

9. Inside the `handleEvent()` method, create an `if` statement that checks if the `type` property of `evtObj` is equal to the string *load*. If it is, call the method `appLoad()`.

```
if(evtObj.type=="load")
{
        appLoad();
}
```

10. Create a private method called `appLoad()`.

Give it no parameters and no return value.

11. Inside the `appLoad()` method, set the font size of the `login_pb` button to *14*. Use the UIObject `setStyle()` method and the `fontSize` property.

```
login.login_pb.setStyle("fontSize",14);
```

This is code associated with the `application` screen, so you must use the correct path to the `login_pb` button in the `login` screen, which is a child of the `application` screen object.

12. Set the font weight of the `login_pb` button to *bold*.

```
login.login_pb.setStyle("fontWeight","bold");
```

13. Declare a private property called `login` of type MmestateLogin.

```
private var login:MmestateLogin;
```

14. Click the Check Syntax button. Save the file.

You should get several errors in the Output panel. The first is: "There is no class or package with the name 'mx.data' found in package 'mx.'" This error appears only when you check the syntax of the external AS file, not when you compile the AS file as part of the application because the data binding class files are compiled and do not reside in the classpath.

The second error is "login_pb member is private and cannot be accessed." You need to change this property declaration in MmestateLogin.as.

15. Return to MmestateLogin.as in /fpad2004/mmestate/classes/.

Return to the file you created in the last exercise or open /fpad2004/lesson09/intermediate/classes/ MmestateLogin_focus.as and save it as *MmestateLogin.as* in /fpad2004/mmestate/classes/.

16. Change `login_pb` to be a public property. Save the file.

```
public var login_pb:mx.controls.Button;
```

The finished file should resemble: /fpad2004/lesson09/intermediate/classes/ MmestateLogin_instancestyle.as.

17. Return to MmestateApp.as and click the Check Syntax button. Save the file.

You should now only get one warning in the Output panel.

The finished file should resemble: /fpad2004/lesson09/intermediate/classes/ MmestateApp_instancestyle.as.

18. Return to mmestate.fla and test the application.

The text on the Login button is now larger and bold.

Setting Style Properties for Multiple Components

If you have styles you want to apply to more than one component (but not all components), you can create a custom style object that you selectively apply to individual component instances. First create a CSSStyleDeclaration object, which is an instance of the mx.styles.CSSStyleDeclaration class.

```
my_style:mx.styles.CSSStyleDeclaration=
  new mx.styles.CSSStyleDeclaration();
```

After you create the style object, you set its style properties. You can set any of the style properties supported by Flash.

```
my_style.color="red";
my_style.textWeight="bold";
```

Next, you must assign the CSSStyleDeclaration object a string name by assigning a value to its styleName property. The name you assign to this property is the one you will use when registering other components to use this custom style.

```
my_style.styleName="errorStyle";
```

Once the object has a string name, you can register it on a global styles list by adding it as a property to the _global.styles object. You do not have to create this object; it exists as soon as a Flash UI component is added to the application. You only need to create properties for it. The name of the property must be the value of the styleName property you set for the custom CSSStyleDeclaration object. You set this property of the _global.styles object equal to the actual CSSStyleDeclaration object.

```
_global.styles.errorStyle=my_style;
```

You can also set properties directly on this object using the setStyle() method.

```
_global.styles.errorStyle.setStyle("borderStyle","none");
_global.styles.errorStyle.borderStyle="none";
```

The final step is to apply the custom style to individual components. To do this, you assign the styleName property of a component instance equal to the property of the _global.styles object that holds your custom CSSStyleDeclaration object. Just as you assigned other properties to component instances, you use the setStyle() method.

```
my_component.setStyle("styleName","errorStyle");
```

In this exercise, you change the appearance of the TextArea components on the home page; you remove their borders and change the background colors.

1. Return to MmestateApp.as in /fpad2004/mmestate/classes/.

Return to the file you created in the last exercise or open /fpad2004/lesson09/intermediate/classes/ MmestateApp_instancestyle.as and save it as *MmestateApp.as* in /fpad2004/mmestate/classes/.

2. Declare a private property called `homeStyle` of type mx.styles.CSSStyleDeclaration.

```
private var homeStyle:mx.styles.CSSStyleDeclaration;
```

3. Inside the constructor, set the `homeStyle` property equal to a new instance of the mx.styles.CSSStyleDeclaration class.

```
homeStyle=new mx.styles.CSSStyleDeclaration();
```

4. Set the `borderStyle` property equal to *none*.

```
homeStyle.borderStyle="none";
```

You are going to register the TextArea components on the home page to use this custom style; this property assignment will remove the borders around them.

5. Set the `backgroundColor` property equal to *0xF6F4F7*.

```
homeStyle.backgroundColor=0xF6F4F7;
```

This is the background color of the background image used in the application.

6. Set the `styleName` property of `homeStyle` equal to *"homeStyle"*.

```
homeStyle.styleName="homeStyle";
```

You can use any name you want; the string name of the custom style does not have to be equal to the actual name of the CSSStyleDeclaration object. Using the same name for both, however, minimizes the number of names floating around.

7. Add your `homeStyle` property to the `_global.styles` object.

```
_global.styles.homeStyle=homeStyle;
```

On the left side of this statement, you are creating a new property of the `_global.styles` object with the string name you assigned to your custom CSSStyleDeclaration object in the previous step. On the right side is the actual name of the CSSStyleDeclaration object.

8. Click the Check Syntax button.

You get two errors: "There is no property with the name 'borderStyle'" and "There is no property with the name 'backgroundColor'." (The first message about the mx.data package is the warning that you saw previously.) Even though you get these errors, your code is actually fine; you can assign `borderStyle` and `backgroundColor` as properties of a CSSStyleDeclaration object. The problem is that they are not defined as properties in the CSSStyleDeclaration class file: /First Run/Classes/mx/styles/CSSStyleDeclaration.as. You can do two things to get the class file to compile. First, you can change the type of the `homeStyle` property to a general Object, thus bypassing the compile-time type checking:

```
private var homeStyle:Object;
```

A second option is to leave `homeStyle` as a CSSStyleDeclaration object and then to assign values for the `borderStyle` and `backgroundColor` properties on the `_global.styles.homeStyle` object instead. You do this in the next step.

9. Move the two lines of code assigning the **borderStyle** and **backgroundColor** properties after the **_global.styles** object statement.

```
11        homeStyle=new mx.styles.CSSStyleDeclaration();
12        homeStyle.styleName="homeStyle";
13        _global.styles.homeStyle=homeStyle;
14        homeStyle.borderStyle="none";
15        homeStyle.backgroundColor=0xF6F4F7;
```

10. Change the two lines of code so they assign properties of the **_global.styles.homeStyle** object and click the Check Syntax button.

```
_global.styles.homeStyle.borderStyle="none";
_global.styles.homeStyle.backgroundColor=0xF6F4F7;
```

You should no longer get errors (you only get the mx.data package warning). You could also use the `setStyle()` method to set these properties:

```
_global.styles.homeStyle.setStyle("borderStyle","none");
```

11. Inside the **appLoad()** method, register the **provide_ta** component to use the properties defined by the **homeStyle** object by setting the **styleName** property of the component using the **setStyle()** method. Use a relative reference to the component from the **application** screen.

```
26        private function appLoad():Void
27        {
28            login.login_pb.setStyle("fontSize",14);
29            login.login_pb.setStyle("fontWeight","bold");
30            main.home.provide_ta.setStyle("styleName","homeStyle");
31        }
```

Just like when you set individual property values, the first argument in the setStyle() method is the name of the property you want to set. You are setting the styleName property for the component equal to the string name of the custom CSSStyleDeclaration object.

12. Similarly, register the `mission_ta` and `info_ta` components to also use the properties defined by the `homeStyle` object.

```
main.home.mission_ta.setStyle("styleName","homeStyle");
main.home.info_ta.setStyle("styleName","homeStyle");
```

13. Declare a private property called `main` of type *MmestateMain*.

```
private var main:MmestateMain;
```

14. Click the Check Syntax button.

You get three instances of the following error: "There is no method with the name 'home'." You get this error because you have not defined the home screen as a public property in the MmestateMain class. If you define that property and then check the syntax again, you will get errors that there are no methods with the names provide_ta, mission_ta, and info_ta. To remedy this, you need to define a class file MmestateHome for the home screen, define provide_ta, mission_ta, and info_ta as public properties in it, link the class to the home screen, and then define the home screen as type MmestateHome in MmestateMain. This solution is the cleanest and most rigorous. In the interest of time, though, you can just change the type of the main property to an Object, thus avoiding the type checking that was producing the error.

15. Change the type of the `main` property to *Object*. Check the syntax and then save the file.

```
private var main:Object;
```

You should get no errors (just the mx.data warning). The finished file should resemble: /fpad2004/lesson09/intermediate/classes/MmestateApp_customstyle.as.

16. Return to mmestate.fla in /fpad2004/mmestate/ and test the application.

Return to the document you created in the last exercise or open /fpad2004/lesson09/intermediate/mmestate_instancestyle.fla and save it as *mmestate.fla* in /fpad2004/mmestate/.

Log in to the application. The TextArea components no longer have borders and they have the same background color as the application. You will learn to remove the scroll bars (which you may or may not see depending on how big you made your TextArea components) in the next lesson.

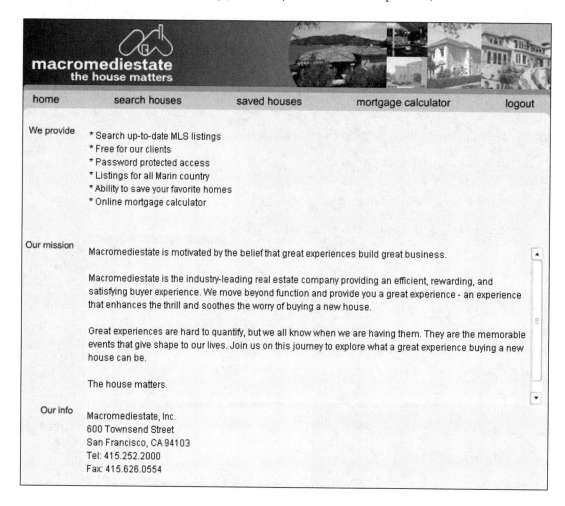

Setting Class Style Properties

If some cases you might want to apply certain styles to *all* the instances of a particular type of component. For example, set the `borderColor` property of *all* TextInput components to one of your company's colors. You do not have to register a custom class to each of the TextInput instances using the method you learned in the last exercise. Instead, you can assign properties for a CSSStyleDeclaration object for the component class.

For some component classes, a default CSSStyleDeclaration object already exists (TextInput, TextArea, NumericStepper, ComboBox, Alert, Accordion, DateChooser, ProgressBar, and Window components). For others, you need to create the CSSStyleDeclaration object for the class (Button, CheckBox, Label, List, and RadioButton components and others). You can see which components have a default object defined by tracing `_global.styles.ComponentName`. If you get [Object object], the CSSStyleDeclaration object already exists, if you get undefined, it does not exist. You can also loop over the `_global.styles` object and trace its properties using a `for-in` loop.

If a default CSSStyleDeclaration object does *not* exist for the class, you need to first create it. You create it by defining a property with the same name as the component class on the `_global.styles` object (the same object used to store your custom CSSStyleDeclaration object in the last exercise).

```
import mx.styles.CSSStyleDeclaration;
_global.styles.Button:CSSStyleDeclaration=new CSSStyleDeclaration();
```

After you create the class style object, you can set style properties for it directly or you can use the `setStyle()` method. You can set any of the supported style properties, though only those supported by that particular class will affect the component.

```
_global.styles.Button.setStyle("textWeight","bold");
```

In this exercise, you change the color of the text for all the TextInput components in the application.

1. Return to MmestateApp.as in /fpad2004/mmestate/classes/.

Return to the document you created in the last exercise or open /fpad2004/lesson09/intermediate/classes/MmestateApp_customstyle.as and save it as *MmestateApp.as* in /fpad2004/mmestate/classes/.

2. Inside the constructor, set the `color` property of all TextInput components equal to *0x007ED6*.

```
_global.styles.TextInput.setStyle("color",0x007ED6);
```

> **Note** *When setting color styles, you can use a string color name ("red") instead of the hex code (0xFF0000) for many of the basic colors. The definitions for the default colors are located in /First Run/Classes/mx/styles/StyleManager.as. If you have a custom color that you plan to use often to set styles, you can register it with the StyleManager class so you can use a string name for it instead of the hex code. To register your custom color, use the static method `registerColorName()` of the StyleManager class: `mx.styles.StyleManager.registerColorName("mmestateBlue",0x007ED6)`.*

3. Save the file.

It should resemble the finished file: /fpad2004/lesson09/intermediate/classes/MmestateApp_classstyle.as.

4. Return to mmestate.fla in /fpad2004/mmestate/ and test the application. Enter text in the input fields.

Return to the document you used in the last exercise or open /fpad2004/lesson09/intermediate/ mmestate_instancestyle.fla and save it as *mmestate.fla* in /fpad2004/mmestate/.

The text you enter in both the TextInput components should now be blue instead of black.

Setting Global Style Properties

You can also set style properties that apply to *all* components in an application by setting properties of a `_global.style` object, which is also an instance of the CSSStyleDeclaration class. This is not the same as the `_global.styles` object (plural!) that holds the custom and class style objects. You do not have to create this `_global.style` object; it exists as soon as a Flash UI component is added to the application. You assign values to specific style properties using the `setStyle()` method.

```
_global.style.setStyle("fontFamily","Arial");
```

A common global style property that you might want to change is `themeColor`, which sets the highlight and focus ring color for the components.

```
_global.style.setStyle("themeColor","haloBlue");
```

There are three possible halo colors you can use: haloGreen (which is the default `themeColor`), haloBlue, and haloOrange. You can set the `themeColor` equal to any other color as well (red, 0x007ED6, and so on). The halo colors, though, implement a fade effect for the highlight and focus rings, which is not available for any other color.

In this exercise, you change the `themeColor` style property for all components to haloOrange.

1. Return to mmestate.fla in /fpad2004/mmestate/ and test the application.

Return to the document you used in the last exercise or open /fpad2004/lesson09/intermediate/ mmestate_instancestyle.fla and save it as */fpad2004/mmestate/mmestate.fla*.

Enter text in both text fields and tab between the components. Look at the color of the default focus ring around each component. Look at the color effects as you mouse over the Login button and then click it.

2. Return to MmestateApp.as in /fpad2004/mmestate/classes/.

Return to the document you created in the last exercise or open /fpad2004/lesson09/intermediate/ classes/MmestateApp_classstyle.as and save it as *MmestateApp.as* in /fpad2004/mmestate/classes/.

3. Inside the constructor, set the `themeColor` property of the `_global.style` class to *green*. Use the `setStyle()` method. Save the file.

```
_global.style.setStyle("themeColor","green");
```

This code changes the focus ring that appears around components from their default color of haloGreen (0x80FF4D) with a fade effect to green (0x00FF00) without a fade effect.

4. Return to mmestate.fla and test the application.

Enter text in both text fields and tab between the components. The focus ring no longer fades away from the component.

5. Return to MmestateApp.as and change the `themeColor` property of the `_global.style` object to *haloOrange*. Save the file.

```
_global.style.setStyle("themeColor","haloOrange");
```

The finished file should resemble: /fpad2004/lesson09/intermediate/classes/ MmestateApp_globalstyle.as.

6. Return to mmestate.fla in /fpad2004/mmestate/ and test the application.

Enter text in both text fields and tab between the components. The focus ring around each component should now be orange instead of green. Click the Login button.

Changing Component Graphics

What if you want to customize a component in a way not accessible by setting a style property? For example, you might want to change the color of the check in a check box or the size of the radio buttons. To make these kinds of changes, you need to revise the source graphics for a component. This process is called **skinning** the component.

Skinning a component is not as straightforward as changing the graphics for one of your MovieClips because when you add a component to your application, it is precompiled. Because of this, the graphics that comprise the MovieClip do not appear in the library. Instead, the class file for the component contains code specifying what skins should be loaded and used. To change the graphics, you can either drag an assets folder for the component which contains the uncompiled graphic pieces that make up the component (the skins) into your application library and then edit them or you can create new MovieClip symbols containing the graphics and then attach them to the component instance with code. The first method is covered in this exercise. For information on the second method, see the Customizing Components chapter in the Using Component book in the Help panel.

The Halo Theme

By default, the skins contained in the HaloTheme.fla are used for all the UI components. The collection of styles and skins contained in this FLA is referred to as a **theme** and the default theme for the UI components is called **Halo**. The HaloTheme.fla is located in the /First Run/ComponentFLA/ folder. On Windows, this folder is <boot drive>\Program Files\Macromedia\Flash MX 2004\ <language>\First Run\ComponentFLA\; on Macintosh, <Macintosh HD>/Applications/ Macromedia Flash MX 2004/<language>/First Run/ComponentFLA/.

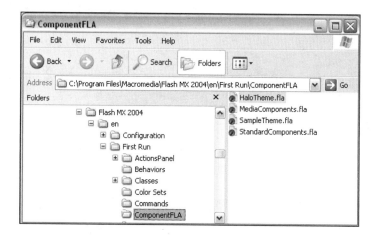

This Halo theme, inspired by the properties of light and human attraction to light, defines the distinctive new look and feel of the Flash MX 2004 components. Halo components feature a glowing ring (the halo) that attracts the eye and encourage user interaction (the amount of glow represents that particular control's "desire" for interaction). You have already seen these halos around the components in the earlier exercises.

Note *Macromedia Breeze and Macromedia Central currently use the Halo components.*

Using a Theme to Skin all Components

You can open the library of any of the theme FLAs and see the MovieClip symbols containing graphics that make up the components. Each component is comprised of many small different graphics pieces—and some of the skins are used by multiple components.

Some of the graphics are symbols that have been created using the drawing tools in Flash, and hence, can be edited in the authoring environment with the drawing tools. Others have been created with code using the Flash drawing API (which is not covered in the book) such as the RectBorder and ButtonSkin elements that have no visual element in the library. To edit these skins, you must edit the source code in their associated class files. All of these MovieClips symbols have been assigned linkage names in the library that are referenced by the class code used to display them in the application.

To apply a different theme (a collection of skins) to all the components in your application, you simply drag the theme's main MovieClip containing all of its assets to the library of your application. When the application is compiled, any component assets included in your application's library will be used instead of the component assets contained in the default HaloTheme.fla.

You can use one of the existing themes or create your own. The SampleTheme.fla theme contains all of the skins available for customizing the components. The default Halo theme uses only a subset of these skins. To create your own theme, make a copy of one of these theme FLA files, save it with a new name, and then edit the graphics of the MovieClip symbols in the library.

In this exercise, you change the theme for your application. You change it from the default Halo theme to the Sample theme and then back again.

1. Return to mmestate.fla in /fpad2004/mmestate/ and test the application.

Return to the document you used in the last exercise or open /fpad2004/lesson09/intermediate/ mmestate_instancestyle.fla and save it as *mmestate.fla* in /fpad2004/mmestate/.

Check out the current color and styles of the various components, especially the Login button.

2. **Return to the FLA and select File > Import > Open External Library. Browse to SampleTheme.Fla in /First Run/ComponentFLA/ and click Open.**

On Windows, this folder is <boot drive>\Program Files\Macromedia\Flash MX 2004\<language>\ First Run\ComponentFLA\; on Macintosh, <Macintosh HD>/Applications/Macromedia Flash MX 2004/<language>/First Run/ComponentFLA/.

3. **In the SampleTheme.fla library, drill down to Flash UI Components 2 > SampleTheme.**

This is the theme's main MovieClip, which contains different assets for all of the UI components.

4. **Drag the SampleTheme MovieClip and drop it into the Library panel for mmestate.fla.**

You might need to open the library if it is closed. The SampleTheme MovieClip and the Themes, Base Classes, and Border Classes folders should all appear in the mmestate.fla library. The assets in these folders will now be used for all the components instead of the ones in the Halo theme.

Your file at this point should resemble: /fpad2004/lesson09/intermediate/mmestate_sampletheme.fla.

5. **Test the application.**

Your components should now look different. They are using the skins and styles specified in the SampleTheme.fla.

6. Select the SampleTheme MovieClip and the Base Classes, Border Classes, and Themes folders in the mmestate.fla library. Right-click/Control-click and select **Delete**.

This returns your application to using the default Halo theme.

Skinning Individual Components

In the last exercise, you applied a new theme to your FLA—which provided new skins for *all* of the components. If you want to change the skins for one or more components (but not all), simply drag Assets folders for individual components from the theme library into your document's library. For example, to skin a RadioButton, drag over the folder called RadioButton Assets.

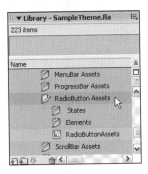

After you add the Assets folder to your application's library, you need to change the linkage property for the new component assets so that they are exported in the first frame. To do this, you change the linkage property of the MovieClip entitled componentNameAssets (for example, RadioButtonAssets) by right-clicking/Control-clicking it in the library and selecting Export in First Frame.

You did not have to change the linkage when you applied the entire theme in the last exercise because the theme's main MovieClip that contained all the assets (for example, SampleTheme) was already set to export in the first frame.

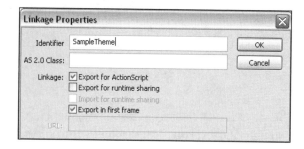

Editing Component Skins

After you have applied a theme or a subset of a theme to a document library, you can edit the graphics skins inside it. To view the skins and the pieces of the skins that comprise a component, drill down into the States and/or Elements folders inside the Assets folder for a component.

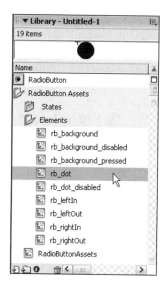

All the pieces that make up a skin are individual MovieClip symbols. To edit a piece of the skin, double-click a specific state or element MovieClip in the library. You enter symbol-editing mode, where you can edit the skin, exactly like you edit any other MovieClip symbol.

In this exercise, you change the style and color of the checkmark displayed for a CheckBox component.

1. Return to mmestate.fla in /fpad2004/mmestate/.

Return to the document you used in the last exercise or open /fpad2004/lesson09/intermediate/ mmestate_instancestyle.fla and save it as *mmestate.fla* in /fpad2004/mmestate/.

2. Select the `search` screen in the Screen Outline pane. From the Components panel, drag out a CheckBox component. Test the application.

Log in to the application and navigate to the search page. Check out the current color and style of the CheckBox component.

☑ CheckBox

3. Return to the FLA and open the document's library.

You can open the library by pressing Ctrl+L (Windows) or Command+L (Macintosh).

4. Return to the SampleTheme.fla library, drill down to Flash UI Components 2 › Themes › MMDefault › CheckBox Assets.

You opened this external library in the last exercise. If you did not do that exercise or closed the library, select File > Import > Open External Library, browse to SampleTheme.Fla in /First Run/ ComponentFLA/, and then click Open.

5. Drag the CheckBox Assets folder to your document's library.

The skins in this CheckBox Assets folder should now be used for all CheckBox components in your document instead of the skins in the default Halo theme.

6. In your document's library, drill down to CheckBox Assets › States and click CheckTrueUp.

This smaller, thicker check mark should now be used inside all the check boxes in your document.

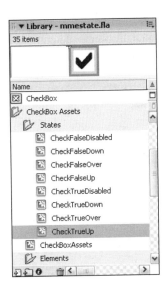

7. Test the application.

Log in to the application and navigate to the search page. Select the check box. You still get the old Halo check mark! Why? Because the CheckBox skin assets were not set to export in the first frame.

8. Right-click/Control-click the CheckBoxAssets MovieClip in the CheckBox Assets folder in your document's library and select Linkage. Select the "Export in first frame" check box and click OK.

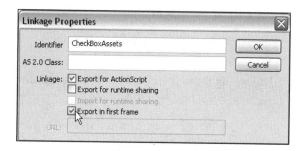

9. Test the application.

Log in to the application and navigate to the search page. Select the check box. Your check mark now has the new style.

10. In your document's library, drill down to CheckBox Assets › Elements and double-click *cb_check_*.

You are now editing the MovieClip symbol that contains the graphic for the check mark.

11. Select *800%* from the drop-down box in the upper right corner of the document.

You are making the check mark larger so you can see and edit it more easily.

12. Double-click the check mark on the Stage to select it. Click the color swatch next to the Fill Color tool in the Tools panel and enter *#007ED6* for a shade of blue.

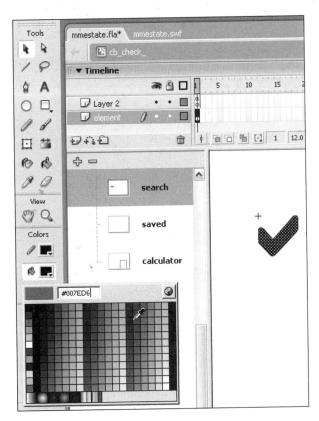

The color of check mark on the Stage should change to blue.

13. Click the `search` screen in the Screen Outline pane to leave symbol-editing mode and return to the `search` screen.

You have now changed the skin that will be used for the check mark in all the CheckBox components.

14. Save the file and test the application.

It should resemble the finished file: /fpad2004/lesson09/intermediate/mmestate_editskin.fla.

Log in to the application and navigate to the search page. Select the check box. Your check mark is now blue.

What You Have Learned

In this lesson, you have:

- Learned about the UIObject and UIComponent component base classes (pages 369–373)
- Used functions and objects to handle component events (pages 373–385)
- Managed focus and tab order for components (pages 385–390)
- Changed the style properties of one component (pages 390–394)
- Applied custom styles to multiple component instances (pages 394–398)
- Applied styles to all components of one class (pages 398–400)
- Set styles for all components in a document (pages 400–401)
- Used a theme to skin all components (pages 401–405)
- Edited component skins (pages 405–409)

10 Using UI Component APIs

Using the prebuilt components that ship with Macromedia Flash MX 2004, ranging from check boxes and buttons to more complicated calendars and accordions, you can now quickly build powerful, effective experiences for your customers. In Lesson 9, "Learning the UI Component Framework," you learned about the component framework and the facets that apply to all the UI components. In this lesson, you use nine of the UI components and manipulate them with code, to become familiar with each of their APIs.

Your goal this lesson is to create the search page for the Macromediestate application where users search for homes that meet their criteria. You implement functionality to populate the controls and capture their selected values. In later lessons, you hook up the interface to server-side data to retrieve and display the results.

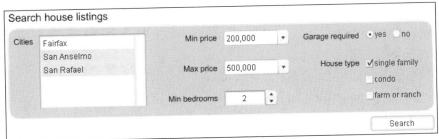

In this lesson, you create an interface using prebuilt UI components to search for houses on the Macromediestate web site.

What You Will Learn

In this lesson, you will:

- Use the Button component
- Use the TextInput component
- Work with the Label component
- Use the TextArea component
- Use the NumericStepper component
- Manage the CheckBox component
- Use the RadioButton component
- Use the ComboBox component
- Manipulate the List component

Approximate Time

This lesson takes approximately 90 minutes to complete.

Lesson Files

Asset Files:

/fpad2004/lesson10/start/assets/houseicon.png

Starting Files:

/fpad2004/lesson10/start/mmestate.fla
/fpad2004/lesson10/start/classes/MmestateLogin.as
/fpad2004/lesson10/start/classes/MmestateHome.as
/fpad2004/lesson10/start/searchHouses.fla
/fpad2004/lesson10/start/classes/Searchform.as

Completed Files:

/fpad2004/lesson10/complete/mmestate.fla
/fpad2004/lesson10/complete/classes/MmestateLogin.as
/fpad2004/lesson10/complete/classes/MmestateHome.as
/fpad2004/lesson10/complete/searchHouses.fla
/fpad2004/lesson10/complete/classes/Searchform.as

Using the Button Component

The Button component is a prebuilt button with a specific look and behavior. It has the same look and feel as an HTML submit button.

If the Button component is suitable for your application and you only need to customize its size, color, label text properties, and so on, it is very quick and easy to use, saving you from building a button from scratch using the native Button class (like you did in Lesson 4, "Creating Button and MovieClip Objects"). If you are building an application with other UI components, another advantage of using the Button component is that it shares the same underlying API as the other components so you can manipulate all the objects using the same event handling, customization framework, and so on.

The Button component is an instance of the mx.controls.Button class with the following inheritance chain: UIObject > UIComponent > SimpleButton > Button. At author time, you can specify the Button component properties in the Property inspector or Component Inspector panels.

You can also set these parameters at runtime by assigning values to properties with the same name using ActionScript.

Note | *Property values set with ActionScript override any values set in the authoring environment.*

The Button component has the following properties for setting the button's label, specifying an image for the button, and setting the button behavior (whether or not it is a toggle button):

label. The text that appears on the button.

icon. An image to display on the button in place of or in addition to text. The value you specify for the icon property is the linkage name of a symbol in the library. Make sure the button and the symbol are the right size; they do not automatically resize to fit the other.

```
my_pb.icon="bike";
```

labelPlacement. Sets the position of the label in relation to an icon (left, right, top, bottom). The default value is right.

toggle. A Boolean indicating whether the button behaves as a toggle switch that stays pressed when you click it until you click it again.

selected. A Boolean indicating whether or not a toggle button is pressed.

enabled. A property of the UIComponent class indicating whether the Button is enabled and can receive focus and be clicked. You set this property for the Login button in Lesson 9.

> **Tip** *You can resize a button using the Free Transform tool or the UIObject setSize() method.*

The Button component has one more event, `click`, in addition to the events from its base UIObject and UIComponent classes. The `click` event is broadcast when the user clicks the button. You used the `click` event when you learned about the component event handling framework in Lesson 9.

> **Tip** *Don't forget that you can set a Button component to be an application's default button so that it broadcasts a click event when the user presses the Enter/Return key in addition to when they click the button. This default button functionality was introduced in Lesson 9.*

The properties, methods, and events for the Button component are in the Actions panel under Components > Button.

In this exercise, you change the label of the Login button at runtime and place an icon on the button.

1. Return to MmestateLogin.as in /fpad2004/mmestate/classes/.

This is the file you created in Lesson 9. If you did not complete that lesson, open /fpad2004/lesson10/ start/classes/MmestateLogin.as and save it as *MmestateLogin.as* in /fpad2004/mmestate/classes/.

2. Inside the `loginReveal()` method, create an `if` statement to check if the `logout` screen is visible. If it is, assign the `login_pb` Button instance a new label of *Relogin*. Use the `setLabel()` method.

```
if (logout.visible)
{
        login_pb.label="Relogin";
}
```

3. Define a private property called `logout` of type *mx.screens.Form*. Save the file.

You will use this file as the starting file for the next exercise. It should resemble the finished file: /fpad2004/lesson10/intermediate/classes/MmestateLogin_button.as.

4. Return to mmestate.fla in /fpad2004/mmestate/ and test the application.

This is the file you created in the last exercise of Lesson 9. If you did not do that exercise, open /fpad2004/lesson10/start/mmestate.fla and save it as *mmestate.fla* in /fpad2004/mmestate/.

> **Note** *To successfully test the application, you also need working versions of MmestateApp.as and MmestateMain.as. If you did not finish Lesson 9, copy these files from the start folder to your /mmestate/classes/ folder.*

Log in to the application and then click the logout button. The Login button should have the new label, Relogin.

5. Return to mmestate.fla and select the `login` screen. Select File › Import › Import to Stage. In the Import dialog box, select houseicon.png from /mmestate/assets/ and click Open. Select "Import as single flattened bitmap" and click OK.

A small house icon with an open door appears on the Stage.

6. Right-click/Control-click the house icon and select Convert to Symbol. In the Convert to Symbol dialog box, name the symbol *houseicon*, make it a Graphic symbol, and select Export for ActionScript. Click OK.

You might need to click the Advanced button if you do not see the Export for ActionScript check box. When you select the Export for ActionScript check box, the linkage name field automatically gets populated with the symbol name, houseicon.

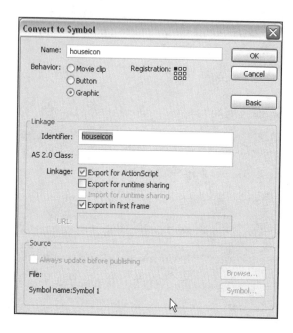

The houseicon symbol appears in the library.

7. Place the house image over the Search button. Use the Free Transform Tool to resize the Button component so the icon fits on it.

If the icon image is larger than the button, the image is displayed outside the button edges. The button will not automatically resize to fit the icon.

8. Delete the house icon from the Stage.

You only need the symbol in the library.

9. Select the Login button. In the Property inspector, set the `icon` parameter to houseicon and leave the `labelPlacement` parameter set to right.

The linkage name of the symbol in the library is houseicon.

You should now see a square on the Button component on the Stage indicating that an image will display on the button at runtime.

10. Save the file and test the application.

You should see the house icon displayed on your Login button.

You will use this file as the starting file for the next exercise. It should resemble the finished file: /fpad2004/lesson10/intermediate/mmestate_button.fla.

Using the TextInput Component

The TextInput component has the same look and feel as an HTML input text field. It is a Flash input text field wrapped with the V2 component architecture so you manipulate it the same way you do the rest of the components: using data binding, using the same event handling and skinning mechanisms, and so on.

A TextInput component can be only a single line. If you need a multiline input text field, you must use the TextArea component.

The TextInput component is an instance of the mx.controls.TextInput class with the following inheritance chain: UIObject > UIComponent > TextInput. You can specify many of the TextInput component properties in the Component Inspector panel.

All of these parameters map to TextInput component properties of the same name; many of the properties in the following list are identical to those for the built-in TextField class.

text. The text to display in the text field. You can set or retrieve the text entered in the TextInput component exactly as you did for Flash input TextField objects.

```
my_ti.text="Alex";
trace(my_ti.text);
```

> **Note** *You do not have to use the suffix _ti when naming TextInput components. Using suffixes is an optional naming methodology used in this book to clearly indicate the type of visual object being referenced in code.*

editable. A Boolean indicating whether the field is editable by the user.

password. A Boolean indicating whether the characters input into the text field are displayed as asterisks. You set the password parameter for the `password_ti` on the login screen in Lesson 8, "Using the Flash Application Framework."

maxChars. The maximum number of characters that a user can enter in the text field.

restrict. A string indicating which characters a user can enter in the text field. You can specify a string of characters or a range of characters.

```
my_ti.restrict="ABCDEFG";
my_ti.restrict="A-G";
```

Events specific for the TextInput component include **change** (broadcast when the user has changed the text) and **enter** (broadcast when the cursor is inside the component and the enter key is pressed). You should use the TextInput component's change event instead of the analogous `onChanged` event native to the underlying TextField class, so that you do not bypass the component's API. UIComponent events commonly used with the TextInput component include `focusIn` and `focusOut`.

In this exercise, you add logic so the user must enter a password containing between 4 and 6 characters.

1. Return to MmestateLogin.as in /fpad2004/mmestate/classes/.

Return to the file you created in the last exercise or open fpad2004/lesson10/intermediate/classes/ MmestateLogin_button.as and save it as *MmestateLogin.as* in /fpad2004/mmestate/classes/.

2. Inside the `loginLoad()` method, set the `maxChars` property of the `password_ti` component to 6.

```
password_ti.maxChars=6;
```

You can also assign this property value in the Component Inspector panel.

3. Place all the existing code inside the `login_pbClick()` method inside an `else` block.

```
53      private function login_pbClick():Void
54      {
55          else
56          {
57              this.visible=false;
58              _parent.main.visible=true;
59          }
60      }
```

4. Before the `else` block, create an `if` block that checks if the `length` of the text entered in the `password_ti` component is less than **4.**

```
if (password_ti.length<4){}
```

5. Inside the `if` block, disable the Login button and trace the text "Your password must be at least **4** characters". Save the file.

```
login_pb.enabled=false;
trace("Your password must be at least 4 characters");
```

You will make this message appear in a Label component instead of in the Output panel in the next exercise.

Your finished file should resemble: /fpad2004/lesson10/intermediate/classes/ MmestateLogin_textinput.as.

6. Return to mmestate.fla in /fpad**2004**/mmestate/ and test the application.

Return to the file you created in the last exercise or open /fpad2004/lesson10/intermediate/ mmestate_button.fla and save it as *mmestate.fla* in /fpad2004/mmestate/.

Enter less than 4 characters in the password text field and try to log in. You should see the message "Your password must be at least 4 characters" in the Output panel and the Login button should be disabled. Try to enter a long password in the password text field; you can no longer enter more than 6 characters.

Working with the Label Component

The Label component is a dynamic TextField object wrapped with the V2 component architecture so you can manipulate it the same way you do the rest of the components: using data binding and the same styles.

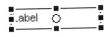

A Label component can be only a single line. If you need a multiline dynamic text field, you must use the TextArea component and hide its borders and scroll bars. The Label component has no borders and broadcasts no events.

The Label component is an instance of the mx.controls.Label class with the following inheritance chain: UIObject > Label. You can specify all the Label component properties in the Property inspector or the Component Inspector panels.

The Label component properties are identical to the properties of the built-in TextField class with the same names.

text. The text to display in the text field. You set or retrieve the text entered in the TextInput component exactly as you did for built-in dynamic TextField objects.

autoSize. A Boolean indicating whether the Label component should resize to fit all the text assigned to its text property. You can specify four values: none (does not resize), left (text is aligned to the left and the component resizes on the right to fit all the text), right (text is aligned to the right and the component resizes on the left to fit all the text), or center (text is aligned in the center and the component resizes on both sides to fit all the text). The default value is none.

html. A Boolean indicating whether the text field should be formatted with any HTML tags that it might contain. The default is false.

In this exercise, you add a Label component to the login screen and dynamically populate it with text.

1. Return to mmestate.fla in /fpad2004/mmestate/.

Return to the file you used in the last exercise or open /fpad2004/lesson10/intermediate/ mmestate_button.fla and save it as *mmestate.fla* in /fpad2004/mmestate/.

2. Select the login screen. From the Components panel, drag out a Label component and place it next to password component.

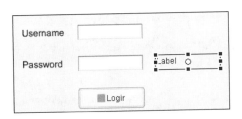

When the user submits the form with less than 4 characters in the password text field, a message will display in the Label component. You could also use a simple dynamic text field instead of a Label component. In this case, there is no advantage of one over the other; in general, you use a Label component when you want to use data binding. If you are a more visual person, you could also place this message on a new screen and make this screen visible when the message needs to be displayed.

3. In the Property inspector, give the Label component the instance name *password_la* and delete the existing value for the `text` parameter.

Nothing will initially be displayed in the component.

Unfortunately, at this time, if you do not have the Label component selected on the Stage it is invisible, making it difficult to work with. (You have to remember where it was on the Stage to select it.) The Label component becomes visible, however, it you turn off Live Preview for the components in the authoring environment. (To disable Live Preview, select Control > Enable Live Preview.) When Live Preview is disabled, all components are represented on the Stage as black squares that you can resize and reposition.

4. Return to MmestateLogin.as in /fpad2004/mmestate/classes/.

Return to the file you created in the last exercise or open fpad2004/lesson10/intermediate/classes/ MmestateLogin_textinput.as and save it as *MmestateLogin.as* in /fpad2004/mmestate/classes/.

5. Declare a private property called *password_la* of type *mx.controls.Label*.

```
private var password_la:mx.controls.Label;
```

6. Inside the `if` statement in the `login_pbClick()` method, change the code so the message "Your password must be at least 4 characters" is displayed in the Label component instead of in the Output panel.

```
38      if (password_ti.length<4)
39      {
40          login_pb.enabled=false;
41          password_la.text="Your password must be at least 4 characters";
42      }
```

7. Inside the loginReveal() method, clear `password_la`. Save the file.

When the user clicks the logout button, the password label needs to be cleared of all text.

```
password_la.text="";
```

Your finished file should resemble: /fpad2004/lesson10/intermediate/classes/MmestateLogin_label.as.

8. Return to mmestate.fla in /fpad2004/mmestate/ and test the application.

Enter less than 4 characters in the password text field and try to log in. You should see the message "Your password must be at least 4 characters" displayed on the right of the password text field, but the message is cut off.

9. Return to mmestate.fla. In the Property inspector for the Label component, set the `autoSize` parameter to left.

You can also set this property via code, setting the `autoSize` property of the Label component equal to true in the `loginLoad()` method.

> **Note** *You cannot make a Label component multiline. If you want multiline text, you must use the TextArea component or a multiline dynamic TextField object.*

10. Save the file and test the application.

Enter less than 4 characters in the password text field and try to log in. You should now see the full message "Your password must be at least 4 characters" displayed to the right of the password text field.

The finished file should resemble: /fpad2004/lesson10/intermediate/mmestate_label.fla.

Using the TextArea Component

The TextArea component has the same look and feel as an HTML textarea control. It is very similar to the TextInput component, except that a *multiline* Flash input TextField object has been wrapped with the V2 component architecture so that you can use data binding and the rest of the component framework.

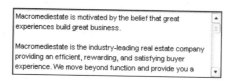

The TextArea component is an instance of the mx.controls.TextArea class with the following inheritance chain: UIObject > UIComponent > View > ScrollView > TextArea. The TextArea component has two additional parameters compared to the TextInput component in the inspector panels: `html` and `wordWrap`.

html. A Boolean indicating whether the text field should be formatted with any HTML tags that it might contain. The default is false. You set the `editable` and `html` properties for the TextArea components on the home page in Lesson 8.

wordWrap. A Boolean indicating whether or not the text wraps. The default is true.

The TextArea component also has additional properties to control scrolling both vertically and horizontally.

hPosition *and* **vPosition.** A number setting the horizontal and vertical scrolling positions, respectively, of the text within the scroll pane.

hScrollPolicy *and* **vScrollPolicy.** A Boolean indicating whether a horizontal or vertical scroll bar, respectively, is displayed. You can specify whether the scroll bar is always displayed (on), never displayed (off), or displayed only when there is text to scroll (auto). The default is auto.

In this exercise, you manipulate the wrapping and scrolling of a TextArea component on the home page.

1. Return to mmestate.fla in /fpad2004/mmestate/.

Return to the file you created in the last exercise or open /fpad2004/lesson10/intermediate/ mmestate_label.fla and save it as *mmestate.fla* in /fpad2004/mmestate/.

2. Select the `mission_ta` component on the `home` screen. In the Property inspector, set `wordWrap` to *false*.

By default, the text in TextArea components wraps to multiple lines.

3. Save the file and test the application.

Each line of text in the `mission_ta` component is displayed on a single line. A horizontal scroll bar is automatically displayed so that you can scroll to the right.

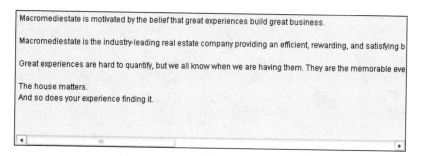

4. Return to mmestate.fla and set the `wordWrap` for `mission_ta` back to *true*.

Next, you will change settings for the scroll bars.

5. If your `mission_ta` component did not have a scroll bar when you tested the application, decrease the size of the component so that a scroll bar is displayed when you test the application.

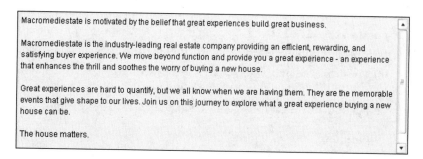

Make sure the other TextArea components are large enough to contain all their text without scroll bars.

6. Open MmestateHome.as in /fpad2004/start/lesson10/classes/ and save it as *MmestateHome.as* in /fpad2004/mmestate/classes/.

The class file for the home screen has been started for you. The file contains skeleton code for the class definition.

7. Create a private property called `mission_ta` of type *mx.controls.TextArea*.

```
private var mission_ta:TextArea;
```

You can use the simple class name; the package mx.controls has been explicitly imported.

8. Inside the `homeLoad()` method, set the `vScrollPolicy` for `mission_ta` to *false*. **Save the file.**

```
misson_ta.vScrollPolicy="off";
```

This code will remove the vertical scroll bar for the `mission_ta` TextArea component.

9. Return to mmestate.fla and link the MmestateHome class to the home screen

Remember, you assign the class file to link to a screen on the Properties tab in the Property inspector.

10. Open the Actions panel for the home screen. Cut the code triggering the XMLConnector component. Delete the remaining event handler code. Save the file.

You are removing the last bit of code remaining in the FLA. The code to cut is shown in the following screenshot.

```
2  on (load) {
3
4      // Trigger Data Source Behavior
5      // Macromedia 2003
6      this.home_xc.trigger();
7
8  }
```

The finished file should resemble: /fpad2004/lesson10/intermediate/mmestate_textarea.fla.

11. Return to MmestateHome.as and paste the code you cut in Step 10 inside the `homeLoad()` method. **Save the file.**

The finished file should resemble: /fpad2004/lesson10/intermediate/classes/ MmestateHome_textarea.as.

12. Return to mmestate.fla and test the application.

You should not see a scroll bar next to the `mission_ta` component. Make sure you can see all the text. If you cannot, change the size and/or position of the components in mmestate.fla to make all the text visible when you test the application.

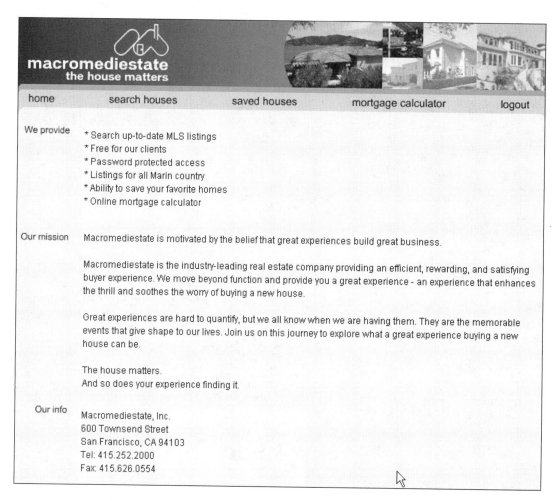

Using the NumericStepper Component

You can provide a control for the user to select a numeric value from a list of values, for example, to select a number 1 through 12 for the month, using a NumericStepper component. The NumericStepper component displays a numeric value with arrow controls to move the selected number up or down.

You specify the minimum and maximum values and the step size to increment the numbers for the NumericStepper component in the inspector panels or using ActionScript.

The NumericStepper component is an instance of the mx.controls.NumericStepper class with the inheritance chain: UIObject > UIComponent > NumericStepper. You use three properties to set your stepper bounds: `minimum` (default is 0), `maximum` (default is 10), and `stepSize` (default is 1). The NumericStepper also has `previousValue` and `nextValue` properties you can use to retrieve the values before and after the selected step.

To set or retrieve the number selected in the NumericStepper, use the `value` property.

```
my_ns.value=4;
trace(my_ns.value);
```

Note *A new value will not be selected if the value assigned does not correspond to a valid value in the stepper.*

You can capture when a user changes the selected number in the NumericStepper using the `change` event.

In this exercise, you add a NumericStepper component to the search application for selecting the number of bedrooms. You set and capture the selected number of bedrooms with ActionScript.

1. Open searchHouses.fla in /fpad2004/lesson10/start/ and save it as *searchHouses.fla* in /fpad2004/mmestate/.

You are going to build the interface to search for houses. This starting file contains the static text for the interface and a Button component.

2. From the Components panel, drag an instance of the NumericStepper component to the Stage.

Place the component next to the Min bedrooms text.

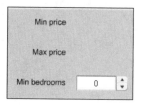

3. In the Property inspector, give the stepper the instance name `bedrooms_ns` and change the `maximum` parameter to 6.

There are no houses in the database with more than 6 bedrooms.

4. Save the file and test the application.

Change the number of bedrooms selected in the NumericStepper.

The finished file should resemble: /fpad2004/lesson10/intermediate/searchHouses_stepper.fla.

5. Open Searchform.as in /fpad2004/lesson10/start/classes/ and save it as *Searchform.as* in /fpad2004/mmestate/classes/.

This class file will contain all the logic for the search houses interface. The file has been started for you; it currently contains the skeleton for the class definition and an event handler for the Search button.

6. Create a private property called `bedrooms_ns` of type NumericStepper.

You can use the simple class name, NumericStepper, because the mx.controls package is explicitly imported at the top of the class file.

7. Inside the `searchformLoad()` method, set the selected value in the NumericStepper to *2*. Use the `value` property.

```
bedrooms_ns.value=2;
```

You can also set this initial value in one of the inspector panels at author time; you are setting the property with code to get experience using the NumericStepper API.

8. Inside the `search_pbClick()` method, trace the selected value in the NumericStepper. Use the `value` property. Save the file.

```
trace(bedrooms_ns.value);
```

The finished file should resemble: /fpad2004/lesson10/intermediate/classes/Searchform_stepper.as.

9. **Return to searchHouses.fla and test the application.**

The initial number of bedrooms selected should now be 2.

Change the number of bedrooms in the NumericStepper and click the Search button. You should see the selected number of bedrooms traced to the output panel.

Utilizing the CheckBox Component

Use a single CheckBox component to collect a true/false value from a user.

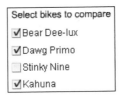

Use a set of CheckBox components if you want to collect a series of true/false values that are not mutually exclusive—more than one check box can be selected.

The CheckBox component has the same look and feel of an HTML check box. Unlike HTML check boxes, though, you do not assign an associated data value for a Flash check box. If a Flash CheckBox component is selected, its value is true or false. As a result, you cannot get a list of selected values for a group of check boxes the same way you can in HTML. In HTML, if you give multiple check boxes the same name and the form is submitted with multiple check boxes selected, the submitted value is a comma-delimited list of the selected check box values. In Flash, you must give each check box instance a unique name, check and see if each check box has been selected, and then manually create a list of selected check boxes.

The CheckBox component is an instance of the mx.controls.CheckBox class with the following inheritance chain: UIObject > UIComponent > SimpleButton > Button > CheckBox. You can use the inspector panels or ActionScript to assign values to its properties:

label. The text that appears next to the box. The default value is CheckBox.

```
my_ch.label="American Express";
trace(my_ch.label);                          //Outputs American Express
```

> **Note** *If the label property is set using one of the inspector panels in the authoring environment, you cannot retrieve the value of the label property in code that is immediately executed when the application loads. You will get an empty string because the component is initialized over multiple frames and the value of the label property is not yet available when the code attempting to access it is executed. Code accessing the label value from within event handlers does not have this problem. If you must access a label value immediately, assign its value with code.*

labelPosition. The position of the label relative to the box (left, right, top, or bottom). The default value is right.

selected. A Boolean indicating whether the CheckBox should be selected (true/false). You can use this property to select a CheckBox or retrieve whether the CheckBox is currently selected. The default value is false.

```
my_ch.selected=true;
trace(my_ch.selected);
```

> **Note** *If you use the Property inspector, the Free Transform tool, or the UIObject API to change the width of a CheckBox component, the width of the CheckBox/label combination changes, not the width of the check box. If you want to change the size of the check box (or its style or the size or style of the check mark), you must edit the component skins as you did in Lesson 9.*

To capture when a user selects a CheckBox component, use the CheckBox component `click` event.

In this exercise, you add three CheckBox components to the search application for selecting the type of house: single family, condo, or farm/ranch. Using ActionScript, you set and capture the CheckBox states and create a comma-delimited list of the selected values.

1. Return to searchHouses.fla in /fpad2004/mmestate/.

Return to the file you created in the last exercise or open /fpad2004/lesson10/intermediate/ searchHouses_stepper.fla and save it as *searchHouses.fla* in /fpad2004/mmestate/.

2. From the Components panel, drag out an instance of the CheckBox component. Name the instance `single_ch` and set the `label` to *single family*.

Place the component next to the House type text.

3. Drag out two more instances of the CheckBox component. Name the first instance `condo_ch` and set the `label` to *condo*. Name the second instance `farm_ch` and set the `label` to *farm or ranch*.

Line up the check boxes vertically next to the House type text.

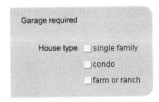

4. Save the file and test the application.

Select and deselect the various check boxes.

The finished file should resemble: /fpad2004/lesson10/intermediate/searchHouses_checkbox.fla.

5. Return to Searchform.as in /fpad2004/mmestate/classes/.

Return to the file you created in the last exercise or open /fpad2004/lesson10/intermediate/classes/ Searchform_stepper.as and save it as *Searchform.as* in /fpad2004/mmestate/classes/.

6. Define the three CheckBox instances as private properties of type *CheckBox*.

```
private var single_ch:CheckBox;
private var condo_ch:CheckBox;
private var farm_ch:CheckBox;
```

7. Inside the `searchformLoad()` method, select the single family home check box. Use the `selected` property.

```
single_ch.selected=true;
```

Although you can also set this initial value in one of the inspector panels at author time, in this step you set it with code to get experience using the API.

8. Inside the `search_pbClick()` method, trace the selected value of the `condo_ch` check box. Save the file.

```
trace(condo_ch.selected);
```

9. Return to searchHouses.fla and test the application.

The single-family home check box should be initially selected. Click the Search button. You should see the value false traced to the Output panel.

10. Return to Searchform.as and delete the `trace()` you added in Step 8.

Instead of capturing the selected state of an individual check box, you are going to capture a string containing a list of the house type IDs for the selected check boxes.

11. Inside the `search_pbClick()` method, create an array called *housetype*.

```
var housetype:Array=new Array();
```

12. Use an `if` statement to check if the `single_ch` check box is selected. If it is selected, add the number 1 to the array.

```
if (single_ch.selected)
{
        housetype.push(1);
}
```

In Lesson 13, "Consuming Web Services," you will search the fpad2004 database for houses with the correct house type. Instead of passing a string to the web service containing the house types, you will pass IDs specifying the house types. You can get the IDs for each house type in a table called housetype in the fpad2004 database. From the database, the IDs for the house types are as follows: single family is 1, condo is 2, and farm/ranch is 3.

13. Check if the `condo_ch` check box is selected. If it is selected, add the number 2 to the array.

```
35      private function search_pbClick():Void
36      {
37          trace(bedrooms_ns.value);
38          var housetype:Array=new Array();
39          if (single_ch.selected)
40          {
41              housetype.push(1);
42          }
43          if (condo_ch.selected)
44          {
45              housetype.push(2);
46          }
47      }
```

14. Check if the `farm_ch` check box is selected. If it is selected, add the number 3 to the array.

```
if (farm_ch.selected)
{
        housetype.push(3);
}
```

15. Trace a comma-delimited list of the house types. Use the Array object `toString()` method.

```
trace(housetype.toString());
```

You don't have to explicitly call the `toString()` method because the `toString()` method is automatically invoked when you try to trace an object. However, you will need to explicitly call this method for this data transformation (an array to a comma-delimited list) when you send this data to a web service in Lesson 13.

16. Save the file.

It should resemble: /fpad2004/lesson10/intermediate/classes/Searchform_checkbox.as.

17. Return to searchHouses.fla and test the application. Select more than one check box and click the Search button.

You should see a comma-delimited list of the selected house type values traced to the Output panel. For example: 1,2,3.

Managing the RadioButton Component

Just like in HTML, you use RadioButton components to create a group of mutually exclusive selectable items (which means only one radio button can be selected at a time).

The RadioButton component is an instance of the mx.controls.RadioButton class with the following inheritance chain: UIObject > UIComponent > SimpleButton > Button > RadioButton. You can use the inspector panels or ActionScript to assign values to its properties.

RadioButton Members

Three of the RadioButton properties are identical to those for the CheckBox: label, `labelPosition`, and `selected`. The RadioButton also has two additional properties you can set for a RadioButton instance.

groupName. The group a RadioButton belongs to. The default value is radioGroup. To make radio buttons mutually exclusive, you must assign all the buttons to the same radio button group. If the user selects a radio button in a group, any other selected radio button is deselected.

```
amex_ch.groupName="creditcard";
trace(amex_ch.groupName);        //Outputs creditcard
```

data. The value associated with a RadioButton instance. The `data` property is similar to the `value` attribute for HTML check boxes and radio buttons.

```
amex_ch.data="AX";
trace(amex_ch.data);             //Outputs AX
```

In addition to the events of its parent classes, the RadioButton also has the `click` event like the CheckBox.

click. Broadcast when a user selects the RadioButton. You use this event with a specific RadioButton instance to capture when that RadioButton is clicked.

```
amex_ch.addEventListener("click",this);
```

> **Note** To change the size and or styles of the RadioButton circles, you must edit the component skins just like you did for the check mark in Lesson 9.

RadioButtonGroup Members

What if you want to find out which radio button is selected in a group? Or get the data for the selected radio button? You don't have to check the `selected` property of each of the individual radio buttons in a group. Instead, you can use two properties of the radio button group.

A RadioButtonGroup is an instance of the mx.controls.RadioButtonGroup class. You can use two of its properties to set or access the selected radio button.

selection. The selected RadioButton component in a group. If you retrieve the `selection` property, a reference to the selected RadioButton object is returned.

```
amex_ch.selected=true;
trace(creditcard.selection);          //Outputs _level0.amex_ch
trace(creditcard.selection.label);    //Outputs American Express
trace(creditcard.selection.data);     //Outputs AX
```

If you assign a value to the `selection` property, the radio button with the corresponding data value is selected.

```
creditcard.selection=visa_ch;        //Selects RadioButton named visa_ch
creditcard.selection="VI";           //Nothing happens
```

selectedData. The data associated with the selected radio button in the group. If you retrieve this property, the `data` value associated with the selected radio button is returned. If the selected RadioButton has no associated `data`, the label `value` is returned.

```
trace(creditcard.selectedData);   //Outputs AX
```

If you assign a value to the `selectedData` property, the radio button with the corresponding `data` value is selected. If none of the RadioButtons has the specified `data` value, the RadioButton with a matching `label` property is selected. If none of the labels match, no RadioButton is selected.

```
creditcard.selectedData="MC";
```

> **Tip** Remember, the *data* and *label* value comparisons are case-sensitive!

You can also use the `click` event with a RadioButtonGroup.

click. Broadcast when a user selects *any* RadioButton in a group.

```
creditcard.addEventListener("click",this);
```

In this exercise, you add two RadioButton components to the search application for selecting whether the house must have a garage. Using ActionScript, you set and capture the RadioButton states.

1. Return to searchHouses.fla in /fpad2004/mmestate/.

Return to the file you created in the last exercise or open /fpad2004/lesson10/intermediate/searchHouses_checkbox.fla and save it as *searchHouses.fla* in /fpad2004/mmestate/.

2. From the Components panel, drag out an instance of the RadioButton component and name the instance yes_rb.

Place the component next to the Garage required text.

3. In the Property inspector, assign a groupName of *garage*, a data value of *1*, a label of *yes*, and a selected value of *true*.

The house table in the fpad2004 database had values of 0 and 1 for the garage field.

4. Use the Free Transform tool to decrease the size of the check box so that it just contains the yes text.

You are making the check box smaller so that the component will be less likely to overlap other components, making it easier for the user to select individual objects.

5. Drag out another instance of the RadioButton component. Name the instance `no_rb` and set the `groupName` to *garage* and the `label` to *no*.

Set the radio buttons next to one another. You will assign the `data` value for this component with code.

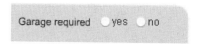

6. Save the file and test the application.

The yes radio button is initially selected. Select one radio button and then the other.

The finished file should resemble: /fpad2004/lesson10/intermediate/searchHouses_radiobutton.fla.

7. Return to Searchform.as in /fpad2004/mmestate/classes/.

Return to the file you created in the last exercise or open /fpad2004/lesson10/intermediate/classes/ Searchform_checkbox.as and save it as *Searchform.as* in /fpad2004/mmestate/classes/.

8. Declare private properties `no_rb` of type *RadioButton* and `garage` of type *RadioButtonGroup*.

You do not need to declare `yes_rb` as a property because you are not going to reference it with code.

9. Inside the `searchformLoad()` method, select the no garage radio button. Use the `selected` property.

```
no_rb.selected=true;
```

Previously, you set the selected radio button at author time. In this step, you are setting the selected button at runtime. The button selected at runtime will be selected in the interface.

10. Inside the `searformLoad()` method, set the `data` property for the `no_rb` button to *0*.

```
no_rb.data=0;
```

You set the data property for `yes_rb` with the Property inspector. You are setting the data property for `no_rb` with code.

11. Inside the `search_pbClick()` method, trace the `selected` value of the `no_rb` radio button.

```
trace(no_rb.selected);
```

12. Trace the `selectedData` property of the `garage` RadioButtonGroup. Save the file.

```
trace(garage.selectedData);
```

13. Return to searchHouses.fla and test the application. Click the Search button.

You should see the values true and 0 traced to the Output panel (after the bedrooms and house type values). Select the yes radio button and click the Search button. You should see the values false and 1 traced to the Output panel.

14. Return to Searchform.as and delete the `trace(no_rb.selected)` statement. Save the file.

The finished file should resemble: /fpad2004/lesson10/intermediate/classes/ Searchform_radiobutton.as.

Working with the ComboBox Component

The ComboBox component has the same look and feel as an HTML select box. You use a ComboBox to create a drop-down list from which the user can select a single item.

Unlike HTML select boxes, you can also make the ComboBox editable so that a user can enter text in a text field in the top row; the ComboBox scrolls to the item with the same text. Only one item is displayed in the closed ComboBox component and a user can only select one item from the list. If you want multiple items initially displayed or you want the user to be able to select multiple items, you must use a List component.

The ComboBox component is an instance of the mx.controls.ComboBox class with the following inheritance chain: UIObject > UIComponent > ComboBase > ComboBox. The ComboBox is made up of a TextInput, a Button, and a List component.

Terminology

The ComboBox has many more properties and methods to manipulate it than the other components covered in the lesson so far. To successfully work with the ComboBox, the most important thing is the terminology. Once you understand the general terminology, all the methods and properties are mostly self-explanatory.

item. Each item in a ComboBox is either a primitive string or an object with `label` and `data` properties.

label. A text string to display for an item in the ComboBox list.

data. The data value to associate with an item in the list.

value. For a noneditable ComboBox, the data for the selected item. For an editable ComboBox, the text entered by the user in the top ComboBox field.

index. Items in a ComboBox are stored in an array. The item displayed at the top of the ComboBox has an index of 0.

Populating a ComboBox

You can populate a ComboBox with values at author time or at runtime. At author time, you enter values for the `labels` parameter and (optionally) the `data` parameter in either of the inspector panels.

Because both the labels and data fields are arrays, you enter individual array items in the fields using a dialog box in which you can add and delete array items as well as change their relative positions.

With code, you can either populate a ComboBox all at once from an array or array of objects or you can add individual items one by one. To populate a ComboBox from an existing array, you use the `dataProvider` property.

```
var bikes:Array=["Kona","Rocky Mountain","VooDoo"];
bikes_cb.dataProvider=bikes;
```

If your data provider is an array of objects, Flash looks for a property of the object called `label` to use to populate the label fields. If no `label` property exists, the ComboBox is populated with a comma-delimited list of all the object properties.

```
var bikes:Array=[{name:"Kona",color:"silver"},{name:"Rocky Mountain",
color:"black"},{name:"VooDoo",color:"green"}];
bikes_cb.dataProvider=bikes;
```

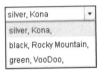

If no `label` field exists in your objects, you can use the ComboBox `labelField` property to specify which object property should be used for the labels.

```
bikes_cb.labelField="name";
```

You can also add individual items to a ComboBox using the `addItem()` and `addItemAt()` methods.

```
var newbike:Object={name:"Intense",color:"silver"};
bikes_cb.addItem(newbike);
```

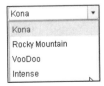

Properties

You can use the Property inspector or Component Inspector panels or ActionScript to assign values to several parameters. `labels` and `data` do not translate directly to properties of the ComboBox: They are properties of individual items in the ComboBox. You assigned values to them in the last section. The `editable` and `rowCount` parameters, however, do correspond to properties of the ComboBox class.

`labels`. An array of text values to populate the ComboBox. The values in the `labels` parameter populate the `label` property of the items in the ComboBox.

`data`. An array of values to associate with items in the ComboBox. The values in the `data` parameter populate the `data` property of the items in the ComboBox.

`editable`. Indicates whether the user can enter text in the first box of the ComboBox.

`rowCount`. The number of items to display in the drop-down list. If there are more items in the list than this value, the drop-down list scrolls.

Some additional ComboBox properties commonly used include the following.

`selectedIndex`. The index of the selected item in the drop-down list. You can set or retrieve the index of the selected item using this property.

```
bikes_cb.selectedIndex=1;
trace(bikes_cb.selectedIndex);         //Outputs 1
```

`selectedItem`. A read-only property that retrieves a reference to the selected item in the drop-down list.

```
trace(bikes_cb.selectedItem);              //Outputs [object Object]
trace(bikes_cb.selectedItem.label);        //Outputs Rocky Mountain
trace(bikes_cb.selectedItem.data);         //Outputs undefined
```

Methods

The ComboBox component also has methods for manipulating and accessing the items in the list. Several methods are listed here:

`addItemAt()`. Adds a new item at a specified index.

`getItemAt()`. Returns the item at a specified index.

`removeAll()`. Removes all items in the list.

`removeItemAt()`. Removes an item at a specified index in the list with another item.

`replaceItemAt()`. Replaces an item at a specified index in the list with another item.

Events

In addition to those of its parent classes, the ComboBox has seven more events. The most commonly used is the `change` event, which is fired when a user changes the item selected in the ComboBox.

There are also `open` and `close` events (fired when the drop-down list starts to open or starts to close), `itemRollOver` and `itemRollOut` events (fired when the pointer rolls over or off an item in the drop-down list; the index of the item is broadcast to the listener), a `scroll` event (fired when the drop-down list is scrolled), and an `enter` event (fired when the Enter/Return key is pressed).

In this exercise, you add two ComboBox components to the search application for selecting the minimum and maximum house prices. You set and capture the selected item. You also create a `change` event handler so that the maximum price displayed is never less than the minimum selected price.

1. Return to searchHouses.fla in /fpad2004/mmestate/.

Return to the file you created in the last exercise or open /fpad2004/lesson10/intermediate/ searchHouses_radiobutton.fla and save it as *searchHouses.fla* in /fpad2004/mmestate/.

2. From the Components panel, drag out an instance of the ComboBox component and name the instance `min_cb`.

Place the component next to the Min price text.

3. In the Property inspector, double-click the field next to the `labels` parameter.

The Values dialog box opens.

You can also open this dialog box by clicking the magnifying glass icon that appears when you select the `labels` parameter field in either of the inspector panels.

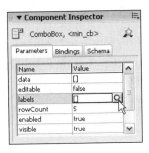

4. In the Values dialog box, click the Add Value button.

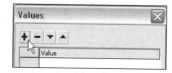

5. Click defaultValue to select it and replace it with the value *100,000*.

6. Repeat Steps 4 and 5 to add several more house prices. For example: 200,000; 300,000; 400,000; and 500,000. Click the OK button.

You should see your new values as an array in the Property inspector.

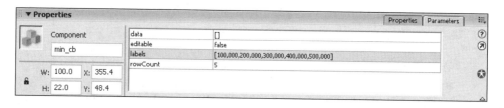

7. From the Components panel, drag out an instance of the ComboBox component and name the instance max_cb.

Place the component next to the Max price text.

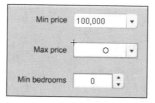

8. Save the file and test the application.

You should see the two combo boxes. Only the minimum price ComboBox should be populated with values. Select a new house price in the minimum price ComboBox.

The finished file should resemble: /fpad2004/lesson10/intermediate/searchHouses_combobox.fla.

9. Return to Searchform.as in /fpad2004/mmestate/classes/.

Return to the file you created in the last exercise or open /fpad2004/lesson10/intermediate/classes/ Searchform_radiobutton.as and save it as *Searchform.as* in /fpad2004/mmestate/classes/.

10. Define two private properties called `min_cb` and `max_cb` of type *mx.controls.ComboBox*.

```
private var min_cb:ComboBox;
private var max_cb:ComboBox;
```

11. Inside the `searchformLoad()` method, create an array called *houseprices* and populate it with the same values you set in the Property inspector for `min_cb`. Use the `selected` property.

```
var prices:Array=["100,000","200,000","300,000","400,000","500,000"];
```

12. Inside the `searchformLoad()` method, populate the `max_cb` ComboBox with the values in the `prices` array. Use the `dataProvider` property.

```
max_cb.dataProvider=prices;
```

13. Inside the `searchformLoad()` method, select the value of 200,000 for `max_cb`. Use the `selectedIndex` property.

```
max_cb.selectedIndex=1;
```

14. Inside the `search_pbClick()` method, trace the `label` property of the selected item for `min_cb`. Use the `selectedItem` property.

```
trace(min_cb.selectedItem.label);
```

15. Inside the `search_pbClick()` method, trace the `value` property for `max_cb`. Save the file.

```
trace(max_cb.value);
```

You cannot use the `selectedItem` property with `max_cb` because you did not populate the `max_cb` ComboBox with objects; you populated the ComboBox with values from a simple array.

As a result, each ComboBox item is a primitive string instead of an object with `label` and `data` properties.

```
trace(max_cb.selectedItem.label); //Returns undefined
```

16. Return to searchHouses.fla and test the application.

The maximum price ComboBox should now be populated with values and should have the price 200,000 initially selected.

17. Select new values in the combo boxes and click the Search button.

You should see the labels for both the selected minimum and maximum prices in the Output panel. For example: 300,000, and 400,000.

18. Return to Searchform.as. Create a new private method called *changeMaxPrice* with no parameters and no return value.

```
private function changeMaxPrice():Void{}
```

Inside this method, you are going to create logic so that if the selected minimum price is changed, the selected maximum price changes so the selected maximum price is never below the selected minimum price.

19. Inside the method, check to see if the selected maximum price is less than the selected minimum price. If it is, set the selected index of `max_cb` equal to the selected index of `min_cb`. Use the `selectedIndex` property.

```
if (min_cb.selectedIndex > max_cb.selectedIndex)
{
        max_cb.selectedIndex=min_cb.selectedIndex;
}
```

The preceding logic assumes that the two lists are populated with the same values in the same indices. You could write more complicated logic so you do not have to make this assumption, but in this application ComboBoxes will always be populated with the same data. They have the same values in this exercise where you populated the ComboBoxes manually and will have the same values in Lesson 12, "Retrieving Data from XML Files," where you populate the two ComboBoxes with values from the same XML file.

20. Inside the `handleEvent()` method, add a new case for when `evtObj.type` is equal to *change*. If this case is true, call the `changeMaxPrice()` method.

```
case ("change"):
        changeMaxPrice();
        break;
```

21. In the `searchformLoad()` method, register the screen as a listener for the `change` event of `min_cb`. Save the file.

```
min_cb.addEventListener("change",this);
```

The finished file should resemble: /fpad2004/lesson10/intermediate/classes/Searchform_combobox.as.

22. Return to searchHouses.fla and test the application. Change the selected minimum price.

The selected maximum price should change to match the selected minimum price.

Using the List Component

The List component has the same look and feel as an HTML multiple select box. You use a List component to create an options list with multiple items displayed or from which the user can select multiple items. The List component is similar to the ComboBox component except that: multiple items are initially displayed, the item list scrolls instead of displayed in a drop-down list, a user can select multiple items instead of just one, and the first row is not editable.

The List component is an instance of the mx.controls.List class with the inheritance chain: UIObject > UIComponent > View > ScrollView > ScrollSelectList > List.

The terminology and methods to populate the List component are identical to those for the ComboBox component. In fact, the two components share almost all the same properties, methods, and events. New parameters in the inspector panels include rowHeight and multipleSelection.

rowHeight. The height of each row in the list.

multipleSelection. Indicates whether the user can select multiple items in the drop-down list using Shift-click or Control-click.

The List component has additional properties for setting scroll properties like those you used for the TextArea component earlier (vScrollPolicy, hScrollPolicy, vPosition, and hPosition). There are also additional properties for selecting multiple items instead of just one.

selectedIndices. An array of indices for the selected items. When the multipleSelection property is true, you can use the selectedIndices property to set or retrieve multiple selected indices in a list; the selectedIndex property sets or retrieves one value.

```
bikes_cb.selectedIndices=[1,2];
trace(bikes_cb.selectedIndices);        //Outputs 1,2
```

selectedItems. Read-only property to retrieve an array of references to the selected items. When the multipleSelection property is true, you can use the selectedItems property to retrieve multiple items selected in a list; the selectedItem property retrieves only one value.

```
trace(bikes_cb.selectedItems);              //Outputs [object Object]
trace(bikes_cb.selectedItems[0].label);     //Outputs Rocky Mountain
trace(bikes_cb.selectedItems[0].data);      //Outputs undefined
```

The List component has less events than the ComboBox because it has no drop-down list. Like the ComboBox, its most commonly used event is the change event, which is fired when a user changes the item selected in the List. There are also itemRollOver and itemRollOut events (fired when the pointer rolls over or off an item in the list; the index of the item is broadcast to the listener) and a scroll event (fired when the drop-down list is scrolled).

In this exercise, you add a List component to the search application for selecting the cities to search. You set and capture the selected items.

1. Return to searchHouses.fla in /fpad2004/mmestate/.

Return to the file you created in the last exercise or open /fpad2004/lesson10/intermediate/searchHouses_combobox.fla and save it as *searchHouses.fla* in /fpad2004/mmestate/.

2. From the Components panel, drag out an instance of the List component and name the instance cities_lb.

Place the component next to the Cities text.

3. Use the Free Transform tool to resize the List component to fill the available space.

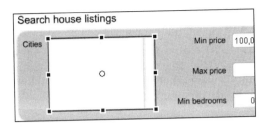

4. In the Property inspector, set the `multipleSelection` parameter to true.

This step enables the user to select multiple cities.

5. Double-click the field next to the `labels` parameter. In the Values dialog box, enter several city names. For example: Fairfax, San Anselmo, and San Rafael.

It does not matter what cities you enter. Before you actually do a search against the database, you will populate the List component with cities from an XML file in Lesson 12.

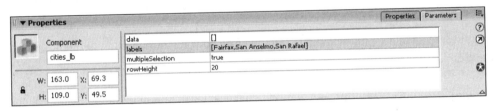

6. Save the file and test the application.

You should see the List component populated with the city names you entered. Select multiple items in the list.

The finished file should resemble: /fpad2004/lesson10/intermediate/searchHouses_list.fla.

7. Return to Searchform.as in /fpad2004/mmestate/classes/.

Return to the file you created in the last exercise or open /fpad2004/lesson10/intermediate/classes/ Searchform_combobox.as and save it as *Searchform.as* in /fpad2004/mmestate/classes/.

8. Define a private property called `cities_lb` of type *mx.controls.List.*

```
private var cities_lb:List;
```

9. Inside the `search_pbClick()` method, trace the indices of the selected items for `cities_lb`. Use the `toString()` method to convert the array to a comma-delimited list.

```
trace(cities_lb.selectedIndices.toString());
```

Just like for the ComboBox exercise, you don't have to explicitly call the `toString()` method because the `toString()` method is automatically invoked when you try to trace an object. You need this data transformation (an array to a comma-delimited list) so you can send this data in a proper format to a web service in Lesson 13.

10. Inside the `search_pbClick()` method, trace the `label` of the first selected item for `cities_lb`.

```
trace(cities_lb.selectedItems[0].label);
```

11. Return to searchHouses.fla and test the application. Select multiple items in the List component and click the Search button.

You should see a list of the selected indices in the Output panel and the label of the first selected item in the list.

12. Return to Searchform.as and delete the `trace()` of `cities_lb.selectedItems[0].label`. Save the file.

The finished file should resemble: /fpad2004/lesson10/intermediate/classes/Searchform_list.as.

What You Have Learned

In this lesson, you have:

- Manipulated the Button component (pages 413–417)
- Worked with the TextInput component (pages 417–419)
- Managed the Label component (pages 419–422)
- Manipulated the TextArea component (pages 422–426)
- Used the NumericStepper component (pages 426–429)
- Manipulated the CheckBox component (pages 429–433)
- Utilized the RadioButton component (pages 433–437)
- Manipulated the ComboBox component (pages 437–445)
- Manipulated the List component (pages 445–448)

11 Creating Visual Objects Dynamically

In addition to adding content directly to the Stage, you can create visual objects dynamically at runtime. Using code, you can create TextField and MovieClip objects, but not Button objects. To create TextField objects dynamically, you use the `createTextField()` method of the MovieClip class. There are several methods to create MovieClip objects dynamically. You can programmatically create new MovieClip instances from existing symbols in the library or you can create and load external JPGs or SWFs into new MovieClips, Loader components, or screens.

There are many scenarios in which you might want to dynamically create visual objects. First, by loading external data, you can update or change a part of the application without changing the FLA file. This is useful for images that need to change periodically because you only need to swap the JPG file. Plus, non-Flash developers can update pictures without having to use Flash or contact a developer. Second, dynamic creation gives you the ability to change the contents of a MovieClip at runtime. For example, in a catalog application, you display the image of a selected item in a particular MovieClip; when the user selects a new item, the image changes to the new item. Third, you can create MovieClips or components dynamically when you don't know ahead of time how many objects you need. For example, you might need one radio button for each type of accepted credit card—where the number and types of credit cards are retrieved from a file or database on the server.

Finally, dynamic object creation lets you break complex applications into smaller SWFs that are downloaded from the server and loaded into the Flash Player only when needed at runtime. This keeps users from waiting for an entire application to download before they can start using the application—which is especially beneficial if the user will not interact with all parts of the

In this lesson, you dynamically load your search-houses application into the Macromediestate application.

application. You should include all the core functionality in the main application and then separate the other pieces into their own SWFs that can be downloaded separately when needed by the user.

In this lesson, you dynamically create MovieClips. First, you attach a MovieClip from the library to display an error icon when the user does not enter a valid password. Next, you attach components from the library, creating check boxes for all the house types dynamically. Then, you dynamically create a MovieClip and load an image of a featured home into it; you do this with code and then using the Loader component. Finally, you load your application into the search screen of the main Macromediestate application.

What You Will Learn

In this lesson, you will:

- Understand and manage object depth
- Attach a MovieClip dynamically from the library
- Create components dynamically
- Create an empty MovieClip dynamically and load a JPG or SWF into it
- Load dynamic content into a Loader component
- Load external content into a screen

Approximate Time

This lesson takes approximately 70 minutes to complete.

Lesson File

Asset Files:

/fpad2004/lesson11/start/assets/erroricon.gif
/fpad2004/lesson11/start/assets/featurehome.jpg

Starting Files:

/fpad2004/lesson11/start/mmestate.fla
/fpad2004/lesson11/start/classes/MmestateLogin.as
/fpad2004/lesson11/start/classes/MmestateHome.as
/fpad2004/lesson11/start/classes/MmestateSearch.as
/fpad2004/lesson11/start/searchHouses.swf

Completed Files:

/fpad2004/lesson11/complete/mmestate.fla
/fpad2004/lesson11/complete/classes/MmestateLogin.as
/fpad2004/lesson11/complete/classes/MmestateHome.as
/fpad2004/lesson11/complete/classes/MmestateSearch.as
/fpad2004/lesson11/complete/createObjects.fla

Understanding Depth

In Flash you can create visual objects that overlap or even completely hide one another. When you create objects in the authoring environment, the way objects are displayed at runtime is determined by either the order of the layers or the screens, or by the order that you dragged items to the Stage within a particular layer or screen. When you create visual objects dynamically with code, you must set this "stacking order" for the objects yourself. You assign relative stacking positions of objects by assigning a numerical value for the **depth** of an object when you create it, much like you assign a z-index property in Cascading Style Sheets.

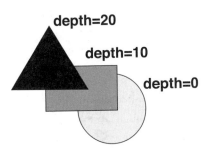

The MovieClip depth you assign must be an integer from –16,383 to +1,048,575. (The document root has a depth of –16,384; higher values are unsupported by the Flash Player.) The relative depths of MovieClips determine how the objects appear in the application at runtime. By default, all objects created at design time, either with tools or by dragging components to the Stage, are located below anything created with ActionScript; objects created at design time are assigned depths at very low negative values. You can retrieve the depth assigned to any object with an instance name using the MovieClip method `getDepth()`.

When you assign depths to objects when you create them with code, you should assign positive values like 100, 200, 300; leaving plenty of space between depths to add additional objects later. If you want objects created with ActionScript to be placed below objects created with the drawing tools, you must use the MovieClip method `swapDepths()`, which lets you swap one object's depth with that of another object. When using `swapDepths()`, the method argument can be either an instance name of a MovieClip with which to swap depths or an integer specifying a depth with which to swap contents. The following code swaps the depths of a Button component and a MovieClip.

```
my_mc.swapDepths(mybutton);
```

This could also be written as follows:

```
var buttondepth:Number=mybutton.getDepth();
my_mc.swapDepths(buttondepth);
```

In this exercise, you use MovieClip methods to get and swap the depths of objects in the Macromedistate application.

1. Return to mmestate.fla in /fpad2004/mmestate/.

This is the file you created in the last lesson. If you did not do that exercise, open /fpad2004/lesson11/ start/mmestate.fla and save it as *mmestate.fla* in /fpad2004/mmestate/.

> **Note** To test the application, you also need working versions of MmestateApp.as, MmestateMain.as, and MmestateHome.as. If you did not finish Lesson 10, copy these files from the start folder to your /mmestate/classes/ folder.

2. On the `login` screen, move the Button component to overlap the password TextInput component.

The button is located on top of the password because you added it to the screen last. You can change the relative order of objects on the Stage within a layer or screen by selecting Modify > Arrange from the main menu and selecting one of the options (Send to Back, Bring to Front, and so on).

3. Return to MmestateLogin.as in /fpad2004/mmestate/classes/.

This is the file you created in the last lesson. If you did not do that exercise, open /fpad2004/lesson11/ start/classes/MmestateLogin.as and save it as *MmestateLogin.as* in /fpad2004/mmestate/classes/.

4. Inside the `loginLoad()` method, trace the depths of `password_ti` and `login_pb`. Use the MovieClip `getDepth()` method. Save the file.

```
trace(password_ti.getDepth());
trace(login_pb.getDepth());
```

Which object do you expect to have a lower depth?

5. Return to mmestate.fla and test the application.

You should get a depth of –16,380 for `password_ti` and a depth of –16,379 for `login_pb`. The button is on top of the password on the Stage, so the button is assigned a less negative depth than the password field.

6. Return to MmestateLogin.as. Inside the `loginLoad()` method, swap the depths of the two components so the button is below the password; use the `swapDepths()` method. Save the file.

```
login_pb.swapDepths(password_ti);
```

7. Return to mmestate.fla and test the application.

The password text field should now appear above the Login button.

8. Return to MmestateLogin.as and delete the `swapDepths()` method. Change the two `getDepth()` methods to get the depths of the `_root` and `application` screens. Add another `getDepth()` method to get the depth of the `login` screen. Save the file.

```
trace(_root.getDepth());
trace(_parent.getDepth());
trace(this.getDepth());
```

How do you expect these depths to compare to those of the Login button and password field?

9. Return to mmestate.fla and move the Login button back to its original position. Save the file and test the application.

You should get a depth of –16,384 for the document root, a depth of –16,383 for the `application` screen, and a depth of –16,382 for the `login` screen.

You will use this file as the starting file for the next exercise. It should resemble the finished file: /fpad2004/lesson11/intermediate/mmestate_depth.fla.

10. Return to MmestateLogin.as. Delete the three `trace()` statements retrieving depths. Save the file.

You will use this file as the starting file for the next exercise. It should resemble the finished file: /fpad2004/lesson11/intermediate/classes/MmestateLogin_depth.as.

Attaching MovieClips Dynamically from the Library

To dynamically create an instance of a MovieClip at runtime from a symbol in the document's library, you must do three things. First, create the MovieClip symbol. If the MovieClip is not initially displayed anywhere in the application, you can delete the instance from the Stage so the symbol exists only in the library. Next, specify a linkage name for the MovieClip in the Library panel. Remember from working with images in Lesson 1, "Learning the Flash Interface," that by default, all symbols in the library that are not used on the Stage are not compiled into the application and are not available for runtime code. To export the MovieClip symbol so it *is* compiled into the application, select Export for ActionScript in the Convert to Symbol dialog box.

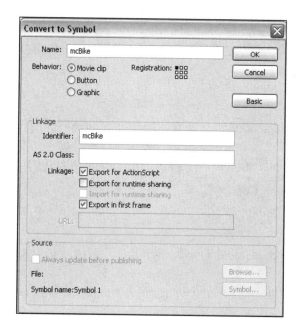

Finally, use the MovieClip `attachMovie()` method, which takes a MovieClip symbol from the library and "attaches it" to a specified MovieClip. The syntax is as follows:

```
my_mc.attachMovie(idName, newName, depth);
```

Where **idName** is the linkage name of the MovieClip symbol in the library, **newname** is the new instance name for the MovieClip being created, and **depth** is an integer specifying the depth into which the new instance is placed. Note that the new MovieClip is always a child of another MovieClip. You can remove a MovieClip attached with `attachMovie()` using the `removeMovieClip()` or `unloadMovie()` methods.

Note *You can also pass an object as a fourth argument to the* `attachMovie()` *method. The object's properties are assigned as properties to the new MovieClip instance. For example, the initialization object could have* `_x` *and* `_y` *properties, which would then be used to set the position of the new MovieClip.*

The following code attaches a MovieClip symbol with the Linkage Identifier mcBike to the main MovieClip instance creating a new MovieClip instance called `bike_mc` at a depth of 10.

```
this.attachMovie("mcBike","bike_mc",10);
```

If no position is specified for the new object, it is placed at (0,0) of the MovieClip it is loaded into.

Note *If you use a depth value already assigned to another object, the new MovieClip will replace the existing object at that depth.*

You can remove the MovieClip with the following code:

```
bike_mc.removeMovieClip();
```

In this exercise, you dynamically attach an error icon next to the error message on the `login` screen when the user enters a password that's less than 4 characters.

1. Return to mmestate.fla in /fpad2004/mmestate/.

Return to the file you used in the last exercise or open /fpad2004/lesson11/intermediate/ mmestate_depth.fla and save it as *mmestate.fla* in /fpad2004/mmestate/.

2. Navigate to the `login` screen and select File › Import › Import to Stage. Browse to erroricon.gif in /mmestate/assets/ and click Open.

The error icon image is placed on the Stage.

3. Place the icon between the `password_ti` and `password_la` components.

Move the `password_la` Label component to the right if necessary.

4. Look at the x and y positions of the error icon in the Property inspector and write down the values.

You will use these positions to place the MovieClip when you attach it via code.

5. Right-click/Control-click the error icon and select Convert to Symbol. In the Symbol Properties dialog box, give the symbol the name *erroricon*, make it a Graphic symbol, and select Export for ActionScript. Click OK.

You might need to click the Advanced button if you do not see the Export for ActionScript check box. When you select the Export for ActionScript check box, the Linkage name is automatically populated with the symbol name, erroricon.

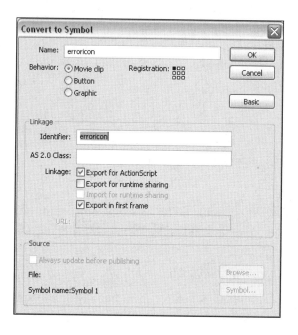

The erroricon symbol appears in the library.

6. Delete the erroricon symbol instance from the Stage. Save the file.

The erroricon MovieClip now exists only in the library.

The finished file should resemble: /fpad2004/lesson11/intermediate/mmestate_attachmovie.fla.

7. Return to MmestateLogin.as in /fpad2004/mmestate/classes/.

Return to the file you created in the last exercise or open /fpad2004/lesson11/intermediate/classes/ MmestateLogin_depth.as and save it as *MmestateLogin.as* in /fpad2004/mmestate/classes/.

8. Create a private property called `erroricon_mc` of type *MovieClip*.

```
private var erroricon_mc:MovieClip;
```

9. Inside the `if` block in the `login_pbClick()` method, use `attachMovie()` to create a MovieClip called `erroricon_mc` at a depth of 10 from the MovieClip symbol with the linkage name *erroricon*.

```
62    private function login_pbClick():Void
63    {
64        if (password_ti.length<4)
65        {
66            login_pb.enabled=false;
67            password_la.text="Your password must be at least 4 characters".
68            this.attachMovie("erroricon","erroricon_mc",10);
69        }
```

10. Still inside the `if` block, set the `_x` and `_y` properties of `erroricon_mc` to the values you wrote down in Step **4**.

```
erroricon_mc._x=401.6;
erroricon_mc._y=307.6;
```

Alternatively, you can set the positions by passing an object with properties `_x` and `_y` to the `attachMovie()` method as a fourth argument:

```
var init:Object={_x:401.6,_y:307.6};
this.attachMovie("erroricon","erroricon_mc",20,init);
```

11. Inside the `else` block in the `login_pbClick()` method, remove `erroricon_mc`. Use the `removeMovieClip()` method. Save the file.

```
erroricon_mc.removeMovieClip();
```

The finished file should resemble: /fpad2004/lesson11/intermediate/classes/
MmestateLogin_attachmovie.as.

12. Return to mmestate.fla and test the application.

Enter a username and one character in the password field. Click the Login button. You should see your error icon and the error message.

13. Successfully log in to the application. Click the Logout button.

You should no longer see your error icon on the login page; the MovieClip was successfully removed.

Creating Components Dynamically

You have attached a MovieClip dynamically, but what if you want to create a component dynamically? For example, you might want to create check boxes dynamically so that their total number and their individual labels are retrieved from a database. Or maybe you want to selectively show an order button only if the user has filled in all of the fields appropriately. Because a component is just an extended MovieClip, you can also use the `attachMovie()` method to dynamically load a component from the library. The UIObject class has a method called `createObject()`, which does the same thing, but wraps it with a more user-friendly name, hiding the word movie. You should use the component API instead of the MovieClip API.

457

When attaching a component dynamically with `createObject()`, the component symbol must exist in the document library, just as it did when using `attachMovie()`. All the prebuilt components have preassigned linkage names that are the same as the component class names.

In the following code, a CheckBox component is dynamically created:

```
this.createObject("CheckBox","email_ch",10);
```

The CheckBox created, though, has no label.

You can assign a `label` after the component is created

```
email_ch.label="Send e-mail?";
```

or you can specify a `label` property in an object passed to `createObject()` as a fourth argument, just as you could with the `attachMovie()` method.

```
var init:Object={label:"Send e-mail?"};
this.createObject("CheckBox","email_ch",10,init);
```

The UIObject class also has a method called `createClassObject()`, which you can use to create a component dynamically. When using this method, you specify the class of the object to create instead of the linkage name of the symbol to attach in the library. The component, though, must still exist in the document library.

```
this.createClassObject(mx.controls.CheckBox,"email_ch",10);
```

In this exercise, you create a group of CheckBox components dynamically, creating one check box for each house type. You set the instance names, positions, and depths of the check boxes dynamically.

1. Create a new Flash document. Save the file as *createObjects.fla* in */fpad2004/mmestate/*.

Instead of working with the existing SearchHouses.fla and Searchform.as files, you will complete this exercise in a separate file so you don't have to worry about positioning the check boxes in the application and working with two files.

2. From the Components panel, drag a CheckBox component to the Stage and then delete it.

This process places a copy of the CheckBox component in the library.

3. Open the Library panel. Right-click/Control-click CheckBox and select Linkage. In the Linkage Properties dialog box, verify that the Identifier name is also CheckBox. Click OK.

The linkage names for the prebuilt components are the same as their class names.

4. Open the Actions panel. Create an array called `housetypes` with three elements: *single family*, *condo*, and *farm or ranch*.

```
var housetypes:Array=new Array("single family","condo","farm or ranch");
```

In this step, you are hard-coding the number of check boxes and their labels. In a real application, this data would come from an external data source. You learn to retrieve data from external data sources in Lesson 12, 13, and 14.

5. Create a variable called `varname` of type *String* that is equal to an empty string.

```
var varname:String="";
```

You will create instance names for the check boxes dynamically. The `varname` variable will hold the current name of a check box.

6. Create a `for` loop that loops from 0 to the length of the `housetypes` array.

```
for (var i=0;i<housetypes.length;i++){}
```

Inside the loop, you will dynamically create a CheckBox for each item in the array.

7. Inside the `for` loop, set `varname` equal to the string "housetype", plus the value of the variable `i`, plus the string "_ch".

```
varname="housetype"+i+"_ch";
```

As you loop through the array, instance names `housetype1_ch`, `housetype2_ch`, and so on are created.

8. Inside the `for` loop, create a new CheckBox with the instance name equal to the value of the `varname` variable. Use the `createObject()` method and set the depth equal to `i` times 10.

```
this.createObject("CheckBox",varname,i*10);
```

If you do not use a new depth for each check box, subsequent check boxes created in the loop will replace one another.

9. After the `createObject()` method inside the `for` loop, set `varname` equal to the *ith* value in the `housetypes` array.

```
this[varname].label=housetypes[i];
```

Note the use of the square bracket notation `this[varname]` to dynamically evaluate the name of the instance. If you used `varname` without `this[]`, the label for the `varname` variable would be set, not the label for `housetype1_ch` or whatever the current value of the `varname` variable is.

10. Save the file and test the application.

Three check boxes are created dynamically, but they appear on top of one another. By default, all the check boxes are positioned at (0,0). You need to set the positions dynamically so the check boxes do not overlap.

11. Before the `for` loop, create a variable called `ypos` of type *Number* that is equal to 0.

```
var ypos:Number=0;
```

You will assign the vertical positions for the check boxes dynamically so they do not appear on top of one another.

12. At the end of the code inside the `for` loop, set the position of the new check box instance using the UIObject `move()` method.

```
this[varname].move(0,ypos);
```

The first time though the loop, the new check box will be positioned at (0,0). For the next position to be different, you need to increment the `ypos` variable before the next loop iteration.

13. At the end of the code inside the `for` loop, increment the `ypos` variable by 20.

```
ypos+=20;
```

Each new check box will be placed 20 pixels below the last.

14. Save the file and test the application.

The check boxes are now aligned vertically.

The finished file should resemble: /fpad2004/lesson11/intermediate/createObjects.fla.

Note *If any of the labels are too long to fit in the default CheckBox width (which is 100), you can use the UIObject* `setSize()` *method to change the width. For example:* `this[varname].setSize(120,22).`

Creating MovieClips with ActionScript

In addition to dynamically loading a MovieClip symbol from the library at runtime, you can also load external images (JPGs) or other Flash applications (SWFs). There are two steps to the process; first, you create an empty MovieClip and then you load content into it.

Creating an Empty MovieClip

You create an empty MovieClip instance using the MovieClip `createEmptyMovieClip()` method, which creates a MovieClip instance with no contents. The syntax is as follows:

```
my_mc.createEmptyMovieClip(instanceName,depth);
```

Where **instancename** is the instance name for the new MovieClip being created, and **depth** is an integer specifying the depth into which the new instance is placed. Note that the new MovieClip is always a child of some other MovieClip.

The following example creates a MovieClip instance called `image_mc` in the main MovieClip instance at a depth of 0:

```
this.createEmptyMovieClip("image_mc",0);
```

If you do not set the _x and _y properties of the MovieClip, it is placed at (0,0) of the MovieClip that it is loaded into.

Note *You can also create empty MovieClips in the authoring environment. Select Insert > New Symbol and create a new MovieClip symbol with no content. You can drag instances of the MovieClip symbol from the library, give them instance names, and then load content into them at runtime using the method in the next section. Empty MovieClip instances appear on the Stage as small circles.*

Loading JPGs or SWFs into a MovieClip

Once you create an empty MovieClip, you load a JPG or SWF into it using the MovieClip `loadMovie()` method. You can load SWFs of JPGs from any location on the Internet into your Flash application. The syntax is as follows:

```
my_mc.loadMovie("URL");
```

The URL can be absolute or relative to the location of the parent SWF:

```
my_mc.loadMovie("http://mysite.com/logo.jpg");
my_mc.loadMovie("../images/logo.jpg");
```

The newly loaded SWF or JPG replaces any existing contents of the MovieClip for which the method was called. The loaded application or image inherits all the position, rotation, and scale properties of the MovieClip. For loaded SWFs, you reference variables of the SWF as properties of that nested MovieClip.

Tip *If you want to access data (like variables, functions, and so on) of the loaded SWF from the parent SWF or data of the parent SWF from the loaded SWF, the two SWFs must originate from exactly the same domain (for example, both from www.macromedia.com; not one from www.macromedia.com and one from mmestate.macromedia.com). If the SWFs are not located on exactly the same domain, you can still exchange data between the two if you add the statement* System.security.allowDomain() *to the Flash application whose data is to be accessed by another SWF. Pass to the* allowDomain() *method the names of the other domains to which you want to give access to the SWF's data. If a SWF is hosted using a secure protocol (HTTPS) and needs to permit access from SWFs hosted in nonsecure protocols, use* System.security.allowInsecureDomain() *instead.*

Events do not fire on a MovieClip created dynamically if you load external content into it. If you want to associate event handlers with the MovieClip, you need to create a wrapper MovieClip object. Create two MovieClips, one nested inside the other, and then load the external content into the nested MovieClip.

```
this.createEmptyMovieClip("wrapper_mc",10);
wrapper_mc.createEmptyMovieClip("nested_mc",20);
wrapper_mc.nested_mc.loadMovie("../images/bikesilver.jpg");
```

You add the event handling on the wrapper MovieClip:

```
wrapper_mc.onRollOver=function():Void
{
    this.nested_mc.loadMovie("../images/bikeblue.jpg");
};
```

You unload the contents of a MovieClip that have been loaded using the loadMovie() method using the unloadMovie() method.

```
my_mc.unloadMovie();
```

Note *There is currently a bug with loading a SWF containing a ComboBox component into a target MovieClip; the ComboBox will not display and work correctly. To fix this, add an instance of the ComboBox component to the target application's library.*

In this exercise, you dynamically create an empty MovieClip on the home page and load an image of a featured home into it.

1. Return to mmestate.fla in /fpad2004/mmestate/.

Return to the file you used in the `attachMovie()` exercise or open /fpad2004/lesson11/ intermediate/mmestate_attachmovie.fla and save it as *mmestate.fla* in /fpad2004/mmestate/.

2. Select the home screen in the Screen Outline pane. Add a new static text field to the right of the "We provide" text field with the text *Featured home*. Use Arial font, black, size 12. Save the file.

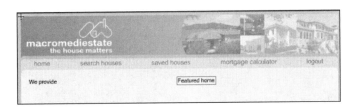

3. Select Window > Design Panels > Info. Place the mouse pointer on the Stage where you want the featured home image. Write down the x and y coordinates from the Info panel. Close the Info panel.

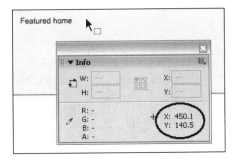

The x and y coordinates of the upper left corner of the image should be somewhere around 450 and 140.

4. Save the file.

The finished file should resemble: /fpad2004/lesson11/intermediate/mmestate_loadjpg.fla.

5. Return to MmestateHome.as.

This is a file you used in the last lesson. If you did not complete that lesson, open /fpad2004/lesson11/ start/classes/MmestateHome.as and save it as *MmestateHome.as* in /fpad2004/mmestate/classes/.

6. Create a private property called `featurehome_mc` of type *MovieClip*.

```
private var featurehome_mc:MovieClip;
```

7. Inside the `homeLoad()` method, create a MovieClip called `featurehome_mc` at a depth of *20*. Use the `createEmptyMovieClip()` method.

```
this.createEmptyMovieClip("featurehome_mc",20);
```

You loaded the erroricon in the first exercise into depth 10. Although you could use a depth of 10 for both MovieClip depths—because the two images are never displayed at the same time, that would be a bad practice. You should always use unique depths for different MovieClip objects.

8. Set the `_x` and `_y` properties to those you wrote down in Step 3.

```
featurehome_mc._x=450;
featurehome_mc._y=140;
```

9. Load the image located at the relative URL /assets/featurehome.jpg into `featurehome_mc`. Use the `loadMovie()` method. Save the file.

```
featurehome_mc.loadMovie("assets/featurehome.jpg");
```

The finished file should resemble: /fpad2004/lesson11/intermediate/classes/ MmestateHome_loadjpg.as.

10. Return to mmestate.fla in /fpad2004/mmestate/ and test the application.

Log in to the application. You should see the feature home image displayed on the home page. If your image and text do not line up properly, change the locations of the components on the home page or the coordinates of the `featurehome_mc` MovieClip.

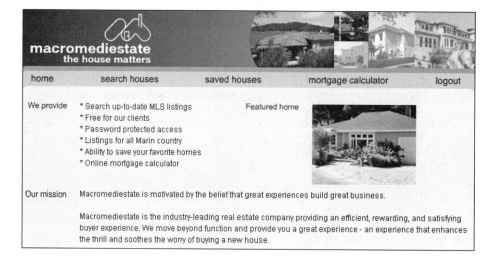

There are two benefits of loading the image dynamically. First, the FLA does not have to be changed if you want to change this image; only the featurehome.jpg image has to be swapped out on the server. Second, the image file size is not part of the application size; the image is downloaded as a separate request.

Managing Depths

In the previous exercises, you specified integer depths for the new objects. It was up to you to keep track of all occupied depths and place new objects accordingly. The built-in MovieClip class has four methods to aid you in manipulating depths. You used `getDepth()` and `swapDepths()` in the first exercise There are two additional methods.

`getInstanceAtDepth()`. Returns either the name of the MovieClip instance at the specified depth or undefined. Use this method to find out if a depth is already occupied before you assign a new object to it.

`getNextHighestDepth()`. Returns a depth value (zero or higher) that you can assign to an object to ensure that it is rendered above all the objects in a particular MovieClip.

```
this.createEmptyMovieClip("bike_mc",getNextHighestDepth());
```

In addition to these four methods, there is also a new DepthManager class, **mx.managers. DepthManager**, which is part of the application framework that has been provided to also help you manage relative depth assignments. The DepthManager class provides additional functionality to the ActionScript MovieClip class for creating and managing depths of objects. See the Help files for more information.

In this exercise, you set the depth of your image MovieClip using the `getNextHighestDepth()` method.

1. Return to MmestateHome.as in /fpad2004/mmestate/classes/.

Return to the file you used in the last exercise or open /fpad2004/lesson11/intermediate/classes/ MmestateHome_loadjpg.as and save it as *MmestateHome.as* in /fpad2004/mmestate/classes/.

2. Inside the `onScreenLoad()` method, change the depth specified in the `createEmptyMovieClip()` method so the next highest depth is used; use the `getNextHighestDepth()` method. Save the file.

```
this.createEmptyMovieClip("featurehome_mc",this.getNextHighestDepth());
```

3. Trace the depth of `featurehome_mc` using `getDepth()`.

```
21    private function homeLoad():Void
22    {
23        mission_ta.vScrollPolicy="off";
24        this.home_xc.trigger();
25        this.createEmptyMovieClip("featurehome_mc",this.getNextHighestDepth())
26        trace(featurehome_mc.getDepth());
27        featurehome_mc.x=450;
```

4. Return to mmestate.fla in /fpad2004/mmestate/ and test the application.

Return to the file you used in the last exercise or open /fpad2004/lesson11/intermediate/ mmestate_loadjpg.fla and save it as *mmestate.fla* in /fpad2004/mmestate/.

Log in to the application. You should still see the featured home image displayed on the home page and you should get a depth value of 0 traced to the Output panel.

5. Return to mmestate.fla and delete the trace you added in Step 3. Save the file.

The finished file should resemble: /fpad2004/lesson11/intermediate/classes/ MmestateHome_managedepth.as.

Monitoring MovieClip Loading Progress

What if you want to monitor the loading process of a MovieClip? Perhaps to display its progress as it proceeds, or to wait and execute some code after the new application has finished loading. The built-in MovieClip class has several class members to use for simple monitoring of the load process, including an `onLoad` event and `getBytesLoaded()` and `getBytesTotal()` methods. To determine what percentage of a MovieClip has loaded, you can compare the value returned by `getBytesLoaded()` with the value returned by `getBytesTotal()`.

There is also a new built-in class for Flash Player 7 called **MovieClipLoader** that broadcasts events providing status information about the file loading process. To implement this functionality for your file loading, you create instances of the MovieClipLoader class instead of the normal MovieClip class. To load and unload JPGs or SWFs, you use the `loadClip()` and `unloadClip()` methods of the MovieClipLoader class.

```
var my_mc:MovieClipLoader;
my_mc.loadClip("search.swf");
my_mc.unloadClip();
```

After the `loadClip()` method is executed, several events are broadcast.

These events include `onLoadStart()` (**when a file starts to download**), `onLoadProgress()` (every time the loading content is written to disk during the loading process), `onLoadComplete()` (when a file download is done), `onLoadInit()` (when actions on the first frame of the loaded MovieClip have been executed at which time you can interact with the loaded application), and `onLoadError()` (when a file fails to load). Just like for normal event handling, you can use the `addListener()` method to register other objects to receive notification when these MovieClipLoader events occur and `removeListener()` to remove them.

To monitor progress during the download, you can either write a MovieClipLoader's `onLoadProgress()` callback function that is invoked periodically during the download process or you can use the `getProgress()` method to explicitly get the download progress at any time; the method returns an object with two properties, `bytesLoaded` and `bytesTotal`.

Using the Loader Component

New to Flash MX 2004, is the ability to load external content into an application without having to write code. The Loader component wraps the creation and loading of content in MovieClips with a visual representation in the authoring environment. To dynamically load content using the Loader component, drag a Loader component to where you want to dynamically add content on the Stage and set parameters in one of the inspector panels.

contentPath. The path to the JPG or SWF to load. The URL can be absolute or relative.

scaleContent. A Boolean indicating whether the content scales to fit the size of the Loader component, or if the Loader scales to fit the content. The default value is true, so the loaded content scales to fit the Loader.

autoLoad. A Boolean indicating whether the content should load automatically. If `autoLoad` is true, the JPG or SWF is downloaded and loaded with the main application. If this JPG or SWF is not needed immediately, you can decrease your initial download time by setting the `autoLoad` parameter to false and then loading the content when necessary using the `load()` method of the Loader screen API, which loads the contents at the URL contained in the `contentPath` property.

Unfortunately, at this time, if you do not have the Loader component selected on the Stage it is invisible (just like the Label component), making it difficult to work with. You have to remember where the Loader component was on the Stage to select it. The Loader becomes visible, though, it you turn off Live Preview in the authoring environment. (To disable Live Preview, select Control > Enable Live Preview.) When Live Preview is disabled, the Loader component is represented on the Stage as a black square that you can resize and reposition.

CREATING VISUAL OBJECTS DYNAMICALLY

Now the Loader component has a visual representation on the Stage. When building the application, you can *see* where dynamic content will be displayed in the application, and visually change its size and position.

The Loader component is an instance of the mx.controls.Loader class, and inherits from UIObject > UIComponent > View > Loader. In addition to the above properties and method, the Loader class API also provides properties (`bytesLoaded`, `bytesTotal`, `percentLoaded`) and events (`progress`, `complete`) for monitoring the loading progress of the content.

In this exercise, you change your application so the featured home is loaded into a Loader component instead of an empty MovieClip.

1. Return to MmestateHome.as in /fpad2004/mmestate/classes/.

Return to the file you created in the last exercise or open /fpad2004/lesson11/intermediate/classes/MmestateHome_managedepth.as and save it as *MmestateHome.as* in /fpad2004/mmestate/classes/.

2. Delete all the code in `homeLoad()` for `featurehome_mc`. Save the file.

Delete the variable declaration and the code shown in the following screenshot.

```
21    private function homeLoad():Void
22    {
23        mission_ta.vScrollPolicy="off";
24        this.home_xc.trigger();
25        this.createEmptyMovieClip("featurehome_mc",this.getNextHighestDepth());
26        featurehome_mc._x=450;
27        featurehome_mc._y=140;
28        featurehome_mc.loadMovie("assets/featurehome.jpg");
29    }
```

The finished file should resemble: /fpad2004/lesson11/intermediate/classes/MmestateHome_loader.as.

3. Return to mmestate.fla in /fpad2004/mmestate/.

Return to the file you used in the last exercise or open /fpad2004/lesson11/intermediate/mmestate_loadjpg.fla and save it as *mmestate.fla* in /fpad2004/mmestate/.

4. Select the home screen. From the Components panel, drag a Loader component to the Stage.

Place it next to the Featured home text. You no longer have to figure out coordinates for where to place the dynamic MovieClip. You just place the Loader component where you want the content to be loaded.

5. Select one of the TextArea objects.

The Loader component is no longer visible.

6. From the main menu, select Control > Enable Live Preview to deselect this option.

The check mark next to Enable Live Preview disappears indicating that this option is no longer selected.

All components are now represented by squares.

7. Select the Loader component. In one of the Inspector panels, set `contentPath` to *assets/featurehome.jpg*.

You are using a relative path to the JPG file from the SWF. You can also specify an absolute URL.

8. Test the application.

Log in to the application. You should see the feature home image displayed on the home page, but it has been scaled to fit inside the Loader component.

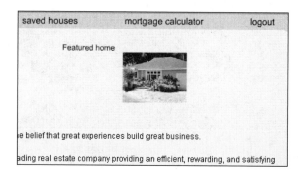

9. Return to mmestate.fla. In one of the Inspector panels, change the `scaleContent` parameter for the Loader component to *false*. Save the file and test the application.

Log in to the application. The image is now displayed in full size. The Loader component has been resized to fit the content. Because you left the `autoLoad` parameter set to true, the content is loaded when the application is loaded. You can defer this loading by setting the `autoLoad` parameter to false, giving the Loader component an instance name, and then loading the content using the `load()` method in code: `home_loader.load()`.

The finished file should resemble: /fpad2004/lesson11/intermediate/mmestate_loader.fla.

10. Select Control > Enable Live Preview to select the option.

This re-enables component live preview so you can see the visual representation of new components in the next lessons.

Loading External Content into a Screen

If you are creating a form-based application, you can bypass the Loader component and load external content directly into the screen. You might recall from Lesson 7, "Building Applications with Screens," that the Screen class actually descends from the Loader class and thus, inherits its properties and methods.

If you look in the Property inspector for a screen, you will see the same `contentPath`, `autoLoad`, and `scaleContent` parameters you saw in the last exercise for the Loader component. (Screen properties are not displayed in the Component Inspector panel.)

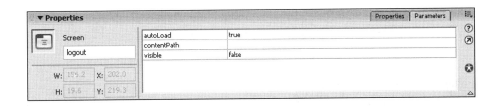

In this exercise, you load your Flash application that searches for houses into the search screen of the Macromediestate application.

1. Return to mmestate.fla in /fpad2004/mmestate/.

Return to the file you created in the last exercise or open /fpad2004/lesson11/intermediate/ mmestate_loader.fla and save it as *mmestate.fla* in /fpad2004/mmestate/.

2. Select the `search` screen in the Screen Outline pane. Delete the check box on the Stage.

This check box is left over from an exercise in Lesson 9, "Learning the UI Component Framework."

3. In the Property inspector, set the `contentPath` parameter for the `search` screen to *searchHouses.swf*. Leave the `autoLoad` parameter set to true.

You created this SWF in the last lesson. If you did not complete lesson, open /fpad2004/lesson11/start/ searchHouses.swf and save it as searchHouses.swf in /fpad2004/mmestate/.

The searchHouses SWF will be downloaded and loaded immediately with the main application and all of its screens. The application does not need to be downloaded immediately, though, because the screen is not shown right away. You can decrease the initial download by deferring the SWF to load later.

4. Test the application.

Log in to the application and navigate to the search page. You should see the search form, though not in an appropriate location. Notice that the components are now using a haloTheme color of orange—the global style set in the mmestate application.

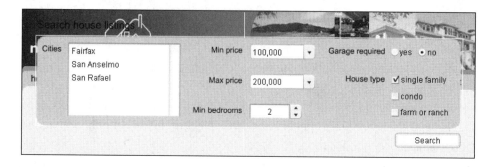

5. Open MmestateSearch.as in /fpad2004/lesson11/start/classes/ save it as *MmestateSearch.as* in /fpad2004/mmestate/classes/.

To change the position of the loaded content, you need to write some code. You will write the code in this MmestateSearch class file and associate this class with the search screen. The class file for the search screen has been started for you. The file contains skeleton code for the class definition. It also sets the initial visibility of the screen to false, because as soon as you associate the class with the screen, you lose the values of the parameters set in the Property inspector (visible was set to false there).

If you were not loading dynamic content into the screen, you could change the screen position simply by using the UIObject move() method to set the x and y positions of the search in the constructor: this.move(0,115);. But you are loading dynamic content, which makes it a little more difficult to change the screen position. You need to create an event handler that fires when the new content has finished loading and then change the position of the loaded content. Although the Loader class hides it from you as much as it can, it actually places loaded content into a new child screen.

6. Inside the searchLoad() method, set the contentPath property to *searchHouses.swf*. Save the file.

```
this.contentPath="searchHouses.swf";
```

You have to set this property in the class file because it too will be lost from the Property inspector when you associate the search screen with the class file.

7. Create a private method called *searchLoadComplete*. Inside, use the UIObject move() method to move the new child screen containing the loaded content to a y position of *115*.

You can get a reference to the new screen containing the loaded content as a MovieClip called contentHolder or using the `getChildScreen()` method of the Screen class, which returns an array of the child screens. The new screen will have an array index of zero.

```
private function searchLoadComplete():Void
{
        this.getChildScreen(0).move(0,115);
}
```

8. Inside the `searchLoad()` method, register the screen as the listener for its `complete` event.

```
this.addEventListener("complete",this);
```

9. Inside the `handleEvent()` method, create an `if` statement to check if `evtObj.type` is equal to *complete*. If it is, call the `searchLoadComplete()` method.

```
if(evtObj.type=="complete")
{
        searchLoadComplete();
}
```

10. Check the syntax and save the file.

The finished file should resemble: /fpad2004/lesson11/intermediate/classes/ MmestateSearch_screenload.as.

11. Return to mmestate.fla. Link the `search` screen to the class MmestateSearch. Test the application.

Log in and navigate to the search page. The SWF should now be loaded into the proper location.

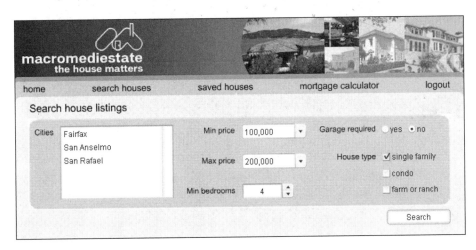

12. Try to change the selected price in a ComboBox.

You can't. The combo boxes no longer work. Remember the bug mentioned earlier this lesson? To get around the bug, you need to drag a copy of the ComboBox component into the mmestate application.

13. Return to mmestate.fla. From the Components panel, drag a ComboBox to the Stage of any screen. Delete the ComboBox. Save the file.

There is now a ComboBox in the parent application's library.

The file should resemble: /fpad2004/lesson11/intermediate/mmestate_screenload.fla.

14. Test the application. Log in and navigate to the search page.

You should now be able to select new prices in the combo boxes. Click the Search button. You should see the selected values for all the components in the Output panel.

> **Note** *You can share library assets between applications by setting up a runtime-shared library so that the assets are not downloaded with each application. In a source FLA, you define assets in the library to be exported (shared as a source for other SWFs) by using the Linkage Properties dialog box to specify a Linkage identifier for the asset and a URL where the source SWF will be posted on the web. Then, you specify assets in the library of another FLA to import these shared assets by assigning a Linkage identifier and URL in the Linkage Properties dialog box identical to those used for the shared asset in the source SWF. When sharing components, you need to use a preloader and manipulate the frames in which components are exported to make sure the components have loaded before you try to use them in your application.*

What You Have Learned

In this lesson, you have:

- Learned about object depth and ways you can manage it (pages 451–453)
- Attached a MovieClip dynamically from the library (pages 454–457)
- Created components dynamically (pages 457–461)
- Created an empty MovieClip and loaded a JPG into it (pages 461–465)
- Loaded dynamic content into a Loader component (pages 467–470)
- Loaded external content into a screen (pages 470–474)

12 Retrieving Data from XML Files

You can retrieve external data to use in a Macromedia Flash application from a variety of remote data sources including text files, XML files, web services, or application server classes. (An overview of each of these methods was presented in the "Retrieving External Data Using Data Connector Components" exercise in Lesson 8.) With so many options for data retrieval, when should you use XML? Use an XML file as a data source instead of a text file when the data is too complex to represent in a simple text file. Use an XML file as a data source instead of accessing "live" data from a web service or application server class when the data you are retrieving can and should be cached in the browser.

You can retrieve data from an XML file two ways: using the native XML class or using the prebuilt XMLConnector data connector. In the first part of this lesson, you use the native XML class to load data to populate the prices in the maximum and minimum combo boxes. In the second part of the lesson, you use the XMLConnector component to retrieve city data and bind it to the List component using data binding. The XMLConnector component, new to Flash MX 2004 and unique to the Professional version, wraps the native XML class allowing you to retrieve and manipulate XML data from the authoring environment without writing any code. It also lets you visually bind data from the XML object to other components so you do not have to manually traverse the XML tree with code.

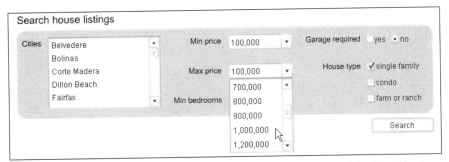

In this lesson, you retrieve data from XML files to populate the price combo boxes and the cities list box in the house-search form.

What You Will Learn

In this lesson, you will:

- Learn to create XML files for data sources
- Retrieve data using the built-in XML class
- Handle results from XML objects requests
- Parse XML objects
- Use the XMLConnector component
- Retrieve data using the XMLConnector component
- Use Data Binding with XMLConnector results
- Handle XMLConnector results
- Retrieve data from other domains

Approximate Time

This lesson takes approximately 80 minutes to complete.

Lesson Files

Asset Files:

/fpad2004/lesson12/start/assets/houseprices.xml
/fpad2004/lesson12/start/assets/cities.xml
/fpad2004/lesson12/start/assets/homepagetext.xml

Starting Files:

/fpad2004/lesson12/start/searchHouses.fla
/fpad2004/lesson12/start/classes/Searchform.as

Completed Files:

/fpad2004/lesson12/complete/searchHouses.fla
/fpad2004/lesson12/complete/classes/Searchform.as

Using XML Files for Data Sources

When moving from static to dynamic applications, you first need to figure out what data you should make dynamic in your application. You should make anything dynamic that might change in the future or for which you need multiple versions (for example, text and/or data for different locales or for different types of users). In both cases, maintaining and updating the application is simplified when the data is not hard-coded in the Flash application. It is easier, faster, and cheaper to change a single data source than it is to change the multiple files and applications that use the data.

Once you figure out what data should be dynamic, you need to decide what method you should use to retrieve the dynamic data. For example, let's take a look at the Macromediestate web application. When do you need dynamic data from the server? For sure, for the login functionality—to check user input values against the values in a database. Also for the search house functionality—to retrieve houses from a database that match user search criteria. In both cases, there is application functionality that must be accessed on the server with each request so you should either call a web service or access an application server class. OK, so no XML there. What else might change in the application? Most likely the text and featured image on the home page (both of which you already made dynamic) and the house prices you use in the combo boxes on the search form (yes, there is inflation) and probably also the cities. You want this data dynamic so it is separated from the application, but you do not need to retrieve a new version of the data from the server every time a user views the search page (which would happen every time the user browsed to a new HTML page and then returned to the page containing the SWF). All that downloading would be a waste of bandwidth because the data has not changed. Instead, you should retrieve this data from XML files, because XML files are cached by the browser like any other HTML page, SWF, JPG, and so on.

But what if the XML file changes? No problem. The browser often checks with the server to see if a locally cached file has changed on the server since the browser cached it. How often this checking occurs is determined by a browser setting specified by the user. A normal default browser setting is to check for new content versions only when you return to a page you viewed in an earlier browser session. Even if the browser checks for a new version, though, the server does not send a new file unless the server file is different than the browser's cached version. This file caching is a great benefit for your Flash applications, allowing you to separate data into external XML (or text) files without having to continually and needlessly download the data with every page you view.

Creating XML Files for Data Sources

In order to use data from XML files, you need to know how to create the XML files. To that end, let's take a look at a simple XML file containing information about bikes.

```
<?xml version="1.0" encoding="UTF-8"?>
<bikes>
      <bike id="1">Kona</bike>
      <bike id="2">VooDoo</bike>
      <bike id="3">Rocky Mountain</bike>
</bikes>
```

The XML document consists of the following:

The first line of code is the XML declaration, which states the type of document it is so XML document readers will know how to process it. The declaration contains information on the type of markup language used (XML), the markup language version (1.0), and the type of character encoding (UTF-8).

Next is the `bikes` root element. The body of an XML document consists of two things: elements (or nodes) and attributes. Elements are tag containers that can hold textual information, attribute name/value pairs, and other elements. Every XML document must have one and only one root element, which is the first element and contains all the other elements.

The rest of the XML document consists of three `bike` elements. Information for each bike is contained in a separate `bike` element with the bike ID specified as an attribute for the node and the bike name as a child text node. The text between the start and end tags of an element is called a text node or the text value of the element.

Note *You must place quotes around all attribute values.*

Instead of placing the bike name in a text node, you can make it another attribute/value pair in the `bike` node.

```
1  <?xml version="1.0" encoding="UTF-8"?>
2  <bikes>
3      <bike id="1" name="Kona"/>
4      <bike id="2" name="VooDoo"/>
5      <bike id="3" name="Rocky Mountain"/>
6  </bikes>
```

It is your choice to place data inside attributes or text nodes.

Note *If you are going to use data binding with the XMLConnector component, the XML data source for the XMLConnector component cannot have a node with both attributes and a child text node as shown in the first example. This restriction is discussed in greater detail in a later exercise, "Using Data Binding with XMLConnector Results."*

In the previous two examples, each node was displayed on a separate line and hierarchically indented with white space between nodes. Using white space in your files makes them easier to read and edit, but you must remember the space is there so that when you load the data into Flash, you can tell Flash to ignore it or the XML document will not be parsed correctly. Here is the previous XML file with no white space.

```
<?xml version="1.0" encoding="UTF-8"?><bikes><bike id="1"
name="Kona"/><bike id="2" name="VooDoo"/><bike id="3" name="Rocky
Mountain"/></bikes>
```

You can also nest nodes. In this example, a `bike` node contains child nodes containing more information about each bike.

```
1   <?xml version="1.0" encoding="UTF-8"?>
2   <bikes>
3       <bike id="1">
4           <brand>Kona</brand>
5           <make>Bear Deluxe</make>
6           <size>17</size>
7           <color>silver</size>
8           <description>A back country dual suspension bike with a
    supreme balance of lightweight performance and out of bounds
    strength. Mid-weight (28-30 lb) with 4 in travel up front and back
    keep you fresh for all day epic adventures. </description>
9       </bike>
10  </bikes>
```

If you want to include HTML data in the XML file, the nodes will contain the special characters, < or >. In order for the XML document to be correctly parsed by an XML reader (Flash in this case), these characters must be escaped. Otherwise when the XML document is parsed, Flash will think the < and > characters are part of the XML markup and that they are start or end characters for XML nodes—which they are not. To keep the XML reader from reading the data inside a node, you can enclose the text inside CDATA tags. CDATA sections begin with the <![CDATA[and end with]]>. Any text inside the CDATA tag will not be parsed.

```
<?xml version="1.0" encoding="UTF-8"?>
<bikes>
    <bike id="1">
        <brand>Kona</brand>
        description><![CDATA[ A <b>back country dual suspension</b> ¬
        bike with a supreme balance of lightweight performance and ¬
        out of bounds strength. <br>Mid-weight (28-30 lb) with 4 in ¬
        travel up front and back keep you fresh for all day epic ¬
        adventures. ]]></description>
    </bike>
</bikes>
```

In this exercise, you examine three XML files. The first two, which contain house prices and city names, will be used later in this lesson. The last one, which contains the HTML text for the home page, you used in Lesson 8.

1. In Flash, select File › Open. Browse to /fpad2004/mmestate/assets/ and open houseprices.xml.

To view XML files in the Open dialog box, you might need to change the type of file displayed by selecting the All Files option in the "Files of type" drop-down (Windows).

The XML file opens in the Flash.

2. Examine the file.

This is a very basic XML file with a root element, one type of child node, and no attributes. Note that there is white space between the nodes; the file has been formatted for easy viewing using tabs and returns. You will use the data in this XML file to populate the search form ComboBoxes with prices in the next several exercises.

3. Open cities.xml in /fpad2004/mmestate/assets/ and examine the file.

This XML file is different, encapsulating all its data as node attributes. No data is contained in text nodes and there is no white space between nodes. You will use this XML data to populate the search form List component with cities later in this lesson.

4. Open homepagetext.xml in /fpad2004/mmestate/assets/ and examine the file.

This XML file contains the HTML text you used in Lesson 8 to populate the TextArea components on the home page. Note the use of <![CDATA[and]]> to surround the text containing HTML tags so the text is not parsed as part of the XML document structure.

Retrieving Data Using the Built-In XML Class

You retrieve XML data from or send XML data to a web server using Flash's built-in XML class. To retrieve data, you create an XML object and then load the remote XML data into it.

The first step is to create a new XML object.

```
var bikes:XML=new XML();
```

> **Note** *You can also pass XML text to the constructor as a source parameter:*
>
> ```
> var bikes:XML=new XML('<bikes><bike id="1" name="Kona"/><bike id="2"
> name="VooDoo"/></bikes>');
> ```
>
> *Or you can create XML objects manually using the XML class* createElement(), createTextNode(), appendChild(), *and* cloneNode() *methods.*

The next step is to load data into the XML object. You use the XML class load() method, which has one argument: the URL for the XML file, which can be an absolute or relative reference. An HTTP request is sent to the URL using a get operation.

```
bikes.load("assets/bikes.xml");
bikes.load("http://www.mmestate.com/assets/bikes.xml");
```

Note *The XML class also has `send()` and `sendAndLoad()` methods which are used to send an XML object to a URL and send an XML object to a URL and then load the server response into another XML object.*

You can also retrieve an XML file generated dynamically at request time from a database on the server by specifying a URL for an application server page, which returns a dynamically created XML file.

```
cities.load("http://www.mmestate.com/coldfusion/getCitiesXml.cfm");
```

Note *For an example, see the ColdFusion file: /fpad2004/mmestate/services/getCitiesXml.cfm. If you don't want the CFM page to ever get cached by the browser, you can append a random number to the end of the URL string.*

The URL must be in exactly the same domain as the SWF file issuing the remote call. If you want to load data from a different domain, the server hosting the XML file you are requesting must have a cross-domain security policy file granting your requesting domain permission. For more information, see the "Requesting Data from other Domains" section at the end of this lesson.

If the XML contains any white space, you must set the white space property to true *before* you load data into the XML object. If you do not, the XML data will not be parsed correctly.

```
bikes.ignoreWhite=true;
```

In this exercise, you create an XML object and load data into it from an XML file containing prices for populating the search form combo boxes, enabling the price ranges and increments to be changed without changing the FLA.

1. Return to searchHouses.fla in /fpad2004/mmestate/.

This is the file you created in the last lesson. If you did not complete that lesson, open /fpad2004/lesson12/start/searchHouses.fla and save it as *searchHouses.fla* in /fpad2004/mmestate/.

2. Select the `min_cb` ComboBox. Double click the `labels` field in the Property inspector to open the Values dialog box. Delete all the values and click OK.

The `labels` parameter should now be an empty array.

3. Save the file.

The finished file should resemble: /fpad2004/lesson12/intermediate/searchHouses_loadxml.fla.

4. Return to Searchform.as in /fpad2004/mmestate/classes/.

This is the file you created in the last lesson. If you did complete that lesson, open /fpad2004/lesson12/ start/classes/Searchform.as and save it as *Searchform.as* in /fpad2004/mmestate/classes/.

5. Delete the code in the `searchformLoad()` method that populates the `max_cb` ComboBox and selects the first index of `max_cb`.

Delete the code shown in the screenshot.

```
36      private function searchformLoad():Void
37      {
38          search_pb.addEventListener("click",this);
39          min_cb.addEventListener("change",this);
40          bedrooms_ns.value=2;
41          single_ch.selected=true;
42          no_rb.selected=true;
43          no_rb.data=0;
44          var prices:Array=["100,000","200,000","300
45          max_cb.dataProvider=prices;
46          max_cb.selectedIndex=1;
47      }
```

6. Create a private method called *populateCombos* with no parameters and no return value. Inside, declare a variable called `prices` of type *XML* that is equal to a new **XML** object.

```
private function populateCombos():Void
{
    var prices:XML=new XML();
}
```

7. Inside the function, set the `ignoreWhite` property of the `prices` XML object to true.

```
prices.ignoreWhite=true;
```

8. At the end of the code inside the function, load the **XML** document located at the relative location */assets/houseprices.xml* into the `prices` XML object. Use the `load()` method.

```
prices.load("assets/houseprices.xml");
```

9. In the `searchformLoad()` method, add a call to the `populateCombos()` method.

```
populateCombos();
```

10. Check the syntax and save the file.

The finished file should resemble: /fpad2004/lesson12/intermediate/classes/Searchform_loadxml.as.

11. Return to searchHouses.fla and test the application.

The combo boxes are not populated with any data. You populate them with the XML data in the next two exercises.

If at this point you want to check and make sure the data was retrieved correctly from the server, you cannot use the method you used in Lesson 8: selecting Debug > List Variables and locating the XML data in the list of application variables because the `prices` variable is local to the `populateCombos()` method. If you really want to see your data in this exercise, you can temporarily change `prices` to a global variable:

```
_global.prices=new XML();
_global.prices.ignoreWhite=true;
_global.prices.load("assets/houseprices.xml");
```

You learn a better way to view your returned data in the next exercise by using an event of the XML class.

Handling Results from XML Object Requests

To access the data returned from the server, you use the `onLoad` event of the XML class. This event is fired when a response is received from the server (either of success or failure). One argument is automatically passed to the callback function and has a value of true if the data was retrieved successfully or false if it was not. Inside the event handler, you use conditional logic to respond accordingly.

```
var bikes:XML=new XML();
bikes.load("assets/bikes.xml");
bikes.onLoad=function(success):Void
{
    if(success)
    {
        [Do something with XML data]
    }
    else
    {
        [Give error message]
    }
};
```

In this exercise, you create an onLoad event handler for the XML object to handle the XML data returned from the server.

1. Return to Searchform.as in /fpad2004/mmestate/classes/.

Return to the file you created in the last exercise or open /fpad2004/lesson12/intermediate/classes/ Searchform_loadxml.as and save it as *Searchform.as* in /fpad2004/mmestate/classes/.

2. Inside the `populateCombos()` method, create a callback function for the `onLoad` event with one parameter called *success*. Place it before the `load()` method.

```
78      private function populateCombos():Void
79      {
80          var pricesML=new XML();
81          prices.ignoreWhite=true;
82          prices.onLoad=function(success)
83          {
84
85          };
86          prices.load("assets/houseprices.xml");
87      }
```

It is a best practice to place event handlers *before* the method calls to which they respond, to ensure that they exist when the event is broadcast.

3. Inside, create the following conditional logic. If the request succeeds, trace the XML object. If the request fails, trace a failure message. Save the file.

```
if (success)
{
    trace(this);
}
else
{
    trace("XML loading failed");
}
```

The finished file should resemble: /fpad2004/lesson12/intermediate/classes/Searchform_handlexml.as.

4. Return to searchHouses.fla in /fpad2004/mmestate/ and test the application.

Return to the file you created in the last exercise or open /fpad2004/lesson12/intermediate/ searchHouses_loadxml.fla and save it as *searchHouses.fla* in /fpad2004/mmestate/.

You should see the cities.xml document in the Output panel. (The XML Object also has a toString() method which renders the complex object to a string so it can be traced.)

```
▼ Output
<?xml version="1.0" encoding="UTF-8"?><prices><price>100,000</
price><price>200,000</price><price>300,000</price><price>400,000</
price><price>500,000</price><price>600,000</price><price>700,000</
price><price>800,000</price><price>900,000</price><price>1,000,000
</price><price>1,200,000</price><price>1,400,000</price><price>1,
600,000</price><price>1,800,000</price><price>2,000,000</price><
price>3,000,000</price><price>4,000,000</price><price>5,000,000</
price></prices>
```

If you want to test a failed request, change the URL specified as an argument to the load() method and retest the application. You should see your "XML loading failed" message in the Output panel.

Parsing XML Objects

To use the data in the XML object, you must learn how to parse an XML object in Flash to access specific node and attribute values. You retrieve specific values using a series of properties of the XML class, which include the following:

childNodes. An array containing references to the child nodes of the specified node.

attributes. An associative array containing all of the attributes of the specified node.

firstChild. The first child in the childNodes array for the specified node.

nodeName. The node name of an XML object.

nodeValue. The text of the specified node if the node is a text node.

Let's look at the following bikes XML document to see how you use these properties to extract values from the XML object.

```
<?xml version="1.0" encoding="UTF-8"?>
<bikes>
    <bike id="1">Kona</bike>
    <bike id="2">VooDoo</bike>
    <bike id="3">Rocky Mountain</bike>
</bikes>
```

If you load this XML document into an XML object called bikes, you can extract the various node and attribute values using the following expressions:

Expression	trace(expression)
bikes.childNodes.length	1
bikes.firstChild.nodeName	bikes
bikes.childNodes[0].nodeName	bikes
bikes.firstChild.childNodes.length	3
bikes.firstChild.firstChild.nodeName	bike
bikes.firstChild.firstChild.attributes.id	1
bikes.firstChild.childNodes[2].attributes.id	3
bikes.firstChild.firstChild.firstChild.nodeValue	Kona
bikes.firstChild.childNodes[2].firstChild.nodeValue	Rocky Mountain

The XML class has additional properties you can use to traverse the XML object including: `nodeType` (the type of the specified node, XML element, or text node), `lastChild` (the last child in the list for the specified node), `nextSibling` (the next sibling in the parent node's child list), `parentNode` (the parent node of the specified node), and `previousSibling` (the previous sibling in the parent node's child list).

> **Note** *If your XML document contains white space and you do not set the `ignoreWhite` property to true before loading the XML data, each white space between nodes is considered a node—and would have to be accounted for in the parsing code.*

In this exercise, you parse the XML object, using node values to populate the price combo boxes.

1. Return to Searchform.as in /fpad2004/mmestate/classes/.

Return to the file you created in the last exercise or open /fpad2004/lesson12/intermediate/classes/ Searchform_handlexml.as and save it as *Searchform.as* in /fpad2004/mmestate/classes/.

2. Change the `if` statement inside the `onLoad` event handler so the number of `price` nodes is traced.

```
trace(this.firstChild.childNodes.length);
```

3. Also inside the **if** statement, trace the value of the first text node, "100,000", in the first **price** node.

Remember that a text node is considered the **firstChild** node of a **ChildNodes** array for its container element.

```
trace(this.firstChild.firstChild.firstChild.nodeValue);
```

You only use the **nodeValue** property with text nodes.

4. Also inside the **if** statement, trace the value of the tenth text node, "1,000,000".

```
trace(this.firstChild.childNodes[9].firstChild.nodeValue);
```

5. Return to searchHouses.fla in /fpad2004/mmestate/ and test the application.

Return to the file you used in the last exercise or open /fpad2004/lesson12/intermediate/ searchHouses_loadxml.fla and save it as *searchHouses.fla* in /fpad2004/mmestate/.

In the Output panel, you should see 18; 100,000; 1,000,000. Now that you know how to get at the data, you are ready to use the data to populate the price combo boxes.

6. Return to Searchform.as. After the **trace()** statements inside the **if** statement of the **onLoad** handler, create a **for** loop that loops over the number of **price** nodes.

```
84    if(success)
85    {
86        trace(this.firstChild.childNodes.length);
87        trace(this.firstChild.firstChild.firstChild.nodeValue);
88        trace(this.firstChild.childNodes[9].firstChild.nodeValue);
89        for (var i=0;i<this.firstChild.childNodes.length;i++)
90        {
91
92        }
93    }
```

7. Inside the **for** loop, add the value contained in the ith **price** text node to the **min_cb** ComboBox. Use the ComboBox **addItem()** method.

You can copy the expression for the 10th **price** text node from the **trace()** statement you added in Step 4 and then replace the number 9 with the variable **i**.

The scope inside this event handler is the XML object the handler is defined for. This means that in order to refer to the **min_cb** ComboBox, you have to use an absolute reference to the component. You cannot use a relative reference (using **_parent**) because the XML object to which the handler belongs is not a MovieClip.

```
_root.application.searchform.min_cb.addItem(this.firstChild. ¬
childNodes[i].firstChild.nodeValue);
```

8. Inside the **for** loop, add the value contained in the ith **price** text node to the **max_cb** ComboBox.

Copy and paste the code from Step 7 and change min_cb to max_cb.

```
_root.application.searchform.max_cb.addItem(this.firstChild. ¬
childNodes[i].firstChild.nodeValue);
```

9. Delete the **trace()** statements you added in Steps 2 through 4. Save the file.

Be sure to check the syntax before you save.

10. Return to searchHouses.fla and test the application.

The price combo boxes should be populated with data from the XML file.

Although the combo boxes are successfully populated when you test this application, they will not be populated when you test the mmestate.swf application, into which the searchHouses.swf application loads. Why? Because _root will have a different value, and your absolute path to the combo boxes is no longer correct.

11. Return to **Searchform.as**. Before the **onLoad** handler inside the **populateCombos()** method, create a variable called **owner** of type *Object* called and set it equal to **this**.

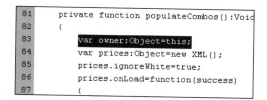

You are grabbing a reference to the current MovieClip in which the XML object resides. The object returned varies depending on whether you have loaded the SWF into any other application. For example, when you test searchHouses by itself, the **owner** property is equal to _level0.application.searchform. When searchHouses.swf is loaded into mmestate.swf, the **owner** property is equal to _level0.application.main.search.contentHolder.application.searchform.

You can refer to the owner property directly inside the onLoad handler because code inside the handler has access to the variables in the function literal's enclosing scope, which is the object in which it is defined.

> **Note** You cannot add the owner property directly to the *prices* XML object, because the XML class is not dynamic. In addition to the method used in Step 11, another option is to subclass the XML class: You define the owner property for the subclass and make your *prices* XML object an instance of this subclass.

12. Inside the onLoad event handler, change the absolute reference to the max_cb and min_cb combo boxes to use a relative reference using the owner property. Save the file.

```
owner.min_cb.addItem(this.firstChild.childNodes[i].firstChild.nodeValue);
owner.max_cb.addItem(this.firstChild.childNodes[i].firstChild.nodeValue);
```

Now your code will still work even if you load the SWF into another SWF.

The finished file should resemble: /fpad2004/lesson12/intermediate/classes/Searchform_parsexml.as.

13. Return to searchHouses.fla and test the application.

The price combo boxes should still be populated.

If you want, you can also test the mmestate.swf application and see that the combo boxes are also populated correctly when loaded into that application.

Using the XMLConnector Component

New to Flash MX Professional 2004, you can now load data from an XML file into an application without having to write code. The XMLConnector component wraps the creation and loading of XML data with a visual representation in the authoring environment. (You were introduced to the XMLConnector component in Lesson 8 as part of an overview for the Flash application framework.) To load data using the XMLConnector component, drag an XMLConnector component to the Stage and set parameters for it in the inspector panels. The XMLConnector component has a visual representation on the Stage at author time allowing you to select and manipulate it, but has no runtime appearance.

A great advantage of using the XMLConnector component is that you can use author time data binding to easily bind values of XML object nodes to other components without having to write the cumbersome code needed to traverse the XML object. Because the returned data is complex, though, you need to learn some new things about data binding (in a later exercise) before you can hook up the XMLConnector to other components.

The XMLConnector component is an instance of the mx.data.components.XMLConnector class, which implements the RPC (Remote Procedure Call) interface. (The WebServiceConnector, which you use in Lesson 13, "Consuming Web Services," also implements the RPC interface so you use an almost identical process to interact with the WebServiceConnector as the XMLConnector.) You can use the inspector panels or ActionScript to assign values to properties (shown below) of an XMLConnector instance:

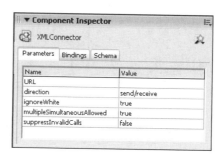

URL. The URL used for the HTTP operation, which can be either absolute or relative. In most cases, the URL must be for the same domain as the SWF the request originates from. Flash Player security is explained in the last section, "Retrieving Data from Other Domains."

direction. Indicates whether XML data is being sent to or received from the server. Possible values include receive, send, and send/receive which use HTTP get, post, and post methods. If you are only retrieving XML data, you must change this property from its default value of send/receive to receive or the call will fail.

ignoreWhite. A Boolean indicating whether white space nodes should be ignored when the XML file is parsed by Flash. This is the same property as for the built-in XML object.

multipleSimultaneousAllowed. A Boolean indicating whether this remote call should occur if other RPC calls (XMLConnector or WebServiceConnector calls) are already in progress. The implications of setting this property are discussed in the next exercise.

suppressInvalidCalls. A Boolean indicating whether to suppress a call if any of the parameters are invalid. This parameter is irrelevant if you are only receiving data from an XML file (as in this lesson).

Note   *If you are going to use data binding with the XMLConnector component, the XML data source for the XMLConnector component cannot have a node with both attributes and a child text node. This restriction is discussed in greater detail in a later exercise, "Using Data Binding with XMLConnector Results."*

In this exercise, you add an XMLConnector component to the searchHouses application that will be used to retrieve data to populate the cities List component.

1. Return to searchHouses.fla in /fpad2004/mmestate/.

Return to the file you used in the last exercise or open /fpad2004/lesson12/intermediate/ searchHouses_loadxml.fla and save it as *searchHouses.fla* in /fpad2004/mmestate/.

2. Select the `searchform` screen. From the Components panel, drag an instance of the XMLConnector component and drop it anywhere on the Stage.

It is common practice to place the data component near the UI component that it will populate.

3. In the Property inspector, give the XMLConnector instance the name `cities_xc`, set the URL parameter to *assets/cities.xml*, and the `direction` parameter to *receive*.

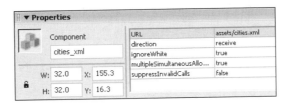

Make sure you set the direction parameter to receive or your call to the XML file will not work!

4. Save the file.

The finished file should resemble: /fpad2004/lesson12/intermediate/searchHouses_xc.fla.

Retrieving Data Using the XMLConnector Component

The XML class (and RPC interface) has one method, `trigger()`, used to initiate remote calls.

```
my_xc.trigger();
```

If the XMLConnector's `multipleSimulataneousAllowed` property is set to true, the call initiates as soon as the `trigger()` method is executed even if another call is already in progress; multiple calls can take place at the same time. Just because you make one RPC call before another call in code, though, does not mean you will get the results of the first call back before you get the results of the second call. If the order that the results are returned matters to your business logic, set `multipleSimultaneousAllowed` to false, so that the call does not occur until all other calls have finished. If a `trigger()` method is executed when `multipleSimultaneousAllowed` is false and another call has already been initiated, the new RPC call is placed in a queue and is sent as soon as the call before it is completed

Compile time debugging. When referencing XMLConnector component instances with code, you should specify the object's type as mx.data.components.XMLConnector. The data component classes, though, are compiled in a SWC, which means you don't have the source code for them. The SWC, however, contains intrinsic class file definitions (remember those ASI files from Lesson 6?). If you place code declaring and referencing an XMLConnector component instance in a FLA, you get compile time type-checking, and the pertinent debugging information. If you place your code in a class file, though, you will not get compile time checking. Instead, you get an error: The class 'mx.data.components.XMLConnector' could not be loaded. This is because there are no class files for the component in the Classes folder in the Flash First Run and User-Specific directories.

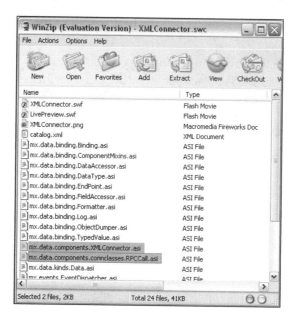

Tip *You can enable type checking for the XMLConnector component in your class files by extracting the relevant intrinsic class file definitions from the XMLConnector SWC and placing them in Flash's Classes folder. You can find XMLConnector.swc in /First Run/ Components/Data Components/. The relevant ASI files to extract using a file extraction program (like WinZip) are mx.data.components.XMLConnector.asi and mx.data.components. connclasses.RPCCall.asi. Create a folder called components in /First Run/Classes/mx/data/ and a folder called connclasses in /First Run/Classes/mx/data/components and then extract mx.data.components.XMLConnector.asi to /First Run/Classes/mx/data/components/ and rename it XMLConnector.as. Extract mx.data.components.connclasses.RPCCall.asi to /First Run/Classes/mx/data/components.connclasses and rename it RPCCall.as. Make sure you change the file endings to AS from ASI or compile time checking will not work. Restart Flash (or copy the new /First Run/Classes/mx/data/components/ folder to the /Classes/mx/data/ folder in the Flash user-specific directory). You will now have compile time checking for the XMLConnector component in your class files.*

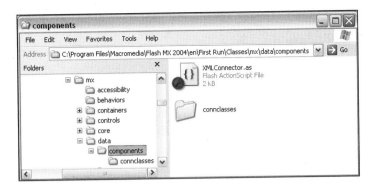

Runtime debugging. To get runtime information about remote procedure calls made with XMLConnector (or WebServicesConnector) components, create an instance of the Log class that is part of the mx.data.binding package. The source files for the data binding class are compiled in the DataBinding component, DataBindingClasses.swc, which is located in /First Run/Data/. The SWC contains an intrinsic class file for the Log class: mx.data.binding.Log.asi.

When you create a new instance of the Log class, you get a detailed log of the remote call operations (and data binding operations) in the Output panel. Place the Log instance in the global scope if you want it to trace events from any of the screens of objects in your application. (Remember that you created a behavior containing this logging code in Lesson 8 and added it to mmestate.fla).

```
_global.__dataLogger=new mx.data.binding.Log();
```

> **Note** *You can name the Log instance any name you want. It does not have to be called __dataLogger.*

You can programmatically turn off the log trace at any time by setting the log instance you created to null, deleting the Log instance it held previously.

```
_global.__dataLogger=null;
```

In this exercise, you retrieve data from the cities.xml file.

1. Return to Searchform.as in /fpad2004/mmestate/classes/.

Return to the file you created in the parsing exercise or open /fpad2004/lesson12/intermediate/classes/Searchform_parsexml.as and save it as *Searchform.as* in /fpad2004/mmestate/classes/.

2. Create a private property called `cities_xc` of type *mx.data.components.XMLConnector*.

```
private var cities_xc:mx.data.components.XMLConnector;
```

3. In the `searchformLoad()` method, initiate the XMLConnector's call to the remote data. Use the `trigger()` method.

```
cities_xc.trigger();
```

4. In the constructor, add code to enable tracing of log operations.

```
_global.__dataLogger=new mx.data.binding.Log();
```

Unfortunately, you cannot insert the code from your snippet in the Behaviors panel. You can only use the Behaviors panel to apply code to objects in the FLA; you cannot use it as a Snippets panel to add code to an ActionScript file.

5. Check the syntax.

You should get a warning message: The class 'mx.data.components.XMLConnector' could not be loaded because there is no intrinsic class definition for this class in the Flash Classes folder.

6. Save the file.

The finished file should resemble: /fpad2004/lesson12/intermediate/classes/Searchform_xctrigger.as.

7. Return to searchHouses.fla and test the application.

Return to the file you created in the last exercise or open /fpad2004/lesson12/intermediate/ searchHouses_xc.fla and save it as *searchHouses.fla* in /fpad2004/mmestate/.

You should see information about the remote call in the Output panel.

```
▼ Output                              ≣,
2/6 12:22:30 application.searchform.
cities_xc: XMLConnector Triggered,
assets/cities.xml
      2/6 12:22:30 application.searchform.
cities_xc: Invoking XMLConnector assets/
cities.xml()
```

You can check to see if the data was retrieved correctly from the server by selecting Debug > List Variables and locating the XML data in the list of application variables (search for the word city).

Using Data Binding with XMLConnector Results

In Lesson 8, you were introduced to data binding; you made a simple binding from a string value to the text property of a text component. When your component contains complex data, like an XML object, though, the data binding process is more complicated; there are many more choices about what you bind to other components and how you do it.

Creating a Schema

The first step in using data binding with the XMLConnector is to create a schema for the return data contained in its `results` property. The schema is a representation of the structure of the `results` object. Instead of manually creating the schema for the XML object as nested arrays and objects, Flash can automatically generate the schema for you from an example XML file. You did this in the "Using Data Binding" exercise in Lesson 8. In the Bindings pane of the Component Inspector panel, you select the `results` property and click the "Import a schema from a sample XML file" button.

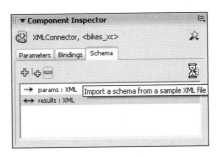

Let's take a look at the schemas resulting from XML files with different structures but containing the same data. First, look at an XML file with all the data contained as node attributes:

```
<bikes>
     <bike id="1" name="Kona"/>
     <bike id="2" name="VooDoo"/>
     <bike id="3" name="Rocky Mountain"/>
</bikes>
```

The generated schema contains a bike schema item of type Array, which has one subfield called [n], which is an object. The object is specified as <empty> because each [n] `bike` node has no child nodes; the `bike` node is empty. Each [n] object, though, has two attributes designated as such by the @ symbol.

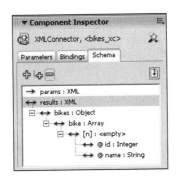

Second, look at an XML file with all the data contained as child nodes (with no attributes):

```
<bikes>
    <bike>
        <id>1</id>
        <name>Kona</name>
    </bike>
    <bike>
        <id>2</id>
        <name>VooDoo</name>
    </bike>
    <bike>
        <id>3</id>
        <name>Rocky Mountain</name>
    </bike>
</bikes>
```

The bike Array schema item has the same subfield called [n], but in this example is of type Object and is not designated as empty because it has child nodes. The [n] object has properties id and name (which are its child nodes).

Next, look at an XML file with data contained as both node attributes and child nodes:

```
<bikes>
    <bike id="1">
        <name>Kona</name
    </bike>
    <bike is="2">
        <name>VooDoo</name>
    </bike>
    <bike id="3">
        <name>Rocky Mountain</name>
    </bike>
</bikes>
```

The [n] object is still of type Object because it has child nodes but in this case, it has both an attribute and a child node designated as subfields.

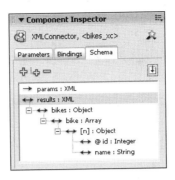

Finally, look at an XML structure containing a combination of attributes and text nodes:

```
<bikes>
    <bike id="1">Kona</bike>
    <bike id="2">VooDoo</bike>
    <bike id="3">Rocky Mountain</bike>
</bikes>
```

Flash cannot generate a schema representing this structure in which a node has both an attribute and a text node. The text nodes are not represented. (You can edit the schema to access the text node instead of the attribute, but not both. It is best not to use this type of structure.)

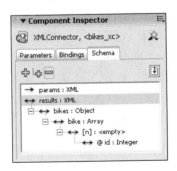

Note *The import schema process might not correctly determine and assign all your data types. You can edit the data type for a schema item in the Schema Attributes pane.*

Creating Bindings with Complex Data

The binding you created in Lesson 8 was very simple: You bound a string value to the text property of a text component. You can also have more complex data as a data source and can bind to more complex components. Array schema items can be bound to UI controls that display arrays of items, like the ComboBox, List, or DataGrid components. To bind an array of items, you select an Array node of the XML object as the data binding source in the Add Binding dialog box:

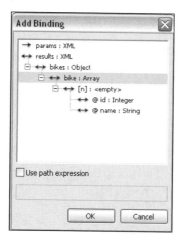

You then select a property of type Array for the component you are binding to in the Bound To dialog box (like the `dataProvider` property):

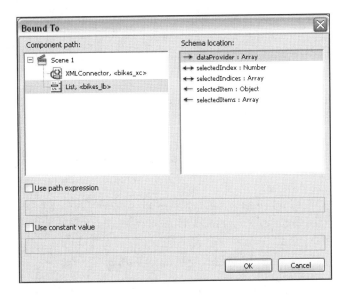

Another possibility is to bind properties of an object in a specific index of a schema item array to a simple component property (like `text` for a Label component or `selected` for a CheckBox control). To create these bindings, you select an item in the array as the binding source.

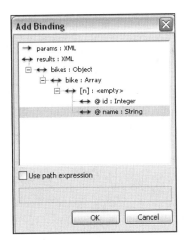

You can then specify an index to use in the Bindings Attribute pane.

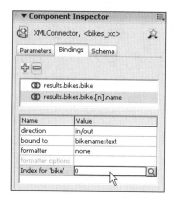

The array index does not have to be a constant; you can assign its value from another component property, like the selected index of a list of ComboBox component.

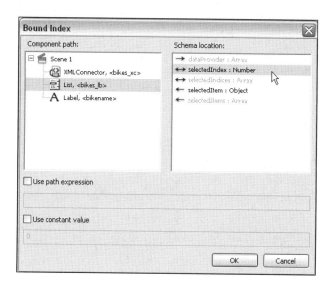

To select a source for the bound index in the Bound Index dialog box, you must uncheck "Use constant value."

Using Binding Formatters

If you bind an object to the dataProvider of a ComboBox or List component, you get a comma-delimited list of all the component properties, just like you did when you used code to bind an object to the ComboBox in Lesson 10, "Using UI Component APIs."

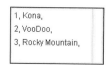

In the ComboBox exercise in Lesson 10, you used code to specify which object property to use for the component display, assigning a value to the `labelField` property. Similarly, you can specify a property of the object to use for the label and data fields from the authoring environment when using visually data binding.

To change how complex data is displayed in a component with data binding, you change the formatter option for the binding in the Bindings pane. When working with arrays of data, you select the Rearrange Fields option.

 *You can also use the Compose String option if the data source is not an array.*

To specify how you want the fields rearranged, you double-click in the formatter options field and enter field definitions where you set properties of the component equal to the names of files in the object. For example, set `label` equal to the `name` attribute and the `data` field equal to the `id` attribute (label=name;data=id;).

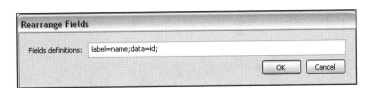

The result is shown in the following screenshot.

If you have a more complex object with more than two properties, you can also specify the entire object as the data property using (.) to represent the object: (label=name;data=.;). For an XML object, though, this data is an XML string.

You can also create a binding assigning a combination of a string and an object property in the Rearrange Fields dialog box by surrounding an expression in single quotation marks and enclosing the names of the object properties in < and >. For example: (label='Bike name is <name>';data=id;).

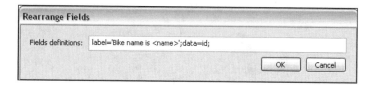

The result is shown in the following screenshot.

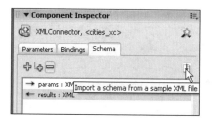

In this exercise, you bind and format the city XML data retrieved by the XMLConnector component to the List component.

1. Return to searchHouses.fla in /fpad2004/mmestate/.

Return to the file you used in the last exercise or open /fpad2004/lesson12/intermediate/ searchHouses_xc.fla and save it as *searchHouses.fla* in /fpad2004/mmestate/.

2. Select the `cities_xc` XMLConnector component and click the Schema tab in the Component Inspector panel. Select the `results` property and click the "Import a Schema from a sample XML file" button.

Make sure you select the `results` property (the object that holds the XML data returned from the server), not the `params` property (the object that holds the XML data to send to the server in a send or send/receive operation).

You need to specify a schema for the return results so that specific node or attribute values can be bound to other components. The schema is specific to your XML file so you need to build the schema yourself. The "Import a Schema from a sample XML file" button lets you automatically construct the schema, or structure, of the returned XML document. You could also create the schema manually using the "Add a field under the selected field" button and specifying values for the schema's attributes in the lower part of the Schema pane of the Component Inspector panel.

3. In the Open dialog box, browse to cities.xml in /fpad2004/mmestate/assets/ and click Open.

You should now see a detailed schema for the `results` property of the XMLConnector component in the Schema pane.

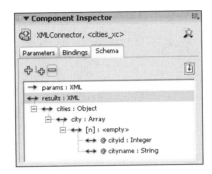

Any of these specific values from the XML object can now be bound to other components.

4. Select the Bindings tab and click the Add Binding button. In the Add Binding dialog box, select city : Array and click OK.

You will bind the values in the `city` nodes of the XML object (which is an array) to the `dataProvider` of the List component.

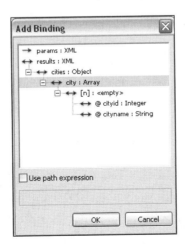

5. In the Binding Attribute pane of the Component Inspector panel, change the `direction` parameter for the binding to *out*.

Now you need to specify what you want to bind the array of `city` nodes to.

6. Double-click the text field next to the `bound to` parameter. In the Bound To dialog box, select the Component path: List, <cities_lb> on the `searchform` screen. Select the Schema location: dataProvider : Array. Click OK.

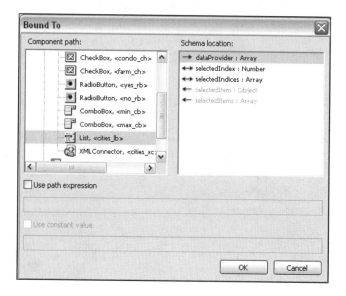

7. Save the file and test the application.

The cities List component should be populated with data. The label field, though, has been assigned as a comma-delimited list of attribute values.

Look at the Output panel. You should see information about the bindings; data binding operations are also traced when you create an instance of the mx.data.binding.Log class.

8. Return to searchHouses.fla and select the `cities_xc` XMLConnector. In the Component Inspector panel, select the Bindings tab and double-click None in the formatter field. From the drop-down menu, select Rearrange Fields.

9. In the Component Inspector panel, double-click None in the formatter options field. In the Rearrange Fields dialog box, enter *label=cityname;data=cityid;*. Click OK.

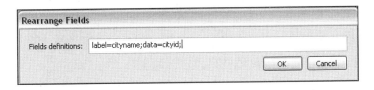

10. Save the file and test the application.

You should now get only the city names in the List component.

The finished file should resemble: /fpad2004/lesson12/intermediate/searchHouses_xcbinding.fla.

11. Select the first city in the List component and click the Search button.

You get the index of the item (0), not its data value (1) displayed in the Output panel. Up to now, the `dataProvider` for the List component was a static simple array, not an object with `label` and `data` properties. You need to change the code to capture data values for the selected cities that you can send to the server.

12. Return to Searchform.as in /fpad2004/mmestate/classes/.

Return to the file you created in the last exercise or open /fpad2004/lesson12/intermediate/classes/ Searchform_xctrigger.as and save it as *Searchform.as* in /fpad2004/mmestate/classes/.

13. In the `search_pbClick()` method, delete the `trace()` of the selected List indices.

Delete the following code:

```
trace(cities_lb.selectedIndices.toString());
```

14. In `search_pbClick()`, create a variable called `cityids` of type *Array*.

```
var cityids:Array=new Array();
```

This array will hold the data values for the selected items in the List component.

15. Create a `for` loop that loops over the number of selected items in the List. Inside the loop, add the `data` property of the selected item to the `cityids` array.

```
for (var i=0;i<cities_lb.selectedIndices.length;i++)
{
        cityids.push(cities_lb.selectedItems[i].data);
}
```

16. After the `for` loop, trace a string version of the `cityids` array.

```
69        trace(max_cb.value);
70        var cityids:Array=new Array();
71        for (var i=0;i<cities_lb.selectedIndices.length;i++
72        {
73            cityids.push(cities_lb.selectedItems[i].data);
74        }
75        trace(cityids.toString());
```

```
trace(cityids.toString());
```

This is the string of city ids you will send the server.

17. Check the syntax. Save the file.

The finished file should resemble: /fpad2004/lesson12/intermediate/classes/Searchform_xcbinding.as.

18. Return to searchHouses.fla and test the application. Select the first two cities in the List component and click the Search button.

You should get the city ids (1,2) instead of indices (0,1) displayed in the Output panel.

Handling XMLConnector Component Results

The XMLConnector class has two events you can use when retrieving data from an XML file: `result` and `status`. To handle these events, you use the same component event-handling framework you used for the UI components.

Handling `result` Events

A `result` event is broadcast when the remote call completes successfully. Here is a simple function handler for a `result` event.

```
function traceResults(evtObj:Object):Void
{
        trace(evtObj.target.results);
}
my_xc.addEventListener("result", traceResults);
```

Just like the UI and screen events you have been working with, the event handler is automatically sent one argument, which has a `type` property (equal to the value "result") and a `target` property (a reference to the object that emitted the event). The `target` event object has a `results` property you can use to reference the actual results returned by the remote call.

As soon as the `result` event for the call is broadcast, the returned XML data is also available as the `results` property of the XMLConnector component (the returned XML is an XML object, not a string).

```
trace(my_xc.results);
```

Inside the `result` event handler, you can call other methods that directly reference the `results` property of the XMLConnector component. Inside the `result` event handler, `evtObj.target.results` and `my_xc.results` can be used interchangeably.

Handling `status` Events

A `status` event is broadcast any time the status of a remote call changes: when it starts, finishes, is placed in a queue, or fails for any reason.

The event object passed to a `status` event handler has the same `type` property (equal to "status") and the `target` property (a reference to the object that emitted the event) of all the V2 component events, but it also has two additional properties: `code` (the name of the specific condition that occurred) and `data` (an object whose properties depend upon the status code generated). Possible `code` values include StatusChange (emitted when a remote call starts or finishes; the `data` property holds the current number of remote calls in progress), CallAlreadyInProgress (emitted if a remote call is initiated and `multipleSimultaneousAllowed` is false, and another call is already in progress), InvalidParamsEmitted (emitted if the `params` property did not contain valid data), and Fault (emitted if any other problems occur during the call).

Here is a simple function handler for a `status` event.

```
function traceStatus(evtObj:Object):Void
{
        trace(evtObj.code);
        trace(evtObj.data.faultcode);
        trace(evtObj.data.faultstring);
}
my_xc.addEventListener("status",traceStatus);
```

If the code value is Fault, the data property is an object with properties: `faultcode` and `faultstring`. When requesting XML files, common `faultcode` values include (with the corresponding `faultstring` value in parentheses):

`XMLConnector.No.Data.Received`. (no data was received from the server). You will get this `faultcode` if the server URL was invalid, not responding, or returned an HTTP error code; or if the server request succeeded but returned 0 bytes of data.

`XMLConnector.Results.Parse.Error`. (received data had an XML parsing error).

> **Note** *If you are sending data to the server using send or send/receive, you might receive* faultcode *values: XMLConnector.Not.XML (params is not an XML object), XMLConnector.Parse.Error (params had XML parsing error), or XMLConnector.Params.Missing (params are null).*

> **Note** *There is also a* send *event you can use when sending XML data to the server, which is broadcast after the parameter data has been gathered but before the data is validated and the remote call is initiated.*

In this exercise, you create a `status` event handler for the `cities_xc` XMLConnector component.

1. **Return to Searchform.as in /fpad2004/mmestate/classes/.**

Return to the file you created in the last exercise or open /fpad2004/lesson12/intermediate/classes/ Searchform_xcbinding.as and save it as *Searchform.as* in /fpad2004/mmestate/classes/.

2. **Create a private method called `cities_xcStatus` with one argument called `evtObj` of type *Object*.**

```
private function cities_xcStatus(evtObj:Object):Void{}
```

3. Inside, trace the event object `code` property and the `faultstring` property of the `data` object.

```
trace(evtObj.code);
trace(evtObj.data.faultstring);
```

4. Inside the `handleEvent()` method, add a new case for when the event object `type` is equal to *status*. For this case, call the `cities_xcStatus()` method.

```
case ("status"):
      cities_xcStatus(evtObj);
      break;
```

5. Inside the `searchformLoad()` method, register the screen instance as the listener for the `status` events of `cities_xc`. Save the file.

```
40        private function searchformLoad():Void
41        {
42            cities_xc.addEventListener("status",this);
43            cities_xc.trigger();
44            populateCombos();
```

The finished file should resemble: /fpad2004/lesson12/intermediate/classes/searchform_xchandle.as.

6. Return to searchHouses.fla in /fpad2004/mmestate/ and test the application.

Return to the file you created in the last exercise or open /fpad2004/lesson12/intermediate/searchHouses_xcbinding.fla and save it as *searchHouses.fla* in /fpad2004/mmestate/.

In the Output panel, you get the values StatusChange and undefined (because `faultstring` is defined only for a `code` value of Fault). A `status` event is emitted every time the status of a call changes.

7. Return to searchHouses.fla and select the **XMLConnector** component. In the Property inspector, misspell the name of the **XML** file.

You are introducing an error, so the remote call will not complete successfully.

8. Test the application.

In the Output panel, you should get a StatusChange code followed by a Fault code with the `faultstring` value: Was expecting data from the server, but none was received.

In this exercise, the `status` handler is simply tracing status codes to the Output panel. In a real application, you could check for a Fault code in the `status` handler and then disable the search button and display a message to the user, attempt to retrieve the data from an alternate data source, or carry out some other appropriate response.

9. Return to searchHouses.fla and fix the misspelling you introduced in Step 7. Save the file.

The finished file should resemble to the starting file: /fpad2004/lesson12/intermediate/searchHouses_xcbinding.fla.

Retrieving Data from Other Domains

Up to now, you were told that in order to retrieve data from an XML file, the XML file had to reside on the same domain as the SWF requesting it. This behavior, though, actually depends on which version of the Flash Player the application is running in. If a Flash application is running in a version of the Flash Player earlier than Flash Player 7, the URL for the XML file must be in the same super-domain as the SWF file initiating the remote call. For example, a SWF file at www.macromedia.com can request XML files posted on mmestate.macromedia.com, because both files are in the same superdomain of macromedia.com. If a Flash application is running in Flash Player 7 or later, though, the XML file must be in *exactly* the same domain as the SWF. For example, a SWF file at www.macromedia.com can only load XML files from www.macromedia.com, not any posted on mmestate.macromedia.com. This is the default security behavior for all remote requests initiated from the Flash Player (to other text files, XML files, and web services).

If you want to access data (including text files, XML files, and web services) from a different domain, you can place a cross-domain policy file on the server the remote XML file (or text file or web service) resides on. A **cross-domain policy file** is an XML file that provides a way for the server to indicate that its files are available to requests from SWF applications from certain domains. When a SWF attempts to access data from another domain, the Flash Player automatically attempts to load a policy file from the other domain. If the domain of the SWF that is attempting to access the data is included in the policy file, the data is automatically accessible and can be downloaded. The policy file must be named crossdomain.xml and it must reside at the root of the web directory.

Here is a security policy file placed on www.macromedia.com that permits requests originating from www.mmestate.com, *. macromedia.com (mmestate.macromedia.com, support.macromedia.com, and so on), and 105.216.0.40 to access its files:

```
<?xml version="1.0"?>
<cross-domain-policy>
     <allow-access-from domain="www.mmestate.com" />
     <allow-access-from domain="*.macromedia.com" />
     <allow-access-from domain="105.216.0.40" />
</cross-domain-policy>
```

Note *A policy file is specific to the port and protocol of the server where it resides. For example, a policy file located at https://www.macromedia.com:8080/crossdomain.xml will apply only to requests made to www.macromedia.com over HTTPS at port 8080. Also, if you specify an IP address in the security policy file, access will be granted only to SWFs loaded from that IP address using IP syntax, not one with the equivalent domain-name syntax; the Flash Player does not perform DNS resolution.*

To allow access to a server's files from all Flash Player requests from any domain, you can create a domain policy with the following node:

```
<allow-access-from domain="*" />
```

Note *The Flash Player security restriction does not apply when you are testing applications in the authoring environment from your desktop. In that case, you can access data from any domain.*

What You Have Learned

In this lesson, you have:

- Learned to create XML files for data sources (pages 476–480)
- Retrieved data using the built-in XML class (pages 480–483)
- Handled results from XML objects requests (pages 483–485)
- Parsed XML objects (pages 485–489)
- Used the XMLConnector component (pages 489–491)
- Retrieved data using the XMLConnector component (pages 491–494)
- Used data binding with XMLConnector results (pages 494–506)
- Handled XMLConnector results (pages 506–510)
- Learned to retrieved data from other domains (pages 510–511)

13 Consuming Web Services

A web service is application functionality that can be published and consumed over the Internet. Web services provide a way for applications to communicate with each other in a platform-independent and programming language-independent manner. In order for this transfer of information to work, there must be a universal language in which the applications can communicate. The most well-known language is SOAP (Simple Object Access Protocol), an XML-based protocol used to write messages to send and receive web service requests and responses over the Internet. A web service, then, is a software interface that describes a collection of operations (to execute procedures or return data) that can be accessed over the network through this standard XML messaging.

In the last few years, web services have become an increasingly popular way to share information between disparate systems, as well as publicly provide (for free or for sale) application functionality to others. For example, web site moguls Google and Amazon both provide web service interfaces. Google provides access to their database so you can send search queries and receive results that you can integrate into your application. Amazon web services give you the ability to search and retrieve product information from their database (including product descriptions, prices, image URLs, and so on) and the ability to add Amazon products to a shopping cart in your application. You can find a list of publicly accessible web services including a list of demo web services to experiment with (such as temperature queries, currency converters, language translators, and so on) at www.xmethods.net.

In this lesson, you use web services to check the user login information and retrieve houses for the search form.

Just as there were two ways to retrieve data from an XML file, there are two ways to retrieve data from a web service: using a WebService class or using the prebuilt WebServiceConnector component. Unlike the XML class, though, the WebService class is not native to the Flash Player. The WebService class is part of a package of compiled classes provided as part of the Flash application framework. The WebServiceConnector component is a wrapper for the WebService class and provides a visual representation for accessing a web service in the authoring environment, along with a way to set parameters without code, data binding capabilities, and the same event handling framework as the rest of the components.

In the first part of this lesson, you use the WebServiceConnector component to implement functionality to check the user login information against a database and grant or deny access to the web site. Because the WebServiceConnector component implements the same RPC interface as the XMLConnector component, using the WebServiceConnector component is almost identical. (This lesson assumes you completed Lesson 12, "Retrieving Data from XML Files," and are familiar with the XMLConnector component.) In the second part of the lesson, you use the WebService class to access a web service with code. You send the user's criteria selected in the house search form to the server and receive matching houses.

What You Will Learn

In this lesson, you will:

- Register a web service in the Flash authoring environment
- Use the WebServiceConnector component
- Use data binding with the WebServiceConnector
- Trigger WebServiceConnector calls and handle its results
- Assign WebServiceConnector parameters with code
- Create a WebService object
- Make the WebService class available at runtime
- Invoke a remote method with a WebService object
- Handle PendingCall object events

Approximate Time

This lesson takes approximately 70 minutes to complete.

Lesson Files

Asset Files:

The web service for your application server

Starting Files:

/fpad2004/lesson13/start/mmestate.fla
/fpad2004/lesson13/start/classes/MmestateLogin.as
/fpad2004/lesson13/start/classes/MmestateMain.as
/fpad2004/lesson13/start/searchHouses.fla
/fpad2004/lesson13/start/classes/Searhform.as

Completed Files:

/fpad2004/lesson13/complete/mmestate.fla
/fpad2004/lesson13/complete/classes/MmestateLogin.as
/fpad2004/lesson13/complete/classes/MmestateMain.as
/fpad2004/lesson13/complete/searchHouses.fla
/fpad2004/lesson13/complete/classes/Searhform.as

Accessing Web Services from Flash

Macomedia Flash MX Professional 2004 provides a way to call web services from your Flash applications using SOAP. The SOAP protocol includes specifications on how to represent complex data as strings, which enables complex data to be sent over HTTP. Thus, any Flash data you send to a web service must be translated into an equivalent string representation as specified by the SOAP protocol. Any data returned to Flash will also be in a SOAP format and must be translated back into ActionScript variables or objects before you can use the data. The generation and translation of SOAP messages is not built into the Flash Player but is provided by a series of ActionScript classes you compile into your Flash applications.

Due to the security restrictions of the Flash Player, you can only directly access web services located on the same server as your SWF (or any server that has a security policy file granting you access). (See the last section of Lesson 12 for more info on Flash Player security.) To access a third-party web service (like the Google or Amazon web services) from Flash, you need to create a proxy service on your application server (which could be an application server class or a web service). The proxy service is the intermediary; you call the proxy server class from your Flash application and the server proxy class calls the third-party web service and returns the results to your Flash application. The bottom line is that you must have an application server to call web services from Flash. If you don't have an application server, however, you can still use web services from Flash because the Flash Player security does not apply when you are testing applications from your desktop. Beware though, that although you can develop and test Flash applications that directly access third-party web services from your desktop, the application will not work when accessed via HTTP in a browser.

Getting Information about a Web Service

In order to use a web service from Flash, you need to know what variables to pass to the web service, including the names and types of data, and what type of data you will get back. Obviously, this is not a problem if you wrote the web service or you have access to the code. If you use a third-party web service (remember, a third-party web service has to be proxied through your application server to the Flash Player!) or you don't have access to the in-house code, you can obtain information about a web service from a WSDL (pronounced "whiz-dull"). A WSDL is an XML document using a standard markup, WSDL (Web Services Description Language), to describe the information a client needs to use the web service (how the server can connect to the remote service, the names of the operations, the names and data types of required parameters, and so on). The web service provider makes the WSDL available on the web for browsing.

Here is part of a WSDL for a currency exchange rate web service (a demo web service located at http://www.xmethods.net/sd/2001/CurrencyExchangeService.wsdl).

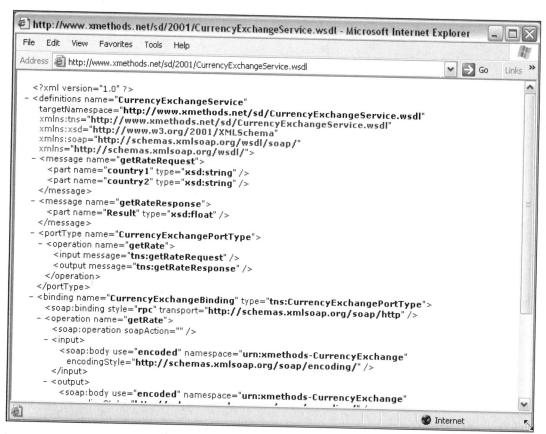

As a developer, you don't need to decipher most of this information; a lot of it is for the server to use when accessing the web service and exchanging information. If you study the WSDL long enough, though, you can probably figure out what information you need: the operation names and the names and types of data needs.

Fortunately you don't have to abstract this information from the WSDL yourself. Instead, you can register a web service in the Web Services panel in the Flash authoring environment. Flash reads the WSDL and displays the names of each remote method (also called an operation) along with the number, names, and types of parameters you need to send to the methods, and the type of value returned from the methods.

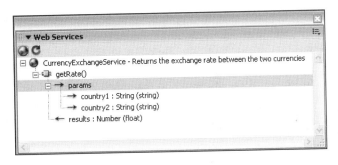

In this exercise, you register a web service in the Web Services panel that you will use in the next exercise to verify user login information.

1. **Verify that House.cfc is located in C:\CFusionMX\wwwroot\fpad2004\mmestate\ services\.**

If you did not place the fpad2004 folder in your web root back in Lesson 1, you need to move House.cfc to this location now. If you are using Java, .NET, or a different ColdFusion setup, make sure the web service is located in the proper location for your server. Instructions are included in the Appendix.

2. **In a browser window, go to http://localhost/fpad2004/mmestate/services/ House.cfc?wsdl.**

If you can successfully view the WSDL, ColdFusion and the web service are correctly installed on your computer. If you are using another platform or port, make sure you can view the WSDL before proceeding with the exercise. For example, if you are using a J2EE server on port 80, browse to http://localhost/fpad2004/mmestate/services/House.jws?wsdl. If you are using .NET, browse to http://localhost/fpad2004/mmestate/services/House.asmx?wsdl.

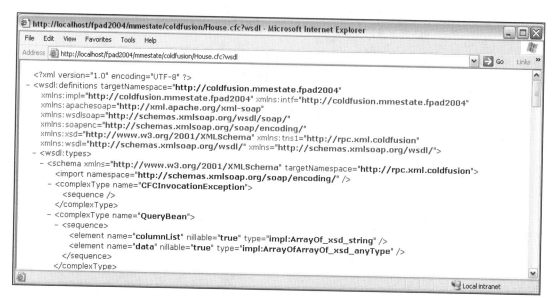

Note *You do not create your own web services in this book; you use a prewritten web service. If you are new to creating web services, you can easily get started using ColdFusion. In ColdFusion, you simply designate which methods of a ColdFusion component (a CFC) you want accessible as a web service by changing the methods' access modifiers to remote. ColdFusion will then generate a WSDL for you. To browse a ColdFusion component containing remote method(s), add "?wsdl" to the end of the URL. You can also use ColdFusion to easily call third-party web services without learning to write SOAP messages using the* `<cfinvoke>` *tag.*

3. **If you are using ColdFusion, register the fpad2004 database in the ColdFusion Administrator.**

Detailed instructions for this process are included in the Appendix. Both a Microsoft Access database and a MySQL database are provided in the /fpad2004/mmestate/data/ folder.

If you are using Java, you need to register the database in the ODBC Administrator. If you are using .NET, the location of the database is hard-coded in the web service and you must either make sure the database is in the correct location or change the location in the web service. Detailed instructions are included in the Appendix.

4. **Return to Flash. From the main menu, select Windows › Development Panels › Web Services. In the Web Services panel, click the Define Web Services button.**

The Define Web Services button is the world icon in the upper left corner of the panel.

5. In the Define Web Services dialog box, click the Add Web Service button.

The Add Web Service button is the plus sign in the upper left corner of the dialog box.

6. In the new line that appears, enter the WSDL for the web service. For example: *http://localhost/fpad2004/mmestate/services/House.cfc?wsdl*.

If you are using a J2EE server on port 80, use http://localhost/fpad2004/mmestate/services/House.jws?wsdl. If you are using .NET, use http://localhost/fpad2004/mmestate/services/House.asmx?wsdl.

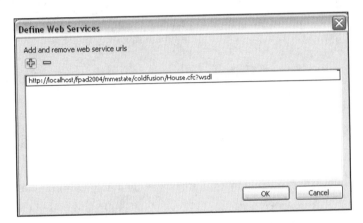

7. Click OK.

You should see the House web service listed in the Web Services panel.

8. Click the + sign next to HouseService to view details about its operations. Drill down to see information about the login operation.

For .NET, the House service appears in the Web Services panel as House instead of HouseService.

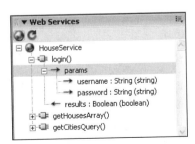

Using the WebServiceConnector Component

New to Flash MX Professional 2004, the WebServiceConnector component lets you consume a web service from Flash without having to write any code. Using the WebServiceConnector component is almost identically to working with the XMLConnector component. You drag a WebServiceConnector component to the Stage and set its properties in one of the inspector panels. The WebServiceConnector component has a visual representation on the Stage allowing you to select and manipulate it, but no runtime appearance.

The WebServiceConnector component is an instance of the mx.data.components. WebServiceConnector class that—like the XMLConnector component—implements the RPC (Remote Procedure Call) interface. You can set parameters for the WebServiceConnector in the Component Inspector panel.

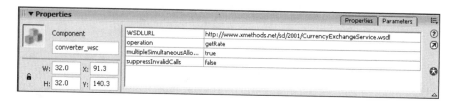

Like the XMLConnector component, the WebServiceConnector component has parameters `multipleSimultaneousAllowed` and `suppressInvalidCalls`. Instead of URL and `direction` parameters, though, it has `WSDLURL` and `operation` parameters.

WSDLURL. The URL of the web service WSDL. In most cases, the URL must be for the same domain as the SWF request originates from. (Flash Player security was explained in the "Retrieving Data from Other Domains" section in Lesson 12.)

operation. The name of the remote operation to call in the web service.

When you enter a URL in the WSDLURL field, Flash introspects the WSDL, adds the web service to the Web Services panel (if it is a valid WSDL URL), and populates a drop-down list next to the operation parameter field from which you select a valid operation for the web service. If you had previously registered web services in the Web Services panel, URLs for valid WSDLs appear in a drop-down list next to the WSDLURL parameter.

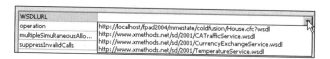

Instead of dragging a WebServiceConnector from the Components panel, you can also add a WebServiceConnector component directly from the Web Services panel. You simply right-click/

Control-click the name of an operation and select Add Method Call. A WebServiceConnector appears on the Stage with its parameters already assigned.

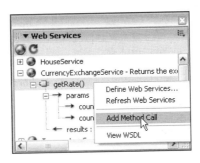

In this exercise, you add a WebServiceConnector component to connect to the login operation of the House web service.

1. Return to mmestate.fla in /fpad2004/mmestate/.

This is the file you created in Lesson 11. If you did complete that lesson, open /fpad2004/lesson13/start/mmestate.fla and save it as *mmestate.fla* in /fpad2004/mmestate/.

> **Note** *There are five versions of the lesson13 folder. Use the folder appropriate for your application server setup. If none of the five folders match your setup and you want to use files in the lesson folders for Lessons 13 through 16 as starting files for later exercises, you need to change two files: the web service URL for the WebServiceConnector on the* login *screen in mmestate.fla and the URL for the web service or Flash Remoting gateway in Searchform.as.*

2. Select the login screen.

You are going to add the WebServiceConnector component to this screen.

3. Expand HouseService in the Web Services panel. Right-click/Control-click the login operation and select Add Method Call.

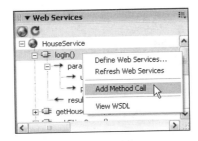

A WebServiceConnector component appears on the Stage.

4. Place the WebServiceConnector component next to the Login button.

It is common practice to place data components next to the components with which they interact, making it easier to decipher and follow program logic.

5. Look at the Property inspector for the WebServiceConnector.

The WSDLURL and operation parameters already have values.

6. In the Property inspector, name the WebServiceConnector instance login_wsc. Save the file.

The finished file should resemble: /fpad2004/lesson13/intermediate/mmestate_wsc.fla.

Using Data Binding with the WebServiceConnector

You can specify the data to send to a web service (if any is required) using data binding or ActionScript. Whenever you use data binding with a component, you need a schema—a representation of the component's associated data. When you used an XMLConnector component, you imported the schema from an XML file. When you use the WebServiceConnector component, the schema is generated automatically. When Flash introspects a WSDL, either when you register a web service in the Web Services panel or when you assign a WSDLURL parameter in an inspector panel, Flash gets all the information it needs to create the schema. The schema contains params and results properties that mirror the schema defined within the WSDL.

To assign values for the data to send to the web service, you bind properties of other components to the WebServiceConnector params property. To bind the data returned from the web service to another component, you bind to the results property.

In this exercise, you use data binding to specify the parameter values to send to the web service using the WebServiceConnector component.

1. Return to mmestate.fla in /fpad2004/mmestate/.

Return to the file you created in the last exercise or open /fpad2004/lesson13/intermediate/ mmestate_wsc.fla and save it as *mmestate.fla* in /fpad2004/mmestate/.

2. Select the WebServiceConnector on the login screen and open the Component Inspector panel. Click the Schema tab.

The number and types of parameters you must send to the web service are displayed, as well as the type of data returned from the web service.

3. Select the Bindings tab and click the Add Binding button. In the Add Binding dialog box, select username : String under params. Click **OK**.

You are going to get the value for this parameter to pass to the web service from the `username_ti` TextField component. Note that when you create this binding, the binding direction is automatically set to the value "in" in the Binding Attributes pane; the binding only needs to be one way, from the TextInput component *to* the WebServiceConnector component.

4. In the Bindings Attribute pane, double-click the text field next to the `bound to` parameter. In the Bound To dialog box, select the `username_ti` TextInput component on the `login` screen and click **OK**.

Note that by default the `text` property of the TextArea component is selected; the TextInput component has only one bindable property.

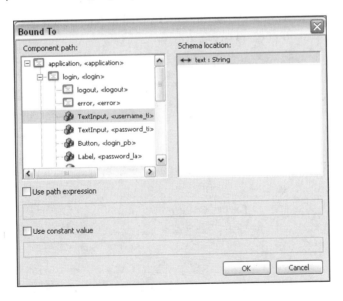

You have now created a binding between the `text` property of the `username_ti` TextInput component and the web service's `password` parameter.

5. Repeat Steps 3 and 4 to add a second binding for the password.

Bind the `text` property of the `password_ti` TextField to the `password` property of the WebServiceConnector's `params` object. You should now have two bindings.

6. Save the file.

The finished file should resemble: /fpad2004/lesson13/intermediate/mmestate_wscbinding.fla.

Triggering WebServiceConnector Calls and Handling Results

You initiate calls to a web service using the WebServiceConnector component and handle its results and status events using the same methods and events of the Remote Procedure Call (RPC) interface you used to interact with the XMLConnector component. The procedure is summarized here and focuses on the differences between the two.

Initiating web service calls. To initiate a call to a web service using the WebServiceConnector component, use the `trigger()` method. (Remember, you can also use a built-in behavior to add the code to trigger a remote call in a FLA.)

```
my_wsc.trigger();
```

> **Note** When testing an application calling a web service, you will get a "file not found" error in the Output panel if there is any problem consuming the web service. For example, if the WSDL does not exist, the number of parameters is wrong, or one of the parameters has the wrong data type. You can use the *status* event described in this exercise to help identify the problem.

If you have multiple WebServiceConnector or XMLConnector components, make sure you set the `multipleSimulataneousAllowed` properties to the appropriate values, so multiple calls are treated in the desired manner.

When referencing WebServiceConnector component instances with code, you should specify the object's type as mx.data.components.WebServiceConnector. For compile time and runtime debugging, implement the same techniques introduced for the XMLConnector component in the "Retrieving Data Using the XMLConnector Component" section in Lesson 12.

Note *Just like for the XMLConnector component, you will get only compile time debugging in a class file if you extract the intrinsic class files from the WebServiceConnector SWC and place them in Flash's Classes folder. To implement, follow the instructions given in Lesson 12 for the XMLConnector component.*

Handling result events. To handle results from a WebServiceConnector call, use the same RPC `result` event with the traditional component event handling framework. Here is a simple function handler for a `result` event.

```
function traceResults(evtObj:Object):Void
{
        trace(evtObj.target.results);
}
my_wsc.addEventListener("result", traceResults);
```

As soon as the `result` event for the call is broadcast, any data returned from the web service is also available as the `results` property of the WebServiceConnector component; other methods called from inside the `result` handler can directly reference the `results` property of the WebServiceConnector component.

```
trace(my_wsc.results);
```

Handling status events. To handle any status events from a WebServiceConnector call, use the same RPC `status` event with the traditional component event handling framework. The event object passed to a `status` event handler has the same `type`, `target`, `code`, and `data` properties as the `status` event handler for the XMLConnector component with the same possible values for the `code` property: StatusChange, CallAlreadyInProgress, InvalidParams, and Fault.

Now that you are sending data to a web service, though, you might want to check for and handle `status` events with an InvalidParams code, which is obtained if a call is initiated and the `params` property contains invalid data (the wrong number of parameters or the wrong data types). If the `suppressInvalidCalls` property for the WebServiceConnector is set to true, the call is ended at this point.

If the remote call fails for any reason, a status event with a Fault code is emitted. For this code, the object held in the `data` property of the event object is an ActionScript mapping of the SOAP Fault XML type, with properties `faultcode`, `faultstring`, `detail`, `element`, and `faultactor` properties. Possible faultcode values include Timeout (timeout when calling method x), Client.Disconnected (could not load WSDL), and Client.NoSuchMethod (couldn't find method x in service). A complete list of fault codes can be found in the Flash Help files for the WebServiceConnector component.

Here is a simple function handler for a status event.

```
function traceStatus(evtObj:Object):Void
{
        trace(evtObj.code);
        if (evtObj.code=="Fault")
        {
                trace(evtObj.data.faultcode);
                trace(evtObj.data.faultstring);
        }
}
my_wsc.addEventListener("status",traceStatus);
```

> **Note** The RPC interface also has a *send* event (briefly mentioned in the last lesson),
> which is broadcast after the parameter data has been gathered but before the data is
> validated and the remote call is initiated. You can use it to perform your own validation
> or manipulation of the parameters before they are sent to the remote operation.

In this exercise, you implement the login functionality. You initiate the remote call, send the web
service the username and password entered by the user, and handle the results, either displaying
the main application screen or an error screen to the user.

1. Return to MmestateLogin.as in /fpad2004/mmestate/classes/.

This is the file you created Lesson 11. If you did complete that lesson, open /fpad2004/lesson13/
start/classes/MmestateLogin.as and save it as *MmestateLogin.as* in /fpad2004/mmestate/classes/.

> **Note** To test your application, you need working versions of MmestateApp.as,
> MmestateMain.as, MmestateHome.as, and MmestateSearch.as. If you did not
> finish Lesson 11, copy these files from the /fpad2004/lesson13/start/classes/
> folder to your /fpad2004/mmestate/classes/ folder.

**2. Declare a private property called `login_wsc` of type
mx.data.components.WebServiceConnector.**

```
private var login_wsc:mx.data.components.WebServiceConnector;
```

**3. Inside the `else` block in the `login_pbClick()` method, call the login operation of the
House web service by triggering the `login_wsc` WebServiceConnector component.**

```
67          else
68          {
69          login_wsc.trigger();
70          this.visible=false;
71          _parent.main.visible=true;
72          erroricon_mc.removeMovieClip();
73          }
```

4. Inside the `handleEvent()` method, add logic so that if the **type** of the event object is *result*, a method called **login_wscResult()** is called. Pass the event object to the method as an argument.

You will create this method in subsequent steps.

```
if(evtObj.type=="result")
{
      login_wscResult(evtObj);
}
```

5. Inside the `loginLoad()` method, register the screen to listen for the **result** event broadcast by the **login_wsc** component.

```
login_wsc.addEventListener("result",this);
```

6. Create a private method called **login_wscResult()** with one parameter called *evtObj* of type *Object* and no return value.

The object automatically sent to the `result` handler has a property called `target` which has a property called `results` which holds the actual results returned by the web service.

```
private function login_wscResult(evtObj:Object):Void{}
```

7. Inside the **login_wscResult()** method, create an **if** statement that checks to see if the value returned from the web service is equal to true.

Remember from examining the schema for the login operation, either in the Web Services panel or in the Component Inspector panel for the WebServiceConnector component, that the data retuned is a Boolean; a value of true is returned if the submitted username and password are valid, false if they are not.

```
if (evtObj.target.results){}
```

You could also refer to the web service return value as `login_wsc.results`.

8. Return to the `login_pbClick()` method, and cut all the code except your WebServiceConnector trigger from inside the `else` block.

Cut the code shown in the following screenshot.

```
67          else
68          {
69              login_wsc.trigger();
70              this.visible=false;
71              _parent.main.visible=true;
72              erroricon_mc.removeMovieClip();
73          }
```

9. Paste the code you cut in Step 8 inside the `if` statement of the `login_wscResult()` method.

If the user has supplied good login credentials, you want to hide the `login` screen and make the `main` screen visible.

```
if (evtObj.target.results)
    {
            this.visible=false;
            _parent.main.visible=true;
            erroricon_mc.removeMovieClip();
    }
```

10. Inside the `login_wscResult()`, create an `else` block. Inside the `else` block, set the `visible` property of the `error` screen to *true*.

If the web service returns a value of false, the user has supplied incorrect login credentials and needs to try again. In this case, you want to display the `error` screen you created in Lesson 7.

```
else
{
    error.visible=true;
}
```

> **Note** *You can also add code inside the else block to clear the username or password text fields after an unsuccessful attempt.*

11. Also inside the `else` block, hide the `logout` screen, remove the `erroricon_mc` MovieClip, and clear the `password_la` Label component.

This is clean up code so that if the `logout` screen or the password error message and image have been displayed, they are hidden or removed when a call is made to the web service. If the web service returns a value of false, you only want the `error` screen displayed.

```
101        else
102        {
103            error.visible=true;
104            erroricon_mc.removeMovieClip();
105            password_la.text="";
106            logout.visible=false;
107        }
```

12. Declare a private property called `error` of type *mx.screens.Form.*

```
private var error:mx.screens.Form;
```

13. Inside the `if` block of the `login_pbClick()` method, make the `error` and `logout` screens invisible.

This is additional clean up code, so conflicting messages are not displayed at the same time.

```
error.visible=false;
logout.visible=false;
```

14. Check the file syntax and save the file.

You should get one warning message: The class 'mx.data.components.WebServiceConnector' could not be loaded. As discussed previously, you do not have compile time checking of the WebServiceConnector in a class file because the WebServiceConnector class files are compiled in the WebServiceConnector component (the SWC) and there are no intrinsic class files for it in the Flash Classes folder. To get compile time checking of your class file, follow the instructions in the "Retrieving Data Using the XMLConnector Component" section in Lesson 12.

The finished file should resemble:
/fpad2004/lesson13/intermediate/classes/MmestateLogin_wscresults.as.

> **Note** *You could (and should!) also create a* status *handler to handle any failed calls to the web service.*

15. Return to mmestate.fla in /fpad2004/mmestate/ and test the application.

Return to the file you created in the last exercise or open /fpad2004/lesson13/intermediate/ mmestate_wscbinding.fla and save it as *mmestate.fla* in /fpad2004/mmestate/.

16. Enter *fpad* for the username and password and click the Login button.

The web service should return a value of true and you should be successfully logged in to the application; you should see the home page of the application.

Look at the Output panel. You should see information describing the binding from the text fields to the WebServiceConnector and the invocation of the web service.

17. Click the Logout button. Enter different values for the username and password and then click the Login button.

Make sure the password you enter is more than 4 characters so the web service call is initiated. You should see the error screen.

Assigning WebServiceConnector Parameters with Code

In the previous exercises, you used data binding to provide the parameters to pass to the web service. You might need to use code to specify parameter values for the web service, though, if you need to pass data that is not gathered from user input or is gathered from user input but needs to be manipulated before sending.

The schemas generated for WebServiceConnector components have two properties, params and results. You can specify parameters to send to the web service by assigning values to the params property with code.

You have two choices when assigning values to the params property.

First, you can set params equal to an object. In this case, the properties of the object must exactly match the names of the web service parameters (which you can get from the Component Inspector panel or the Web Services panel).

```
var countries:Object={country1:"united states",country2:"germany"};
this.converter_wsc.params=countries;
this.converter_wsc.trigger();
```

You can also set params directly.

```
this.converter_wsc.params=
{country1:"united states",country2:"germany"};
```

The second option is to set params equal to an array. In this case, the order of the items in the array must correspond to the order the web service parameters are specified (which you can get from the Component Inspector panel or the Web Services panel).

```
var countries:Array=["united states","germany"];
this.converter_wsc.params=countries;
```

In this example, you would not get an error if you swapped the order of the arguments—you would get the inverse of the currency exchange rate. But in most cases, you will get an error (or at least an incorrect result) if the arguments are not in the correct order.

Note *Even if the web service has a single parameter, you must set* params *equal to either an array with one element or an object with one property. You cannot set* params *equal to the primitive value.*

In this exercise, you remove the data binding for the WebServiceConnector component and instead use code to specify parameters to send to the web service.

1. Return to mmestate.fla in /fpad2004/mmestate/.

Return to the file you used in the last exercise or open /fpad2004/lesson13/intermediate/ mmestate_wscbinding.fla and save it as *mmestate.fla* in /fpad2004/mmestate/.

2. Select the `login_wsc` component on the `login` screen. Delete its two bindings in the Component Inspector panel. Save the file.

You will replace the functionality of the bindings with code.

The finished file should resemble: /fpad2004/lesson13/intermediate/mestate_wscparams.fla.

3. Return to MmestateLogin.as in /fpad2004/mmestate/classes/.

Return to the file you created in the last lesson or open /fpad2004/lesson13/intermediate/classes/ MmestateLogin_wscresults.as and save it as *MmestateLogin.as* in /fpad2004/mmestate/classes/.

4. At the beginning of the code inside the `else` block of the `login_pbClick()` method, set the `params` property of `login_wsc` equal to an array containing the username and password input to the text fields. Save the file.

Make sure you place this code *before* the WebServiceConnector trigger.

```
76        else
77        {
78            login_wsc.params=[username_ti.text,password_ti.text];
79            login_wsc.trigger();
80        }
```

The finished file should resemble: /fpad2004/lesson13/intermediate/classes/ MmestateLogin_wscparams.as.

5. Return to mmestate.fla and test the application. Log in to the application.

You should still be able to log in successfully using fpad as the username and password.

Using the WebService Class

The WebServiceConnector component's underlying functionality is provided by the WebService class, just as the XMLConnector component was a wrapper for the XML class. Unlike the XML class, though, the WebService class is not native to the Flash Player. The WebService class is part of the mx.services package of compiled classes provided as part of the Flash application framework. The benefits of using one versus the other are listed below.

Reasons to use the WebServiceConnector component:

1. Provides a visual way to set up access to a web service in the authoring environment and a way to set its parameters without code.

2. Can use data binding to assign values for the web service parameters or to handle the web service results.

3. Can handle events associated with the remote call using the same event handling framework as the rest of the components.

Reasons to use the WebService class:

1. Can create all logic to call a web service with code.

2. More suitable for applications that call a lot of web services. You can use a single WebService object to make multiple web service calls.

3. Gives you more flexibility. You must use the WebService class in applications that need custom data handling (processing that cannot be handled by data binding and the data components).

4. Have more control over the remote call. You can change the SOAP header, view the raw SOAP messages sent and received, set the concurrency of all calls made with that WebService object, and change, delay or turn off SOAP decoding.

5. Can use the mx.services.Log class to get more detailed log information than that provided by the data binding Log class used for the WebServiceConnector.

To call a web service using the mx.services package of classes, you first create a WebService object. When you create a new WebService object, the WSDL file that defines the web service gets downloaded, parsed, and all necessary information stored in the object. You can then call the methods of the web service directly on the WebService object, and handle any callbacks from the web service. The WebService object is called a **proxy** object because it mimics the structure of the remote object so you can call methods of the remote object as if they were local. The mx.services package consists of four classes: WebService, PendingCall, Log, and SOAPCall.

WebService. An instance of this class is the proxy for the remote web service from which you invoke methods.

PendingCall. An instance of this class is created when you invoke a web service operation and is used to handle the result and faults of that call.

Log. An instance of this class is used to record log activity related to the web service call.

SOAPCall. An instance of this class is used to set advanced properties of the WebService object.

Creating a WebService Object

The first step in calling a web service using the WebService class is to create an instance of the WebService class (mx.services.WebService), which acts as a local reference to a remote web service. To create an instance of the WebService class, you pass the URL of the WSDL to the constructor as an argument.

```
var my_ws:mx.services.WebService=new mx.services.WebService(WSDLURL);
```

When this code is executed, the WSDL is parsed (by the code contained in the WebService class). If the parsing is successful, an onLoad event is emitted and the WebService object is ready to use. (The WSDL contains the information needed to correctly encode and send a SOAP request.) You can place calls to web service operations inside the onLoad callback, but it is not necessary. Any operations invoked before the WSDL has been parsed are queued and transmitted after the WSDL is parsed. If the WSDL parsing fails (the WSDL is not found or is not well-formed), an onFault event is broadcast. Just as for the built-in events, you handle the events by creating callbacks with the same names. (This class is not part of the component framework, so you do not need to register listeners using addEventListener().)

```
my_ws.onLoad()=function:Void
{
  [invoke some web service methods]
};
my_ws.onFault()=function:Void
{
  trace("Server unavailable. Try again later…");
};
```

In this exercise, you create a WebService object in the searchHouses application that will be used to access a web service that retrieves houses matching the user's search criteria.

1. Return to Searchform.as in /fpad2004/mmestate/classes/.

This is the file you created in the last lesson. If you did complete that lesson, open /fpad2004/lesson13/ start/classes/Searchform.as and save it as *Searchform.as* in /fpad2004/mmestate/classes/.

2. Declare a private property called search_ws of type *mx.services.WebService*.

```
private var search_ws:mx.services.WebService;
```

3. In the constructor, create a new WebService object called `search_ws` with a WSDL located at http://localhost/fpad2004/mmestate/services/House.cfc?wsdl.

```
search_ws=new mx.services.WebService("http://localhost/fpad2004/
mmestate/services/House.cfc?wsdl");
```

If you are using a different platform or port, use the appropriate WSDL.

> **Note** *In general, you should try to minimize the amount of code in the constructor. You could place the code contained in the constructor in an* init() *method and then call the* init() *method from the constructor.*

4. Check the syntax and save the file.

You get the warning: "The class 'mx.services.WebService' could not be loaded," because there is no actual or intrinsic class file in the Flash Classes folder, just as there were no class files in that folder for the data connector components. When working with the XMLConnector and WebServiceConnector components, though, you *did* get compile time checking when you compiled the FLA that used the class file referencing the compiled XMLConnector or WebServiceConnector class—because the SWC in the FLA library contained the class files being referenced. Similarly, although you are not using a visual connector component on the Stage, you still need to get the compiled versions of the mx.services.WebService class into the library of the FLA so it is compiled into the SWF.

The finished file should resemble: /fpad2004/lesson13/intermediate/classes/Searchform_wscreate.as.

Making the WebService Class Available at Runtime

To make the mx.services package of web service classes available at runtime, you must have a component containing the compiled web service classes in your FLA file's library. The WebServiceConnector SWC contains these compiled classes, so the classes will be available if you have a WebServiceConnector component in your library. If you are not using the WebServiceConnector in your application, you can instead add a slimmed-down SWC called WebServiceClasses to your library that contains only the mx.services package of classes.

To add the WebServiceClasses SWC to your library, open Classes.fla (provided with Flash MX 2004), by selecting Window > Other Panels > Common Libraries > Classes. Classes.fla contains SWCs for any compiled classes provided for Flash without their source code.

Next, drag an instance of the WebServiceClasses symbol from the library of Classes.fla to your document's library.

Note *If you drag an instance of the WebServiceClasses symbol to your document's Stage instead, the WebServiceClasses symbol is represented on the Stage by a world icon (the WebServiceConnector component icon missing the plug). You need to delete this instance from the Stage because the icon will appear in your published application, unlike the WebServiceConnector symbol, which has no runtime appearance.*

In this exercise you add the WebServiceClasses SWC to the library of the searchHouses FLA.

1. Return to searchHouses.fla in /fpad2004/mmestate/.

This is the file you created in the last lesson. If you did complete that lesson, open /fpad2004/lesson13/start/searchHouses.fla and save it as *searchHouses.fla* in /fpad2004/mmestate/.

2. Select Window > Other Panels > Common Libraries > Classes.

The library of Classes.fla opens.

3. Drag an instance of the WebServiceClasses symbol from the library of Classes.fla to the library of searchHouses.fla. Save the file.

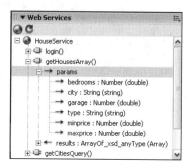

The finished file should resemble: /fpad2004/lesson13/intermediate/searchHouses_wslibrary.fla.

Invoking a Remote Method with a WebService Object

The WebService object you create is a proxy for the actual web service. To invoke methods of the remote web service, you invoke methods of the WebService object with the same name as those of the web service. When you invoke a method of the WebService object, a PendingCall object is created, which represents the remote call in progress. The PendingCall class is part of the mx.services package of classes and has properties, methods, and events you can use to access the web service return results as well as information about the SOAP request. You do not explicitly create a PendingCall object, you just set the return value of a remote method invocation equal to it as shown (making sure to include values for all the parameters in the correct order and with the right data type).

```
myPendingCallObject=myWebServiceObject.myOperation(param1,param2,…);
```

You can give the PendingCall object any name; you use this name to access the web service results after the call is complete (or emits an onFault event). For example, to call the currency converter web service that has an operation called getRate() with two parameters, country1 and country2, use the following code:

```
getRateCall=converter_ws.getRate("united states","italy");
```

Tip *You can get detailed information during a web service request by creating an instance of the mx.services.Log class and passing the name of the Log object as a second argument to the WebService object constructor. You then write an* onLog *event handler for the Log object in which you specify what to do with the log messages as they are received. See the Log class in the Flash Help files for more details.*

In this exercise, you invoke the `getHousesArray()` method of the House web service, sending the information the user selected in the search form to it.

1. Return to searchHouses.fla in /fpad2004/mmestate/.

Return to the file you created in the last exercise or open /fpad2004/lesson13/intermediate/ searchHouses_wslibrary.fla and save it as *searchHouses.fla* in /fpad2004/mmestate/.

2. In the Web Services panel, drill down to HouseService › getHousesArray() › params.

Look at the names, data types, and order of the parameters. Leave this panel open so you can see it when editing the ActionScript file. Although, the entire authoring environment becomes grayed out and fuzzy when you are editing a class file, you can still partially see the contents of the panel, so you know what order to specify your parameters to the web service operation.

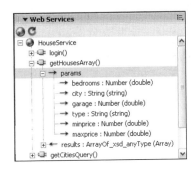

3. Return to Searchform.as in /fpad2004/mmestate/classes/.

Return to the file you created in a previous exercise this lesson or open /fpad2004/lesson13/ intermediate/classes/Searchform_wscreate.as and save it as *Searchform.as* in /fpad2004/ mmestate/classes/.

4. Define a private property called `searchWsCall` of type *mx.services.PendingCall*.

```
private var searchWsCall:mx.services.PendingCall;
```

5. At the end of the code inside the `search_pbClick()` method, create a PendingCall object called *searchWsCall* by invoking the `getHousesArray()` method of the WebService object search_ws.

```
searchWsCall=search_ws.getHousesArray();
```

```
78        for (var i=0;i<cities_lb.selectedIndices.length;i++
79        {
80            cityids.push(cities_lb.selectedItems[i].data);
81        }
82        trace(cityids.toString());
83        searchWsCall=search_ws.getHousesArray();
84    }
```

6. Look at the Web Services panel to see the order the parameters need to be passed to the operation. Copy and paste the appropriate expressions from inside the `trace()` statements to be arguments for the method invocation.

For example, the first parameter for the operation is called bedrooms and is of type Number. Copy the expression, bedrooms_ns.value, from the `trace()` statement and paste it so it is the first argument in the method invocation.

```
searchWsCall=search_ws.getHousesArray(bedrooms_ns.value,
cityids.toString(),garage.selectedData,housetype.toString(),
min_cb.selectedItem.label, max_cb.value);
```

Notice the maximum and minimum parameters required by the operation are numbers, but the values you are sending are strings, for example, 100,000 or 1,00,000. You will format this data correctly in the next step.

> **Note** If you want, you can delete all the `trace()` statements when you are finished.

7. At the top of the file, import the Formatters class.

This is a class you created in Lesson 5 to remove all non-numeric characters from strings. If you did not complete that lesson and do not have Formatters.as in /fpad2004/mmestate/classes/, open /fpad2004/lesson13/start/classes/Formatters.as and save it as *Formatters.as* in /fpad2004/mmestate/classes/.

Because the class resides in the same folder as Searchform.as, this import statement is not necessary, but it is a good practice to add it so you can easily see what external classes are being referenced.

```
import Formatters;
```

8. Format the values for the price combo boxes passed to the web service using the `formatNumber()` method of the Formatters class. Cast `max_cb.value` to a String before using it as an argument to the `formatNumber()` method.

If you don't cast max_cb to a String, you get a type mismatch error.

```
searchWsCall=search_ws.getHousesArray(bedrooms_ns.value,
cityids.toString(),garage.selectedData,housetype.toString(),
Formatters.formatNumber(min_cb.selectedItem.label),
Formatters.formatNumber(String(max_cb.value)));
```

9. Check the syntax and save the file.

You should get only the four errors stating that the compiler cannot find the compiled classes referenced.

The finished file should resemble: /fpad2004/lesson13/intermediate/classes/Searchform_wsinvoke.as.

10. Return to searchHouses.fla and test the application. Select some cities and click the Search button.

Nothing should happen; you have not handled the return results yet.

Make sure you do not get an "Error opening URL" message in the Output panel. If you get this error, you have a problem with your code; you are probably not passing the correct number of parameters, have them in the wrong order, or have not cast them to the correct data types. To get more detailed information, you need to capture and read the Faults emitted during the remote call invocation. You learn how to handle invocation events in the next exercise.

Handling PendingCall Object Events

When a WebService operation completes, the properties of the PendingCall object are assigned values, and an onResult or an onFault event is broadcast. You capture these events by creating callbacks of the PendingCall object with the same name as the event.

The onResult event is broadcast when a web service invocation has succeeded and returned a result. The onResult event handler is passed one argument: the variable returned by the web service, which can be a complex variable like an object or an array of objects.

```
myPendingCallObject=myWebServiceObject.myOperation(param1,param2,…);
myPendingCallObject.onResult=function(result):Void
{
      trace(result);
};
```

> **Tip** *Inside the onResult event handler, you can also access properties of the PendingCall object including response and request, which contain the SOAP request sent and returned in raw XML format.*

The onFault event is broadcast when a web service invocation fails. The onFault event handler is passed one argument: a SOAPFault object with properties faultcode, faultstring, detail, element, and faultactor properties. Possible faultcode values are the same values you get for the WebServiceConnector component and include Timeout (timeout when calling method x), Client.Disconnected (could not load WSDL), and Client.NoSuchMethod (couldn't find method x in service). (A complete list of fault codes can be found in the Flash Help files for the WebServiceConnector component.)

```
myPendingCallObject.onFault=function(fault:Object):Void
{
      trace(fault.faultcode+","+fault.faultstring);
};
```

In this exercise, you create an `onResult` handler for the PendingCall object, which is passed the results returned from the web service.

1. Return to Searchform.as in /fpad2004/mmestate/classes/.

Return to the file you created in the last exercise or open /fpad2004/lesson13/intermediate/classes/ Searchform_wsinvoke.as and save it as *Searchform.as* in /fpad2004/mmestate/classes/.

2. At the end of the code inside the `search_pbClick()` method, set the `onResult` event of `searchWsCall` equal to a function literal with one parameter called `result` of type *Array*.

```
searchWsCall.onResult=function(result:Array):Void();
```

The ColdFusion web service returns an array of structures which become an ActionScript array of objects. The Java web service returns an ArrayList of HashMaps which also becomes an ActionScript array of objects. The C# web service returns an ArrayList of custom objects which becomes an ActionScript array of XML objects; you cannot return a Hashtable from a C# web service.

> **Tip** *Trace `this.response` inside `searchWsCall.onResult` to view the raw SOAP returned by the web service.*

3. If you are using .NET, copy NetConverter.as from /fpad2004/lesson13 (.NET port 80)/ start/classes/ to /fpad2004/mmestate/classes/.

The NetConverter class has been prewritten. It contains one static method, `xmlToObject()`, which converts the array of XML objects returned from the .NET web service to an array of general ActionScript objects.

4. If you are using .NET, return to Searchform.as and inside `searchWsCall.onResult`, set the `result` variable equal to the value returned from calling the `xmlToObject()` method of the NetConverter class.

```
result=NetConverter.xmlToObject(result);
```

5. Inside `searchWsCall.onResult`, trace `result`. Save the file.

```
trace(result);
```

6. Return to searchHouses.fla in /fpad2004/mmestate/ and test the application.

Return to the file you used in the last exercise or open /fpad2004/lesson13/intermediate/ searchHouses_wslibrary.fla and save it as *searchHouses.fla* in /fpad2004/mmestate/.

7. Select some cities, select a maximum price, and set any other parameter. Click the Search button.

Make sure you select a large maximum price; houses are expensive in California.

You should see an [object Object] traced to the Output panel for each house returned from the web service that matches your search criteria.

8. Return to Searchform.as. Inside the `searchWsCall.onResult` handler, trace the `DESCRIPTION` property of the item in the first array element of `result`. Save the file.

```
trace(result[0].DESCRIPTION);
```

You can get a list of all the properties of the objects returned by the web service by using a `for-in` loop to loop over `result[0]`.

> **Note** *The properties of objects returned by ColdFusion web services are always all capital letters.*

The finished file should resemble: /fpad2004/lesson13/intermediate/classes/Searchform_wshandle.as.

9. Return to searchHouses.fla. Select some cities and a new maximum price and then click the Search button.

You should see the description of the first house returned displayed in the Output panel. You will learn to display and manipulate sets of data (like this) in Lesson 15, "Using the DataGrid Component."

```
[object Object],[object Object],[object Object],[object Object]
A great place above the crashing waves in desirable Duxbury Reef
neighborhood. Three-building cluster offers main house, guest qtrs and
office on half acre+. Also, potting & storage sheds, gazebo, seasonal
pond & established gardens & landscaping. Fully fenced, totally private
; good offstreet parking; paved roads all the way. Perfect for full-
time, part-time or shared ownership. Among the most delightful
properties around.
```

> **Tip** *If you want control over the SOAP that is generated and how the SOAP is handled by Flash, you can set properties of a mx.services.SOAPCall object. When you create a WebService object, a SOAPCall object is created for each operation in the WSDL and contains all the information about that particular operation (how the XML should look that is sent over the network, the operation style, and so on). For example, you can set the concurrency of all calls made with that WebService object and change, delay, or turn off SOAP decoding. For more information, see the SOAPCall class in the Flash Help files.*

What You Have Learned

In this lesson, you have:

- Registered a web service in the Flash authoring environment (pages 515–519)
- Used the WebServiceConnector component (pages 520–522)
- Used data binding with the WebServiceConnector (pages 522–524)
- Triggered WebServiceConnector calls and handled its results (pages 524–530)
- Assigned WebServiceConnector parameters with code (pages 530–533)
- Created a WebService object (pages 533–534)
- Made the WebService class available at runtime (pages 534–536)
- Invoked a remote method with a WebService object (pages 536–539)
- Handled PendingCall object events (pages 539–541)

14 Accessing Remote Services Using Flash Remoting

In the last lesson, you learned to access remote application functionality as web services using SOAP over HTTP. If you have existing server-side functionality (ColdFusion CFCs, Java classes, Java beans, C# classes, and so on), you don't have to convert all your classes into web services to access them from Flash. You can access them directly using Macromedia Flash Remoting MX, a programming tool and runtime environment for connecting Flash directly to remote application server services. Flash Remoting is a separate product from Macromedia Flash MX 2004 and is available for ColdFusion, J2EE, and .NET platforms. (It is built into ColdFusion MX and JRun4.) Flash Remoting has two pieces: a client side piece that includes the necessary classes and debugging tools for developing remoting applications in the Flash authoring environment and a server piece that serves as the gateway for all remoting requests from the Flash Player to the application server.

So when do you use Flash Remoting to access application server functionality and when do you use web services? It all depends. Some developers and businesses prefer to use web services because they use a standard protocol for communication. Others prefer to use Flash Remoting because remoting does not require application server functionality to be exposed as web services. Flash Remoting can also be significantly faster when handling large sets of data; Flash Remoting communicates using binary messages that require less bandwidth and are more efficient than the more verbose text-based SOAP messages. In addition, the client-side message generation and serialization/deserialization of data is built into the Flash Player for Flash Remoting. With web services, you have to include a package of classes with every application to perform these functions. Including this code adds to the application's size and results in slower processing because the functionality is not built into the Flash Player.

```
Searchform.as*                                                          _ 🗗 ×
🕀 🔎 🎲 ✓ 🗏 🖵                                                          ◈ 🔃
74              cityids.push(cities_lb.selectedItems[i].data);
75          }
76          var net_conn:Object= NetServices.createGatewayConnection(
        "http://localhost/flashservices/gateway");
77          var houseService:Object=net_conn.getService(
        "fpad2004.mmestate.services.House",this);
78          houseService.getHousesArray(bedrooms_ns.value,cityids.toString(), garage.
        selectedData,housetype.toString(),Formatters.formatNumber(min_cb.selectedItem.
        label),Formatters.formatNumber(String(max_cb.value)));
79      }
80
```

In this lesson, you use Flash Remoting to retrieve houses matching the user's search criteria.

At the time of this book's publication, the only way to communicate with a remote service using Flash Remoting is with code, using a package of remoting classes that are written with ActionScript 1.0. (Flash Remoting is on a different product cycle release than the Flash authoring tool.) The remoting classes do not come with Flash MX 2004; they are part of the Flash Remoting Components, which you install as an add-on to the Flash authoring environment. New authoring components for Flash Remoting, however, will be available soon. Keep an eye out for new remoting classes written in ActionScript 2.0 as well as a visual data connector component to use with Flash Remoting (similar to the WebServiceConnector and XMLConnector components) later this year.

In this lesson, you retrieve the houses matching the user search criteria using Flash Remoting instead of web services, rewriting the code used in Lesson 13, "Consuming Web Services." This code rewrite enables readers who do not have Flash Remoting to still be able to complete the exercises in Lessons 15, "Using the DataGrid Component," and Lesson 16, "Persisting Data on the Client." In order to complete the exercises in this lesson, you must have an application server with Flash Remoting installed. Installation details are included in the Appendix.

What You Will Learn

In this lesson, you will:

- Check the Flash Remoting installation
- Include the remoting class files
- Create a NetConnection object
- Use the NetConnection Debugger
- Create service proxy objects
- Invoke remote service methods
- Handle responses from remote services
- Handle responses for multiple calls from the same service proxy object
- Use a general responder class for handling events
- Learn how Flash Remoting converts data between ActionScript and your application server

Approximate Time

This lesson takes approximately 90 minutes to complete.

Lesson Files

Asset Files:

The class file or assembly for your application server

Starting Files:

/fpad2004/lesson14/start/searchHouses.fla
/fpad2004/lesson14/start/classes/Searchform.as
/fpad2004/lesson14/start/classes/NetResponder.as

Completed Files:

/fpad2004/lesson14/complete/searchHouses.fla
/fpad2004/lesson14/complete/classes/Searchform.as

Understanding Flash Remoting

Using Flash Remoting, data is exchanged between the Flash Player and the application server using a binary format called AMF (Action Message Format) that was developed by Macromedia and is based on SOAP. On the client side, ActionScript variables are translated into AMF by the Flash Player. The data is sent over HTTP to the Flash Remoting gateway on the server, which translates the AMF data into native objects for the specific application server and invokes the requested method. Any data returned by the application is converted back into AMF by the Flash Remoting gateway and then sent via HTTP to the Flash Player, which deserializes the AMF into ActionScript variables and makes them available to the Flash application. The process is shown in the following picture.

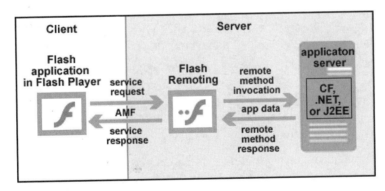

Note *To view an application using Flash Remoting, the user must have Flash Player 6 version r40 or later.*

Setting Up Flash Remoting

Flash Remoting has two parts: the Flash authoring add-ons and the server-side piece.

For the authoring environment, you must install the Flash Remoting Components. The Flash Remoting Components are not included with Flash MX 2004; they must be downloaded from http://www.macromedia.com/software/flashremoting/downloads/components/. The Flash Remoting Components extend the Flash authoring environment, providing tools to use remoting and the key ActionScript files needed to enable Flash Remoting from Flash. The remoting add-ons include ActionScript APIs for invoking remote services from within Flash, several Flash Remoting menu options within Flash, Flash Remoting options in the ActionScript toolbox, and a NetConnection Debugger, which enables you to watch and trace events across both the client and server.

For the server side, you must install Flash Remoting on your application server. Flash Remoting is built into ColdFusion MX and JRun4 and is available as a separate product for all other J2EE servers and for the .NET platform. The server piece of Flash Remoting is the gateway between Flash and the application server. It sits on top of your application server and handles the requests from Flash to the application server and handles the data translation from AMF to your application server variables and vice versa.

> **Note** Alternatives to Macromedia's Flash Remoting gateway are also available. The OpenAMF Project is a free open-source alternative to Flash Remoting using Java (www.openamf.org). AMFPHP is an open source project for Flash Remoting using PHP (www.amfphp.org) and FLAP is an open source project for adding Flash Remoting to Perl (www.simonf.com/flap).

In this exercise, you make sure the Flash Remoting Components are installed in the Flash authoring environment and the Flash Remoting gateway is installed on your application server.

1. Follow the setup instructions in the Appendix for your server.

Make sure the appropriate server classes are installed in the correct location for your application server and that the Flash Remoting Components and the Flash Remoting gateway are installed.

For ColdFusion, House.cfc is located in the same place as it was to access it as a web service. The class file for Java and the assembly file for .NET, however, are located in a different locations than the analogous web service files.

2. In Flash, select Window › Other Panels.

If you see listings for NetConnection Debugger and Service Browser, the Flash Remoting Components are installed.

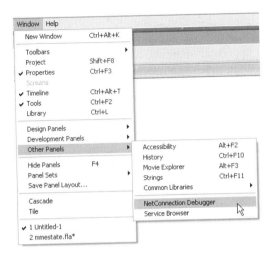

3. Browse to http://localhost/flashservices/gateway/ (or the URL for your application server's gateway).

Possible other gateway locations include http://localhost/flashremoting/gateway.aspx (.NET server using the preinstalled flash remoting application), http://localhost:8500/flashservices/gateway/ (stand-alone version of ColdFusion using a built-in server on port 8500), http://localhost:8100/flashservices/gateway/ (JRun4 using the default server on port 8100), or http://{application context}/flashsevices/gateway/ (any J2EE server with Flash Remoting installed).

If Flash Remoting is correctly installed on your application server, you should get a blank page, not a "The page cannot be found" error or any other error.

The URL of the Flash Remoting gateway does not translate to a directory on the application server. Rather, it is a mapping that points to a Java servlet or an ASP.NET page in a .NET assembly that provides the gateway between Flash and the application server. For ColdFusion MX or J2EE servers, the general URL for the Flash Remoting gateway is http://webserver[:port]/flashservices/gateway/ where flashservices is the name of the Java application context and gateway is the servlet mapping. For .NET servers, the Flash gateway URL is http://webserver[:port]/{assembly root directory}/gateway.aspx where a flashgateway.dll file resides in a bin directory beneath the assembly root directory and gateway.aspx is a blank page Flash uses to access the application. When you install Flash Remoting for .NET, a flashremoting application is automatically created and you can use Flash Remoting immediately with no additional setup by adding your compiled assemblies in the C:\Inetpub\wwwroot\flashremoting\bin\ directory. Instructions for using Flash Remoting in your .NET application with assemblies not located in /flashremoting/bin are included in the Appendix.

547

Including the Remoting Class Files

To enable an application to use Flash Remoting, you need to include the code for the ActionScript remoting classes. Definitions for the NetConnection and NetServices classes are contained in a file called NetServices.as, which was installed to the \Flash\<language>\First Run\Include\ folder when you installed the Flash Remoting Components.

At the time of this book's publication, the Flash Remoting Components had not yet been updated for ActionScript 2.0, which means the remoting classes cannot be imported into your class files. Instead, you have to use #include to include the code defining the remoting class definitions.

```
#include "NetServices.as"
```

When you include the NetServices.as file, you don't have to specify a path in the include statement. Flash automatically looks in the \First Run\Include\ directory for any ActionScript files not found in the current FLA directory.

So where do you place the include statement? If you place it in a class file, you get a lot of compile-time errors. Until ActionScript 2.0 remoting classes are available, the cleanest way to include the remoting class definitions is to include NetServices.as in the Timeline of the FLA. Even though the class definitions are in the FLA, you can write the code creating instances and handling events of the remoting objects in external class files.

Note *At this time, you should check the Macromedia web site and see if ActionScript 2.0 versions of the remoting classes are available so you can properly import the class definitions into class files instead of having to include them in the FLA.*

In this exercise, you include the remoting classes in your application.

1. Return to searchHouses.fla in /fpad2004/mmestate/.

This is the file you created in the last lesson. If you did complete that lesson, open /fpad2004/lesson14/start/searchHouses.fla and save it as *searchHouses.fla* in /fpad2004/mmestate/.

Note *There are five versions of the lesson14 folder. Use the folder appropriate for your application server setup. If none of the five folders match your setup and you want to use files in the lesson folders for Lessons 13 through 16 as starting files for any exercises, you need to change two files: the web service URL for the WebServiceConnector on the* login *screen in mmestate.fla and the URL for the web service or Flash Remoting gateway in Searchform.as.*

2. Open the Timeline panel (if it is closed) and select the `application` screen. Select Layer 1 in the Timeline panel and open the Actions panel.

Make sure the title of the Actions panel is Actions – Frame and not Actions – Screen. You are going to add code to the Timeline, not on the screen object.

3. Open the Actions toolbox and expand the Remoting branch.

When you installed the Flash Remoting Components, entries for the remoting classes were added to the Actions toolbox.

4. Double-click #include NetServices.as in the Actions toolbox. Save the file.

The `include` statement is added to the Actions panel. Remember, you do not put semicolons at the end of `include` statements.

The finished file should resemble: /fpad2004/lesson14/intermediate/searchHouses_netservices.fla.

Creating a NetConnection Object

The next step is to create a Flash Remoting connection object (an instance of the NetConnection class) that contains all the information needed to connect to the Flash Remoting gateway. You create a NetConnection object using the static method `createGatewayConnection()` of the NetServices class (one of the remoting classes contained in NetServices.as). You pass one argument to the method, the URL of the Flash remoting gateway on the server.

```
var my_conn:NetConnection=NetServices.createGatewayConnection(URL);
```

The URL you specify must have the same domain as your SWF; the same security policy applies for remoting as it did for accessing remote data from the Flash Player. (See the "Retrieving Data from Other Domains" section in Lesson 12 for more details.)

Note *An intrinsic class definition for the NetConnection class is included in the Flash /First Run/Classes/ folder. You can also use a _conn suffix in the NetConnection object name to enable code-hinting in the ActionScript editor.*

Setting a default gateway. In addition to setting the URL for the gateway in the `createGatewayConnection()` method, you can also specify a default gateway URL using the NetServices class static method `setDefaultGatewayURL()`.

```
NetServices.setDefaultGatewayURL(URL);
```

If you set a remoting gateway using the `setDefaultGateway()` method, you do not have to specify a URL argument in `createGatewayConnection()`. It you specify a URL in both the `setDefaultGateway()` and `createGatewayConnection()` methods, the URL in the `createGatewayConnection()` methods overrides the URL set in the `setDefaultGateway()` method.

Specifying the remoting gateway from outside the FLA. Because your Flash Remoting gateway URL might change—for example, when you move code from a development to a production server—you might not want to hard-code the URL in the FLA. To separate the gateway URL from the FLA, you have several choices. You can set the gateway as a variable in a separate AS file and then include the AS file. Another option is to create a class containing static properties (your application "constants"), one of which is the gateway URL, and then use that class property in your application. Finally, you can set the gateway in the web page in which the SWF is embedded. To set the gateway variable in the web page that loads the SWF, define a variable called `gatewayURL` in the `<object>` tag that calls the SWF. The gateway specified in the `gatewayURL` variable is then used by any `createGatewayConnection()` method in the Flash application that has no URL argument. If you combine any of these methods for defining the gateway URL, the hierarchy from highest precedence to lowest is: URL specified in a `createGatewayConnection()` > URL specified in a web page as a `gatewayURL` variable > default gateway specified in the `setDefaultGatewayURL()`.

In this exercise, you create a NetConnection object that contains the information needed to connect to the remote server.

1. Return to Searchform.as in /fpad2004/mmestate/classes/.

This is the file you created in the last lesson. If you did complete that lesson, open /fpad2004/lesson14/start/classes/Searchform.as and save it as *Searchform.as* in /fpad2004/mmestate/classes/.

2. Delete the property declarations for `search_ws` and `searchWsCall` and the code creating the WebService object `search_ws` inside the constructor.

You no longer need the code for the web service invocation.

3. Comment out all the code in the `search_pbClick()` method for the searchWsCall object.

You should comment out this code instead of deleting it so you can, in a later exercise, copy the values of the arguments you passed to the web service and pass them to the remote service you access with Flash Remoting. Comment out the code shown in the following screenshot.

```
75          for (var i=0;i<cities_lb.selectedIndices.length;i++)
76          {
77              cityids.push(cities_lb.selectedItems[i].data);
78          }
79          searchWsCall=search_ws.getHousesArray(bedrooms_ns.value,cityids.toString
            (),garage.selectedData,housetype.toString(),Formatters.formatNumber(min_cb.
            selectedItem.label),Formatters.formatNumber(String(max_cb.value)));
80          searchWsCall.onResult=function(result:Array):Void
81          {
82              trace(result);
83              trace(result[0].DESCRIPTION);
84          };
85      }
```

4. Declare a private property called **net_conn** of type *NetConnection*.

```
private var net_conn:NetConnection;
```

5. Inside **searchformLoad()**, set the **net_conn** property equal to a **NetConnection object.**
Use the **createGatewayConnection()** method of the **NetServices class.**

```
net_conn=NetServices.createGatewayConnection();
```

6. Inside the parentheses for **createGatewayConnection()**, enter the **URL of the remoting**
gateway: *http://localhost/flashservices/gateway/*.

Use the appropriate Flash Remoting gateway URL for your server set-up. (For JRun4 using the
default server, the URL is http://localhost:8100/flashservices/gateway/. For .NET using the
flashremoting application, the URL is http://localhost/flashremoting/gateway.aspx.)

7. Save the file.

The finished file should resemble: /fpad2004/lesson14/intermediate/classes/
Searchform_netconnection.as.

Using the NetConnection Debugger

You can debug your Flash Remoting applications during development using the NetConnection
Debugger panel. The NetConnection Debugger panel is not part of the Flash MX 2004; it was added
as a tool to the authoring environment when you installed the Flash Remoting Components. The
NetConnection Debugger lets you monitor traffic between Flash and Flash Remoting on your application server, so you can see if data is being sent and received correctly by your Flash application.

To set-up your application to send and receive events in the NetConnection Debugger, include the
file NetDebug.as in your FLA.

```
#include "NetDebug.as"
```

The NetDebug.as file was added to the \First Run\Include\ directory when you installed the Flash Remoting Components (just like the NetServices.as file). Similarly, at the time of this book's publication, only an ActionScript 1.0 version of the Debugger code is available, so you need to include the file in your FLA instead of importing a class into your application class files.

Note *NetDebug.as is not required for Flash Remoting to work. You should remove or comment out the include statement once your application is working properly. Leaving the code enabling the NetConnection Debugger in a deployed application adds file size and can create security risks.*

To use the NetConnection Debugger, select Window > NetConnection Debugger before you test your application. Like the Output panel, this panel stays visible when testing applications in the authoring environment. When you test the application, Flash Remoting events are displayed in the NetConnection Debugger panel when remote service methods are called or data is returned. Example results from a remote method call are displayed in the NetConnection Debugger panel in the following screenshot.

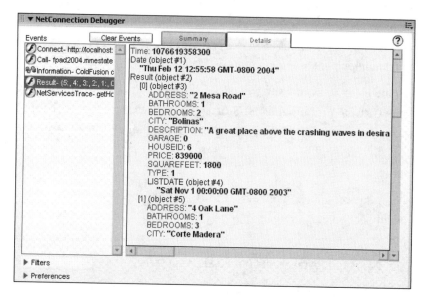

You can click events in the left panel of the NetConnection Debugger panel to see either summary or detailed information for the event in the right panel. If you click a Call event, you can see the actual parameter values sent to the remote method and if you click a Result method, you can see what values are returned. If you have debugging enabled for a ColdFusion MX application server, these events also include server activities, such as includes and SQL queries.

The NetConnection Debugger provides a quick way to check for errors in your remote methods. For example, if you have an error in a query in your remote method and you invoke the remote method from your Flash application, you do not get an error. The Flash application just doesn't work. If you examine the information in the NetConnection Debugger, you find helpful information, such as the following debug message that a query did not execute successfully: "Service threw an exception during method invocation: Error Executing Database Query."

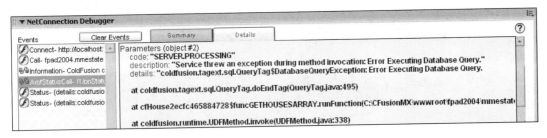

In this exercise, you enable and use the NetConnection Debugger to monitor Flash Remoting events.

1. Return to searchHouses.fla in /fpad2004/mmestate/.

Return to the file you created in an earlier exercise or open /fpad2004/lesson14/intermediate/searchHouses_netservices.fla and save it as *searchHouses.fla* in /fpad2004/mmestate/.

2. Select the `application` screen and open the Actions panel. Select Layer 1: Frame 1 under application in the Actions panel Script Navigator.

Make sure you are editing the code for the Timeline of the `application` screen. You should see the line of code including the NetServices.as file.

3. Include the NetDebug.as file. Save the file.

```
#include "NetDebug.as"
```

The finished file should resemble: /fpad2004/lesson14/intermediate/searchHouses_netdebug.fla.

4. Select Window > Other Panels > NetConnection Debugger.

You must open the NetConnection Debugger panel *before* you test the application. You cannot open the NetConnection Debugger panel when viewing a SWF.

5. Test the application. Click the Search button.

You should see one Connect event listed in the NetConnection Debugger panel.

> **Note** *The* `createGatewayConnection()` *method sets up the connection object, but the Flash client does not actually communicate with the server until a remote method is invoked.*

6. Click the Details tab in the NetConnection Debugger panel.

Details for the NetConnection object are displayed.

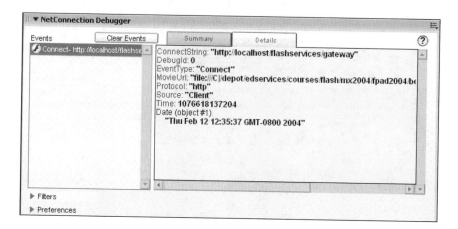

Tip   *You can drag the borders of the panes in the NetConnection Debugger panel to change their size.*

Creating Service Proxy Objects

Once you have created the NetConnection object (which contains only the information needed to make a connection to the gateway), the next step is to create a local proxy object for a remote service. You invoke methods of the remote service using the proxy object.

You create a proxy object using the `getService()` method of the NetConnection class.

```
var myService:Object=my_conn.getService(serviceName,defaultResponder);
```

`serviceName` is the fully qualified service name of the remote service and `defaultResponder` is the ActionScript object that handles the results returned from the remote service. In many cases, you can set the default responder object equal to `this`. In Timeline based development, `this` refers to the main Timeline and you can build your event handlers as functions or function literals on the main Timeline. In class-based screen development, `this` refers to the screen in which the NetConnection object is defined and you can build your event handlers as methods of the class.

The proxy objects created for a NetConnection object are analogous to the WebService objects, which contained all the information for connecting to a particular web service. You created a WebService object using the `new` keyword to invoke the class constructor in the last lesson. You create a Flash Remoting proxy object differently, using the `getService()` method of the NetConnection class.

So what exactly do you enter for the name of the service? Let's look at each server in turn.

ColdFusion MX. Flash Remoting can access ColdFusion components (CFCs) and ColdFusion pages (CFMs) located in the web root. (It is easiest and most common to access CFCs.) For a ColdFusion component Bike.cfc located in C:\CFusionMX\wwwroot\fpad2004\, the service name is fpad2004.Bike.

J2EE servers. Flash Remoting can access Java classes (POJOs), Java Beans, Java servlets, EJBs, and JMXs (JRun4 only) located in a Java application classpath. The package of a Java class must mirror the directory structure from the classpath. For a Java class Bike.class located in C:\JRun4\servers\default\SERVER-INF\classes\fpad2004\, the package name is fpad2004.Bike.

.NET. Flash Remoting can access DLLs and ASP.NET pages (ASPX) located in assembly folders for which Flash Remoting is installed. Only the assembly library for the remote service is required for the deployed Flash application. (Services are compiled in the assembly library from one or more class files; the assembly library, resides in the bin directory beneath the assembly root folder.) For .NET, the namespace for service classes typically mirrors the directory structure from the web root, but this is not necessary. For example, consider a Bike.cs class located in C:\Inetpub\wwwroot\flashremoting\fpad2004\. The corresponding assembly library fpad2004.dll is located in C:\Inetpub\wwwroot\flashremoting\bin\fpad2004.dll and the package name for the service in Flash is fpad2004.Bike.

> **Note** *You can also call third-party web services directly from a Flash application using Flash Remoting (by specifying the web service WSDL) if you are using a ColdFusion or .NET server. Both servers have the ability to create automatic proxies for web services, though by default, this ability is turned off. (It was on by default for ColdFusion MX before Updater 3.) For ColdFusion, you can re-enable the automatic proxy generation by creating a DISABLE_CFWS_ADAPTERS servlet init-param entry in the web.xml file in the flashgateway.ear archive. For .NET, you must give the ASP.NET user write permissions for the flashremoting application.*

In addition to the `getService()` method, the NetConnection class also has methods to retrieve debug events for the connection and communicate with the NetConnection Debugger as well as a `setCredentials()` method for passing username and password credentials for secured services.

In this exercise, you create a proxy object for the remote House service.

1. In Flash, return to Searchform.as in /fpad2004/mmestate/classes/.

Return to the file you created in the NetConnection exercise or open /fpad2004/lesson14/intermediate/classes/Searchform_netconnection.as and save it as *Searchform.as* in /fpad2004/mmestate/classes/.

2. At the end of the code inside the `search_pbClick()` method, create a variable named `houseService` and set it equal to the object returned from invoking the `getService()` method of the `net_conn` NetConnection object.

```
79          trace(result);
80          trace(result[0].DESCRIPTION);
81      };*/
82      var net_conn:Object=NetServices.createGatewayConnection(
"http://localhost/flashservices/gateway");
83      var houseService:Object= net_conn.getService();
84  }
```

3. Pass two arguments to the `getService()` method. For the service name, use *fpad2004.mmestate.services.House* and for the default responder object, use the screen instance.

```
var houseService:Object= net_conn.getService ¬
("fpad2004.mmestate.services.House",this);
```

4. Save the file.

The finished file should resemble: /fpad2004/lesson14/intermediate/classes/Searchform_proxyobject.as.

Invoking Remote Service Methods

The service proxy object you created (using the `getService()` method of a NetConnection object) is a proxy for the actual remote service. To invoke methods of the remote service, you simply invoke methods of the service proxy object with the same names as the methods of the remote services. The general syntax to call a remote method is:

```
myServiceObject.myOperation();
```

You do not set the invocation equal to anything. The events broadcast by the call when it succeeds or fails are handled by the object you specified as the default responder object when you created the service proxy object. (This process is a bit different than what you did for web services. For web services, you created a PendingCall object by setting it equal to the invocation of a remote method and you handled the results of the remote service call on the PendingCall object.)

If the remote service requires parameters, you simply pass them to the method, making sure to place them in the correct order and with the right data type.

```
myServiceObject.myOperation(param1,param2,…);
```

> **Note** If you are using .NET or Java and you make changes to your class files, you must recompile the class. In addition, for Java, you must also restart the server and for .NET, you must also re-create the assembly.

In this exercise, you invoke the getHousesArray() method of the remote House service.

1. Return to Searchform.as in /fpad2004/mmestate/classes/.

Return to the file you created in the last exercise or open /fpad2004/lesson14/intermediate/classes/
Searchform_proxyobject.as and save it as *Searchform.as* in /fpad2004/mmestate/classes/.

2. At the end of the code inside the search_pbClick() method, invoke the getHousesArray() method of the houseService object.

```
houseService.getHousesArray();
```

3. Copy the parameters you sent to the getHousesArray() operation using the search_ws object and paste them inside the getHousesArray() method call.

```
houseService.getHousesArray(bedrooms_ns.value,cityids.toString(), ¬
garage.selectedData,housetype.toString(),Formatters.formatNumber ¬
(min_cb.selectedItem.label),Formatters.formatNumber(String ¬
(max_cb.value)));
```

You commented out rather than deleted the web service code in the previous exercise so you didn't
have to retype all these arguments in this step.

4. Save the file.

The finished file should resemble: /fpad2004/lesson14/intermediate/classes/Searchform_invoke.as.

5. Make sure the NetConnection Debugger panel is open and click its Clear Events button.

The entries in the NetConnection Debugger panel are not automatically cleared when you retest
the application.

6. Return to searchHouses.fla in /fpad2004/mmestate/ and test the application.

Return to the file you created in an earlier exercise or open /fpad2004/lesson14/intermediate/
searchHouses_netdebug.fla and save it as *searchHouses.fla* in /fpad2004/mmestate/.

7. Select some cities and a maximum price and then click the Search button. Look at the NetConnection Debugger panel.

You should see Call and Result events. Select the Call event and click the Details tab. You should see the values of the arguments you sent to the remote service.

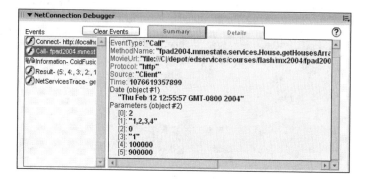

Select the Result event. You should see the values of the result returned to the Flash application.

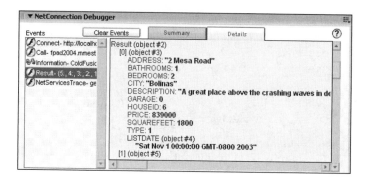

8. Look at the Output panel.

The Output panel should display the message: NetServices info 1: getHousesArray_Result was received from server: ,,,,,,,

If you test an application from within Flash and you have not written any code to handle the result returned from a remoting call, Flash displays the result in the Output panel. In this case, an array of objects was returned, which cannot be converted to a string, so you get commas with no values in between.

Handling Responses

When a Flash Remoting call to a remote operation completes, an `onResult` or an `onStatus` event is broadcast. (The WebService class broadcast `onResult` and `onFault` events.) You capture these events by creating callbacks of the default responder object with the same name as the event.

Remember the default responder object is the object you specified when creating the service proxy object using the `getService()` method of the NetConnection object.

Handling result events. The `onResult` event is broadcast when a remote call invocation has succeeded and returned a result. The `onResult` event handler is passed one argument: the variable returned by the remote service, which can be a complex variable like an object or an array of objects.

```
var myService:Object=my_conn.getService("fpad2004.Myclass",
defaultResponder);
myService.myOperation(param1,param2,…);
defaultResponder.onResult=function(result):Void
{
      trace(result);
};
```

Handling status events. The `onStatus` event is broadcast when a remote call invocation fails, either because the gateway encounters an error or the remote service encounters an error and throws an exception. The `onStatus` event handler is passed an event object with the following properties: `code` (equal to "SERVER.PROCESSING"), `level` (equal to "error"), `type` (the type of exception thrown; for example, flashgateway.adapter.NoSuchServiceException if the service does not exist or coldfusion.tagext.sql.QueryTag$DatabaseQueryException if there is a problem in a query), `description` (a sentence describing the exception), and `details` (the full details of the exception returned from the application server).

```
var myService:Object=my_conn.getService("fpad2004.Myclass",
defaultResponder);
myService.myOperation(param1,param2,…);
defaultResponder.onStatus=function(evtObj:Object):Void
{
      trace(evtObj.description);
};
```

When a call fails, a Status event is displayed in the NetConnection Debugger where you can see all the values of the properties of the status event object.

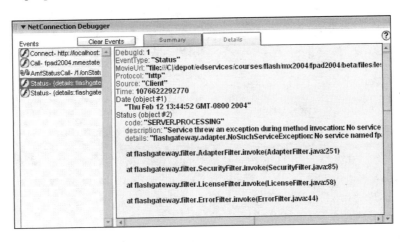

If the default responder object does not have an `onStatus` handler defined, Flash looks for an `onStatus` event handler on `_root` and then on `_global.System`. This behavior gives the ability to create a catchall type error handler.

> **Note** *You can also create event handlers with the name of the remote service method with an _Result and _Status suffix. If you have both an `onResult` handler, and a `_Result()` function, the `_Result()` function is executed. The same is true if you have both `_Status` and `onStatus` handlers. Also, be aware that, all of the current documentation for Flash Remoting is for Timeline-based development in Flash MX and often depicts the event callbacks defined as stand-alone functions `methodName_Result()` and `methodName_Status()` on the main Timeline. For example: `var bikeServ: Object=my_conn.getService("fpad2004.Bike",this); bikeServ.getAll(); function getAll_Result(result):Void{};`.*

In this exercise, you create `onResult` and `onStatus` handlers as methods of the screen class to handle results from calls from the houseService proxy object.

1. Return to Searchform.as in /fpad2004/mmestate/classes/.

Return to the file you created in the last exercise or open /fpad2004/lesson14/intermediate/classes/Searchform_invoke.as and save it as *Searchform.as* in /fpad2004/mmestate/classes/.

2. Cut the code for the `searchWsCall onResult` handler from inside the `search_pbClick()` method, and paste it at the end of the class definition.

Your remoting handler will be almost identical, so there is no need to retype the whole method. Instead, you just convert it to a method of the screen, which is the default responder object for the call. Cut the code shown in the following screenshot.

```
76        /*searchWsCall=search_ws.getHousesArray(bedrooms_n
    garage.selectedData,housetype.toString(),Formatters.format
    String(max_cb.value)});
77        searchWsCall.onResult=function(result:Array):Void
78        {
79            trace(result);
80            trace(result[0].DESCRIPTION);
81        };*/
82        var net_conn:Object=NetServices.createGatewayConne
83        var houseService:Object= net_conn.getService("fpad
84        houseService.getHousesArray(bedrooms_ns.value,city
    Formatters.formatNumber(min_cb.selectedItem.label),Formatt
85    }
```

The return variable from the ColdFusion CFC, the Java class, and the .NET assembly is an ActionScript array of associative arrays. The ColdFusion CFC returns an array of structures, the Java class returns an ArrayList of HashMaps, and the C# class used to create the .NET assembly returns an ArrayList of Hashtables. For more details on Flash Remoting data conversion, see the last section in this lesson.

3. If you are using .NET, delete the line of code inside searchWsCall.onResult converting the result variable.

Here is the line of code to delete.

```
result=NetConverter.xmlToObject(result)
```

Using Flash Remoting, you can return an ArrayList of Hashtables (which you could not do with a web service) which is converted to an ActionScript array of associative arrays.

4. Change the code you pasted in Step 2 to be a *private* method of the class called onResult. Save the file.

```
private function onResult(result:Array):Void
{
    trace(result);
    trace(result[0].DESCRIPTION);
}
```

That's it for the onResult handler. You will display the data returned from the remote method in a DataGrid component in the next lesson.

5. Return to searchHouses.fla in /fpad2004/mmestate/ and test the application.

Return to the file you used in the last exercise or open /fpad2004/lesson14/intermediate/ searchHouses_netdebug.fla and save it as *searchHouses.fla* in /fpad2004/mmestate/.

6. Select some cities and a maximum price and then click the Search button. Look at the Output panel.

You should no longer see the message: NetServices info 1: getHousesArray_Result was received from server: „„„„. Instead, you should see empty commas (the objects which cannot be translated to strings—one for each house returned) and the description for one of the houses.

7. Return to Searchform.as. Create a new private method called onStatus with one argument called evtObj of type *Object* that traces the description property.

```
private function onStatus(evtObj:Object):Void
{
    trace(evtObj.description);
}
```

> **Note** *If there is a problem with a remote method invocation in a real application, you should display a message to the user and disable the search interface.*

8. Change the code creating the proxy object in the `search_pbClick()` method so the service package name is incorrect. Save the file.

For example, leave the e off the end of House.

```
var houseService:Object=
net_conn.getService("fpad2004.mmestate.services.Hous",this);
```

9. Return to searchHouses.fla. Make sure you have the NetConnection Debugger panel open and test the application.

You might want to clear the events in the NetConnection Debugger panel so you can easily discern the new events generated.

10. Select some cities and a maximum price and then click the Search button.

You should see a description of the error traced to the Output panel: Service threw an exception during method invocation: No service named fpad2004.mmestate.services.Hous is known to Flash Remoting MX. You should also see in the NetConnection Debugger panel a Status event instead of a Result event. Look at the details of one of the Status events. You get the error description along with more details.

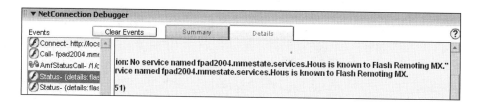

11. Return to Searchform.as. Undo the error you introduced in Step 8. Save the file.

```
var houseService:Object=
net_conn.getService("fpad2004.mmestate.services.House",this);
```

The finished file should resemble: /fpad2004/lesson14/intermediate/classes/Searchform_handle.as.

Handling Responses for Multiple Calls from the Same Service Proxy Object

So far you handled the events broadcast from one remote service call from a service proxy object. If the service has multiple methods, though, and you want to call more than one, how do you handle the results? Or what if you want to make multiple calls to the same remote method and handle them differently? If the remote methods you call are from different remote classes, the

operations would be invoked by different service proxy objects and you could specify different responder objects when creating the service proxy objects.

```
var bikeServ:Object=my_conn.getService("fpad2004.Bike",responder1);
bikeServ.getAll();
responder1.onResult=function(result):Void{};
var wineServ:Object=my_conn.getService("fpad2004.Wine",responder2);
wineServ.getAll();
responder2.onResult=function(result):Void{};
```

This doesn't work if you are calling multiple methods from the same service proxy object and you want to handle the results with different handlers.

```
var bikeServ:Object=my_conn.getService("fpad2004.Bike",responder);
bikeServ.getAll();
bikeServ.updateBike("id","name","description");
```

Yes, you could create two different proxy objects for the same service, but that's unnecessary and causes extra overhead. There is a better alternative. Instead of specifying a default responder object when you create the service proxy object, you can specify responder objects in the remote method invocations. You specify the responder object as the first argument to the method call, before any other arguments.

```
var bikeServ:Object=my_conn.getService("fpad2004.Bike");
bikeServ.getAll(responder1);
bikeServ.updateBike(responder2,"id","name","description");
```

Do not specify a default responder object in both the `getService()` method and in a service operation call; you will get an error.

Note *You cannot specify responder objects in service calls that are handled by `_Result()` and `_Status()` handlers.*

In this exercise, you specify a responder object in a remote method invocation instead of specifying a default responder for all methods of a service proxy object.

1. Return to Searchform.as in /fpad2004/mmestate/classes/.

Return to the file you created in the last exercise or open /fpad2004/lesson14/intermediate/classes/ Searchform_handle.as and save it as *Searchform.as* in /fpad2004/mmestate/classes/.

2. In the `search_pbClick()` method, remove the second argument to the `getService()` method.

```
var houseService:Object=
net_conn.getService("fpad2004.mmestate.services.House");
```

3. In the `search_pbClick()` method, add **this** as the first argument to the `getHousesArray()` call. Save the file.

```
houseService.getHousesArray(this,bedrooms_ns.value,cityids.toString(), ¬
garage.selectedData,housetype.toString(),Formatters.formatNumber ¬
(min_cb.selectedItem.label),Formatters.formatNumber(String ¬
(max_cb.value)));
```

This exercise is purely instructional. Because you are only making a call to one remote method, there is no need to specify a responder object in the method invocation instead of specifying one responder object for all calls made with the service proxy object.

The finished file should resemble: /fpad2004/lesson14/intermediate/classes/Searchform_responder.as.

4. Return to searchHouses.fla in /fpad2004/mmestate and test the application.

Return to the file you used in the last exercise or open /fpad2004/lesson14/intermediate/ searchHouses_netdebug.fla and save it as *searchHouses.fla* in /fpad2004/mmestate/.

5. Select some cities and a maximum price and then click the Search button.

You should get results, exactly as you did before.

Creating a General Responder Class

What if you have a more complicated system and you want more flexibility? Say you want the same result handler to be used by two different calls, but want to use different status handlers? For example, you might have a single dynamic text field or Label that you want to populate with data returned from various remote methods but you want different behaviors if the invocations fail.

If you want to have a small group of versatile error handlers that handle any errors from many different responder objects, you must break the dependency of the same responder object handling both the events for an invocation. You can accomplish this by creating a general responder class to which you pass names of methods that you want to handle each of the events.

In the following code, a general responder class called NetResponder is created.

```
NetResponder.as
 1  class NetResponder
 2  {
 3          private var onResult:Function;
 4          private var onStatus:Function;
 5          function NetResponder(resultMethod,statusMethod)
 6          {
 7                  this.onResult=function(result):Void
 8                  {
 9                          resultMethod(result);
10                  };
11                  this.onStatus=function(result):Void
12                  {
13                          statusMethod(result);
14                  };
15          }
16  }
```

> **Note** The two parameters *resultMethod* and *statusMethod* are object references to the functions that should handle the results and errors.

You then create result and event handlers for all different types of responses:

```
this.resultHandler1=function(){};
this.resultHandler2=function(){};
this.resultHandler3=function(){};
this.statusHandler1=function(){};
this.statusHandler2=function(){};
```

Next, you create service proxy objects without default responders:

```
var bikeServ:Object=my_conn.getService("fpad600.Bike");
```

Finally, invoke remote methods; specify for each invocation a custom responder object that specifies the methods you want to use to handle its result and any errors:

```
bikeServ.getAll(new NetResponder(resultHandler1,statusHandler1));
bikeServ.updateBike(new NetResponder(resultHandler1,statusHandler2), ¬
"id","name","description");
bikeServ.addBike(new NetResponder(resultHandler3,statusHandler1), ¬
"id","name","description");
```

> **Note** You can also use object.method notation when specifying the handlers as arguments for the NetResponder class: *bikeServ.getAll(new NetResponder(object2.resultHandler, object1.statusHandler));*.

In this exercise, you use an instance of a general responder class to specify what methods should handle the onResult and onStatus events.

1. Open NetResponder.as in /fpad2004/lesson14/start/classes/ and save it as *NetResponder.as* **in /fpad2004/mmestate/classes/.**

The NetResponder class has been written for you.

2. Return to Searchform.as in /fpad2004/mmestate/classes/.

Return to the file you created in the last exercise or open /fpad2004/lesson14/intermediate/classes/ Searchform_responder.as and save it as *Searchform.as* in /fpad2004/mmestate/classes/.

3. At the top of the class, import the NetResponder class.

```
import NetResponder;
```

This import statement is not necessary, but it is helpful to list at the top of a class file all the classes you are referencing within it.

4. Change the name of the onResult() method to *getHousesResult* **and the name of the** onStatus() **method to** *getHousesStatus.*

You are changing the names so the methods are not automatically invoked, but are instead passed as arguments to the NetResponder class constructor.

```
119    private function getHousesResult(result:Array):Void
120    {
121        trace(result);
122        trace(result[0].DESCRIPTION);
123    }
124    private function getHousesStatus(evtObj:Object):Void
125    {
126        trace(evtObj.description);
127    }
```

Like the last exercise, this exercise is also purely instructional because you are only making a call to one remote method.

5. In the search_pbClick() **method, change the first argument** this **to be a new instance of the NetResponder class. Pass** this.getHousesResult **as the first argument and** this.getHousesStatus **as the second argument. Save the file.**

```
houseService.getHousesArray(new NetResponder(this.getHousesResult, ¬
this.getHousesStatus),bedrooms_ns.value,cityids.toString(), ¬
garage.selectedData,housetype.toString(), ¬
Formatters.formatNumber(min_cb.selectedItem.label), ¬
Formatters.formatNumber(String(max_cb.value)));
```

The finished file should resemble: /fpad2004/lesson14/intermediate/classes/
Searchform_responderclass.as.

6. **Return to searchHouses.fla in /fpad2004/mmestate and test the application.**

Return to the file you used in the last exercise or open /fpad2004/lesson14/intermediate/
searchHouses_netdebug.fla and save it as *searchHouses.fla* in /fpad2004/mmestate/.

7. **Select some cities and a maximum price and then click the Search button.**

You should get results, exactly as you did before.

Converting Data for Flash and the Application Server

Because the remote service you used in this lesson was written for you, you did not have to think about how the data was translated between the Flash Player and the application server; the remote method just worked. The last thing to look at in this lesson is exactly how this translation occurs: What types of variables do ActionScript variables become when passed to your application server and what types of ActionScript variables do your native application variables become when passed back to Flash? Though we will not delve into this topic too deeply, a brief overview is presented to get you thinking in the right direction when you start building your remote classes for exchanging data with Flash.

ActionScript and ColdFusion

Because ActionScript and ColdFusion are both loosely typed languages, the conversion between the two is pretty straightforward: Number to Number, Boolean to Boolean, String to String, Date to Date, and XML to XML. Arrays and objects are a little trickier: An ActionScript array with contiguous numeric indices becomes a ColdFusion array, an ActionScript associative array becomes a ColdFusion structure, but an ActionScript object becomes name/value argument pairs for a CFC.

Thus, if your CFC takes a structure as an argument, you must pass an ActionScript associative array, not an object.

```
var bike:Array=new Array();
bike["name"]="Kona";
bike["color"]="silver";
bike["size"]=17;
bikeService.addNew(bike);
```

The CFC method that handles this call might look like the following:

```
<cffunction name="addNew" access="remote" returntype="void">
    <cfargument name="newItem" type="struct" required="true">
    [other code]
</cffunction>
```

If you pass an object to the method instead:

```
var bike:Object={name:"Kona",color:"silver",size:17};
bikeService.addNew(bike);
```

The CFC must look like this:

```
<cffunction name="addNew" access="remote" returntype="void">
    <cfargument name="name" type="string" required="true">
    <cfargument name="color" type="string" required="true">
    <cfargument name="size" type="numeric" required="true">
    [other code]
</cffunction>
```

If you pass an array of objects from Flash rather than a single object, it becomes an array of structures for the CFC method—there is no need to convert the objects into named arrays.

Going in the other direction, from ColdFusion to ActionScript, a ColdFusion array becomes an ActionScript ordered array and a ColdFusion structure becomes an ActionScript associative array. You also need to be careful returning numeric and Boolean values. Make sure you explicitly specify the return type of the CFC to numeric or Boolean (or use the `Val()` function or return only the numbers 0 or 1) or your data will become a string in ActionScript.

Note   *The names of structure keys become all uppercase when you return them to Flash.*

You can also pass back query objects from ColdFusion; they become RecordSet objects in Flash. The RecordSet object is not native to the Flash Player; its class definition is included in the file RecordSet.as, which is included in the NetServices.as file. The RecordSet object has many methods for manipulating its data including `addItem()`, `getItemAt()`, `getLength()`, `sort()`, and so on. You can use a RecordSet returned from a remote class as a data provider to components exactly as you did arrays of objects. The Flash Remoting Components also includes a DataGlue API, which provides methods for binding RecordSet data to components via code. You cannot return RecordSet objects from Flash to ColdFusion, they do not become ColdFusion query objects.

Note   *It is a good idea to return arrays of objects from remote methods instead of RecordSets for greater flexibility and reusability. RecordSets are not a supported SOAP data type.*

ActionScript and Java

Conversion from ActionScript to Java is a bit different than from ActionScript to ColdFusion because Java is not a loosely type language. The following table shows what ActionScript variables become in Java.

ActionScript Data Type	Java Data Type
Number	java.lang.Double
Boolean	java.lang.Boolean
String	java.lang.String
Date	java.lang.Date
Array	java.util.ArrayList
Associative array	flashgateway.util.CaseInsensitiveMap which implements java.util.Map
RecordSet	Cannot send to server
Object	flashgateway.io.ASObject which implements java.util.Map
XML	org.w3c.dom.Document

The two interesting items are the Java flashgateway objects that get created. When an associative array is sent to the server, it becomes a flashgateway.util.CaseInsensitiveMap. This is essentially a case-insensitive version of a java.util.Map. Thus, you don't have to worry about case-matching your arguments and properties between Flash and Java. Otherwise it behaves exactly like a java.util.Map.

When an object is sent to the server, it becomes a flashgateway.io.ASObject, which implements java.util.Map and is a class provided by the Flash Remoting install. Like flashgateway.util.CaseInsensitiveMap, it provides case-insensitivity but also has additional methods, getType() and setType(). You use getType() to get the type of the ActionScript object (if it is an instance of a class) and process it accordingly. You can use setType() to set the type of ActionScript object you want the Java object to become when it is returned to Flash—instead of just being created as an instance of the general Object class. When the Flash client receives the typed object from the remote service, Flash runs the constructor for the type and attaches all the object's methods.

Going in the other direction, from Java to ActionScript, the translation is pretty straightforward: Any Java number types to an ActionScript Number, Booleans to Booleans, strings to strings, and dates to dates (whether they are primitives or objects). For collections of data, a java.util.Collection becomes an ActionScript array, a java.util.Map an ActionScript associative array, and an org.w3c.dom.Document an ActionScript XML object. You can also return an object that implements the java.io.Serializable interface; both the public and private properties are available as ActionScript properties.

You cannot, however, return a java.sql.ResultSet to Flash. ResultSets are live, connected objects associated with pooled and I/O socket resources (like Statements and Connections). Thus, when a Statement or Connection is closed, the associated ResultSet is also closed and, therefore, not available to Flash Remoting. Even if you leave a Statement or Connection open, there is no guarantee you can retrieve a populated ResultSet instance because the connections can be closed and reclaimed by the application server at any time. In JDBC 3.0, however, there is a new interface javax.sql.RowSet (which is a disconnected ResultSet) that is supported by some JDBC drivers. (This class is not included in JRun4 but is available from Sun.)

ActionScript and C#

Conversion from ActionScript to C# is much like the translation between ActionScript to Java. The following table shows what ActionScript variables become in C#.

ActionScript Data Type	C# Data Type
Number	System.Double
Boolean	System.Boolean
String	System.String
Date	System.DateTime
Array	System.Collections.ArrayList
Associative array	System.Collections.Hashtable
RecordSet	Cannot be sent to server
Object	FlashGateway.IO.ASObject which implements ICollection interface
XML	System.Xml.XmlDocument

The interesting item here is the FlashGateway.IO.ASObject, which is created when an ActionScript object is sent to the server. The FlashGateway.IO.ASObject implements the ICollection interface and allows you to create a Hashtable (or other ICollection implementation), and then give that Hashtable a type property so that when it is returned to Flash, it can be associated with a specific type of object. In order to use the ASObject type in C#, you need to include FlashGateway.IO in the namespace for your class files. You then create an instance of ASObject and set the object type using an ASType property. When the Flash client receives the typed object from the remote service, Flash runs the constructor for the type and attaches all the object's methods.

Going in the other direction, from C# to ActionScript, the translation is pretty straightforward: Any C# number types to an ActionScript Number, Booleans to Booleans, strings to strings, and dates to dates (whether they are primitives or objects). For collections of data, a System.Collections.ICollection becomes an ActionScript array, a System.Collections.Hashtable becomes an ActionScript associative array, a System.Data.DataTable an ActionScript RecordSet, a System.Data.DataSet an associative array of ActionScript RecordSets, and an System.Xml.XmlDocument an ActionScript XML object.

What You Have Learned

In this lesson, you have:

- Checked the Flash Remoting installation (pages 545–547)
- Included the remoting class files (pages 548–549)
- Created a NetConnection object (pages 549–551)
- Used the NetConnection Debugger (pages 551–554)
- Created service proxy objects (pages 554–556)
- Invoked remote service methods (pages 556–558)
- Handled responses from remote services (pages 558–562)
- Handled responses for multiple calls from the same service proxy object (pages 562–564)
- Used a general responder class for handling events (pages 564–567)
- Learned how Flash Remoting converts data between ActionScript and your application server (pages 567–570)

15 Using the DataGrid Component

In the last two lessons, you retrieved an array of objects from the server but had no way to display the data. You cannot use the List or ComboBox components because they can display only a single field of data. To display multiple columns of data, you use the DataGrid component. The DataGrid component displays data in a normal table layout. You can specify what columns are displayed and customize how the grid appears, setting borders, grid lines, headers, row heights, column widths, and so on. The DataGrid is not just a simple display tool; it also provides built-in data scrolling, sorting, column resizing, and cell edit capabilities. In addition, you can customize the data values displayed in a column; you can format the data, display combinations of multiple data fields, or create virtual columns that contain data not available in any field in the DataGrid's data source. And to top this, you aren't limited to displaying simple strings. You can display a MovieClip in a grid column whose appearance is customized based on the row in the grid it occupies.

In this lesson, you display the house results retrieved from the server in the last two lessons in a DataGrid component. You select what data to display and format the prices and the Boolean garage values. You also learn to load MovieClips in a DataGrid column. To each row in the grid, you add a check box (for the user to save that house) and a small picture of the house. You also create an event handler so that when the user selects a row in the grid, details for that house are displayed.

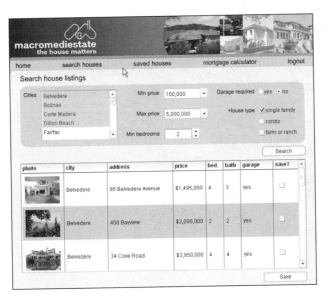

In this lesson, you display the house search results in a DataGrid component.

What You Will Learn

In this lesson, you will:

- Display data in a DataGrid component
- Use DataGrid properties to customize a DataGrid
- Customize DataGrid columns
- Set column properties that depend on DataGrid properties
- Respond to DataGrid events
- Customize the data displayed in a column
- Display a CheckBox in a DataGrid column
- Display an image in a DataGrid column

Approximate Time

This lesson takes approximately 100 minutes to complete.

Lesson files

Asset Files:

JPG files in /fpad2004/lesson15/start/assets/house/ folder

Starting Files:

/fpad2004/lesson15/start/searchHouses.fla
/fpad2004/lesson15/start/classes/Searchform.as
/fpad2004/lesson15/start/classes/Searchresults.as
/fpad2004/lesson15/start/classes/Showhouse.as
/fpad2004/lesson15/start/classes/Formatters.as
/fpad2004/lesson15/start/houseDetails.swf

Completed Files:

/fpad2004/lesson15/complete/searchHouses.fla
/fpad2004/lesson15/complete/classes/Searchform.as
/fpad2004/lesson15/complete/classes/Searchresults.as
/fpad2004/lesson15/complete/classes/Showhouse.as
/fpad2004/lesson15/complete/classes/Formatters.as
/fpad2004/lesson15/complete/classes/CheckCellRenderer.as
/fpad2004/lesson15/complete/classes/ImageRenderer.as

Using the DataGrid Component

You use a DataGrid component to create a two-dimensional display of data which the user can scroll, select rows or individual cells, edit, resort, and resize.

The DataGrid component is an instance of the mx.controls.DataGrid class with the inheritance chain: UIObject > UIComponent > View > ScrollView > ScrollSelectList > List > DataGrid.

Terminology

The DataGrid component is quite complex and has many more properties and methods than the other components. To use the DataGrid's API, the first thing you need to do is figure out the terminology; then the properties, methods, and events are generally self-explanatory.

Just like a table, a DataGrid consists of rows and columns of data. You do not, however, have to display all the data associated with the DataGrid in the table; you can select which columns you want to display. The data associated with the DataGrid is called the **data model**. The data displayed in the grid is called the **data view**. It is important to keep the distinction between the data model and data view in mind when examining the DataGrid terminology and the API; some DataGrid manipulations are performed on the data displayed in the grid while others affect all the data associated with the DataGrid.

The terms used when referring to the data model include:

item. A DataGrid is made up of items and each item is an object with properties. Each object property can be displayed as a column of data in the grid.

index. Items in a DataGrid are stored in an array. The first item has an index of 0.

The terms used when referring to the data view include:

row. A row of data displayed in the grid.

column. A column of data displayed in the grid. Each column is also an object that can be manipulated with ActionScript. By default, the name of the column object is the name of the property in the item object.

cell. The data cell at a particular row index and column index.

header. The header for a column. By default, the header text is the name of the column.

Populating a DataGrid

Because the data for a DataGrid component is two-dimensional, you cannot set labels and data at author time as you can for the ComboBox and List Box components. Instead, you must populate the DataGrid either by setting up data bindings in the authoring environment (supplying an array of objects as the data source) or using ActionScript.

With code, you populate a DataGrid just as you did ComboBox and List components: either all at once from an array of objects or by adding individual items one by one. To populate a DataGrid from an existing array of objects, you use the `dataProvider` property.

```
var bikes:Array=[{name:"Kona",color:"silver"},{name:"Rocky Mountain",
color:"black"},{name:"VooDoo",color:"green"}];
bikes_dg.dataProvider=bikes;
```

Each object becomes an item in the DataGrid and each object property becomes a column in the DataGrid.

name	color
Kona	silver
Rocky Mountain	black
VooDoo	green

You can also add individual items to a DataGrid using the `addItem()` and `addItemAt()` methods.

```
var newbike:Object={name:"Intense",color:"silver"};
bikes_dg.addItem(newbike);
```

name	color
Kona	silver
Rocky Mountain	black
VooDoo	green
Intense	silver

In this exercise, you populate a DataGrid component with the results returned by the house search form.

1. Open searchHouses.fla in /fpad2004/lesson15/start/ and save it as *searchHouses.fla* in /fpad2004/mmestate/.

This is the ending file from Lesson 13, "Consuming Web Services." The web service files were chosen as the starting files for this lesson for wider reader accessibility; anyone who has the application web service can complete the exercises, not just those who have Flash Remoting installed. See the Appendix for more details on the server and file location requirements.

If you prefer, you can use your searchHouses.fla and Searchform.as files you created last lesson, but you will have to rewrite some of the steps in this lesson to apply to the code in your file.

2. Select the `searchresults` screen. From the Components panel, drag out an instance of the DataGrid component and name it `houses_dg`.

Place the component under the search form.

3. Use the Free Transform tool to increase the size of the DataGrid so it fills the empty space on the Stage.

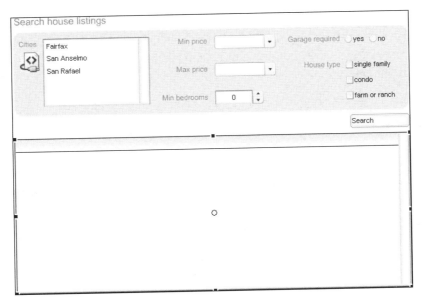

4. In the Property inspector, set the `visible` parameter for the `searchresults` screen to *false*. Save the file.

You do not want the DataGrid on the `searchresults` screen to be displayed until after the search results are returned.

The finished file should resemble: /fpad2004/lesson15/intermediate/searchHouses_dgpopulate.fla.

5. Open Searchform.as in **/fpad2004/lesson15/start/classes/** and save it as *searchHouses.fla* in **/fpad2004/mmestate/classes/**.

This is the ending file from Lesson 13. If you prefer, you can use the Searchform.as file you created last lesson, but you will have to rewrite a couple of the steps in this lesson to apply to the code in your file.

6. Inside the `search_pbClick()` method before the `searchWsCall onResult` handler, create a variable called **owner** of type *Object* and set it equal to *this*.

In this step, `this` refers to the screen instance. You need to create a reference to the object in which the function lives so that you can reference the components from inside the event handler. This is exactly what you did in Lesson 12, "Retrieving Data From XML Files," as well when setting component properties from inside an XML `onLoad` handler.

```
79          searchWsCall=search_ws.getHousesArray(bedrooms_ns.value,cityids
   .toString(),garage.selectedData,housetype.toString(),Formatters.formatNumber
   (min_cb.selectedItem.label),Formatters.formatNumber(String(max_cb.value)));
80          var owner:Object=this;
81          searchWsCall.onResult=function(result:Array):Void
82          {
```

7. Inside the `onResult` handler for `searchWsCall`, delete the two `trace` statements and set the `dataProvider` property of the DataGrid in the `searchresults` screen to `result`. Use the variable `owner` to reference the DataGrid.

```
owner._parent.searchresults.houses_dg.dataProvider=result;
```

If you are using .NET, place this code after the remaining line of code in the event handler which reformats the `result` variable to an array of objects.

8. Inside the onResult handler for searchWsCall, set the visibility of the seachresults screen to true. Save the file.

```
owner._parent.searchresults.visible=true;
```

The finished file should resemble: /fpad2004/lesson15/intermediate/classes/ Searchform_dgpopulate.as.

9. Return to searchHouses.fla and test the application. Select some cities and a maximum price and then click the Search button.

You should see your search results displayed in the DataGrid component.

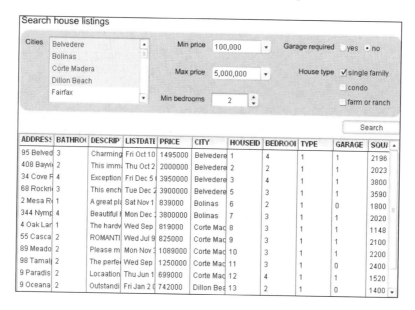

You customize the DataGrid, specifying what columns you want displayed, the width of columns, and so on in a later exercise.

10. **Click a header in the DataGrid.**

The data in the grid is reordered by the data in the column you selected. By default, you can reorder the data by clicking any of the column headers.

11. Click and drag the border between two headers.

This process changes the width of a column. By default, you can change the width of all the columns.

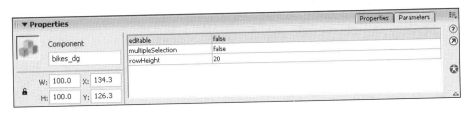

Using DataGrid Properties to Customize a DataGrid

Interaction with the DataGrid in the inspector panels is limited; you can set three DataGrid properties.

Properties you can set in the inspector panels include:

editable. A Boolean indicating whether the cells in the DataGrid are editable. The default value is false.

multipleSelection. A Boolean indicating whether multiple items in the grid can be selected. The default value is false.

rowHeight. The height of each row in pixels. The default value is 20 pixels. All rows must have the same height and the row height does not change automatically to fit the size of the text that a row contains.

Other properties you can use to customize the DataGrid with ActionScript include:

showHeaders. A Boolean indicating whether column headers are displayed. The default value is true. By defaults, column headers are shaded a light gray to differentiate them from the other rows in the grid.

headerHeight. The height of the header row in pixels. The default value is 20 pixels.

selectable. A Boolean indicating whether a user can select a row (or rows) in the grid. The default value is true. If you want the user to be able to select multiple rows, you must also set the `multipleSelection` property to true.

You can make the DataGrid scrollable in both the vertical and horizontal directions. To manipulate the scrolling behavior, you use the `hScrollPolicy` and `vScrollPolicy` properties (which you used in Lesson 10, "Using UI Component APIs," for the TextArea component). By default, the DataGrid has no horizontal scrolling (`hScrollPolicy` is off) and vertical scrolling when necessary (`vScrollPolicy` is auto). You can set horizontal and vertical positions using the `hPosition` and `vPosition` properties.

To change the appearance of the DataGrid, you use the component style API introduced in Lesson 9, "Learning the UI Component Framework." Styles that are often used to customize the DataGrid include `alternatingRowColors` (two row colors to alternate), `vGridLines` and `hGridLines` (whether to show grid lines), `vGridLineColor` and `hGridLineColor` (the color of the grid lines), `headerColor` (the color of the column headers), `headerStyle` (a custom CSSStyleDeclaration object to set the styles for the headers), `borderColor` and `borderStyle` (the color and style of the grid border), `selectionColor` and `rollOverColor` (the color of a selected or rolled over row), and `textSelectedColor` and `textRollOverColor` (the color of the text in a selected or rolled over row).

The effects of applying the styles in this code to a DataGrid are shown in the following screenshot.

```
bikes_dg.setStyle("vGridLines",false);
bikes_dg.setStyle("hGridLines",false);
bikes_dg.setStyle("borderStyle","none");
bikes_dg.setStyle("headerColor",0xFFFFFF);
bikes_dg.vScrollPolicy="off";
```

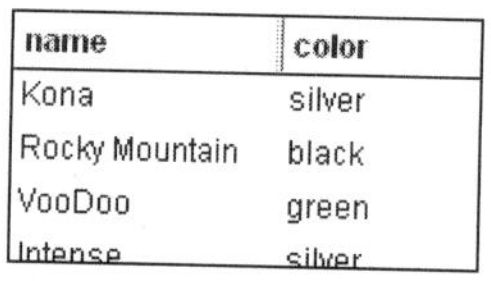

Note *You can also apply styles to individual columns. You learn to reference and manipulate individual columns in the next exercise.*

In this exercise, you use properties of the DataGrid API to customize the DataGrid.

1. Open Searchresults.as in **/fpad2004/lesson15/start/classes/** and save it as *Searchresults.as* in **/fpad2004/mmestate/classes/**.

This class file will contain the code for the `searchresults` screen. It has been started for you; it contains the skeleton code for the class, a `load` event handler, and a `click` event handler for a Save button you will add in a later exercise.

2. Return to searchHouses.fla in **/fpad2004/mmestate/**.

Return to the file you created in the last exercise or open /fpad2004/lesson15/intermediate/ searchHouses_dgpopulate.fla and save it as *searchHouses.fla* in /fpad2004/mmestate/.

3. Select the `searchresults` screen. In the Property inspector, link the screen to the Searchresults class. Save the file.

The finished file should resemble: /fpad2004/lesson15/intermediate/searchHouses_dgproperties.fla.

4. Return to Searchresults.as. Create a public property called **houses_dg** of type *mx.controls.DataGrid*.

```
public var houses_dg:mx.controls.DataGrid;
```

5. Inside the `customizeDataGrid()` method, set the `rowHeight` to 74.

```
houses_dg.rowHeight=74;
```

The default row height is 20 pixels. You are increasing the height of each row so that an image will fit in each row. (You add an image to each row in a later exercise.)

> **Note** *You cannot change the height of individual rows. Each row in a DataGrid (and List) component must have the same height.*

6. Inside the `customizeDataGrid()` method, set the DataGrid to alternate row columns between white (0xFFFFFF) and gray (0xCECECE). Use the UIComponent `setStyle()` method to set the `alternatingRowColors` property. Save the file.

When you set the `alternatingRowColors` property, you set the value equal to an array with two elements, which are the two colors you want to alternate.

```
houses_dg.setStyle("alternatingRowColors", [0xFFFFFF,0xCECECE]);
```

7. Return to searchHouses.fla and test the application. Select some cities and a maximum price and then click the Search button.

Your rows should be much taller, but there is now a partial row displayed at the bottom of the grid.

ADDRESS	BATHRO(	DESCRIP	LISTDATE	PRICE	CITY	HOUSEID	BEDROOI	TYPE	GARAGE	SQU/
95 Belved	3	Charming	Fri Oct 10	1495000	Belvedere	1	4	1	1	2196
408 Baywi	2	This imm:	Thu Oct 2	2000000	Belvedere	2	2	1	1	2023
34 Cove F	4	Exception	Fri Dec 5	3950000	Belvedere	3	4	1	1	3800

8. Return to Searchresults.as. Inside the `customizeDataGrid()` method, set the size of the DataGrid to **656** pixels wide and **3** times the row height plus the header height high. Use the UIObject `setSize()` method and the DataGrid `rowHeight` and `headerHeight` properties. Save the file.

```
houses_dg.setSize(656,houses_dg.rowHeight*3+houses_dg.headerHeight);
```

You are matching the DataGrid width to the width of the gray box containing the search form. You are setting the DataGrid height so that exactly three rows are displayed at a time. You do not want partial rows of data displayed.

The finished file should resemble: /fpad2004/lesson15/intermediate/classes/ Searchresults_dgproperties.as.

9. Return to searchHouses.fla and test the application. Select some cities and a maximum price and then click the Search button.

You should see exactly three rows displayed in the DataGrid.

ADDRESS	BATHRO(	DESCRIP	LISTDATE	PRICE	CITY	HOUSEID	BEDROOI	TYPE	GARAGE	SQU/
95 Belved	3	Charming	Fri Oct 10	1495000	Belvedere	1	4	1	1	2196
408 Baywi	2	This imm:	Thu Oct 2	2000000	Belvedere	2	2	1	1	2023
34 Cove F	4	Exception	Fri Dec 5	3950000	Belvedere	3	4	1	1	3800

Customizing DataGrid Columns

When you add items to a DataGrid, columns are created and displayed for every item property. The order of the columns and the column headers are set automatically. In most cases, you will want to change which columns are displayed, the order the columns are displayed, and how the columns are labeled. You can manipulate the columns in a DataGrid two ways: using properties and methods of the DataGrid class or using methods of the DataGridColumn class, which apply to a specific column.

Each column in the DataGrid is an instance of the mx.controls.gridclasses.DataGridColumn class. By default, one DataGridColumn instance is automatically created for each item property when you populate a DataGrid. The name of each column is the name of the corresponding item property. The column objects are stored in an array. The column on the left side of the DataGrid has an index of 0. The index increments by 1 as you move to the right in the DataGrid.

Using the DataGrid `columnNames` Property

You can change the order of the columns, hide columns, or add new columns using the `columnNames` property of the DataGrid class.

Setting column order. To set the order the columns are displayed, use the DataGrid `columnNames` property. Set the property equal to an array of the column names. The columns will be displayed in the order they are listed in the array. In the following example, a DataGrid is populated with information about bikes and the columns are listed in the order they were added to the data provider.

```
var bikes:Array=[{name:"Kona",color:"silver",id:1},{name:"Rocky
Mountain",color:"black",id:2},{name:"VooDoo",color:"green",id:3}];
bikes_dg.dataProvider=bikes;
```

name	color	id
Kona	silver	1
Rocky Mounta	black	2
VooDoo	green	3

To change the order, set the `columnNames` property. You must assign the column order before you assign the data provider (or columns will be added instead of reordered).

```
bikes_dg.columnNames=["id","name","color"];
```

id	name	color
1	Kona	silver
2	Rocky M	black
3	VooDoo	green

Note *Make sure the case and spelling of the column names match the names of the corresponding item properties exactly.*

Hiding columns. You can also use the DataGrid `columnNames` property to display a subset of the properties instead of all the properties. To hide columns, specify a subset of the column names in the array for the `columnNames` property.

```
bikes_dg.columnNames=["name","color"];
```

name	color
Kona	silver
Rocky M	black
VooDoo	green

Adding columns. You can also use the DataGrid `columnNames` property to add new columns to the DataGrid, properties that are not contained in the items used to populate the grid. To add columns, specify the names of new columns in the array for the `columnNames` property. You can populate the new column with values from components using data binding or from calculated values using either code or data bindings.

```
bikes_dg.columnNames=["name","color","code"];
```

name	color	code
Kona	silver	
Rocky M	black	
VooDoo	green	

Using DataGrid Methods

You can use methods of the DataGrid class to add and remove columns including `addColumn()`, `addColumnAt()`, `removeAllColumns()`, and `removeColumnAt()`. When using the `addColumn()` and `addColumnAt()` methods, you can specify either the name for the new column object to be created or the name of an existing DataGridColumn object (which is covered in the next section).

There are also DataGrid methods to retrieve a specific column or the index of a column, `getColumnAt()` and `getColumnIndex()`, and a method to space all the columns equally, `spaceColumnsEqually()`. You use the `getColumnAt()` method to return a column object, which can then be manipulated using properties of the DataGridColumn class.

Using the DataGridColumn Class API

You use properties of the DataGridColumn class API to get or set properties of a specific column, like the column's width or its header text.

width. The width of the column in pixels. The default value is 50 pixels.

headerText. The text displayed in the column header. The default value is the name of the column object.

columnName. The read-only name of the item property associated with a column.

You use the DataGrid getColumnAt() method to retrieve a reference to a specific column.

```
bikes_dg.getColumnAt(0).width=100;
bikes_dg.getColumnAt(0).headerText="Name";
bikes_dg.getColumnAt(1).headerText="Color";
```

Name	Color
Kona	silver
Rocky Mountain	black
VooDoo	green

You cannot set a DataGridColumn property directly on the name of a column that was automatically created.

```
name.headerText="Name"; //does not work
```

Note *You should set the proper sizing and formatting of the DataGrid columns before the DataGrid is populated.*

Using the constructor. In the previous examples, instances of the mx.controls.gridclasses.DataGridColumn class were automatically created, either when you assigned a value to the dataProvider property or when you added a new column using the DataGrid columnNames property or the addColumn() and addColumnAt() methods. You can also explicitly create an instance of the DataGridColumn class using the new keyword to call the class constructor, which has one parameter, the name of the column that then becomes the name of the DataGridColumn instance.

```
import mx.controls.gridclasses.DataGridColumn;
var code_dgc:DataGridColumn=new DataGridColumn("Code");
```

You can then add the column to the DataGrid using the addColumn() or addColumnAt() method of the DataGrid class.

```
bikes_dg.addColumnAt(0,code_dgc);
```

Code	Name	Color
	Kona	silver
	Rocky Mountain	black
	VooDoo	green

An advantage of explicitly creating a column instance is that you can set properties of the column using the column name instead of using the DataGrid getColumnAt() method. This enables you to specify the column size and formats before the DataGrid columns are created instead of after, which reduces processor demand.

```
code_dgc.width=70;
```

Code	Name	Color
	Kona	silver
	Rocky Mountain	black
	VooDoo	green

Setting Column Styles

You can apply styles to individual columns using the component style API. In the following example, the text in one column is centered and the background color of another column is set to green.

```
bikes_dg.getColumnAt(1).setStyle("textAlign","center");
bikes_dg.getColumnAt(2).setStyle("backgroundColor","green");
```

Code	Name	Color
	Kona	silver
	Rocky Mountain	black
	VooDoo	green

In this exercise, you customize the houses_dg DataGrid, displaying only a subset of the data and changing the column widths.

1. Return to Searchresults.as in /fpad2004/mmestate/classes/.

Return to the file you created in the last exercise or open /fpad2004/lesson15/intermediate/classes/ Searchresults_dgproperties.as and save it as *Searchresults.as* in /fpad2004/mmestate/classes/.

2. Inside the customizeDataGrid() method, change the DataGrid display so only the HOUSEID, CITY, ADDRESS, PRICE, BEDROOMS, BATHROOMS, and GARAGE columns are displayed. Use the DataGrid columnNames property. Save the file.

Remember that you set the columnNames property equal to an array of names.

```
houses_dg.columnNames=["HOUSEID","CITY","ADDRESS","PRICE","BEDROOMS",
"BATHROOMS","GARAGE"];
```

> **Note** *To get the names and cases of the fields returned from the server, you can use a* for-in *loop inside the web service* onResult *handler.*

3. Return to searchHouses.fla and test the application. Select some cities and a maximum price and then click the Search button.

Return to the file you created in the last exercise or open /fpad2004/lesson15/intermediate/searchHouses_dgproperties.fla and save it as *searchHouses.fla* in /fpad2004/mmestate/.

Only the columns you specified are displayed, but they are too narrow.

4. Return to Searchresults.as. Add a new column to the DataGrid called *SAVE* by modifying the `columnNames` property. Make it the last column.

```
houses_dg.columnNames=["HOUSEID","CITY","ADDRESS","PRICE","BEDROOMS",
"BATHROOMS","GARAGE","SAVE"];
```

In a later exercise, you are going to place a check box in the SAVE column that the user can select to add that house to his or her saved houses list.

5. At the end of the code inside the `customizeDataGrid()` method, change the width of the first column to *100*. Use the DataGrid `getColumnAt()` method and the DataGridColumn `width` property.

```
houses_dg.getColumnAt(0).width=100;
```

6. Change the width of the remaining columns to *100, 150, 75, 40, 40, 75,* and *45*, respectively.

```
houses_dg.getColumnAt(1).width=100;
houses_dg.getColumnAt(2).width=150;
houses_dg.getColumnAt(3).width=75;
houses_dg.getColumnAt(4).width=40;
houses_dg.getColumnAt(5).width=40;
houses_dg.getColumnAt(6).width=75;
houses_dg.getColumnAt(7).width=45;
```

7. Change the header text of the first column to *photo*. Use the DataGrid `getColumnAt()` method and the DataGridColumn `headerText` property.

```
houses_dg.getColumnAt(0).headerText="photo";
```

In a later exercise, you will display a photo in this column instead of a house ID.

8. Change the header text of the remaining columns to *city*, *address*, *price*, *bed*, *bath*, *garage*, and *save?*, respectively. Save the file.

```
houses_dg.getColumnAt(1).headerText="city";
houses_dg.getColumnAt(2).headerText="address";
houses_dg.getColumnAt(3).headerText="price";
houses_dg.getColumnAt(4).headerText="bed";
houses_dg.getColumnAt(5).headerText="bath";
houses_dg.getColumnAt(6).headerText="garage";
houses_dg.getColumnAt(7).headerText="save?";
```

The finished file should resemble: /fpad2004/lesson15/intermediate/classes/ Searchresults_dgcolumns.as.

9. Return to searchHouses.fla and test the application. Select some cities and a maximum price and then click the Search button.

The columns now have appropriate widths and there is a new empty column with the header "save?".

photo	city	address	price	bed	bath	garage	save?
1	Belvedere	95 Belvedere Avenue	1495000	4	3	1	
2	Belvedere	408 Bayview	2000000	2	2	1	
3	Belvedere	34 Cove Road	3950000	4	4	1	

Setting Column Properties that Depend on DataGrid Properties

In the last exercise, you set properties to change the width and header text of individual columns in a DataGrid. You can also set whether columns are editable, resizable, or sortable by setting the DataGridColumn class properties `editable`, `resizable`, or `sortable` to true or false. These three properties, however, must be set in conjunction with a corresponding property for the DataGrid: `editable`, `resizableColumns`, and `sortableColumns`, respectively. Setting one of these properties to true for an individual column will have no affect unless the property for the DataGrid is also true. By default, columns in a DataGrid are resizable and sortable but are not editable.

For example, if you want to make only one column in a DataGrid editable, you must make all the columns editable (by setting the DataGrid `editable` property to true) and then setting the `editable` properties of individual columns to false.

```
bikes_dg.editable=true;
bikes_dg.getColumnAt(0).editable=false;
bikes_dg.getColumnAt(1).editable=false;
```

In this exercise, you make only certain columns in the DataGrid sortable.

1. Return to Searchresults.as in /fpad2004/mmestate/classes/.

Return to the file you created in the last exercise or open /fpad2004/lesson15/intermediate/classes/ Searchresults_dgcolumns.as and save it as *Searchresults.as* in /fpad2004/mmestate/classes/.

2. In the `customizeDataGrid()` method, make the first column nonsortable. Use the DataGridColumn `sortable` property.

```
houses_dg.getColumnAt(0).sortable=false;
```

You will be displaying an image in this column and it does not make sense to sort the images by the underlying house IDs.

You do not have to first set the DataGrid `sortable` property to true, because it is true by default.

3. Save the file.

The finished file should resemble: /fpad2004/lesson15/intermediate/classes/ Searchresults_dgsortable.as.

4. Return to searchHouses.fla in /fpad2004/mmestate/ and test the application. Select some cities and a maximum price and then click the Search button.

Return to the file you used in the last exercise or open /fpad2004/lesson15/intermediate/ searchHouses_dgproperties.fla and save it as *searchHouses.fla* in /fpad2004/mmestate/.

5. Click the photo header.

The photo column (currently displaying house IDs) should no longer be sortable.

6. Click the price header.

The prices are not sorted numerically. By default, the data in a DataGrid column is sorted using character Unicode code points (just as the items in arrays were sorted). This means numbers come first, followed by upper-case letters, then lowercase letters. To change how the data in a column is sorted, you capture the DataGrid `headerRelease` event and use the `sortItemsBy()` method of the List class (which the DataGrid inherits from). A code snippet for numeric sorting is provided in the section on DataGrid events.

Manipulating DataGrid Data

Earlier you learned to manipulate columns in the DataGrid using DataGrid methods: `addColumn()`, `addColumnAt()`, `removeAllColumns()`, `removeColumnAt()`, `getColumnAt()`, and `getColumnIndex()`. In addition to customizing the data view of a DataGrid, you can also manipulate the data model: retrieving, replacing, and removing items in a DataGrid. You can manipulate a grid using many of the same methods you used to manipulate the data in a List component:

getItemAt(). Returns the item at a specified index.

removeAll(). Removes all items in the list.

removeItemAt(). Removes an item at a specified index in the list with another item.

replaceItemAt(). Replaces an item at a specified index in the list with another item.

In addition, the DataGrid class has a method for replacing the data in one particular cell.

editField(). Replaces the data in a particular cell. You pass three arguments to the method: the row index, the column name, and the new data for the cell.

In addition to using the `getItemAt()` method to retrieve data at a specific index value, you can retrieve selected items in the DataGrid using the same properties you used to retrieve selected items in a List component: `selectedItem`, `selectedItems`, `selectedIndex`, and `selectedIndices`.

Responding to DataGrid Events

Like the ComboBox and List components, the most commonly used DataGrid event is `change`, which is fired when a user changes the item selected in the component; in the DataGrid, the `change` event is fired when the user selects a new row. The DataGrid also has events for individual cells or columns.

When the user clicks in a cell (either an editable or noneditable cell), a `cellPress` event is fired. The event handler is passed an event object with properties `type` (the string cellPress), `itemIndex` (the item index of the cell pressed), and `columnIndex` (the column index of the cell pressed). If a cell is editable, there are three additional events which can be fired: `cellEdit` (when the user changes a cell's value), `cellFocusIn` (when the user clicks in or tabs to an editable cell), and `cellFocusOut` (when the user leaves an editable cell either by clicking another cell or tabbing out). The event handlers for each of these events also receive an event object with `type`, `itemIndex`, and `columnIndex` properties. The `cellEdit` handler also receives an `oldValue` property that contains the previous value of the cell.

For columns, there are two events: `columnStretch` (when the user resizes a column) and `headerRelease` (when the user presses and releases a column header).

Creating custom sorts for data in a DataGrid column. To change how the data in a column is sorted, you capture the DataGrid `headerRelease` event and perform a custom sort. Inside the event handler, you determine which column was clicked (using the event object's `columnIndex` property), which direction the sort arrow is pointing (using the undocumented DataGrid `sortDirection` property which is equal to the string ASC or DESC), and the `sortItemsBy()` method of the List class (which the DataGrid inherits from). The `sortItemsBy()` method takes two arguments; the first is the name of the item property to sort by and the second is either an order string (ASC or DESC) or the Array sort flags (which you used in Lesson 3, "Learning the Flash Player Object Model," when sorting arrays.) Here is the code for sorting a DataGrid column numerically.

```
bikes_dg.addEventListener("headerRelease",this);
function headerRelease(evtObj:Object):Void
{
    if (evtObj.columnIndex==0)
    {
        var arrayFlags:Number=Array.NUMERIC; //make sort numeric
        if (bikes_dg.sortDirection=="DESC")  //make sort descending
        {
        arrayFlags=arrayFlags|Array.DESCENDING;
        }
        bikes_dg.sortItemsBy(bikes_dg.getColumnAt(0).columnName, ¬
        arrayFlags);
    }
}
```

In this exercise, you display the details for a house when a user selects it in the DataGrid. When the DataGrid `change` event fires, you retrieve the selected item and send it to a prebuilt application that displays the house details.

1. Return to searchHouses.fla in /fpad2004/mmestate/.

Return to the file you used in the last exercise or open /fpad2004/lesson15/intermediate/ searchHouses_dgproperties.fla and save it as *searchHouses.fla* in /fpad2004/mmestate/.

2. Create a new screen called *showhouse*.

You are going to load a prebuilt application that displays the details for a particular house into this screen. When the user selects a row in the DataGrid, this screen will be made visible and the appropriate house details displayed.

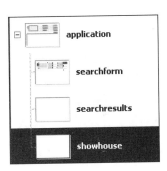

3. Return to Searchresults.as in /fpad2004/mmestate/classes/.

Return to the file you created in the last exercise or open /fpad2004/lesson15/intermediate/classes/Searchresults_dgsortable.as and save it as *Searchresults.as* in /fpad2004/mmestate/classes/.

4. Inside the `searchresultsLoad()` method, register the screen to listen for the `houses_dg` change event.

```
houses_dg.addEventListener("change",this);
```

When the user selects a row, you want the details for that house to display.

5. Copy houseDetails.swf from /fpad2004/lesson15/start/ to /fpad2004/mmestate/.

This Flash application displays the details for a single house. The file has been created for you; it uses principles you have already learned. The source files for the application, houseDetails.fla and Housedetails.as, are also located in the /fpad2004/lesson15/start/ folder if you want to examine them. The application is Form-based with an `application` screen and a `housedetails` child screen. A class called Housedetails.as is linked to the `housedetails` screen and contains a method called `displayItem()`, which has one argument, an object containing the fields to display. You will call the `displayItem()` method from the searchHouses application, passing to it the selected item in the DataGrid. The `housedetails` screen also has a "hide details" button which when pressed, hides the screen of the calling application.

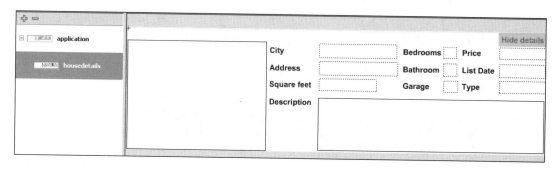

6. Return to Searchresults.as. Inside the `searchresultsLoad()` method, load *houseDetails.swf* into the `showhouse` screen.

```
_parent.showhouse.load("houseDetails.swf");
```

You are loading the houseDetails application into the `showhouse` screen when the `searchresults` screen loads. The `showhouse` screen is initially hidden. When the user selects a row in the DataGrid, the selected house is passed to a method of the houseDetails application that displays it. You do not want to load the application in the `change` event handler, because then the house display application would flicker as it reloads for every house. Instead, you simply change the data displayed in the already loaded application.

7. Create a new private method called *showhouseDetail* with no parameters or return value.

```
private function showhouseDetail():Void{}
```

This method will be called when the user selects a row.

8. Inside `showhouseDetail()`, hide the `searchform` screen and make the `showhouse` screen visible.

```
_parent.searchform.visible=false;
_parent.showhouse.visible=true;
```

When the user selects a house, you want the search form hidden and the `showhouse` screen displayed.

9. Inside `showhouseDetail()`, call the `displayItem()` method of the loaded application. Pass the selected house in the DataGrid to the method. Use the `selectedItem` property.

You need to use an appropriate relative reference to the `housedetails` screen in the loaded application. Remember from Lesson 11, "Creating Visual Objects Dynamically," that when you load a SWF into a screen, it gets placed in a new screen called `contentHolder`.

```
_parent.showhouse.contentHolder.application.housedetails.displayItem(house
s_dg.selectedItem);
```

10. Inside the `handleEvent()` method, create logic so the method `showhouseDetail()` is called when a `change` event is fired.

```
if (evtObj.type=="change")
{
        showhouseDetail();
}
```

11. Save the file.

The finished file should resemble: /fpad2004/lesson15/intermediate/classes/Searchresults_dgchange.as.

12. Open Showhouse.as in /fpad2004/lesson15/start/classes/ and save it as *Showhouse.as* in /fpad2004/mmestate/classes/.

This class file contains code for the `showhouse` screen. The file has been written for you; it contains code to place the SWF in the proper location on the screen once it has finished loading and code to display the `searchform` screen whenever the `visible` property of the `showhouse` screen is changed to false.

13. Return to searchHouses.fla. Link the `showhouse` screen to the Showhouse class. Save the file.

The finished file should resemble: /fpad2004/lesson15/intermediate/searchHouses_dgchange.fla.

14. Test the application. Select some cities and a maximum price and then click the Search button. Select a house in the DataGrid.

You should see the details for the selected house displayed.

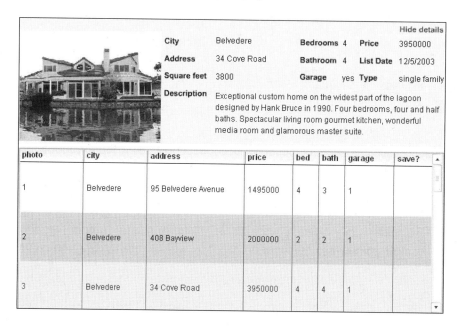

15. Select another house in the DataGrid.

You should see the details for the new house displayed.

16. Click the Hide details button.

The details for the house should disappear and you should see the search form.

Customizing the Data Displayed in a Column

What if you need the data in a column displayed in a different format than it exists in the data provider? For example, you might want to format numbers and prices or display a combination of several item properties in a column. Or you might want to create a virtual column, one containing a calculated value that may or may not be based on other grid fields.

To control how the data is displayed in a column, you use the DataGridColumn class `labelFunction` property to specify the name of a function to pass the data through before it is displayed. When you define this function, it must have one parameter of type Object (which is the item in the DataGrid that is passed to the function) and it must return a String. The returned string value is displayed in the column for that item.

> **Note** *You can also specify a* `labelFunction` *property for ComboBox and List components.*

```
function createCode(item:Object):String
{
      return item.name+item.id;
}
bikes_dg.getColumnAt(0).labelFunction=createCode;
```

> **Tip** *You can also customize the data displayed in a column using data binding in the authoring environment. You used one column formatter, Rearrange Fields, in Lesson 12 to specify the data to display in a ComboBox label field. There are additional built-in formatters (that are defined in XML files in the Flash /First Run/Formatters/ folder) including: Boolean (formats a Boolean as a String whose value you can specify), Number (formats the number to have a specified number of fractional digits), and Compose String (converts a data object to a string). You can also create your own formatter by creating an analogous XML file. To use binding in conjunction with a DataGrid component, you insert a data component (either a DataHolder or a DataSet component) between the data provider and the DataGrid. You bind (or assign) the results to the data component and then bind the data component to the DataGrid. You build a schema for the data component and then specify formatters for specific fields. See the Flash Help files for more details on working with these data components.*

In this exercise, you customize the data display in the DataGrid garage column to show yes or no instead of 1 or 0. You also customize the price column so that the house price is formatted with commas and a dollar sign.

1. Return to Searchresults.as in /fpad2004/mmestate/classes/.

Return to the file you created in the last exercise or open /fpad2004/lesson15/intermediate/classes/ Searchresults_dgchange.as and save it as *Searchresults.as* in /fpad2004/mmestate/classes/.

2. Create a new private method called **formatGarage** with one argument called **item** of type *Object* and a return value of type *String*.

```
private function formatGarage(item:Object):String{}
```

This method will return a value of either yes or no for display in the garage column of the DataGrid.

3. Inside **formatGarage()**, return the string *"yes"* if **item.GARAGE** is true and *"no"* if it is not true.

The value of **item.GARAGE** is either 0 or 1. If the value is 1, the Boolean equivalent is true and if the value is 0, the equivalent is false.

```
73      private function formatGarage(item:Object):String
74      {
75          if(item.GARAGE)
76          {
77              return "yes";
78          }
79          else
80          {
81              return "no";
82          }
83      }
```

4. At the end of the code inside the **customizeDataGrid()** method, set the **labelFunction** property for the GARAGE column equal to the **formatGarage()** method.

```
houses_dg.getColumnAt(6).labelFunction=formatGarage;
```

Make sure you do not use parentheses after the method name because you are referencing the method, not calling it.

5. Create a new private method called **formatPrice** with one argument called **item** of type *Object* and a return value of type *String*.

```
private function formatPrice(item:Object):String{}
```

This method adds commas and a dollar sign to the prices. A format price function is a good general function that you should define in your Formatters class.

6. Inside **formatPrice()**, return the value returned from a static method of the Formatters class called **formatPrice()**. Pass to the method the value contained in the **item.PRICE** field.

Use the **String()** method to first cast the **item.Price** value to a String. This ensures that the price is a String even if it is returned from the remote service as a Number.

```
return Formatters.formatPrice(String(item.PRICE));
```

You can create the `formatPrice()` method of the Formatters class yourself (using methods of the String and Array classes) or you can use the Formatters class provided in the /fpad2004/lesson15/start/classes/ folder. The following steps use the prewritten method of the Formatters class.

Note *It is a good practice to explicitly import the Formatter class at the top of the class file so all the external class files referenced in the class are listed at the top of the file.*

7. At the end of the code inside the `customizeDataGrid()` method, set the `labelFunction` property for the **PRICE** column equal to the `formatPrice()` method. Save the file.

```
houses_dg.getColumnAt(3).labelFunction=formatPrice;
```

8. Open Formatters.as in /fpad2004/lesson15/start/classes/ and save it as *Formatters.as* in /fpad2004/mmestate/classes/. Look at the `formatPrice()` method.

The method can format prices that need up to two commas. If you want, you can rewrite the function to use a general algorithm so the method can be used to format a price of any size.

9. Return to searchHouses.fla and test the application. Select some cities and a maximum price and then click the Search button.

Return to the file you created in the last exercise or open /fpad2004/lesson15/intermediate/searchHouses_dgchange.fla and save it as *searchHouses.fla* in /fpad2004/mmestate/.

The values in the garage columns should now be yes or no instead of 1 or 0, and the prices should be formatted with commas and a dollar sign.

photo	city	address	price	bed	bath	garage	save?
3	Belvedere	34 Cove Road	$3,950,000	4	4	yes	
5	Belvedere	68 Rockridge Avenue	$3,900,000	3	3	yes	
6	Bolinas	2 Mesa Road	$839,000	2	1	no	

10. Scroll down to the bottom of the DataGrid.

You should see values for the garage and price fields in an empty row.

			$und,efi,ned			no	

The formatting function is applied to every row in the DataGrid, even if the underlying item to populate the row is undefined. You need to check and see if an item is undefined before assigning it a value.

11. Return to Searchresults.as. In the `formatGarage()` method, change the `else` block to an `else if` block that checks if `item.GARAGE` is equal to *0*.

By using this condition instead of the catchall `else` block, values will be assigned only to items in the grid that have an existing GARAGE property value of 0 or 1.

```
else if (item.GARAGE==0)
{
      return "no";
}
```

12. In the `formatPrice()` method, surround the `return` statement with conditional logic so it is executed only if `item` is not undefined. Save the file.

```
if(item!=undefined)
{
      return Formatters.formatPrice(String(item.PRICE));
}
```

The finished file should resemble: /fpad2004/lesson15/intermediate/classes/ Searchresults_customcol.as.

13. Return to searchHouses.fla and test the application. Select some cities and a maximum price and then click the Search button.

You should no longer have the extra garage and price values in the empty row(s) at the bottom of the grid.

Displaying MovieClips in DataGrid Columns

In the previous exercise, you learned to format the data displayed in a column, displaying a modified or calculated string value. You are, however, not constrained to displaying strings in DataGrid columns. You can also display MovieClips. There are three steps to using a MovieClip to render the contents of cells in a DataGrid. First, you create a cell renderer class that specifies what content to display in a cell. Next, you create a MovieClip symbol in the FLA library and link the symbol to the cell renderer class. Third, you specify a column in the DataGrid to use the MovieClip symbol.

Tip   *You can also display MovieClips in ComboBox and List components.*

The first step is to write a class that uses properties and methods of the CellRenderer class (an API specified by Macromedia) to communicate and exchange data with the DataGrid in which the

MovieClip is being placed. The most important of these methods is `setValue()`, which you use to set the content to be displayed in the cell. You can display an image, a component, a combination of text and graphics, and so on. The `setValue()` method is executed every time the contents of a cell needs to be rendered—which is when the user scrolls the list or rolls over or selects a row.

The `setValue()` method automatically receives three arguments when it is invoked. You can give these parameters any name you want when you define them in your method definition, but they are called `suggested`, `item`, and `selected` in the Flash documentation and those names are used here for consistency.

```
function setValue(suggested:String,item:Object,selected:String){}
```

suggested. A string equal to the value of the data associated with the column cell.

item. An object equal to the item in the DataGrid that is currently being rendered. You can access and use any of the item's properties in the `setValue()` method.

selected. A string with the following possible values: normal, highlighted, and selected. If the user is not currently interacting with the cell being rendered, `selected` is equal to normal. If the user's mouse is over a row, `selected` has a value of highlighted and if the user selects the row, the `selected` parameter has a value of selected.

> **Note** *The Flash Help documentation erroneously states that the selected parameter is a Boolean with true or false values.*

In addition to the `setValue()` method, you can also implement `setSize()`, `getPreferredHeight()`, and `getPreferredWidth()` methods, which are used to position and constrain the loaded content within the DataGrid cell.

The Cell Renderer class has three properties you can declare and use in your cell render class to retrieve information about the cell that is being rendered.

listOwner. A reference to the DataGrid (or List) component that contains the cell being rendered.

getCellIndex. A function used to return the current location of the cell being rendered. The function returns an object with two properties: `columnIndex` and `itemIndex`.

getDataLabel. A function used to get the name of the column being rendered.

Note that the CellRenderer class is not an actual interface; it simply provides a set of properties and methods that you can use in your cell renderer class to communicate with the DataGrid container. You do not have to implement all of the CellRenderer class properties and methods, and you do not use the `implements` keyword when creating your renderer class.

Once you have your cell renderer class written, the second step is to create a MovieClip symbol in the FLA. This MovieClip often has no content on its Stage, and instead creates objects or components to display in the cell dynamically with code. You must assign the MovieClip symbol a linkage identifier and link it to an ActionScript 2.0 cell renderer class.

The final step is to specify a column in the DataGrid that is to use the MovieClip symbol to display the content in each of its cells. To do this, you set the `cellRenderer` property of the DataGridColumn class equal to the linkage identifier for a MovieClip symbol in the FLA library.

```
bikes_dg.getColumnAt(3).cellRenderer="bikeRenderer";
```

Tip *You can also display a MovieClip in a column header using the DataGridColumn class headerRenderer property.*

In this exercise, you use a prebuilt cell renderer class that comes with Flash MX 2004 to display a check box in a column of the DataGrid.

1. Open CheckCellRenderer.as in ‹Flash›/First Run/Classes/mx/controls/cells/ and save it as *CheckCellRenderer.as* in /fpad2004/mmestate/classes/. Examine the code.

When the class is instantiated, the `createChildren()` method is automatically called. (This method is part of the component-building framework.) It loads a CheckBox component, names the instance `check`, registers a `click` handler for the CheckBox, and places the CheckBox in the middle of the cell.

The `setValue()` method is called every time a cell in the grid is rendered. If the current item being rendered is not equal to undefined, the CheckBox is made visible and the CheckBox is selected if the current value of the data in the column being rendered is equal to true. The `getDataLabel()` function is used to retrieve the name of the column being rendered and `item[getDataLabel()]` evaluates the current value of the cell data (true or false).

When a CheckBox is selected, the `click` handler is called and the data provider for the DataGrid is edited to set the underlying data associated with the cell equal to true or false depending on if the user has selected or deselected the CheckBox. The `listOwner` property retrieves a reference to the DataGrid container and then the `editField()` method of the dataProvider class is used to change the data in one field of an item in the DataGrid's data provider. You pass three values to the `editField()` method, the index of the item, the name of the property in the item to modify, and the new data value. You get all of these values for the current cell being rendered using the CellRenderer `getCellIndex()` and `getDataLabel()` function properties.

Note *The CheckCellRenderer class incorrectly specifies the third argument to the* `setValue()` *method as a Boolean instead of a String.*

2. Change the class definition so the class is not part of the mx.controls.cell package. Save the file.

The class definition should appear as shown.

```
class CheckCellRenderer extends UIComponent
```

3. Return to searchHouses.fla in /fpad2004/mmestate/.

Return to the file you used in the last exercise or open /fpad2004/lesson15/intermediate/ searchHouses_dgchange.fla and save it as *searchHouses.fla* in /fpad2004/mmestate/.

4. Select Insert › New Symbol from the main menu. In the Create New Symbol dialog box, name the symbol *CheckCellRenderer*, assign a *MovieClip* behavior, and select the Export for ActionScript check box.

If you do not see the Export for ActionScript check box, click the Advanced button to see the linkage options. When you select Export for ActionScript, the Linkage Identifier field is populated with the name of the symbol.

5. Enter *CheckCellRenderer* in the AS 2.0 Class field and click OK.

You are linking the new symbol to the CheckCellRenderer class you copied in Step 1. When you click OK, you enter symbol-editing mode for the MovieClip symbol.

6. Click the `searchresults` screen in the Screen Outline pane to leave symbol-editing mode. Open the Library panel.

You should see the CheckCellRenderer symbol in the library. This is an empty MovieClip symbol with no content on its Stage. The CheckCellRenderer class dynamically loads the content, a CheckBox component, using `createObject()`. Because the class attaches a CheckBox component from the library, you would also need to add a CheckBox symbol to the library if you did not already have one.

7. From the Components panel, drag a Button component to the Stage. Place it under the right corner of the DataGrid.

You might need to decrease the size of the DataGrid so the two components are not overlapping on the Stage. Remember the height and width of the DataGrid component are being set with code so the relative locations of the DataGrid and Button you see on the Stage will not be the same at runtime.

8. Name the Button `save_pb` and assign a label of *Save*. Save the file.

In the next lesson, you will save information for the selected houses to the user's computer, much like you save cookies from HTML pages. In this lesson, you are going to output the values of the SAVE property when the user clicks the button, verifying that the `click` handler of the CheckCellRenderer class is working.

The finished file should resemble: /fpad2004/lesson15/intermediate/searchHouses_dgcheckbox.fla.

9. Return to Searchresults.as in /fpad2004/mmestate/classes/.

Return to the file you created in the last exercise or open /fpad2004/lesson15/intermediate/classes/ Searchresults_dgcustomcol.as and save it as *Searchresults.as* in /fpad2004/mmestate/classes/.

10. At the end of the code inside the `customizeDataGrid()` method, set the `cellRenderer` property for the SAVE column equal to the string *CheckCellRenderer*. Save the file.

```
houses_dg.getColumnAt(7).cellRenderer="CheckCellRenderer";
```

You set the `cellRenderer` property equal to the name of the Linkage Identifier for the MovieClip symbol.

11. Inside the `save_pbClick()` method, loop over the items in the DataGrid and display the value of the SAVE property.

```
for (var i=0;i<houses_dg.length;i++)
{
        trace(houses_dg.getItemAt(i).SAVE);
}
```

The skeleton of this method was created for you in the starting file for Searchresults.as.

12. Save the file.

The finished file should resemble: /fpad2004/lesson15/intermediate/classes/ Searchresults_checkbox.as.

13. Return to searchHouses.fla and test the application. Select some cities and a maximum price and then click the Search button.

You should see check boxes in the SAVE column of the DataGrid.

photo	city	address	price	bed	bath	garage	save?	
1	Belvedere	95 Belvedere Avenue	$1,495,000	4	3	yes	☐	
2	Belvedere	408 Bayview	$2,000,000	2	2	yes	☐	
3	Belvedere	34 Cove Road	$3,950,000	4	4	yes	☐	

Save

14. Select the save check box for several houses and click the Save button.

You should get a value of true for each house with the save check box selected and undefined for the rest.

Displaying an Image in a DataGrid Column

In the last exercise, you used a prebuilt cell renderer class to load a CheckBox component into a cell, to select the check box based on the underlying column data, and to modify the underlying DataGrid data when the user selected or deselected the check box in that cell. In this exercise, you are going to write your own cell renderer class to load a new image into each cell of the DataGrid, displaying a small image of a house in each row of the DataGrid. Because the content of cells are continually being re-rendered (as the user scrolls, mouses over, or selects a row), you need to add logic to load and unload the images being displayed.

1. Return to searchHouses.fla in /fpad2204/mmestate/.

Return to the file you created in the last exercise or open /fpad2004/lesson15/intermediate/ searchHouses_dgcheckbox.fla and save it as searchHouses.fla in /fpad2004/mmestate/.

2. Right-click/Control-click the CheckCellRender in the library and select Duplicate.

This is a quicker way to create a new symbol than creating it from scratch.

3. In the Duplicate Symbol dialog box, change the symbol name to *ImageRenderer*, select the Export for ActionScript check box, enter *ImageRenderer* in the AS 2.0 Class field, and click OK.

The new symbol appears in the library.

4. Save the file.

The finished file should resemble: /fpad2004/lesson15/intermediate/searchHouses_dgimage.fla.

5. Create a new ActionScript file. Create a class called *ImageRenderer* that extends the *MovieClip* class and has an empty constructor.

```
class ImageRenderer extends MovieClip
{
        function ImageRenderer(){}
}
```

6. Save the file as ImageRenderer.as in /fpad2004/mmestate/classes/.

You will write this cell renderer class to load an image in the following steps.

7. Define a private property called `image_mc` of type MovieClip.

```
private var image_mc:MovieClip;
```

You are going to create this MovieClip and load a house image into it.

8. Inside the constructor, create a new MovieClip called `image_mc` at depth of *100*.

```
this.createEmptyMovieClip("image_mc",100);
```

9. Inside the constructor, scale the MovieClip to *25%*. Use the MovieClip `_xscale` and `_yscale` properties.

```
image_mc._xscale=25;
image_mc._yscale=25;
```

All the house images are 320-by-240 pixels. You need to scale the MovieClip so the image is small enough to appear in the DataGrid row. If you were not also displaying the full size image elsewhere (in the houseDetails application), it would be better to change the actual image sizes instead of scaling them in the Flash Player to decrease download bandwidth.

10. Inside the constructor, set the MovieClip position's x and y position to *7* and *-30*, respectively. Use the MovieClip's `_x` and `_y` properties.

```
image_mc._x=7;
image_mc._y=-30;
```

You are changing the image location within the cell in this step, so the image is centered in the cell and has a little extra space around it. By default, the top of the image is displayed at the centerline of the cell, and the left edge is at the left side of the cell. You have set the cell to have a height of 74 and a width of 100. The scaled image is 80-by-60 pixels.

11. Create a private method called `setValue()` with three arguments: `suggested` of type *String*, `item` of type *Object*, and `selected` of type *String*, and no return value.

```
function setValue(suggested:String,item:Object,selected:String):Void{}
```

You are only going to use the item Object argument in this cell renderer.

12. Inside `setValue()`, create an `if` statement checking to see if `item` is defined.

```
if(item!=undefined){}
```

You want to make sure the item is defined before loading an image, just like you did when formatting the price and garage fields.

13. Inside the `if` block, load the image house1.jpg which is located in the /fpad**2004**/ mmestate/assets/houses/ folder into the `image_mc` MovieClip. Use the MovieClip's `loadMovie()` method.

```
this.image_mc.loadMovie("assets/houses/house1.jpg");
```

Images for all the houses are contained in the /fpad2004/mmestate/assets/houses/ folder. There is one image for each house in the database and the images are named using their HOUSEID property: house1.jpg, house2. jpg, and so on.

14. Change the `loadMovie()` method so you load the image for the grid row being rendered. Reference the HOUSEID property of the `item` object passed to the `setValue()` method. Save the file.

```
this.image_mc.loadMovie("assets/houses/house"+item.HOUSEID+".jpg");
```

For an item with HOUSEID equal to 1, the image assets/houses/house1.jpg is loaded; for an item with HOUSEID equal to 2, the image assets/houses/house2.jpg is loaded; and so on.

15. Return to Searchresults.as in /fpad**2004**/mmestate/classes/.

Return to the file you created in the last exercise or open /fpad2004/lesson15/intermediate/classes/ Searchresults_dgcheckbox.as and save it as *Searchresults.as* in /fpad2004/mmestate/classes/.

16. At the end of the code inside the `customizeDataGrid()` method, set the `cellRenderer` property for the HOUSEID column equal to *ImageRenderer*. Save the file.

```
houses_dg.getColumnAt(0).cellRenderer="ImageRenderer";
```

The finished file should resemble: /fpad2004/lesson15/intermediate/classes/Searchresults_dgimage.as.

17. Return to searchHouses.fla and test the application. Select some cities and a maximum price and then click the Search button.

You should see a small image of a house in each row of the DataGrid.

photo	city	address	price	bed	bath	garage	save?
	Belvedere	95 Belvedere Avenue	$1,495,000	4	3	yes	☐
	Belvedere	408 Bayview	$2,000,000	2	2	yes	☐
	Belvedere	34 Cove Road	$3,950,000	4	4	yes	☐

18. Roll over the rows in the DataGrid.

The house images flicker—the images are constantly being reloaded as the contents of the cells are re-rendered. To avoid flickering, you need to check if an image has already loaded in the cell and if the right image is being displayed (the cells are re-rendered as they are scrolled, moused over, or selected).

19. Scroll to the bottom of the DataGrid.

You should see an image all by itself without any other data in the last row. This is the same image you see if you scroll up one row in the grid. This image should not be displayed; you will have to write some code to keep it from appearing. To avoid this extra image, you need to unload the image in a row if the new item being displayed does not have a HOUSEID. (This is good code to add anyway because it would be necessary if the user removed an item from the grid.)

photo	city	address	price	bed	bath	garage	save?	
	Corte Madera	98 Tamalpais	$1,250,000	3	2	no	☐	
	Corte Madera	9 Paradise Way	$699,000	4	2	yes	☐	

20. Return to ImageRenderer.as. Create a private property called `imageID` of type *Number*.

When an image is loaded, you are going to store the HOUSEID for the item being rendered in this property. You can then compare the stored `imageID` to the HOUSEID of the current item being rendered and see if they are the same.

```
private var imageID:Number;
```

21. Inside the `if` statement in the `setValue()` method, set the `imageID` property equal to the HOUSEID property of the `item` object passed to the method.

```
this.imageID=item.HOUSEID;
```

22. Change the `if` statement in the `setValue()` method to also make sure the `imageID` is not equal to `item.HOUSEID`.

```
if (item!=undefined && this.imageID!=item.HOUSEID)
```

The first time you view a new item in the grid, the `imageID` property is not yet defined, so a new image is loaded. Every time you scroll in the grid, the `setValue()` method is called to re-render the cells' contents. If the house image has already been loaded for an item being displayed, the value of the `imageID` property will already be equal to the `item.HOUSEID` so a new image will not be loaded for that row.

23. At the top of the code inside the `setValue()` method, create a new `if` statement that checks if `item.HOUSEID` is undefined and if it is, unloads the image and sets the `imageID` property to *undefined*.

```
if(item.HOUSEID==undefined)
{
        this.image_mc.unloadMovie();
        this.imageID=undefined;
}
```

This code takes care of unloading an image in a row that previously held data but now does not contain any data. The last thing you need to do is re-render a cell if you scroll back up in the other direction. Right now, you have removed an image and that image will not be re-rendered as you scroll back up.

photo	city	address	price	bed	bath	garage	save?
	Corte Madera	89 Meadow Court	$1,089,000	3	2	yes	☐
	Corte Madera	98 Tamalpais	$1,250,000	3	2	no	☐
	Corte Madera	9 Paradise Way	$699,000	4	2	yes	☐

24. Change the previous `if` statement in the `setValue()` method so that the code inside is executed if `this.imageID` is not equal to `item.HOUSEID` or if `image_mc` has been unloaded.

You can use the MovieClip `getBytesLoaded()` method to check if the MovieClip has been unloaded. If the image has been unloaded, the MovieClip will have a size of zero.

```
if (item!=undefined &&
(this.imageID!=item.HOUSEID || image_mc.getBytesLoaded()==0))
```

25. Save the file.

The finished file should resemble: /fpad2004/lesson15/intermediate/classes/ImageRenderer.as.

26. Return to searchHouses.fla and test the application. Select some cities and a maximum price and then click the Search button. Roll over the rows in the DataGrid.

The house images should no longer flicker, and you should not have an extra image at the bottom of the grid.

Using the DataGrid Component with the DataSet Component

You can also use a DataSet component in conjunction with a DataGrid component. The DataSet component is a nonvisual component that helps you manage data and provides advanced sorting, filtering, and edit-tracking mechanisms. The DataSet is the intermediary between the data source and the data display. You can use it to keep track of changes a user makes to the data in the grid, and on your command, works with a Resolver component to create an XML file containing the changes (the XML file is called an Update packet) which you can send to the server. On the server, you need to write a server class to parse the XML and make the specified changes to the database: modifying, adding, or deleting records. For more information on using the DataSet component, see the Flash Help files and the tutorials provided on the Macromedia Developer Center at http://www.macromedia.com/devnet/.

What You Have Learned

In this lesson, you have:

- Displayed data in a DataGrid component (pages 575–579)
- Used DataGrid properties to customize a DataGrid (pages 579–582)
- Customized DataGrid columns (pages 583–588)
- Set column properties that depended upon DataGrid properties (pages 588–589)
- Responded to DataGrid events (pages 590–594)
- Customized the data displayed in a column (pages 595–598)
- Displayed a CheckBox in a DataGrid column (pages 598–603)
- Displayed an image in a DataGrid column (pages 603–608)

16 Persisting Data on the Client

Just as with HTML-based web applications, there are two ways to persist data from Flash applications: on the client side and on the server side. Whether you store data on the server or the client, depends on the data and the purpose. Data that needs to be stored permanently, such as customer contact information, should be stored on the server. Information that is persisted primarily as a convenience for users, such as a username or application preferences, can be stored on the client to save the overhead of transmitting the data back to the server and putting it in a database.

In Lessons 12 through 14, you learned to persist data on the server, sending data as XML over HTTP, or using web services or Flash Remoting. In this lesson, you learn to store data on the client using SharedObjects. SharedObjects are Macromedia Flash's version of cookies. You create an ActionScript SharedObject in a Flash application and then store it on the user's computer (in a file with the extension SOL). The data in the SharedObject file can be accessed by any Flash application from the same domain as the SWF that created the SharedObject. SharedObjects are more powerful than cookies, allowing you to directly store complex data; Flash serializes and deserializes the data for you. SharedObjects are not stored in the same location as cookies on the user's computer and are not deleted when the user deletes cookies from their browser.

In this lesson, you store the user's favorite houses on their computer and then display them on the Macromediestate saved page.

You have 10 saved houses

city	address	price	bed	bath	garage	sq ft	list date
Belvedere	95 Belvedere Avenue	$1,495,000	4	3	yes	2196	10/10/200
Belvedere	34 Cove Road	$3,950,000	4	4	yes	3800	12/5/2003
Belvedere	68 Rockridge Avenue	$3,900,000	3	3	yes	3590	12/2/2003
Corte Madera	9 Paradise Way	$699,000	4	2	yes	1520	6/12/2003
Dillon Beach	89 Dillon Beach Road	$775,000	4	3	yes	3100	12/3/2003
Dillon Beach	32 Kahilana Road	$999,500	3	2	yes	4480	11/28/200
Bolinas	2 Mesa Road	$839,000	2	1	no	1800	11/1/2003
Bolinas	344 Nymph Road	$3,800,000	3	4	yes	2020	12/22/200
Corte Madera	4 Oak Lane	$819,000	3	1	yes	1148	9/17/2003
Dillon Beach	9 Oceana Way	$742,000	2	2	no	1400	1/2/2004

In this lesson, you store the username and saved house data on the user's computer as SharedObjects. You store the username when the user logs into the Macromediestate application and you retrieve the username and redisplay it when the user returns to the Flash application. To finish the application, you store the houses the user saves on the house search page in a SharedObject and then retrieve the houses and display them in a DataGrid on the saved page in the Macromediestate application.

What You Will Learn

In this lesson, you will:

- View SharedObject files on your computer
- Change Flash Player settings for SharedObjects
- Create SharedObjects
- Save SharedObjects to disk
- Access data in a SharedObject
- Handle SharedObject events
- Save complex data in a SharedObject

Approximate Time

This lesson takes approximately 70 minutes to complete.

Lesson Files

Asset Files:

Starting Files:

/fpad2004/lesson16/start/mmestate.fla
/fpad2004/lesson16/start/classes/MmestateLogin.as
/fpad2004/lesson16/start/classes/MmestateSaved.as
/fpad2004/lesson16/start/searchHouses.fla
/fpad2004/lesson16/start/classes/Searchresults.as

Completed Files:

/fpad2004/lesson16/complete/mmestate.fla
/fpad2004/lesson16/complete/classes/MmestateLogin.as
/fpad2004/lesson16/complete/classes/MmestateSaved.as
/fpad2004/lesson16/complete/searchHouses.fla
/fpad2004/lesson16/complete/classes/Searchresults.as

Viewing SharedObject Files

For applications that run in a version of the Flash Player before 7.0.r19, SOL files are written to the following directory: /<application data>/Macromedia/Flash Player/<path to the SWF on the domain> where the location of the <application data> directory varies with operating system. An example location for a SharedObject from macromedia.com on a Windows computer is: C:\Documents and Settings\<user>\Application Data\Macromedia\Flash Player\macromedia.com\support\ flashplayer\sys\settings.sol. The URL of the SWF is included to avoid name collisions between SOL files with the same names from different locations.

Starting with Flash Player 7.0.r19, SharedObjects are still written to the /<user>/Application Data/ Macromedia/Flash Player/ directory but are now stored in a randomly named subdirectory in a #SharedObjects directory. Thus, SOL files can be found in the following location: /<application data>/ Macromedia/Flash Player/#SharedObjects/<randomly named directory>/<path to the SWF on the domain>. The insertion of a randomly generated directory name in the SOL location enhances client-side web security.

SharedObject files must be deleted by the end user—either by manually deleting the SOL files from his or her computer or by using the Flash Player Settings Manager (which you use in the next exercise). Clearing cookies from the browser does not delete Flash SharedObjects.

In this exercise, you locate and view existing SOL files on your computer.

1. Search for files on your machine with the extension SOL.

On Windows, select Start > Search > For Files or Folders and enter *.SOL in the search field. Files with any name that have an SOL extension are returned.

If you completed Lesson 14, "Accessing Remote Services Using Flash Remoting," you should see a TestMovie_Config_Info.sol file. This SOL file is generated and used by the NetConnection Debugger.

2. Open one of the SOL files with a text editor.

Although the file contains many characters that cannot be interpreted by the text editor, you can still see the names and values of the variables stored in the SOL file.

Changing Flash Player Settings for SharedObjects

By default, all Flash applications can save SharedObject files to your computer and each domain is allowed 100KB. A user can adjust this storage limit and also deny or approve requests to store objects exceeding the set storage limit.

As a user, you can set the storage limits on a per-domain or a global basis. To change per-domain values, you right-click/Control-click anywhere on a Flash application and select Settings. In the Flash Player Settings dialog box that appears, you set a value from none to unlimited. To change the global storage value for all domains you have not visited yet, click the Advanced button on the first tab of the Flash Player Settings dialog box. A browser window opens for the Flash Player Settings Manager, a Flash application with functionality that allows you to change the global storage limit for your Flash Player and to modify individual storage limits for domains currently storing data on your computer.

In this exercise, you change the Flash Player settings for SharedObjects on your computer.

1. Return to mmestate.fla in /fpad2004/mmestate/ and test the application.

This is the file you used in the Lesson 15. If you did not complete that lesson, open /fpad2004/lesson16/start/mmestate.fla and save it as *mmestate.fla* in /fpad2004/mmestate/.

2. Right-click/Control-click anywhere on the application and select Settings.

A dialog box opens in which you can change the settings for how the Flash Player interacts with your computer (camera, microphone, and SharedObject settings).

3. Select the Local Storage tab.

The Local Storage tab has a folder icon. The amount of space currently used by the application domain (local in this case) is displayed. If you want to be prompted every time an application from this domain wants to store data, select None (move the slider all the way to the left). If you want to let applications from this domain store data on your computer without you ever being prompted, select Unlimited (move the slider all the way to the right). Select the Never Ask Again check box if you don't want applications from this domain to ever save information on your computer and you don't want to be asked again.

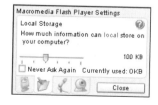

If a Flash application attempts to save a larger SharedObject file than the size specified for its domain, the Flash Player displays a Local Storage dialog box, which lets the user allow or deny local storage for the domain requesting access. (You will see this dialog box in a later exercise.)

In addition to using this method to set the storage limit for the domain of an application you are currently viewing, you can also change the default storage limits for all domains you have not visited yet.

4. Select the Privacy tab and click the Advanced button.

The Privacy tab is the first tab at the bottom of the Flash Player Settings dialog box. A macromedia.com web page is displayed in your browser and contains information about the Settings Manager, a Flash application hosted on macromedia.com that lets you manage global privacy settings, storage settings, security settings, and automatic notification settings for your Flash Player.

5. Click the Global Storage Settings Panel link on the left side of the page.

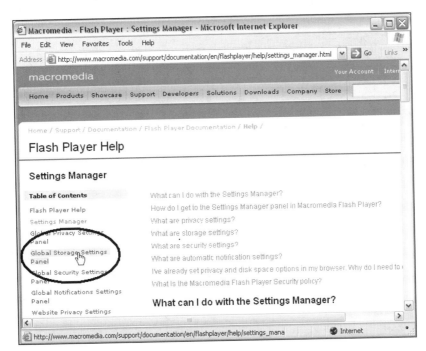

The Global Storage Settings Panel appears. This panel lets you change the default global storage limit from 100KB to any value from none to unlimited.

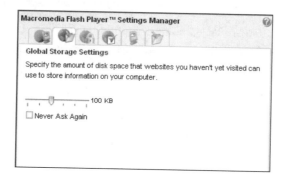

Select the Never Ask Again check box if you don't want applications from any domain to ever save information on your computer and you don't want to be asked again. If you want to be prompted every time an application wants to store data, select None. If you want to let all domains store data on your computer without you ever being prompted, select Unlmited.

The value you select in this panel applies to all domains that have not yet stored any data on your computer. It does not apply to domains which already have data stored locally. To change the values for the domains that have already stored data, you use the Website Storage Settings Panel.

6. Click the Website Storage Settings Panel link on the left side of the page.

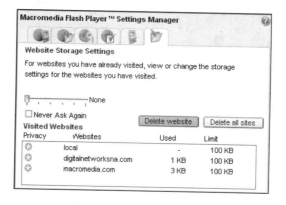

Using the Website Storage Settings panel, you can view a list of all domains currently storing data on your computer; the amount of data each currently has stored, as well as the storage limit of each, are displayed. You can change individual domain storage limits, delete the SharedObjects for one domain, or for all domains (which would be the equivalent of clearing browser cookies).

7. Close the Settings Manager browser window. Return to your SWF in Flash and click the Close button in the Flash Player Settings dialog box

The Flash Player Settings dialog box closes.

Creating SharedObjects

There are two steps involved in creating SharedObject files. First, you must write ActionScript to create and populate an ActionScript SharedObject. Second, you must save a file on the user's computer that contains the SharedObject.

You implement both steps using methods of the built-in SharedObject class.

getLocal(). Creates a SharedObject if it does not yet exist or retrieves the SharedObject from disk if it already exists. This is a static method of the SharedObject class, with one argument, the name of the SharedObject file on the user's computer.

flush(). Immediately writes a SharedObject to a file on the user's computer. This method is covered in detail in the next exercise.

> **Note** *The SharedObject class also has* `clear()` *and* `getSize()` *methods as well as additional methods you can use when you are using the Macromedia Flash Communication server.*

Here is the code to create a SharedObject:

```
var my_so:SharedObject=SharedObject.getLocal("username");
```

A new SOL file, username.sol, will be created (exactly when the file is created is discussed in the next exercise) if a file with the same name has not yet been created by this application. If a file with the same name and location (which depends upon the saving application's domain) already exists, the Flash Player retrieves the local data and stores it in the `my_so` SharedObject, which you can then manipulate with ActionScript just like any other object.

To populate a SharedObject with the data that you want stored on the user's computer, create properties of the SharedObject `data` property (the only defined property of the SharedObject class). Any properties added to this `data` object will be later stored in the SOL file. The following ActionScript code adds a property called `user` with a value of John to the SharedObject.

```
my_so.data.user="John";
```

> **Note** *Only properties of the* `data` *object of the SharedObject are saved to disk. You can create new properties directly on the SharedObject (not as properties of the* `data` *object), but these properties will not be saved to disk.*

You can store complex data structures in a SharedObject, by assigning a complex variable to a property of the `data` object.

```
var people:Array=["Robert","Sue","Matt","James"];
my_so.data.users=people;
```

In this exercise, you create and populate a SharedObject to save the username entered by the user when they log in to the Macromediestate application.

1. Return to MmestateLogin.fla in /fpad2004/mmestate/classes/.

Return to the file you created in the last lesson or open /fpad2004/lesson16/start/classes/ MmestateLogin.as and save it as *MmestateLogin.as* in /fpad2004/mmestate/classes/.

2. Define a private property `username_so` of type *SharedObject*.

```
private var username_so:SharedObject;
```

3. Inside the constructor, set the `username_so` property equal to the SharedObject from an SOL file called *username*. Use the `getLocal()` method.

```
username_so=SharedObject.getLocal("username");
```

4. Before the `if` block in the `login_pbClick()` method, create a property called `username` on the `data` property of the SharedObject. Set it equal to the username entered in the text field.

```
username_so.data.username=username_ti.text;
```

When the user clicks the Login button, the username he or she enters is saved to the ActionScript SharedObject and will be written to disk on his or her computer.

5. Save the file.

It should resemble the finished file: /fpad2004/lesson16/intermediate/classes/ MmestateLogin_createso.as.

Saving SharedObjects to Disk

Now that you have created the SharedObject in ActionScript, how do you save it to an SOL file on the user's computer? There are two ways a SharedObject can be written to disk: automatically when the SWF is removed from the Flash Player or explicitly in response to an ActionScript statement. In both cases, the user must have approved enough space for the SharedObject to be written to disk.

If an application attempts to save an object that exceeds the storage limit specified by the user for that application domain, the Flash Player displays the Local Storage dialog box, which lets the user allow or deny additional storage for that domain.

If the user clicks Allow, the SharedObject is saved to file and a success event is generated. If the user clicks Deny, the SharedObject is not saved to file and a failed event is generated. (You learn to handle these events with code later in this lesson.)

Automatically Saving SharedObjects

Once the SharedObject is created and populated, it is automatically written to disk when the SWF is unloaded from the Flash Player—if the SharedObject is under the storage limit specified by the user. The SWF is unloaded when a page is refreshed, a new page is requested, the browser is closed, or via an ActionScript `unloadMovie()` method.

If the SharedObject is over the allowed storage limit, the user will get the size prompt box if the page is refreshed or the application is unloaded via ActionScript. If the user browses to a new page or closes the browser window, however, the SharedObject write fails silently. The user is not prompted to allow additional space and the SharedObject is not written to disk. For this reason, it is better to always explicitly write SharedObjects to disk using the ActionScript `flush()` method whenever possible.

Explicitly Saving SharedObjects

Instead of relying on the SharedObject to be automatically saved, you can use the SharedObject `flush()` method to explicitly save the SharedObject to a file, for example, in response to a user event:

```
my_so.flush();
```

When this code is executed, the SharedObject is written to disk—if it is below the allowed file size. If it is above the allowed file size, the user will be prompted to allow additional space to save the SharedObject. After the user responds to the dialog box, the `flush()` method is called again and emits an `onStatus` event. Using the`flush()` method, you can programmatically capture the success or failure of the writing of the SharedObject to file and respond accordingly. (Events are handled in a later exercise.)

You can also specify one argument for the `flush()` method, a `minimumDiskSpace` parameter, which specifies the size of the SOL file to be created on the user's computer—instead of simply letting the file size be set by the actual size of the data being written. By creating a SOL file that is larger than the data being written to it, you build in the ability for the SharedObject data size to increase without prompting the user for approval every time the file exceeds the storage limit. For example, if a SharedObject is currently 100 bytes but you expect it might grow to a maximum of 500 bytes, create it with a value of 500 for the `minimumDiskSpace` parameter:

```
my_so.flush(500);
```

In this exercise, you save the SharedObject containing the username to disk.

1. Return to MmestateLogin.as in /fpad2004/mmestate/classes/.

Return to the file you created in the last exercise or open /fpad2004/lesson16/intermediate/classes/ MmestateLogin_createso.as and save it as *MmestateLogin.as* in /fpad2004/mmestate/classes/.

2. After the code assigning the `username` SharedObject property in the `login_pbClick()` method, explicitly save the SharedObject to disk. Use the `flush()` method.

```
username_so.flush();
```

```
66    private function login_pbClick():Void
67    {
68        username_so.data.username=username_ti.text
69        username_so.flush();
70        if (password_ti.length<4)
71        {
```

3. Save the file.

It should resemble the finished file: /fpad2004/lesson16/intermediate/classes/ MmestateLogin_storeso.as.

4. Return to mmestate.fla in /fpad2004/mmestate/ and test the application.

Return to the file you used in the earlier exercise this lesson or open /fpad2004/lesson16/start/ mmestate.fla and save it as *mmestate.fla* in /fpad2004/mmestate/.

5. Enter any values in the username and password text fields and click the Login button.

The SharedObject is written to disk when you click the Login button. If you had not added a `flush()` method to the code, the SharedObject would not be written to disk until you close the SWF.

6. Right-click/Control-click the SWF and select Settings. On the Local Storage tab, move the slider all the way to the left (to select None).

If you completed the Flash Remoting lesson, you will already have SharedObjects for the local domain on your computer and will receive a dialog box warning you that all existing SharedObjects will be deleted.

7. If you get a Local Storage dialog box asking you to approve SharedObject deletion, click **OK**.

All existing SharedObjects are deleted.

8. In the Flash Player Setting dialog box, click the **Close** button.

Now you will be prompted for permission before the Flash Player can save a SharedObject to disk.

9. Enter a new username and password and click the Login button.

The Local Storage dialog box opens and you are asked to allow or deny the request by the local domain to store data.

10. Click Allow. Close the SWF.

The new username value is stored to a SharedObject file called username.sol.

If you did not have a `flush()` method and you closed the SWF, you would not have received the dialog box requesting more space and the save would have silently failed.

11. Test the application again.

You should not see an initial value in the username text field. The value was actually retrieved from the username.sol file on your computer by the `getLocal()` method, but you have not used the value yet to initially populate the text field.

12. Using your computer's file browser, browse to (or search for) the username.sol file.

The exact location of the SOL will depend on your computer. If you have your files installed in the ColdFusion web root on Windows, the path should be similar to the following: C:\Documents and Settings\<user>\Application Data\Macromedia\Flash Player\localhost\CFusionMX\wwwroot\ fpad2004\mmestate\mmestate.swf.

Note *A stand-alone version of the Flash Player is used when testing applications from the authoring environment. Flash MX 2004 shipped with version 7.0 r14 of the stand-alone Flash Player, which is earlier than Flash Player 7.0.r19 that began storing SharedObjects in a location including a randomly named directory in the #SharedObjects folder.*

13. Open the file with a text editor.

You should see the value of the username you entered in the text field.

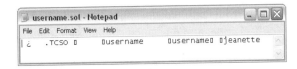

Accessing Data from a SharedObject

The getLocal() method—which you used to create a SharedObject—is also used to read data from the SharedObject. When the following code is executed, there are two possible outcomes.

```
var my_so:SharedObject=SharedObject.getLocal("mySO");
```

If a SharedObject file with the same name (mySO.sol) does not already exist (from the same application domain), a new SharedObject is created (at the appropriate time). If the SharedObject file already exists, its contents are read into the data property of the SharedObject my_so.

Just as with cookies, it is a best practice to test for the existence of a SharedObject before referencing it. Once you know the SharedObject exists, you can reference its properties just like any other object in Flash. In the following example, a message stating the number of items you have already selected (which was previously stored or will be stored in the file count.sol) is only displayed if a value has been previously saved.

```
var count_so:SharedObject=SharedObject.getLocal("count");
if (count_so.data.count!=undefined)
{
        trace("You have already selected "+count_so.data.count+" items");
}
```

If you store an object in a SharedObject property (instead of a primitive value), you can reference all the object's methods and properties exactly as you reference members of any other object. For example, to reference the length property of an Array object contained in the SharedObject, you can use the following syntax:

```
for (var i=0;i<cart_so.data.cart_array.length;i++) {
            [statements]
}
```

Like cookies, SharedObjects cannot be read from different domains. The Flash Player only has the capability of reading SharedObject files if the SharedObject was created from the same domain as the SWF requesting the data.

In this exercise, you retrieve the username stored in the SharedObject and use it to pre-populate the username text field in the login form.

1. Return to MmestateLogin.as in /fpad2004/mmestate/classes/.

Return to the document you created in the last exercise or open /fpad2004/lesson16/intermediate/classes/MmestateLogin_storeso.as and save it as *MmestateLogin.as* in /fpad2004/mmestate/classes/.

2. In the `loginLoad()` method, populate the username text field from the SharedObject.

```
username_ti.text=username_so.data.username;
```

Even in this simple case, you should surround this statement accessing a SharedObject value with conditional logic. If the user does not allow SharedObjects from this domain to be saved on his or her computer, a value of undefined will be displayed in the text field the next time the application is tested.

3. Surround the code from Step 2 with an `if` statement to make sure the SharedObject property exists.

```
if(username_so.data.username!=undefined)
{
        username_ti.text=username_so.data.username;
}
```

4. Save the file.

It should resemble the finished file: /fpad2004/lesson16/intermediate/classes/ MmestateLogin_accessso.as.

5. Return to mmestate.fla and test the application. Enter a username and password and click the Login Button. Close the SWF.

Return to the file you used in the last exercise or open /fpad2004/lesson16/start/mmestate.fla and save it as *mmestate.fla* in /fpad2004/mmestate/.

6. Test the application again.

The username text field should be populated with the last value that you used to log in to the application. This value was retrieved from the SOL file on your computer.

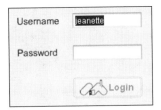

Handling SharedObject Events

When a flush() method is executed, it returns either a Boolean value of true or false, or a string value of "pending."

true. Returned if the user is allowing local storage from the domain and there is enough space allotted for the SharedObject to be saved without prompting the user.

false. Returned if the user is not allowing local storage from the domain or if Flash is unable to save the SharedObject for any reason.

pending. Returned if the user has permitted local storage from this domain but the amount of space is not sufficient to store the SharedObject.

The return value is immediately available to code after the flush() method.

```
soSuccess=my_so.flush();
if(!soSuccess)
{
      message.text=("Your data could not be saved");
}
else if(soSuccess=="pending")
{
      message.text=("You need to approve more storage...");
}
```

If the flush() method returns "pending," the user is presented with the Local Storage Settings dialog box to approve or deny more storage space. After the user responds to the dialog box, the flush() method is called again and returns either true or false and an onStatus event is broadcast.

The event object passed to the onStatus event handler has a level property (equal to "Status" or "Error") and a code property equal to SharedObject.Flush.Failed (the user did not allot additional disk space) or SharedObject.Flush.Success (the user allotted additional disk space for the SharedObject).

```
my_so.onStatus=function(evtObj:Object):Void
{
      if(evtObj.code=="SharedObject.Flush.Failed")
      {
            message.text=("Your data could not be saved");
      }
      else if(evtObj.code=="SharedObject.Flush.Success")
      {
            message.text=("Your data was saved successfully");
      }
};
```

In this exercise, you use the return values from the `flush()` method and the SharedObject `onStatus` event to capture whether or not the writing of the SharedObject to disk was successful.

1. Return to MmestateLogin.as in /fpad2004/mmestate/classes/.

Return to the file you created in the last exercise or open /fpad2004/lesson16/intermediate/classes/ MmestateLogin_accessso.as and save it as *MmestateLogin.as* in /fpad2004/mmestate/classes/.

2. In the `login_pbClick()` method, set the return value from the `flush()` method equal to a variable called `soSuccess`.

```
var soSuccess=username_so.flush();
```

Make sure you declare the variable as local to the method, but don't declare a data type because the `flush()` method can return a Boolean or a String.

3. After the `flush()` method, trace `soSuccess`.

```
74    private function login_pbClick():Void
75    {
76        username_so.data.username=username_ti.text
77        var soSuccess=username_so.flush();
78        trace(soSuccess);
79        if (password_ti.length<4)
```

4. At the end of the code inside the constructor, create an `onStatus` handler for `username_so` with one parameter called `evtObj` of type *Object*. Inside, trace the `code` property of `evtObj`. Save the file.

```
username_so.onStatus=function(evtObj:Object):Void
{
    trace(evtObj.code)
};
```

Although not the most elegant, it is most expedient to define this event handler inside another method like this.

The finished file should resemble: /fpad2004/lesson16/intermediate/classes/ MmestateLogin_handleso.as.

5. Return to mmestate.fla and test the application. Enter a username and password and click the Login Button.

Return to the file you used in the last exercise or open /fpad2004/lesson16/start/mmestate.fla and save it as *mmestate.fla* in /fpad2004/mmestate/.

You should get a value of true in the Output panel. The SharedObject was successfully saved.

6. Right-click/Control-click the SWF and select Settings. On the Local Storage tab, select the Never Ask Again check box. Click OK and then Close.

The existing SharedObject is deleted and you will never be asked again to allow SharedObjects to be stored from this domain.

7. Change the username and click the Login button again.

You should get a value of false in the Output panel. The Local Storage dialog box does not open asking you to allow more space.

8. Right-click/Control-click the SWF and select Settings. On the Local Storage tab, deselect the Never Ask Again check box. Click Close.

A value of None is now selected. You should be prompted to allow more storage space when a flush() method is executed.

9. Change the username and click the Login button again.

You should get a value of pending in the Output panel and you should be prompted to allow more storage.

10. Click Deny.

You should get a value of SharedObject.Flush.Failed in the Output panel.

11. Click the Login button again.

You should get a value of pending in the Output panel and should be prompted to allow more storage.

12. Click Allow.

You should get a value of SharedObject.Flush.Success in the Output panel and your username is stored locally on disk.

13. Close the SWF. Retest the application.

You should see the last username you entered.

Saving Complex Data in a SharedObject

In the exercises so far, you have been storing a simple string value in a SharedObject. What do you need to do differently if you want to store something more complicated, like the contents of a DataGrid? Not much. The Flash Player performs all the serialization and deserialization of the complex data for you. As mentioned earlier, you store complex data structures in a SharedObject exactly as you do simple strings, by assigning a property of the `data` object.

```
my_so.data.users=["Russ","Pete","Maureen","Ron","Kim","Noah"];
```

In some cases, you might need to add additional loops to your code when generating or using the data in the complex SharedObject. In other cases, the code you write is no more difficult than for simple stings; for example, if you are assigning the retrieved data to the `dataProvider` property of a component.

> **Tip** *If you use a DataSet component to manage your complex data, you can also use the DataSet class methods `saveToSharedObject()` and `loadFromSharedObject()`, which simplify writing and retrieving of sets of data to a SharedObject.*

In this exercise, you save the houses to disk in the searchHouses application and then retrieve and display them on the saved houses page in the mmestate application.

1. Return to Searchresults.as.

Return to the file you created in the last lesson or open /fpad2004/lesson16/start/classes/Searchresults.as and save it as *Searchresults.as* in /fpad2004/mmestate/classes/.

2. Define a public property called `houses_so` of type *SharedObject*.

```
public var houses_so:SharedObject;
```

You want this property to be public so you can directly access it from a class associated with the `saved` screen of the mmestate application.

3. Inside the constructor, set `houses_so` equal to a SharedObject that stores its data in a local file named *savedhouses*. Use the SharedObject `getLocal()` method.

```
houses_so=SharedObject.getLocal("savedhouses");
```

You are placing this code in the constructor so any data already saved in the SharedObject file is immediately loaded into the `houses_so` property when the screen loads and is, therefore, immediately accessible to any classes that want to use its data. Specifically, when you load the searchHouses application into the mmestate application, you want to be able to load the saved house data from the SharedObject into a DataGrid on the `saved` screen.

4. Inside the constructor, check to see if the savedhouses.sol file already has data in a property called **houses**. If it does not, create an Array property called **houses** on the SharedObject **data** object.

```
if (houses_so.data.houses==undefined)
{
        houses_so.data.houses=new Array();
}
```

If the savedhouses.sol file already has data in it, the houses_so.data property will be populated with this data when the getLocal() method of Step 3 is executed. If the SOL file does not contain any house data, you need to define the houses property for the SharedObject as an Array so you can use the methods of the Array class to populate it (which you do in Steps 5 and 6).

5. Inside the **save_pbClick()** method, change the existing trace of the house **SAVE** property to an **if** statement with the same argument.

```
74      private function save_pbClick():Void
75      {
76          for (var i=0;i<houses_dg.length;i++)
77          {
78              if(houses_dg.getItemAt(i).SAVE)
79              {
80              }
81          }
82      }
```

Instead of tracing the value of the SAVE property of each house item, you want to check and see if the property has a value of true. If it does, then you want to add the house item to the SharedObject so it can be saved to disk.

6. Inside the **if** statement, use the Array **push()** method to add the new item to the **houses** property of the **houses_so.data** property.

```
houses_so.data.houses.push(houses_dg.getItemAt(i));
```

This code will add the new item to the items already stored in the SharedObject (if any). This means you can get duplicate houses stored. A selected house will be added, regardless if it is already saved. To prevent this from occurring, you need to make sure a house with the HOUSEID of the selected house in the DataGrid is not already in the SharedObject before you add it.

7. Create logic to make sure an item with the **HOUSEID** of the selected house item is not already in the SharedObject.

For each selected house (inside the if statement), set a Boolean flag to true (call it savehouse). Then loop through the houses array in the SharedObject and compare the HOUSEID values in the houses SharedObject array to the HOUSEID for the selected house in the DataGrid. If you get a match of HOUSEID values, set savehouse to false. After the loop, add the selected house to the SharedObject houses array if savehouse is still true.

```
78          if(houses_dg.getItemAt(i).SAVE)
79          {
80              var savehouse:Boolean=true;
81              for (var j=0;j<houses_so.data.houses.length;j++)
82              {
83                  if(houses_dg.getItemAt(i).HOUSEID==houses_so.data.houses[j].HOUSEID
84                  {
85                      savehouse=false;
86                  }
87              }
88              if (savehouse)
89              {
90                  houses_so.data.houses.push(houses_dg.getItemAt(i));
91              }
92          }
```

8. After the outer **for** loop, save the SharedObject to disk.

```
houses_so.flush();
```

9. After the **flush()**, method, trace the number of items in the SharedObject's **houses** property. Save the file.

```
trace(houses_so.data.houses.length);
```

This code lets you see that something has happened when you test the application. It also lets you verify that the same house is not added to the SharedObject more than once.

The finished file should resemble: /fpad2004/lesson16/intermediate/classes/Searchresults_houseso.as.

10. Return to searchHouses.fla in /fpad2004/mmestate/ and test the application. Retrieve some houses from the database, check the save check box for several of the houses in the DataGrid, and click the Save button.

Return to the file you used in the last lesson or open /fpad2004/lesson16/start/searchHouses.fla and save it as *searchHouses.fla* in /fpad2004/mmestate/.

You should see the number of saved houses displayed in the Output panel.

11. Keep the same houses selected and click the Save button again.

You should see the same number of saved houses displayed in the Output panel. The number should not have increased.

12. Browse to (or search for) savedhouses.sol on your computer. Open the file in a text editor.

You should see the data for the houses.

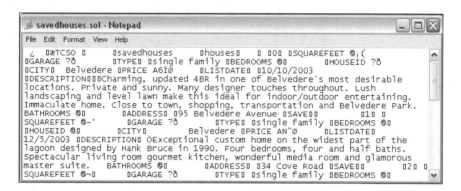

Next you will create the code for the `saved` screen in the Macromediestate application to display the data contained in the SharedObject.

13. Open MmestateSaved.as in /fpad2004/lesson16/start/classes/ and save it as *MmestateSaved.as* in /fpad2004/mmestate/classes/.

This class file contains code for the `saved` screen of the Macromediestate application. The file has been started for you; it contains code for the event-handling skeleton and for customizing the DataGrid—all code you have written before. Note that the code for customizing the DataGrid looks much the same as the code for customizing the DataGrid in Searchresults.as. Instead of having duplicate code, it would be better to create a new class containing the similar functionality and could be used by both screen classes. Right now, the houses are simply displayed on the `saved` screen. You could also show house details by loading the showDetails.swf application into a Loader component or a new screen and invoking the `displayItem( )` method just like you did in the `searchresults` screen of searchHouses.fla.

14. Return to mmestate.fla and select the `saved` screen. From the Components panel, drag out a DataGrid component and give it the name `savedhouses_dg.` Use the Free Transform tool to resize the DataGrid to take up most of the screen space.

Return to the file you used in the last exercise or open /fpad2004/lesson16/start/mmestate.fla and save it as *mmestate.fla* in /fpad2004/mmestate/.

15. Above the grid, create a dynamic TextField called `message_txt`. Use a black, bold, Arial font of size 16. Use the text handle to make the TextField about as wide as the DataGrid.

16. Link the **saved** screen to the MmestateSaved class. Save the file.

The finished file should resemble: /fpad2004/lesson16/intermediate/mmestate_houseso.fla.

17. Return to MmestateSaved.as. Inside the `savedReveal()` method, create an `if/else` construct that checks to see if the SharedObject in the loaded searchHouses application has any houses stored in it.

You need to use an appropriate relative reference to the `searchresults` screen in the loaded application. Remember from Lesson 11, "Creating Visual Objects Dynamically," that when you load a SWF into a screen it gets placed in a new screen called `contentHolder`.

```
if(_parent.search.contentHolder.application.searchresults.houses_so. ¬
data.houses.length!=0 && _parent.search.contentHolder.application. ¬
searchresults.houses_so.data.houses.length!=undefined)
{}
else
{}
```

18. If the SharedObject contains saved houses, make the DataGrid visible, set the `dataProvider` of the DataGrid, and populate the `message_txt` TextField with a message stating the number or saved houses.

```
savedhouses_dg.visible=true;
savedhouses_dg.dataProvider=_parent.search.contentHolder.application. ¬
searchresults.savedhouses_so.data.houses;
message_txt.text="You have "+_parent.search.contentHolder.application. ¬
searchresults.savedhouses_so.data.houses.length+" saved houses";
```

19. If the SharedObject does not contain any houses, hide the DataGrid and populate the `message_txt` TextField with an appropriate message. Save the file.

```
else
{
    savedhouses_dg.visible=false;
    message_txt.text="You have no saved houses";
}
```

The finished file should resemble: /fpad2004/lesson16/intermediate/classes/ MmestateSaved_houseso.as.

20. Return to mmestate.fla and test the application. Click the Saved button.

You should see your saved houses displayed in the DataGrid.

macromediestate
the house matters

home | search houses | saved houses | mortgage calculator | logout

You have 10 saved houses

city	address	price	bed	bath	garage	sq ft	list date
Belvedere	95 Belvedere Avenue	$1,495,000	4	3	yes	2196	10/10/200
Belvedere	34 Cove Road	$3,950,000	4	4	yes	3800	12/5/2003
Belvedere	68 Rockridge Avenue	$3,900,000	3	3	yes	3590	12/2/2003
Corte Madera	9 Paradise Way	$699,000	4	2	yes	1520	6/12/2003
Dillon Beach	89 Dillon Beach Road	$775,000	4	3	yes	3100	12/3/2003
Dillon Beach	32 Kahilana Road	$999,500	3	2	yes	4480	11/28/200
Bolinas	2 Mesa Road	$839,000	2	1	no	1800	11/1/2003
Bolinas	344 Nymph Road	$3,800,000	3	4	yes	2020	12/22/200
Corte Madera	4 Oak Lane	$819,000	3	1	yes	1148	9/17/2003
Dillon Beach	9 Oceana Way	$742,000	2	2	no	1400	1/2/2004

21. Return to the search page and save more houses. Return to the saved page.

You should see the houses you just saved in the DataGrid as well.

Congratulations, you have completed building the application! You can now create your own rich Internet applications with Flash. Of course, you have not learned everything there is to know about Flash and you are bound to have some questions as you start developing your own applications. There are a plethora of Flash resources for you to use including web sites, forums, blogs, and e-mail lists; a small number are listed here. For tutorials and articles, check out the Macromedia Developer Center (http://www.macromedia.com/devnet/) and the MX Developers Journal (http://sys-con.com/mx/). For online support, use the Macromedia Flash Support forum (http://webforums.macromedia.com/flash) and the Macromedia Flash blog aggregator (http://www.markme.com/mxna/index.cfm?category=Flash). Additional tutorials and forums are available at http://www.were-here.com and http://www.actionscript.com. Several e-mail lists include Flashcoders, a high-volume advanced list for ActionScript (http://chattyfig.figleaf.com) and flashfusion, a list for Flash and ColdFusion integration (http://flashcfm.com). Thanks for reading and now get out there are build some great web applications!

What You Have Learned

In this lesson, you have:

- Viewed SharedObject files on your computer (page 611)

- Changed the Flash Player settings for SharedObjects (pages 612–614)

- Created SharedObjects (pages 615–616)

- Saved SharedObjects to disk using `flush()` (pages 616–619)

- Accessed data in a SharedObject and used it populate UI components (pages 620–621)

- Responded to SharedObject events (pages 622–624)

- Saved complex data in a SharedObject (pages 625–631)

A Setup Instructions

This appendix contains instructions for installing the appropriate software on your computer so you can complete all the exercises in this book.

General Requirements

Minimum system requirements include:

Windows

- 600MHz Intel Pentium III processor or equivalent
- Windows 98 SE (4.10.2222 A), Windows 2000, or Windows XP

Macintosh

- 500MHz PowerPC G3 processor
- Mac OS X 10.2.6 and later, 10.3

Cross-Platform

- 256 MB RAM (512 MB recommended)
- 600 MB available disk space
- DVD-ROM drive

To perform the first 12 lessons, you need Macromedia Flash MX 2004 Professional. To perform Lessons 13 through 16, you also need a web server, an application server, and either Microsoft Access or MySQL. You can use a ColdFusion, .NET, or J2EE application server; ColdFusion, C#, and Java files are provided.

The following software is required:

- Macromedia Flash MX Professional 2004
- One or more of the following application servers: ColdFusion MX, JRun4, J2EE server and Flash Remoting for J2EE, .NET server and Flash Remoting for .NET

- Microsoft Access or MySQL

- A text editor

- (Optional) Macromedia Dreamweaver MX 2004 (used for embedding Flash applications in an HTML page in one exercise in Lesson 1, "Learning the Flash Interface")

- A web browser with the Macromedia Flash Player 7. The latest Flash Player version is available from: http://www.macromedia.com/software/flashplayer/.

- A file extraction program like WinZip or StuffIt

Follow the setup instructions for one of the following application servers.

ColdFusion MX

The following instructions are for setting up the book files on a ColdFusion server on Windows. You will need to modify the instructions appropriately for Macintosh. Flash Remoting is built into ColdFusion MX.

1. Install ColdFusion MX.

A single IP developer edition of ColdFusion is available from: http://www.macromedia.com/downloads/.

The exercise instructions assume you have installed ColdFusion to use your web server on port 80. If you install ColdFusion with its own built-in web server (which by default uses port 8500), you will need to use the appropriate URLs in the exercise instructions. For example, instead of using the URL http://localhost/fpad2004/mmestate/services/House.cfc?wsdl, you should use http://localhost:8500/fpad2004/mmestate/services/House.cfc?wsdl. Solution files for both ports have been provided.

2. Browse the page at the following URL: http://localhost/flashservices/gateway/.

If a blank page is returned, ColdFusion and Flash Remoting are running and working properly. (Flash Remoting is built into ColdFusion MX, you do not need to install it separately.)

If you are using ColdFusion with the built-in server, browse to http://localhost:8500/flashservices/gateway/. The Flash Remoting gateway URL is http://webserver[:port]/flashservices/gateway/ where flashservices is the name of the Java application and gateway is the servlet mapping.

3. Install the Flash Remoting MX Components.

These components are an add-on for the Flash MX 2004 authoring environment. They can be downloaded from: http://www.macromedia.com/software/flashremoting/downloads/components/. Make sure Flash is installed but is not open before installing the components.

4. Copy the fpad2004 folder from the DVD to the web root for your ColdFusion installation.

If you used the default values during the ColdFusion installation, the web root is C:\CFusionMX\webroot\.

This step places all the working files for this book in the web root. However, if you prefer to have the fpad2004 folder on your desktop (or any other location), you can just place the ColdFusion CFC (which is used by the lessons which connect to remote data) in the web root. In that case, copy House.cfc from /fpad2004/services/coldfusion/ and place it in C:\CFusionMX\wwwroot\ fpad2004\mmestate\services\. If you do not use this exact path, you will have to modify the instructions in the lessons accordingly.

The fpad2004 folder is over 400 MB in size. To save space, keep only one lesson folder for lessons 13 through 16. (There are multiple versions of these folders for different application server setups.)

5. Browse to http://localhost/fpad2004/mmestate/services/House.cfc.

You should see information about the House component displayed. This step confirms that the ColdFusion component is in the correct location for Lessons 13 through 16.

If you are using ColdFusion's built-in server, browse to http://localhost:8500/fpad2004/mmestate/ services/House.cfc.

6. Create a ColdFusion data source called *fpad2004* that points to the provided database.

Two versions of the database are included in the /fpad2004/data/ folder: Microsoft Access and MySQL. Use the ColdFusion Administrator to point to one of these databases.

Steps for using Microsoft Access

    a. Open the ColdFusion Administrator. (On Windows, select Start > Programs > Macromedia > Macromedia ColdFusion MX > Administrator.)

    b. Click the Data Sources link on the left side of the web page. (It's under the Data & Services category.)

    c. In the Add New Data Source box, enter *fpad2004* for the data source name and select Microsoft Access for the driver. Click Add.

    d. Enter (or browse to) the location of the database file: /fpad2004/data/fpad2004.mdb. If you placed the fpad2004 folder in the CFusionMX web root, this path will be: C:\CFusionMX\ wwwroot\fpad2004\data\fpad2004.mdb.

    e. Leave "Use Default username" selected and click Submit. You should get a "datasource updated successfully" message and fpad2004 should appear in the list of data sources.

Steps for using MySQL

   a. Copy the fpad2004 folder located in /fpad2004/data/ to your /mysql/data/ folder.

   b. Open the ColdFusion Administrator. (On Windows, select Start > Programs > Macromedia > Macromedia ColdFusion MX > Administrator.)

   c. Click the Data Sources link on the left side of the web page. (It's under the Data & Services category.)

   d. In the Add New Data Source box, enter *fpad2004* for the data source name and select MySQL for the driver. Click Add.

   e. Enter fpad2004 in the Database field.

   f. Click Submit. You should get a "datasource updated successfully" message and fpad2004 should appear in the list of data sources.

Note *MySQL is free. You can get a copy from http://www.mysql.com.*

JRun4

The following instructions are for setting up the book files on the default JRun server.

1. Install JRun4.

Make sure you have the latest version, which includes JRun4 Updater 2 (which upgrades JRun4, JRun4 SP1, and JRun 4 SP1a installations). A single IP developer edition is available from: http://www.macromedia.com/software/jrun/trial/.

2. Start the default JRun server.

Select Start > Programs > Macromedia JRUN4 > JRUN Launcher and then select the default JRun server and click Start.

The instructions in the next step assume you are using the default server. If you use a different JRun server, modify the instructions and file locations appropriately.

3. (Optional) Configure the default JRun server to use port 80.

The exercise instructions assume you have configured JRun to use a web server on port 80. By default, the JRun server uses port 8100. You can leave the default server using port 8100, but you will need to change the URLs in the exercise instructions to use port 8100. For example, instead of using the URL http://localhost/fpad2004/mmestate/services/House.jws?wsdl, you should use http://localhost:8100/fpad2004/mmestate/services/House.jws?wsdl. Solution files for both ports have been provided.

4. Make sure Flash Remoting is working by browsing to http://localhost/flashservices/gateway/.

If a blank page is returned, JRun4 and Flash Remoting are running and working properly. Flash Remoting is built into JRun4.

If you use a server on any other port, modify the URL appropriately. For example for the default server using port 8100, use http://localhost:8100/flashservices/gateway/. The Flash Remoting gateway URL is http://webserver[:port]/flashservices/gateway/ where flashservices is the name of the Java application context and gateway is the servlet mapping.

5. Install the Flash Remoting MX Components.

These components are an add-on for the Flash MX 2004 authoring environment. They can be downloaded from: http://www.macromedia.com/software/flashremoting/downloads/components/. Make sure Flash is installed but is not open before installing the components.

6. Copy the fpad2004 folder from the DVD to your computer.

You can place the files anywhere you want, even on your desktop. In the following steps, though, you will need to copy the Java class files and the Java web service file to the appropriate locations.

The fpad2004 folder is over 400 MB in size. To save space, keep only one lesson folder for lessons 13 through 16. (There are multiple versions of these folders for different application server setups.)

7. Create an ODBC data source called *fpad2004* that points to the provided database.

Two versions of the database are provided: Microsoft Access and MySQL. Use the ODBC Administrator to point to one of the databases. If you are using MySQL, you must first copy the fpad2004 folder located in /fpad2004/data/ to your /mysql/data/ folder.

8. Copy the House.jws file in /fpad2004/services/java/ and place it in C:\JRun4\servers\ default\default-ear\default-war\fpad2004\mmestate\services\.

If you are not using the default JRun server, modify the path accordingly.

This file is used in Lesson 13, "Consuming Web Services," for connecting to web services. You can test the web service by browsing to http://localhost/fpad2004/mmestate/services/House.jws?wsdl (or http://localhost:8100/fpad2004/mmestate/services/House.jws?wsdl). You should get a page displaying XML.

9. Copy the files in /fpad2004/services/java/ (except the JWS file) and place them in C:\JRun4\servers\default\server-inf\classes\fpad2004\mmestate\services\.

If you are not using the default JRun server, modify the path accordingly.

These files are used for Flash Remoting in Lesson 14, "Accessing Remote Services Using Flash Remoting." Although you only need the class file, the Java source file and two BAT files (for compiling and testing the code) are also included. To test the code, place testFpad2004HouseClass.bat in C:\JRun4\servers\default\SERVER-INF\classes\ and run the BAT file from there.

> **Note** *You use prewritten Java classes for the exercises in this book. If you are going create and compile your own Java class files, you need to make sure the current directory path (.) is in the system classpath. You can check your classpath variables from a command line prompt using: echo %CLASSPATH%. To add the entry to your classpath, use the following command: set CLASSPATH=.;%CLASSPATH%. To create your own Java web service proxies for third-party web services (not covered in this book), you also need to place webservices.jar in the system classpath: set CLASSPATH=C:\jrun4\lib\webservices.jar;.;%CLASSPATH%.*

Other J2EE servers

The following instructions are for setting up the book files on a J2EE server.

1. Install a J2EE server.

You can use any J2EE server that is supported by Flash Remoting including Windows, Linux, and Solaris J2EE servers that meet the J2EE 1.2, 1.3 and Servlet 2.2, 2.3 specifications. You can find the J2EE server requirements listed at:
http://www.macromedia.com/software/flashremoting/productinfo/system_reqs/.

> **Note** *All exercises in this book assume you have your application server configured to use port 80.*

2. Install Flash Remoting for J2EE.

A 30-day trial version is available from: http://www.macromedia.com/downloads/.

3. Install Flash Remoting MX Updater Release 1 for Java.

The Java remoting updater is available from http://www.macromedia.com/software/flashremoting/.

    a. Extract the contents of the updater flashremoting-java-updater-r1.zip file to a temporary location.

    b. Follow the installation instructions in the FRUpdaterRelease1Install.html file for your particular configuration; this HTML file is contained in the updater ZIP file.

4. Make sure Flash Remoting is working by browsing to: http://{webserver}[:port]/flashremoting/flashsevices/gateway/.

If a blank page is returned, Flash Remoting is working properly.

The Flash Remoting gateway URL is http://webserver[:port]/flashservices/gateway/ where flashservices is the name of the Java application context and gateway is the servlet mapping.

5. Install the Flash Remoting MX Components.

These components are an add-on for the Flash MX 2004 authoring environment. They can be downloaded from: http://www.macromedia.com/software/flashremoting/downloads/components/. Make sure Flash is installed but is not open before installing the components.

6. Copy the fpad2004 folder from the DVD to your computer.

You can place the files anywhere you want, even on your desktop. In the following steps, though, you need to copy the Java class files and the Java web service file to the appropriate locations.

The fpad2004 folder is over 400 MB in size. To save space, keep only one lesson folder for lessons 13 through 16. (There are multiple versions of these folders for different application server setups.)

7. Create an ODBC data source called *fpad2004* that points to the provided database.

Two versions of the database are provided: Microsoft Access and MySQL. Use the ODBC Administrator to point to one of these databases. If you are using MySQL, you must first copy the fpad2004 folder located in /fpad2004/data/ to your /mysql/data/ folder.

8. Copy the House.jws file in /fpad2004/services/java/ and place it in a /fpad2004/mmestate/services/ directory in the context root for your application.

For example: C:\JRun4\servers\default\default-ear\default-war\fpad2004\mmestate\services\.

This file is used in Lesson 13 for connecting to web services. You can test the web service by browsing to http://localhost/fpad2004/mmestate/services/House.jws?wsdl. You should get a page displaying XML.

9. Copy the files in /fpad2004/services/java/ (except the JWS file) and place them in a /fpad2004/mmestate/services/ directory in the classes directory for your server.

For example: C:\JRun4\servers\default\server-inf\classes\fpad2004\mmestate\services\.

These files are used for Flash Remoting in Lesson 14. Although you only need the class file, the Java file and two BAT files (for compiling and testing the code) are also included. To test the code, place testFpad2004HouseClass.bat in the classes folder (for example, C:\JRun4\servers\default\SERVER-INF\classes\ ) and run the BAT file from there.

.NET

The following instructions are for setting up the book files on a .NET server.

1. Install Microsoft .NET Framework v1.0 or later.

The .NET framework is available from http://msdn.microsoft.com/downloads/.

> **Note** *You use a prewritten .NET assembly for the exercises in this book. If you are going to create your own assemblies, you need to make sure the location of the .NET framework is in the system path variable. To check, right-click My Computer (or your appropriate computer name) on your desktop and select Properties. Select the Advanced tab. Click the Environment Variables button. Under System variables, select the Path variable and click Edit. Add C:\WINNT\Microsoft.NET\Framework\v1.1.4322; (or the appropriate location for your installation) to the Variable Value and click OK. Click OK to leave the Environment Variables dialog box and click OK again to leave the System Properties dialog box.*

2. Install Flash Remoting for .NET.

A 30-day trial version is available from http://www.macromedia.com/downloads/.

> **Note** *When you install Flash Remoting, a default .NET application called flashremoting is created.*

3. Install Flash Remoting MX Updater Release 1 for .NET.

The .NET remoting updater is available from: http://www.macromedia.com/software/flashremoting/.

    a. Extract the contents of the flashremoting-net-updater-r1.zip file to a temporary location.

    b. In Windows Explorer, locate flashgateway.dll in C:\Inetpub\wwwroot\flashremoting\bin\.

    c. Replace the existing flashgateway.dll file in the bin directory with the one you extracted from the flashremoting-net-updater-r1.zip file.

4. Make sure Flash Remoting is working by browsing to: http://localhost/flashremoting/gateway.aspx.

If a blank page is returned, Flash Remoting is working properly.

If you want to use Flash Remoting in a .NET application other than the default flashremoting application (with assemblies not located in <web root>/flashremoting/bin/), use the following steps:

    a. In the top-level directory for the assembly, create a page called gateway.aspx, which contains only a single ASP.NET tag: <%@ Page %>.

b. In the bin directory where the assembly is compiled, place a copy of the flashgateway.dll file, which can be found in C:\Inetpub\wwwroot\flashremoting\bin\.

c. In the web.config file for the assembly, embed the following code somewhere inside the <system.web> tag:

```
<httpModules>
<add name="GatewayController" type="FlashGateway.Controller. ¬
GatewayController, flashgateway" />
</httpModules>
```

5. **Change the security of the Access database to give the ASPNET user Read permissions.**

If you want the Flash Remoting client to read from any file in the application, you must change the Security settings for the file or a parent folder to give the ASPNET user Read permissions.

a. Right-click the fpad2004.mdb file in C:\Inetpub\wwwroot\flashremoting\fpad2004\ mmestate\services\ and select Properties.

b. Click the Security tab and then click Add.

c. Select the ASPNET user from the list, click Add, then click OK.

Note *You might need to change the selected item in the "Look in" drop-down box so your computer name is selected.*

d. Leave the Read and Read & Execute check boxes selected for the ASPNET user.

Note *Give the ASPNET user Write permissions if you want the Flash Remoting client to also write to the database.*

e. Click OK.

6. **Install the Flash Remoting MX Components.**

These components are an add-on for the Flash MX 2004 authoring environment. They can be downloaded from: http://www.macromedia.com/software/flashremoting/downloads/components/. Make sure Flash is installed but is not open before installing the components.

7. **Copy the fpad2004 folder from the DVD to your computer.**

You can place the files anywhere you want, even on your desktop. In the following steps, though, you need to copy the C# class file, the assembly, and the web service file to the appropriate locations.

The fpad2004 folder is over 400 MB in size. To save space, keep only one lesson folder for lessons 13 through 16. (There are multiple versions of these folders for different application server setups.)

8. Copy the House.asmx file from /fpad2004/services/net/ and place it in C:\Inetpub\ wwwroot\fpad2004\mmestate\services\.

This file is used in Lesson 13 for connecting to web services. You can test the web service by browsing to http://localhost/fpad2004/mmestate/services/House.asmx?wsdl. You should get a page displaying XML.

9. Copy the fpad2004.mmestate.services.dll file from /fpad2004/services/net/ and place it in C:\Inetpub\wwwroot\flashremoting\bin\.

If you are using Flash Remoting with another .NET application, modify the path accordingly.

10. Copy the files in /fpad2004/services/net/ (except the ASMX and DLL files) and place them in C:\Inetpub\wwwroot\flashremoting\fpad2004\mmestate\services\.

If you are using Flash Remoting with another .NET application, modify the path accordingly.

These files include the source and compiled C# files (the source files for the assembly used for Flash Remoting in Lesson 14), two BAT files (for compiling the class and creating the assembly), an Access database, and the assembly manifest XML file.

> **Note** The House class and House web service are hard-coded to use the Microsoft Access database: C:\Inetpub\wwwroot\flashremoting\fpad2004\mmestate\services\fpad2004.mdb. If you change the location of the database, you need to change the CS file code, recompile the class, and re-create the assembly as well as change the code in the ASMX file. You can also change the code to use the MySQL version of the database provided in /fpad2004/data/. (You need to copy this folder to your /mysql/data/ folder.)

General Notes for All Servers

If you want to use any of the files in the lesson folders for Lessons 13 through 16 as starting files, you will need to make changes to two files if your application server setup does not match one of the five for which solutions are provided. You must change the web service URL for the WebServiceConnector on the login screen in mmestate.fla and the URL for the web service or Flash Remoting gateway in Searchform.as.

To complete the exercises in Lesson 6 or later, you must have completed the Setting Classpaths exercise in Lesson 5, which sets the classes folder to be a Flash classpath.

Index

AS (ActionScript) files, Flash file types, 3
AsBroadcaster class, 103–104
ASC (ActionScript Communication) files, Flash file types, 3
ASSetPropFlags() function, 120
assignment operator (=), 63, 64
associative array data types
    data conversion between ActionScript
       and C#, 570
       and ColdFusion, 567–568
       and Java, 568–570
      toString() method, 125
associative arrays, 123–126
attachMovie() method, 454, 457
attributes property, XML objects, 485
authoring classes, 103
authoring environment, 4–6
autoSize property, 137–140
    Label component, 420

B

background images, importing, 38–41
Bandwidth Profiler, 38–39, 41
behaviors, 346–351
    custom behaviors, 352–355
bindable metadata tag, 359
Boolean class, 103–104
    wrappers, 111
Boolean data types, 61
    data conversion between ActionScript
       and C#, 570
       and ColdFusion, 567–568
       and Java, 568–570
borderColor and borderStyle properties, 391
bottom properties, 370
_btn suffix, code hinting, 155
Button class, 103–104
Button components, 339–341, 413–417
    versus Button objects, 153
    component architecture, 369
    CSSStyleDeclaration objects, 398
Button objects
    basics, 153
    versus Button components, 153
    button symbols, 154
      editing Timeline, 158–164
    code-hinting, 154–155
    event handlers
      on Button objects, 167–170
      in Timeline, 164–166
    naming, 154–155
    properties, 155–158
    states, 158–161

C

C# programming language, data conversion with
    ActionScript, 570
CalcError class, 255–256
calcMortgage() function
    calculations inside functions, 85
    changing from standalone functions to methods,
      131–134
    placing in external AS files, 88–89
callback functions. *See* event handlers
CallRenderer class, MovieClip display in DataGrid
    columns, 598–603
Camera class, 103–104
Cascading Style Sheets (CSS), setting style properties
    classes, 398–400
    components, 390–394
case-sensitivity, 54
    string comparisons, 73
    variables, 61–62
catch keyword, exception handling, 89–95
cellEdit event, 590
cellFocusIn event, 590
CellPress event, 590
change event, List component, 446
charAt() method, 111–114
CheckBox components, 429–433
    creating dynamically, 458–461
    CSSStyleDeclaration objects, 398
    displaying in DataGrid column, 600–603
child classes, 238–240
child objects, MovieClips, 183–189
childNodes property, XML objects, 485
class keyword, 201–207, 288
classes, 99
    built-in classes
      classes unique to Flash, 103–104
      core classes, 103–104
      dynamic, 254–256
    children and parent classes, 238–240
      calling parent class constructors, 240–244
    constructors, 226–227
      overloaded, 227
      this identifier, reference class properties, 228–232
    creating, 201–207
    crosspaths
      global, 208, 209–212
      per-FLA, 208–209
    importing
      implicitly and explicitly, 214
      with wildcards, 215–218
    inheritance, 238–240
    interfaces, 244–250
    intrinsic classes, 287–290

numChildForms property, 323, 326–328
NumericStepper components, 426–429
    component architecture, 369
    CSSStyleDeclaration objects, 398

O

Object class, 254
    custom objects, 126–128
        data typing, 130–134
        defining methods, 128–129
        loops, 130
    hierarchy model, 103
Object data types, data conversion between ActionScript
    and C#, 570
    and ColdFusion, 567–568
    and Java, 568–570
object-oriented programming. *See* OOP
<object> tags, Flash Player version detection, 25
objects, 100. *See also* specific objects
    copying, 19
    depth, 451–453
        Depth Manager, 465–466
    selecting multiple, 13
onChanged event, 144–145, 147–148
onFault event, 539
onKillFocus event, 142–145
onRelease event, 164, 182, 189
onReleaseOutside event, 164, 182
onResult event, 539, 558
onRollout and onRollover events, 164, 182
onSetFocus event, 142–145
OOP (object-oriented programming), terminology,
    99–102
Open state, panels, 6–10
OpenAMF Project, 546
operation property, WebServiceConnector component,
    520
operators
    arithmetic, 64
    comparison, 73–75
    conditional, 75–76
    logical, 75
Options menu, Actions panel, 51
order of precedence, arithmetic operators, 64
Other panels, 6
Output panel, 57
Over state, buttons, 159, 161–163
overloaded constructors, 227
overloaded methods, 233

P

panels
    authoring environment, 4–5
    Design, 6
    Development, 6
    docked/undocked, 7
    gripper, 8
    hiding/restoring, 10
    Other, 6
    saving panel sets, 11
    states, 6–10
    Window menu (list), 6
params property, WebServiceConnector component, 530
parent classes, 238–244
parent objects, MovieClips, 183–189
parseFloat() function, data typing, 66
parseInt() function, data typing, 66
password property, 137–140
    TextInput component, 418
PendingCall objects
    event handlers, 539–541
    invoking remote methods, 536
per-FLA crosspaths, 208–209
pop() method, 117
populateCombos() method, 484
pow() method, 105–107
previousValue property, NumericStepper component,
    425
price property, 279–283
private methods, 233–236
ProgressBar components
    component architecture, 369
    CSSStyleDeclaration objects, 398
project files. *See* FLP (Flash project) files
Project panel, 10
    version control status icons, 43
properties, 100–101
    TextField objects, 136–140
Public API, 270–273
public methods, 233–236
push() method, 117

R

RadioButton components, 433–437
    CSSStyleDeclaration objects, 398
rate property, 279–283
RateError class, 202, 206–207
RDS version control, 42
RecordSet data types, data conversion between
    ActionScript
    and C#, 570
    and ColdFusion, 567–568
    and Java, 568–570
relative paths, MovieClip objects, 183–189
removeAll() and removeItemAt() methods, 440, 590
removeAllColumns() and removeAllColumnsAt() methods,
    DataGrid component, 584
removeMovieClip() method, 454

real world. real training. real results.

Get more done in less time with
Macromedia Training and Certification.

Two Types of Training

Roll up your sleeves and get right to work with authorized training
from Macromedia.

1. **Classroom Training**
    Learn from instructors thoroughly trained and certified by
    Macromedia. Courses are fast-paced and task-oriented to get
    you up and running quickly.

2. **Online Training**
    Get Macromedia training when you want with affordable, interactive online
    training from Macromedia University.

Stand Out from the Pack

Show your colleagues, employer, or prospective clients that you
have what it takes to effectively develop, deploy, and maintain dynamic
applications—become a Macromedia Certified Professional.

Learn More

For more information about authorized training or to find a class near you,
visit **www.macromedia.com/go/training1**

Macromedia Tech Support: http://www.macromedia.com/support

Licensing Agreement

The information in this book is for informational use only and is subject to change without notice. Macromedia, Inc., and Macromedia Press assume no responsibility for errors or inaccuracies that may appear in this book. The software described in the book is furnished under license and may be used or copied only in accordance with terms of the license.

The software files on the DVD-ROM included here are copyrighted by Macromedia, Inc. You have the non-exclusive right to use these programs and files. You may use them on one computer at a time. You may not transfer the files from one computer to another over a network. You may transfer the files onto a single hard disk so long as you can prove ownership of the original DVD-ROM.

You may not reverse engineer, decompile, or disassemble the software. You may not modify or translate the software or distribute copies of the software without the written consent of Macromedia, Inc.

Opening the disc package means you accept the licensing agreement. For installation instructions, see the ReadMe file on the DVD-ROM.